FOUNDATIONS OF
GENETIC ALGORITHMS•4

FOUNDATIONS OF GENETIC ALGORITHMS •4

EDITED BY

RICHARD K. BELEW

AND

MICHAEL D. VOSE

MORGAN KAUFMANN PUBLISHERS, INC.
SAN FRANCISCO, CALIFORNIA

Sponsoring Editor   Michael B. Morgan
Production Manager   Yonie Overton
Production Editor   Cheri Palmer
Editorial Coordinator   Marilyn Alan
Production Artist/Cover Design   Susan M. Sheldrake
Printer   Edwards Brothers, Inc.

Morgan Kaufmann Publishers, Inc.

Editorial and Sales Office

340 Pine Street, Sixth Floor
San Francisco, CA 94104-3205
USA

Telephone   415 / 392-2665
Facsimile   415 / 982-2665
E-mail   mkp@mkp.com
Web site   http://www.mkp.com

ISSN 1081-6593
ISBN 1-55860-460-X

FOGA–96

THE PROGRAM COMMITTEE

Lee Altenberg, *Maui High Performance Computing Center*

Thomas Baeck, *Informatik Centrum Dortmund, and Leiden University*

Wolfgang Banzhaf, *Dortmund University*

Eric Baum, *NEC*

Richard Belew, *University of California, San Diego*

Lashon Booker, *MITRE Corporation*

Kenneth DeJong, *George Mason University*

Larry Eshelman, *Philips Laboratories*

David E. Goldberg, *University of Illinois*

Andrew B. Kahng, *University of California, Los Angeles*

Sam Mahfoud, LBS *Capitol Management, Inc.*

Worthy Martin, *University of Virginia*

Melanie Mitchell, *Santa Fe Institute*

Heinz Muehlenbein, *German National Research Center for Information Technology*

Kihong Park, *Purdue University*

Nick Radcliffe, *Quadstone Ltd.*

Dave Rogers, *Molecular Simulations, Inc.*

Stephen Smith, *Carnegie Mellon University*

William Spears, *Naval Research Laboratory*

Michael D. Vose, *University of Tennessee*

Darrell Whitley, *Colorado State University*

Alden Wright, *University of Montana*

Contents

Introduction

The fourth Foundations of Genetic Algorithms workshop (FOGA) was held August 2 through August 5, 1996, in Alcala Park, San Diego. These workshops have been held biennially, starting in 1990. FOGA alternates with the International Conference on Genetic Algorithms (ICGA) which is held in odd years (ICGA's European sister conference, Parallel Problem Solving from Nature, is held in even years). Both the FOGA and ICGA events are sponsored and organized under the auspices of the International Society for Genetic Algorithms.

In keeping with past tradition, the papers in this proceedings are longer than typical conference papers, and were subjected to two rounds of reviewing to improve clarity. This has not dampened, however, the spirit which FOGA embraces as a venue where researchers can advance hypotheses and discuss ideas, interacting openly – and often spiritedly – with colleagues. Principally limited by the range of submissions, the workshop proceedings still manage to reflect a healthy diversity in the field. The following overview attempts to organize the contributions thematically.

An active research area is the mathematization of the simple genetic algorithm, in which the goal is to *prove theorems* relating to the nature of genetic search. Two papers in this category are "Diagonalizing the Simple GA Mixing Matrix" and "A Further Result on the Markov Chain Model of Genetic Algorithms and Its Application to a Simulated Annealing-like Strategy". The first shows how a sparse similarity transformation diagonalizes the simple GA's mixing matrix. The second paper illustrates tools and techniques associated with proving, from first principles, properties about genetic search based on Markov chain definitions.

Empirical work relating to fundamental objects involved in the mathematization of genetic search are "A Search for Counterexamples to Two Conjectures on the Simple Genetic Algorithm" and "Analyzing GAs Using Markov Models with Semantically Ordered and Lumped States". The first paper has to do with properties of the signal component of the simple genetic algorithm, as opposed to its stochastic aspects. It sheds light on a fundamental conjecture, and provides a nontrivial example of cyclic behavior in the infinite population case. The second paper touches on the inherent emergent behavior of genetic search and reports on preliminary empirical inquiry into the effects of aggregating states in the exact Markov chain model.

In contrast, the next group of papers aims at *modeling* selected statistics of GA behavior. Here, rather than theorem proving or investigating basic mathematical objects, the goals are model simplicity, computational efficiency, and qualitative agreement of modeled statistics to actual or average observed behavior. "Genetic Algorithm Dynamics in a Two-well Potential" uses a model of key population statistics to investigate genetic algorithm dynamics and contrast it with simulated annealing on a sample problem. The model is motivated by heuristic principles from statistical mechanics and is experimentally verified. The paper "Noisy Fitness Evaluation in Genetic Algorithms and the Dynamics of Learning" uses similar modeling techniques to predict population statistics for two sample problems involving a stochastic fitness measure. "Probing Genetic Algorithm Performance of Fitness Landscapes" is similar in spirit, except that fitness is deterministic and model parameters are experimentally calibrated to observed behavior.

The paper "Replicators, Majorization and Genetic Algorithms: New Models and Analytical tools" lies somewhere between the work described in the previous paragraphs. It advocates a class of models based on replicator equations for the analysis of evolutionary algorithms, and suggests operators which have improved analytical tractability.

The analysis of schemata continues to be a theme in work looking at how patterns of features in the problem representation come to impact genetic search by being selected and recombined with one another. "Nonlinearity, Hyperplane Ranking and the Simple Genetic Algorithm" is aimed at shedding light on how hyperplane rankings correlate with nonlinearity of the objective function and relate to the convergence of the simple genetic algorithm. "Convergence Controlled Variation" investigates advantages pair-wise crossover may have over pool-wise and other convergence controlled reproductive mechanisms, revisiting the concepts of exploration, schemata propagation, and hitchhiking. "Fitness Landscape Characterization by Variance of Decompositions" presents a framework in which a variety of schema-based statistics are defined/reviewed, and some are related to Walsh coefficients. Crossover correlation is defined, related to variance coefficients, and used to contrast various crossover types. Crossover is known to favor the linkages of some representational features over others (typically, those closer together on the genome). "Learning Linkage" applies facet-wise analysis to a crossover operator designed to facilitate the learning of appropriate linkage. "SEARCH, Blackbox Optimization, and Sample Complexity" suggests a framework within which the design and analysis of blackbox optimization algorithms in qualitative and quantitative terms can be approached and related to other symbolic learning methods.

The next group of papers deal with a fairly broad class of search strategies. The paper "On Searching α-ary Hypercubes and Related Graphs" develops the theme of landscapes being induced by operators and fitness functions together with how the operator is used within the algorithm. The main objective is to raise questions concerning fundamental analysis rather than presenting a design methodology. The paper "A Stationary Point Convergence Theory for Evolutionary Algorithms" adapts the convergence theory for generalized pattern search methods to a class of real-coded stochastic algorithms for which generally effective stopping rules may be available.

Representation and operators have an enormous impact on performance. Progress has been made in describing genetic search in a representation independent manner, and a number of representation independent operators have been defined. The paper "Real Representations" advances the perspective that representation independent characterizations of genetic search can be specialized to particular problems such that relevant problem features are captured. The paper "A Study of Fixed-Length Subset Recombination" relates to these issues in that it considers alternate representations for subset problems and investigates operators designed for or that were specialized to them.

The final category of papers is more applications oriented (the last paper mentioned above could be included here). "Fitness Functions for Multiple Objective Optimization Problems: Combining Preferences with Pareto Rankings" illustrates a design methodology for representing a multiple objective function by a single value which incorporates some preferences between Pareto optimal solutions. "Exact Uniform Initialization For Genetic Programming" solves the problem of initialization, given no a priori information, of a population of complete derivation trees from a bounded context-free language. Applications to genetic programming are given. "Stochastic Context-Free Grammar Induction with a Genetic Algorithm Using Local Search" relies on knowledge of formal languages to couple a evolutionary search process for good stochastic grammars with local tuning of the probabilities associated with the rules of the grammar. The paper also touches upon the issues of representation, operators, and cross-generational sampling.

In summary, this volume echoes themes that have surfaced at earlier FOGA workshops, extends them in new directions, further develops conceptual tools we can expect to see again, and identifies issues of growing importance. Many people played a part in FOGA's success and deserve mention, but none more so than the authors, participants, and program committee.

Michael D. Vose
C. S. Dept., 107 Ayres Hall
The University of Tennessee
Knoxville, TN 37996-1301
vose@cs.utk.edu

Richard K. Belew
Computer Science & Engr. Dept.
Univ. California – San Diego
La Jolla, CA 92093-0114
rik@cs.ucsd.edu

Diagonalizing the Simple GA Mixing Matrix

Gary J. Koehler
Department of Decision and Information Sciences
College of Business Administration, 351 BUS
University of Florida
Gainesville, FL 32611
koehler@nervm.nerdc.ufl.edu

Abstract

The simple GA mixing matrix, M, is diagonalized by a congruence transformation involving a lower-triangular matrix, L. L is sparse. Several applications using L are given. One application gives the rank of M under various choices of GA parameter values. A second application shows how L might prove useful in studying the GA Fixed Point Problem. In this problem L is used to change a quadratic equation having $2^\ell(2^\ell+1)/2$ terms to one having no cross terms and only 2ℓ squared terms.

1 INTRODUCTION

Vose and Liepins (1991) presented an infinite-sized population model for simple Genetic Algorithms (GAs). Nix and Vose (1992) extended this model to the finite population case. In both cases, a mixing matrix, M, plays a key roll. The Walsh transform, W, has been used to simplify calculations involving M because pre and post-multiplication by W produces a sparse matrix. A sparse matrix is one having a small percentage of nonzero elements (see Tewarson 1973).

We develop a congruence transformation involving a lower-triangular matrix, L, which can be used to completely diagonalize M. L is sparse. After developing L, we provide several applications. One application gives the rank of M under various choices of parameter values. A second application shows how L might prove useful in studying the GA Fixed Point Problem. In this problem L is used to change a quadratic equation having $2^{\ell}\left(2^{\ell}+1\right)/2$ terms to one having no cross terms and only 2ℓ squared terms (where ℓ is the string size.)

In Section 2 we give notation and background material. In Section 3 L is given and certain properties presented. Applications of L are given in Section 4. Most proofs are given in the Appendix.

2 NOTATION AND BACKGROUND MATERIAL

We consider a population of binary strings of length $\ell > 1$ which we represent by integers $0,1,...,2^{\ell}-1$. The lowest order bit is at position 0, the next at position 1, etc. The following notation will be used:

$i \oplus j$	is the bitwise "exclusive-or" of i and j;
$i \otimes j$	is the bitwise "and" of i and j;
$\lvert j \rvert$	is the number of non-zero bits of j;
hi(j)	is the position of the highest non-zero bit (for j>0) and 0 otherwise;
lo(j)	is the position of the lowest non-zero bit (for j>0) and 0 otherwise;
$\delta(a)$	is 1 if expression a evaluates to TRUE, and 0 otherwise;
F	is a diagonal matrix with $F_{i,i} > 0$ ($F_{i,i}$ is the fitness of string i);
P_i	is a permutation matrix with $\left(P_i\right)_{s,t} \equiv \delta\left(i \oplus s = t\right)$;
x^T, X^T	is the transpose of vector x (matrix X);
1	is a vector of ones (when used as a vector);
1_k	is a unit vector with a one in position k; and
I	is an identity matrix of appropriate size.

Matrix and vector subscripting starts with index 0.

Vose and Liepins (1991) derived an exact expression for the probability of generating an offspring, 0, by recombination of parents i and j using one point crossover with rate χ and uniform mutation with rate $\mu < 1$. That probability is given by

$$M_{i,j} = \frac{(1-\mu)^{\ell}}{2}\left[\eta^{|i|}\left(1-\chi+\frac{\chi}{\ell-1}\sum_{k=1}^{\ell-1}\eta^{-\Delta_{i,j,k}}\right)+\eta^{|j|}\left(1-\chi+\frac{\chi}{\ell-1}\sum_{k=1}^{\ell-1}\eta^{\Delta_{i,j,k}}\right)\right]$$

where

$$\Delta_{i,j,k} = \left\lvert(2^k-1)\otimes i\right\rvert - \left\lvert(2^k-1)\otimes j\right\rvert \qquad \eta = \frac{\mu}{1-\mu}$$

and $\eta^0 \equiv 1$ even when $\eta = 0$.

In the next section we develop a congruence transformation which diagonalizes the matrix M of probabilities.

3 A SPARSE LOWER TRIANGULAR CONGRUENCE TRANSFORM

Let L be lower triangular with unit diagonal. Since we want LML^T to be diagonal, all off-diagonal terms need to be zero. For term $\left(LML^T\right)_{s,t}$ with $s > t$, this requires that

$$\left(LML^T\right)_{s,t} = 0 = \sum_{i=0}^{s}\sum_{j=0}^{t} L_{s,i}M_{i,j}L_{t,j} = \sum_{i=0}^{s}\left(\sum_{j=0}^{t-1} L_{s,i}M_{i,j}L_{t,j} + L_{s,i}M_{i,t}\right)$$

$$= \sum_{i=0}^{s-1}\left(\sum_{j=0}^{t-1} L_{s,i}M_{i,j}L_{t,j} + L_{s,i}M_{i,t}\right) + \sum_{j=0}^{t-1} M_{s,j}L_{t,j} + M_{s,t}$$

so

$$\sum_{i=0}^{s-1} L_{s,i}\left(\sum_{j=0}^{t-1} L_{t,j}M_{i,j} + M_{i,t}\right) + \sum_{j=0}^{t-1} L_{t,j}M_{s,j} = -M_{s,t}\,.$$

Let

$$A_{i,t} = \sum_{j=0}^{t-1} L_{t,j}M_{i,j} + M_{i,t} \qquad\qquad \sum_{i=0}^{s-1} L_{s,i}A_{i,t} = -A_{s,t}\,.$$

Thus, the L values can be computed sequentially by the algorithm given below. This algorithm roughly follows ideas found in Tcwarson (1973). Notice that no value of L is used before it is defined.

1. Set $k = 0$.
2. For $t = k$ to $2^\ell\ 1$

$$A_{t,k} = \sum_{j=0}^{k-1} L_{k,j}M_{t,j} + M_{t,k}$$

3. For $s = k$ to 0

$$L_{k+1,s} = \begin{cases} -\dfrac{\left(A_{k+1,s} + \sum\limits_{i=s+1}^{k} L_{k+1,i}A_{i,s}\right)}{A_{s,s}} & A_{s,s} \neq 0 \\ 0 & \end{cases}$$

4. Set k to k+1. If $k < 2^\ell - 1$ go to 2, else stop

For example, going through the algorithm we get:

1. Set $k = 0$.

2. For $t = k$ to $2^{\ell} - 1$

$$A_{t,k} = \sum_{j=0}^{k-1} L_{k,j} M_{t,j} + M_{t,k}$$

With k=0, this gives

$$A_{0,0} = M_{0,0}, \quad A_{1,0} = M_{1,0}, \quad A_{2,0} = M_{2,0}, \text{ etc.}$$

3. For $s = k$ to 0

$$L_{k+1,s} = \begin{cases} -\dfrac{\left(A_{k+1,s} + \sum\limits_{i=s+1}^{k} L_{k+1,i} A_{i,s}\right)}{A_{s,s}} & A_{s,s} \neq 0 \\ 0 \end{cases}$$

With k=0 and $A_{0,0} \neq 0$, this gives:

$$L_{1,0} = -\frac{A_{1,0}}{A_{0,0}}$$

4. Set k to k+1. If $k < 2^{\ell} - 1$ go to 2, else stop.

Now k is 1 and we return to step 2.

2. For $t = k$ to $2^{\ell} - 1$

$$A_{t,k} = \sum_{j=0}^{k-1} L_{k,j} M_{t,j} + M_{t,k}$$

This gives:

$$A_{1,1} = L_{1,0} M_{1,0} + M_{1,1}, \quad A_{2,1} = L_{1,0} M_{2,0} + M_{2,1}, \text{ etc.}$$

And so on.

The above process is tedious and of little practical value except to gain insights into the structure of L. With such insights, the following result was obtained that shows how to compute L directly.

Theorem 1: *(L Computation)*

Cases (1)-(7) define L such that LML^{T} is diagonal. Compute these values in the order of cases and within each case, in the order specified. Once an element is computed, later cases giving the same element subscripts are to be ignored.

1. $L_{s,t} = 0 \qquad s < t$

2. $L_{s,s} = 1$

3. $L_{s,t} = 0 \qquad s > t,\ t \notin \left\{0, 2^{k}, 2^{k} + 1 : k = 0, \ldots, 2^{\ell-1}\right\}$

4. Special cases

$$L_{1,0} = L_{3,1} = -\frac{(1+\eta)}{2} \qquad L_{2,1} = \frac{2\chi - \ell + 1}{\ell - 1}$$

$$L_{3,0} = \eta + \frac{\chi(1-\eta)^2}{2(\ell - 1)}$$

5. $s = 2^k \qquad k \geq 1$

$$L_{s,0} = \frac{\chi(1+\eta)}{(k-1)\chi - \ell + 1} \qquad L_{s,1} = -\frac{\chi}{(k-1)\chi - \ell + 1}$$

$$L_{s,2^{k-1}} = -\frac{k\chi - \ell + 1}{(k-1)\chi - \ell + 1} \qquad L_{s,t} = 0$$

6. $s = 2^k + 1 \qquad k \geq 1$

$$L_{s,0} = \frac{-\chi(1+\eta^2)}{2[(k-1)\chi - \ell + 1]} \qquad L_{s,1} = \frac{\chi(1+\eta)}{2[(k-1)\chi - \ell + 1]}$$

$$L_{s,2^k} = -\frac{(1+\eta)}{2} \qquad L_{s,2^{k-1}} = \frac{(1+\eta)(k\chi - \ell + 1)}{2[(k-1)\chi - \ell + 1]}$$

$$L_{s,2^{k-1}+1} = -\frac{k\chi - \ell + 1}{(k-1)\chi - \ell + 1} \qquad L_{s,t} = 0$$

7. $s \notin \{0, 2^k, 2^k + 1: k = 0, \ldots, 2^{\ell-1}\}$

(a) $t \in \{0,1\} \qquad L_{s,t} = \delta(s \otimes 1 = t) \sum_{h=1}^{|s|-1-t\otimes 1} \eta^h$

(b) $t \in \{2^k, 2^k + 1: k = 1, \ldots, 2^{\ell-1}\}$

$$m \equiv |s \otimes (2^k - 1)| \quad \text{where k satisfies} \quad t \otimes 2^k = 1$$

$$L_{s,t} = (-1)^{t \otimes 1} \delta(s \otimes 2^k \neq 0) \left[\sum_{h=0}^{m-1} \eta^h - \sum_{h=0}^{|s|-1-m-t\otimes 1} \eta^h \right]$$

(c) $L_{s,t} = 0$

The proof of Theorem 1 is in the Appendix. Figure 1 shows the lower triangular portion of the first 16 rows and columns of L for $\ell \geq 4$. The calculation order for L is important. For example, under Case (6), $L_{s,2^k}$ must be computed before $L_{s,2^{k-1}+1}$ since, for k=1, the former gives the correct value even though both sets of subscripts give $L_{s,2}$.

$$
\begin{bmatrix}
1 \\
-\dfrac{(1+\eta)}{2} & 1 \\
-\dfrac{\chi(1+\eta)}{\ell-1} & \dfrac{2\chi-\ell+1}{\ell-1} & 1 \\
\eta+\dfrac{\chi(1-\eta)^2}{2(\ell-1)} & -\dfrac{(1+\eta)}{2} & -\dfrac{(1+\eta)}{2} & 1 \\
\dfrac{\chi(1+\eta)}{\chi-\ell+1} & \dfrac{-\chi}{\chi-\ell+1} & -\dfrac{2\chi-\ell+1}{\chi-\ell+1} & 0 & 1 \\
-\dfrac{\chi(1+\eta^2)}{2(\chi-\ell+1)} & \dfrac{\chi(1+\eta)}{2(\chi-\ell+1)} & \dfrac{(1+\eta)(2\chi-\ell+1)}{2(\chi-\ell+1)} & -\dfrac{(2\chi-\ell+1)}{\chi-\ell+1} & -\dfrac{(1+\eta)}{2} & 1 \\
\eta & 0 & -1-\eta & 1 & 0 & -1 & 1 \\
0 & \eta & -\eta & 0 & \eta & -1-\eta & 0 & 1 \\
\dfrac{\chi(1+\eta)}{2\chi-\ell+1} & \dfrac{-\chi}{2\chi-\ell+1} & 0 & 0 & -\dfrac{(3\chi-\ell+1)}{2\chi-\ell+1} & 0 & 0 & 0 & 1 \\
-\dfrac{\chi(1+\eta^2)}{2(2\chi-\ell+1)} & \dfrac{\chi(1+\eta)}{2(2\chi-\ell+1)} & 0 & 0 & \dfrac{(1+\eta)(3\chi-\ell+1)}{2(2\chi-\ell+1)} & -\dfrac{(3\chi-\ell+1)}{2\chi-\ell+1} & 0 & 0 & -\dfrac{(1+\eta)}{2} & 1 \\
\eta & 0 & -1-\eta & 1 & 0 & 0 & 0 & 0 & 0 & -1 & 1 \\
0 & \eta & -\eta & 0 & 0 & 0 & 0 & 0 & \eta & -1-\eta & 0 & 1 \\
\eta & 0 & 0 & 0 & -1-\eta & 1 & 0 & 0 & 0 & -1 & 0 & 0 & 1 \\
0 & \eta & 0 & 0 & -\eta & 0 & 0 & 0 & \eta & -1-\eta & 0 & 0 & 0 & 1 \\
\eta+\eta^2 & 0 & -1-\eta-\eta^2 & 1+\eta & -\eta & 0 & 0 & 0 & \eta & -1-\eta & 0 & 0 & 0 & 0 & 1 \\
0 & \eta+\eta^2 & -\eta-\eta^2 & \eta & 0 & -\eta & 0 & 0 & \eta+\eta^2 & -1-\eta-\eta^2 & 0 & 0 & 0 & 0 & 0 & 1
\end{bmatrix}
$$

Figure 1. First 16 rows by 16 columns of matrix L $\left(\ell \geq 4\right)$.

It is of value to note the density of L. Consider first only the strictly lower triangular portion of L. For $\ell \geq 2$ we have the following upper bounds on the number of non-zero components (depending on the crossover rate, additional terms may become zero):

Rows 0-3:   6 non-zero components

For $k = 2,\dots,\ell-1$:

Row 2^k: 3 non-zero components (Case 5)

Row $2^k +1$:   5 non-zero components (Case 6)

For rows $s = 2^k +2$ to $2^{k+1} -1$:

1 non-zero component (Case 7a)

$$2\sum_{h=1}^{k}\delta\left(s \otimes 2^h \neq 0\right) \text{ non-zero components (Case 7b)}$$

-1 non-zero component (Case 7b explained below).

Case (7b) has that

$$m \equiv \left|s \otimes \left(2^k -1\right)\right|$$

$$L_{s,t} = (-1)^{t\otimes 1}\,\delta\left(s \otimes 2^k \neq 0\right)\left[\sum_{h=0}^{m-1}\eta^h - \sum_{h=0}^{|s|-1-m-t\otimes 1}\eta^h\right]$$

which is zero when the two sums cancel out. This happens when

$$2\left|s \otimes \left(2^k - 1\right)\right| = |s| - t \otimes 1.$$

For each s, this will occur at least once. If s is odd, then let $t = 2^k + 1$ where k gives $\left|s \otimes \left(2^k - 1\right)\right| = (|s| - 1)/2$. Similarly, if s is even, let $t = 2^k$ where k gives $\left|s \otimes \left(2^k - 1\right)\right| = |s|/2$. These t values will always satisfy $t \in \left\{2^k, 2^k + 1: k = 1,\ldots,2^{\ell-1}\right\}$ since $s \notin \left\{0, 2^k, 2^k + 1: k = 0,\ldots,2^{\ell-1}\right\}$ requires that $|s| \geq 2$ and, hence, that $t \geq 2$.

Collecting terms gives the maximum number of nonzero components below the diagonal as

$$6 + \sum_{k=2}^{\ell-1}\left(8 + \sum_{s=2^k+2}^{2^{k+1}-1} 2\sum_{h=1}^{k}\delta\left(s \otimes 2^h \neq 0\right)\right) = 6 + \sum_{k=2}^{\ell-1}\left(8 + \sum_{s=2^k+2}^{2^{k+1}-1}\left(2|s| - 2(s \otimes 1)\right)\right)$$

Substituting

$$\sum_{s=2^k+2}^{2^{k+1}-1}(s \otimes 1) = \frac{2^{k+1} - 2^k - 2}{2}$$

gives

$$6 + \sum_{k=2}^{\ell-1}\left(8 - \left(2^{k+1} - 2^k - 2\right) + 2\sum_{s=2^k+2}^{2^{k+1}-1}|s|\right) = 6 + \sum_{k=2}^{\ell-1}\left(10 - 2^{k+1} + 2^k + 2\sum_{s=2^k+2}^{2^{k+1}-1}|s|\right).$$

But

$$\sum_{s=2^k+2}^{2^{k+1}-1}|s| = \sum_{h=0}^{k}\binom{k}{h}(h+1) - 3 = 2^k - 3 + \sum_{h=0}^{k}\binom{k}{h}h = 2^k - 3 + k2^{k-1}$$

giving

$$6 + \sum_{k=2}^{\ell-1}\left(10 - 2^{k+1} + 2^k + 2\sum_{s=2^k+2}^{2^{k+1}-1}|s|\right) = 6 + \sum_{k=2}^{\ell-1}\left(10 - 2^{k+1} + 2^k + 2\left(2^k - 3 + k2^{k-1}\right)\right)$$

$$= 6 + \sum_{k=2}^{\ell-1}\left(4 + (k+1)2^k\right) = 6 + 4(\ell - 2) + 2^\ell - 4 + (\ell - 2)2^\ell = (\ell - 1)\left(2^\ell + 4\right) - 2.$$

Adding in the 2^ℓ diagonal components gives an upper bound on the total number of non-zero components of L as $\ell\left(2^\ell + 4\right) - 6$. Collecting the above results gives the following.

Theorem 2: *(Number of Nonzero Components of L)*

L has, at most, $\ell\left(2^\ell + 4\right) - 6$ non-zero components. At most, $(\ell - 1)\left(2^\ell + 4\right) - 2$ are below the diagonal. The density of non-zero components is asymptotically $O\left(\ell / 2^\ell\right)$.

In certain situations it is of value to know the row sums of L. Row sums of L are given below.

Theorem 3:

$$(L1)_s = \begin{cases} 1 & s = 0 \\[4pt] \dfrac{1-\eta}{2} & s = 1 \\[6pt] -\dfrac{\chi(1-\eta)}{(k-1)\chi - \ell + 1} & s = 2^k, \quad k \geq 1 \\[8pt] \dfrac{1-\eta}{2}(L1)_{2^k} & s = 2^k + 1, \quad k \geq 1 \\[6pt] 0 & \text{otherwise} \end{cases}$$

Proof:

Case 1: $(L1)_0$ is 1 by definition.

Case 2: $(L1)_1 = 1 - \dfrac{1+\eta}{2} = \dfrac{1-\eta}{2}$

Case 3: $(L1)_2 = 1 - \dfrac{\chi(1+\eta)}{\ell-1} + \dfrac{2\chi - \ell + 1}{\ell-1}$

$$= \frac{\ell-1}{\ell-1} - \frac{\chi(1+\eta)}{\ell-1} + \frac{2\chi - \ell + 1}{\ell-1} = \frac{\chi(1-\eta)}{\ell-1}$$

Case 4: $(L1)_3 = 1 + \eta + \dfrac{\chi(1-\eta)^2}{2(\ell-1)} - 2\dfrac{1+\eta}{2} = \dfrac{\chi(1-\eta)^2}{2(\ell-1)}.$

Case 5: $(L1)_{2^k} = 1 + \dfrac{\chi(1+\eta)}{(k-1)\chi - \ell + 1} - \dfrac{\chi}{(k-1)\chi - \ell + 1} - \dfrac{k\chi - \ell + 1}{(k-1)\chi - \ell + 1}$

$$= -\frac{\chi(1-\eta)}{(k-1)\chi - \ell + 1}.$$

Case 6: $(L1)_{2^k+1}$

$$= 1 + \frac{-\chi(1+\eta^2)}{2[(k-1)\chi - \ell + 1]} + \frac{\chi(1+\eta)}{2[(k-1)\chi - \ell + 1]} - \frac{(1+\eta)}{2}$$

$$+ \frac{(1+\eta)(k\chi - \ell + 1)}{2[(k-1)\chi - \ell + 1]} - \frac{k\chi - \ell + 1}{(k-1)\chi - \ell + 1}$$

$$= -\frac{\chi(1-\eta)^2}{2[(k-1)\chi - \ell + 1]}$$

Case 7: Let $s \notin \{0, 2^k, 2^k + 1: k = 0, \ldots, 2^{\ell-1}\}$. Then

$$(\mathrm{L1})_s = 1 + \delta(s \otimes 1 = 0)\sum_{h=1}^{|s|-1}\eta^h + \delta(s \otimes 1 = 1)\sum_{h=1}^{|s|-2}\eta^h$$

$$+ \sum_{k=1}^{\ell-1}\left(\delta(s \otimes 2^k \neq 0)\left[\sum_{h=0}^{|s\otimes(2^k-1)|-1}\eta^h - \sum_{h=0}^{|s|-1-|s\otimes(2^k-1)|}\eta^h \right]\right)$$

$$- \sum_{k=1}^{\ell-1}\left(\delta(s \otimes 2^k \neq 0)\left[\sum_{h=0}^{|s\otimes(2^k-1)|-1}\eta^h - \sum_{h=0}^{|s|-2-|s\otimes(2^k-1)|}\eta^h \right]\right)$$

If s is even then

$$(\mathrm{L1})_s = 1 + \sum_{h=1}^{|s|-1}\eta^h + \sum_{k=1}^{\ell-1}\left(\delta(s \otimes 2^k \neq 0)\left[\sum_{h=0}^{|s\otimes(2^k-1)|-1}\eta^h - \sum_{h=0}^{|s|-1-|s\otimes(2^k-1)|}\eta^h \right]\right)$$

$$- \sum_{k=1}^{\ell-1}\left(\delta(s \otimes 2^k \neq 0)\left[\sum_{h=0}^{|s\otimes(2^k-1)|-1}\eta^h - \sum_{h=0}^{|s|-2-|s\otimes(2^k-1)|}\eta^h \right]\right)$$

Using Lemma A2 from the Appendix gives

$$(\mathrm{L1})_s = 1 + \sum_{h=1}^{|s|-1}\eta^h - \eta^{|s|-1}\sum_{k=1}^{\ell-1}\left(\delta(s \otimes 2^k \neq 0)\eta^{-|s\otimes(2^k-1)|}\right)$$

$$(\mathrm{L1})_s = 1 + \frac{1-\eta^{|s|}}{1-\eta} - 1 - \frac{\eta^{|s|}-1}{\eta-1} = 0$$

Similarly, if s is odd

$$(\mathrm{L1})_s = 1 + \sum_{h=1}^{|s|-?}\eta^h - \eta^{|s|-1}\sum_{k=1}^{\ell-1}\left(\delta(s \otimes 2^k \neq 0)\eta^{-|s\otimes(2^k-1)|}\right)$$

$$(\mathrm{L1})_s = 1 + \frac{1-\eta^{|s|-1}}{1-\eta} - 1 - \eta^{|s|-1}\frac{1-\eta^{-|s|-1}}{\eta-1} = 0.$$

4 APPLICATIONS

In this section we give some uses of L. The first results give properties of M.

4.1 DIAGONALIZED FORM AND RANK OF M

The first result uses L to diagonalize M.

Theorem 4: *(Diagonalized form of M)*

Let $D = LML^T$. Then

$$D_{s,s} = (1-\mu)^{\ell}\begin{cases} 1 & s = 0 \\[2mm] -\dfrac{(1-\eta)^2}{4} & s = 1 \\[4mm] -\dfrac{\chi(1-\eta)^2}{[(k-1)\chi - \ell + 1]}\left[\dfrac{k\chi}{\ell-1} - 1\right] & s = 2^k,\ \ k \geq 1 \\[4mm] \dfrac{\chi(1-\eta)^4}{4[(k-1)\chi - \ell + 1]}\left[\dfrac{k\chi}{\ell-1} - 1\right] & s = 2^k + 1,\ \ k \geq 1 \\[4mm] 0 & \text{otherwise} \end{cases}$$

The proof of this Theorem is in the Appendix. Notice that D has only 2ℓ non-zero components. This fact is used later to greatly simplify a quadratic equation involving M.

An immediate result of Theorem 4 follows from the fact that L is non-singular.

Corollary 5: *(Rank of M)*
>   The rank of M is:
>   a. 2ℓ when $\chi > 0$ and $\mu \neq 0.5$;
>   b.   2 when $\chi = 0$ and $\mu \neq 0.5$;
>   c.   1 when $\mu = 0.5$.

4.2 SIMPLIFYING THE GA FIXED POINT PROBLEM

Let z^k be a vector whose components are the proportion of strings in the kth population. The simple GA moves from one population to another stochastically. The expected behavior can be modeled (Vose, 1993) by

$$z^{k+1} = G_1(z^k) = \mathcal{M}\left(\frac{Fz^k}{1'Fz^k}\right)$$

where

$$\mathcal{M}(y) \equiv \begin{pmatrix} y^T P_0^T M P_0 y \\ y^T P_1^T M P_1 y \\ \cdot \\ \cdot \\ \cdot \\ y^T P_{2^\ell - 1}^T M P_{2^\ell - 1} y \end{pmatrix}.$$

A fixed point of $G_1(\ )$ is then $z = G_1(z) = \mathcal{M}\left(\dfrac{Fz^k}{1'Fz^k}\right)$. Alternatively, z is a fixed point of

$G_1(\ )$ if and only if (see Vose 1993) $Fz/(1'Fz)^2$ is a fixed point of $G_2(x) = F\mathcal{M}(x)$. Working with $G_2(\ )$ is more convenient since we avoid the division in $G_1(\ )$. Note that each row of $x = G_2(x) = F\mathcal{M}(x)$ is a quadratic equation having $2^\ell(2^\ell + 1)/2$ quadratic terms. L can be used to simplify one of these.

Component k of $x = F\mathcal{M}(x)$ is

$$x_k = F_{k,k}x^T P_k^T M P_k x = F_{k,k}x^T P_k^T L^{-1} D (L^T)^{-1} P_k x.$$

Let

$$y(k) = (L^T)^{-1} P_k x.$$

Then

$$1_k^T P_k L^T y(k) = 1_0^T L^T y(k) = F_{k,k} y(k)^T D y(k).$$

This quadratic form has no cross terms and only 2ℓ squared terms. This may prove useful in exploring properties of $G(\ )$.

5 SUMMARY AND FUTURE DIRECTIONS

A sparse lower triangular matrix, L, is given that diagonalizes the single GA mixing matrix. L is sparse and trivially inverted. This congruence transform was used to show the rank of M under various parameter choices. Also, the GA fixed-point problem involves quadratic equations having $2^\ell(2^\ell + 1)/2$ terms. L can be used to simplify one of these to a quadratic form having no cross terms and only 2ℓ squared terms which may prove useful.

Future work will focus on using L to gain insights to the GA fixed-point problem. Also, diagonalizing M reveals that M has an underlying structure that has not clearly understood. M has low rank and can be represented by the product of three sparse matrices (L^{-1}, D and $(L^T)^{-1}$). Furthermore, D has non-zero values having the following relationship

$$D_{i+1,i+1} = -\frac{(1-\eta)^2}{4} D_{i,i} \qquad i \in \{0, 2^k : k \geq 1\}.$$

Furthermore

$$D_{i,i} = \frac{(1-\mu)^\ell \chi (1-\eta)^2}{\ell - 1}\, \frac{k\chi - \ell + 1}{k\chi \quad \chi - \ell \, | \, 1} \qquad i = 2^k, \quad k \geq 1.$$

What these structures signify is not understood.

Another area of future work would be to determine a general form of L corresponding to the general form of a mixing matrix given by Vose and Wright (1995).

References

A. Nix & M. D. Vose. (1992) Modeling Genetic Algorithms with Markov Chains. *Annals of Mathematics and Artificial Intelligence*, 5, 79-88.

R. P. Tewarson. (1973) *Sparse Matrices*, New York: Academic Press.

M. D. Vose. (1993) Modeling Simple Genetic Algorithms., *Foundations of Genetic Algorithms*, II, 63-73, San Mateo, CA: Morgan Kaufmann.

M. D. Vose & G. E. Liepins. (1991) Punctuated Equilibria in Genetic Search. *Complex Systems*, 5, 31-44.

M. D. Vose & A. H. Wright. (1995) Simple Genetic Algorithms with Linear Fitness. *Evolutionary Computation*, 2(4): 347-368.

Appendix

The proofs in this section will be sketched. They are not hard, just tedious. A few preliminary results will help in our proofs. The first results of Lemma A1 follow easily from the definition of M.

Lemma A1: *(Values of M)*
The following expressions hold:

$$M_{s,s} = (1-\mu)^\ell \eta^{|s|} \qquad M_{0,2^v} = (1-\mu)^\ell \frac{1 \pm \eta}{2}$$

$$M_{0,2^v+1} = (1-\mu)^\ell \frac{(1+\eta^2)(\ell-1) - v\chi(1-\eta)^2}{2(\ell-1)}, \quad v \geq 1$$

$$M_{2^v,2^k} = (1-\mu)^\ell \left(\eta + \frac{(k-v)\chi(\eta-1)^2}{2(\ell-1)} \right), \quad k \geq v$$

$$M_{2^v,2^k+1} = (1-\mu)^\ell \frac{(1+\eta)\eta}{2}, \quad k \geq v$$

$$M_{2^v,2^k+1} = \frac{(1-\mu)^\ell}{2} \left(\eta + \eta^2 + \frac{\chi(v-k)(\eta^3 - \eta^2 - \eta + 1)}{\ell-1} \right), \quad k \leq v$$

$$M_{2^v+1,2^k+1} = (1-\mu)^\ell \left(\eta^2 + \frac{(k-v)\chi\eta(\eta-1)^2}{2(\ell-1)} \right), \quad k \geq v$$

The proofs of Theorems 1 and 2 are aided by noting that, for $T = \left\{ 0, 2^k, 2^k + 1 : k = 0, \ldots, 2^{\ell-1} \right\}$, column t of LM looks like

$$
\left[
\begin{array}{l}
\text{Row} \\[4pt]
0 \qquad M_{0,t} \\[6pt]
1 \qquad M_{1,t} - \dfrac{(1+\eta)}{2} M_{0,t} \\[10pt]
2 \qquad M_{2,t} - \dfrac{\chi(1+\eta)}{\ell-1} M_{0,t} + \dfrac{2\chi - \ell + 1}{\ell-1} M_{1,t} \\[10pt]
3 \qquad M_{3,t} + \left(\eta + \dfrac{\chi(1-\eta)^2}{2(\ell-1)}\right) M_{0,t} - \dfrac{(1+\eta)}{2} M_{1,t} - \dfrac{(1+\eta)}{2} M_{2,t} \\[10pt]
s = 2^k \qquad M_{s,t} + \dfrac{\chi(1+\eta)}{(k-1)\chi - \ell + 1} M_{0,t} - \dfrac{\chi}{(k-1)\chi - \ell + 1} M_{1,t} - \dfrac{k\chi - \ell + 1}{(k-1)\chi - \ell + 1} M_{s/2,t} \\[12pt]
s = 2^k + 1 \qquad M_{s,t} - \dfrac{\chi(1+\eta^2)}{2[(k-1)\chi - \ell + 1]} M_{0,t} + \dfrac{\chi(1+\eta)}{2[(k-1)\chi - \ell + 1]} M_{1,t} + \dfrac{(1+\eta)(k\chi - \ell + 1)}{2[(k-1)\chi - \ell + 1]} M_{2^{k-1},t} \\[10pt]
\qquad\qquad - \dfrac{k\chi - \ell + 1}{(k-1)\chi - \ell + 1} M_{2^{k-1}+1,t} - \dfrac{(1+\eta)}{2} M_{s-1,t} \\[12pt]
\qquad\qquad M_{s,t} + \delta(s \otimes 1 = 0) M_{0,t} \displaystyle\sum_{h=1}^{|s|-1} \eta^h + \delta(s \otimes 1 = 1) M_{1,t} \displaystyle\sum_{h=1}^{|s|-2} \eta^h \\[10pt]
s \notin T \qquad + \displaystyle\sum_{k=1}^{hi(s)} \delta(s \otimes 2^k \neq 0) \left[\sum_{h=0}^{|s\otimes(2^k-1)|-1} \eta^h - \sum_{h=0}^{|s|-1-|s\otimes(2^k-1)|} \eta^h \right] M_{2^k,t} \\[10pt]
\qquad\qquad - \displaystyle\sum_{k=1}^{hi(s)} \delta(s \otimes 2^k \neq 0) \left[\sum_{h=0}^{|s\otimes(2^k-1)|-1} \eta^h - \sum_{h=0}^{|s|-2-|s\otimes(2^k-1)|} \eta^h \right] M_{2^k+1,t}
\end{array}
\right]
$$

We start by showing that elements in the rows $s \notin T$ are zero valued. The following simple result helps.

Lemma A2:

The following identity holds for any s, non-negative a and $\eta \neq 0$:

$$
\sum_{k=1}^{a} \delta(s \otimes 2^k \neq 0)\, \eta^{-|s\otimes(2^k-1)|} =
$$

$$
\begin{cases}
\eta^{-|1\otimes s|} \displaystyle\sum_{k=1}^{|s\otimes(2^{a+1}-1)|-|1\otimes s|} \dfrac{1}{\eta^{k-1}} = \dfrac{\eta^{-|1\otimes s|} - \eta^{-|s\otimes(2^{a+1}-1)|}}{1 - \eta^{-1}} & \left| s \otimes \left(2^{a+1} - 1\right) \right| \geq 1 + |1 \otimes s| \\[18pt]
0 & \text{Otherwise}
\end{cases}
$$

Lemma A3:

For $s \notin T$, $(LM)_{s,t} = 0$.

Proof (sketch):

When $\mu = 0.5$, $L_{s,t} = 0$ for $s \notin T$ and so the result is trivial. Assume in the following that $\mu \neq 0.5$. The proof will be by induction on $|s| - |s \otimes 1|$.

Part (a):

Clearly, since $s \notin T$, $|s| - |s \otimes 1| \geq 2$. We start with the case where s is even and $|s| = 2$. The case where s is odd and $|s| - |s \otimes 1| = 2$ follows similarly. Let $s = 2^x + 2^y, y > x > 0$. Substituting, gives

$$(LM)_{s,t} = M_{s,t} + \eta M_{0,t} - [1 + \eta] M_{2^x,t} + M_{2^x+1,t} - M_{2^y+1,t}$$

$$\frac{2}{(1-\mu)^\ell} \left(M_{2^y+1,t} + [1+\eta] M_{2^x,t} - \eta M_{0,t} - M_{2^x+1,t} \right)$$

$$= \eta^2 \left(1 - \chi + \frac{\chi}{\ell-1} \sum_{k=1}^{\ell-1} \eta^{-\Delta_{2^y+1,t,k}} \right) + \eta^{|t|} \left(1 - \chi + \frac{\chi}{\ell-1} \sum_{k=1}^{\ell-1} \eta^{\Delta_{2^y+1,t,k}} \right)$$

$$+ [1+\eta]\eta \left(1 - \chi + \frac{\chi}{\ell-1} \sum_{k=1}^{\ell-1} \eta^{-\Delta_{2^x,t,k}} \right) + [1+\eta]\eta^{|t|} \left(1 - \chi + \frac{\chi}{\ell-1} \sum_{k=1}^{\ell-1} \eta^{\Delta_{2^x,t,k}} \right)$$

$$- \eta \left(1 - \chi + \frac{\chi}{\ell-1} \sum_{k=1}^{\ell-1} \eta^{-\Delta_{0,t,k}} \right) - \eta\eta^{|t|} \left(1 - \chi + \frac{\chi}{\ell-1} \sum_{k=1}^{\ell-1} \eta^{\Delta_{0,t,k}} \right)$$

$$- \eta^2 \left(1 - \chi + \frac{\chi}{\ell-1} \sum_{k=1}^{\ell-1} \eta^{-\Delta_{2^x+1,t,k}} \right) - \eta^{|t|} \left(1 - \chi + \frac{\chi}{\ell-1} \sum_{k=1}^{\ell-1} \eta^{\Delta_{2^x+1,t,k}} \right)$$

$$= \eta^2 \left(1 - \chi + \frac{\chi}{\ell-1} \left[\sum_{k=1}^{\ell-1} \eta^{-\Delta_{2^y+1,t,k}} + [1+\eta]\eta^{-1} \sum_{k=1}^{\ell-1} \eta^{-\Delta_{2^x,t,k}} - \eta^{-1} \sum_{k=1}^{\ell-1} \eta^{-\Delta_{0,t,k}} - \sum_{k=1}^{\ell-1} \eta^{-\Delta_{2^x+1,t,k}} \right] \right)$$

$$+ \eta^{|t|} \left(1 - \chi + \frac{\chi}{\ell-1} \left[\sum_{k=1}^{\ell-1} \eta^{\Delta_{2^y+1,t,k}} + [1+\eta]\sum_{k=1}^{\ell-1} \eta^{\Delta_{2^x,t,k}} - \eta \sum_{k=1}^{\ell-1} \eta^{\Delta_{0,t,k}} - \sum_{k=1}^{\ell-1} \eta^{\Delta_{2^x+1,t,k}} \right] \right)$$

The term in the first bracket expands to:

$$\sum_{k=1}^{\ell-1} \eta^{-\Delta_{1+2^y,t,k}} + [1+\eta]\eta^{-1} \sum_{k=1}^{\ell-1} \eta^{-\Delta_{2^x,t,k}} - \eta^{-1} \sum_{k=1}^{\ell-1} \eta^{-\Delta_{0,t,k}} - \sum_{k=1}^{\ell-1} \eta^{-\Delta_{2^x+1,t,k}}$$

$$= \sum_{k=1}^{\ell-1} \left[\eta^{-\Delta_{1+2^y,t,k}} + [1+\eta]\eta^{-1}\eta^{-\Delta_{2^x,t,k}} - \eta^{-1}\eta^{-\Delta_{0,t,k}} - \eta^{-\Delta_{2^x+1,t,k}} \right]$$

$$= \sum_{k=1}^{\ell-1} \eta^{-\Delta_{2^x+2^y,t,k}} \left[\begin{array}{l} \eta^{-\left|(2^h-1)\oplus(1+2^y)\right|+\left|(2^h-1)\oplus(2^x+2^y)\right|} + [1+\eta]\eta^{-1}\eta^{-\left|(2^h-1)\oplus 2^x\right|+\left|(2^h-1)\oplus(2^x+2^y)\right|} \\[2mm] -\eta^{-1}\eta^{\left|(2^h-1)\oplus(2^x+2^y)\right|} - \eta^{-\left|(2^h-1)\oplus(2^x+1)\right|+\left|(2^h-1)\oplus(2^x+2^y)\right|} \end{array} \right]$$

The following cases hold for the term in the brackets:

$$k \le x: \quad \eta^{-1} + [1+\eta]\eta^{-1} - \eta^{-1} - \eta^{-1} = 1$$

$$x < k \le y: \quad 1 + [1+\eta]\eta^{-1} - \eta^{-1}\eta^{1} - \eta^{-1} = 1$$

$$k > y: \quad 1 + [1+\eta]\eta^{-1}\eta^{1} - \eta^{-1}\eta^{2} - 1 = 1$$

Using a similar approach

$$\frac{2}{(1-\mu)^\ell}\left(M_{2^y+1,t} + [1+\eta]M_{2^x,t} - \eta M_{0,t} - M_{2^x+1,t}\right)$$

$$= \eta^2\left(1-\chi + \frac{\chi}{\ell-1}\sum_{k=1}^{\ell-1}\eta^{-\Delta_{2^x+2^y,t,k}}\right) + \eta^{|t|}\left(1-\chi+\frac{\chi}{\ell-1}\sum_{k=1}^{\ell-1}\eta^{\Delta_{2^x+2^y,t,k}}\right)$$

$$= \frac{2}{(1-\mu)^\ell}\left(M_{2^x+2^y,t}\right)$$

which proves that

$$M_{s,t} + \eta M_{0,t} - [1+\eta]M_{2^x,t} + M_{2^x+1,t} - M_{2^y+1,t} = 0.$$

Part (b):

Now assume that $(LM)_{s,t} = 0$ for all rows where $\left|s\right| - \left|s\otimes 1\right| = z$, $s \notin T$ and consider rows with index $s+2^v$, $v > hi(s)$, $s \notin T$. Row $s+2^v$ of LM has elements that look like:

$$(LM)_{2^v+s,t} = M_{2^v+s,t} + M_{s,t} - M_{s,t} + \delta(s\otimes 1 = 0)M_{0,t}\left(\sum_{h=1}^{|s|-1}\eta^h + \eta^{|s|}\right)$$

$$+ \delta(s\otimes 1 = 1)M_{1,t}\left(\sum_{h=1}^{|s|-2}\eta^h + \eta^{|s|-1}\right)$$

$$+ \sum_{k=1}^{hi(s)}\delta\left((2^v+s)\otimes 2^k \ne 0\right)\left[\sum_{h=0}^{\left|(2^v+s)\otimes(2^k-1)\right|-1}\eta^h - \sum_{h=0}^{\left|(2^v+s)\right|-1-\left|(2^v+s)\otimes(2^k-1)\right|}\eta^h\right]M_{2^k,t}$$

$$+ \left[\sum_{h=0}^{\left|(2^v+s)\otimes(2^v-1)\right|-1}\eta^h - \sum_{h=0}^{\left|(2^v+s)\right|-1-\left|(2^v+s)\otimes(2^v-1)\right|}\eta^h\right]M_{2^v,t}$$

$$-\sum_{k=1}^{hi(s)}\delta\left((2^v+s)\otimes 2^k\neq 0\right)\left[\sum_{h=0}^{\left|(2^v+s)\otimes(2^k-1)\right|-1}\eta^h \;-\sum_{h=0}^{\left|(2^v+s)\right|-2-\left|(2^v+s)\otimes(2^k-1)\right|}\eta^h\right]M_{2^k+1,t}$$

$$-\left[\sum_{h=0}^{\left|(2^v+s)\otimes(2^v-1)\right|-1}\eta^h \;-\sum_{h=0}^{\left|(2^v+s)\right|-2-\left|(2^v+s)\otimes(2^v-1)\right|}\eta^h\right]M_{2^v+1,t}$$

which simplifies to

$$(LM)_{2^v+s,t}=(LM)_{s,t}+M_{2^v+s,t}-M_{s,t}+\delta(s\otimes 1=0)M_{0,t}\,\eta^{|s|}+\delta(s\otimes 1=1)M_{1,t}\,\eta^{|s|-1}$$

$$+\sum_{k=1}^{hi(s)}\delta\left(s\otimes 2^k\neq 0\right)\left(\eta^{|s|-1-\left|s\otimes(2^k-1)\right|}M_{2^k+1,t}-\eta^{|s|-\left|s\otimes(2^k-1)\right|}M_{2^k,t}\right)$$

$$+\left[\frac{\eta-\eta^{|s|}}{1-\eta}\right]M_{2^v,t}-\left[\frac{1-\eta^{|s|}}{1-\eta}\right]M_{2^v+1,t}$$

We will now give intermediate results. First

$$\left[\frac{\eta-\eta^{|s|}}{1-\eta}\right]M_{2^v,t}-\left[\frac{1-\eta^{|s|}}{1-\eta}\right]M_{2^v+1,t}$$

$$=\frac{(1-\mu)^\ell}{2}\left[-\eta\left(\frac{\chi}{\ell-1}\sum_{k=1}^{\ell-1}\eta^{-\Delta_{2^v,t,k}}\right)-\eta^{|s|}(1-\chi)\eta-\eta^{|t|}(1-\chi)\atop -\eta^{|s|}\eta^{|t|}\left(\frac{\chi}{\ell-1}\sum_{k=1}^{\ell-1}\eta^{\Delta_{2^v,t,k}}\right)\right]$$

and, using Lemma A2

$$\frac{2}{(1-\mu)^\ell}\sum_{k=1}^{hi(s)}\delta\left(s\otimes 2^k\neq 0\right)\left(\eta^{|s|-1-\left|s\otimes(2^k-1)\right|}M_{2^k+1,t}-\eta^{|s|-\left|s\otimes(2^k-1)\right|}M_{2^k,t}\right)$$

$$=-\eta\eta^{|s|}\frac{\chi}{\ell-1}\left[\left[\eta^{-|1\otimes s|}-\eta^{-|s|}\right]\sum_{h=1}^{lo(s-s\otimes 1)}\eta^{\left|(2^h-1)\otimes t\right|}\atop +\sum_{h=lo(s-s\otimes 1)+1}^{hi(s)}\eta^{\left|(2^h-1)\otimes t\right|}\left[\eta^{-\left|s\otimes(2^h-1)\right|}-\eta^{-|s|}\right]\atop +\eta^{-1}\sum_{h=lo(s-s\otimes 1)+1}^{\ell-1}\eta^{\left|(2^h-1)\otimes t\right|}\left[\eta^{-|1\otimes s|}-\eta^{-\left|s\otimes(2^h-1)\right|}\right]\right]$$

$$-\eta^{|t|}(1-\chi)\left(\eta^{|s|-|1\otimes s|}-1\right)$$

which together give

$$\frac{2(\mathrm{LM})_{2^v+s,t}}{(1-\mu)^\ell}=\frac{2}{(1-\mu)^\ell}\left(\begin{array}{c}\mathrm{M}_{2^v+s,t}-\mathrm{M}_{s,t}\\[4pt]+\delta(s\otimes 1=0)\mathrm{M}_{0,t}\eta^{|s|}+\delta(s\otimes 1=1)\mathrm{M}_{1,t}\eta^{|s|-1}\end{array}\right)$$

$$-\eta\eta^{|s|}\frac{\chi}{\ell-1}\left[\begin{array}{c}\left[\eta^{-|1\otimes s|}-\eta^{-|s|}\right]\sum_{h=1}^{lo(s-s\otimes 1)}\eta^{|(2^h-1)\otimes t|}\\[8pt]+\sum_{h=lo(s-s\otimes 1)+1}^{hi(s)}\eta^{|(2^h-1)\otimes t|}\left[\eta^{-|s\otimes(2^h-1)|}-\eta^{-|s|}\right]\\[8pt]+\eta^{-1}\sum_{h=lo(s-s\otimes 1)+1}^{\ell-1}\eta^{|(2^h-1)\otimes t|}\left[\eta^{-|1\otimes s|}-\eta^{-|s\otimes(2^h-1)|}\right]\end{array}\right]$$

$$-\eta^{|t|}(1-\chi)\left(\eta^{|s|-|1\otimes s|}-1\right)-\eta\left(\frac{\chi}{\ell-1}\sum_{h=1}^{\ell-1}\eta^{-\Delta_{2^v,t,h}}\right)-\eta^{|s|}(1-\chi)\eta-\eta^{|t|}(1-\chi)$$

$$-\eta^{|s|}\eta^{|t|}\left(\frac{\chi}{\ell-1}\sum_{h=1}^{\ell-1}\eta^{\Delta_{2^v,t,h}}\right)$$

At this point, it is easier to consider two cases, the case for s even and s odd and then to expand and collect the terms in a manner similar to that done in Part (a). This gives

$$\frac{2(\mathrm{LM})_{2^v+s,t}}{(1-\mu)^\ell}=-\eta\eta^{|s|}\frac{\chi}{\ell-1}\Big[$$

$$-\eta^{-1}\sum_{h=1}^{\ell-1}\eta^{-\Delta_{0,t,h}}-\eta^{-1}\eta^{|t|}\sum_{h=1}^{\ell-1}\eta^{\Delta_{0,t,h}}-\sum_{h=1}^{\ell-1}\eta^{-\Delta_{s+2^v,t,h}}-\eta^{-1}\eta^{-|s|}\eta^{|t|}\sum_{h=1}^{\ell-1}\eta^{\Delta_{s+2^v,t,h}}$$

$$+\eta^{-1}\sum_{h=1}^{\ell-1}\eta^{-\Delta_{s,t,h}}+\eta^{-1}\eta^{-|s|}\eta^{|t|}\sum_{h=1}^{\ell-1}\eta^{\Delta_{s,t,h}}\left[1-\eta^{-|s|}\right]\sum_{h=1}^{lo(s)}\eta^{|(2^h-1)\otimes t|}$$

$$+\sum_{h=lo(s)+1}^{hi(s)}\eta^{|(2^h-1)\otimes t|}\left[\eta^{-|s\otimes(2^h-1)|}-\eta^{-|s|}\right]+\eta^{-1}\sum_{h=lo(s)+1}^{\ell-1}\eta^{|(2^h-1)\otimes t|}\left[1-\eta^{-|s\otimes(2^h-1)|}\right]$$

$$+\eta^{-|s|}\sum_{h=1}^{\ell-1}\eta^{-\Delta_{2^v,t,h}}+\eta^{-1}\eta^{|t|}\sum_{h=1}^{\ell-1}\eta^{\Delta_{2^v,t,h}}\Big]$$

Focus on the term in brackets. Converting exponents to deltas and pulling together similar sums gives four different partial sums.

$$1]: \quad -\eta^{-1}\sum_{h=1}^{\ell-1}\eta^{-\Delta_{0,t,h}} +\left[1-\eta^{-|s|}\right]\sum_{h=1}^{lo(s)}\eta^{-\Delta_{0,t,h}} -\eta^{-|s|}\sum_{h=lo(s)+1}^{hi(s)}\eta^{-\Delta_{0,t,h}}$$

$$+\eta^{-1}\sum_{h=lo(s)+1}^{\ell-1}\eta^{-\Delta_{0,t,h}} +\eta^{-|s|}\sum_{h=1}^{v}\eta^{-\Delta_{0,t,h}} +\eta^{-|s|}\eta^{-1}\sum_{h=v+1}^{\ell-1}\eta^{-\Delta_{0,t,h}}$$

$$2]: \quad -\eta^{-1}\eta^{|t|}\sum_{h=1}^{\ell-1}\eta^{\Delta_{0,t,h}} +\eta^{-1}\eta^{|t|}\sum_{h=1}^{v}\eta^{\Delta_{0,t,h}} +\eta^{|t|}\sum_{h=v+1}^{\ell-1}\eta^{\Delta_{0,t,h}}$$

$$3]: \quad -\sum_{h=1}^{v}\eta^{-\Delta_{s,t,h}} -\eta^{-1}\sum_{h=v+1}^{\ell-1}\eta^{-\Delta_{s,t,h}} +\eta^{-1}\sum_{h=1}^{\ell-1}\eta^{-\Delta_{s,t,h}} +\sum_{h=lo(s)+1}^{hi(s)}\eta^{-\Delta_{s,t,h}}$$

$$-\eta^{-1}\sum_{h=lo(s)+1}^{\ell-1}\eta^{-\Delta_{s,t,h}}$$

$$4]: \quad -\eta^{-1}\eta^{-|s|}\eta^{|t|}\sum_{h=1}^{v}\eta^{\Delta_{s,t,h}} -\eta^{-|s|}\eta^{|t|}\sum_{h=v+1}^{\ell-1}\eta^{\Delta_{s,t,h}} +\eta^{-1}\eta^{-|s|}\eta^{|t|}\sum_{h=1}^{\ell-1}\eta^{\Delta_{s,t,h}}$$

These further simplify to:

$$-\eta^{-1}\sum_{h=1}^{lo(s)}\eta^{-\Delta_{0,t,h}} +\sum_{h=1}^{lo(s)}\eta^{-\Delta_{0,t,h}} +\eta^{-|s|}\sum_{h=hi(s)+1}^{v}\eta^{-\Delta_{0,t,h}} +\eta^{-|s|}\eta^{-1}\sum_{h=v+1}^{\ell-1}\eta^{-\Delta_{0,t,h}}$$

$$+\eta^{|t|}\left(1-\eta^{-1}\right)\sum_{h=v+1}^{\ell-1}\eta^{\Delta_{0,t,h}}$$

$$-\sum_{h=1}^{lo(s)}\eta^{-\Delta_{0,t,h}} -\eta^{-|s|}\sum_{h=hi(s)+1}^{v}\eta^{-\Delta_{0,t,h}} -\eta^{-1}\eta^{-|s|}\sum_{h=v+1}^{\ell-1}\eta^{-\Delta_{0,t,h}} +\eta^{-1}\sum_{h=1}^{lo(s)}\eta^{-\Delta_{0,t,h}}$$

$$+\left(\eta^{-1}-1\right)\eta^{|t|}\sum_{h=v+1}^{\ell-1}\eta^{\Delta_{0,t,h}}$$

which clearly give a sum of zero.

$\square$

Proof of Theorem 1:

We show that the off diagonal elements of LML^{T} are zero. Each case is considered in turn. The following six cases are true due to a direct application of Lemma A3.

(a) Row 0 of LM times column $x \notin T$ of L^{T}.

(b) Row 2^{k} of LM times column $x \notin T$ of L^{T}.

(c) Row $2^{v}+1 \quad (v \geq 2)$ of LM times column $x \notin T$ of L^{T}.

(d) Row 1 of **LM** times column $x \notin T$ of $\mathbf{L}^T$.

(e) Row 2 of **LM** times column $x \notin T$ of $\mathbf{L}^T$.

(f) Row 3 of **LM** times column $x \notin T$ of $\mathbf{L}^T$.

(g) Row 0 of **LM** times column 1 of $\mathbf{L}^T$:

$$M_{0,1} - \frac{(1+\eta)}{2} M_{0,0} = (1-\mu)^\ell \frac{1+\eta}{2} - \frac{(1+\eta)}{2}(1-\mu)^\ell = 0.$$

(h) Row 0 of **LM** times column 2 of $\mathbf{L}^T$:

$$M_{0,2} - \frac{\chi(1+\eta)}{\ell-1} M_{0,0} + \frac{2\chi - \ell + 1}{\ell-1} M_{0,1}$$

$$= (1-\mu)^\ell \frac{1+\eta}{2} - \frac{\chi(1+\eta)}{\ell-1}(1-\mu)^\ell + \frac{2\chi-\ell+1}{\ell-1}(1-\mu)^\ell \frac{1+\eta}{2}$$

$$= (1-\mu)^\ell \frac{1+\eta}{2}\left[1 - \frac{2\chi}{\ell-1} + \frac{2\chi-\ell+1}{\ell-1}\right] = 0.$$

(i) Row 0 of **LM** times column 3 of $\mathbf{L}^T$:

$$M_{0,3} + \left(\eta + \frac{\chi(1-\eta)^2}{2(\ell-1)}\right) M_{0,0} - \frac{(1+\eta)}{2} M_{0,1} - \frac{(1+\eta)}{2} M_{0,2}$$

$$= (1-\mu)^\ell \frac{1 + \eta^2 - \dfrac{\chi(\eta-1)^2}{\ell-1}}{2} + \left(\eta + \frac{\chi(1-\eta)^2}{2(\ell-1)}\right)(1-\mu)^\ell$$

$$- \frac{(1+\eta)}{2}(1-\mu)^\ell \frac{1+\eta}{2} - \frac{(1+\eta)}{2}(1-\mu)^\ell \frac{1+\eta}{2}$$

$$= \frac{(1-\mu)^\ell}{2}\left[1 + \eta^2 - \frac{\chi(\eta-1)^2}{\ell-1} + 2\eta + \frac{\chi(1-\eta)^2}{\ell-1} - \frac{(1+\eta)^2}{2} - \frac{(1+\eta)^2}{2}\right]$$

$$= \frac{(1-\mu)^\ell}{2}\left[1 + \eta^2 + 2\eta - 1 - 2\eta - \eta^2\right] = 0.$$

(j) Row 0 of **LM** times column $t = 2^v$ $(v \geq 2)$ of $\mathbf{L}^T$:

$$M_{0,t} + \frac{\chi(1+\eta)}{(v-1)\chi - \ell + 1} M_{0,0} - \frac{\chi}{(v-1)\chi - \ell + 1} M_{0,1} - \frac{v\chi - \ell + 1}{(v-1)\chi - \ell + 1} M_{0,t/2}$$

$$= (1-\mu)^\ell \frac{1+\eta}{2} + \frac{\chi(1+\eta)}{(v-1)\chi - \ell + 1}(1-\mu)^\ell - \frac{\chi}{(v-1)\chi - \ell + 1}(1-\mu)^\ell \frac{1+\eta}{2}$$

$$- \frac{v\chi - \ell + 1}{(v-1)\chi - \ell + 1}(1-\mu)^\ell \frac{1+\eta}{2}$$

$$= (1-\mu)^{\ell}\,\frac{1+\eta}{2}\left[1+\frac{2\chi}{(v-1)\chi-\ell+1}-\frac{\chi}{(v-1)\chi-\ell+1}-\frac{v\chi-\ell+1}{(v-1)\chi-\ell+1}\right]$$

$$= (1-\mu)^{\ell}\,\frac{1+\eta}{2}\left[1+\frac{\chi-v\chi+\ell-1}{(v-1)\chi-\ell+1}\right]=0.$$

(k) Row 0 of LM times column $t = 2^{v}+1$ $(v \ge 2)$ of L^{T}:

$$M_{0,t}-\frac{\chi(1+\eta^{2})}{2[(v-1)\chi-\ell+1]}M_{0,0}+\frac{\chi(1+\eta)}{2[(v-1)\chi-\ell+1]}M_{0,1}-\frac{(1+\eta)}{2}M_{0,2^{v}}$$

$$+\frac{(1+\eta)(v\chi-\ell+1)}{2[(v-1)\chi-\ell+1]}M_{0,2^{v-1}}-\frac{v\chi-\ell+1}{(v-1)\chi-\ell+1}M_{0,2^{v-1}+1}.$$

$$M_{0,t}-\frac{v\chi-\ell+1}{(v-1)\chi-\ell+1}M_{0,2^{v-1}+1}$$

$$= (1-\mu)^{\ell}\,\frac{(1+\eta^{2})(\ell-1)-v\chi(1-\eta)^{2}}{2(\ell-1)}$$

$$-\frac{v\chi-\ell+1}{(v-1)\chi-\ell+1}(1-\mu)^{\ell}\,\frac{(1+\eta^{2})(\ell-1)-(v-1)\chi(1-\eta)^{2}}{2(\ell-1)}$$

$$= \frac{(1-\mu)^{\ell}}{2(\ell-1)((v-1)\chi-\ell+1)}\left[\begin{array}{l}\left[(1+\eta^{2})(\ell-1)-v\chi(1-\eta)^{2}\right]((v-1)\chi-\ell+1)\\ -(v\chi-\ell+1)\left((1+\eta^{2})(\ell-1)-(v-1)\chi(1-\eta)^{2}\right)\end{array}\right]$$

$$= \frac{(1-\mu)^{\ell}}{2(\ell-1)((v-1)\chi-\ell+1)}\left[-2\eta\chi(\ell-1)\right]$$

Thus

$$M_{0,t}-\frac{\chi(1+\eta^{2})}{2[(v-1)\chi-\ell+1]}M_{0,0}+\frac{\chi(1+\eta)}{2[(v-1)\chi-\ell+1]}M_{0,1}-\frac{(1+\eta)}{2}M_{0,2^{v}}$$

$$+\frac{(1+\eta)(v\chi-\ell+1)}{2[(v-1)\chi-\ell+1]}M_{0,2^{v-1}}-\frac{v\chi-\ell+1}{(v-1)\chi-\ell+1}M_{0,2^{v-1}+1}$$

$$= \frac{(1-\mu)^{\ell}}{2(\ell-1)((v-1)\chi-\ell+1)}\left[-2\eta\chi(\ell-1)\right]$$

$$-\frac{\chi(1+\eta^{2})}{2[(v-1)\chi-\ell+1]}(1-\mu)^{\ell}+\frac{\chi(1+\eta)}{2[(v-1)\chi-\ell+1]}(1-\mu)^{\ell}\,\frac{1+\eta}{2}$$

$$-\frac{(1+\eta)}{2}(1-\mu)^{\ell}\frac{1+\eta}{2}+\frac{(1+\eta)(v\chi-\ell+1)}{2[(v-1)\chi-\ell+1]}(1-\mu)^{\ell}\frac{1+\eta}{2}$$

$$=\frac{(1-\mu)^{\ell}}{2((v-1)\chi-\ell+1)}\left[-2\eta\chi-\chi(1+\eta^2)\right]$$

$$+(1-\mu)^{\ell}\frac{1+\eta}{2}\left[\frac{\chi(1+\eta)}{2[(v-1)\chi-\ell+1]}-\frac{(1+\eta)}{2}+\frac{(1+\eta)(v\chi-\ell+1)}{2[(v-1)\chi-\ell+1]}\right]$$

$$=\frac{-(1-\mu)^{\ell}\chi(1+\eta)^2}{2((v-1)\chi-\ell+1)}+\frac{(1-\mu)^{\ell}(1+\eta)^2}{4((v-1)\chi-\ell+1)}\left[\chi-((v-1)\chi-\ell+1)+v\chi-\ell+1\right]$$

$$=\frac{-(1-\mu)^{\ell}\chi(1+\eta)^2}{2((v-1)\chi-\ell+1)}+\frac{(1-\mu)^{\ell}(1+\eta)^2}{4((v-1)\chi-\ell+1)}\left[2\chi\right]=0$$

(l) Row 1 of **LM** times column 2 of $\mathbf{L}^T$:

$$-\frac{\chi(1+\eta)}{\ell-1}\left[M_{1,0}-\frac{(1+\eta)}{2}M_{0,0}\right]+\frac{2\chi-\ell+1}{\ell-1}\left[M_{1,1}-\frac{(1+\eta)}{2}M_{0,1}\right]+\left[M_{1,2}-\frac{(1+\eta)}{2}M_{0,2}\right]$$

$$-(1-\mu)^{\ell}\left(\frac{2\chi-\ell+1}{\ell-1}\left[\eta-\frac{(1+\eta)^2}{4}\right]+\left[\eta+\frac{\chi(\eta-1)^2}{2(\ell-1)}-\frac{(1+\eta)^2}{4}\right]\right)$$

$$-\frac{(1-\mu)^{\ell}}{4(\ell-1)}\left[4\eta(\ell-1)+2\chi(\eta-1)^2-(1+\eta)^2(\ell-1)+(2\chi-\ell+1)4\eta-(1+\eta)^2(2\chi-\ell+1)\right]$$

$$=\frac{(1-\mu)^{\ell}}{4(\ell-1)}\left[(2\chi-\ell+1)(\eta-1)^2+(2\chi-\ell+1)4\eta-(1+\eta)^2(2\chi-\ell+1)\right]$$

$$=\frac{(1-\mu)^{\ell}(2\chi-\ell+1)}{4(\ell-1)}\left[(\eta-1)^2+4\eta-(1+\eta)^2\right]=0.$$

(m) Row 1 of **LM** times column 3 of $\mathbf{L}^T$:

$$\left(\eta+\frac{\chi(1-\eta)^2}{2(\ell-1)}\right)\left[M_{1,0}-\frac{(1+\eta)}{2}M_{0,0}\right]-\frac{1+\eta}{2}\left[M_{1,1}-\frac{(1+\eta)}{2}M_{0,1}\right]$$

$$-\frac{1+\eta}{2}\left[M_{1,2}-\frac{(1+\eta)}{2}M_{0,2}\right]+\left[M_{1,3}-\frac{(1+\eta)}{2}M_{0,3}\right].$$

Substituting for the **M** values and dividing by $(1-\mu)^{\ell}$ gives

$$-\frac{1+\eta}{2}\left[\eta-\frac{(1+\eta)^2}{4}\right]-\frac{1+\eta}{2}\left[\eta+\frac{\chi(\eta-1)^2}{2(\ell-1)}-\frac{(1+\eta)^2}{4}\right]$$

$$+\left[\frac{(1+\eta)\eta}{2}-\frac{(1+\eta)}{2}\frac{1+\eta^2-\chi(\eta-1)^2/(\ell-1)}{2}\right]$$

Factoring out $(1+\eta)/2$ gives

$$-\eta+\frac{(1+\eta)^2}{4}-\eta-\frac{\chi(\eta-1)^2}{2(\ell-1)}+\frac{(1+\eta)^2}{4}+\eta-\frac{1+\eta^2-\dfrac{\chi(\eta-1)^2}{\ell-1}}{2}$$

$$=\frac{(1+\eta)^2}{2}-\eta-\frac{1+\eta^2}{2}=0.$$

(n) Row 1 of $\mathbf{LM}$ times column $t=2^v$ $(v\geq 2)$ of $\mathbf{L^T}$:

$$\left(\mathbf{M}_{1,0}-\frac{(1+\eta)}{2}\mathbf{M}_{0,0}\right)\frac{\chi(1+\eta)}{(v-1)\chi-\ell+1}-\left(\mathbf{M}_{1,1}-\frac{(1+\eta)}{2}\mathbf{M}_{0,1}\right)\frac{\chi}{(v-1)\chi-\ell+1}$$

$$-\left(\mathbf{M}_{1,2^{v-1}}-\frac{(1+\eta)}{2}\mathbf{M}_{0,2^{v-1}}\right)\frac{v\chi-\ell+1}{(v-1)\chi-\ell+1}+\left(\mathbf{M}_{1,2^v}-\frac{(1+\eta)}{2}\mathbf{M}_{0,2^v}\right).$$

Expanding terms after dividing through by $(1-\mu)^\ell$ gives

$$\left(\frac{(1+\eta)}{2}-\frac{(1+\eta)}{2}\right)\frac{\chi(1+\eta)}{(v-1)\chi-\ell+1}-\left(\eta-\frac{(1+\eta)}{2}\frac{(1+\eta)}{2}\right)\frac{\chi}{(v-1)\chi-\ell+1}$$

$$-\left(\eta+\frac{(v-1)\chi(\eta-1)^2}{2(\ell-1)}-\frac{(1+\eta)}{2}\frac{(1+\eta)}{2}\right)\frac{v\chi-\ell+1}{(v-1)\chi-\ell+1}$$

$$+\left(\eta+\frac{v\chi(\eta-1)^2}{2(\ell-1)}-\frac{(1+\eta)}{2}\frac{(1+\eta)}{2}\right)$$

$$=\frac{(1-2\eta+\eta^2)}{4}\frac{\chi}{(v-1)\chi-\ell+1}-\left(\eta+\frac{(v-1)\chi(\eta-1)^2}{2(\ell-1)}-\frac{(1+\eta)^2}{4}\right)\frac{v\chi-\ell+1}{(v-1)\chi-\ell+1}$$

$$+\left(\frac{v\chi(\eta-1)^2}{2(\ell-1)}-\frac{(1-2\eta+\eta^2)}{4}\right)$$

$$=\frac{(1-\eta)^2}{4[(v-1)\chi-\ell+1]}\left[\chi-\left(\frac{2(v-1)\chi}{(\ell-1)}-1\right)(v\chi-\ell+1)+\left(\frac{2v\chi}{(\ell-1)}-1\right)[(v-1)\chi-\ell+1]\right]$$

$$= \frac{(1-\eta)^2}{4[(v-1)\chi-\ell+1]}\left[\begin{array}{l}\chi-\left(\dfrac{2v\chi}{(\ell-1)}-1\right)(v\chi-\ell+1)+\left(\dfrac{2\chi}{(\ell-1)}\right)(v\chi-\ell+1)\\[2mm]+\left(\dfrac{2v\chi}{(\ell-1)}-1\right)[v\chi-\ell+1]-\chi\left(\dfrac{2v\chi}{(\ell-1)}-1\right)\end{array}\right]$$

$$= \frac{(1-\eta)^2}{4[(v-1)\chi-\ell+1]}\left[\chi+\left(\frac{2\chi}{(\ell-1)}\right)(v\chi-\ell+1)-\chi\left(\frac{2v\chi}{(\ell-1)}-1\right)\right]$$

$$= \frac{(1-\eta)^2}{4[(v-1)\chi-\ell+1]}\left[\chi+\frac{2v\chi^2}{(\ell-1)}-2\chi-\frac{2v\chi^2}{(\ell-1)}+\chi\right]=0.$$

(o) Row 1 of **LM** times column 2^v+1 $(v\geq 2)$ of $\mathbf{L}^{\mathrm{T}}$:

$$-\left(M_{1,0}-\frac{(1+\eta)}{2}M_{0,0}\right)\frac{\chi(1+\eta^2)}{2[(v-1)\chi-\ell+1]}+\left(M_{1,1}-\frac{(1+\eta)}{2}M_{0,1}\right)\frac{\chi(1+\eta)}{2[(v-1)\chi-\ell+1]}+$$

$$-\left(M_{1,2^v}-\frac{(1+\eta)}{2}M_{0,2^v}\right)\frac{(1+\eta)}{2}+\left(M_{1,2^{v-1}}-\frac{(1+\eta)}{2}M_{0,2^{v-1}}\right)\frac{(1+\eta)(v\chi-\ell+1)}{2[(v-1)\chi-\ell+1]}$$

$$-\left(M_{1,2^{v-1}+1}-\frac{(1+\eta)}{2}M_{0,2^{v-1}+1}\right)\frac{v\chi-\ell+1}{(v-1)\chi-\ell+1}+\left(M_{1,2^v+1}-\frac{(1+\eta)}{2}M_{0,2^v+1}\right).$$

Expanding terms after dividing through by $(1-\mu)^\ell$ gives

$$-\left(\frac{(1+\eta)}{2}-\frac{(1+\eta)}{2}\right)\frac{\chi(1+\eta^2)}{2[(v-1)\chi-\ell+1]}+\left(\eta-\frac{(1+\eta)}{2}\frac{(1+\eta)}{2}\right)\frac{\chi(1+\eta)}{2[(v-1)\chi-\ell+1]}$$

$$-\left(\eta+\frac{v\chi(\eta-1)^2}{2(\ell-1)}-\frac{(1+\eta)}{2}\frac{(1+\eta)}{2}\right)\frac{(1+\eta)}{2}$$

$$+\left(\eta+\frac{(v-1)\chi(\eta-1)^2}{2(\ell-1)}-\frac{(1+\eta)}{2}\frac{(1+\eta)}{2}\right)\frac{(1+\eta)(v\chi-\ell+1)}{2[(v-1)\chi-\ell+1]}$$

$$-\left(\frac{(1+\eta)\eta}{2}-\frac{(1+\eta)}{2}\frac{(1+\eta^2)(\ell-1)-(v-1)\chi(1-\eta)^2}{2(\ell-1)}\right)\frac{v\chi-\ell+1}{(v-1)\chi-\ell+1}$$

$$+\left(\frac{(1+\eta)\eta}{2}-\frac{(1+\eta)}{2}\frac{(1+\eta^2)(\ell-1)-v\chi(1-\eta)^2}{2(\ell-1)}\right)$$

$$=\frac{(1-\eta)^2(1+\eta)}{4}\left[\begin{array}{l}-\dfrac{\chi}{2[(v-1)\chi-\ell+1]}+\left(\dfrac{2(v-1)\chi}{(\ell-1)}-1\right)\dfrac{(v\chi-\ell+1)}{2[(v-1)\chi-\ell+1]}\\[3mm]-\left(\dfrac{2v\chi}{(\ell-1)}-1\right)\dfrac{1}{2}+\left(1-\dfrac{(v-1)\chi}{(\ell-1)}\right)\dfrac{v\chi-\ell+1}{(v-1)\chi-\ell+1}+\left(\dfrac{v\chi}{(\ell-1)}-1\right)\end{array}\right].$$

The term in brackets becomes

$$\frac{1}{2[(v-1)\chi-\ell+1]}\left[-\chi+\left(\frac{2(v-1)\chi}{(\ell-1)}-1\right)(v\chi-\ell+1)+2\left(1-\frac{(v-1)\chi}{(\ell-1)}\right)(v\chi-\ell+1)\right]-\frac{1}{2}$$

$$=\frac{1}{2[(v-1)\chi-\ell+1]}\left[-\chi+(v\chi-\ell+1)\right]-\frac{1}{2}=0$$

(p) Row 2 of **LM** times column 3 of $\mathbf{L}^T$:

$$\left(\eta+\frac{\chi(1-\eta)^2}{2(\ell-1)}\right)\left(\mathbf{M}_{2,0}-\frac{\chi(1+\eta)}{\ell-1}\mathbf{M}_{0,0}+\frac{2\chi-\ell+1}{\ell-1}\mathbf{M}_{1,0}\right)$$

$$-\frac{(1+\eta)}{2}\left(\mathbf{M}_{2,1}-\frac{\chi(1+\eta)}{\ell-1}\mathbf{M}_{0,1}+\frac{2\chi-\ell+1}{\ell-1}\mathbf{M}_{1,1}\right)$$

$$-\frac{(1+\eta)}{2}\left(\mathbf{M}_{2,2}-\frac{\chi(1+\eta)}{\ell-1}\mathbf{M}_{0,2}+\frac{2\chi-\ell+1}{\ell-1}\mathbf{M}_{1,2}\right)$$

$$\left(\mathbf{M}_{2,3}-\frac{\chi(1+\eta)}{\ell-1}\mathbf{M}_{0,3}+\frac{2\chi-\ell+1}{\ell-1}\mathbf{M}_{1,3}\right).$$

Expanding terms after dividing through by $(1-\mu)^\ell$ gives

$$\left(\eta+\frac{\chi(1-\eta)^2}{2(\ell-1)}\right)\left(\frac{(1+\eta)}{2}-\frac{\chi(1+\eta)}{\ell-1}+\frac{2\chi-\ell+1}{\ell-1}\frac{(1+\eta)}{2}\right)$$

$$-\frac{(1+\eta)}{2}\left(\eta+\frac{\chi(\eta-1)^2}{2(\ell-1)}-\frac{\chi(1+\eta)}{\ell-1}\frac{(1+\eta)}{2}+\frac{2\chi-\ell+1}{\ell-1}\eta\right)$$

$$-\frac{(1+\eta)}{2}\left(\eta-\frac{\chi(1+\eta)}{\ell-1}\frac{(1+\eta)}{2}+\frac{2\chi-\ell+1}{\ell-1}\left(\eta+\frac{\chi(\eta-1)^2}{2(\ell-1)}\right)\right)$$

$$\left(\frac{(1+\eta)\eta}{2}-\frac{\chi(1+\eta)}{\ell-1}\frac{(1+\eta^2)(\ell-1)-\chi(1-\eta)^2}{2(\ell-1)}+\frac{2\chi-\ell+1}{\ell-1}\frac{(1+\eta)\eta}{2}\right)$$

$$=-\frac{(1+\eta)}{2}\left(\frac{\chi(\eta-1)^2}{2(\ell-1)}-\frac{\chi(1+\eta)^2}{2(\ell-1)}+\frac{4\chi\eta}{2(\ell-1)}\right)$$

$$-\frac{(1+\eta)}{2}\left(-\frac{\chi(1+\eta)^2}{2(\ell-1)}+\frac{4\chi\eta}{2(\ell-1)}+\frac{2\chi}{\ell-1}\frac{\chi(\eta-1)^2}{2(\ell-1)}-\frac{\chi(\eta-1)^2}{2(\ell-1)}\right)$$

$$\left(-\frac{\chi(1+\eta)(1+\eta^2)}{2(\ell-1)}+\frac{\chi^2(1-\eta)^2(1+\eta)}{2(\ell-1)^2}+\frac{2\chi(1+\eta)\eta}{2(\ell-1)}\right)$$

$$= -\frac{(1+\eta)}{2}\left(-\frac{2\chi(1+\eta)^2}{2(\ell-1)}+\frac{8\chi\eta}{2(\ell-1)}+\frac{2\chi^2(\eta-1)^2}{2(\ell-1)^2}+\frac{\chi(1+\eta^2)}{(\ell-1)}-\frac{\chi^2(1-\eta)^2}{(\ell-1)^2}-\frac{2\chi\eta}{(\ell-1)}\right)$$

$$= -\frac{(1+\eta)}{4(\ell-1)}\left(-2\chi(1+\eta)^2+8\chi\eta+2\chi(1+\eta^2)-4\chi\eta\right)$$

$$= -\frac{(1+\eta)\chi}{4(\ell-1)}\left(-2-4\eta-2\eta^2+8\eta+2+2\eta^2-4\eta\right)=0.$$

(q) Row 2 of LM times column $t=2^v$ $(v\geq 2)$ of L^T:

$$\left(M_{2,0}-\frac{\chi(1+\eta)}{\ell-1}M_{0,0}+\frac{2\chi-\ell+1}{\ell-1}M_{1,0}\right)\frac{\chi(1+\eta)}{(v-1)\chi-\ell+1}$$

$$-\left(M_{2,1}-\frac{\chi(1+\eta)}{\ell-1}M_{0,1}+\frac{2\chi-\ell+1}{\ell-1}M_{1,1}\right)\frac{\chi}{(v-1)\chi-\ell+1}$$

$$-\left(M_{2,2^{v-1}}-\frac{\chi(1+\eta)}{\ell-1}M_{0,2^{v-1}}+\frac{2\chi-\ell+1}{\ell-1}M_{1,2^{v-1}}\right)\frac{v\chi-\ell+1}{(v-1)\chi-\ell+1}$$

$$+\left(M_{2,2^v}-\frac{\chi(1+\eta)}{\ell-1}M_{0,2^v}+\frac{2\chi-\ell+1}{\ell-1}M_{1,2^v}\right).$$

Expanding terms after dividing through by $(1-\mu)^\ell$ gives

$$\left(\frac{1+\eta}{2}-\frac{\chi(1+\eta)}{\ell-1}+\frac{2\chi-\ell+1}{\ell-1}\frac{1+\eta}{2}\right)\frac{\chi(1+\eta)}{(v-1)\chi-\ell+1}$$

$$-\left(\left(\eta+\frac{\chi(\eta-1)^2}{2(\ell-1)}\right)-\frac{\chi(1+\eta)}{\ell-1}\frac{1+\eta}{2}+\frac{2\chi-\ell+1}{\ell-1}\eta\right)\frac{\chi}{(v-1)\chi-\ell+1}$$

$$-\left(\begin{array}{l}\left(\eta+\frac{(v-2)\chi(\eta-1)^2}{2(\ell-1)}\right)-\frac{\chi(1+\eta)}{\ell-1}\frac{1}{2}\eta\\[2mm]+\frac{2\chi-\ell+1}{\ell-1}\left(\eta+\frac{(v-1)\chi(\eta-1)^2}{2(\ell-1)}\right)\end{array}\right)\frac{v\chi-\ell+1}{(v-1)\chi-\ell+1}$$

$$+\left(\left(\eta+\frac{(v-1)\chi(\eta-1)^2}{2(\ell-1)}\right)-\frac{\chi(1+\eta)}{\ell-1}\frac{1+\eta}{2}+\frac{2\chi-\ell+1}{\ell-1}\left(\eta+\frac{v\chi(\eta-1)^2}{2(\ell-1)}\right)\right)$$

$$= -\left(\frac{\chi(\eta-1)^2}{2(\ell-1)}-\frac{\chi(1+\eta)^2}{2(\ell-1)}+\frac{2\chi}{\ell-1}\eta\right)\frac{\chi}{(v-1)\chi-\ell+1}$$

$$-\left(-\frac{\chi(\eta-1)^2}{2(\ell-1)}-\frac{\chi(1+\eta)^2}{2(\ell-1)}+\frac{2\chi\eta}{\ell-1}+\frac{2(v-1)\chi^2(\eta-1)^2}{2(\ell-1)^2}\right)\frac{v\chi-\ell+1}{(v-1)\chi-\ell+1}$$

$$+\left(-\frac{\chi(\eta-1)^2}{2(\ell-1)}-\frac{\chi(1+\eta)^2}{2(\ell-1)}+\frac{2\chi\eta}{\ell-1}+\frac{2\nu\chi^2(\eta-1)^2}{2(\ell-1)^2}\right)$$

$$=-\left(-\frac{\chi(\eta-1)^2}{2(\ell-1)}-\frac{\chi(1+\eta)^2}{2(\ell-1)}+\frac{2\chi\eta}{\ell-1}+\frac{2(v-1)\chi^2(\eta-1)^2}{2(\ell-1)^2}\right)$$

$$-\left(-\frac{\chi(\eta-1)^2}{2(\ell-1)}-\frac{\chi(1+\eta)^2}{2(\ell-1)}+\frac{2\chi\eta}{\ell-1}+\frac{2(v-1)\chi^2(\eta-1)^2}{2(\ell-1)^2}\right)\frac{\chi}{(v-1)\chi-\ell+1}$$

$$+\left(-\frac{\chi(\eta-1)^2}{2(\ell-1)}-\frac{\chi(1+\eta)^2}{2(\ell-1)}+\frac{2\chi\eta}{\ell-1}+\frac{2\nu\chi^2(\eta-1)^2}{2(\ell-1)^2}\right)$$

$$=\frac{2\chi^2(\eta-1)^2}{2(\ell-1)^2}-\left(-\frac{\chi(\eta-1)^2}{2(\ell-1)}-\frac{\chi(1+\eta)^2}{2(\ell-1)}+\frac{2\chi\eta}{\ell-1}+\frac{2(v-1)\chi^2(\eta-1)^2}{2(\ell-1)^2}\right)\frac{\chi}{(v-1)\chi-\ell+1}$$

$$=\frac{\chi^2}{2(\ell-1)[(v-1)\chi-\ell+1]}\left[\frac{2\chi(\eta-1)^2(v-1)}{(\ell-1)}-(\eta-1)^2+(1+\eta)^2-4\eta-\frac{2(v-1)\chi(\eta-1)^2}{2(\ell-1)}\right]$$

$$=\frac{\chi^2}{2(\ell-1)[(v-1)\chi-\ell+1]}\left[\frac{2\chi(\eta-1)^2(v-1)}{(\ell-1)}-(\eta-1)^2+(1+\eta)^2-4\eta-\frac{2(v-1)\chi(\eta-1)^2}{2(\ell-1)}\right]$$

$$=0$$

(r) Row 2 of **LM** times column 2^v+1 $\left(v\geq 2\right)$ of $\mathbf{L}^\mathsf{T}$:

$$-\left(M_{2,0}-\frac{\chi(1+\eta)}{\ell-1}M_{0,0}+\frac{2\chi-\ell+1}{\ell-1}M_{1,0}\right)\frac{\chi(1+\eta^2)}{2[(v-1)\chi-\ell+1]}$$

$$+\left(M_{2,1}-\frac{\chi(1+\eta)}{\ell-1}M_{0,1}+\frac{2\chi-\ell+1}{\ell-1}M_{1,1}\right)\frac{\chi(1+\eta)}{2[(v-1)\chi-\ell+1]}$$

$$-\left(M_{2,2^v}-\frac{\chi(1+\eta)}{\ell-1}M_{0,2^v}+\frac{2\chi-\ell+1}{\ell-1}M_{1,2^v}\right)\frac{(1+\eta)}{2}$$

$$+\left(M_{2,2^{v-1}}-\frac{\chi(1+\eta)}{\ell-1}M_{0,2^{v-1}}+\frac{2\chi-\ell+1}{\ell-1}M_{1,2^{v-1}}\right)\frac{(1+\eta)(v\chi-\ell+1)}{2[(v-1)\chi-\ell+1]}$$

$$-\left(M_{2,2^{v-1}+1}-\frac{\chi(1+\eta)}{\ell-1}M_{0,2^{v-1}+1}+\frac{2\chi-\ell+1}{\ell-1}M_{1,2^{v-1}+1}\right)\frac{v\chi-\ell+1}{(v-1)\chi-\ell+1}$$

$$+\left(M_{2,2^v+1}-\frac{\chi(1+\eta)}{\ell-1}M_{0,2^v+1}+\frac{2\chi-\ell+1}{\ell-1}M_{1,2^v+1}\right)$$

Expanding terms after dividing through by $(1-\mu)^\ell$ gives

$$-\left(\frac{1+\eta}{2}-\frac{\chi(1+\eta)}{\ell-1}\eta+\frac{2\chi-\ell+1}{\ell-1}\frac{1+\eta}{2}\right)\frac{\chi(1+\eta^2)}{2[(v-1)\chi-\ell+1]}$$

$$+\left(\left(\eta+\frac{\chi(\eta-1)^2}{2(\ell-1)}\right)-\frac{\chi(1+\eta)}{\ell-1}\frac{1+\eta}{2}+\frac{2\chi-\ell+1}{\ell-1}\eta\right)\frac{\chi(1+\eta)}{2[(v-1)\chi-\ell+1]}$$

$$-\left(\left(\eta+\frac{(v-1)\chi(\eta-1)^2}{2(\ell-1)}\right)-\frac{\chi(1+\eta)}{\ell-1}\frac{1+\eta}{2}+\frac{2\chi-\ell+1}{\ell-1}\left(\eta+\frac{v\chi(\eta-1)^2}{2(\ell-1)}\right)\right)\frac{(1+\eta)}{2}$$

$$+\left(\left(\eta+\frac{(v-2)\chi(\eta-1)^2}{2(\ell-1)}\right)-\frac{\chi(1+\eta)^2}{2(\ell-1)}+\frac{2\chi-\ell+1}{\ell-1}\left(\eta+\frac{(v-1)\chi(\eta-1)^2}{2(\ell-1)}\right)\right)\frac{(1+\eta)(v\chi-\ell+1)}{2[(v-1)\chi-\ell+1]}$$

$$-\left(\frac{(1+\eta)\eta}{2}-\frac{\chi(1+\eta)}{\ell-1}\frac{(1+\eta^2)(\ell-1)-(v-1)\chi(1-\eta)^2}{2(\ell-1)}+\frac{2\chi-\ell+1}{\ell-1}\frac{(1+\eta)\eta}{2}\right)\frac{v\chi-\ell+1}{(v-1)\chi-\ell+1}$$

$$+\left(\frac{(1+\eta)\eta}{2}-\frac{\chi(1+\eta)}{\ell-1}\frac{(1+\eta^2)(\ell-1)-v\chi(1-\eta)^2}{2(\ell-1)}+\frac{2\chi-\ell+1}{\ell-1}\frac{(1+\eta)\eta}{2}\right)$$

$$=+\left(\frac{\chi(\eta-1)^2}{2(\ell-1)}-\frac{\chi(1+\eta)^2}{2(\ell-1)}+\frac{2\chi\eta}{\ell-1}\right)\frac{\chi(1+\eta)}{2[(v-1)\chi-\ell+1]}$$

$$-\left(-\frac{\chi(\eta-1)^2}{2(\ell-1)}-\frac{\chi(1+\eta)^2}{2(\ell-1)}+\frac{2\chi\eta}{\ell-1}+\frac{2v\chi^2(\eta-1)^2}{2(\ell-1)^2}\right)\frac{(1+\eta)}{2}$$

$$+\left(-\frac{\chi(\eta-1)^2}{2(\ell-1)}-\frac{\chi(1+\eta)^2}{2(\ell-1)}+\frac{2\chi\eta}{\ell-1}+\frac{2(v-1)\chi^2(\eta-1)^2}{2(\ell-1)^2}\right)\frac{(1+\eta)(v\chi-\ell+1)}{2[(v-1)\chi-\ell+1]}$$

$$-\left(-\frac{\chi(1+\eta)(1+\eta^2)}{2(\ell-1)}+\frac{(v-1)(1+\eta)\chi^2(1-\eta)^2}{2(\ell-1)^2}+\frac{2\chi(1+\eta)\eta}{2(\ell-1)}\right)\frac{v\chi-\ell+1}{(v-1)\chi-\ell+1}$$

$$+\left(-\frac{\chi(1+\eta)(1+\eta^2)}{2(\ell-1)}+\frac{v(1+\eta)\chi^2(1-\eta)^2}{2(\ell-1)^2}+\frac{2\chi(1+\eta)\eta}{2(\ell-1)}\right)$$

$$=\left(\frac{\chi(\eta-1)^2}{2(\ell-1)}-\frac{\chi(1+\eta)^2}{2(\ell-1)}+\frac{2\chi\eta}{\ell-1}\right)\frac{\chi(1+\eta)}{2[(v-1)\chi-\ell+1]}$$

$$-\left(-\frac{\chi(\eta-1)^2}{2(\ell-1)}-\frac{\chi(1+\eta)^2}{2(\ell-1)}+\frac{\chi(1+\eta^2)}{(\ell-1)}\right)\frac{(1+\eta)}{2}$$

$$+\left(-\frac{\chi(\eta-1)^2}{2(\ell-1)}-\frac{\chi(1+\eta)^2}{2(\ell-1)}+\frac{\chi(1+\eta^2)}{(\ell-1)}\right)\frac{(1+\eta)(v\chi-\ell+1)}{2\left[(v-1)\chi-\ell+1\right]}$$

$$=-\left(-(\eta-1)^2-(1+\eta)^2+2(1+\eta^2)\right)\frac{\chi(1+\eta)}{4(\ell-1)}$$

$$+\left(-(\eta-1)^2-(1+\eta)^2+2(1+\eta^2)\right)\frac{(1+\eta)\chi(v\chi-\ell+1)}{4(\ell-1)\left[(v-1)\chi-\ell+1\right]}=0.$$

(s) Row 3 of LM times column $t = 2^v$ $(v \geq 2)$ of L^T:

$$\left[M_{3,0}+\left(\eta+\frac{\chi(1-\eta)^2}{2(\ell-1)}\right)M_{0,0}-\frac{(1+\eta)}{2}M_{1,0}-\frac{(1+\eta)}{2}M_{2,0}\right]\frac{\chi(1+\eta)}{(v-1)\chi-\ell+1}$$

$$-\left[M_{3,1}+\left(\eta+\frac{\chi(1-\eta)^2}{2(\ell-1)}\right)M_{0,1}-\frac{(1+\eta)}{2}M_{1,1}-\frac{(1+\eta)}{2}M_{2,1}\right]\frac{\chi}{(v-1)\chi-\ell+1}$$

$$-\left[M_{3,2^{v-1}}+\left(\eta+\frac{\chi(1-\eta)^2}{2(\ell-1)}\right)M_{0,2^{v-1}}-\frac{(1+\eta)}{2}M_{1,2^{v-1}}-\frac{(1+\eta)}{2}M_{2,2^{v-1}}\right]\frac{v\chi-\ell+1}{(v-1)\chi-\ell+1}$$

$$+\left[M_{3,2^v}+\left(\eta+\frac{\chi(1-\eta)^2}{2(\ell-1)}\right)M_{0,2^v}-\frac{(1+\eta)}{2}M_{1,2^v}-\frac{(1+\eta)}{2}M_{2,2^v}\right]$$

Expanding terms after dividing through by $(1-\mu)^\ell$ gives

$$\left[\begin{array}{c}\dfrac{(1+\eta^2)(\ell-1)-\chi(1-\eta)^2}{2(\ell-1)}+\left(\eta+\dfrac{\chi(1-\eta)^2}{2(\ell-1)}\right)\\[2mm]-\dfrac{(1+\eta)}{2}\dfrac{(1+\eta)}{2}-\dfrac{(1+\eta)}{2}\dfrac{(1+\eta)}{2}\end{array}\right]\frac{\chi(1+\eta)}{(v-1)\chi-\ell+1}$$

$$-\left[\begin{array}{c}\dfrac{(1+\eta)\eta}{2}+\left(\eta+\dfrac{\chi(1-\eta)^2}{2(\ell-1)}\right)\dfrac{(1+\eta)}{2}\\[2mm]-\dfrac{(1+\eta)}{2}\eta-\dfrac{(1+\eta)}{2}\left(\eta+\dfrac{\chi(\eta-1)^2}{2(\ell-1)}\right)\end{array}\right]\frac{\chi}{(v-1)\chi-\ell+1}$$

$$-\left[\begin{array}{l}\dfrac{1}{2}\left(\eta+\eta^2+\dfrac{\chi(v-2)\left(\eta^3-\eta^2-\eta+1\right)}{\ell-1}\right)+\left(\eta+\dfrac{\chi(1-\eta)^2}{2(\ell-1)}\right)\dfrac{(1+\eta)}{2}\\[2mm] -\dfrac{(1+\eta)}{2}\left(\eta+\dfrac{(v-1)\chi(\eta-1)^2}{2(\ell-1)}\right)-\dfrac{(1+\eta)}{2}\left(\eta+\dfrac{(v-2)\chi(\eta-1)^2}{2(\ell-1)}\right)\end{array}\right]\dfrac{v\chi-\ell+1}{(v-1)\chi-\ell+1}$$

$$+\left[\begin{array}{l}\dfrac{1}{2}\left(\eta+\eta^2+\dfrac{\chi(v-1)\left(\eta^3-\eta^2-\eta+1\right)}{\ell-1}\right)+\left(\eta+\dfrac{\chi(1-\eta)^2}{2(\ell-1)}\right)\dfrac{(1+\eta)}{2}\\[2mm] -\dfrac{(1+\eta)}{2}\left(\eta+\dfrac{v\chi(\eta-1)^2}{2(\ell-1)}\right)-\dfrac{(1+\eta)}{2}\left(\eta+\dfrac{(v-1)\chi(\eta-1)^2}{2(\ell-1)}\right)\end{array}\right]$$

$$=+\left[\begin{array}{l}-\dfrac{\chi(v-2)\left(\eta^3-\eta^2-\eta+1\right)}{2(\ell-1)}-\dfrac{\chi(1-\eta)^2(1+\eta)}{4(\ell-1)}\\[2mm] +\dfrac{(2v-3)\chi(\eta-1)^2(1+\eta)}{4(\ell-1)}\end{array}\right]\dfrac{v\chi-\ell+1}{(v-1)\chi-\ell+1}$$

$$+\left[\dfrac{\chi(v-1)\left(\eta^3-\eta^2-\eta+1\right)}{2(\ell-1)}+\dfrac{\chi(1-\eta)^2(1+\eta)}{4(\ell-1)}-\dfrac{(2v-1)\chi(\eta-1)^2(1+\eta)}{4(\ell-1)}\right]$$

$$=+\left[-\dfrac{2\chi(\eta-1)^2(1+\eta)}{4(\ell-1)}+\dfrac{2\chi\left(\eta^2-1\right)(\eta-1)}{4(\ell-1)}\right]$$

$$+\left[-\dfrac{2\chi(v-2)}{4(\ell-1)}-\dfrac{\chi}{4(\ell-1)}+\dfrac{(2v-3)\chi}{4(\ell-1)}\right]\dfrac{\chi(1+\eta)(\eta-1)^2}{(v-1)\chi-\ell+1}=0$$

(l) Row 3 of LM times column 2^v+1 $\left(v\geq 2\right)$ of L^T:

$$-\left[M_{3,0}+\left(\eta+\dfrac{\chi(1-\eta)^2}{2(\ell-1)}\right)M_{0,0}-\dfrac{(1+\eta)}{2}M_{1,0}-\dfrac{(1+\eta)}{2}M_{2,0}\right]\dfrac{\chi\left(1+\eta^2\right)}{2\left[(v-1)\chi-\ell+1\right]}$$

$$+\left[M_{3,1}+\left(\eta+\dfrac{\chi(1-\eta)^2}{2(\ell-1)}\right)M_{0,1}-\dfrac{(1+\eta)}{2}M_{1,1}-\dfrac{(1+\eta)}{2}M_{2,1}\right]\dfrac{\chi(1+\eta)}{2\left[(v-1)\chi-\ell+1\right]}$$

$$-\left[M_{3,2^v}+\left(\eta+\dfrac{\chi(1-\eta)^2}{2(\ell-1)}\right)M_{0,2^v}-\dfrac{(1+\eta)}{2}M_{1,2^v}-\dfrac{(1+\eta)}{2}M_{2,2^v}\right]\dfrac{(1+\eta)}{2}$$

$$+\left[M_{3,2^{v-1}}+\left(\eta+\dfrac{\chi(1-\eta)^2}{2(\ell-1)}\right)M_{0,2^{v-1}}-\dfrac{(1+\eta)}{2}M_{1,2^{v-1}}-\dfrac{(1+\eta)}{2}M_{2,2^{v-1}}\right]\dfrac{(1+\eta)(k\chi-\ell+1)}{2\left[(v-1)\chi-\ell+1\right]}$$

$$-\left[M_{3,2^{\nu-1}+1} + \left(\eta + \frac{\chi(1-\eta)^2}{2(\ell-1)}\right)M_{0,2^{\nu-1}+1} - \frac{(1+\eta)}{2}M_{1,2^{\nu-1}+1} - \frac{(1+\eta)}{2}M_{2,2^{\nu-1}+1}\right]\frac{\nu\chi-\ell+1}{(\nu-1)\chi-\ell+1}$$

$$+\left[M_{3,2^{\nu}+1} + \left(\eta + \frac{\chi(1-\eta)^2}{2(\ell-1)}\right)M_{0,2^{\nu}+1} - \frac{(1+\eta)}{2}M_{1,2^{\nu}+1} - \frac{(1+\eta)}{2}M_{2,2^{\nu}+1}\right].$$

Expanding terms after dividing through by $(1-\mu)^\ell$ gives

$$-\left[\frac{(1+\eta^2)(\ell-1)-\chi(1-\eta)^2}{2(\ell-1)} + \left(\eta + \frac{\chi(1-\eta)^2}{2(\ell-1)}\right) - \frac{(1+\eta)}{2}\frac{(1+\eta)}{2} - \frac{(1+\eta)}{2}\frac{(1+\eta)}{2}\right]\frac{\chi(1+\eta^2)}{2[(\nu-1)\chi-\ell+1]}$$

$$+\left[\frac{(1+\eta)\eta}{2} + \left(\eta + \frac{\chi(1-\eta)^2}{2(\ell-1)}\right)\frac{(1+\eta)}{2} - \frac{(1+\eta)}{2}\eta - \frac{(1+\eta)}{2}\left(\eta + \frac{\chi(\eta-1)^2}{2(\ell-1)}\right)\right]\frac{\chi(1+\eta)}{2[(\nu-1)\chi-\ell+1]}$$

$$-\left[\frac{1}{2}\left(\eta+\eta^2 + \frac{\chi(\nu-1)(\eta^3-\eta^2-\eta+1)}{\ell-1}\right) + \left(\eta + \frac{\chi(1-\eta)^2}{2(\ell-1)}\right)\frac{(1+\eta)}{2} - \frac{(1+\eta)}{2}\left(\eta + \frac{\nu\chi(\eta-1)^2}{2(\ell-1)}\right) - \frac{(1+\eta)}{2}\left(\eta + \frac{(\nu-1)\chi(\eta-1)^2}{2(\ell-1)}\right)\right]\frac{(1+\eta)}{2}$$

$$+\left[\frac{1}{2}\left(\eta+\eta^2 + \frac{\chi(\nu-2)(\eta^3-\eta^2-\eta+1)}{\ell-1}\right) + \left(\eta + \frac{\chi(1-\eta)^2}{2(\ell-1)}\right)\frac{(1+\eta)}{2} - \frac{(1+\eta)}{2}\left(\eta + \frac{(\nu-1)\chi(\eta-1)^2}{2(\ell-1)}\right) - \frac{(1+\eta)}{2}\left(\eta + \frac{(\nu-2)\chi(\eta-1)^2}{2(\ell-1)}\right)\right]\frac{(1+\eta)(k\chi-\ell+1)}{2[(\nu-1)\chi-\ell+1]}$$

$$-\left[\left(\eta^2 + \frac{(\nu-2)\chi\eta(\eta-1)^2}{2(\ell-1)}\right) + \left(\eta + \frac{\chi(1-\eta)^2}{2(\ell-1)}\right)\frac{(1+\eta^2)(\ell-1)-(\nu-1)\chi(1-\eta)^2}{2(\ell-1)}\frac{\nu\chi-\ell+1}{(\nu-1)\chi-\ell+1} - \frac{(1+\eta)}{2}\frac{(1+\eta)\eta}{2} - \frac{(1+\eta)}{2}\frac{(1+\eta)\eta}{2}\right]$$

$$+\begin{bmatrix}\left(\eta^2+\dfrac{(v-1)\chi\eta(\eta-1)^2}{2(\ell-1)}\right)\\[2ex]+\left(\eta+\dfrac{\chi(1-\eta)^2}{2(\ell-1)}\right)\dfrac{(1+\eta^2)(\ell-1)-v\chi(1-\eta)^2}{2(\ell-1)}\\[2ex]-\dfrac{(1+\eta)}{2}\dfrac{(1+\eta)\eta}{2}-\dfrac{(1+\eta)}{2}\dfrac{(1+\eta)\eta}{2}\end{bmatrix}.$$

But

$$\frac{(1+\eta^2)(\ell-1)-\chi(1-\eta)^2}{2(\ell-1)}+\left(\eta+\frac{\chi(1-\eta)^2}{2(\ell-1)}\right)-\frac{(1+\eta)}{2}\frac{(1+\eta)}{2}-\frac{(1+\eta)}{2}\frac{(1+\eta)}{2}$$

$$=\frac{(1+\eta^2)}{2}-\frac{\chi(1-\eta)^2}{2(\ell-1)}+\eta+\frac{\chi(1-\eta)^2}{2(\ell-1)}-\frac{(1+\eta)^2}{2}=0.$$

$$\frac{(1+\eta)\eta}{2}+\left(\eta+\frac{\chi(1-\eta)^2}{2(\ell-1)}\right)\frac{(1+\eta)}{2}-\frac{(1+\eta)}{2}\eta-\frac{(1+\eta)}{2}\left(\eta+\frac{\chi(\eta-1)^2}{2(\ell-1)}\right)=0.$$

$$\frac{1}{2}\left(\eta+\eta^2+\frac{\chi(v-1)(\eta^3-\eta^2-\eta+1)}{\ell-1}\right)+\left(\eta+\frac{\chi(1-\eta)^2}{2(\ell-1)}\right)\frac{(1+\eta)}{2}$$

$$-\frac{(1+\eta)}{2}\left(\eta+\frac{v\chi(\eta-1)^2}{2(\ell-1)}\right)-\frac{(1+\eta)}{2}\left(\eta+\frac{(v-1)\chi(\eta-1)^2}{2(\ell-1)}\right)$$

$$=\frac{2\chi(v-1)(1+\eta)(\eta-1)^2}{4(\ell-1)}+\frac{\chi(1-\eta)^2(1+\eta)}{4(\ell-1)}-\frac{v\chi(\eta-1)^2(1+\eta)}{4(\ell-1)}-\frac{(v-1)\chi(\eta-1)^2(1+\eta)}{4(\ell-1)}$$

$$=\frac{\chi(1+\eta)(\eta-1)^2}{4(\ell-1)}\left[2(v-1)+1-v-(v-1)\right]=0.$$

$$\frac{1}{2}\left(\eta+\eta^2+\frac{\chi(v-2)(\eta^3-\eta^2-\eta+1)}{\ell-1}\right)+\left(\eta+\frac{\chi(1-\eta)^2}{2(\ell-1)}\right)\frac{(1+\eta)}{2}$$

$$-\frac{(1+\eta)}{2}\left(\eta+\frac{(v-1)\chi(\eta-1)^2}{2(\ell-1)}\right)-\frac{(1+\eta)}{2}\left(\eta+\frac{(v-2)\chi(\eta-1)^2}{2(\ell-1)}\right)$$

$$=+\frac{2\chi(v-2)(1+\eta)(\eta-1)^2}{4(\ell-1)}+\frac{\chi(1-\eta)^2(1+\eta)}{4(\ell-1)}$$

$$-\frac{(v-1)\chi(\eta-1)^2(1+\eta)}{4(\ell-1)}-\frac{(v-2)\chi(\eta-1)^2(1+\eta)}{4(\ell-1)}$$

$$= \frac{\chi(1+\eta)(\eta-1)^2}{4(\ell-1)}\left[2(v-2)+1-(v-1)-(v-2)\right]=0.$$

$$\left(\eta^2+\frac{(v-2)\chi\eta(\eta-1)^2}{2(\ell-1)}\right)+\left(\eta+\frac{\chi(1-\eta)^2}{2(\ell-1)}\right)\frac{(1+\eta^2)(\ell-1)-(v-1)\chi(1-\eta)^2}{2(\ell-1)}$$

$$-\frac{(1+\eta)}{2}\frac{(1+\eta)\eta}{2}-\frac{(1+\eta)}{2}\frac{(1+\eta)\eta}{2}$$

$$=\eta^2-\frac{\chi\eta(\eta-1)^2}{2(\ell-1)}+\frac{\eta(1+\eta^2)}{2}+\frac{\chi(1-\eta)^2(1+\eta^2)}{4(\ell-1)}-\frac{(v-1)\chi(1-\eta)^2\chi(1-\eta)^2}{4(\ell-1)^2}-\frac{(1+\eta)^2\eta}{2}$$

$$=\frac{\chi(\eta-1)^2}{4(\ell-1)}\left[-2\eta+(1+\eta^2)-\frac{(v-1)\chi(1-\eta)^2}{(\ell-1)}\right]=\frac{\chi(\eta-1)^4}{4(\ell-1)^2}\left[\ell-1-(v-1)\chi\right]$$

$$\eta^2+\frac{(v-1)\chi\eta(\eta-1)^2}{2(\ell-1)}+\left(\eta+\frac{\chi(1-\eta)^2}{2(\ell-1)}\right)\frac{(1+\eta^2)(\ell-1)-v\chi(1-\eta)^2}{2(\ell-1)}$$

$$-\frac{(1+\eta)}{2}\frac{(1+\eta)\eta}{2}-\frac{(1+\eta)}{2}\frac{(1+\eta)\eta}{2}$$

$$=-\frac{2\chi\eta(\eta-1)^2}{4(\ell-1)}+\frac{\chi(1-\eta)^2(1+\eta^2)}{4(\ell-1)}-\frac{\chi(1-\eta)^2 v\chi(1-\eta)^2}{4(\ell-1)^2}$$

$$\eta=\frac{\chi(\eta-1)^2}{4(\ell-1)}\left[-2\eta+(1+\eta^2)-\frac{v\chi(1-\eta)^2}{(\ell-1)}\right]=\frac{\chi(\eta-1)^4}{4(\ell-1)^2}\left[\ell-1-v\chi\right].$$

Thus the original expression becomes

$$-\frac{\chi(\eta-1)^4}{4(\ell-1)^2}\left[\ell-1-(v-1)\chi\right]\frac{v\chi-\ell+1}{(v-1)\chi-\ell+1}+\frac{\chi(\eta-1)^4}{4(\ell-1)^2}\left[\ell-1-v\chi\right]=0.$$

(u) Row 2^k of LM times column 2^v+1 $\quad(v\geq k\geq 2)$ of L^T:

$$-\left[\begin{array}{c}M_{2^k,0}+\dfrac{\chi(1+\eta)}{(k-1)\chi-\ell+1}M_{0,0}-\dfrac{\chi}{(k-1)\chi-\ell+1}M_{1,0}\\[2ex]-\dfrac{k\chi-\ell+1}{(k-1)\chi-\ell+1}M_{2^{k-1},0}\end{array}\right]\frac{\chi(1+\eta^2)}{2\left[(v-1)\chi-\ell+1\right]}$$

$$+\left[\begin{array}{c}M_{2^k,1}+\dfrac{\chi(1+\eta)}{(k-1)\chi-\ell+1}M_{0,1}-\dfrac{\chi}{(k-1)\chi-\ell+1}M_{1,1}\\[2ex]-\dfrac{k\chi-\ell+1}{(k-1)\chi-\ell+1}M_{2^{k-1},1}\end{array}\right]\frac{\chi(1+\eta)}{2\left[(v-1)\chi-\ell+1\right]}$$

$$-\left[\begin{array}{l} M_{2^k,2^v} + \dfrac{\chi(1+\eta)}{(k-1)\chi-\ell+1}M_{0,2^v} - \dfrac{\chi}{(k-1)\chi-\ell+1}M_{1,2^v} \\ -\dfrac{k\chi-\ell+1}{(k-1)\chi-\ell+1}M_{2^{k-1},2^v} \end{array}\right]\dfrac{(1+\eta)}{2}$$

$$+\left[\begin{array}{l} M_{2^k,2^{v-1}} + \dfrac{\chi(1+\eta)}{(k-1)\chi-\ell+1}M_{0,2^{v-1}} - \dfrac{\chi}{(k-1)\chi-\ell+1}M_{1,2^{v-1}} \\ -\dfrac{k\chi-\ell+1}{(k-1)\chi-\ell+1}M_{2^{k-1},2^{v-1}} \end{array}\right]\dfrac{(1+\eta)(v\chi-\ell+1)}{2[(v-1)\chi-\ell+1]}$$

$$-\left[\begin{array}{l} M_{2^k,2^{v-1}+1} + \dfrac{\chi(1+\eta)}{(k-1)\chi-\ell+1}M_{0,2^{v-1}+1} - \dfrac{\chi}{(k-1)\chi-\ell+1}M_{1,2^{v-1}+1} \\ -\dfrac{k\chi-\ell+1}{(k-1)\chi-\ell+1}M_{2^{k-1},2^{v-1}+1} \end{array}\right]\dfrac{v\chi-\ell+1}{(v-1)\chi-\ell+1}$$

$$+\left[M_{2^k,2^v+1} + \dfrac{\chi(1+\eta)}{(k-1)\chi-\ell+1}M_{0,2^v+1} - \dfrac{\chi}{(k-1)\chi-\ell+1}M_{1,2^v+1} - \dfrac{k\chi-\ell+1}{(k-1)\chi-\ell+1}M_{2^{k-1},2^v+1} \right].$$

Expanding each bracketed term after dividing through by $(1-\mu)^\ell$ gives

$$M_{2^k,0} + \dfrac{\chi(1+\eta)}{(k-1)\chi-\ell+1}M_{0,0} - \dfrac{\chi}{(k-1)\chi-\ell+1}M_{1,0} - \dfrac{k\chi-\ell+1}{(k-1)\chi-\ell+1}M_{2^{k-1},0}$$

$$= \dfrac{1+\eta}{2} + \dfrac{\chi(1+\eta)}{(k-1)\chi-\ell+1} - \dfrac{\chi}{(k-1)\chi-\ell+1}\dfrac{1+\eta}{2} - \dfrac{k\chi-\ell+1}{(k-1)\chi-\ell+1}\dfrac{1+\eta}{2}$$

$$\dfrac{1+\eta}{2} + -\dfrac{\chi(1+\eta)}{2[(k-1)\chi-\ell+1]} - \dfrac{1+\eta}{2} - \dfrac{\chi}{(k-1)\chi-\ell+1}\dfrac{1+\eta}{2} = 0.$$

$$M_{2^k,1} + \dfrac{\chi(1+\eta)}{(k-1)\chi-\ell+1}M_{0,1} - \dfrac{\chi}{(k-1)\chi-\ell+1}M_{1,1} - \dfrac{k\chi-\ell+1}{(k-1)\chi-\ell+1}M_{2^{k-1},1}$$

$$= \left(\eta + \dfrac{k\chi(\eta-1)^2}{2(\ell-1)}\right) + \dfrac{\chi(1+\eta)}{(k-1)\chi-\ell+1}\dfrac{1+\eta}{2} - \dfrac{\chi}{(k-1)\chi-\ell+1}\eta$$

$$-\dfrac{k\chi-\ell+1}{(k-1)\chi-\ell+1}\left(\eta + \dfrac{(k-1)\chi(\eta-1)^2}{2(\ell-1)}\right)$$

$$= \eta + \dfrac{k\chi(\eta-1)^2}{2(\ell-1)} + \dfrac{\chi(1+\eta)^2}{2[(k-1)\chi-\ell+1]} - \dfrac{2\chi\eta}{2[(k-1)\chi-\ell+1]} - \dfrac{2[k\chi-\ell+1]\eta}{2[(k-1)\chi-\ell+1]}$$

$$-\dfrac{k\chi-\ell+1}{(k-1)\chi-\ell+1}\dfrac{(k-1)\chi(\eta-1)^2}{2(\ell-1)}$$

$$= \eta + \frac{k\chi(\eta-1)^2}{2(\ell-1)} + \frac{\chi(1+\eta^2)}{2[(k-1)\chi-\ell+1]} - \frac{[k\chi-\ell+1]\eta}{[(k-1)\chi-\ell+1]} - \frac{(k\chi-\ell+1)(k-1)\chi(\eta-1)^2}{2[(k-1)\chi-\ell+1](\ell-1)}$$

$$= + \frac{k\chi(\eta-1)^2}{2(\ell-1)} + \frac{\chi(\eta-1)^2}{2[(k-1)\chi-\ell+1]} - \frac{(k\chi-\ell+1)(k-1)\chi(\eta-1)^2}{2[(k-1)\chi-\ell+1](\ell-1)}$$

$$= + \frac{k\chi(\eta-1)^2[(k-1)\chi-\ell+1]+\chi(\eta-1)^2(\ell-1)}{2[(k-1)\chi-\ell+1](\ell-1)} - \frac{(k\chi-\ell+1)(k-1)\chi(\eta-1)^2}{2[(k-1)\chi-\ell+1](\ell-1)}$$

$$= \frac{\chi(\eta-1)^2}{2[(k-1)\chi-\ell+1](\ell-1)}\big[k[(k-1)\chi-\ell+1]+(\ell-1)-(k\chi-\ell+1)(k-1)\big]$$

$$= \frac{\chi(\eta-1)^2}{2[(k-1)\chi-\ell+1](\ell-1)}\big[k[(k-1)\chi-\ell+1]+(\ell-1)-(k\chi-\ell+1)(k-1)\big] = 0.$$

$$M_{2^k,2^v} + \frac{\chi(1+\eta)}{(k-1)\chi-\ell+1}M_{0,2^v} - \frac{\chi}{(k-1)\chi-\ell+1}M_{1,2^v} - \frac{k\chi-\ell+1}{(k-1)\chi-\ell+1}M_{2^{k-1},2^v}$$

$$= \left(\eta + \frac{(v-k)\chi(\eta-1)^2}{2(\ell-1)}\right) + \frac{\chi(1+\eta)}{(k-1)\chi-\ell+1}\frac{(1+\eta)}{2}$$

$$\quad - \frac{\chi}{(k-1)\chi-\ell+1}\left(\eta+\frac{v\chi(\eta-1)^2}{2(\ell-1)}\right)$$

$$\quad - \frac{k\chi-\ell+1}{(k-1)\chi-\ell+1}\left(\eta+\frac{(v-k+1)\chi(\eta-1)^2}{2(\ell-1)}\right)$$

$$= \eta + \frac{(v-k)\chi(\eta-1)^2}{2(\ell-1)} + \frac{\chi(1+\eta)^2}{2[(k-1)\chi-\ell+1]} - \frac{\chi\eta}{(k-1)\chi-\ell+1}$$

$$\quad - \frac{v\chi^2(\eta-1)^2}{2[(k-1)\chi-\ell+1](\ell-1)} - \frac{(k\chi-\ell+1)\eta}{(k-1)\chi-\ell+1}$$

$$\quad - \frac{(v-k+1)\chi(\eta-1)^2(k\chi-\ell+1)}{2[(k-1)\chi-\ell+1](\ell-1)}$$

$$= \frac{(v-k)\chi(\eta-1)^2}{2(\ell-1)} + \frac{\chi(1-\eta)^2}{2[(k-1)\chi-\ell+1]} - \frac{v\chi^2(\eta-1)^2}{2[(k-1)\chi-\ell+1](\ell-1)}$$

$$-\frac{(v-k+1)\chi(\eta-1)^2(k\chi-\ell+1)}{2[(k-1)\chi-\ell+1](\ell-1)}$$

$$=\frac{\chi(\eta-1)^2}{2[(k-1)\chi-\ell+1](\ell-1)}\left[\begin{array}{l}(v-k)[(k-1)\chi-\ell+1]+(\ell-1)\\-v\chi-(v-k+1)(k\chi-\ell+1)\end{array}\right]$$

$$=-\frac{\chi(\eta-1)^2[v\chi-\ell+1]}{[(k-1)\chi-\ell+1](\ell-1)}.$$

$$M_{2^k,2^{v-1}}+\frac{\chi(1+\eta)}{(k-1)\chi-\ell+1}M_{0,2^{v-1}}-\frac{\chi}{(k-1)\chi-\ell+1}M_{1,2^{v-1}}-\frac{k\chi-\ell+1}{(k-1)\chi-\ell+1}M_{2^{k-1},2^{v-1}}$$

Case 1: $v>k$

$$M_{2^k,2^{v-1}}+\frac{\chi(1+\eta)}{(k-1)\chi-\ell+1}M_{0,2^{v-1}}-\frac{\chi}{(k-1)\chi-\ell+1}M_{1,2^{v-1}}$$

$$-\frac{k\chi-\ell+1}{(k-1)\chi-\ell+1}M_{2^{k-1},2^{v-1}}$$

$$=\left(\eta+\frac{(v-1-k)\chi(\eta-1)^2}{2(\ell-1)}\right)+\frac{\chi(1+\eta)}{(k-1)\chi-\ell+1}\frac{(1+\eta)}{2}$$

$$-\frac{\chi}{(k-1)\chi-\ell+1}\left(\eta+\frac{(v-1)\chi(\eta-1)^2}{2(\ell-1)}\right)$$

$$-\frac{k\chi-\ell+1}{(k-1)\chi-\ell+1}\left(\eta+\frac{(v-k)\chi(\eta-1)^2}{2(\ell-1)}\right)$$

$$-\frac{\chi(\eta-1)^2}{2(\ell-1)}+\frac{\chi(1-\eta)^2}{2[(k-1)\chi-\ell+1]}-\frac{(2v-k-1)\chi^2(\eta-1)^2}{2(\ell-1)[(k-1)\chi-\ell+1]}$$

$$=\frac{\chi(\eta-1)^2}{2(\ell-1)[(k-1)\chi-\ell+1]}\left[-[(k-1)\chi-\ell+1]+\ell-1-(2v-k-1)\chi\right]$$

$$=-\frac{\chi(\eta-1)^2[(v-1)\chi-\ell+1]}{(\ell-1)[(k-1)\chi-\ell+1]}.$$

Case 2: $v=k$

$$=\left(\eta+\frac{\chi(\eta-1)^2}{2(\ell-1)}\right)+\frac{\chi(1+\eta)}{(k-1)\chi-\ell+1}\frac{(1+\eta)}{2}$$

$$-\frac{\chi}{(k-1)\chi-\ell+1}\left(\eta+\frac{(k-1)\chi(\eta-1)^2}{2(\ell-1)}\right)-\frac{k\chi-\ell+1}{(k-1)\chi-\ell+1}(\eta)$$

$$= +\frac{\chi(\eta-1)^2}{2(\ell-1)} + \frac{\chi(1-\eta)^2}{2[(k-1)\chi-\ell+1]} - \frac{(k-1)\chi^2(\eta-1)^2}{2(\ell-1)[(k-1)\chi-\ell+1]}$$

$$= \frac{\chi(\eta-1)^2}{2(\ell-1)[(k-1)\chi-\ell+1]}\left[[(k-1)\chi-\ell+1]+\ell-1-(k-1)\chi\right]=0$$

$$M_{2^k,2^{v-1}+1} + \frac{\chi(1+\eta)}{(k-1)\chi-\ell+1}M_{0,2^{v-1}+1} - \frac{\chi}{(k-1)\chi-\ell+1}M_{1,2^{v-1}+1} - \frac{k\chi-\ell+1}{(k-1)\chi-\ell+1}M_{2^{k-1},2^{v-1}+1}$$

Case 1: $v > k$

$$= \frac{(1+\eta)\eta}{2} + \frac{\chi(1+\eta)}{(k-1)\chi-\ell+1}\frac{(1+\eta^2)(\ell-1)-(v-1)\chi(1-\eta)^2}{2(\ell-1)}$$

$$- \frac{\chi}{(k-1)\chi-\ell+1}\frac{(1+\eta)\eta}{2} - \frac{k\chi-\ell+1}{(k-1)\chi-\ell+1}\frac{(1+\eta)\eta}{2}$$

$$= +\frac{\chi(1+\eta)}{(k-1)\chi-\ell+1}\frac{(1+\eta^2)(\ell-1)-(v-1)\chi(1-\eta)^2}{2(\ell-1)} - \frac{2\chi}{(k-1)\chi-\ell+1}\frac{(1+\eta)\eta}{2}$$

$$= +\frac{\chi(1+\eta)(1-\eta)^2}{2[(k-1)\chi-\ell+1]} - \frac{(v-1)\chi^2(1+\eta)(1-\eta)^2}{2(\ell-1)[(k-1)\chi-\ell+1]}$$

$$= -\frac{\chi(1+\eta)(1-\eta)^2[(v-1)\chi-\ell+1]}{2[(k-1)\chi-\ell+1](\ell-1)}$$

Case 2: $v = k$

$$= \frac{1}{2}\left(\eta+\eta^2 + \frac{\chi(\eta^3-\eta^2-\eta+1)}{\ell-1}\right)$$

$$+ \frac{\chi(1+\eta)}{(k-1)\chi-\ell+1}\frac{(1+\eta^2)(\ell-1)-(k-1)\chi(1-\eta)^2}{2(\ell-1)}$$

$$- \frac{\chi}{(k-1)\chi-\ell+1}\frac{(1+\eta)\eta}{2} - \frac{k\chi-\ell+1}{(k-1)\chi-\ell+1}\frac{1}{2}(\eta+\eta^2)$$

$$= \frac{1}{2}\left((1+\eta)\eta + \frac{\chi(1+\eta)(\eta-1)^2}{\ell-1}\right)$$

$$+ \frac{\chi(1+\eta)}{(k-1)\chi-\ell+1}\frac{(1+\eta^2)}{2} - \frac{\chi(1+\eta)}{(k-1)\chi-\ell+1}\frac{(k-1)\chi(1-\eta)^2}{2(\ell-1)}$$

$$- \frac{\chi(1+\eta)\eta}{2[(k-1)\chi-\ell+1]} - \frac{(k\chi-\ell+1)(1+\eta)\eta}{2[(k-1)\chi-\ell+1]}$$

$$= \frac{\chi(1+\eta)(\eta-1)^2}{2(\ell-1)} + \frac{\chi(1+\eta)(1-\eta)^2}{2\left[(k-1)\chi-\ell+1\right]} - \frac{(k-1)(1-\eta)^2\chi^2(1+\eta)}{2\left[(k-1)\chi-\ell+1\right](\ell-1)}$$

$$= \frac{(1-\eta)^2\chi(1+\eta)}{2\left[(k-1)\chi-\ell+1\right](\ell-1)}\left[(k-1)\chi-\ell+1+\ell-1-(k-1)\chi\right]=0.$$

$$= M_{2^k,2^v+1} + \frac{\chi(1+\eta)}{(k-1)\chi-\ell+1}M_{0,2^v+1} - \frac{\chi}{(k-1)\chi-\ell+1}M_{1,2^v+1} - \frac{k\chi-\ell+1}{(k-1)\chi-\ell+1}M_{2^{k-1},2^v+1}$$

$$\frac{(1+\eta)\eta}{2} + \frac{\chi(1+\eta)}{(k-1)\chi-\ell+1}\frac{\left(1+\eta^2\right)(\ell-1)-v\chi(1-\eta)^2}{2(\ell-1)}$$

$$-\frac{\chi}{(k-1)\chi-\ell+1}\frac{(1+\eta)\eta}{2}-\frac{k\chi-\ell+1}{(k-1)\chi-\ell+1}\frac{(1+\eta)\eta}{2}$$

$$= +\frac{\chi(1+\eta)(1-\eta)^2}{2\left[(k-1)\chi-\ell+1\right]} - \frac{(1+\eta)v\chi^2(1-\eta)^2}{2\left[(k-1)\chi-\ell+1\right](\ell-1)}$$

$$= \frac{\chi(1+\eta)(1-\eta)^2}{2\left[(k-1)\chi-\ell+1\right]}\left[\ell-1-v\chi\right] = -\frac{\chi(1+\eta)(1-\eta)^2\left[v\chi-\ell+1\right]}{2\left[(k-1)\chi-\ell+1\right]}.$$

Gathering intermediate results gives

Case 1: $v > k$

$$= \frac{\chi(\eta-1)^2\left[v\chi-\ell+1\right]}{\left[(k-1)\chi-\ell+1\right](\ell-1)}\frac{(1+\eta)}{2} - \frac{\chi(\eta-1)^2\left[(v-1)\chi-\ell+1\right]}{(\ell-1)\left[(k-1)\chi-\ell+1\right]}\frac{(1+\eta)(v\chi-\ell+1)}{2\left[(v-1)\chi-\ell+1\right]}$$

$$+ \frac{\chi(1+\eta)(1-\eta)^2\left[(v-1)\chi-\ell+1\right]}{2\left[(k-1)\chi-\ell+1\right](\ell-1)}\frac{v\chi-\ell+1}{(v-1)\chi-\ell+1} - \frac{\chi(1+\eta)(1-\eta)^2\left[v\chi-\ell+1\right]}{2\left[(k-1)\chi-\ell+1\right]} = 0.$$

Case 2: $v = k$ This case is 0.

$\square$

Proof of Theorem 4:
The proof method is similar to that used in Theorem 1.

(a) Row 0 of $\mathbf{LM}$ times column 0 of $\mathbf{L}^T$:

$$M_{0,0} = (1-\mu)^\ell$$

(b) Row 1 of $\mathbf{LM}$ times column 1 of $\mathbf{L}^T$:

$$-\frac{(1+\eta)}{2}\left[M_{1,0} - \frac{(1+\eta)}{2}M_{0,0}\right] + \left[M_{1,1} - \frac{(1+\eta)}{2}M_{0,1}\right] = (1-\mu)^\ell\left[\eta - \frac{(1+\eta)^2}{4}\right]$$

$$= -\frac{(1-\mu)^{\ell}(1-\eta)^2}{4}$$

(c) Row 2 of **LM** times column 2 of $\mathbf{L}^{\mathrm{T}}$:

$$-\frac{\chi(1+\eta)}{\ell-1}\left(\mathbf{M}_{2,0} - \frac{\chi(1+\eta)}{\ell-1}\mathbf{M}_{0,0} + \frac{2\chi-\ell+1}{\ell-1}\mathbf{M}_{1,0}\right)$$

$$+\frac{2\chi-\ell+1}{\ell-1}\left(\mathbf{M}_{2,1} - \frac{\chi(1+\eta)}{\ell-1}\mathbf{M}_{0,1} + \frac{2\chi-\ell+1}{\ell-1}\mathbf{M}_{1,1}\right)$$

$$+\left(\mathbf{M}_{2,2} - \frac{\chi(1+\eta)}{\ell-1}\mathbf{M}_{0,2} + \frac{2\chi-\ell+1}{\ell-1}\mathbf{M}_{1,2}\right)$$

$$= -\frac{\chi(1+\eta)}{\ell-1}\left(2\mathbf{M}_{2,0} - \frac{\chi(1+\eta)}{\ell-1}\mathbf{M}_{0,0} + 2\frac{2\chi-\ell+1}{\ell-1}\mathbf{M}_{1,0}\right)$$

$$+\frac{2\chi-\ell+1}{\ell-1}\left(2\mathbf{M}_{2,1} + \frac{2\chi-\ell+1}{\ell-1}\mathbf{M}_{1,1}\right) + \mathbf{M}_{2,2}$$

Substituting for the M values and (temporarily) dividing by $(1-\mu)^{\ell}$ gives

$$= -\frac{\chi(1+\eta)^2}{2(\ell-1)}\left(2 - \frac{2\chi}{\ell-1} + 2\frac{2\chi-\ell+1}{\ell-1}\right) + \frac{2\chi-\ell+1}{\ell-1}\left(2\eta + \frac{\chi(\eta-1)^2}{(\ell-1)} + \frac{2\chi-\ell+1}{\ell-1}\eta\right) + \eta$$

$$= -\frac{\chi^2(1+\eta)^2}{(\ell-1)^2} + \frac{2\chi-\ell+1}{(\ell-1)^2}\left(\eta(\ell-1) + \chi(\eta-1)^2 + 2\chi\eta\right) + \eta$$

$$= -\frac{\chi^2(1+\eta)^2}{(\ell-1)^2} + \frac{2\chi-\ell+1}{(\ell-1)^2}\left(\eta(\ell-1) + \chi(\eta^2+1)\right) + \eta$$

$$= \frac{1}{(\ell-1)^2}\left[-\chi^2(1+\eta)^2 + 2\chi\eta(\ell-1) + 2\chi^2(\eta^2+1) - (\ell-1)\chi(\eta^2+1)\right]$$

$$= \frac{1}{(\ell-1)^2}\left[\chi^2(\eta-1)^2 - (\ell-1)\chi(\eta-1)^2\right]$$

Multiplying by $(1-\mu)^{\ell}$ and simplifying gives

$$\frac{\chi(\eta-1)^2(1-\mu)^{\ell}}{(\ell-1)}\left[\frac{\chi}{\ell-1}-1\right].$$

(d) Row 3 of **LM** times column 3 of $\mathbf{L}^{\mathrm{T}}$:

$$\left(\eta + \frac{\chi(1-\eta)^2}{2(\ell-1)}\right)\left(\mathbf{M}_{3,0} + \left(\eta + \frac{\chi(1-\eta)^2}{2(\ell-1)}\right)\mathbf{M}_{0,0} - \frac{(1+\eta)}{2}\mathbf{M}_{1,0} - \frac{(1+\eta)}{2}\mathbf{M}_{2,0}\right)$$

$$-\frac{(1+\eta)}{2}\left(M_{3,1}+\left(\eta+\frac{\chi(1-\eta)^2}{2(\ell-1)}\right)M_{0,1}-\frac{(1+\eta)}{2}M_{1,1}-\frac{(1+\eta)}{2}M_{2,1}\right)$$

$$-\frac{(1+\eta)}{2}\left(M_{3,2}+\left(\eta+\frac{\chi(1-\eta)^2}{2(\ell-1)}\right)M_{0,2}-\frac{(1+\eta)}{2}M_{1,2}-\frac{(1+\eta)}{2}M_{2,2}\right)$$

$$+\left(M_{3,3}+\left(\eta+\frac{\chi(1-\eta)^2}{2(\ell-1)}\right)M_{0,3}-\frac{(1+\eta)}{2}M_{1,3}-\frac{(1+\eta)}{2}M_{2,3}\right)$$

$$=\left(\eta+\frac{\chi(1-\eta)^2}{2(\ell-1)}\right)\left(2M_{3,0}+\left(\eta+\frac{\chi(1-\eta)^2}{2(\ell-1)}\right)M_{0,0}-2\frac{(1+\eta)}{2}M_{1,0}-2\frac{(1+\eta)}{2}M_{2,0}\right)$$

$$-\frac{(1+\eta)}{2}\left(2M_{3,1}-\frac{(1+\eta)}{2}M_{1,1}-2\frac{(1+\eta)}{2}M_{2,1}\right)$$

$$-\frac{(1+\eta)}{2}\left(2M_{3,2}-\frac{(1+\eta)}{2}M_{2,2}\right)+M_{3,3}$$

Substituting for the M values and (temporarily) dividing by $(1-\mu)^\ell$ gives

$$=\left(\eta+\frac{\chi(1-\eta)^2}{2(\ell-1)}\right)\left(1+\eta^2-\frac{\chi(\eta-1)^2}{\ell-1}+\left(\eta+\frac{\chi(1-\eta)^2}{2(\ell-1)}\right)-(1+\eta)^2\right)$$

$$-\frac{(1+\eta)}{2}\left(2\frac{(1+\eta)\eta}{2}-\frac{(1+\eta)}{2}\eta-2\frac{(1+\eta)}{2}\left(\eta+\frac{\chi(\eta-1)^2}{2(\ell-1)}\right)\right)$$

$$-\frac{(1+\eta)}{2}\left(2\frac{(1+\eta)\eta}{2}-\frac{(1+\eta)}{2}\eta\right)+\eta^2$$

$$=-\left(\eta+\frac{\chi(1-\eta)^2}{2(\ell-1)}\right)\left(\frac{\chi(1-\eta)^2}{2(\ell-1)}+\eta\right)-\frac{(1+\eta)^2}{4}\left(-\eta-\frac{\chi(\eta-1)^2}{(\ell-1)}\right)-\frac{(1+\eta)^2\eta}{4}+\eta^2$$

$$=-\frac{\eta\chi(1-\eta)^2}{(\ell-1)}-\left(\frac{\chi(1-\eta)^2}{2(\ell-1)}\right)^2+\frac{(1+\eta)^2}{4}\left(\frac{\chi(\eta-1)^2}{(\ell-1)}\right)=\frac{\chi(1-\eta)^4}{4(\ell-1)}-\frac{\chi^2(1-\eta)^4}{4(\ell-1)^2}$$

Multiplying by $(1-\mu)^\ell$ and simplifying gives

$$-\frac{\chi(1-\mu)^\ell(1-\eta)^4}{4(\ell-1)}\left[\frac{\chi}{\ell-1}-1\right]$$

(e) Row 2^k of **LM** times column 2^k of $\mathbf{L}^T$:

$$\frac{\chi(1+\eta)}{(k-1)\chi-\ell+1}\left(M_{2^k,0}+\frac{\chi(1+\eta)}{(k-1)\chi-\ell+1}M_{0,0}-\frac{\chi}{(k-1)\chi-\ell+1}M_{1,0}-\frac{k\chi-\ell+1}{(k-1)\chi-\ell+1}M_{2^{k-1},0}\right)$$

$$
-\frac{\chi}{(k-1)\chi-\ell+1}\left(\begin{array}{l} M_{2^k,1}+\dfrac{\chi(1+\eta)}{(k-1)\chi-\ell+1}M_{0,1}-\dfrac{\chi}{(k-1)\chi-\ell+1}M_{1,1} \\[2ex] -\dfrac{k\chi-\ell+1}{(k-1)\chi-\ell+1}M_{2^{k-1},1} \end{array}\right)
$$

$$
-\frac{k\chi-\ell+1}{(k-1)\chi-\ell+1}\left(\begin{array}{l} M_{2^k,2^{k-1}}+\dfrac{\chi(1+\eta)}{(k-1)\chi-\ell+1}M_{0,2^{k-1}}-\dfrac{\chi}{(k-1)\chi-\ell+1}M_{1,2^{k-1}} \\[2ex] -\dfrac{k\chi-\ell+1}{(k-1)\chi-\ell+1}M_{2^{k-1},2^{k-1}} \end{array}\right)
$$

$$
+\left(M_{2^k,2^k}+\frac{\chi(1+\eta)}{(k-1)\chi-\ell+1}M_{0,2^k}-\frac{\chi}{(k-1)\chi-\ell+1}M_{1,2^k}-\frac{k\chi-\ell+1}{(k-1)\chi-\ell+1}M_{2^{k-1},2^k}\right)
$$

$$
=\frac{\chi(1+\eta)}{(k-1)\chi-\ell+1}\left(\begin{array}{l} 2M_{2^k,0}+\dfrac{\chi(1+\eta)}{(k-1)\chi-\ell+1}M_{0,0}-2\dfrac{\chi}{(k-1)\chi-\ell+1}M_{1,0} \\[2ex] -2\dfrac{k\chi-\ell+1}{(k-1)\chi-\ell+1}M_{2^{k-1},0} \end{array}\right)
$$

$$
-\frac{\chi}{(k-1)\chi-\ell+1}\left(2M_{2^k,1}-\frac{\chi}{(k-1)\chi-\ell+1}M_{1,1}-2\frac{k\chi-\ell+1}{(k-1)\chi-\ell+1}M_{2^{k-1},1}\right)
$$

$$
-\frac{k\chi-\ell+1}{(k-1)\chi-\ell+1}\left(2M_{2^k,2^{k-1}}-\frac{k\chi-\ell+1}{(k-1)\chi-\ell+1}M_{2^{k-1},2^{k-1}}\right)+M_{2^k,2^k}
$$

Substituting for the M values and (temporarily) dividing by $(1-\mu)^{\ell}$ gives

$$
=\frac{\chi(1+\eta)}{(k-1)\chi-\ell+1}\left(\begin{array}{l} 2\dfrac{1+\eta}{2}+\dfrac{\chi(1+\eta)}{(k-1)\chi-\ell+1}-2\dfrac{\chi}{(k-1)\chi-\ell+1}\dfrac{1+\eta}{2} \\[2ex] -2\dfrac{k\chi-\ell+1}{(k-1)\chi-\ell+1}\dfrac{1+\eta}{2} \end{array}\right)
$$

$$
-\frac{\chi}{(k-1)\chi-\ell+1}\left(\begin{array}{l} 2\left(\eta+\dfrac{k\chi(\eta-1)^2}{2(\ell-1)}\right)-\dfrac{\chi}{(k-1)\chi-\ell+1}\eta \\[2ex] -2\dfrac{k\chi-\ell+1}{(k-1)\chi-\ell+1}\left(\eta+\dfrac{(k-1)\chi(\eta-1)^2}{2(\ell-1)}\right) \end{array}\right)
$$

$$
-\frac{k\chi-\ell+1}{(k-1)\chi-\ell+1}\left(2\left(\eta+\frac{\chi(\eta-1)^2}{2(\ell-1)}\right)-\frac{k\chi-\ell+1}{(k-1)\chi-\ell+1}\eta\right)+\eta
$$

$$
=-\frac{\chi(k\chi-\ell+1)}{(\ell-1)[(k-1)\chi-\ell+1]}\left[-\frac{\chi(1+\eta)^2(\ell-1)}{((k-1)\chi-\ell+1)(k\chi-\ell+1)}+\frac{\chi(1+\eta)^2(\ell-1)}{((k-1)\chi-\ell+1)(k\chi-\ell+1)}\right.
$$

$$-\frac{(1+\eta)^2(\ell-1)}{(k\chi-\ell+1)}+\frac{(1+\eta)^2(\ell-1)}{(k-1)\chi-\ell+1}-\frac{2(\ell-1)}{(k-1)\chi-\ell+1}\left(\eta+\frac{(k-1)\chi(\eta-1)^2}{2(\ell-1)}\right)$$

$$-\frac{\chi\eta(\ell-1)}{((k-1)\chi-\ell+1)(k\chi-\ell+1)}+\frac{2\eta(\ell-1)}{(k\chi-\ell+1)}+\frac{k\chi(\eta-1)^2}{(k\chi-\ell+1)}$$

$$+\frac{2(\ell-1)}{\chi}\left(\eta+\frac{\chi(\eta-1)^2}{2(\ell-1)}\right)-\frac{k\chi-\ell+1}{(k-1)\chi-\ell+1}\frac{\eta(\ell-1)}{\chi}-\frac{\eta((k-1)\chi-\ell+1)(\ell-1)}{\chi(k\chi-\ell+1)}\Bigg].$$

The term in brackets can be simplified as follows.

$$-\frac{(1+\eta)^2(\ell-1)-2\eta(\ell-1)-k\chi(\eta-1)^2}{(k\chi-\ell+1)}+\frac{(1+\eta)^2(\ell-1)-(k-1)\chi(\eta-1)^2-2(\ell-1)\eta}{(k-1)\chi-\ell+1}$$

$$-\frac{\chi\eta(\ell-1)}{((k-1)\chi-\ell+1)(k\chi-\ell+1)}+\frac{\eta(\ell-1)}{\chi}\left[2-\frac{k\chi-\ell+1}{(k-1)\chi-\ell+1}-\frac{(k-1)\chi-\ell+1}{(k\chi-\ell+1)}\right]+(\eta-1)^2$$

But

$$2-\frac{k\chi-\ell+1}{(k-1)\chi-\ell+1}-\frac{(k-1)\chi-\ell+1}{(k\chi-\ell+1)}=\frac{-\chi^2}{(k\chi-\ell+1)((k-1)\chi-\ell+1)}$$

and

$$-\frac{(1+\eta)^2(\ell-1)-2\eta(\ell-1)-k\chi(\eta-1)^2}{(k\chi-\ell+1)}+\frac{(1+\eta)^2(\ell-1)-(k-1)\chi(\eta-1)^2-2(\ell-1)\eta}{(k-1)\chi-\ell+1}$$

$$=-\frac{(1+\eta^2)(\ell-1)-k\chi(\eta-1)^2}{(k\chi-\ell+1)}+\frac{(1+\eta^2)(\ell-1)-(k-1)\chi(\eta-1)^2}{(k-1)\chi-\ell+1}$$

$$=\frac{2\eta\chi(\ell-1)}{(k\chi-\ell+1)((k-1)\chi-\ell+1)}.$$

So the bracketed term is equal to

$$\frac{2\eta\chi(\ell-1)}{(k\chi-\ell+1)((k-1)\chi-\ell+1)}-\frac{\chi\eta(\ell-1)}{((k-1)\chi-\ell+1)(k\chi-\ell+1)}-\frac{\chi\eta(\ell-1)}{(k\chi-\ell+1)((k-1)\chi-\ell+1)}+(\eta-1)^2$$

$$=(\eta-1)^2$$

Collecting terms, we have our result

$$-\frac{\chi(k\chi-\ell+1)(\eta-1)^2(1-\mu)^\ell}{(\ell-1)[(k-1)\chi-\ell+1]}$$

(f) Row 2^k+1 of **LM** times column 2^k+1 of $\mathbf{L}^{\mathrm{T}}$:

$$\frac{-\chi(1+\eta^2)}{2[(k-1)\chi-\ell+1]}\left(\begin{array}{l}M_{2^k+1,0}-\dfrac{\chi(1+\eta^2)}{2[(k-1)\chi-\ell+1]}M_{0,0}+\dfrac{\chi(1+\eta)}{2[(k-1)\chi-\ell+1]}M_{1,0}\\[2ex]+\dfrac{(1+\eta)(k\chi-\ell+1)}{2[(k-1)\chi-\ell+1]}M_{2^{k-1},0}-\dfrac{k\chi-\ell+1}{(k-1)\chi-\ell+1}M_{2^{k-1}+1,0}-\dfrac{(1+\eta)}{2}M_{2^k,0}\end{array}\right)$$

$$+\frac{\chi(1+\eta)}{2[(k-1)\chi-\ell+1]}\left(\begin{aligned}&M_{2^k+1,1}-\frac{\chi(1+\eta^2)}{2[(k-1)\chi-\ell+1]}M_{0,1}+\frac{\chi(1+\eta)}{2[(k-1)\chi-\ell+1]}M_{1,1}\\&+\frac{(1+\eta)(k\chi-\ell+1)}{2[(k-1)\chi-\ell+1]}M_{2^{k-1},1}-\frac{k\chi-\ell+1}{(k-1)\chi-\ell+1}M_{2^{k-1}+1,1}-\frac{(1+\eta)}{2}M_{2^k,1}\end{aligned}\right)$$

$$+\frac{(1+\eta)(k\chi-\ell+1)}{2[(k-1)\chi-\ell+1]}\left(\begin{aligned}&M_{2^k+1,2^{k-1}}-\frac{\chi(1+\eta^2)}{2[(k-1)\chi-\ell+1]}M_{0,2^{k-1}}+\frac{\chi(1+\eta)}{2[(k-1)\chi-\ell+1]}M_{1,2^{k-1}}\\&+\frac{(1+\eta)(k\chi-\ell+1)}{2[(k-1)\chi-\ell+1]}M_{2^{k-1},2^{k-1}}-\frac{k\chi-\ell+1}{(k-1)\chi-\ell+1}M_{2^{k-1}+1,2^{k-1}}-\frac{(1+\eta)}{2}M_{2^k,2^{k-1}}\end{aligned}\right)$$

$$-\frac{k\chi-\ell+1}{(k-1)\chi-\ell+1}\left(\begin{aligned}&M_{2^k+1,2^{k-1}+1}-\frac{\chi(1+\eta^2)}{2[(k-1)\chi-\ell+1]}M_{0,2^{k-1}+1}+\frac{\chi(1+\eta)}{2[(k-1)\chi-\ell+1]}M_{1,2^{k-1}+1}\\&+\frac{(1+\eta)(k\chi-\ell+1)}{2[(k-1)\chi-\ell+1]}M_{2^{k-1},2^{k-1}+1}-\frac{k\chi-\ell+1}{(k-1)\chi-\ell+1}M_{2^{k-1}+1,2^{k-1}+1}-\frac{(1+\eta)}{2}M_{2^k,2^{k-1}+1}\end{aligned}\right)$$

$$-\frac{(1+\eta)}{2}\left(\begin{aligned}&M_{2^k+1,2^k}-\frac{\chi(1+\eta^2)}{2[(k-1)\chi-\ell+1]}M_{0,2^k}+\frac{\chi(1+\eta)}{2[(k-1)\chi-\ell+1]}M_{1,2^k}\\&+\frac{(1+\eta)(k\chi-\ell+1)}{2[(k-1)\chi-\ell+1]}M_{2^{k-1},2^k}-\frac{k\chi-\ell+1}{(k-1)\chi-\ell+1}M_{2^{k-1}+1,2^k}-\frac{(1+\eta)}{2}M_{2^k,2^k}\end{aligned}\right)$$

$$+\left(\begin{aligned}&M_{2^k+1,2^k+1}-\frac{\chi(1+\eta^2)}{2[(k-1)\chi-\ell+1]}M_{0,2^k+1}+\frac{\chi(1+\eta)}{2[(k-1)\chi-\ell+1]}M_{1,2^k+1}\\&+\frac{(1+\eta)(k\chi-\ell+1)}{2[(k-1)\chi-\ell+1]}M_{2^{k-1},2^k+1}-\frac{k\chi-\ell+1}{(k-1)\chi-\ell+1}M_{2^{k-1}+1,2^k+1}-\frac{(1+\eta)}{2}M_{2^k,2^k+1}\end{aligned}\right)$$

We will first show that the first five terms sum to zero. They simplify to

$$\frac{-\chi(1+\eta^2)}{2[(k-1)\chi-\ell+1]}\left(\begin{aligned}&M_{2^k+1,0}-\frac{\chi(1+\eta^2)}{2[(k-1)\chi-\ell+1]}M_{0,0}+2\frac{\chi(1+\eta)}{2[(k-1)\chi-\ell+1]}M_{1,0}\\&+2\frac{(1+\eta)(k\chi-\ell+1)}{2[(k-1)\chi-\ell+1]}M_{2^{k-1},0}-2\frac{k\chi-\ell+1}{(k-1)\chi-\ell+1}M_{2^{k-1}+1,0}-2\frac{(1+\eta)}{2}M_{2^k,0}\end{aligned}\right)$$

$$+\frac{\chi(1+\eta)}{2[(k-1)\chi-\ell+1]}\left(\begin{aligned}&M_{2^k+1,1}+\frac{\chi(1+\eta)}{2[(k-1)\chi-\ell+1]}M_{1,1}\\&+2\frac{(1+\eta)(k\chi-\ell+1)}{2[(k-1)\chi-\ell+1]}M_{2^{k-1},1}-2\frac{k\chi-\ell+1}{(k-1)\chi-\ell+1}M_{2^{k-1}+1,1}-2\frac{(1+\eta)}{2}M_{2^k,1}\end{aligned}\right)$$

$$+\frac{(1+\eta)(k\chi-\ell+1)}{2[(k-1)\chi-\ell+1]}\left(\begin{array}{l}M_{2^k+1,2^{k-1}}+\dfrac{(1+\eta)(k\chi-\ell+1)}{2[(k-1)\chi-\ell+1]}M_{2^{k-1},2^{k-1}}\\[2mm]-2\dfrac{k\chi-\ell+1}{(k-1)\chi-\ell+1}M_{2^{k-1}+1,2^{k-1}}-2\dfrac{(1+\eta)}{2}M_{2^k,2^{k-1}}\end{array}\right)$$

$$-\frac{k\chi-\ell+1}{(k-1)\chi-\ell+1}\left(\begin{array}{l}M_{2^k+1,2^{k-1}+1}\\[1mm]-\dfrac{k\chi-\ell+1}{(k-1)\chi-\ell+1}M_{2^{k-1}+1,2^{k-1}+1}-2\dfrac{(1+\eta)}{2}M_{2^k,2^{k-1}+1}\end{array}\right)-\frac{(1+\eta)}{2}\left(M_{2^k+1,2^k}-\frac{(1+\eta)}{2}M_{2^k,2^k}\right)$$

Divide through by $(1-\mu)^{\ell}$ and then consider each large bracket term, in order.

(Term 1)

$$\frac{1}{(1-\mu)^{\ell}}\left[\begin{array}{l}M_{2^k+1,0}-\dfrac{\chi(1+\eta^2)}{2[(k-1)\chi-\ell+1]}M_{0,0}+2\dfrac{\chi(1+\eta)}{2[(k-1)\chi-\ell+1]}M_{1,0}\\[3mm]+2\dfrac{(1+\eta)(k\chi-\ell+1)}{2[(k-1)\chi-\ell+1]}M_{2^{k-1},0}-2\dfrac{k\chi-\ell+1}{(k-1)\chi-\ell+1}M_{2^{k-1}+1,0}-2\dfrac{(1+\eta)}{2}M_{2^k,0}\end{array}\right]$$

$$=\frac{(1+\eta^2)(\ell-1)-k\chi(1-\eta)^2}{2(\ell-1)}-\frac{\chi(1+\eta^2)}{2[(k-1)\chi-\ell+1]}+2\frac{\chi(1+\eta)}{2[(k-1)\chi-\ell+1]}\frac{(1+\eta)}{2}$$

$$+2\frac{(1+\eta)(k\chi-\ell+1)}{2[(k-1)\chi-\ell+1]}\frac{(1+\eta)}{2}-2\frac{k\chi-\ell+1}{(k-1)\chi-\ell+1}\frac{(1+\eta^2)(\ell-1)-(k-1)\chi(1-\eta)^2}{2(\ell-1)}-2\frac{(1+\eta)}{2}\frac{(1+\eta)}{2}$$

$$=\frac{(1+\eta^2)(\ell-1)-k\chi(1-\eta)^2}{2(\ell-1)}+\frac{\chi2\eta}{2[(k-1)\chi-\ell+1]}-\frac{(1-\eta)^2(k\chi-\ell+1)}{2[(k-1)\chi-\ell+1]}$$

$$-\frac{(1+\eta)^2}{2}+\frac{k\chi-\ell+1}{(k-1)\chi-\ell+1}\frac{(k-1)\chi(1-\eta)^2}{(\ell-1)}$$

$$=\frac{1}{2(\ell-1)[(k-1)\chi-\ell+1]}\left[\begin{array}{l}\chi2\eta(\ell-1)-(1-\eta)^2(\ell-1)(k\chi-\ell+1)\\[1mm]-k\chi(1-\eta)^2[(k-1)\chi-\ell+1]+2(k\chi-\ell+1)(k-1)\chi(1-\eta)^2\\[1mm]-2\eta(\ell-1)[(k-1)\chi-\ell+1]\end{array}\right]$$

(Term 2)

$$\frac{1}{(1-\mu)^{\ell}}\left[\begin{array}{l}M_{2^k+1,1}+\dfrac{\chi(1+\eta)}{2[(k-1)\chi-\ell+1]}M_{1,1}+2\dfrac{(1+\eta)(k\chi-\ell+1)}{2[(k-1)\chi-\ell+1]}M_{2^{k-1},1}\\[3mm]-2\dfrac{k\chi-\ell+1}{(k-1)\chi-\ell+1}M_{2^{k-1}+1,1}-2\dfrac{(1+\eta)}{2}M_{2^k,1}\end{array}\right]$$

$$=\frac{(1+\eta)\eta}{2}+\frac{\chi(1+\eta)}{2[(k-1)\chi-\ell+1]}\eta+2\frac{(1+\eta)(k\chi-\ell+1)}{2[(k-1)\chi-\ell+1]}\left(\eta+\frac{(k-1)\chi(\eta-1)^2}{2(\ell-1)}\right)$$

$$-2\frac{k\chi-\ell+1}{(k-1)\chi-\ell+1}\frac{(1+\eta)\eta}{2}-2\frac{(1+\eta)}{2}\left(\eta+\frac{k\chi(\eta-1)^2}{2(\ell-1)}\right)$$

$$= \frac{(1+\eta)\eta}{2} + \frac{\chi(1+\eta)\eta}{2[(k-1)\chi - \ell + 1]} + \frac{(1+\eta)\eta(k\chi - \ell + 1)}{[(k-1)\chi - \ell + 1]} + \frac{(1+\eta)(k\chi - \ell + 1)}{2[(k-1)\chi - \ell + 1]}\left(\frac{(k-1)\chi(\eta-1)^2}{(\ell-1)}\right)$$

$$- (1+\eta)\eta\frac{k\chi - \ell + 1}{(k-1)\chi - \ell + 1} - (1+\eta)\eta - (1+\eta)\left(\frac{k\chi(\eta-1)^2}{2(\ell-1)}\right)$$

$$= -\frac{(1+\eta)\eta}{2} + \frac{\chi(1+\eta)\eta}{2[(k-1)\chi - \ell + 1]} + \frac{(1+\eta)(k\chi - \ell + 1)}{2[(k-1)\chi - \ell + 1]}\left(\frac{(k-1)\chi(\eta-1)^2}{(\ell-1)}\right) - (1+\eta)\left(\frac{k\chi(\eta-1)^2}{2(\ell-1)}\right)$$

$$= \chi(1+\eta)\frac{\eta(\ell-1) + (k\chi - \ell + 1)(k-1)(\eta-1)^2 - k(\eta-1)^2[(k-1)\chi - \ell + 1]}{2(\ell-1)[(k-1)\chi - \ell + 1]} - \frac{(1+\eta)\eta}{2}$$

$$= \frac{\chi[\eta^3 + 1]}{2[(k-1)\chi - \ell + 1]} - \frac{(1+\eta)\eta}{2}$$

(Term 3)

$$\frac{1}{(1-\mu)^\ell}\left[M_{2^k+1,2^{k-1}} + \frac{(1+\eta)(k\chi - \ell + 1)}{2[(k-1)\chi - \ell + 1]}M_{2^{k-1},2^{k-1}} - 2\frac{k\chi - \ell + 1}{(k-1)\chi - \ell + 1}M_{2^{k-1}+1,2^{k-1}} - 2\frac{(1+\eta)}{2}M_{2^k,2^{k-1}}\right]$$

$$= \frac{(1+\eta)\eta}{2} + \frac{(1+\eta)(k\chi - \ell + 1)}{2[(k-1)\chi - \ell + 1]}\eta - 2\frac{k\chi - \ell + 1}{(k-1)\chi - \ell + 1}\frac{(1+\eta)\eta}{2} - 2\frac{(1+\eta)}{2}\left(\eta + \frac{\chi(\eta-1)^2}{2(\ell-1)}\right)$$

$$= \frac{(1+\eta)\eta}{2} + \frac{(1+\eta)(k\chi - \ell + 1)}{2[(k-1)\chi - \ell + 1]}\eta - \frac{k\chi - \ell + 1}{(k-1)\chi - \ell + 1}(1+\eta)\eta - (1+\eta)\eta - \frac{\chi(1+\eta)(\eta-1)^2}{2(\ell-1)}$$

$$= -\frac{(1+\eta)\eta}{2} - \frac{(1+\eta)(k\chi - \ell + 1)}{2[(k-1)\chi - \ell + 1]}\eta - \frac{\chi(1+\eta)(\eta-1)^2}{2(\ell-1)}$$

(Term 4)

$$\frac{1}{(1-\mu)^\ell}\left[M_{2^k+1,2^{k-1}+1} - \frac{k\chi - \ell + 1}{(k-1)\chi - \ell + 1}M_{2^{k-1}+1,2^{k-1}+1} - 2\frac{(1+\eta)}{2}M_{2^k,2^{k-1}+1}\right]$$

$$= \left(\eta^2 + \frac{\chi\eta(\eta-1)^2}{2(\ell-1)}\right) - \frac{k\chi - \ell + 1}{(k-1)\chi - \ell + 1}\eta^2 - 2\frac{(1+\eta)}{2}\frac{\left(\eta + \eta^2 + \frac{\chi(\eta^3 - \eta^2 - \eta + 1)}{\ell-1}\right)}{2}$$

$$= \eta^2 + \frac{\chi\eta(\eta-1)^2}{2(\ell-1)} - \frac{k\chi - \ell + 1}{(k-1)\chi - \ell + 1}\eta^2 - \frac{(1+\eta)}{2}\left(\eta + \eta^2 + \frac{\chi(\eta^3 - \eta^2 - \eta + 1)}{\ell-1}\right)$$

(Term 5)

$$\frac{1}{(1-\mu)^\ell}\left[M_{2^k+1,2^k} - \frac{(1+\eta)}{2}M_{2^k,2^k}\right] = \frac{(1+\eta)\eta}{2} - \frac{(1+\eta)}{2}\eta = 0.$$

Pulling these terms together gives

$$-\frac{\chi(1+\eta^2)}{2[(k-1)\chi-\ell+1]}\frac{1}{2(\ell-1)[(k-1)\chi-\ell+1]}\begin{bmatrix}\chi2\eta(\ell-1)-(1-\eta)^2(\ell-1)(k\chi-\ell+1)\\-k\chi(1-\eta)^2[(k-1)\chi-\ell+1]\\+2(k\chi-\ell+1)(k-1)\chi(1-\eta)^2\\-2\eta(\ell-1)[(k-1)\chi-\ell+1]\end{bmatrix}$$

$$+\frac{\chi(1+\eta)}{2[(k-1)\chi-\ell+1]}\left(\frac{\chi[\eta^3+1]}{2[(k-1)\chi-\ell+1]}-\frac{(1+\eta)\eta}{2}\right)$$

$$-\frac{(1+\eta)(k\chi-\ell+1)}{2[(k-1)\chi-\ell+1]}\left(\frac{(1+\eta)\eta}{2}+\frac{(1+\eta)(k\chi-\ell+1)}{2[(k-1)\chi-\ell+1]}\eta+\frac{\chi(1+\eta)(\eta-1)^2}{2(\ell-1)}\right)$$

$$-\frac{k\chi-\ell+1}{(k-1)\chi-\ell+1}\left(\begin{array}{c}\eta^2+\dfrac{\chi\eta(\eta-1)^2}{2(\ell-1)}-\dfrac{k\chi-\ell+1}{(k-1)\chi-\ell+1}\eta^2\\[2mm]-\dfrac{(1+\eta)}{2}\left(\eta+\eta^2+\dfrac{\chi(\eta^3-\eta^2-\eta+1)}{\ell-1}\right)\end{array}\right)$$

which gives

$$-\frac{\chi(1+\eta^2)}{4[(k-1)\chi-\ell+1]^2}\begin{bmatrix}\chi2\eta-(1-\eta)^2(k\chi-\ell+1)-k\chi(1-\eta)^2\dfrac{[(k-1)\chi-\ell+1]}{\ell-1}\\[2mm]+2\dfrac{(k\chi-\ell+1)}{\ell-1}(k-1)\chi(1-\eta)^2-2\eta[(k-1)\chi-\ell+1]\end{bmatrix}$$

$$+\frac{\chi(1+\eta)}{4[(k-1)\chi-\ell+1]^2}\left(\chi[\eta^3+1]-(1+\eta)\eta[(k-1)\chi-\ell+1]\right)$$

$$-\frac{(1+\eta)(k\chi-\ell+1)}{4[(k-1)\chi-\ell+1]^2}\left(\begin{array}{c}(1+\eta)\eta[(k-1)\chi-\ell+1]+(\overline{1+}\,\eta)(k\chi-\ell+1)\eta\\[2mm]+\dfrac{\chi(1+\eta)(\eta-1)^2[(k-1)\chi-\ell+1]}{(\ell-1)}\end{array}\right)$$

$$-\frac{k\chi-\ell+1}{4[(k-1)\chi-\ell+1]^2}\left(\begin{array}{c}4\eta^2[(k-1)\chi-\ell+1]+\dfrac{2\chi\eta(\eta-1)^2}{(\ell-1)}[(k-1)\chi-\ell+1]-4(k\chi-\ell+1)\eta^2\\[2mm]-2(1+\eta)[(k-1)\chi-\ell+1]\left(\eta+\eta^2+\dfrac{\chi(\eta^3-\eta^2-\eta+1)}{\ell-1}\right)\end{array}\right)$$

Dividing by $4[(k-1)\chi-\ell+1]^2$ and expanding terms gives

$$-\chi^2 2\eta(1+\eta^2)+(1-\eta)^2(k\chi-\ell+1)\chi(1+\eta^2)+k\chi^2(1-\eta)^2\frac{[(k-1)\chi-\ell+1]}{\ell-1}(1+\eta^2)$$

$$-2\frac{(k\chi-\ell+1)}{\ell-1}(k-1)\chi^2(1-\eta)^2(1+\eta^2)+2\eta[(k-1)\chi-\ell+1]\chi(1+\eta^2)+\chi^2[\eta^3+1](1+\eta)$$

$$-(1+\eta)^2\,\eta\big[(k-1)\chi-\ell+1\big]\chi-(1+\eta)^2\,\eta\big[(k-1)\chi-\ell+1\big](k\chi-\ell+1)-(1+\eta)^2(k\chi-\ell+1)^2\eta$$

$$-\frac{\chi(1+\eta)^2(\eta-1)^2\big[(k-1)\chi-\ell+1\big](k\chi-\ell+1)}{(\ell-1)}-4\eta^2\big[(k-1)\chi-\ell+1\big](k\chi-\ell+1)$$

$$-\frac{2\chi\eta(\eta-1)^2}{(\ell-1)}\big[(k-1)\chi-\ell+1\big](k\chi-\ell+1)+4(k\chi-\ell+1)^2\eta^2$$

$$+2(1+\eta)\big[(k-1)\chi-\ell+1\big]\left(\eta+\eta^2+\frac{\chi\big(\eta^3-\eta^2-\eta+1\big)}{\ell-1}\right)(k\chi-\ell+1)$$

Simplifying gives

$$+\chi^2\big[\eta^3+1\big](1+\eta)-\chi^2 2\eta\big(1+\eta^2\big)+(k\chi-\ell+1)\left[\chi\big(1+\eta^2\big)(1-\eta)^2-\frac{2(k-1)\chi^2(1-\eta)^2\big(1+\eta^2\big)}{\ell-1}\right]$$

$$+\big[(k-1)\chi-\ell+1\big]\left[\frac{k\chi^2(1-\eta)^2\big(1+\eta^2\big)}{\ell-1}+2\eta\chi\big(1+\eta^2\big)-(1+\eta)^2\eta\chi\right]$$

$$-\big[(k-1)\chi-\ell+1\big](k\chi-\ell+1)\left[\begin{array}{c}\dfrac{\chi(1+\eta)^2(\eta-1)^2}{(\ell-1)}+\dfrac{2\chi\eta(\eta-1)^2}{(\ell-1)}+4\eta^2+(1+\eta)^2\eta\\[2ex]-2(1+\eta)\left(\eta+\eta^2+\dfrac{\chi\big(\eta^3-\eta^2-\eta+1\big)}{\ell-1}\right)\end{array}\right]$$

$$+(k\chi-\ell+1)^2\big[4\eta^2-(1+\eta)^2\eta\big]+\chi^2\big(\eta^3-1\big)(\eta-1)$$

$$+(k\chi-\ell+1)\left[\chi\big(1+\eta^2\big)(1-\eta)^2-\frac{2(k-1)\chi^2(1-\eta)^2\big(1+\eta^2\big)}{\ell-1}\right]$$

$$+\big[(k-1)\chi-\ell+1\big]\left[\frac{k\chi^2(1-\eta)^2\big(1+\eta^2\big)}{\ell-1}+\eta\chi(1-\eta)^2\right]$$

$$-\big[(k-1)\chi-\ell+1\big](k\chi-\ell+1)\left[\frac{\chi(\eta-1)^2\big(1+4\eta+\eta^2\big)-2(1+\eta)\chi(\eta-1)\big(\eta^2-1\big)}{(\ell-1)}-\eta(1-\eta)^2\right]$$

$$+(k\chi-\ell+1)^2\big[-\eta(1-\eta)^2\big].$$

Factoring out $(1-\eta)^2$ and reducing terms with $\big[(k-1)\chi-\ell+1\big]$ to $\big[k\chi-\ell+1\big]$ and $-\chi$ gives, after simplifying terms,

$$+\chi^2\big(1+\eta^2\big)-\chi\left[\frac{k\chi^2\big(1+\eta^2\big)}{\ell-1}\right]+(k\chi-\ell+1)\left[\chi\big(1+\eta^2\big)-\frac{k\chi^2\big(1+\eta^2\big)}{\ell-1}+\frac{\chi^2\big(1+\eta^2\big)}{(\ell-1)}\right]+(k\chi-\ell+1)^2\left[\frac{\chi\big(1+\eta^2\big)}{(\ell-1)}\right]$$

Factoring out $\chi\big(1+\eta^2\big)$ gives

$$+\chi - \frac{k\chi^2}{\ell-1} + (k\chi - \ell + 1)\left[1 - \frac{k\chi}{\ell-1} + \frac{\chi}{(\ell-1)}\right] + (k\chi - \ell + 1)^2\left[\frac{1}{(\ell-1)}\right]$$

which gives

$$+\chi - \frac{k\chi^2}{\ell-1} + (k\chi - \ell + 1)\left[1 - \frac{k\chi}{\ell-1} + \frac{\chi}{(\ell-1)} + \frac{(k\chi - \ell + 1)}{\ell-1}\right].$$

which sums to zero. Now we consider the last term of the original expression. Dividing through by $(1-\mu)^\ell$ gives

$$\frac{1}{(1-\mu)^\ell}\left(\begin{array}{l} M_{2^k+1,2^k+1} - \dfrac{\chi(1+\eta^2)}{2[(k-1)\chi - \ell + 1]}M_{0,2^k+1} + \dfrac{\chi(1+\eta)}{2[(k-1)\chi - \ell + 1]}M_{1,2^k+1} \\[2ex] + \dfrac{(1+\eta)(k\chi - \ell + 1)}{2[(k-1)\chi - \ell + 1]}M_{2^{k-1},2^k+1} - \dfrac{k\chi - \ell + 1}{(k-1)\chi - \ell + 1}M_{2^{k-1}+1,2^k+1} - \dfrac{(1+\eta)}{2}M_{2^k,2^k+1} \end{array}\right)$$

$$= \frac{1}{[(k-1)\chi - \ell + 1]}\left(\begin{array}{l} [(k-1)\chi - \ell + 1]\eta^2 - \dfrac{\chi(1+\eta^2)}{2}\dfrac{(1+\eta^2)(\ell-1) - k\chi(1-\eta)^2}{2(\ell-1)} \\[2ex] + \dfrac{\chi(1+\eta)}{2}\dfrac{(1+\eta)\eta}{2} + \dfrac{(1+\eta)(k\chi - \ell + 1)}{2}\dfrac{(1+\eta)\eta}{2} \\[2ex] -(k\chi - \ell + 1)\left(\eta^2 + \dfrac{\chi\eta(\eta-1)^2}{2(\ell-1)}\right) - \dfrac{(1+\eta)}{2}[(k-1)\chi - \ell + 1]\dfrac{(1+\eta)\eta}{2} \end{array}\right)$$

$$= \frac{1}{[(k-1)\chi - \ell + 1]}\left(\begin{array}{l} -\chi\eta^2 - \dfrac{\chi(1+\eta^2)^2}{4} + \dfrac{k\chi^2(1+\eta^2)(1-\eta)^2}{4(\ell-1)} \\[2ex] + \dfrac{\chi(1+\eta)^2\eta}{2} - \dfrac{k\chi^2\eta(\eta-1)^2}{2(\ell-1)} + \dfrac{\chi\eta(\eta-1)^2}{2} \end{array}\right)$$

Multiplying by $(1-\mu)^\ell$ and then reorganizing gives the final result of

$$= \frac{(1-\mu)^\ell \chi(1-\eta)^4}{4[(k-1)\chi - \ell + 1]}\left(\frac{k\chi}{(\ell-1)} - 1\right)$$

(g) Row $x \notin T$ of LM times column $x \notin T$ of L^T:

    This is zero using Lemma A3.

A Further Result on the Markov Chain Model of Genetic Algorithms and Its Application to a Simulated Annealing-like Strategy

Joe Suzuki*
Department of Mathematics
Osaka University
Toyonaka, Osaka 560, JAPAN

Abstract

T. E. Davis studied genetic algorithms where mutation rates were reduced to an arbitrarily small positive value. This paper provides two generalizations of these results. We too let mutation reduce to an arbitrarily small positive value but also let crossover probabilities go to zero and selective pressure go to infinity. We show that the stationary distribution focuses on an optimal uniform population. We also give sufficient conditions for ergodicity for a simulated annealing-like strategy. As an aside, the uniform crossover counterpart of the Vose-Liepins formula is derived using the Markov chain model.

1 INTRODUCTION

Genetic algorithms (GAs) are stochastic search techniques widely applied to combinatorial optimization problems [11, 14, 29, 30, 31, 32, 33]. GAs move from population to population. Each population consists of chromosomes (individuals) which represent candidate solutions to the optimization problem. A new population is formed by transforming individuals of the current population using stochastic operators (genetic operators) that emulate evolution in biological systems.

Our discussion is based on T. E. Davis's work [1, 5] on a simulated annealing (SA) like strategy for simple GAs [11] in which a rigorous theoretical basis was constructed in addition to some empirical experiments. As usual, the following three basic genetic operations are

---

Part of this work was done while the author visited Stanford University (Sept. '95 -March '97).

applied to each generation change: selection, mutation, and crossover. However, intuitively, a wide space of solutions should be searched in the earlier generations while a region including an optimal solution should be converged in the latter generations. Some authors have addressed the possibility of SA-like strategies which allow some control parameters to be variant during the generation changes. SA [9, 16, 19] is also a stochastic search technique with applications to combinatorial optimization problems based on the annealing of crystalline solids, where the algorithm is implemented by generating a sequence of trial solutions and reducing the absolute temperature so that the trial solution sequence converges to an optimal solution. In particular, D. E. Goldberg's paper on Boltzmann tournament selection [13] was the first to explicitly outline the close correspondence between SA and GAs.

Many theoretical results are available for GAs. Holland [14] presented the well-known schemata theorem and minimal deceptive problems [3] have been analyzed using Walsh functions [12]. To a limited extent, Markov chains have been used to analyze GAs [6, 7, 10, 20]. More recently, Markov chains giving exact expected GA behavior have been specified by E. A. Nix and M. D. Vose [26] and T. E. Davis [4, 5], and have been studied intensively [4, 5, 20, 26, 27]. The state space of these Markov chains consist of tuples representing populations by the frequency of each individual therein. In this paper we first generalize this Markov model to include a parameterized uniform crossover [22, 25] and use this model to extend results by Davis [4, 5].

Davis [4] studied an SA-like strategy [9, 16, 19], where the mutation rate is reduced slow enough to an arbitrarily small positive value to maintain ergodicity (Section 3 summarizes this result.) This ensured that the Markov chain's stationary distribution focused on some uniform population (a population consisting of identical individuals). Although this result is important, it leaves several problems:

1. the probability that an optimal individual is obtained in a GA is strictly less than one although the population converges to uniformity asymptotically;

2. the resulting condition on the variant mutation probability for ergodicity is to assure an asymptotic, not finite time convergence; and

3. the crossover probability is invariant.

As for the first problem, in general, as the variant mutation probability diminishes, one of the populations with an optimal individual cannot be necessarily generated although some uniform population is obtained. In that case, it seems to be useless to keep the condition on the variant mutation probability so that we can obtain some uniform population rather than some population with an optimal individual. For the second and third problems, it seems that the convergence to the stationary probability distribution could be faster by considering some variant crossover probability for each generation.

In Section 4, we shall prove the following claim (Theorem 2): the stationary distribution focuses on the uniform population with an optimal solution (the best population) as mutation and crossover probabilities and a fitness ratio go to zero, where the fitness ratio is defined in Section 4 (Roughly speaking, the less the fitness ratio is, the more the so-called selective pressure is.) In the SA-like strategy of Section 5, the fitness ratio is decreased (the selective pressure is increased) by boosting the power of the fitness function.

Although Theorem 2 improves on the Davis algorithm [4, 5] by guaranteeing asymptotic focus on the best population, the resulting convergence rate is slower. We rectify this by also reducing the crossover probability and the fitness ratio to zero. Although we do not provide optimal parameter schedules, nor any definite functions for changing the three parameters, we do avoid introducing a SA-like temperature schedule (and so we can use Theorem 2). This is unlike a procedure used by Mahfoud and Goldberg [17, 18], where the parameters are invariant but temperature changes determine the survival probability between two pairs of parents and children.

NOTATION

The following notation will be used. At generation t, individuals, each having L genes, are randomly chosen. Subsequent generations at $t = 1, 2, \cdots$ are formed using crossover, mutation and selection operators. Let

γ: the number of possible values which each gene takes;

$G = \{0, 1, \cdots, \gamma - 1\}$: a set of possible values which each gene takes;

L: the number of genes contained in each individual;

$N = \gamma^L$: the number of possible individuals;

$J = \{0, 1, , \cdots, N - 1\}$: a set of individuals;

$i_l, l = 1, 2, \cdots, N$: the individual with the l-th largest fitness value;

$g[j] \in G, j = 0, 1, \cdots, L - 1$: the value of the j-th gene;

$i \in J$: an individual (represented as both the string $g[0]g[1] \cdots g[L - 1]$ and the integer $0 \leq \sum_{j=0}^{L-1} \gamma^j g[L - 1 - j] \leq N - 1$);

$f(i), i \in J$: the fitness value of an individual i;

μ: a mutation probability;

χ: a crossover probability;

$F = \max\{f(i_{j+1})/f(i_j) : f(i_{j+1}) \neq f(i_j), 1 \leq j \leq N - 1\}$: a fitness ratio;

$p = (\mu, \chi, F)$: invariant parameters;

M: the number of individuals contained in each population;

0^+: an arbitrarily small positive value;

$\det A$: the determinant of a matrix A;

$|S|$: the cardinality of a set S;

$\delta(E)$: 1 (if E is true), 0 (otherwise);

$H(i, i'), i, i' \in J$: the Hamming distance between two individuals i and i';

$|i|, i \in J$: the number of ones in an individual i;

$i \otimes i', i, i' \in J$: the bitwise multiplication of two individuals i and i';

$i \oplus i', i, i' \in J$: the bitwise exclusive-or of two individuals i and i';

$\bar{i}, i \in J$: the one's complement of an individual i;

$\mu(t), t = 1, 2, \cdots$: a mutation probability of a generation t;

$\chi(t), t = 1, 2, \cdots$: a crossover probability of a generation t;

$m(t)$: a non-decreasing function of each generation t.

$F(t) = F^{m(t)}, t = 1, 2, \cdots$: the $m(t)$ power of F; and

$p(t) = (\mu(t), \chi(t), F(t))$: variant parameters;

2   THE MARKOV CHAIN MODEL

In this section, we summarize the basic Markov chain model and provide a preliminary result (Theorem 1).

The probability of which population is generated at the next generation depends on the number of occurrences of each individual in the current population rather than the population itself. We collect populations with the number of occurrences vector $z[s]$ as a group called a state $s \in S$, where $z[s] = (z[0, s], z[1, s], \cdots, z[N - 1, s])$, $z[i, s]$ is the number of occurrence of an individual $i \in J$ in a state $s \in S$, and S is the set of states. It is known [26] that the cardinality $|S|$ of states is given by

$$|S| = \binom{M + N - 1}{M} ,$$

and that the transition probability $Q(s'|s)$ from one state $s \in S$ to another $s' \in S$ is expressed by a multinomial distribution as

$$Q(s'|s) = \frac{M!}{\prod_{i' \in J} z[i', s']!} \prod_{i \in J} P(i|s)^{z[i, s']}, \tag{1}$$

where $P(i|s)$ is the probability of generating an individual $i \in J$ from a state $s \in S$. When only the selection operation is applied, i.e., for $\mu = \chi = 0$ (one operator algorithms), if the roulette wheel selection (page 237 in Goldberg [11]) is assumed, the probability $P(i|s)$, $i \in J, s \in S$, yields

$$P_1(i|s) = \frac{z[i, s]f(i)}{\sum_{i' \in J} z[i', s]f(i')} .$$

When the mutation operation is also applied, i.e., for $\mu > 0, \chi = 0$ (two operator algorithms), the probability $P(i|s)$, $i \in J, s \in S$, becomes

$$P_2(i|s) = \sum_{i' \in J} \mu^{H(i, i')}(1 - \mu)^{L - H(i, i')} P_1(i'|s) .$$

It is known that the transition matrix Q in Eq. (1) is primitive as long as the mutation probability μ is positive [15, 20].

Definition 1 ([21]) *A square nonnegative matrix A is* **primitive** *if there exists a positive integer k such that $A^k > 0$, where $X \geq 0$ refers to the fact that all the elements of a matrix X are nonnegative while $X > 0$ refers to the fact that all the elements of X are positive.*

Primitivity intuitively refers to the property that all the states in S can communicate with each other in finite transitions. Throughout the paper, we assume $\mu > 0$ so that the Markov chain is primitive.

When the mutation and crossover operations can be also applied i.e., for $\mu > 0, \chi > 0$ (three operator algorithms), the probability

$$P_3(k|s) = \sum_{i,j \in J} P_1(i|s)P_1(j|s)r_{i,j}(k), \ k \in J \ , \ s \in S \ ,$$

depends on what type of crossover operations is used, where $r_{i,j}(k)$ is the probability that $k \in J$ is generated from $i, j \in J$ via the crossover and mutation operations, and $r_{i,j}(k) = r_{i \oplus k, j \oplus k}(0)$ holds. It is known that for the traditional one-point crossover with $\gamma = 2$ [27],

$$r_{i,j}(0) \ = \ \frac{1-\chi}{2}[\mu^{|i|}(1-\mu)^{L-|i|} + \mu^{|j|}(1-\mu)^{L-|j|}] + \frac{\chi}{2}\sum_{k=1}^{L-1}\frac{1}{L-1}$$
$$\cdot [\mu^{|i|-\Delta(i,j,k)}(1-\mu)^{L-|i|+\Delta(i,j,k)} + \mu^{|j|+\Delta(i,j,k)}(1-\mu)^{L-|j|-\Delta(i,j,k)}] \ , \quad (2)$$

where

$$\Delta(i,j,k) = |(2^k - 1) \otimes i| - |(2^k - 1) \otimes j| \ .$$

For the traditional one-point crossover with $\gamma \geq 3$, see Koehler, Bhattacharyya, and Vose [1], and Bhattacharyya and Koehler [2].

The following formula is on uniform crossover (See Appendix A for the proof of Theorem 1, and Corollaries 1 and 2.), where, unlike the traditional uniform crossover ($\chi = 1/2$) [25], we consider the parameterized uniform crossover [22] for $\gamma = 2$ and each crossover probability χ. In the remainder of the paper, $\gamma = 2$ is assumed.

Theorem 1 *When the (parameterized) uniform crossover is applied, for $i, j, \in J$,*

$$r_{i,j}(0) \ = \ \frac{1}{2}\sum_{t=0}^{|i \oplus j|}\chi^t(1-\chi)^{|i \oplus j|-t}\sum_{s=0}^{t}\binom{|(i \oplus j) \otimes i|}{t-s}\binom{|(i \oplus j) \otimes j|}{s}$$
$$\cdot [\mu^{|i|+2s-t}(1-\mu)^{L-|i|-2s+t} + \mu^{|j|-2s+t}(1-\mu)^{L-|j|+2s-t}] \ . \quad (3)$$

Corollary 1 *For $i, j, k \in J$ such that $|i \oplus k| = 0$ and $|j \oplus k| = L$,*

$$r_{ij}(k) = \frac{1}{2}\{[\chi\mu + (1-\chi)(1-\mu)]^L + [\chi(1-\mu) + (1-\chi)\mu]^L\} \ . \quad (4)$$

Note that $|i \oplus k| = 0$ and $|j \oplus k| = L$ imply $i = \bar{j} = k$.

Corollary 2 *For $i, j, k \in J$ such that $|i \oplus k| = |j \oplus k| = L$,*

$$r_{ij}(k) = \mu^L \ . \quad (5)$$

Evidently, $r_{ij}(k) = r_{ii}(\bar{i}) = \mu^L$ since $|i \oplus k| = |j \oplus k| = L$ implies $i = j = \bar{k}$ (Crossover does not have any effect, which is very reasonable since the parents are identical and the child has no bits in common with them.)

Quite recently, Vose [28] expressed the following formula for any type of crossover operations

$$r_{i,j}(0) = \sum_{u,v,w} \mu_u \mu_v \frac{\chi_w + \chi_{\bar{w}}}{2},\tag{6}$$

where the summation ranges over $u, v, w \in J$ such that

$$(i \oplus u) \otimes w \oplus (j \oplus v) \otimes \bar{w} = 0,\tag{7}$$

χ_w, $w \in J$, is a crossover probability with which $w \otimes i \oplus \bar{w} \otimes j$ is generated from $i, j \in J$, and μ_u, $u \in J$, is a mutation probability with which $i \oplus u$ is generated from $i \in J$. However, the formula in Eqs. (6) and (7) is not explicitly expressed in terms of χ and μ but evident from the definition of $r_{ij}(0)$ and the procedure of simple GAs. In fact, the derivations of Eqs. (2) and (3) from Eqs. (6) and (7) are not straightforward.

The formulae in this section provide an understanding of how simple GAs work under each condition whereas the equations themselves have no direct practical merit.

Throughout the paper, our discussion excludes some elitist strategies [6], which can also be expressed as a form of Markov chain but which are not primitive in general [23, 24].

3   THE DAVIS ALGORITHM

Davis [4] determined an expression for the stationary distribution, $q^{(u)}$, over S for a fixed positive μ and its limit, q, as $\mu \to 0^+$. For state s, we have

$$q^{(\mu)}[s] = \frac{\det(Q[s] - I)}{\displaystyle\sum_{s' \in S} \det(Q[s'] - I)}$$

by solving the linear equation $q^{(\mu)} Q = q^{(\mu)}$ using Cramer's rule, where the (s', s)-element of Q is the transition probability $Q(s|s')$. The matrix $Q[s]$, $s \in S$, is derived from Q by replacing the row indexed by a state s with the zero row vector $(0, 0, \cdots, 0)$. Note that the transition matrix Q depends on the mutation probability μ for the two and three operator algorithms.

Let $S[u]$ be the set of states $s' \in S$ such that for some $i' \in J$, when $u = u(i) \in U$,

1. $z[i, s'] = M - 1$;

2. $z[i', s'] = 1$; and

3. $H(i, i') = 1$,

where $U \subset S$ is the set of uniform populations $u(i)$, $i \in J$, consisting of an individual i. The limit is given as

$$q[s] = \lim_{\mu \to 0+} q^{(\mu)}[s] = \begin{cases} \dfrac{\lim\limits_{\mu \to 0+} \det(Q^*[s] - I)}{\sum\limits_{s' \in U} \lim\limits_{\mu \to 0+} \det(Q^*[s'] - I)} & [s \in U] \\[4mm] 0 & [s \in S - U] \end{cases} \quad , \tag{8}$$

where the elements of $Q^*[u]$, $u \in U$, are defined by

$$Q^*[u](s'|s) = \begin{cases} 0 & [s = u] \\ Q(s'|s) + \sum_{u' \in U - \{u\}} \delta(s' \in S[u'])Q(u'|s)/L & [s \neq u] \end{cases} \tag{9}$$

for $s, s' \in S - U + \{u\}$, Note that $|S[u]| = L$ for $u \in U$, and that the matrix $Q^*[u]$ has the following property:

$$\begin{aligned} \sum_{s' \in S-U+\{u\}} Q^*[u](s'|s) &= \sum_{s' \in S-U+\{u\}} Q(s'|s) + \sum_{u' \in U-\{u\}} \sum_{s' \in S[u']} Q(u'|s)/L \\ &= \sum_{s' \in S-U+\{u\}} Q(s'|s) + \sum_{u' \in U-\{u\}} Q(u'|s) \\ &= \sum_{s' \in S} Q(s'|s) = 1 \end{aligned} \tag{10}$$

for $s \in S - U$. Note also that Eq. (8) depends on a crossover probability χ for the three operator algorithms.

Example 1 $L = 2$ and $M = 2$.

Then, $N = 4$ and $|S| = 10$. Let $s_0, s_1, \cdots, s_9$ be the ten states in S such that $z[i, s]$, $i = 00, 01, 10, 11$, $s = s_0, s_1, \cdots, s_9$, are given as

i	s_0	s_1	s_2	s_3	s_4	s_5	s_6	s_7	s_8	s_9
00	2	1	1	1	0	0	0	0	0	0
01	0	1	0	0	2	1	1	0	0	0
10	0	0	1	0	0	1	0	2	1	0
11	0	0	0	1	0	0	1	0	1	2

The uniform populations are $u(00) = s_0$, $u(01) = s_4$, $u(10) = s_7$, $u(11) = s_9$ and then, $U = \{s_0, s_4, s_7.s_9\}$. Set $S[u]$ for $u \in U$ are as follows: $S[s_0] = \{s_1, s_2\}$, $S[s_4] = \{s_1, s_6\}$, $S[s_7] = \{s_2, s_8\}$, $S[s_9] = \{s_6, s_8\}$. Finally, the $Q^*[s_0]$ matrix is given as below. For compactness we write $Q(s_i|s_j)$ as $Q_{j,i}$.

$$\begin{bmatrix} 0 & 0 & 0 & 0 & 0 & 0 & 0 \\ Q_{1,0} & Q_{1,1} + Q_{1,4}/2 & Q_{1,2} + Q_{1,7}/2 & Q_{1,3} & Q_{1,5} & Q_{1,6} + (Q_{1,4} + Q_{1,9})/2 & Q_{1,8} + (Q_{1,7} + Q_{1,9})/2 \\ Q_{2,0} & Q_{2,1} + Q_{2,4}/2 & Q_{2,2} + Q_{2,7}/2 & Q_{2,3} & Q_{2,5} & Q_{2,6} + (Q_{2,4} + Q_{2,9})/2 & Q_{2,8} + (Q_{2,7} + Q_{2,9})/2 \\ Q_{3,0} & Q_{3,1} + Q_{3,4}/2 & Q_{3,2} + Q_{3,7}/2 & Q_{3,3} & Q_{3,5} & Q_{3,6} + (Q_{3,4} + Q_{3,9})/2 & Q_{3,8} + (Q_{3,7} + Q_{3,9})/2 \\ Q_{4,0} & Q_{4,1} + Q_{4,4}/2 & Q_{4,2} + Q_{4,7}/2 & Q_{4,3} & Q_{4,5} & Q_{4,6} + (Q_{4,4} + Q_{4,9})/2 & Q_{4,8} + (Q_{4,7} + Q_{4,9})/2 \\ Q_{5,0} & Q_{5,1} + Q_{5,4}/2 & Q_{5,2} + Q_{5,7}/2 & Q_{5,3} & Q_{5,5} & Q_{5,6} + (Q_{5,4} + Q_{5,9})/2 & Q_{5,8} + (Q_{5,7} + Q_{5,9})/2 \\ Q_{6,0} & Q_{6,1} + Q_{6,4}/2 & Q_{6,2} + Q_{6,7}/2 & Q_{6,3} & Q_{6,5} & Q_{6,6} + (Q_{6,4} + Q_{6,9})/2 & Q_{6,8} + (Q_{6,7} + Q_{6,9})/2 \\ Q_{8,0} & Q_{8,1} + Q_{8,4}/2 & Q_{8,2} + Q_{8,7}/2 & Q_{8,3} & Q_{8,5} & Q_{8,6} + (Q_{8,4} + Q_{8,9})/2 & Q_{8,8} + (Q_{8,7} + Q_{8,9})/2 \end{bmatrix}$$

Another result (Section 8 in [4]) is the derivation of a sufficient condition that assures the strong ergodicity of the inhomogeneous Markov chain as the mutation probability $\mu(t)$ is reduced to zero.

Definition 2 (ergodicity [15]) *An inhomogeneous Markov chain is weakly ergodic if* $\lim_{t\to\infty}[Q_{mt}(s|s') - Q_{mt}(s|s'')] = 0$ *for any* $s, s', s'' \in S$ *and* $m = 1, 2, \cdots$, *where* $Q_{mt} = \prod_{h=m}^{t} Q_h$, *and* Q_h *is a transition matrix over a state set* S *at a time instance* $h = 1, 2, \cdots$. *An inhomogeneous Markov chain is strongly ergodic for a probability vector* q *if* $\lim_{t\to\infty} Q_{mt}(s|s') = q[s]$ *for any* $s, s' \in S$ *and* $m = 1, 2, \cdots$.

Letting $m = 1$ in Definition 2, we suppose that the initial distribution over S is given as

$$q_0 = (q_0[0], q_0[1], \cdots, q_0[|S| - 1]) \ .$$

Then the distributions at the time instances $1, 2, \cdots, t$ are obtained as $q_1 = q_0 Q_1$, $q_2 = q_1 Q_2 = q_0 Q_1 Q_2, \cdots, q_t = q_0 \prod_{h=1}^{t} Q_h$. However, q_t does not necessarily converge to q in Eq. (8) for any q_0 when $\mu(t) \to 0^+$ during the generation changes $t = 1, 2, \cdots$ because, at this point, we are not sure whether the strong ergodicity of the Markov chain holds. In fact, the transition matrix Q_t depends on the mutation probability $\mu(t)$ for each generation $t = 1, 2, \cdots$. It is shown [4] that the Markov chain is weakly ergodic if

$$\mu(t) \geq \frac{1}{2} t^{-1/ML} \ . \tag{11}$$

when the mutation probability $\mu(t)$, $t = 1, 2, \cdots$, is reduced to zero. In addition, strong ergodicity is also proved for the q in Eq. (8) if $\mu(t)$ is monotone non-increasing as well. In other words, the distribution over S converges to $q[s]$, $s \in S$, in Eq. (8) when $\mu(t) \to 0^+$ if $\mu(t)$ is monotone non-increasing and satisfies Eq. (11).

However, as seen in Eq. (8), all the distribution limit components $r[i] = q[u(i)]$ corresponding to each solution, $i \in J$, are positive, where $q[s], s \in S$, are computed from Eq. (8), and $r[i], i \in J$, is the probability that the uniform population $u(i)$ occurs as $\mu \to 0^+$. In that sense, it seems that it is useless to assure ergodicity. However, both the empirical evidence (Section 5 in [4]) and theoretical development (Section 9 in [4]) suggest that $r[i_1]$ is numerically close to one in most cases and that the desired limiting behavior can be obtained as the population size M goes to infinity, although the mathematical proof is not established.

It should be noted that the results hold for any regular crossover operation that generates two identical individuals if the two individuals picked via the selection operation are identical, thus the result is applicable to the two-point traditional crossover, the multi-point traditional crossover, the segmented crossover, the uniform crossover, the shuffle crossover etc. [8] as well. The reason is that the derivation [4] for the three operator algorithms depends on just the property that no crossover occurs among any two identical individuals. Summarizing the above, we get the following statement.

Lemma 1 *The mutation bound in Eq. (11) is valid for any regular crossover operation and any crossover probability* χ.

Since Eq. (11) is not dependent on the crossover rate, one might suspect that Lemma 1 is self-evident. However, Davis's results [4] were obtained using only a one-point crossover operator with fixed probability. Lemma 1 provides the necessary confirmation of its generality. This will be needed to apply Theorem 2 in this paper.

4   MAIN THEOREM

Our attempt here is to prove optimality as stated in Theorem 2.

Theorem 2 *For the three operator algorithms, the stationary distribution focuses on the best population* $(\sum_{j=1}^{l} r[i_j] \to 1)$ *as the crossover probability* $\chi \to 0$ *and the fitness ratio*

$$F = \max_{1 \le j \le N-1, f(i_j) \ne f(i_{j+1})} f(i_j)/f(i_{j+1}) \to 0 \,,$$

where l *is such that* $f(i_1) = \cdots = f(i_l) > f(i_{l+1}) \ge \cdots \ge f(i_N)$. *More precisely,*

$$\sum_{s \in \{u(i_1) \cdots u(i_l)\}} \lim_{F \to 0} \lim_{\chi \to 0} [\lim_{\mu \to 0+} q^{(\mu)}[s]] = \sum_{s \in \{u(i_1) \cdots u(i_l)\}} \lim_{p \to (0+,0,0)} q_p[s] = 1 \,, \qquad (12)$$

where q_p *is the stationary distribution over* S *when the three parameters are* $p = (\mu, \chi, F)$.

Remark 1 *Intuitively, any population approaches uniformity as* $\mu \to 0^+$ *in the Davis algorithm, and* $F \to 0$ *makes the algorithm adapt the elitist strategies [6], which insures that the individual with the highest fitness value in the current population appears in the successor population. Therefore, the population inevitably converges to a uniform population of optimal solutions.*

The following example illustrates the results of Theorem 2.

Example 2 $L = 1$, $M = 2$, $\gamma = 2$, *and* $F = f(1)/f(0) < 1$

Then, $N = 2$ and $|S| = 3$. Let $s_0, s_1, \cdots, s_9$ be the three states such that $z[i, s]$, $i = 0, 1$, $s = s_0, s_1, s_2$, are given as

i	s_0	s_1	s_2
0	2	1	0
1	0	1	2

The corresponding transition matrix is

$$Q = \begin{pmatrix} (1-\mu)^2 & 2\mu(1-\mu) & \mu^2 \\ \frac{[(1-\mu)+F\mu]^2}{[1+F]^2} & \frac{[(1-\mu)+F\mu][\mu+F(1-\mu)]}{[1+F]^2} & \frac{[\mu+F(1-\mu)]^2}{[1+F]^2} \\ \mu^2 & 2\mu(1-\mu) & (1-\mu)^2 \end{pmatrix} \,,$$

where each row (column) is indexed by s_0, s_1, s_2 from the first to the third. Therefore, the limit of the stationary distribution as $\mu \to 0$ becomes, from Eq. (8), $q = (1/(1 + F^2), 0, F^2/(1 + F^2))$ since

$$Q^*[s_0] = \begin{pmatrix} 0 & 0 \\ \frac{[(1-\mu)+F\mu]^2}{[1+F]^2} & 1 - \frac{[(1-\mu)+F\mu]^2}{[1+F]^2} \end{pmatrix} \,, \quad \det(Q^*[s_0] - I) = \frac{[(1-\mu)+F\mu]^2}{[1+F]^2}$$

and

$$Q^*[s_2] = \begin{pmatrix} 1 - \frac{[\mu+F(1-\mu)]^2}{[1+F]^2} & \frac{[\mu+F(1-\mu)]^2}{[1+F]^2} \\ 0 & 0 \end{pmatrix} \,, \quad \det(Q^*[s_2] - I) = \frac{[\mu + F(1-\mu)]^2}{[1+F]^2} \,.$$

Obviously, $q \to (1,0,0)$ as $F \to 0$.

Proof of Theorem 2: It is sufficient to show that $\lim_{p\to(0+,0,0)} \det(Q^*[u(i_j)] - I) \neq 0, j = 1, 2, \cdots, l$, and $\lim_{p\to(0+,0,0)} \det(Q^*[u(i_j)] - I) = 0, j = l+1, l+2, \cdots, N$.

Letting V denote the set of $s \in S$ such that $1 \leq z[i_j, s] \leq M - 1$ for some $j = 1, 2, \cdots, l$, we obtain the following lemma at once.

Lemma 2 *For any* $s \in V + \cup_{j=1}^{l}\{u(i_j)\}$

$$\lim_{p\to(0+,0,0)} \sum_{s' \in V + \cup_{j=1}^{l}\{u(i_j)\}} Q(s'|s) = 1 , \tag{13}$$

and for any pair of $s' \in S - V - \cup_{j=1}^{l}\{u(i_j)\}$ *and* $s \in V + \cup_{j=1}^{l}\{u(i_j)\}$

$$\lim_{p\to(0+,0,0)} Q(s'|s) = 0 . \tag{14}$$

Eq. (13) holds because

$$\lim_{p\to(0+,0,0)} \sum_{s \in V + \cup_{j=1}^{l}\{u(i_j)\}} Q(s'|s)$$

$$= \lim_{F\to 0}[1 - \{1 - \sum_{k=1}^{l} P_1(i_k|s)\}^M] = \lim_{F\to 0}[1 - \{\frac{\sum_{k=l+1}^{N} z[i_k, s]f(i_k)}{\sum_{i\in J} z[i, s]f(i)}\}^M] = 1 .$$

For Eq. (14), note

$$\lim_{p\to(0+,0,0)} \sum_{s' \in S - V - \cup_{j=1}^{l}\{u(i_j)\}} Q(s'|s) = 1 - \lim_{p\to(0+,0,0)} \sum_{s' \in V + \cup_{j=1}^{l}\{u(i_j)\}} Q(s'|s) = 0 .$$

Eq. (14) follows because $Q(s'|s) \geq 0$ for any s, s'.

Lemma 3 *If an individual i has the largest fitness value in a state s, then* $\lim_{F\to 0} P_1(i|s) > 0$.

Let W_p^1 and D_p^1 be the submatrices of $Q^*[u(i_1)]$ which consist of rows and columns indexed by the states in V and $S - U - V$, respectively. In the following, we denote $\lim_{p\to(0+,0,0)} W_p^1$ and $\lim_{p\to(0+,0,0)} D_p^1$ as W^1 and D^1, respectively. Then,

$$\lim_{p\to(0+,0,0)} \det(Q^*[u(i_1)] - I) = -\det(W^1 - I_{|V|}) \cdot \det(D^1 - I_{|S-U-V|})$$

holds. In fact, from definition, $\{u(i_1)\} \cap S[u] = \phi$ for any $u \in U$ ($S[u]$ refers to a set of non-uniform populations.), and $S[u(i_j)] \subset V \subset S$ for any $j = 1, 2, \cdots, l$. Thus,

$$\sum_{s' \in V + \{u(i_1)\}} Q^*[u(i_1)](s'|s)$$

$$= \sum_{s' \in V + \{u(i_1)\}} Q(s'|s) + \sum_{u'=U-\{u(i_1)\}} \sum_{s' \in (V+\{u(i_1)\})\cap S[u']} Q(u'|s)/L$$

$$= \sum_{s' \in V + \{u(i_1)\}} Q(s'|s) + \sum_{u'=U-\{u(i_1)\}} \sum_{s' \in V \cap S[u']} Q(u'|s)/L$$

and

$$\sum_{u'\in U-\{u(i_1)\}}\sum_{s'\in V\cap S[u']} Q(u'|s)/L$$

$$= \sum_{j=2}^{l}\sum_{s'\in S[u(i_j)]} Q(u(i_j)|s)/L + \sum_{u'\in U-\cup_{j=1}^{l}\{u(i_j)\}}\sum_{s'\in V\cap S[u']} Q(u'|s)/L$$

$$= \sum_{j=2}^{l} Q(u(i_j)|s) + \sum_{j=l+1}^{N} |V\cap S[u(i_j)]|Q(u(i_j)|s)/L$$

hold, where $|S[u]| = L$ for any $u \in U$ has been applied. Therefore, for any $s \in V$,

$$\sum_{s'\in V+\{u(i_1)\}} Q^*[u(i_1)](s'|s)$$

$$= \sum_{s\in V+\cup_{j=1}^{l}\{u(i_j)\}} Q(s'|s) + \sum_{j=l+1}^{N} (|V\cap S[u(i_j)]|/L)Q(u(i_j)|s) \to 1$$

from Lemma 1 and $u(i_j) \in S - V - \cup_{j'=1}^{l}\{u_{j'}\}$, $j = l+1, l+2, \cdots, N$. Combining this with Eq. (10), it turns out that any (s, s')-element of $Q^*[u(i_1)]$, $s \in V, s' \in S - V - \{u(i_1)\}$, diminishes as in Figure 1.

In addition, if all the spectral radii of W^1 and D^1 are less than one, then $\det(W^1 - I_{|V|}) \neq 0$ and $\det(D^1 - I_{|S-U-V|}) \neq 0$. In fact, then $\det(W^1 - \lambda I_{|V|}) = \prod_{\lambda'\in\Lambda_{W^1}}(\lambda' - \lambda) \neq 0$ and $\det(D^1 - \lambda I_{|S-U-V|}) = \prod_{\lambda'\in\Lambda_{D^1}}(\lambda' - \lambda) \neq 0$, for $\lambda \geq 1$, where Λ_{W^1} and Λ_{D^1} are the sets of eigenvalues for the matrices W^1 and D^1, respectively. We shall show all the spectral radii of the matrices are less than one by applying the Perron-Frobenius theorem [21] (See Appendix B.) Then to show that the spectral radii of W^1 and D^1 are less than one, it is sufficient to prove that there exist stochastic primitive matrices W^* and D^* such that $0 \leq W^1 \leq W^*$ and $W^1 \neq W^*$, and $0 \leq D^1 \leq D^*$ and $D^1 \neq D^*$. Note that the sums for any row in W^1 and D^1 are less than or equal to one from Eq. (10).

1. The sum for some row in W^1 turns out to be strictly less than one because, from Eq. (9) and Lemma 3,

$$\lim_{p\to(0^+,0,0)} Q^*[u(i_1)](u(i_1)|s) = \lim_{p\to(0^+,0,0)} Q(u(i_1)|s) = \lim_{F\to 0} P_1(i_1|s)^M > 0 ,$$

   where s is a non-uniform population such that the individual i_1 is contained ($s \in V$ holds.) Therefore, we can define W^* so that $0 \leq W^1 \leq W^*$, and $W^1 \neq W^*$. Thus, W^* can be selected such that W^* is stochastic. Moreover, since W^1 is primitive, so is W^* because $W^* \geq W^1$. From the fifth item of Appendix B, all the spectral radii of W^1 are less than 1.

2. The sum for some row in D turns out to be strictly less than one because, from Eq. (9) and Lemma 3,

$$\lim_{p\to(0^+,0,0)} Q^*[u(i_1)](s'|s)$$

$$= \lim_{p\to(0^+,0,0)} [Q(s'|s) + Q(u(i)|s)/L] = \lim_{p\to(0^+,0,0)} Q(u(i)|s)/L = \lim_{F\to 0} P_1(i|s)^M/L > 0$$

for $i \in J$ such that $H(i_j, i) = 1$ and $f(i_j) > f(i)$ for some $j = 1, 2, \cdots, l$, where s refers to a non-uniform population such that the individual i has the largest fitness value in the population ($s \in S - U - V$ holds.), and $s' \in V \cap S[u(i)]$ ($z[i, s'] = M - 1$ and $z[i_j, s'] = 1$). If $f(i_j) = f(i)$ holds for all i such that $H(i_j, i) = 1$ for any $i = 1, 2, \cdots, l$, then $f(i_1) = f(i_2) = \cdots = f(i_N)$ and $\det(D^1 - I_{|S-U-V|}) = 1$ ($|S - U - V| = 0$). Therefore, we can define D^* so that $0 \le D^1 \le D^*$, and $D^1 \ne D^*$. Thus, D^* can be selected such that D^* is stochastic. Moreover, since D^1 is primitive, so is D^* because $D^* \ge D^1$. From the fifth item of Appendix B, all the spectral radii of D^1 are less than one.

These complete the proof of $\det(Q^*[u(i_1)] - I) \ne 0$. A similar technique can be applied for the proof of $\det(Q^*[u(i_j)] - I) \ne 0$, $j = 2, 3, \cdots, l$.

Next, we shall prove that the determinant $\det(Q^*[u(i_{l+1})] - I)$ diminishes to zero as $p \to (0^+, 0, 0)$.

Let W_p^{l+1} and D_p^{l+1} be the submatrices of $Q^*[u(i_{l+1})]$ which consist of rows and columns indexed by the states in V and $S - U - V$, respectively. In the following, we denote $\lim_{p \to (0^+, 0, 0)} W_p^{l+1}$ and $\lim_{p \to (0^+, 0, 0)} D_p^{l+1}$ as W^{l+1} and D^{l+1}, respectively.

If we can prove

$$\lim_{p \to (0^+, 0, 0)} \det(Q^*[u(i_{l+1})] - I) = -\det(W^{l+1} - I_{|V|}) \cdot \det(D^{l+1} - I_{|S-U-V|}) ,$$

then it is sufficient to show $\det(W^{l+1} - I_{|V|}) = 0$. Thus, all we have to prove is

$$\lim_{p \to (0^+, 0, 0)} \sum_{s' \in V} Q^*[u(i_{l+1})](s'|s) = 1$$

for any $s \in V$. In fact, then, W^{l+1} is a stochastic matrix, and thus includes one as an eigenvalue by the first item of Appendix B. From Eq. (9), and $S[u(i_j)] \subset V \subset S$ for any $j = 1, 2, \cdots, l$,

$$\sum_{s' \in V} Q^*[u(i_{l+1})](s'|s) = \sum_{s' \in V} Q(s'|s) + \sum_{u' = U - \{u(i_{l+1})\}} \sum_{s' \in V \cap S[u']} Q(u'|s)/L$$

and

$$\sum_{u' \in U - \{u(i_{l+1})\}} \sum_{s' \in V \cap S[u']} Q(u'|s)/L$$

$$= \sum_{j=1}^{l} \sum_{s' \in S[u(i_j)]} Q(u(i_j)|s)/L + \sum_{u' \in U - \cup_{j=1}^{l}\{u(i_j)\} - \{u(i_{l+1})\}} \sum_{s' \in V \cap S[u']} Q(u'|s)/L$$

$$= \sum_{j=1}^{l} Q(u(i_j)|s) + \sum_{j=l+2}^{N} |V \cap S[u(i_j)]| Q(u(i_j)|s)/L$$

hold, where $|S[u]| = L$ for any $u \in U$ has been applied. Therefore, for $s \in V$,

$$\sum_{s' \in V} Q^*[u(i_{l+1})](s'|s) = \sum_{s \in V + \cup_{j=1}^{l}\{u(i_j)\}} Q(s'|s) + \sum_{j=l+2}^{N} (|V \cap S[u(i_j)]|/L) Q(u(i_j)|s) \to 1$$

from Lemma 1.

This completes the proof of $\det(Q^*[u(i_{l+1})] - I) = 0$. A similar technique can be applied for the proof of $\det(Q^*[u(i_j)] - I) = 0$, $j = l+2, l+3, \cdots, N$.

Q. E. D.

We are not sure from Theorem 1 how fast the distribution of states converges to the stationary distribution because asymptotic analysis does not address convergence rate. In a sense, the fact that the stationary distribution is optimal does not necessarily imply that the parameters have some optimal values for a given GA. As $p \to (0^+, 0, 0)$, the Markov chain stays primitive but convergence may be slow since early populations may not contain an optimal solution and spend considerable time in a non-optimal basin of attraction.

However, this property would not cause any serious problem in the later generations of some SA-like strategy which shall be introduced in Section 5 because, in the later generations, the solution is unlikely to fall in a local optima. Instead, the truly optimal solution should be selected among promising candidates.

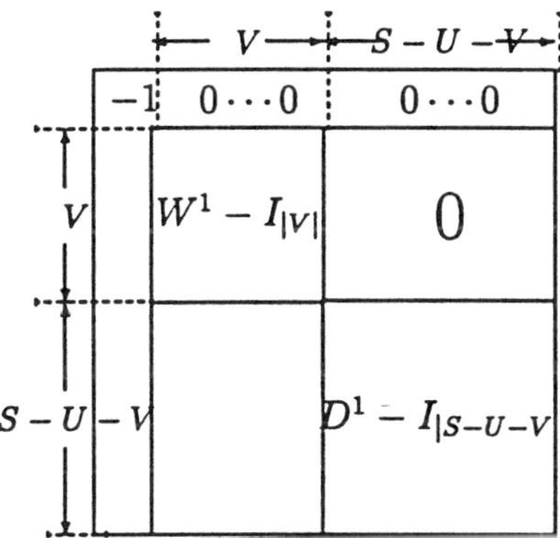

Any (s, s')-element, $s \in V, s' \in S - U - V$, of $Q^*[u(i_1)] - I$ diminish.

Figure 1: The matrix $\lim_{\mu \to 0^+} Q^*[u(i_1)] - I$

5   SA-LIKE STRATEGY

The following SA-like strategy could be considered.

Algorithm 1 *Generate some population at each* $t = 0, 1, \cdots$ *using the following operations:*

1. *Selection with probability* $z[i, s] f(i)^{m(t)} / [\sum_{i' \in J} z[i', s] f(i')^{m(t)}]$ *for* $i \in J$;

2. *Crossover with probability* $\chi(t)$;

3. *Mutation with probability* $\mu(t)$.

Remark 2 *The Davis algorithm is the specific case where $\chi(t) \equiv \chi$ and $m(t) \equiv 1$.*

In this section, the Markov chain is a function of $\chi(t)$, $F(t)$, and $\mu(t)$. In the following result, we provide sufficient conditions to ensure ergodicity.

Theorem 3 *The limit in Eq. (12) is obtained for any crossover as long as $p(t) = (\mu(t), \chi(t), F(t))$ is monotone non-increasing to $(0^+, 0, 0)$, and $\mu(t)$ satisfies Eq. (11).*

Remark 3 *The strategy does not rely on crossover and selective pressure for search in the sense that setting $\chi(t) \equiv 0$ and $F \equiv 0$ for all generations would not change any of the asymptotic results. However, the crossover probability and the fitness ratio should be positive, even if they are reduced to an arbitrarily small value, because they are expected to enhance the finite time convergence behavior of the algorithm.*

For Example 2, the bound reduces to $\mu(t) \geq 1/(2\sqrt{t})$.

Proof of Theorem 3: Weak ergodicity is obtained because the mutation bound remains the same for any crossover (by Lemma 1) and any fitness ratio as well, even when they are variant. The bound in Eq. (11) turns out to depend on M and L rather than $\chi(t)$ and $F(t)$ from the derivation [4]. What we need to prove here is that the bound satisfies strong ergodicity if $\chi(t)$ and $F(t)$ are monotone non-increasing. So, we note the following lemma.

Lemma 4 ([15]) *An inhomogeneous Markov chain is strongly ergodic if it is weakly ergodic and if for each transition matrix Q_t there exists a stationary distribution q_t, $t = 0, 1, \cdots$, and*

$$\sum_{t=0}^{\infty} \sum_{s \in S} |q_t[s] - q_{t+1}[s]| < \infty . \tag{15}$$

Further, if $q = \lim_{t \to \infty} q_t$, then q is the unique vector in Definition 2.

From the mean value theorem, the difference between the corresponding components of any two consecutive vectors in the sequence can be written as

$$q_{t+1}[s] - q_t[s] = \frac{\partial q_p[s]}{\partial \mu}\Big|_{p=p^*(t)}[\mu(t+1) - \mu(t)] + \frac{\partial q_p[s]}{\partial \chi}\Big|_{p=p^*(t)}[\chi(t+1) - \chi(t)]$$
$$+ \frac{\partial q_p[s]}{\partial F}\Big|_{p=p^*(t)}[F(t+1) - F(t)]$$

for $s \in S$, where $p(t) = (\mu(t), \chi(t), F(t))$, and $p^*(t)$ satisfies $p(t+1) < p^*(t) < p(t)$. Then, as proved for $\mu(t)$ in Ref. [4], we have $\sum_{t=0}^{\infty} |\chi(t+1) - \chi(t)| = \chi(0) - \chi(\infty) \leq 1$, and $\sum_{t=0}^{\infty} |F(t+1) - F(t)| = F(0) - F(\infty) \leq 1$ because $\chi(t)$ and $F(t)$ are monotone non-increasing.

Therefore, we have

$$\sum_{t=0}^{\infty} \sum_{s \in S} |q_{t+1}[s] - q_t[s]|$$
$$= \sum_{t=0}^{\infty} \sum_{s \in S} \Big|\frac{\partial q_p[s]}{\partial \mu}\Big|_{p=p^*(t)}[\mu(t+1) - \mu(t)]\Big| + \sum_{t=0}^{\infty} \sum_{s \in S} \Big|\frac{\partial q_p[s]}{\partial \chi}\Big|_{p=p^*(t)}[\chi(t+1) - \chi(t)]\Big|$$

$$+ \sum_{t=0}^{\infty} \sum_{s \in S} |\frac{\partial q_p[s]}{\partial F}|_{p=p^*(t)} [F(t+1) - F(t)]|$$

$$\leq |S|(C_\mu + C_\chi + C_F) \,,$$

where

$$C_\mu = \sup_{s \in S, p} |\frac{\partial q_p[s]}{\partial \mu}| \,, \quad C_\chi = \sup_{s \in S, p} |\frac{\partial q_p[s]}{\partial \chi}| \,, \quad C_F = \sup_{s \in S, p} |\frac{\partial q_p[s]}{\partial F}| \,.$$

In addition, we have the following lemma.

Lemma 5 $C_\mu, C_\chi, C_F < \infty$ for $0 \leq \mu(t), \chi(t), F(t) \leq 1$.

$C_\mu < \infty$ was proved in Ref. [4]. $C_\chi < \infty$ and $C_F < \infty$ are proved quite similarly.

Q. E. D.

The sufficient conditions in Theorem 3 are for asymptotic optimality, not for each finite generation $t = 1, 2, \cdots$. In addition, the condition in Eq. (11) is still strong, and some improvement (sacrificing the theoretical condition for practical effectiveness, finding some new tighter bound which replaces the existing condition, etc.) might be required for practical algorithms.

One reason why the bound to assure ergodicity remains the same ($\chi(t)$ and $F(t)$ should be monotone non-increasing) when χ and F are also variant is that ergodicity assures the asymptotic, not finite time convergence. If $\chi(t)$ and $F(t)$ decrease slowly until $\mu(t)$ is sufficiently small and they decrease very fast suddenly after that, the stationary distribution can be obtained when $\chi(t)$ and $F(t)$ diminish because $\mu(t)$ is still positive for a finite generation t. However, the desired distribution may not be obtained immediately [19].

Refinement of the bound (Eq. (11)) would be important as a future work. Davis suggests (Section 10.4 in Ref. [4]) the possibility that the bound could be improved up to $O(1/t)$ by successfully applying the general sufficient condition [15] for weak ergodicity to the Markov chain.

6   CONCLUDING REMARKS

This paper explores the theoretical properties of the Markov model for GAs which are applicable to SA-like strategies. These include

1. the derivation of the uniform crossover counterpart of the Vose-Liepins formula [27] (Theorem 1);

2. the proof that a population asymptotically goes to the uniform population with an optimal solution (the best population) as the three parameters diminish (Theorem 2); and

3. the derivation of a sufficient condition of strong ergodicity for the Markov chain that represents a SA-like strategy (Theorem 3).

In particular, the main theorem (Theorem 2) has been obtained by extending and improving Davis's work [4, 5], and gives an idea on how to get the best population in actual situations, which is required in several areas of GAs.

When comparing GAs with variant and invariant parameters, evidently a GA with some variant parameters would outperform any GA with invariant parameters. The problem lies in the lack of a general rule on how to control the parameters. Considering few theoretical results which have been developed thus far, we would argue that theoretical approaches such as Theorems 2 and 3 have an important significance as initial steps. We expect the SA-like GAs to be addressed intensively from both theoretical and practical aspects.

Acknowledgement: The author would like to thank Dr.   Thomas E. Davis of AFOSR/AOARD, Mr.   Takahiko Murata of Fujitu Research Corp., and Prof.   Gary J. Koehler of University of Florida for their helpful suggestions.

References

[1] Koehler, G. J., Bhattacharyya, S. and Vose, M. D, unpublished manuscript 1996.

[2] Bhattacharyya, S. and Koehler, G. J., "An Analysis of Non-Binary Genetic Algorithms with Cardinality 2^{U^n}", *Complex Systems*, vol. 8, pages 227-256, 1994.

[3] Bethke, A. D., *Genetic Algorithms as Function Optimizers*. PhD thesis, University of Michigan, 1981.

[4] Davis, T. E., *Toward an Extrapolation of the Simulated Annealing Convergence Theory onto the Simple Genetic Algorithm*. PhD thesis, Gainesville: University of Florida, 1991.

[5] Davis, T. E. and Principe J. C., "A Simulated Annealing Like Convergence Theory for the Simple Genetic Algorithm", in [30], pages 174-181.

[6] De Jong, K. A., *An Analysis of the Behavior of a Class of Genetic Adaptive Systems*. PhD thesis, University of Michigan, Ann Arbor, Mich., 1975.

[7] Eiben, A. E., Aarts, E. H. L. and Van Hee, K. M., "Global Convergence of Genetic Algorithms: A Markov Chain Analysis", in [32], pages 4-12.

[8] Eshelman, L. J., Caruana, R. A., and Schaffer, J. D., "Biases in the Crossover Landscape", in [29], pages 10-19.

[9] Geman S., & Geman, D., "Stochastic Relaxation, Gibbs Distributions and the Bayesian Restoration of Images", *IEEE Trans. Patt. Anal. Mach. Intel.*, vol. 6, no. 6, pages 721-741, Nov. 1984.

[10] Goldberg, D. E. and Segrest, P., "Finite Markov Chain Analysis of Genetic Algorithms", in Grefenstette, J. J. (Ed.), *Proceedings of an International Conference on Genetic Algorithms '87*. Hillsdale, NJ: Lawrence Earlbaum Associates, 1987.

[11] Goldberg, D. E., *Genetic Algorithms in Search, Optimization, and Machine Learning*. Reading, MA: Addison-Wesley, 1989.

[12] Goldberg, D. E., "Genetic Algorithm and Walsh Functions: Part I, A Gentle Introduction; Part II, Deception and Its Analysis", *Complex Systems*, vol. 3, pages 129-171, 1990.

[13] Goldberg, D, E., "A note on Boltzmann tournament selection for genetic algorithms and population-oriented simulated annealing", *Complex Systems*, vol. 4, pages 445-460, 1990.

[14] Holland, J. H., *Adaptation in Natural and Artificial Systems*. Ann Arbor: The University of Michigan Press, 1975.

[15] Iosifescu, M., *Finite Markov Processes and Their Applications*. Chichester: Wiley, 1980.

[16] Kirkpatrick, S., Gelatt, C. D., & Vecci, M. P., "Optimization by Simulated Annealing", *Science*, vol. 220, no. 4598, pages 671-680, May 1983.

[17] Mahfoud, S. W., and Goldberg, D. E., "A Genetic Algorithm for Parallel Simulated Annealing", in [33], pages 302-310.

[18] Mahfoud, S. W., and Goldberg, D. E., "Parallel Recombinative Simulated Annealing: a Genetic Algorithm", *Parallel Computing 21*, pages 1-28, 1995.

[19] Romeo, F. and Sangiovanni-Vincentelli, A, "A Theoretical Framework for Simulated Annealing", *Algorithm*, vol. 6, pages 302-345, 1991.

[20] Rudolph, G. "Convergence Analysis of Canonical Genetic Algorithms". *IEEE Trans. on Neural Networks, special issue on Evolutionary Computation*, vol. 5, no. 1, pages 96-101, Jan. 1994.

[21] Seneta, E., *Non-negative Matrices and Markov Chains*. New York, NY: Springer Verlag, 1981.

[22] Spears, W. M. and DeJong, K. A., "On the virtues of parametrized uniform crossover", in [30], pages 230-236.

[23] Suzuki, J., "A Markov Chain Analysis on a Genetic Algorithm", in [31], pages 146-153.

[24] Suzuki, J., "A Markov Chain Analysis on a Simple Genetic Algorithm", *IEEE Trans. on Systems, Man, and Cybernetics*, vol. SMC-25, no. 4, pages 655-659, April 1995.

[25] Syswerda, G., "Uniform Crossover in Genetic Algorithms", in [29], pages 2-9.

[26] Nix, E. A. and Vose, M. D., "Modeling Genetic Algorithms with Markov chains", Annals of Math. and Artificial Intelligence, vol. 5, pages 79-88, 1992.

[27] Vose, M. D. and Liepins, G. E., "Punctuated Equilibria in Genetic Search", *Complex Systems*, vol. 5, pages 31-44, 1991.

[28] Vose, M. D., "Advanced GA Theory", *ICGA-95 Tutotial*, page 8, 1995.

[29] Schaffer, J. D. (Ed.), *Procoodings of International Conference on Genetic Algorithms '89*, George Mason University, VA, San Mateo: Morgan Kaufmann, 1989.

[30] Belew, R. K. and Booker, L. B. (Eds.), *Proceedings of the Fourth International Conference on Genetic Algorithms '91*. San Diego: Univ. of California, CA, San Mateo: Morgan Kaufmann, 1991.

[31] Forrest, S. (Ed.), *Proceedings of the Fifth International Conference on Genetic Algorithms '93*. Urabana-Champaign: Univ. of Illinois, IL, San Mateo: Morgan Kaufmann, 1993.

[32] Schwefel, H. P. and Männer, R. (Eds.), *Parallel Problem Solving from Nature*, Berlin and Heidelberg: Springer, 1990.

[33] Reinhard Männer and Bernard Manderick (Ed.), *Parallel Problem Solving from Nature, 2*, Amsterdam: North-Holland, 1992.

Appendix A: the Markov chain model of GAs

Proof of Theorem 1

Suppose that t bit positions ($0 \leq t \leq |i \oplus j|$) exchange bits by uniform crossover since the exchanges occur at the positions where the two individuals i and j have different values. The probability is expressed as $\chi^t(1 - \chi)^{|i \oplus j| - t}$.

The $|i \oplus j|$ positions (before uniform crossover) are classified into two groups:

1. the positions at which individual i and j have genes 1 and 0, respectively ($|(i \oplus j) \otimes i|$ bits); and

2. the positions at which individual i and j have genes 0 and 1, respectively ($|(i \oplus j) \otimes j|$ bits).

Without loss of generality, it is supposed that $t - s$ and s bits ($0 \leq s \leq t$) out of the $|(i \oplus j) \otimes i|$ and $|(i \oplus j) \otimes j|$ bits, respectively, are exchanged by uniform crossover. This event can occur in

$$\binom{|(i \oplus j) \otimes i|}{t - s} \binom{|(i \oplus j) \otimes j|}{s} \tag{16}$$

different ways.

Consider the child individual i' of $i \in J$ such that i and i' have different and same values at the exchanged and unexchanged bit positions, respectively. By uniform crossover, the number of 1's in the $|(i \oplus j) \otimes i|$ positions of i is decreased by $t - s$ while the number of 1's in the $|(i \oplus j) \otimes j|$ positions of i is decreased by s. Therefore, the number of 1's in i is increased by $2s - t$, thus the number of 1's and 0's in i' are $|i| + 2s - t$ and $L - |i| - 2s + t$, respectively. Similarly, the number of 1's and 0's in j' are $|j| - 2s + t$ and $L - |j| + 2s - t$, respectively, for the child individual j' of $j \in J$. Therefore, the probability that one of the two crossed individuals (one of the two is randomly selected with probability 1/2.) becomes the zero string is

$$\frac{1}{2}[\mu^{|i|+2s-t}(1 - \mu)^{L-|i|-2s+t} + \mu^{|j|-2s+t}(1 - \mu)^{L-|j|+2s-t}] . \tag{17}$$

The sum over all the products of Eqs. (16) and (17) ranging $0 \leq s \leq t$ yields

$$\frac{1}{2}\sum_{s=0}^{t} \binom{|(i \oplus j) \otimes i|}{t - s} \binom{|(i \oplus j) \otimes j|}{s}$$
$$\cdot [\mu^{|i|+2s-t}(1 - \mu)^{L-|i|-2s+t} + \mu^{|j|-2s+t}(1 - \mu)^{L-|j|+2s-t}] .$$

when the number of exchanged bits via uniform crossover, t, is given. Taking into account the probability $\chi^t(1 - \chi)^{|i \oplus j| - t}$ for $0 \le t \le |i \oplus j|$, we obtain the claim.

Q. E. D.

Proof of Corollary 1

Since $i \oplus k = 0$ and $j \oplus k = 2^L - 1$, we have

$$(i \oplus k) \oplus (j \oplus k) = 2^L - 1$$

$$[(i \oplus k) \oplus (j \oplus k)] \otimes (i \oplus k) = 0$$

$$[(i \oplus k) \oplus (j \oplus k)] \otimes (j \oplus k) = 2^L - 1 .$$

Thus,

$$
\begin{aligned}
& r_{i,j}(k) \\
= \; & r_{i \oplus k, j \oplus k}(0) \\
= \; & \frac{1}{2}\sum_{t=0}^{L} \chi^t(1-\chi)^{L-t} \sum_{s=0}^{t} \binom{0}{t-s}\binom{L}{s} [\mu^{2s-t}(1-\mu)^{L-2s+t} + \mu^{L-2s+t}(1-\mu)^{2s-t}] \\
= \; & \frac{1}{2}\sum_{t=0}^{L} \chi^t(1-\chi)^{L-t} \binom{L}{t} [\mu^t(1-\mu)^{L-t} + \mu^{L-t}(1-\mu)^t] \\
= \; & \frac{1}{2}[\sum_{t=0}^{L} \binom{L}{t}\chi^t(1-\chi)^{L-t}\mu^t(1-\mu)^{L-t} + \sum_{t=0}^{L}\binom{L}{t}\chi^t(1-\chi)^{L-t}\mu^{L-t}(1-\mu)^t] \\
= \; & \frac{1}{2}\{[\chi\mu + (1-\chi)(1-\mu)]^L + [\chi(1-\mu) + (1-\chi)\mu]^L\} .
\end{aligned}
$$

Q. E. D.

Proof of Corollary 2

Since $i \oplus k = 2^L - 1$ and $j \oplus k = 2^L - 1$, we have

$$(i \oplus k) \oplus (j \oplus k) = 0$$

$$[(i \oplus k) \oplus (j \oplus k)] \otimes (i \oplus k) = 0$$

$$[(i \oplus k) \oplus (j \oplus k)] \otimes (j \oplus k) = 0 .$$

Thus,

$$
\begin{aligned}
& r_{i,j}(k) \\
= \; & r_{i \oplus k, j \oplus k}(0) \\
= \; & \frac{1}{2}\sum_{t=0}^{0} \chi^t(1-\chi)^{-t} \sum_{s=0}^{t} \binom{0}{t-s}\binom{0}{s} [\mu^{L+2s-t}(1-\mu)^{-2s+t} + \mu^{L-2s+t}(1-\mu)^{2s-t}] \\
= \; & \mu^L
\end{aligned}
$$

Q. E. D.

Appendix B: the Perron-Frobenius theorem

Let A be a stochastic primitive matrix. Then [21],

1. $\alpha = 1$ is an eigenvalue of A;

2. $\alpha = 1$ has corresponding left and right eigenvectors with strictly positive components;

3. $\alpha = 1 > |\alpha'|$ for any eigenvalue $\alpha' \neq \alpha$;

4. the eigenvector associated with $\alpha = 1$ are unique to constant multiples;

5. If $0 \leq B \leq A$ and β is an eigenvalue of B, then $|\beta| \leq \alpha = 1$. Moreover, $|\beta| = \alpha = 1$ implies $B = A$; and

6. $\alpha = 1$ is a simple root of the characteristic polynomial of A.

A Search for Counterexamples to Two Conjectures on the Simple Genetic Algorithm

Alden H. Wright
Computer Science Dept.
The University of Montana
Missoula, MT 59812-1008
wright@cs.umt.edu

Garrett Bidwell*
BBN Systems and Technologies
Cambridge, MA bidwell@cs.umt.edu

Abstract

We empirically searched for cycling and chaotic behavior in the infinite population Simple Genetic Algorithm. We found examples of period 2 cycling (which we expected) and long period cycling (which we didn't expect). These examples had mutation and crossover distributions which do not correspond to the way that mutation and crossover are normally used in practice. We also searched unsuccessfully for stable polymorphic fixed points in the zero mutation case.

1   Introduction

Vose (1990) introduced a rigorous dynamical system model for the binary-representation genetic algorithm with proportional selection, with the simplifying assumption of an infinite population size. This model has been further extended in Vose & Liepins (1991), Vose & Wright (1994), and Vose (1996). If the string length is ℓ, the model is defined in terms of a differentiable mapping $\mathcal{G}$ from R^n into itself, where $n = 2^\ell$. The mapping $\mathcal{G}$ describes how a population changes from one generation to the next.

Conjecture 1: The iterates of $\mathcal{G}$ always converge to a fixed point.

This conjecture was posed in Vose & Wright (1995b). The conjecture is known to be true when the fitness function is linear or very close to linear, as shown in Vose & Wright (1994).

Hastings (1981) gives an empirically derived counterexample for the diploid discrete-time model of biological population genetics, and Akin (1982) proves the existence of cycling for the continuous-time diploid model.

---

*This work was done while this author was a Master's student at the University of Montana

The conjecture is obviously false for general mutation. To illustrate, consider a 1-bit model with a mutation rate of 1. Then on each generation, each 0 individual will be mutated to a 1 individual and vice versa. Thus, under any nonzero fitnesses, $\mathcal{G}$ will map the vector population $[1, 0]^T$ to $[0, 1]^T$ and vice versa, giving a stable cycle of period 2.

We empirically show the existence of more complex cycling behavior.

Conjecture 2: If mutation is zero, the only asymptotically stable fixed points of $\mathcal{G}$ correspond to populations containing a single type of individual.

This conjecture was also stated as Conjecture 4.4 in Vose and Wright (1995b). A fixed point x of $\mathcal{G}$ is *asymptotically stable* if if there is a neighborhood V of x such that $lim_{t\to\infty}\mathcal{G}^t(y) = x$ for all $y \in V$. If every eigenvalue of the differential matrix $d\mathcal{G}_x$ has modulus less than one, then x is asymptotically stable, see Guckenheimer (1983).

Our empirical search for counterexamples of this conjecture was unsuccessful.

There has been extensive work on methods for maintaining diversity in genetic algorithms. The dissertation of Mahfoud (1995) gives an excellent survey of this work. If conjecture 2 is true, this suggests that a "standard" genetic algorithm cannot maintain a stable population that includes individuals near two or more local maxima of the fitness function. (While the results of this paper are for infinite populations and no mutation, one should expect that increasing the population size and removing mutation would decrease noise and hence lead to an improved ability to maintain stable populations near two or more local maxima of the fitness function.) This gives justification for special techniques, such as sharing and niching methods, for maintaining stable diverse populations on multimodal fitness landscapes.

2 The Simple Genetic Algorithm

The Simple Genetic Algorithm is a standard genetic algorithm over fixed length binary strings that uses proportional selection and various types of crossover and mutation.

2.1 The Vose Model

We consider a generalization of the infinite population model of the Simple Genetic Algorithm introduced in Vose (1990), which is the theoretical framework used in Vose (1996). Other references include Vose and Wright (1994) and Vose (1995). The domain Ω is the set of length ℓ binary strings. Let $n = 2^\ell$ and note that elements of Ω correspond to integers in the range $[0, n)$. They are thereby thought of interchangeably as integers or as bit strings or as column vectors with entries from $\{0, 1\}$. Let $\mathbf{1}$ denote the vector of all ones (which corresponds to the integer $n - 1$). Let e_k denote the kth column of the $n \times n$ identity matrix.

Let $\oplus$ denote the bitwise exclusive-OR operation, and let $\otimes$ denote the bitwise AND operation on Ω. For $x \in \Omega$, the one's-complement of x is denoted by $\bar{x}$. Note that $\bar{x} = \mathbf{1} \oplus x$. If $expr$ is an expression that is either true or false, then $[expr] = 1$ if $expr$ is true and $[expr] = 0$ otherwise. Let $\delta_{ij} = [i = j]$. The $n \times n$ permutation matrix whose i, j th entry is $\delta_{i\oplus k,j}$ is denoted by σ_k. Note that $(\sigma_k x)_i = x_{i\oplus k}$.

A *population* is a real-valued probability vector x indexed over Ω; the probability (or fraction) of string i in population x is x_i. The set of all populations is the *unit simplex* $\Lambda = \{x \in (R^{\geq 0})^n : \mathbf{1}^T x = 1\}$, where $R^{\geq 0}$ denotes the non-negative reals. The e_k are vertices of Λ and correspond to populations consisting entirely of one string type (namely k).

A $n \times n$ *mixing matrix* M encodes mutation and crossover. M is defined so that $M_{i,j}$ is the probability of obtaining the 0 string by doing mutation and crossover on the parent strings i and j. Thus, $x^T M x$ is the probability (or fraction) of the 0 string as a the result of doing crossover and mutation to population x. The formula for the M matrix is given in Vose (1996) and is repeated here for completeness.

Considering $k \in \Omega$ as a *crossover mask* used with parents $i, j \in \Omega$, the children are $(i \otimes k) \oplus (j \otimes \overline{k})$ and $(j \otimes k) \oplus (i \otimes \overline{k})$. We assume one child is kept (with equal probability). Let χ_k denote the probability that mask k is used. Let μ_k, $k \in \Omega$, be the probability that a string x is mutated into the string $x \oplus k$. Under general crossover and mutation, referred to as *mixing*, M is given by:

$$M_{i,j} = \sum_{u,v,k \in \Omega} \mu_u \mu_v \frac{\chi_k + \chi_{\overline{k}}}{2} [((i \oplus u) \otimes k) \oplus ((j \oplus v) \otimes \overline{k}) = 0] \qquad (1)$$

Note that M is symmetric and nonnegative.

We will refer to the vector $\chi \in \Lambda$ as a *crossover probability distribution*, or just as a *crossover distribution*. The crossover distribution is determined by the type of crossover. For example, one-point crossover with a crossover rate of C corresponds to the crossover distribution

$$\chi_i = \begin{cases} 1 - C & \text{if } i = 0 \\ C/(\ell - 1) & \text{if } \exists k = 1, 2, \ldots \ell - 1 \text{ such that } i = 2^k - 1 \\ 0 & \text{otherwise} \end{cases}$$

Similarly, uniform crossover with a crossover rate of C is given by

$$\chi_i = \begin{cases} 1 - C + C 2^{-\ell} & \text{if } i = 0 \\ C 2^{-\ell} & \text{if } i > 0 \end{cases}$$

We will refer to the vector $\mu \in \Lambda$ as a *mutation probability distribution*, or just as a *mutation distribution*. The mutation distribution is determined by the type of mutation. For example, mutation defined by a per-bit mutation rate R corresponds to the mutation distribution given by

$$\mu_i = R^{1^T i} (1 - R)^{\ell - 1^T i}$$

The *mixing function* $\mathcal{M} : \Lambda \longrightarrow \Lambda$ gives the population after crossover and mutation. (If x corresponds to a finite population, then $\mathcal{M}(x)$ is the expected population after crossover and mutation.) $\mathcal{M}$ has component functions defined by:

$$\mathcal{M}_i(x) = x^T \sigma_i M \sigma_i x$$

The mixing function can also be written in the form:

$$\mathcal{M}_i(x) = e_i^T \mathcal{M}(x) = \sum_{u,v \in \Omega} x_{u \oplus i} x_{v \oplus i} M_{u,v} = \sum_{u,v \in \Omega} x_u x_v M_{u \oplus i, v \oplus i} \qquad (2)$$

It is shown in Vose (1996) that $\mathcal{M}_k(x)$ can be interpreted as the probability of string k in the population that is obtained by applying mutation and crossover to population x.

Note that $\mathcal{M}$ is *homogeneous of degree 2*, i.e., $\mathcal{M}(\alpha x) = \alpha^2 \mathcal{M}(x)$ for any scalar α.

The formula for the entries of the differential $d\mathcal{M}_x$ follows by direct computation from equation (2).

$$
\begin{aligned}
(d\mathcal{M}_x)_{i,j} &= \frac{\partial}{\partial x_j} \sum_{u,v \in \Omega} x_u x_v M_{u \oplus i, v \oplus i} \\
&= \sum_{u,v} (\delta_{u,j} x_v + \delta_{v,j} x_u) M_{u \oplus i, v \oplus i} \\
&= \sum_{u} x_v M_{j \oplus i, v \oplus i} + \sum_{u} x_u M_{u \oplus i, j \oplus i} \\
&= 2 \sum_{u} x_u M_{i \oplus j, u \oplus i}
\end{aligned}
$$

where $\delta_{u,j} = 1$ if $u = j$ and $\delta_{u,j} = 0$ otherwise.

Assuming a *fitness function* $f : \Omega \longrightarrow R^+$, proportional selection is the mapping $\mathcal{F} : \Lambda \longrightarrow \Lambda$ defined by $\mathcal{F}(x) = Fx/1^T Fx$, where F is the $n \times n$ diagonal matrix $F_{i,j} = \delta_{i,j} f(i)$. The fitness function is regarded as a vector through the correspondence $f_i = f(i)$.

The transition from one generation to the next of the infinite population simple genetic algorithm is given by the mapping

$$
\mathcal{G} = \mathcal{M} \circ \mathcal{F} : \Lambda \longrightarrow \Lambda.
$$

The Vose infinite population model described above has a close relationship to earlier population genetics models. For example, Geiringer (1944) described a multilocus model based on recombination (crossover) only. She introduced the concept of a "linkage distribution", which is essentially another name for a probability distribution over crossover masks. Some more recent papers that describe related work in population genetics include Karlin and Liberman (1978), (1979), and (1990). These models are diploid models that do not include mutation, whereas the Vose model is haploid and does include mutation.

2.2   The differential of $\mathcal{G}$

In order to determine the stability of fixed points of $\mathcal{G}$, we need to be able to compute the differential of $\mathcal{G}$ at fixed points.

The material in this section is derived from Vose (1996).

Let P denote the projection

$$
I - x \frac{1^T F}{1^T Fx}
$$

Lemma 2.1

$$
d\mathcal{G}_x = \frac{1}{1^T Fx} d\mathcal{M}_{Fx/1^T Fx} FP
$$

Proof. Consider the function $h(x) = x/1^T x$. Its differential is

$$
dh_x = \frac{I}{1^T x} - x \frac{1^T}{(1^T x)^2}
$$

Since $\mathcal{G}(x) = \mathcal{M}(h(Fx))$, the chain rule gives

$$
\begin{aligned}
d\mathcal{G}_x &= d\mathcal{M}_{h(Fx)} dh_{Fx} F \\
&= d\mathcal{M}_{h(Fx)} \left(\frac{I}{1^T Fx} - Fx \frac{1^T}{(1^T Fx)^2} \right) F \\
&= \frac{1}{1^T Fx} d\mathcal{M}_{h(Fx)} FP
\end{aligned}
$$

$\square$

3   Constructing Fixed Points

Let y be a fixed point of $\mathcal{G}$. Then we have:

$$
\mathcal{G}(y) = \mathcal{M}\left(\frac{Fy}{1^T Fy} \right) = y
$$

Let $x = Fy/(1^T Fy)^2$. Then $1^T x = 1^T Fy/(1^T Fy)^2 = 1/(1^T Fy)$ and

$$
\begin{aligned}
\mathcal{M}(x) &= \mathcal{M}\left(\frac{Fy}{(1^T Fy)^2} \right) = \frac{1}{(1^T Fy)^2} \mathcal{M}\left(\frac{Fy}{1^T Fy} \right) \\
&= \frac{y}{(1^T Fy)^2} = F^{-1} \frac{Fy}{(1^T Fy)^2} = F^{-1} x
\end{aligned} \tag{3}
$$

Let X be the $n \times n$ diagonal matrix $X_{i,j} = \delta_{i,j} x_i$. and let g be the n vector $g_i = 1/f_i = 1/f(i)$. Then this equation can be rewritten as

$$
\mathcal{M}(x) = F^{-1} x = Xg
$$

Our method for generating random fixed points is to start with a random point x in the simplex. (The detailed methodology for choosing x will be given later.) Given x, we can compute g by $g = X^{-1} \mathcal{M}(x)$. The fitnesses are easily computed by $f(i) = g_i^{-1}$.

From x, we also compute the corresponding fixed point y by

$$
y = F^{-1} x / (1^T x)^2
$$

Finally, we note that if a point y of the simplex is to be a fixed point of $\mathcal{G}$, then $x = Fy/(1^T Fy)^2$ must satisfy equation (3), so the fitness f as computed above must be the unique fitness that will make y a fixed point.

4   Searching for Cyclic Behavior

4.1   Methodology

Hastings (1981) demonstrated stable cyclic behavior in a discrete-time, constant fitness, two-locus, two-allele, diploid, infinite-population model. This model includes crossover but not mutation. His methodology was to do a numerical search for a stable Hopf bifurcation. In other words, he searched over populations and crossover rates for a point where the differential of the transition map had a real eigenvalue between -1 and 1 and a pair of complex eigenvalues with modulus close to 1. For each population and crossover rate, he generated a corresponding fitness. When he found a stable Hopf bifurcation, he parameterized the system over the crossover rate, and then iterated the system to look for stable cycling behavior. He found several examples, some of which are described in detail in Hastings (1981).

Our procedure for looking for a counterexample to conjecture 1 followed a methodology similar to that of Hastings. For each trial, we generated random mutation and crossover distributions, and a random population vector x. We computed the mixing matrix M that corresponds to the mutation and crossover distributions, and followed the procedure given at the end of Section 2 to compute the fitness and fixed point y corresponding to M and x. We found the eigenvalues of of $d\mathcal{G}_y$ using the QR algorithm as implemented following Chapter 11 of Press (1992). If all real eigenvalues had absolute value less than 1 and some complex eigenvalue had modulus greater than 1, we iterated the system 30 times starting from perturbations of the fixed point y. We detected three kinds of outcomes from the iteration: convergence to a fixed point, convergence to a cycle of period 2, and non-convergence. In cases of non-convergence, we then looked in more detail for interesting behavior.

The intuitive motivation for this procedure is as follows. We are searching for an unstable fixed point where the behavior near the fixed point is cyclic and repelling in 2 (or possibly more) dimensions and is contracting in the remaining dimensions. The behavior would be cyclic and repelling in the eigenspace of the complex eigenvalues with modulus greater than 1, and contracting in the eigenspace of the remaining eigenvectors. The hope is that trajectories starting near this unstable fixed point will converge to a stable periodic cycle.

We used two procedures for generating random mutation/crossover distributions and random population vectors. The first method was to generate the n components of the vector randomly from a uniform distribution over $[0, 1]$, and then normalize the vector so that the sum of the components was 1. For the second method, we first randomly chose between 1 and $n - 2$ components of the vector to be zero, and then chose the remaining components as with the first method. When we applied this method to choosing the population vector x, the "zero" components were set to 10^{-8}, which avoided overflow problems with finding eigenvalues.

4.2   Results

We found examples of both approximate period 2 cycling and longer period cycling. All examples of cycling were for genetic algorithms with 3 bits or more, and were generated by using mutation distributions that had many zero components.

To guard against the possibility that these examples were the artifacts of finite precision floating point arithmetic, these examples were run on Maple using 200 decimal-digit precision arithmetic. It should be noted that all quantities involved in the computation are positive, so there should be no possibility of "catastrophic cancelation".

To guard against the possibility that there were small divergent components in the results, the examples were run for 100,000 generations. After a convergence period of a few thousand generations, the graphs look the same at the beginning of the simulation as at the end.

Of course, computer floating-point computations cannot mathematically prove the existence of cycling.

We give two specific examples.

First is a 3-bit example that exhibits both approximate period 2 cycling and longer period cycling. Figure 1 shows the long-period cycling by plotting of the odd numbered generations from generation 1 to generation 1500. The long period length is approximately 800 generations. A plot of the even numbered generations would look essentially the same, except shifted by half of the long period. Figure 2 shows the odd-numbered generations from 98,500 to 100,000.

This example was generated using the following parameters:

Mutation distribution: $[0, 0, 0, 0, 0, 0.92431012295, 0.07568987705, 0]$.

Crossover distribution: $[0, 0, 0.00045333862, 0.18649248799, 0.402363733, 0, 0, 0.403053606]$

Fitness: $[1.14095516458, 1.54743922498, 0.21910897310, 0.11026697012,$
$0.60205233386, 1.11500442255, 0.43395246731, 3.27024330619]$

Fixed point: $[0.20829345545, 0.15689801943, 0.09281778305, 0.03711709950,$
$0.22026606341, 0.19491636472, 0.05222667592, 0.03746453852]$

We did not find any 3-bit examples that did not converge whose first component of the mutation distribution was not zero.

The second example, shown in Figure 2, is a 4-bit example that exhibits long period cycling without period 2 cycling. Figure 3 shows every generation from generation 99,500 to generation 100,000. The period length is approximately 200 generations. This example was generated using the following parameters:

Mutation distribution: $[0.163082130, 0, 0, 0, 0.56124617479, 0, 0.27574300391, 0,$
$0, 0, 0, 0, 0, 0, 0, 0]$.

Crossover distribution: $[0.07413297401, 0, 0, 0, 0.06496689448, 0.17438274378, 0, 0,$
$0.12760739880, 0, 0.27383219607, 0.28507779287, 0, 0, 0, 0]$

Fitness: $[0.26931619062, 0.00000011160, 0.82567205904, 0.00000013171,$
$3.73619740388, 5.41096045807, 0.00000044376, 5.94155773254,$
$0.00000007687, 0.06241539118, 0.00000008612, 0.00000012359,$
$3.75146639703, 6.96087252897, 5.18366848032, 0.00000060560]$

Fixed point: $[0.08262271198, 0.08960499858, 0.06337908163, 0.07592443302,$
$0.02850140995, 0.02188019848, 0.02253466654, 0.01719816329,$
$0.13009475647, 0.14208881473, 0.11611842899, 0.08091208872,$
$0.04073704669, 0.03601416632, 0.03587653907, 0.01651249549,]$

This example has nonzero first component of the mutation distribution.

5   Stable Fixed points with No Mutation

We followed almost the same methodology as in the previous section. The mutation distribution was always $[1, 0, 0, \ldots, 0]$. We generated the crossover distribution, the random population vector x, and the fitness in the same way. The fixed point generated in this way always had more than one nonzero component, and so was not at a vertex of the simplex. We looked for cases where all eigenvalues had modulus less than or equal to 1, and where all components of the fitness vector were not equal. In other words, this was a direct search for counterexamples, rather than the more indirect search of the previous section.

We ran 4,000,000 trials with each of 3 bits, 4 bits, and 5 bits. We did not find any counterexamples to conjecture 2.

We did find a number of "almost" counterexamples: fixed points in the interior of the simplex with real eigenvalues whose absolute values were equal to 1. In these examples, all nonzero components of the fixed point vector corresponded to a component of the fitness vector of value 1, which was the maximum fitness value. These fixed points correspond to populations consisting entirely of individuals of equal and maximum fitness. These fixed points are "nonhyperbolic". In other words, the linear approximation determined by the differential does not determine the stability. We would guess that there is a space (such as a curve or surface) of such fixed points that connects vertices of the simplex corresponding to the strings of maximum fitness.

6 Conclusion

We searched for counterexamples to conjectures 1 and 2. We found empirical counterexamples to conjecture 1: namely a number of instances of stable cycling of both period 2 and longer periods for the infinite population simple genetic algorithm with mutation. These examples have mutation distributions that do not correspond to the way that mutation is normally used in genetic algorithms. We did not find any counterexamples to conjecture 2. Thus, our results give empirical evidence that both conjectures are true for models that correspond to genetic algorithms as they are normally used in practice.

A finite population GA that used the same parameters (crossover and mutation distributions and fitness function) as the infinite population cycling examples should also exhibit cycling behavior if the population size is sufficiently large. It is unclear whether this could happen for population sizes as they are currently used in practice. It may well be that the "noise" due to the finite population size would quickly move the system away from the stable cyclic attractor of the infinite population system.

This work suggests that a rigorous proof of cycling behavior might be possible.

Acknowledgments

This research was partially supported by a Montana's NSF EPSCoR Program grant and a University of Montana grant.

References

Akin, E. (1982) "Cycling in Simple Genetic Systems", *J. Math. Biology, 13*, 305-324.

Geiringer, H. (1944) "On the probability theory of linkage in Mendelian heredity", *Annals of Mathematical Statistics, 15*, 25-57.

Guckenheimer, J., & Holmes, P. (1983). *Nonlinear Oscillations, Dynamical Systems, and Bifurcations of Vector Fields*, Springer Verlag.

Hastings, A. (1981). "Stable cycling in discrete-time genetic models", *Proc. Nat. Acad. Sci. USA, 78*, 7224-7225.

Karlin, S. & Liberman, U. (1978) "Classifications and comparisons of multilocus recombination distributions", *Proc. Nat. Acad. Sci. USA, 75*, 6332-6336.

Karlin, S. & Liberman, U. (1979) "Central equilibria in multilocus systems I. Generalized nonepistatic selection regimes", *Genetics, 91*, 777-798.

Karlin, S. & Liberman, U. (1990) "Global convergence properties in multilocus viability selection models: the additive model and the Hardy-Weinberg law", *Mathematical Biology, 29*, 161-176.

Mahfoud, S. (1995). "Niching Methods for Genetic Algorithms", IlliGAL Technical Report No. 95001, Illinois Genetic Algorithms Laboratory, University of Illinois at Urbana-Champaign, Urbana, IL 61801.

Nagylaki, T. (1992). *Introduction to Theoretical Population Genetics*, Springer Verlag.

Press, W. H., Teukolsky, S. A, Vetterling, W. T., & Flannery, B. P. (1982). *Numerical Recipes in C: The Art of Scientific Computing*, second edition, Cambridge University Press.

Vose, M. D. (1990). "Formalizing Genetic Algorithms", *Proc. IEEE wksp. on G.A.s, N.N.s, & S.A. applied to problems in Signal & Image Processing*, May 1990, Glasgow, U.K.

Vose, M. D. (1995). "Modeling Simple Genetic Algorithms", *Evolutionary Computation, 3*, 453-472.

Vose, M. D. (1996). *The Simple Genetic Algorithm: foundations and theory*. MIT Press, (to appear).

Vose, M. D. & Liepins, G. E. (1991). "Punctuated Equilibria In Genetic Search", *Complex Systems, 5*, 31-44.

Vose, M. D. & Wright, A. H. (1994). "Simple Genetic Algorithms with Linear Fitness", *Evolutionary Computation, 2*(4), 347-368.

Wright, A. H. & Vose, M. D. (1995a). "Finiteness of the Fixed Point Set for the Simple Genetic Algorithm", *Evolutionary Computation, 3*(3).

Vose, M. D. & Wright, A. H. (1995b). "Stability of Vertex Fixed Points and Applications", *Foundations of Genetic Algorithms 3*, edited by L. D. Whitley and M. D. Vose, Morgan Kaufmann Publishers, Inc., San Francisco, CA.

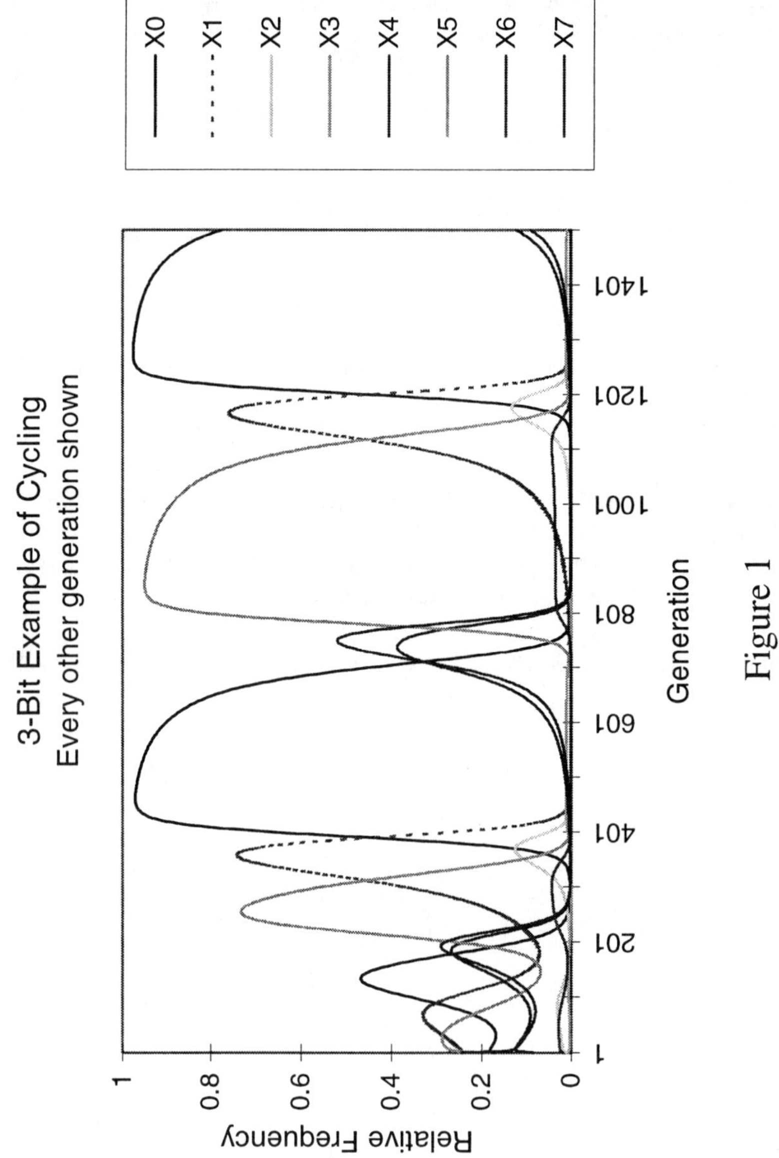

3-Bit Example of Cycling
Every other generation shown
Relative Frequency
1
0.8
0.6
0.4
0.2
0
1
201
401
601
801
1001
1201
1401
Generation
X0
X1
X2
X3
X4
X5
X6
X7

Figure 1

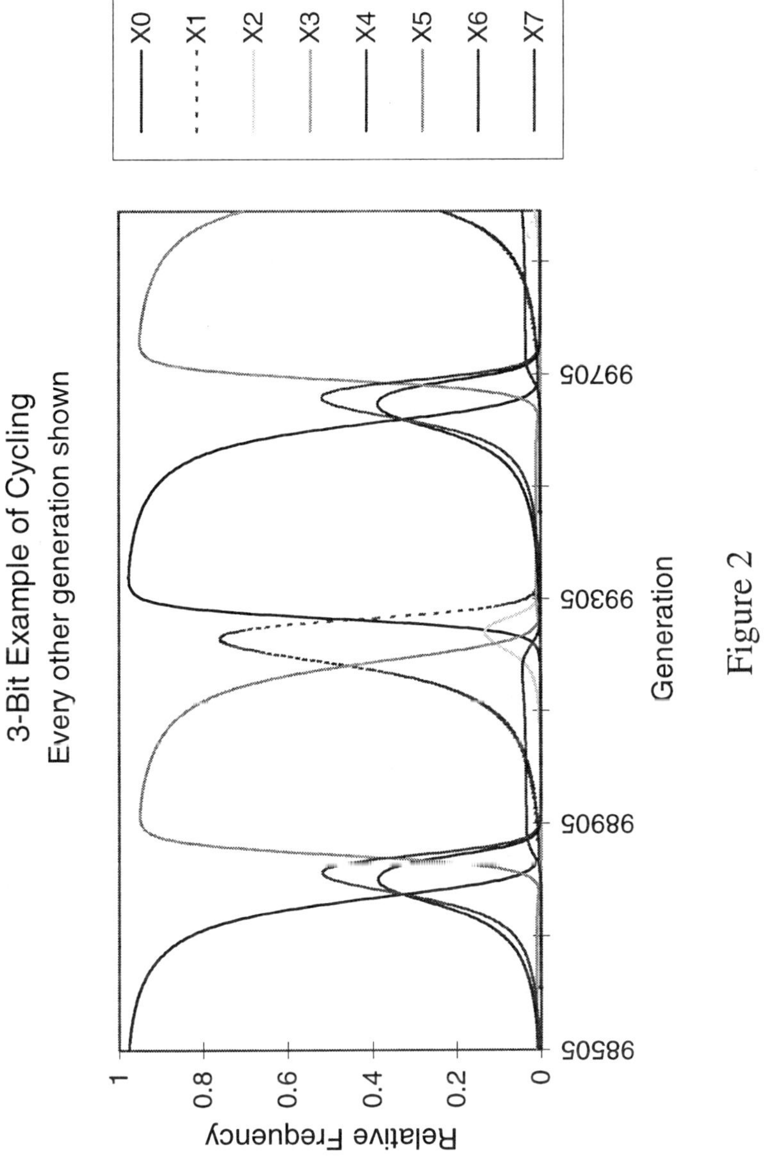

3-Bit Example of Cycling
Every other generation shown
X0
X1
X2
X3
X4
X5
X6
X7
Relative Frequency
1
0.8
0.6
0.4
0.2
0
Generation
98505
98905
99305
99705

Figure 2

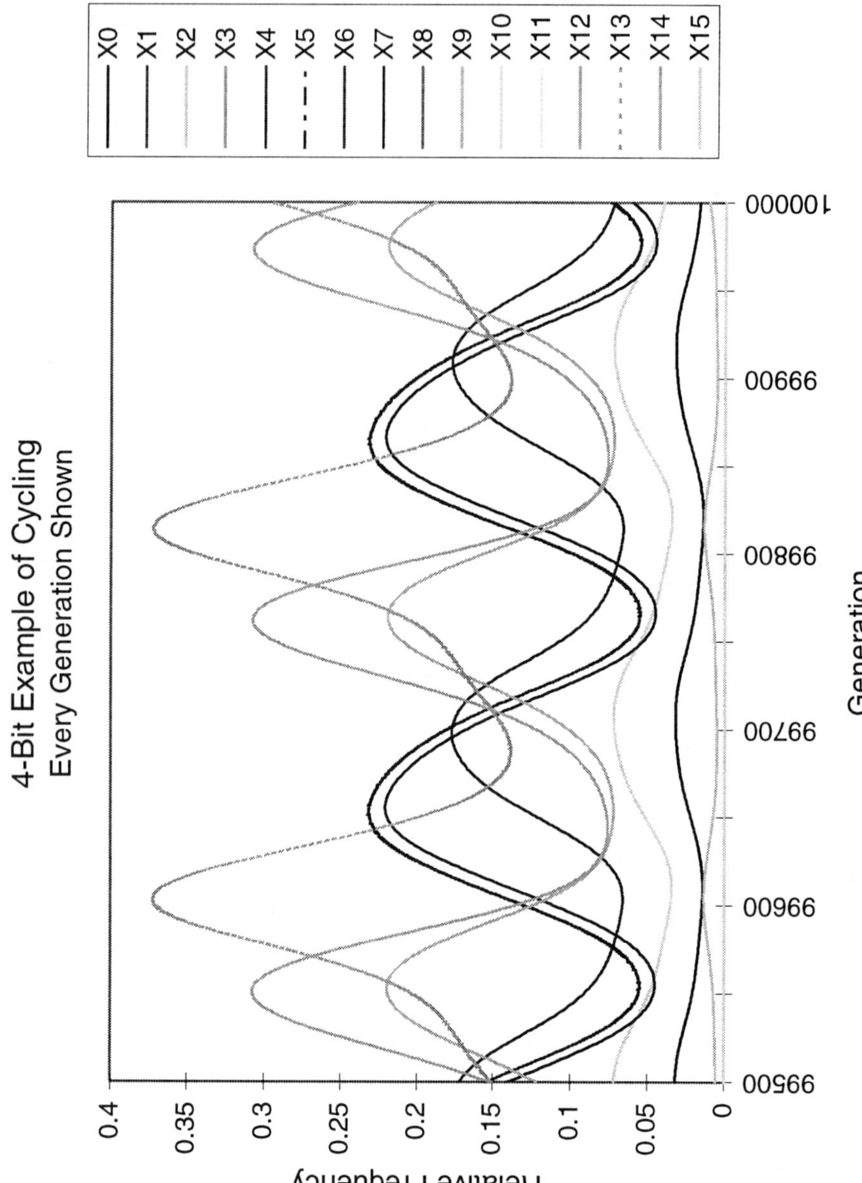

4-Bit Example of Cycling
Every Generation Shown
Relative Frequency
Generation
X0
X1
X2
X3
X4
X5
X6
X7
X8
X9
X10
X11
X12
X13
X14
X15

Figure 2

Analyzing GAs Using Markov Models with Semantically Ordered and Lumped States

William M. Spears
Code 5510 - AI Center
Naval Research Laboratory
Washington, DC 20375-5337
spears@aic.nrl.navy.mil

Kenneth A. De Jong
Computer Science Department
George Mason University
Fairfax, VA 22030
kdejong@gmu.edu

Abstract

At the previous FOGA workshop, we presented some initial results on using Markov models to analyze the transient behavior of genetic algorithms (GAs) being used as function optimizers (GAFOs). In that paper, the states of the Markov model were ordered via a simple and mathematically convenient lexicographic ordering used initially by Nix and Vose. In this paper, we explore alternative orderings of states based on interesting semantic properties such as average fitness, degree of homogeneity, average attractive force, etc. We also explore lumping techniques for reducing the size of the state space. Analysis of these reordered and lumped Markov models provides new insights into the transient behavior of GAs in general and GAFOs in particular.

1 INTRODUCTION

Considerable progress has been made in recent years regarding the use of Markov models to analyze the behavior of evolutionary algorithms. In this paper, we extend and expand on the results we presented in the previous FOGA workshop concerning the use of Markov models to analyze the transient behavior of GAs being used for function optimization (De Jong, Spears and Gordon, 1994). First, we abandon the mathematically convenient lexicographic ordering of the states of the Markov models and explore alternative orderings of states which have interesting semantic properties, and which provide new insight into the transient behavior of GAFOs. In addition, we explore various lumping techniques for reducing the size of the Markov models and evaluate the effects of lumping on model accuracy.

Our work continues to be based on the Nix and Vose Markov model (Nix and Vose, 1992) of a simple GA using fixed-length binary strings, 1-point crossover, bit-flipping mutation, and fitness proportional selection. If l is the length of the binary strings, then there are $r = 2^l$ possible strings. If n is the population size, then the number of possible populations, N, corresponding to the number of possible states is:

$$N = \binom{n + r - 1}{r - 1} \tag{1}$$

The possible populations are described by the matrix Z, which is an $N \times r$ matrix. [1] The ith row $\phi_i =< z_{i,0}, ..., z_{i,r-1} >$ of Z is the incidence vector for the ith population. In other words, $z_{i,y}$ is the number of occurrences of string y in the ith population, where y is the integer representation of the binary string. For example, suppose $l = 2$ and $n = 2$. Then $r = 4$, $N = 10$, and the Z matrix would be as shown in Table 1.

Table 1: The Z Matrix when $n = 2$ and $l = 2$

State	Binary	String		
	00	01	10	11
P1	0	0	0	2
P2	0	0	1	1
P3	0	0	2	0
P4	0	1	0	1
P5	0	1	1	0
P6	0	2	0	0
P7	1	0	0	1
P8	1	0	1	0
P9	1	1	0	0
P10	2	0	0	0

Nix and Vose then define two mathematical operators, F and M, where F is determined from the fitness function, and M depends on the mutation rate μ, crossover rate χ, and form of crossover and mutation used. [2] With F and M defined, it is now possible to calculate exact state transition probabilities $Q_{i,j}$, which specify how likely it is that a simple GA in state i (the current population) will be in state j in the next generation:

$$Q_{i,j} = n! \prod_{y=0}^{r-1} \frac{\left[M\left(\frac{F\phi_i}{|F\phi_i|}\right)_y \right]^{z_{j,y}}}{z_{j,y}!} \tag{2}$$

As we showed in our previous paper (De Jong, Spears and Gordon, 1994), the resulting state transition matrix Q can be used in a variety of ways to gain important insights about the transient behavior of GAFOs. One of the techniques introduced was the idea of visualizing the change in the distribution of probability mass of Q^k as k increases. Figure 1 illustrates

---

[1] For programming convenience we transpose the Z matrix of Nix and Vose (1992).

[2] In their paper they assume a standard bit flipping mutation operator and a 1-point crossover which produces a single offspring, although M can be generalized to other operators.

one of these visualizations for the case of $n = 3$, $l = 3$, a mutation rate of $\mu = 0.01$, a crossover rate of $\chi = 1.0$, and a ramp fitness function of $f(y) = integer(y) + 1$. Since $n = 3$ and $l = 3$, there are 120 states in this example.

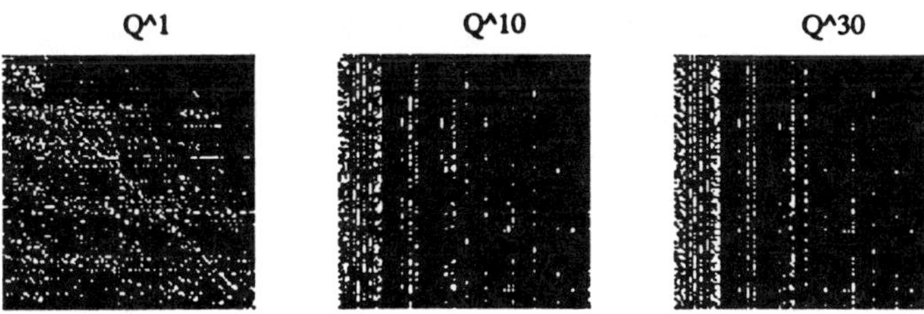

Figure 1: Q^k for Ramp Function with $\mu = 0.01$ and $\chi = 1.0$

The visualization of the probability mass distribution is achieved by mapping each entry $Q_{i,j}$, the probability of moving from state i to state j in one generation, onto a gray scale in which black represents low probability and white high probability. As k increases, the emerging vertical lines in Q^k represent the states (populations) at which the steady state distribution will accumulate most of its probability mass.

2   SEMANTICALLY ORDERED STATES

One of the surprising features brought out with these visualizations is how quickly the probability mass shifts left to a relatively small number of states. However, because the Q matrix uses the lexicographic ordering of the states generated by the Z matrix, it is not easy to get a sense of the characteristics of this set of emerging high probability states.

To remedy this, we have explored a variety of alternative orderings of the states based on interesting semantic properties of the underlying populations they represent such as average fitness, presence of the global optimum, and degree of homogeneity. In this section, results are presented which provide additional insight into the transient behavior of GAFOs, and which tie in nicely with other recent mathematical results such as (Vose, 1995).

2.1   ORDERING STATES BY AVERAGE FITNESS

Perhaps the most intuitive hypothesis as to the character of this emerging set of high probability states is that they correspond to states (populations) with high average fitness. Our visualization technique makes it easy to test this hypothesis by calculating the average fitness of each population in the Z matrix, and then reordering the states of the Q matrix in decreasing order of fitness (left to right and top to bottom). If this hypothesis is correct, we should see a strong shift of probability mass to the left into states with the highest average fitness. Figure 2 illustrates the effects of this reordering for the same model used in Figure 1.

Although there is clear visual evidence of a shift of probability mass to the left, the trend does not seem as strong as the one observed in Figure 1 using the lexicographic ordering, suggesting that high average fitness is not a dominant property of these emerging high

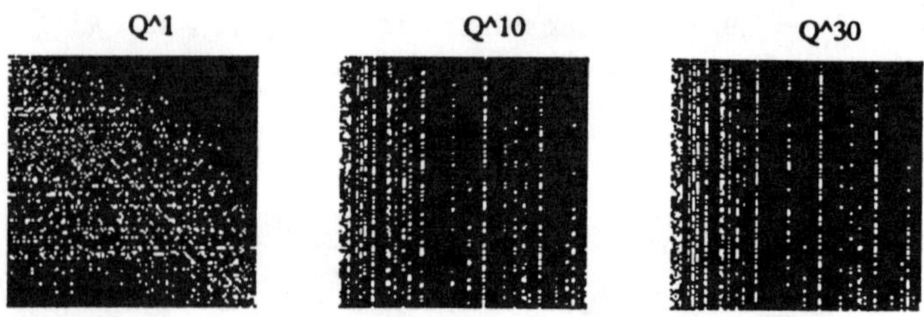

Figure 2: Q^k with States in Decreasing Order of Average Fitness

probability states.

An alternative hypothesis is that these emerging states contain a large number of copies of the global optimum. Sorting the states on this basis produces a somewhat different ordering, but yields only minor differences in the visualizations, indicating that it is also not a strong predictor of these emerging states.

Since we have the Q^k data available, it is possible to identify and track the specific states that are accumulating significant amounts of probability mass. This is illustrated in Figure 3.

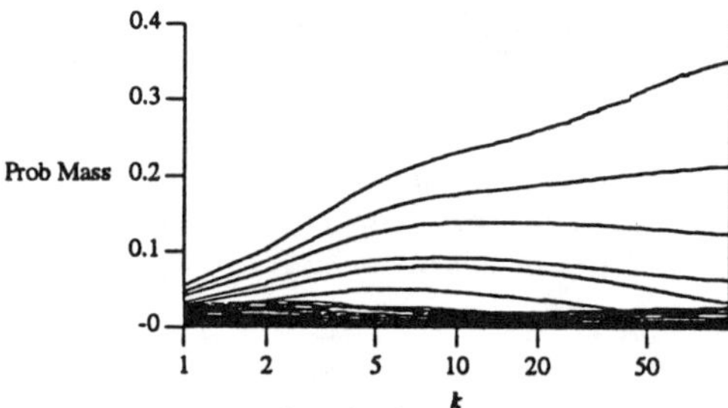

Figure 3: Probability Mass Curves Associated with Figure 2

Each curve in Figure 3 represents the total probability mass in a column of Q^k as a function of k, the number of generations. The x-axis is depicted using a log scale in order to focus on the transient behavior. Viewed in this way one can see very clearly the emergence of a few dominant high probability states already by generation 2 and these states maintain that dominance for large values of k. Since there are 120 states in this example, it can be seen that the vast majority of states have low probability mass.

The state accumulating the most probability mass is the one representing the population consisting entirely of duplicate copies of the most fit individual. The second most dominant state consists entirely of duplicate copies of the second most fit individual. The third state contains only copies of the third most fit individual, and so on. So, in this particular case, the emerging states are best described as homogeneous populations of highly fit individuals that act as "basins of attraction" in which mutation is the only source of variation.

2.2   ORDERING BASED ON HAMMING DISTANCE

To test this hypothesis further, we used the average Hamming distance between all pairs of individuals in a population as a measure of homogeneity, and ordered the states by increasing average Hamming distance (decreasing homogeneity). If this hypothesis is correct, then we should see a strong shift to the left in our visualizations over a broad range of models. Figure 4 illustrates the results for the ramp function.

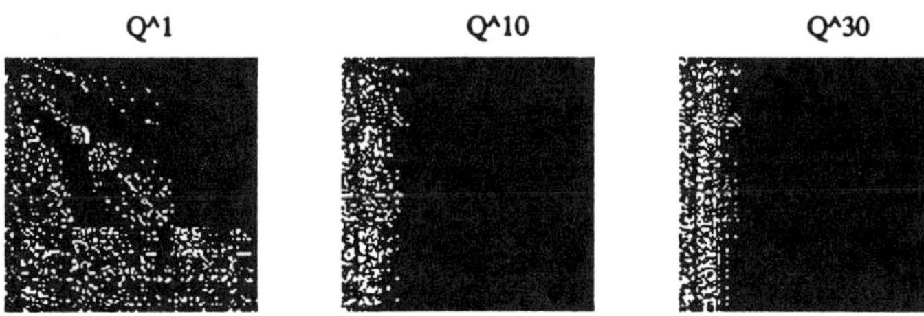

Figure 4: Q^k with States in Increasing Order of Average Hamming Distance

As one can see, the results are quite striking and show a very strong correlation between homogeneity and accumulating probability mass.

2.3   ORDERING STATES BY PROBABILITY MASS

One of the striking features of Figure 3 is how early these attracting states emerge. This suggests that the original state transition matrix Q contains evidence of these states. One way of interpreting the total probability mass of column j in $Q_{i,j}$ is that it provides a measure of the attractive force of state j. That is, given a GA in any arbitrary state i, the total probability mass in column j represents how strongly a GA is "pulled" into state j. Intuitively, columns with more probability mass are states defining basins of attraction.

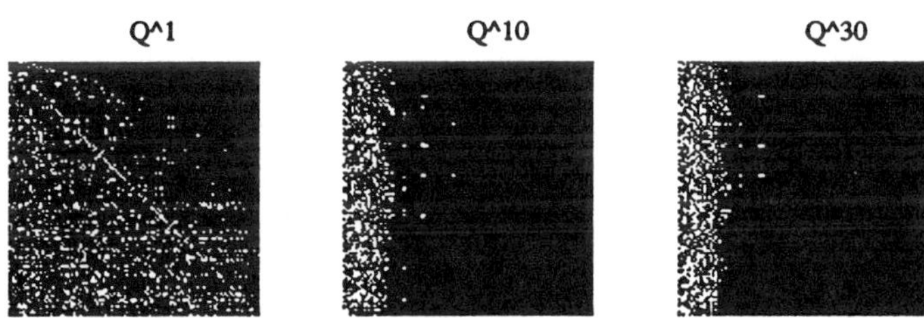

Figure 5: Q^k with States in Decreasing Order of Probability Mass

Given a particular Q matrix, it is quite straightforward to compute the column mass and to reorder the states in descending order of probability mass. Figure 5 illustrates this for the ramp function used in the previous examples.

Again, the results are quite striking. There is very strong correlation between the initial attracting states and those which persist and strengthen.

2.4   A QUANTITATIVE ANALYSIS OF THE ORDERING RESULTS

Visually displaying the results in the preceding sections provides useful qualitative evidence concerning which states accumulate probability mass over time. It is also instructive to analyze these results quantitatively, as follows. If a particular ordering of states is a perfect predictor of the shifting of probability mass to the left, then Q^k would have the property that the column mass of each succeeding state will decrease (from left to right). A simple metric Ψ that measures how well the initial ordering of states predicts decreasing column mass in Q^k is give by:

```
Ψ = 0.0;
for (i = 1; i < N; i++) {
    for (j = i + 1; j ≤ N; j++) {
        if (m_i < m_j) Ψ = Ψ + m_j − m_i;
    }
}
```

The probability mass of state (column) i in Q^k is denoted m_i. If the initial (Q^1) ordering is a perfect predictor of the shifting of the probability mass to the left in Q^k, then the column mass of each succeeding state in Q^k will not increase and $\Psi = 0$. Ψ will be greater than 0 if the prediction is not perfect (e.g., if the column mass of some state in Q^k is greater than the column mass of some preceding state), and the penalty for an incorrect prediction is weighted by the amounts of column mass involved.

Applying this metric to the ramp function at $k = 100$ yields the results shown in Table 2. These results confirm the earlier visual results, indicating that ordering states by initial probability mass or Hamming distance provide strong predictors for those states that persist and strengthen in probability mass as k increases.

Table 2: Ψ Values for Different Orderings of the Ramp Function

Ordering	Ψ
Lexicographic	5.18
Average Fitness	9.40
Hamming Distance	0.54
Probability Mass	0.10

The results in Table 2 are for one particular Markov model involving a ramp function where $n = 3$, $l = 3$, $\mu = 0.01$, and $\chi = 1.0$. To get a better sense of the generality of these results we also computed Ψ for those models investigated in our earlier paper (De Jong, Spears and Gordon, 1994). Table 3 summarizes some representative results at $k = 100$. For these particular functions $l = 2$, $n = 10$, $N = 286$, and $\chi = 1.0$. We analyzed two settings for μ as indicated in the table.

Table 3: Ψ Values for Different Functions

Function	Ordering	μ	Ψ
Class 2	Lexicographic	0.1	22.54
	Average Fitness	0.1	8.75
	Hamming Distance	0.1	59.75
	Probability Mass	0.1	15.73
Class 3	Lexicographic	0.1	26.15
	Average Fitness	0.1	24.34
	Hamming Distance	0.1	53.44
	Probability Mass	0.1	22.20
Type 1 Deceptive	Lexicographic	0.01	55.44
	Average Fitness	0.01	19.35
	Hamming Distance	0.01	7.44
	Probability Mass	0.01	1.52
Type 2 Deceptive	Lexicographic	0.01	45.32
	Average Fitness	0.01	25.17
	Hamming Distance	0.01	5.32
	Probability Mass	0.01	2.18

The results indicate that ordering states by initial probability mass consistently provides a good predictor of the relative importance of states as k increases. Not surprisingly, the lexicographic ordering is of little use. Also, as one might expect, the usefulness of ordering by Hamming distance appears to be tied to the mutation rate. At low mutation rates Hamming distance provides a good ordering, but degrades significantly at higher mutation rates. It is also interesting to note that ordering by average fitness is a much better predictor at higher mutation rates. This agrees with the results presented in our earlier paper (De Jong, Spears and Gordon, 1994) which suggested that optimal GAFO performance is frequently obtained using higher mutation rates than those traditionally used.

The quantitative and qualitative analyses of these Markov models provide a simple intuitive picture of the transient behavior of a GA. A GA is pulled quite early towards homogeneous basins of attraction and, once in a particular basin, is not likely to leave it. This complements nicely the more formal results obtained by Vose (1995).

3   REDUCED MARKOV MODELS

Since the number of states N grows extremely fast as n or l increases, we are currently limited to Markov models involving small population sizes and small string lengths. To address this issue, we have explored several approaches for reducing the size of the state space in order to allow us to scale to larger GA models.

In keeping with the theme of our earlier paper (De Jong, Spears and Gordon, 1994), we are interested in having models make predictions about GAFO behavior, that is, predictions appropriate to the use of GAs as optimizers. To answer such questions, we need only combine Q^k with a set of initial conditions concerning a GA at generation 0. For this paper we make the reasonable assumption that GA populations are randomly initialized. Thus, the *a priori* probability of the GA being in state i at time 0, denoted as $P(i @ 0)$, is:

$$P(i @ 0) = \frac{n!}{z_{i,0}! \; \ldots \; z_{i,r-1}!} \left[\frac{1}{r}\right]^n \tag{3}$$

Given this, we can now compute the probability that the GA will be in a particular state at time k:

$$P(j @ k) = \sum_i P(i @ 0) \, Q_{i,j}^k \tag{4}$$

by simply considering the probability of each possible k-step transition, appropriately weighted by the *a priori* probabilities. We can also compute probabilities over a set of states. Define a predicate $Pred_J$ and the set J of states that make $Pred_J$ true. Then the probability that the GA will be in one of the states of J at time k is:

$$P(J @ k) = \sum_{j \in J} P(j @ k) \tag{5}$$

In this paper, we let J represent the set of all states which contain at least one copy of the optimum, and then use a Markov model to compute $P(J @ k)$, the probability of having at least one copy of the optimum in the population at generation k.

The models we have constructed so far are exact models and give precise values for such probabilities. One approach to estimating the accuracy of a reduced model is to compare $P(J @ k)$ values for both the exact and the reduced models. We have used this technique to evaluate the merits of various state reduction techniques and present our initial results in this section.

3.1   REMOVING LOW PROBABILITY STATES

One of the most striking features of the Q matrix visualizations is how quickly the probability mass accumulates in the form of a relatively small number of vertical stripes. These columns of high probability mass correspond to the set of attractor states in which the GA being modeled is most likely to be as evolution proceeds. If we sort the states by "column mass" we observe a fair number of states with very small amounts of probability mass in Q^1 and that mass continues to decrease over time (Q^k, $k > 1$). Intuitively, such states are candidates to be eliminated if we want a reduced model that still has good predictive accuracy.

We tested this intuition in the following manner. We iteratively deleted the state containing the smallest column mass from the model by removing the corresponding row and column from the Q matrix. Since the rows must sum to 1.0, we distributed the small amount of deleted probability mass uniformly to all remaining states. After removing a state, we compared $P(J @ k = 100)$ for both the exact and the reduced model.

Table 4 gives an example of the typical results obtained, namely, that the accuracy of the $P(J @ k)$ values degrades rather rapidly even when a relatively small proportion of the states is removed.

Table 4: Ramp Function, $n = 5$, $l = 2$, $\mu = 0.1$, $\chi = 1.0$, $k = 100$, $N = 56$

Number (%) of States Removed	$P(J @ k = 100)$
0 (0.0%)	0.920196
1 (1.8%)	0.915596
2 (3.6%)	0.905835
3 (5.4%)	0.897447
4 (7.1%)	0.890103

3.2 LUMPED STATES

In addition to introducing significant $P(J @ k)$ errors, simply deleting a state from the model also has the conceptual difficulty that the GA being modeled can still visit states which have been deleted from the model. A more satisfying approach would be to reduce the number of states by lumping multiple states into a single state, thus maintaining the direct correspondence between the GA and its model. The issues to be resolved are: 1) how is lumping achieved computationally (i.e., what changes are made to the Q matrix), and 2) what states should be lumped together?

To get an intuitive sense of these issues, consider an arbitrary Q matrix obtained from a Markov chain of 3 states:

$$Q = \begin{bmatrix} p_{1,1} & p_{1,2} & p_{1,3} \\ p_{2,1} & p_{2,2} & p_{2,3} \\ p_{3,1} & p_{3,2} & p_{3,3} \end{bmatrix}$$

The entries in the Q matrix, $p_{i,j}$, represent the probability that the system will transition to state j, given that it currently is in state i.

Suppose the goal is to lump states 2 and 3 together. How can this be accomplished? Consider how state 1 transitions to states 2 and 3 ($p_{1,2}$ and $p_{1,3}$). Lumping states 2 and 3 together means that the combined state represents being in either state 2 or state 3 (and it is impossible to tell which of those two states the system is in). Since this is a disjunctive situation, the probability of transition from state 1 to the lumped state is simply the sum $p_{1,2} + p_{1,3}$. In general, transitions *into* a lumped state are easily computed as the sum of the transitions into each state of the lumped state. Stated another way, column 3 can be removed by adding its values to column 2.

However, transitions *from* lumped states (removing a row) are more complicated. In the above example, the simplest case to analyze is when the probability of transitioning from state 2 to state 1 is the same as the probability of transitioning from state 3 to state 1 ($p_{2,1} = p_{3,1}$). Thus the probability of transitioning from the lumped state to state 1 must still be $p_{2,1} = p_{3,1}$, since it doesn't matter whether the system is in state 2 or 3 of the lumped state.

In general, however, the probability of transitioning from states 2 and 3 to state 1 will not be the same. A reasonable first thought is that in this case the appropriate lumped transition probability is just the average of the two: $(p_{2,1} + p_{3,1})/2$. However, a simple average of row entries will not work well in general. This is because the Markov chain might spend much more time in one of the two states that are being lumped. Thus a weighted average of row entries is called for. The weights should reflect the relative amount of time spent in each of the two states being lumped. Unfortunately, this data is not known in general, and is frequently a function of time. However, recall that the column masses provide reasonable estimates of the relative amount of time spent in particular states, and hence are good candidates for the weights to be used for lumping (for a mathematical treatment of this lumping algorithm see Spears, 1996). Mathematically, the lumping algorithm can be described as follows.

Assume that two states have been chosen for lumping. Let S denote the set of N states, and let the non-empty sets $S_1, ..., S_{N-1}$ partition S such that one S_i contains the two chosen states, while each other S_i is composed of exactly one state. Let m_i denote the column mass of state i. Then the lumped matrix Q' is:

$$Q'_{i,j} = p'_{i,j} = \frac{1}{\sum_{x \in S_i} m_x} \sum_{x \in S_i} m_x \sum_{y \in S_j} p_{x,y} \tag{6}$$

This corresponds to taking a weighted average of the two rows corresponding to the two chosen states, while summing the two corresponding columns. The other entries in the Q matrix remain unchanged. This can be illustrated by continuing the previous example, which lumps states 2 and 3. In that case $S_1 = \{1\}$ and $S_2 = \{2, 3\}$. The lumped matrix Q' is described by:

$$
\begin{aligned}
p'_{1,1} &= p_{1,1} \\
p'_{1,2} &= p_{1,2} + p_{1,3} \\
p'_{2,1} &= \frac{1}{m_2 + m_3}[m_2 p_{2,1} + m_3 p_{3,1}] \\
p'_{2,2} &= \frac{1}{m_2 + m_3}[m_2(p_{2,2} + p_{2,3}) + m_3(p_{3,2} + p_{3,3})]
\end{aligned}
$$

Applying this to a specific example where $m_1 = 1.2$, $m_2 = .6$, and $m_3 = 1.2$ yields:

$$Q = \begin{bmatrix} .7 & .1 & .2 \\ .4 & .2 & .4 \\ .1 & .3 & .6 \end{bmatrix}$$

$$Q' = \begin{bmatrix} .7 & .3 \\ .2 & .8 \end{bmatrix}$$

Note how the .7 does not change ($p_{1,1} = p'_{1,1}$). This makes sense, since the lumping of states 2 and 3 should have no affect on this value. The rest of the values in Q' (which refer to states 2 and 3) are weighted averages (sometimes trivial) of sums of the values in the 2nd and 3rd rows and columns of Q.

In general, the exact lumping of arbitrary states is not always possible (see Spears, 1996). So we are left with a situation in which states with identical rows can be combined without difficulty, but is not likely to result in a significant reduction in the number of states since identical rows are encountered relatively infrequently. However, since we are interested in reduced models which give good, but not necessarily perfect $P(J @ k)$ values, it seems plausible that states with "nearly identical" rows could be combined without introducing too much error into a model. The most straightforward measure of row similarity is the sum of the squared error (SSE):

$$SSE(i, j) = \sum_k (p_{i,k} - p_{j,k})^2 \tag{7}$$

Such a measure together with a similarity threshold ϵ can be used to identify states to be lumped. At a high level, the full lumping algorithm is:

Lump()
    Repeat as long as possible
        Find a pair of states i and j for which $SSE(i, j) < \epsilon$.
        Lump-states(i,j) by taking a weighted average of rows i
        and j, and by summing the ith and jth columns.

3.3   ONE-PASS LUMPING

In order to get a sense of the viability of this approach, we first implemented a one-pass lumping algorithm, and compared the results with those produced by the unlumped models. Since our goal is to compute probabilities involving states containing the optimum (the J set), we don't want to lump J states with non-J states. Consequently, the lumping algorithm is run separately for both sets of states, making a single pass over the unlumped states and allowing only the lumping of pairs of unlumped states. Hence, the maximum reduction in the number of states will be 50%. In addition, the amount of lumping will be a function of ϵ, the similarity measure threshold value. More specifically, our one-pass algorithm is:

For a given ϵ
    For each unlumped state i in the J set
        Find the most similar unlumped state j in the J set.
        If $SSE(i, j) < \epsilon$, Lump-states(i,j).
    Repeat this process for non-J states.

Table 5: Ramp Function, $n = 5$, $l = 2$, $\mu = 0.1$, $\chi = 1.0$, $k = 100$, $N = 56$

ϵ	Number (%) of States Removed	$P(J @ k = 100)$
.000	0 (0%)	0.920196
.010	14 (25%)	0.918322
.020	22 (39%)	0.919037
.030	23 (41%)	0.918995
.040	25 (45%)	0.918810
.090	26 (46%)	0.917849

Table 5 gives the results on the same model used in section 3.1. Notice the rather dramatic difference in the results in comparison with Table 4. It is not difficult to obtain greater than

40% (out of a possible 50%) reduction in the number of states while still producing accurate $P(J @ k)$ values.

3.4 MULTI-PASS LUMPING

It is not hard to extend one-pass lumping to multi-pass lumping which produces lumped states involving more than just pairs of unlumped states:

> For a given ϵ
> > Repeat until no new lumped states are created
> > > For each state i in the J set of the current lumped model
> > > > Find the most similar state j in the J set.
> > > > If $SSE(i,j) < \epsilon$, Lump-states(i,j).
> > > Repeat this process for non-J states.

In theory multi-pass lumping could result in a lumped two state model involving just J and non-J. In practice, this would require large values of ϵ and unacceptable reductions in $P(J @ k)$ accuracy.

Table 6: Ramp Function, $n = 5$, $l = 2$, $\mu = 0.1$, $\chi = 1.0$, $k = 100$, $N = 56$

ϵ	Number (%) of States Removed	$P(J @ k = 100)$
.000	0 (0%)	0.920196
.010	19 (34%)	0.917328
.020	28 (50%)	0.912407
.030	33 (59%)	0.914112
.040	36 (64%)	0.911954
.090	44 (79%)	0.897008

Table 6 gives an example of typical results obtained with multi-pass lumping. In this case the model can be reduced by as much as 79% and still produce $P(J @ k)$ values within 3% of the values produced by the full model.

Table 7: Ramp Function, $n = 10$, $l = 2$, $\mu = 0.1$, $\chi = 1.0$, $k = 100$, $N = 286$

ϵ	Number (%) of States Removed	$P(J @ k = 100)$
.000	0 (0%)	0.995170
.010	225 (79%)	0.993724
.020	245 (86%)	0.992398
.030	256 (90%)	0.991835
.045	265 (93%)	0.990371

Another interesting property that we have observed is that, as the size of the state space increases, models can generally be reduced even further. Table 7 shows the results obtained on a model identical to the previous one except that the population size is 10 rather than 5, increasing the number of states from 56 to 286. In this case over 90% of the states can be removed with less than 1% loss in accuracy. Similar results on other models suggest that the lumping algorithm actually performs better as the number of states increases (in terms of the percentage of states that can be removed without significant losses in numerical accuracy).

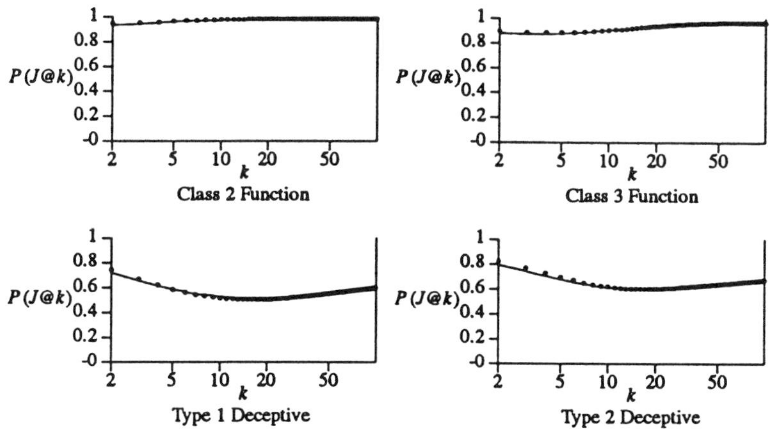

Figure 6: $P(J @ k)$ where ϵ is 0.0 and 0.030 for Several Functions

So far we have been using $P(J @ k = 100)$ as a measure of the accuracy of reduced models. In point of fact we would like $P(J @ k)$ to be accurate for all values of k, particularly those representing transient behavior, since that is where most of the interesting GAFO behavior occurs. Figure 6 graphs the transient behavior for the four functions used in Table 2. The dotted curves represents the exact $P(J @ k)$ values for k ranging from 2 to 100. The solid curves represent the values computed for the lumped model when $\epsilon = .030$. The x-axis is depicted using a log scale in order to focus on the transient behavior. Roughly 80% of the states have been removed, yet the lumped models are predicting transient behavior extremely well.

3.5   SEMANTIC LUMPING

We have seen in the preceding section that we can significantly reduce the size of a Markov model without significant loss of accuracy. This is quite encouraging and allows us to scale to larger models. This was achieved with a lumping strategy based on properties of the Q matrix without any reference to GA semantics. That is, except for the J set partition of the state space, the lumping procedure could be used on arbitrary Markov models.

The next step is to understand better from a GA point of view the properties of the states being lumped. The approach we are taking is to work backwards from the data obtained in the previous section, which provides examples of effective lumping of states. If the states being lumped share any obvious properties, these properties could be used to develop semantically based lumping strategies, which could allow us to perform lumping without having to compute the full Q matrix. We are currently exploring these ideas and briefly summarize our work in progress in this section.

Recall that the states in these Markov models represent the set of all possible populations of size n of binary strings of length l, as enumerated by the incidence matrix Z (e.g., Table 1). One pattern that shows up quite clearly is that states (populations) that are nearly identical to each other in their Z row entries are frequently lumped. This is particularly true if populations differ only on strings with low fitness. Hence one could imagine a similarity measure based on Hamming distance and fitness alone without any reference to the Q matrix at all.

How effective is this? Preliminary results suggest that measures based on these two properties alone are not sufficient. This appears to be due to the fact that there must be some accounting for the amount of time spent in states to be lumped. Recall that column mass estimates the relative amount of time spent in a given state. We have been able to obtain reasonably effective results by adding column mass weighting, but that involves the Q matrix. If time spent in a state could be characterized via GA semantics, then we would have a promising basis for purely semantic lumping. We are currently pursuing this possibility.

4   RELATED WORK

There is a considerable body of literature involving both lumped Markov models and transient behavior. We briefly summarize in this section that work which is most closely related to the work presented here.

Vose (1995) describes an "aggregation" (lumping) theorem, which arbitrarily partitions the set of states S into s non-empty sets $S_1, ..., S_s$. Denoting the steady state probability of state i as π_i, this theorem states that if

$$Q'_{i,j} = \frac{1}{\sum_{x \in S_i} \pi_x} \sum_{x \in S_i} \pi_x \sum_{y \in S_j} p_{x,y} \tag{8}$$

then $\pi'_j = \sum_{x \in S_j} \pi_x$.

This theorem states that if lumping is performed in this manner, the steady state behavior of the lumped system is the same as the original system. Interestingly, this form of aggregation has also been applied in the Markov community (e.g., see Stewart and Wu, 1992). In both cases the emphasis has been on examining steady state behavior. Note that one difference between our method of lumping and the more traditional method is the choice of weights - we focus on column mass instead of steady state values. This leads to the intriguing hypothesis that our lumping algorithm will be more accurate when describing transient behavior. Preliminary results appear to confirm this hypothesis.

Transient behavior has also been investigated by the Markov community, but traditional techniques often involve the computation of "matrix exponentials", in which the Markov chain is described by a system of ordinary differential equations (e.g., see Sidje and Stewart, 1996). Although these techniques are not related to our lumping algorithm, it is possible that they could answer the same types of questions. Future work will focus on this possibility.

Finally, it has been noted in the literature (Dayar and Stewart, 1996; Kemeny and Snell, 1960) that perfect lumping can occur if there exists a partition of the states into "blocks" such that:

$$\forall S_i, S_j \subset S, \forall x \in S_i : \sum_{y \in S_j} p_{x,y} = k_{i,j} \tag{9}$$

where $k_{i,j}$ is a constant value that depends only on i and j. This means that the probability of transitioning from each state in any block S_i to any other block S_j must be the same. Since this is related to our notion of "row similarity", being more general but harder to compute, it raises the interesting possibility of a more general version of the sum of the squared error (SSE) metric that will still yield good results.

5   SUMMARY AND CONCLUSIONS

In this paper, we have explored alternative orderings of the states of Markov models of GAs based on interesting semantic properties such as average fitness, degree of homogeneity, average attractive force, etc. We have also explored lumping techniques for reducing the size of the state space and the corresponding Markov models. Analysis of these reordered and lumped Markov models provides new insights into the transient behavior of GAs in general and GAFOs in particular. The emerging picture is one in which a relatively small number of states dominate the transient behavior of GAs and serve as basins of attraction. The characteristics of these basins of attraction are states (populations) which are nearly homogeneous and contain copies of high fitness individuals.

As we have seen, further analysis of Markov models involving the full state space is not likely to scale to "real world" configurations. However, the results obtained from these smaller models have provided some insights into how one might obtain useful semantically lumped models which would scale better. We are currently pursuing these ideas.

Acknowledgements

We would like to thank Diana Gordon and the anonymous referees for their constructive comments which were quite helpful in improving the paper.

References

T. Dayar & W. J. Stewart. (1996) Quasi-lumpability, lower bounding coupling matrices, and nearly completely decomposable Markov chains. To appear in the *SIAM Journal on Matrix Analysis and Applications.*

K. A. De Jong, W. M. Spears, & D. F. Gordon. (1994) Using Markov chains to analyze GAFOs. *Proceedings of the Foundations of Genetic Algorithms Workshop.* Estes Park, CO: Morgan Kaufmann, 115 - 137.

J. Kemeny & J. Snell. (1960) *Finite Markov Chains.* D. Van Nostrand, New York.

A. E. Nix & M. D. Vose. (1992) Modelling genetic algorithms with Markov chains. *Annals of Mathematics and Artificial Intelligence #5,* 79 - 88.

R. Sidje & W. J. Stewart. (1996) A survey of methods for computing large sparse matrix exponentials arising in Markov chains. *Submitted for publication.*

W. M. Spears. (1996) A compression algorithm for probability transition matrices. *NRL-AIC Technical Report.* In preparation.

W. J. Stewart & W. Wu. (1992) Numerical experiments with iteration and aggregation for Markov chains. *ORSA Journal on Computing*, Volume 4, #3, 336 - 350.

M. Vose. (1995) Modeling Simple Genetic Algorithms. *Evolutionary Computation*, Volume 3, #4, 453-472.

Genetic Algorithm Dynamics in a Two-well Potential

Jonathan Shapiro[*]
Department of Computer Science
The University, Manchester M13 9PL U.K.

Adam Prügel-Bennett
NORDITA Blegdamsvej 17,
DK-2100 Copenhagen Ø, Denmark

Abstract

The dynamics of a simple genetic algorithm is analyzed on a simple two-well function of
unitation. In the infinite population limit, there are phase transitions in the dynamics as
the selection strength and the crossover probability are changed. In one phase, the system
always evolves to a population consisting only of strings from the local well starting from
any initial population containing some strings from the local well. In the second phase, the
genetic algorithm can evolve to a population consisting of strings from the global well, but
only if a finite fraction of the initial population was from the global well. In the third phase,
the algorithm will evolve to a population consisting of strings from the global well from
any initial population. For a finite population, the increasing correlation of the population
changes the nature of the transition; this is analysed in a weak selection limit where the
effects are small. Fluctuation effects, which cause the transition to be smooth in a finite
population and are important, are not analysed here. Comparisons with simulations show
that the results of the theory are qualitatively correct. There is a phase in which the GA
evolves quickly to the global minimum, which can be orders of magnitude faster than a
Monte Carlo algorithm; and another phase in which it evolves to a population dominated
by strings from the local well. Quantitatively, the simulations and theory are not in good
agreement due to the simplifications of the theory.

1 Introduction

There are many ways in which optimization problems in high dimensional spaces can be hard to
solve. Three issues which can contribute to intractability are well-known: there can be a huge
number of local optima, there can be large barriers between local optima, and there can be large
relative differences between the size of the basins of attraction of the optima. It is clear how these

---

[*]Internet address: jls@cs.man.ac.uk

can contribute to the difficulty of search. If there are a large number of local optima, there may not be an efficient way to look in each; if there are large barriers between the local optima there may be no efficient way to increase the move set of the search algorithm to allow it to move from one optima to another; if the basin of attraction of the local optima constitutes most of the search space, it may take an enormous amount of time to generate states in the basin of a good or global optima. Although in no sense are these the only reasons that hard problems are hard, these features have been shown to be important in a wide range of combinatorial optimization problems such as the travelling salesman (Mezard et al., 1986) problem, machine learning problems such as learning in a Ising perceptron (Rattray, 1995), and in many other problems.

In this paper, we consider the latter two of these issues in a simple manifestation. We consider a problem consisting of two wells, a true minimum and a local minimum, and consider what determines whether the algorithm will find the global minimum and on what time-scale. In order to compare the effectiveness of a genetic algorithm with that of simulated annealing, we consider a simple problem on which the dynamics of both algorithms can be studied mathematically. We argue that there are situations in which the genetic algorithm considerably outperforms simulated annealing. That is, the GA goes from the local optima to the global optima orders of magnitude faster than simulated annealing does. For other situations, however, the reverse is true, simulated annealing finds the global optima from the local one efficiently, whereas the GA only finds it in a time comparable to the ergodic time-scale. It is hoped that these results can help understand how GAs behave in more general multi-optimal potentials, and what properties of the search space may cause one algorithm to be more effective than the other.

Search spaces with basins and barriers reveal important differences between genetic algorithms and stochastic hill-climbing or simulated annealing type algorithms in ways that problems like *ones-counting* do not. It is clear that barriers will have different effects on the two types of algorithms. Simulated annealing uses local moves. Thus, a barrier must be surmounted and the time to do so is determined by the (low) probability of a sequence of moves which does so. This gives rise to the well-known exponential dependence on the barrier height (van Kampen, 1981). Genetic algorithms use crossover which can be very nonlocal. Thus, the genetic algorithm can move between basins without populating the intermediate states. If so, the characteristic time will be set by transition rates between these states and entropy factors. There is a more subtle difference between genetic algorithms and simulated annealing, which relates to detailed balance. In simulated annealing search, the relative transition rates between states is a function of the potential difference. In genetic algorithms is not simply a function of the potential differences, it depends upon the population as well. A result of this is that something like a noised-induced transition (Landauer, 1996) can occur in which it is impossible for the genetic algorithm to leave a local optima in the large population limit. Alternatively, this can also result in situations in which the rate of transition from the local optima is much greater than the rate back as predicted by detailed balance. This effect can be seen in the problem analyzed below.

The methods used in this study rely on results of the statistical mechanics and maximum entropy approaches to genetic algorithms developed elsewhere. The statistic mechanics approach has been applied to random problems with no epistatis (Prügel-Bennett and Shapiro, 1996), problems with exponential numbers of local optima but small barriers (Prügel-Bennett and Shapiro, 1994; Shapiro et al., 1994; Shapiro and Prügel-Bennett, 1995), weakly NP-complete problems (Rattray, 1996) and noisy fitness evaluation in a simple learning problem (Rattray and Shapiro, 1996) This method has been shown to accurately predict the dynamical behaviour of genetic algorithms. It includes effects of finite population, deviation from Gaussian distribution of fitness distributions, and the effect of correlation of the population due to selection. However, here we will use a very simplified approach which we hope makes the system transparent, but which will not be as accurate as previous applications of this approach. There are important reasons why a simplified approach is required; these are discussed in section 2.

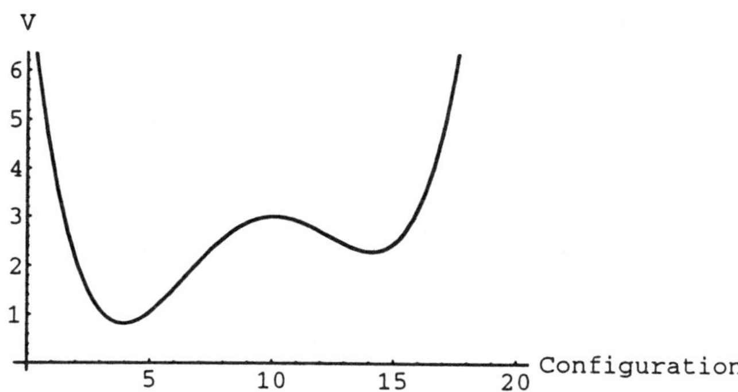

Figure 1: The goal is to study the evolution of a genetic algorithm on a potential looking like this. The horizontal axis is a slice through configuration space; the vertical axis is the potential which the algorithm is to minimize

The dynamics of activation over a barrier via local noise processes has been widely studied, going back to (Kramers, 1940), and is important in chemistry and biology (Fleming and Hänggi, 1993) as well as being fundamental to the behavior of a simulated annealing algorithm. This problem has not been so widely studied in genetic algorithms, however. The reason for this may be because simulated annealing is thought to be appropriate for problems with barriers, whereas GAs are thought to be appropriate for other types of problems (e.g. building blocks). In practice, however, both algorithms are applied to similar problems. Two previous researches are worthy of mention. First, Wright's Shifting Balance Theory (Wright, 1970) describes the transition of a population from one peak in a fitness landscape to another due to immigration, drift, and selection pressure. This pertains to biological populations; for current views of this work, see (Volkenstein, 1994) or (Coyne et al., 1996). This theory is quite relevant to the question discussed here; however, the model we consider is (ostensibly) simpler than the three phases of the dynamics suggested by Wright. More specifically about genetic algorithms is the study of trapping functions in (Deb and Goldberg, 1993). These researchers studied the conditions for the problem to be fully deceptive. This work does not answer the questions about dynamics which we feel are essential in understanding the behavior of the different algorithms.

2   The Statistical Mechanics Approach For Macroscopically Separated Minima

The statistical mechanics formulation for studying genetic algorithm dynamics has been proposed and developed elsewhere. There are three elements to this. First, it describes the population at a given time in terms of a few macroscopic quantities. Second, techniques from statistical mechanics are used to average over the stochasticity to get the average evolution of these macroscopic quantities. In this regard, it is closely related to the work of Vose and Wright (Vose and Wright, 1995) on describing the GA via sampling from a parent population, except in the statistical mechanics approach it is macroscopic quantities which are sampled. Finally, a maximum entropy assumption is used to infer properties of the population which are required to determine the evolution but are not simply related to the macroscopics which are known.

There is a difficulty in applying this approach to the current problem. In the past work, cumulants of the distribution of some quantity of the strings, such as the unitation or the fitness, were used as the cumulants. For a unimodal distribution, a cumulant expansion can be truncated at a small number of cumulants without great loss of accuracy in many cases. This provided a way to convert the problem to one of low dimension which could be easily solved. However, to use a cumulant expansion to describe a multi-modal distribution, many high cumulants are required; this would offer no simplification. It is important to emphasize that it is not the fact that there are many optima which causes the problem. The statistical mechanics approach has already been applied successfully to situations in which there a large number of local optima, and produced accurate results. In those cases quantities could be found whose distribution in the population was unimodal and could be described by a cumulant expansion. In this problem, where the optima are macroscopically separated, no uni-modally distributed quantity is known.

To get around this problem, we model the distribution of fitnesses in the population as the sum of two unimodal distributions, one distribution corresponding to each well,

$$\rho(m) = f\rho^g(m) + (1-f)\rho^l(m). \tag{1}$$

Here, the superscript g (or l) denotes the global (or local) well, f is the fraction of the population in the global well, m is some macroscopic quantity which is uni-modally distributed in the subpopulations of each well, and $\rho(m)$ is the normalized distribution of m in the appropriate subpopulation. The two distributions are then characterized by cumulants as in earlier work, and we can derive equations for the evolution of the cumulants of the two distributions and the evolution of f under selection and crossover. High cumulants may still be required if there is appreciable overlap between the two distributions; we assume there is not. We will focus most attention on the evolution of f. Much of the behavior of this system can be understood by studying this quantity.

An additional difficulty is that the entropy maximization step becomes more difficult in a multi-modal system. There may be a rigorous way to get around this problem, however, here we will take a simpler and less rigorous approach. It remains an open question, however, how to apply the statistical mechanics approach to a system with macroscopically separated minima in a well-founded manner.

3 Crossover-Induced Transitions in Multi-Well Potentials

Before presenting calculations on a specific model, the general effects of crossover in multi-well potentials are discussed.

Consider first the case of two minima, each of which is defined by a single string X^0 and X^1. Suppose there is a local minimum at X^0, a global minimum at X^1 and a barrier along the direction between them. The importance question for this problem is: how long does it take the search algorithm to move from the local minima to the global one? For simulated annealing this translates into the question: how long does it take for the algorithm to reach the global minimum at such a temperature that transitions back to the local minimum are unlikely? For the GA this translates into: given a population consisting of strings in the local well, how long does it take to reach a population with many strings in the global well? One could also ask for the time to get a single global string for a single time-step. The former question will help to understand what happens in multi-well potentials, where the algorithm may have to move from one minima to the next incrementally.

Start a GA with a fraction f of the population in the local minima and a fraction $1 - f$ in the global one and ask what happens to f. Clearly, selection alone would rapidly de-populate the local well and populate the global one. Crossover between strings in different wells, however, can de-populate the global minimum and populate the local one. One way to see this is to consider a very high barrier. In that case, both children are likely to die. Renormalizing the population size increases the fraction in the *most populated* well. Another aspect of problem which influences the direction of the transition induced by crossover between wells is the relative widths of the potential around each minimum. Thus, crossover and selection can be in competition. When so, there will be a critical fraction f_c which depends upon the selection strength and crossover rate, properties of the potential, and the form of crossover. If f starts above f_c, it evolves *in the mean* to 1; if f starts below f_c, it evolves in the mean to 0. In other words, if sufficient number are in the global minimum, the algorithm depletes the local minimum, otherwise it depletes the global one. It is also possible for f_c to be 0 or 1 for other parameter values. Such a system can have a phase transition in the infinite population limit like that discussed in section 4.5.

Consider the implications of this result for the search time of the genetic algorithm. For those parameters for which $f_c = 0$, the search is much like that of simulated annealing, it is dominated by the time to produce a string in the global well. Once it produces a single string in the global well the population will evolve to the state dominated by global minima. However, when $0 < f_c < 1$, to make progress to the global minimum, the algorithm must produce a fraction of the population (at least $f_c P$) in the other well in one generation. This time-scale is exponential in P. Of course, when $f_c = 1$, only the local minimum is a stable solution to the genetic algorithm – it will never find the global one.

The effects of mutation and crossover between strings in the same well have not been consider yet. If the minima consist of single strings, crossover within a well will have small local effects, since the strings will be very similar. The search time will be determined by the time to produce a single string in the global well under these two operators if $f_c = 0$, the time to produce fP global strings otherwise. This calculation will be presented elsewhere (Shapiro and Prügel-Bennett, 1996).

In the next section, we consider a model in the minima are not single strings, however, but they have have some entropy, or some (approximately) neutral volume. Then, the strings in each well can be very different from one another, and crossover between strings in the local well can produces strings in the global well at a much higher rate than local changes can. This effect will depend upon the relative entropies of the two wells, and on the correlation (or similarity) between strings in the population.

Thus, simulated annealing and genetic algorithms can behave very differently in multi-well potentials. For different values of the selection strength and crossover probability, and depending on the properties of the potential, the GA can be in a phase in which the transition time to the global well is very fast, or one in which it is very slow as compared to the noise-induced transition between wells. This is shown in a specific instance in the next section.

4 The Model

We consider functions of unitation

$$m = \frac{1}{N} \sum_{i=1}^{N} x_i \tag{2}$$

which have two minima. The generic problem is,

$$V(m) \approx \begin{cases} Nw_l(m - m_l)^2/2 + Nv_l; & \text{if } m \geq m_b \\ Nw_g(m - m_g)^2/2; & \text{if } m < m_b \end{cases} \tag{3}$$

with the center of the local well closer to $1/2$ than is the center of the global one, for example, $m_l = 0.2, m_b = 0.1$. It is important to note the entropy difference between the two wells. There are many more states in the local minima than in the global one.

A particularly tractable case has $w_g = 0$. Here the goal is to find a state with less than Nm_b ones in it. We use this particular simple form because it is obviously much simpler to calculate; however, it is possible to do the calculations for quadratic or linear global potentials. The potential is shown in figure 2.

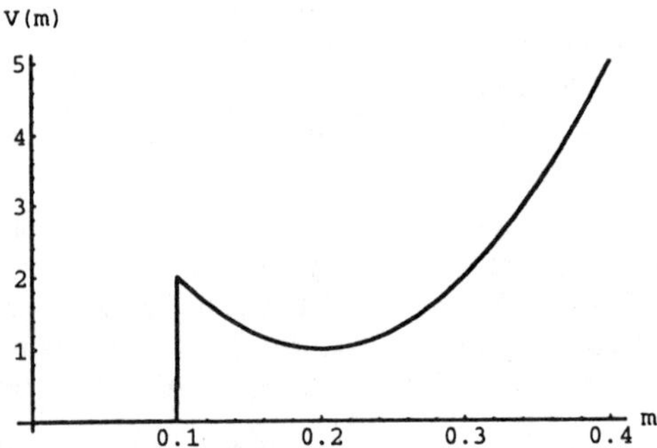

Figure 2: The form of the potential which is simplest for calculational purposes is shown. The local well is quadratic; the global well is square.

4.1 The search time for a simulated annealing algorithm

In order to model the search time for simulated annealing on this problem, the first passage time to get to the global well can be computed for a Monte Carlo dynamics with fixed temperature. Strictly speaking, this is a lower bound on the search time, since there is some probability of moving from the global to the local minimum which means that the global minimum may be found more than once in an actual annealed search. However, it is useful to compare the genetic algorithm to the best that the simulated annealing algorithm can do.

We consider the average time to get a string with Nm_g 1's in it starting with one with Nm 1's. Let $T(m)$ denote the average time to get to m_b starting from m. Clearly, $T(m)$ obeys

$$
\begin{aligned}
T(m) \;=\; & 1 + (1-m)\left\{W_+(m)T(m+\varepsilon) + [1-W_+(m)]T(m)\right\} \\
& + \; m\left\{W_-(m)T(m-\varepsilon) + [1-W_-(m)]T(m)\right\}.
\end{aligned}
\tag{4}
$$

Here $W_\pm(m)$ is the transition probability of the transition from m to $m\pm\varepsilon$ under the algorithm, where $\varepsilon = 1/N$. Under Glauber dynamics,

$$
W_\pm(m) = \frac{1}{2}\left\{1 - \tanh b\,[V(m\pm\varepsilon) - V(m)]\right\}
\tag{5}
$$

with b the inverse temperature. The boundary conditions are

$$
T(m_g) \;=\; 0;
\tag{6}
$$
$$
T(1) - T(1-\varepsilon) \;=\; W_-(1)^{-1}.
\tag{7}
$$

This linear difference equation is easily solved by elementary methods. Because there is only one barrier, there is a temperature which minimizes the transition time between barriers. This is because at too low a temperature there is insufficient noise to move the system far from $m = m_l$, whereas at too high a temperature the system spends most time around m near to $1/2$ which is farther from the global minimum. An example of the search time between barriers is shown in figure 3. This shows the time to get from m_l to m_b; this is the relevant time for the $w_g = 0$ model. One could also average $T(m)$ over starting values of m. (Note: The search time here is measured in the number of Monte Carlo steps, which is comparable to the number of function evaluations. In certain circumstances, function evaluations might be more efficient for algorithms using local moves such as simulated annealing than for algorithms using non-local moves such as crossover. This possibility will be ignored).

4.2 The Genetic Algorithm

First the infinite population limit is considered. It is shown that the two competing effects discussed in section 3 lead to a phase transition in the dynamics – as the search parameters are changed, the dynamics can change abruptly from being a system which always evolves to the local well, to one which always evolves to the global one. In this limit, correlation effects can be ignored and sufficiently strong selection results a population dominated by strings from the global well.

The finite population effects include effect of correlations on the rate of crossover-induced transitions between wells, and fluctuations in the expected number of strings which move between the wells in each generation. Correlation effects can be calculated in the weak selection limit. We have not calculated the fluctuations. Both of these effects are discussed in more detail subsequently.

The genetic algorithm will consist of Boltzmann selection and uniform crossover; no mutation effects will be treated. The genetic algorithm will start with population uniformly distributed with in the suboptimal subspace, rather than a random start. These conditions are chosen to bring the focus primarily on crossover driven transition between the wells. Uniform crossover has stronger effects and is less dependent upon the particulars of the potential. Starting the population uniformly distributed on the optimal subspace allows us to ignore history effects. In general, the properties of the population in the well will depend upon how the population evolved to that well. This choice of initial conditions is optimal for the effectiveness of the GA, however, since it assumes that the

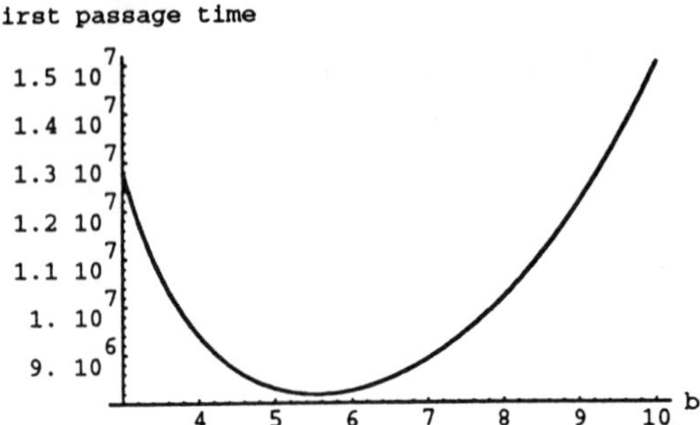

Figure 3: The mean time for a Monte Carlo algorithm to find the global well starting in the local well as a function of the inverse temperature b. No annealing is required, as there is only one barrier. Here $N = 50, m_l = 0.2, m_b = 0.1, w_l = 1, w_g = 0$. The minimum time is about $8.18(10^6)$ function evaluations for $b = 5.6$.

population is as uncorrelated as possible in the suboptimal subspace. Had the population had to find the local well via GA search, the population would be more highly correlated and crossover would be less effective at causing transitions between wells.

4.3 Infinite Population Limit

In the infinite population limit, the population distributions in each well can be taken as approximately Gaussian (which is not strictly true unless the infinite N limit is also taken). Fluctuations can be ignored so all stochastic quantities take their expected values. In addition, all terms higher than zeroth order in $1/P$ expansions are ignored.

4.3.1 The Initial Population and Dynamics Within the Wells

First, we review the behavior of a genetic algorithm within a quadratic well. This was studied by (Rattray, 1996) using the statistical mechanics formalism for more general quadratic minima in a finite population. The infinite population results can be derived by a variety of methods, however.

The population will be characterized by two (reduced) cumulants: the mean unitation

$$k_1 = \frac{1}{P}\frac{1}{N}\sum_i \sum_\alpha X_i^\alpha, \tag{8}$$

the variance about this mean

$$k_2 = \frac{1}{P}\sum_\alpha \left(\frac{1}{N}\sum_i X_i^\alpha - k_1\right)^2, \tag{9}$$

and by the correlation between strings

$$q = \frac{1}{P(P-1)} \sum_{\alpha} \sum_{\beta \neq \alpha} \frac{1}{N} \sum_{i} (2X_i^{\alpha} - 1)(2X_i^{\beta} - 1). \tag{10}$$

Note that the cumulants as defined here do not scale with N. The correlation measure is an number between -1 and 1 where 1 denotes all strings identical, 0 denotes all strings mutually orthogonal, etc.

Under Boltzmann selection, where the probability of choosing a string with potential E is proportional to $\exp(-\beta E)$, the cumulants evolve as follows,

$$k_1 \quad \rightarrow \quad \frac{k_1 + \beta w_l k_2 m_l}{1 + \beta w_l k_2} \tag{11}$$

$$k_2 \quad \rightarrow \quad \frac{k_2}{1 + \beta w_l k_2}. \tag{12}$$

Here β is the selection strength for Boltzmann selection. The effect on q of selection will be discussed momentarily.

Uniform crossover, with crossover probability p_c results in

$$k_1 \quad \rightarrow \quad k_1 \tag{13}$$

$$q \quad \rightarrow \quad q \tag{14}$$

$$k_2 \quad \rightarrow \quad k_2 - \frac{p_c}{2}\left[k_2 - \frac{(1-q)}{4}\right]. \tag{15}$$

The correlation, which is undetermined in the above equations, can be determined from k_1 and k_2 via a maximum entropy assumption (Shapiro and Prügel-Bennett, 1995). It is computed by averaging the correlation over all populations which have the same k_1 and k_2 weighted by the entropy of the population. (An example being a binomial distribution $k_2 = m(1 - m); q = 1 - 4k_2$.) The interpretation of this is that in an infinite population, the correlation is always the expected correlation of a population with the given mean and variance. Selection only changes it indirectly through changes to the mean and the variance.

In an infinite population, these evolve to fixed points $k_1^* = m_l$, k_2^* and q^*, which are easily computed (k_2^* is found by solving the quadratic fixed-point equation of selection - crossover; q^* is found by the maximum entropy calculation described in references (Prügel-Bennett and Shapiro, 1996; Rattray, 1996)). The initial population will be taken to be this fixed-point population is a single well.

4.4 Movement Across Wells

In order to calculate the rate transitions across wells, several simplifying assumptions will be made. First, we assume that within the local well, the population is always at the fixed-point distribution. This is not true; once there are strings from both wells, they are no longer fixed-points. However, it may be true through most of the evolution, if, for example, the time in which the fraction in each well is changing is short compared to the time to find a string in the global well. Second, we assume that the population in the global well has a mean very close to m_b and a very small variance. This can be argued by entropy considerations, most of the volume of the well has that value of unitation.

By making these two assumptions, all of the dynamics of this evolving population can be subsumed into the dynamics of an iterative map acting on the variable f, which denotes the fraction in the global well. It is not necessary to simplify the system to this extent; It is possible derive the dynamical acting on the system consisting of several cumulants and a correlation for each well's subpopulation as well as f, but it is not necessary to do this to understand the qualitative behavior of this system.

Selection changes the proportion of strings in each well. The general effect can be expressed,

$$f \to \frac{f}{f + a(1-f)}. \tag{16}$$

Here a is ratio of the probability of selecting from the local well to that of the global well. In the infinite population limit, with $\rho^l(m)$ defined as the normalized distribution of m values in the local well as in equation 1,

$$a = \frac{\int \rho^l(m) S[V(m)]\, dm}{\int \rho^g(m) S[V(m)]\, dm} \tag{17}$$

where $S(V)$ is the selection probability for a string with potential V. Note that the normalization condition for the ρs is that the integral over the well is one, e.g.

$$\int_{m_b}^{\infty} \rho^l(m)\, dm = 1. \tag{18}$$

The quantity a can be thought of as a measure of the selection strength – it is 1 for random selection and 0 for infinite selection strength.

Crossover is performed in two stages. First, $P/2$ pairs are picked from the population and uniform crossover with probability p_c occurs between the pairs. Next this is done again with $P/2$ new pairings to get the population to P. This avoids a correlation effect which would be harder to analyse. Crossover can cause transitions between wells. Define transition probabilities W_{ll}^g to be the probability of producing a string in the global well from two strings in the local well, and likewise for W_{gg}^l, W_{lg}^g. The subscripts denote the source of the parents, the superscript the location of the child. The transition probabilities can be found by averaging the population statistics over binomial factors. Using a Gaussian approximation to the binomial, the probability of crossing m^α with m^β that are correlated with correlation $q^{\alpha\beta}$ and producing a child m is approximately Gaussian in m with mean $(m^\alpha + m^\beta)/2$ and variance $(1 - q^{\alpha\beta})/(4N)$. This is averaged over the population in the local well to find W_{ll}^g.

The effect of crossover on the fraction in the global well is computed by averaging the average transition rates over the fractions of each type of crossover (between two strings from the global well occurs with fraction f^2, etc.). Putting this together, an equation for the evolution of f can be found,

$$f \to p_c W_{ll}^g/2 + f\left[1 - p_c(1 - W_{lg}^g + W_{ll}^g)\right] + f^2 p_c(1 - W_{gg}^l/2 + W_{ll}^g/2 - W_{lg}^g). \tag{19}$$

During the period when there is appreciable occupancy of both wells, crossover will affect the within well statistics, as the mean in the local well moves closer to the global well. This has the effect of changing the transition probabilities dynamically. We will ignore this effect here under the assumption that the time when this effect is important is short. Putting this effect in will be important in getting accurate predictions of the dynamics, but by ignoring it, it is easy to get a simple qualitative picture of what governs the behavior of this system. This is the assumption of constant within well statistics mentioned above.

4.5   Infinite Population Phase Transition

We focus our attention on the dynamics of f. This variable follows an iterative map determined by the equations of crossover and selection the composition of equation 16 with equation 19. This map has three fixed points; the dynamics is governed by these fixed points. A possible situation is shown in figure 4 a). There are stable fixed points near $f \approx 0$ and for $f > 1$ (which is unphysical) and an unstable fixed point at $f = 1$. In this case, the system always evolves to the local well, unless the system is completely in the global well to start. This is comparable to the situation discussed at the outset of the paper, selection is unable to overcome the disruptive effects of crossover.

As the selection strength is increased (a decreased) and/or the crossover probability is decreased, a transition occurs. Here the fixed points above $f = 1$ and at $f = 1$ change position. Now $f = 1$ is stable and the unstable fixed point is less than 1. Thus, if the initial value of f is large enough, the dynamics evolves to the state $f = 1$. Figures 4 b) and c) show this transition.

The most important transition occurs when the stable fixed point near $f = 0$ and the unstable one coalesce and undergo a tangent bifurcation, as seen in figures 4 d), e) and f). Beyond this point, only the fixed point at $f = 1$ is stable (the other fixed points are now complex) and even starting at $f = 0$ the genetic algorithm evolves to the global well. The time to do this in generations can be small. This can be seen as the zig-zag lines, which show a graphical iteration of the map starting from $f = 0$.

Thus, there are three distinct phases of parameter space. In one, the GA always evolves to a population consisting only of locally optimal strings whether or not there were globally optimal strings in the population initially. In the second phase, the GA will evolve to the globally optimal solution only if there are a sufficient number of globally optimal strings initially. In the final phase, the GA will evolve to a population dominated by globally optimal strings. In the first two phases, the GA will never find the global optimum, because in this infinite population limit, the time to find it due to fluctuations diverges. In the final phase, the GA finds the global optimum in (possibly) a small number of iterations. However, each iteration takes an infinite number of function evaluations (since there are infinite number of strings). In order to make sense of this system, the finite population must be considered.

4.6   Finite Population Effects

A number of finite population effects will change these results. An important effect is the increasing correlation and the decreasing variance in the population. In a finite population, the population in the local well will correlate due to duplication effects caused by selection. The variance will decrease due to selection, and crossover will be continuously less effective at restoring the variance due to the correlating population. A consequence of these two effects is that the rate of transitions between the local well and the global well goes to zero over time. If selection is too strong, the population will correlate before it has time to evolve to the global minimum. To get this effect, we must be able to calculate how W_{ll}^g changes over time.

In order to deal with this, the dynamics of the cumulants and the correlation are reintroduced. This is still treated in a quadratic well limit, interactions between wells are ignored except as they affect f.

Finite population dynamics in a quadratic well was treated by (Rattray, 1996); it will not be reproduced here. The effect on the cumulants can be treated very accurately, but the increased correlation due to duplication of strings under selection, was treated only in a weak selection limit. The change

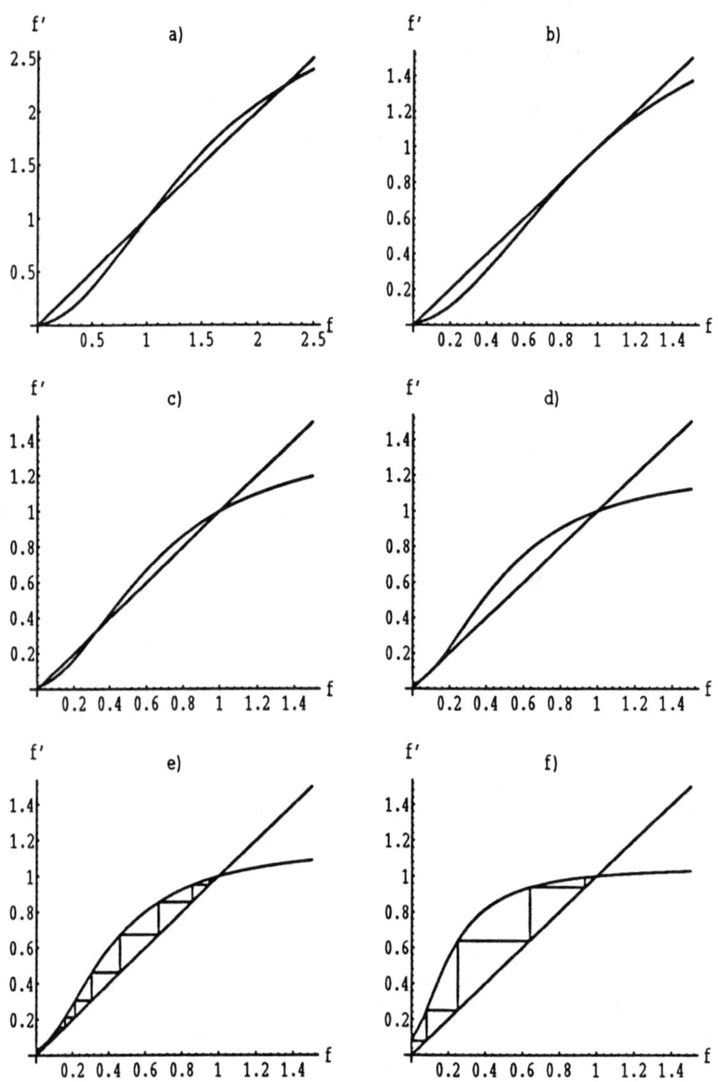

Figure 4: Infinite population dynamics of f occur as an iterative map. These figures show the fraction of the population in the global well after selection and crossover, f', versus the fraction in the global well before. The crossover probability, p_c, is 1 throughout, the selection strength parameter (defined in equations 16 and 17)) is varying: a) $a = 0.7$, b) $a = 0.5$, c) $a = 0.3$, d) $a = 0.2$, e) $a = 0.15$, f) $a = 0.05$. There are three fixed points (although they need not be real); their locations depend upon the selection strengths, crossover rates, string size and properties of the potential. There are two transitions, which are discussed in the text.

in correlation due to duplication can be expressed,

$$\Delta q_{dup} = \frac{1}{P_{eff}},$$ (20)

where P_{eff} is an effective population size. For random selection, it is the population size, since under selection one population member is lost per generation on average due to sampling drift. For weak selection, it can be approximated by

$$P_{eff} = P \frac{\sqrt{1 + 2\beta k_2}}{1 + \beta k_2}$$ (21)

The finite population decrease in the variance which we use is the small β expansion of (Rattray, 1996) under the assumption the distribution within the well is approximately at m_l. From the dynamics of the cumulants and the correlation, the dynamics of W_{ll}^g is computed.

The strength of selection in correlated the population within the local well is set by βk_2^*. The selection strength which determines the change in the fraction in each well is set by $N v_l \beta$. Thus, unless v_l is taken to be extremely small, the small selection limit is the appropriate one.

In addition to the correlation of the locally optimal population, the population in the global well de-correlates. At any given time, there will be a small number which were generated from crossings between parents in the local well; the rest are duplicates of those. As this small number increases, the population in this well de-correlates. As W_{gg}^l is small, this is a less important effect. We have not attempted to calculate it.

There will be fluctuation effects which will smooth out the transition. Although the expected value of f may evolve to a fixed point, due to fluctuations the population may not end up at that fixed point in all cases. This effect will be most important near the transition points, and will smooth out the transitions. It is important to put in these fluctuation terms, but we have not done so.

Finally, there are the effects due to the non-Gaussian nature of the distribution of m's within each well. The evolution of higher cumulants may have important effects. Since the transition probabilities between between the wells depend upon the tails of the distributions of m's in the populations, there is no reason to think that these can be ignored. However, they make the computation considerable more complicated, and we have not yet considered them.

4.7   Simulations, Results, and Comparisons with Simulated Annealing

The infinite population model predicts that there will be a sharp transition between a system which evolves to the global minimum to one which stays in the local one forever. The finite population effects which we have put in do not change the sharpness of the transition. They change the location of the transition point and change the course of the dynamics. Figure 5 show the evolution of f for a simulated GA as predicted by the finite population dynamics and for a real GA. It shows typical strengths and weaknesses of the theory. There is a region in which the GA evolves quickly to a population of globally optimal solutions. There is also a region in which the GA stays in the local well for a very long time. Thus, the theory is qualitatively correct. However, many quantitative differences are apparent from the example shown. The most important weakness is that the transition is smooth, whereas the theory predicts an abrupt transition. The theory predicts that as the transition point is approached in parameter space, the time to move between wells diverges. However, in the simulations, the this time appears relatively constant. Finally, the curves do not lie on top of one another, the theory predicts a different time course than is followed by the simulations. This is particularly noticeable in figure 5 d). Here, the theory predicts that f reaches a maximum and then decreases. This is due to the correlation of the population. There is no sign of this in the simulations (at least at the predicted time-scale).

5 Conclusions and Future Work

We have argued that the dynamics of a genetic algorithm in a two well potential can be very different from that of local stochastic hill-climbers such as simulated annealing. There are two competing effects. Crossover between strings from different wells can be deleterious. Thus, considering this effect alone would suggest that a GA would only populated the global well in a time of the order of the ergodic time, which is exponential in the population size. Thus, a stochastic hill-climber would be much more effective. However, if the strings within a well can be different, because there are many dissimilar strings with the same fitness and the population has not correlated, then crossover within a well can be much more effective than local moves. We have shown a very simple model in which these two competing effects result in a phase transition in the infinite population limit. In the finite population, there is no sharp transition. There are still regimes of parameter space for which the GA is much faster than simulated annealing and those for which it is much slower.

There are a number of unanswered questions. First, we have not characterized the parameter space. Thus, we do not know whether these results are typical. It was surprising that the correlation of the population did not have a bigger effect, for example by making it hard to find a value of the selection strength which was strong enough to be within the phase where the global well is stable, but not so strong as to correlated the population too fast. Perhaps the weak selection limit is not typical. In addition, the scaling of the search times with N and P need to be studied.

The biggest calculational challenge is to put in the fluctuations in f which lead to the smoothing of the transition. It would be reasonably straight-forward to consider a more realistic two-well potential, and to put in the dynamics of the cumulants and the transition rates more accurately, although it would be more involved numerically. It does not seem worth pursuing this without or until a method predicting how fluctuations smooth the transition.

Another interesting question which has not been considered here is the importance of mutation. If the population *is* correlated, mutation can de-correlate it somewhat. Suppose one considers the time-scale for mutation to make the population sufficiently de-correlated so that crossover can cause rapid transitions to the global well; can that time-scale be short compared to the time for simulated annealing to find the global minimum? This question is important for more realistic situations where mutation is used, and where the population will typically be more correlated than we have assumed here.

References

Coyne, J. A., Barton, N. H., and Turelli, M. (1996). A critique of Sewall Wright's shifting balance theory of evolution, preprint.

Deb, K. and Goldberg, D. E. (1993). Analyzing deception in trap functions. In Whitley, L. D., editor, *Foundations of Genetic Algorithms 2*. Morgan Kaufmann.

Fleming, G. R. and Hänggi, P. (1993). *Activated Barrier Crossing*. World Scientific.

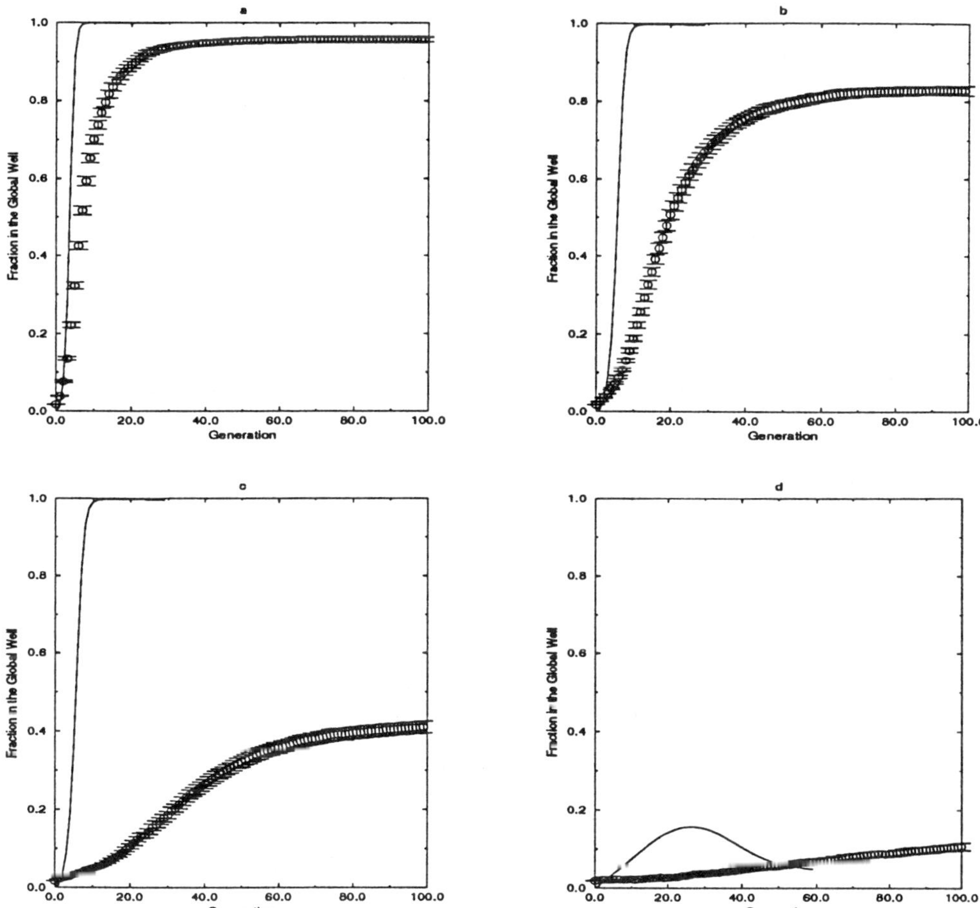

Figure 5: The evolution of the GA for varying values of the selection strength, β, defined in section 4.3.1. In all graphs, the solid line is the evolution of f with time-dependent transition rates computed through the correlation in a weak selection limit, and the circles are simulations of a GA averaged over 1000 runs. In all cases, population size is 50, N is 50, $p_c = 0.5$, $m_l = 0.2$ and $m_b = 0.1$. The selection strengths are: a) $\beta = 1.0$, b) $\beta = 0.5$, c) $\beta = 0.25$, d) $\beta = 0.1$.

Kramers, H. A. (1940). *Physica (Utrecht)*, 7:284.

Landauer, R. (1996). State-dependent noise and interface propagation. In Millonas, M., editor, *Fluctuations and Order*. Springer.

Mezard, M., Parisi, G., and Virasoro, M. (1986). *Spin-Glass Theory and Beyond*. World Scientific.

Prügel-Bennett, A. and Shapiro, J. L. (1994). An analysis of genetic algorithms using statistical mechanics. *Phys. Rev. Letts.*, 72(9):1305–1309.

Prügel-Bennett, A. and Shapiro, J. L. (1996). Dynamics of genetic algorithms for the ising spin-glass chain. *Physica D*, to appear.

Rattray, M. (1995). An analysis of a genetic algorithm training the binary perceptron. Master's thesis, University of Manchester.

Rattray, M. (1996). The dynamics of a genetic algorithm under stabilizing selection. *Complex Systems*, 9:213–234.

Rattray, M. and Shapiro, J. (1996). Noisy fitness evaluation in genetic algorithms and the dynamics of learning. These proceedings.

Shapiro, J. L. and Prügel-Bennett, A. (1995). Maximum entropy analysis of genetic algorithm operators. *Lecture Notes in Computer Science*, 864:14–24.

Shapiro, J. L. and Prügel-Bennett, A. (1996). Genetic algorithms in multi-well potentials. in preparation.

Shapiro, J. L., Prügel-Bennett, A., and Rattray, M. (1994). A statistical mechanical formulation of the dynamics of genetic algorithms. *Lecture Notes in Computer Science*, 864:17–27.

van Kampen, N. (1981). *Stochastic Processes in Physics and Chemistry*. North-Holland.

Volkenstein, M. V. (1994). *Physical Approaches to Biological Evolution*. Springer-Verlag.

Vose, M. D. and Wright, A. H. (1995). Simple genetic algorithms with linear fitness. *Evolutionary Computation*, 2:347–368.

Wright, S. (1970). Random drift and the shifting balance theory of evolution. In Kojima, K., editor, *Mathematical Topics in Population Genetics*. Springer-Verlag. and references therein.

Noisy Fitness Evaluation in Genetic Algorithms and the Dynamics of Learning

Magnus Rattray * **and Jonathan Shapiro** [†]
Computer Science Department,
University of Manchester,
Oxford Road,
Manchester M13 9PL, U.K.

Abstract

A theoretical model is presented which describes selection in a genetic algorithm (GA) under a stochastic fitness measure and correctly accounts for finite population effects. Although this model describes a number of selection schemes, we only consider Boltzmann selection in detail here as results for this form of selection are particularly transparent when fitness is corrupted by additive Gaussian noise. Finite population effects are shown to be of fundamental importance in this case, as the noise has no effect in the infinite population limit. In the limit of weak selection we show how the effects of any Gaussian noise can be removed by increasing the population size appropriately. The theory is tested on two closely related problems: the one-max problem corrupted by Gaussian noise and generalization in a perceptron with binary weights. The averaged dynamics can be accurately modelled for both problems using a formalism which describes the dynamics of the GA using methods from statistical mechanics. The second problem is a simple example of a learning problem and by considering this problem we show how the accurate characterization of noise in the fitness evaluation may be relevant in machine learning. The training error (negative fitness) is the number of misclassified training examples in a batch and can be considered as a noisy version of the generalization error if an independent batch is used for each evaluation. The noise is due to the finite batch size and in the limit of large problem size and weak selection we show how the effect of this noise can be removed by increasing the population size. This allows the optimal batch size to be determined, which minimizes computation time as well as the total number of training examples required.

---

* Internet address: rattraym@cs.man.ac.uk.
[†] Internet address: jls@cs.man.ac.uk.

1   INTRODUCTION

Genetic algorithms (GAs) are adaptive search techniques which can be used to find good solutions to problems with poorly characterized and high-dimensional search spaces (Goldberg, 1989; Holland, 1975). They have been successfully applied in a large range of domains, including a number of machine learning problems. The GA differs from other stochastic search techniques, such as simulated annealing, because solutions evolve in parallel within a population. It is hoped that this may lead to improvement through the recombination of mutually useful features from different population members.

The relative merit of each solution within the population is usually determined through a fitness measure. The fitness evaluation may be noisy due to measurement limitations or incomplete training data and it is important to understand and predict the effects of such noise. In some machine learning and optimization applications there may be a tradeoff between improved fidelity in evaluating fitness and the increased computational cost this requires. It has been suggested that GAs are suitable in this domain, since they are relatively robust against the effects of noise (Fitzpatrick & Grefenstette, 1988). Indeed, GAs have recently been shown to deal better with noise than competing local search algorithms on a class of simple additive problems (Baum *et al*, 1995).

In (Miller & Goldberg, 1995), noise corrupted fitness was modelled in terms of its effect on the mean fitness after selection from a continuous and Gaussian distribution of fitness. This is effectively an infinite population assumption and leads to the conclusion that proportionate selection is unaffected by noise. In a finite population, the tails of the distribution will be sparsely populated and this will prove to be of fundamental importance when accounting for the effects of noise. Although Miller and Goldberg sized the population to account for increased finite population effects due to noise, their choice of population size was based on a conservative predictor rather than an exact result (Goldberg *et al*, 1992). Their calculation of the variance for the one-max domain assumes a binomial distribution of alleles within the population and this assumption is also made in a number of other predictive models (Mühlenbein & Schlierkamp-Voosen, 1995; Srinivas & Patnaik, 1995; Thierens & Goldberg, 1995). In a finite population this assumption breaks down, because the population becomes more correlated under selection than predicted by a binomial distribution and this results in a reduced variance.

In this work, a theoretical model is presented which describes selection under a general stochastic fitness measure and correctly accounts for finite population effects. Although this model can be applied to a number of selection schemes and noise distributions, Boltzmann selection is considered in greatest detail here as the results in this case are transparent. This is not the most common selection scheme used in GAs, but it seems an appropriate scheme for problems where the distribution of fitness is close to Gaussian, as it conserves the population's shape in this case. It is also easy to choose the selection strength so that the population makes continued progress under selection. For weak Boltzmann selection and Gaussian noise, it is shown how an increase in population size removes the effects of noise on selection. Noise only affects a finite population under this form of selection, which emphasizes the need for any theory to properly account for finite population effects.

The theory is applied to two problems for which the full dynamics can be solved, extending a formalism developed by Prügel-Bennett, Shapiro, and Rattray for modelling the dynamics of the GA using methods from statistical mechanics (Prügel-Bennett & Shapiro, 1994; Prügel-Bennett & Shapiro, 1995; Rattray, 1995; Rattray & Shapiro, 1996; Shapiro *et al*, 1994). This formalism does not require that the population be sufficiently large to ensure convergence to the global optimum and properly accounts for correlations accumulated under selection. Under this formalism, the population is described by a small number of macroscopic statistics and a maximum entropy assumption is used to determine anything not trivially related to these macroscopics. Difference equations are derived which determine the mean change to each macroscopic under each genetic operator and these can be iterated in sequence to simulate the averaged dynamics. A more exact approach also follows fluctuations from mean behaviour by following an ensemble of populations (Prügel-Bennett, 1996). However, mean behaviour alone is sufficient to accurately describe the problems under consideration here. The macroscopics which have proved most successful to date are cumulants of some appropriate quantity within the population and the mean correlation (closely related to the mean Hamming distance). The first two cumulants are the mean and variance respectively while higher cumulants describe deviations from a Gaussian distribution.

The first case considered is the one-max problem corrupted by Gaussian noise. To simplify the discussion, bit-simulated crossover is used (Syswerda, 1993) and this allows the dynamics to be modelled by iterating only two macroscopics: the mean fitness and correlation within the population. A maximum entropy assumption is required to determine the higher cumulants before selection and to evolve the correlation under selection. Relevant results from other studies are reproduced where necessary in order to make the discussion self-contained. Simulation results show very good correspondence to the theory for a range of noise strengths and the theory accurately predicts the evolution of each macroscopic, averaged over many runs of the GA.

The second case considered is a simple problem from learning theory, generalization by a binary perceptron. A perceptron with binary weights is trained to learn a teacher perceptron by training on examples produced by the teacher. This has previously been shown to be equivalent to a noisy version of one-max if a new batch of examples are presented each time the training error is calculated (Baum *et al*, 1995). This problem was solved under the statistical mechanics formalism in (Rattray & Shapiro, 1996) and those results are reviewed here. The training error is well approximated by a Gaussian distribution whose mean is the the generalization error and whose variance increases as the batch size is reduced. The theory is shown to agree closely with simulation results averaged over many runs of the GA. In the limit of large problem size and weak selection an increase in population size removes the effects of noise due to the finite size of each training batch and this allows the optimal batch size to be determined.

2 NOTATION

Notation will follow GA conventions where appropriate and therefore differs from a number of related publications which use conventions from statistical physics (Prügel-Bennett & Shapiro, 1994; Prügel-Bennett & Shapiro, 1995; Rattray, 1995; Rattray & Shapiro, 1996). The population size is N and each population member, labelled α, has two associated fitness measures. The ideal fitness f_α is some deterministic function of the genotype, while the noisy fitness F_α is related to this through a conditional probability distribution $p(F|f)$. For example, in a supervised learning problem f_α might be the fitness evaluated over all possible training examples and F_α might be the best estimate given a small training batch. When we refer to the fitness this will usually be the ideal fitness and the noisy fitness will always be referred to explicitly.

In the cases under consideration here, each population member's genotype is a string of binary alleles of length l. The usual convention in GA theory is to take alleles $x_i^\alpha \in \{0, 1\}$ where i labels the site and α labels the population member. Here, however, we choose alleles $S_i^\alpha \in \{-1, 1\}$ which are more appropriate for the binary perceptron problem. A trivial change in variables maps one convention onto the other.

2.1 CUMULANTS

Throughout this paper the population will be described by a number of macroscopic variables, the cumulants of the ideal fitness distribution within the population and the mean correlation within the population. Cumulants are statistics which describe the population shape and are often reasonably stable to fluctuations between runs of the GA, so that they average well (Prügel-Bennett & Shapiro, 1995). The first two cumulants are the mean and variance respectively, while higher cumulants describe deviations from a Gaussian distribution. The third and fourth cumulants are related to the skewness and kurtosis of the population, respectively. The nth cumulant of a finite population is denoted κ_n.

If f_α is the fitness of population member α then the cumulants of fitness within a finite population are given by,

$$\kappa_n = \lim_{\gamma \to 0} \frac{\partial^n}{\partial \gamma^n} \ln Z; \qquad Z = \sum_{\alpha=1}^{N} e^{\gamma f_\alpha}. \tag{1}$$

Here, Z is called the partition function and holds all the information required to determine the population's cumulants. So, for example, the first two cumulants (the mean and variance) are,

$$\kappa_1 \;=\; \lim_{\gamma \to 0} \frac{\sum_\alpha f_\alpha e^{\gamma f_\alpha}}{\sum_\alpha e^{\gamma f_\alpha}} = \frac{1}{N} \sum_{\alpha=1}^{N} f_\alpha \tag{2a}$$

$$\kappa_2 \;=\; \lim_{\gamma \to 0} \frac{\sum_\alpha f_\alpha^2 e^{\gamma f_\alpha} \left(\sum_\alpha e^{\gamma f_\alpha} \right) - \left(\sum_\alpha f_\alpha e^{\gamma f_\alpha} \right)^2}{\left(\sum_\alpha e^{\gamma f_\alpha} \right)^2}$$

$$\;=\; \frac{1}{N} \sum_{\alpha=1}^{N} (f_\alpha)^2 - \left(\frac{1}{N} \sum_{\alpha=1}^{N} f_\alpha \right)^2. \tag{2b}$$

In order to model selection on a finite population, N population members are randomly sampled from an infinite population before selection (this procedure is described in greater detail in section 3). It is well known that the expected variance of a finite sample is reduced by a factor of $1 - 1/N$ and similar corrections occur for the higher cumulants. If K_n is the nth cumulant of an infinite population, then expectation values for the first four cumulants of a finite sample are given by,

$$\kappa_1 \;=\; K_1 \tag{3a}$$
$$\kappa_2 \;=\; \mathcal{N}_2 K_2 \tag{3b}$$
$$\kappa_3 \;=\; \mathcal{N}_3 K_3 \tag{3c}$$
$$\kappa_4 \;=\; \mathcal{N}_4 K_4 - 6\mathcal{N}_2 (K_2)^2 / N. \tag{3d}$$

Here, $\mathcal{N}_2$, $\mathcal{N}_3$ and $\mathcal{N}_4$ give the finite population corrections (Prügel-Bennett & Shapiro, 1995),

$$\mathcal{N}_2 = 1 - \frac{1}{N} \qquad \mathcal{N}_3 = 1 - \frac{3}{N} + \frac{2}{N^2} \qquad \mathcal{N}_4 = 1 - \frac{7}{N} + \frac{12}{N^2} - \frac{6}{N^3}. \tag{4}$$

If $p(f)$ is the distribution of fitness in an infinite population, then the infinite population cumulants can be generated from a characteristic function (analogous to the partition function)[1],

$$K_n = \lim_{\gamma \to 0} \frac{\partial^n}{\partial \gamma^n} \ln \rho(\gamma); \qquad \rho(\gamma) = \int df\, p(f) e^{\gamma f}. \tag{5}$$

---

[1] This is usually written with an explicitly imaginary argument to ensure convergence of the integral, in which case it is a Fourier transform.

The characteristic function can also be written in terms of a cumulant expansion,

$$\rho(\gamma) = \exp\left(\sum_{n=1}^{\infty} \frac{K_n \gamma^n}{n!}\right). \tag{6}$$

It is often useful to parameterize the fitness distribution by expanding around a Gaussian distribution. In this case we choose a Gram-Charlier expansion (see, for example, (Stuart & Ord, 1987)),

$$p(f) = \frac{1}{\sqrt{2\pi K_2}} \exp\left(\frac{-(f - K_1)^2}{2K_2}\right) \left[1 + \sum_{n=3}^{n_c} \frac{K_n}{n! K_2^{n/2}} H_n\left(\frac{f - K_1}{\sqrt{K_2}}\right)\right], \tag{7}$$

where $H_n(x) = (-1)^n e^{x^2/2} \frac{d^n}{dx^n} e^{-x^2/2}$ are Hermite polynomials and n_c is the number of cumulants used. Four cumulants were used in this work and the third and fourth Hermite polynomials are $H_3(x) = (x^3 - 3x)$ and $H_4(x) = (x^4 - 6x^2 + 3)$. This function is not a well defined probability distribution since it is not necessarily positive, but it has the correct cumulants and provides a very good approximation in many cases.

2.2 CORRELATION

The correlation is a measure of genotype similarity. The simplest measure of correlation between two population members, α and β, is given by,

$$q_{\alpha\beta} = \frac{1}{l} \sum_{i=1}^{l} S_i^{\alpha} S_i^{\beta}. \tag{8}$$

Recall that $S_i^{\alpha} \in \{-1, 1\}$ so that this quantity equals one when two population members are identical and is zero on average for two randomly generated population members. This is closely related to the Hamming distance between two binary sequences. To get the mean correlation within the population one averages this quantity over each distinct pair of population members,

$$q = \langle q_{\alpha\beta} \rangle_{\alpha \neq \beta} = \frac{2}{N(N-1)} \sum_{\alpha=1}^{N} \sum_{\beta > \alpha} q_{\alpha\beta}. \tag{9}$$

The expected correlation of a finite sample is equal to the correlation in an infinite population.

3 SELECTION

To describe a general selection scheme it is instructive to separate the sampling process from the weighting process. Each population member is assigned a selection weight w_α, which is generally some non-decreasing function of fitness (this is the measured, noisy fitness F_α). For fitness proportionate selection the selection weight is simply equal to the fitness. Selection weights can also be defined for ranking, tournament and truncation selection, and the general method described here can be applied to these cases (Rattray, 1996). We will consider Boltzmann selection in greatest detail, as this provides a transparent result for Gaussian noise (De la Maza & Tidor, 1991; Prügel-Bennett & Shapiro, 1994). For Boltzmann selection the selection weight is defined,

$$w_\alpha = \exp(\beta F_\alpha), \tag{10}$$

where β is the selection strength which determines the relative probability of selection for each population member. By scaling the selection strength inversely with the population's standard deviation one avoids the problem of long convergence times, often cited as a problem with using fitness-proportionate forms of selection. This scaling is used in section 3.3.

To select a new population it is necessary to take a weighted sample from the population before selection. Ideally, the proportion of each population member in the new population is given by,

$$p_\alpha = \frac{w_\alpha}{\sum_\alpha w_\alpha}. \tag{11}$$

However, it is not possible to choose exactly this amount in a finite population. We will consider Roulette wheel sampling, as this provides an analytically tractable model for finite population effects. Other, less noisy forms of sampling are often preferred in practice (see, for example, (Baker, 1987)) and a challenging task would be to extend the present analysis to these cases.

Under Roulette wheel sampling, N new population members are selected with replacement, with probability p_α. Following the discussion in (Prügel-Bennett, 1996), this process can be divided into two stages,

1. Select an infinite population from a finite population, so that p_α is exactly the proportion of population member α in the infinite population after selection.

2. Randomly sample N population members from the infinite population to make up the new finite population.

Mutation and crossover do not involve sampling and can therefore be carried out during the infinite population stage of the dynamics without any loss of generality. A similar sampling procedure is used in (Vose & Wright, 1994), but there they follow an exact microscopic description of the population while we only consider a small number of macroscopic statistics. This simplification makes our prescription less general, but allows us to capture a number of interesting and non-trivial features of the dynamics in a natural way.

3.1 GENERATING THE CUMULANTS AFTER SELECTION

The cumulants of an infinite population after selection can be generated from the logarithm of a selection partition function. If K_n^s is the nth cumulant of an infinite population after selection then,

$$K_n^s = \lim_{\gamma \to 0} \frac{\partial^n}{\partial \gamma^n} \ln Z_s; \qquad Z_s = \sum_{\alpha=1}^{N} w_\alpha e^{\gamma f_\alpha}. \tag{12}$$

For example,

$$\begin{aligned} K_1^s &= \lim_{\gamma \to 0} \frac{\sum_\alpha w_\alpha f_\alpha e^{\gamma f_\alpha}}{\sum_\alpha w_\alpha e^{\gamma f_\alpha}} \\ &= \sum_{\alpha=1}^{N} p_\alpha f_\alpha, \end{aligned} \tag{13a}$$

where we have used the definition of p_α in equation (11). Similarly one finds,

$$K_2^s = \sum_{\alpha=1}^{N} p_\alpha f_\alpha^2 - \left(\sum_{\alpha=1}^{N} p_\alpha f_\alpha \right)^2. \tag{13b}$$

These are exactly the cumulants of an infinite population after selection, since p_α is exactly the proportion of each population member in this case. The expected cumulants of a finite population after selection can be found by applying equations (3a) to (3d).

The exact fitness of each population member is not known in general, only the cumulants of the distribution from which they are sampled. The selection weight also has a stochastic component due to variance in the conditional probability distribution relating the measured fitness to the ideal fitness $p(F|f)$. Therefore, it is necessary to average over the sampling procedure and the noise in fitness evaluation in order to determine the expected cumulants after selection. Instead of averaging over the cumulants directly, it is more convenient to average over the logarithm of the partition function defined in equation (12),

$$\langle \ln Z_s \rangle = \left(\prod_{\alpha=1}^{N} \int df_\alpha\, p(f_\alpha) \int dF_\alpha\, p(F_\alpha|f_\alpha) \right) \ln Z_s. \tag{14}$$

Following the discussion in (Prügel-Bennett & Shapiro, 1994) we use Derrida's trick to express the logarithm as an integral[2] (Derrida, 1981).

$$\langle \ln Z_s \rangle = \int_0^\infty dt\, \frac{e^{-t} - \langle e^{-tZ_s} \rangle}{t}. \tag{15}$$

If the selection weight associated with population member α is a function of F_α alone then the averages on the right hand side decouple from one another,

$$\begin{aligned}
\langle e^{-tZ_s} \rangle &= \left(\prod_{\alpha=1}^{N} \int df_\alpha\, p(f_\alpha) \int dF_\alpha\, p(F_\alpha|f_\alpha) \right) \exp\left(-t \sum_{\alpha=1}^{N} w(F_\alpha) e^{\gamma f_\alpha} \right) \\
&= \left(\int df\, p(f) \int dF\, p(F|f) \exp\left(-t w(F) e^{\gamma f} \right) \right)^N.
\end{aligned} \tag{16}$$

3.2 BOLTZMANN SELECTION

Consider Boltzmann selection, in which case the selection weight is defined in equation (10). The above expression can be substituted into equation (15) and equation (12) then provides the expected cumulants of an infinite population after Boltzmann selection (the term in the integrand of equation (15) which does not involve γ is not required for $n > 0$),

$$K_n^s = -\lim_{\gamma \to 0} \frac{\partial^n}{\partial \gamma^n} \int_0^\infty dt\, \frac{g^N(t,\gamma,\beta)}{t}, \tag{17}$$

where

$$g(t,\gamma,\beta) = \int df\, p(f) \int dF\, p(F|f) \exp\left(-t e^{\beta F + \gamma f} \right). \tag{18}$$

Notice that although these are cumulants of an infinite population after selection, they depend on N which is the population size *before* selection (see section 3). In general these integrals have to be determined numerically and for the simulation results presented in this paper the integrals were computed by Gaussian quadratures (Press *et al*, 1992). The ideal fitness distribution can be parameterized by the Gram-Charlier expansion in equation (7).

---

[2] To see this, notice that $\frac{1}{Z} = \int_0^\infty dt\, e^{-Zt}$, integrate both sides with respect to Z and swap the order of integration (as long as $Z > 0$).

3.3 WEAK SELECTION AND GAUSSIAN NOISE

An analytically tractable case is for weak selection corrupted by additive Gaussian noise, in which case $p(F|f)$ is given by a Gaussian distribution centred around f,

$$p(F|f) = \frac{1}{\sqrt{2\pi\sigma^2}} \exp\left(\frac{-(F-f)^2}{2\sigma^2}\right). \tag{19}$$

Here, σ^2 is the variance of the noise. As shown in (Prügel-Bennett & Shapiro, 1994), one can express the logarithm of the partition function analytically for small β. This limit is accurate for sufficiently small $\beta\sqrt{K_2+\sigma^2}$ and is instructive as it shows the relevant effects of selection for each cumulant.

For small β and γ, $g(t,\gamma,\beta)$ which is defined in equation (18) can be expanded in $te^{\beta F+\gamma f}$. Exponentiating this expansion one finds,

$$g^N(t,\gamma,\beta) \simeq \exp(-tN\psi(\gamma,\beta))\left(1+\frac{Nt^2}{2}\left(\psi(2\gamma,2\beta)-\psi^2(\gamma,\beta)\right)\right), \tag{20}$$

where

$$\begin{aligned}
\psi(\gamma,\beta) &= \int df\, p(f)\int dF\, p(F|f)\, e^{\beta F+\gamma f} \\
&= \exp\left(\tfrac{1}{2}(\beta\sigma)^2\right)\rho(\beta+\gamma).
\end{aligned}$$

Here, $\rho(\gamma)$ is the characteristic function defined in equation (5) which can be written in terms of the cumulant expansion defined in equation (6). Completing the integral in equation (17), one finds that the cumulants after selection up to $O(1/N)$ are given by,

$$K_n^s = \lim_{\gamma\to 0}\frac{\partial^n}{\partial\gamma^n}\left[\sum_{i=1}^{\infty}\frac{(\gamma+\beta)^i K_i}{i!} - \frac{e^{(\beta\sigma)^2}}{2N}\exp\left(\sum_{i=1}^{\infty}\frac{(2^i-2)(\gamma+\beta)^i K_i}{i!}\right) + O\left(\frac{1}{N}\right)\right]. \tag{21}$$

The leading term here is the infinite population result.

Expanding the first three cumulants after selection in β, for fixed $\beta\sigma$, one finds,

$$K_1^s = K_1 + \beta\left(1-\frac{e^{(\beta\sigma)^2}}{N}\right)K_2 + \frac{\beta^2}{2}\left(1-\frac{3e^{(\beta\sigma)^2}}{N}\right)K_3 + \cdots \tag{22a}$$

$$K_2^s = \left(1-\frac{e^{(\beta\sigma)^2}}{N}\right)K_2 + \beta\left(1-\frac{3e^{(\beta\sigma)^2}}{N}\right)K_3 + \cdots \tag{22b}$$

$$K_3^s = \left(1-\frac{3e^{(\beta\sigma)^2}}{N}\right)K_3 + \beta\left[\left(1-\frac{7e^{(\beta\sigma)^2}}{N}\right)K_4 - \frac{6e^{(\beta\sigma)^2}}{N}(K_2)^2\right] + \cdots. \tag{22c}$$

For zero noise ($\sigma = 0$) one retrieves the result in (Prügel-Bennett & Shapiro, 1994). As in the zero noise case, finite population effects lead to a reduced variance and a negative third cumulant[3], related to the population's skewness, which leads to an accelerated reduction in variance under further selection. Notice that a normally distributed infinite population remains Gaussian under selection and does not lose variance. This is clearly an idealization which cannot be achieved in a finite population,

---

[3]The third cumulant typically becomes negative even in an infinite population because of an initially negative fourth cumulant (for finite l) – however, finite population effects are often more significant.

where tails of the population are sparsely populated and no progress can be made beyond the best solution. The other genetic operators are required to reduce the magnitude of the higher cumulants by repopulating the tails of the population.

The noise in selection increases the magnitude of the finite population terms by reducing the accuracy of sampling, resulting in a faster loss of variance and less improvement under selection. Clearly, noise has no effect in the infinite population limit. This is because the effect of noise over-estimating and under-estimating the value of f exactly cancels in this limit. This again emphasizes the need for accurate characterization of finite population effects.

It can be seen from equation (21) that in the weak selection limit the effects of Gaussian noise can be removed by increasing the population size appropriately. If N_0 is the population size for zero noise, then the effects of any Gaussian noise which is introduced can be removed by setting,

$$N = N_0 \exp\left((\beta\sigma)^2\right). \tag{23}$$

It is remarkable that the effects of noise on selection can be removed for *every* cumulant by this simple increase in population size. This population resizing proves to be particularly of interest in the context of the binary perceptron problem discussed in section 5.

Notice that this population resizing only holds if selection strength is independent of the noise variance, so that only finite population terms in equations (21) involve the noise variance. For example, this is not the case if selection strength is scaled according to statistics from the measured, noise corrupted fitness distribution (although the equations describing the dynamics would still hold). Here, we scale selection strength inversely to the standard deviation of the ideal fitness distribution $\beta = \beta_s/\sqrt{\kappa_2}$, which ensures a constant selection pressure. This is a rather artificial choice, as ideal fitness statistics would not be known in a real noise corrupted problem. However, the results derived here describe a GA with any fixed schedule for determining the selection strength each generation. The scaling used here is equivalent (on average) to an appropriate schedule for the associated noise less problem.

4   ONE-MAX WITH GAUSSIAN NOISE

The dynamics for the one-max problem can be modelled using a statistical mechanics formalism developed in (Prügel-Bennett & Shapiro, 1995; Rattray, 1995; Rattray & Shapiro, 1996). This discussion will follow that presented in (Rattray & Shapiro, 1996) most closely. To simplify matters bit-simulated crossover is used, where the population is completely shuffled during crossover so that a child's alleles come from any population member with equal probability (Syswerda, 1993). This brings the population straight to the fixed point of standard uniform crossover (without selection) and allows the population to be accurately described by only two macroscopics: the mean fitness and correlation. Under more general forms of crossover it is necessary to follow the evolution of the higher cumulants, as described in (Prügel-Bennett & Shapiro, 1995; Rattray, 1995). Here, we only wish to consider the simplest GA (from a theoretical perspective) compatible with the problems under consideration.

The formalism used here differs from the models described in (Muhlenbein & Schlierkamp-Voosen, 1995; Srinivas & Patnaik, 1995; Thierens & Goldberg, 1995) by the inclusion of a constraint on the mean correlation within the population. In these models the population was considered to be binomially distributed, and this assumption breaks down when a finite population correlates under selection. This is especially important here, as noise has no effect in the infinite population limit. Unfortunately, the inclusion of an extra constraint means that the dynamic trajectory for the macroscopics can no longer be described analytically. However, the description is still compact in the sense that there are few degrees of freedom and any numerical computation which is required does not depend on population size or genotype length.

In the following sections difference equations are derived for the change in mean fitness and correlation within the population under the action of each genetic operator. To describe the population before selection it is necessary to determine terms which are not trivially related to these two macroscopics. In order to calculate these terms a maximum entropy calculation is introduced, which is described in the appendix. Finally, the theory is compared to simulation results averaged over many runs, showing excellent agreement and accurately predicting the averaged evolution of each macroscopic.

4.1 THE MACROSCOPICS

The ideal fitness for one-max is given by,

$$f_\alpha = \sum_{i=1}^{l} S_i^\alpha. \tag{24}$$

Here, the alleles are $S_i^\alpha \in \{-1, 1\}$, which is most convenient for the binary perceptron problem considered in section 5. This can easily be converted to the standard binary convention under a linear transformation. The mean and variance of an infinite population are,

$$K_1 = \sum_{i=1}^{l} \langle S_i^\alpha \rangle_\alpha \tag{25a}$$

$$K_2 = \left\langle \left(\sum_{i=1}^{l} S_i^\alpha \right)^2 \right\rangle_\alpha - \left(\sum_{i=1}^{l} \langle S_i^\alpha \rangle_\alpha \right)^2$$

$$= l(1-q) + \sum_{i=1}^{l} \sum_{j \neq i} \langle S_i^\alpha S_j^\alpha \rangle_\alpha - \langle S_i^\alpha \rangle_\alpha \langle S_j^\alpha \rangle_\alpha, \tag{25b}$$

where the angled brackets denote population averages and we have used an infinite population expression for the correlation,

$$q = \frac{1}{l} \sum_{i=1}^{l} \langle S_i^\alpha S_i^\beta \rangle_{\alpha \neq \beta} \stackrel{N \to \infty}{=} \frac{1}{l} \sum_{i=1}^{l} \langle S_i^\alpha \rangle_\alpha^2. \tag{26}$$

The finite population correction to the second cumulant is given in equation (3b).

Equation (25b) shows how an increase in correlation results in a reduced variance, all other terms being equal. The $i \neq j$ term in this expression is related to the linkage disequilibrium in population genetics (Ewens, 1979) and disappears after bit-simulated crossover. In this case the correlation can be deduced directly from the variance after crossover.

4.2 MUTATION

Under mutation, bits are flipped throughout the population with probability p_m. Introducing an independent binary variable for each allele within the population provides a natural way of describing this operator,

$$S_i^\alpha \to M_i^\alpha S_i^\alpha; \qquad M_i^\alpha = \left\{ \begin{array}{ll} 1 & \text{with probability } 1 - p_m \\ -1 & \text{with probability } p_m. \end{array} \right. \tag{27}$$

So, for example, the mean fitness of an infinite population after mutation is,

$$K_1^m = \sum_{i=1}^{l} \langle M_i^\alpha S_i^\alpha \rangle_\alpha \tag{28}$$

and averaging over all mutations gives the expectation value for the mean after mutation,

$$\langle K_1^m \rangle = (1 - 2p_m)K_1. \tag{29}$$

This calculation can be generalized to the higher cumulants (Prügel-Bennett & Shapiro, 1995). The correlation after mutation is similarly found to be,

$$q_m = (1 - 2p_m)^2 q. \tag{30}$$

4.3 CROSSOVER

Under bit-simulated crossover, the population is brought straight to the fixed point of standard uniform crossover (without selection). Notice that averages between and within population members are equal on average after this form of crossover; so, for example, terms like $\langle S_i^\alpha S_j^\beta \rangle_{i \neq j}$ and $\langle S_i^\alpha S_j^\alpha \rangle_{i \neq j}$ are equal (where brackets now denote site averages) and the second term in equation (25b) disappears. Similar cancellations are possible in the higher cumulants, as described in (Prügel-Bennett & Shapiro, 1995). To accurately model selection we describe the population by four cumulants after crossover,

$$K_1^c = K_1 \tag{31a}$$

$$K_2^c = l(1-q) \tag{31b}$$

$$K_3^c = -2K_1 + 2\sum_{i=1}^{l} \langle S_i^\alpha \rangle_\alpha^3 \tag{31c}$$

$$K_4^c = -2l(1-4q) - 6\sum_{i=1}^{l} \langle S_i^\alpha \rangle_\alpha^4. \tag{31d}$$

The terms in the expressions for the third and fourth cumulants which are not trivially related to known macroscopics are calculated through a maximum entropy assumption, as described in the appendix. The correlation does not change under crossover, since the mean number of alleles at each site is conserved. In (Prügel-Bennett & Shapiro, 1995) it is shown how the cumulants relax towards this fixed point under more standard crossover schemes.

4.4 SELECTION

The cumulants after Boltzmann selection are given in equation (17). It only remains to calculate the correlation after selection. This is a difficult task in general, as it requires some knowledge of the mapping between genotype and fitness and we will again make use of the maximum entropy calculation described in the appendix.

It is instructive to divide the correlation after selection into two contributions: a duplication term and a natural increase term. The duplication term gives the increased correlation due to the duplication of existing population members required in a finite population. The natural increase term is due to the natural increase in correlation as the population moves into a region of higher fitness. The following results were derived in full in (Rattray, 1995; Rattray & Shapiro, 1996) and here we only provide an outline of the derivation.

The correlation in an infinite population after selection is,

$$
\begin{aligned}
q_s &= \sum_{\alpha=1}^{N} p_\alpha^2 (1 - q_{\alpha\alpha}) + \sum_{\alpha=1}^{N} \sum_{\beta=1}^{N} p_\alpha p_\beta q_{\alpha\beta} \\
&= \Delta q_d + q_\infty,
\end{aligned}
\tag{32}
$$

where $q_{\alpha\alpha}$ are dummy variables which are assumed to come from the same statistics as $q_{\alpha\beta}$. Thus, $q_{\alpha\alpha}$ is the expected correlation between two distinct population members both with fitness f_α. The first term here is arrived at by noting that duplicates have a correlation of unity and replace a pair in the matrix of correlations which would otherwise have expected correlation $q_{\alpha\alpha}$. The second term is the natural increase in correlation as fitness increases (and entropy lowers) and is the sole contribution in the infinite population limit (these definitions differ slightly from those used in (Rattray, 1995)).

4.4.1 Natural Increase Term

We estimate the conditional probability distribution for correlation given two fitness values before selection $p(q_{\alpha\beta}|f_\alpha, f_\beta)$ by assuming the alleles within the population are distributed according to the maximum entropy distribution described in the appendix. Then q_∞ is simply the correlation averaged over this distribution and the distribution of fitness after selection, $p_s(f)$.

$$
q_\infty = \int dq_{\alpha\beta} \, df_\alpha \, df_\beta \, p_s(f_\alpha) p_s(f_\beta) p(q_{\alpha\beta}|f_\alpha, f_\beta) \, q_{\alpha\beta}.
\tag{33}
$$

This integral can be calculated for large l by the saddle point method[4] and we find that in this limit the result depends only on the mean fitness after selection (Rattray, 1995),

$$
q_\infty(y) = \frac{1}{l} \sum_{i=1}^{l} \left(\frac{\tau_i + \tanh(y)}{1 + \tau_i \tanh(y)} \right)^2 ,
\tag{34a}
$$

where y is implicitly related to the mean fitness after selection through,

$$
K_1^s = \sum_{i=1}^{l} \frac{\tau_i + \tanh(y)}{1 + \tau_i \tanh(y)}.
\tag{34b}
$$

Here, τ_i is the mean allele at site i before selection and for a distribution at maximum entropy one finds (see equation (59) in the appendix),

$$
\tau_i = \tanh(z + x\eta_i).
$$

The Lagrange multipliers, z and x, are chosen to enforce constraints on the mean overlap and correlation within the population before selection and η_i is drawn from a Gaussian distribution with zero mean and unit variance.

---

[4] For weak selection the large l restriction can be dropped (Rattray, 1996).

It is instructive to expand in y, which is appropriate in the weak selection limit. In this case one finds,

$$K_1^s = K_1^c + yK_2^c + \frac{y^2}{2}K_3^c + \frac{y^4}{3!}K_4^c + \cdots \tag{35a}$$

$$q_\infty(y) = q - \frac{y}{l}K_3^c - \frac{y^2}{2l}K_4^c + \cdots, \tag{35b}$$

where K_n^c are the cumulants after bit-simulated crossover, when the population is assumed to be at maximum entropy (defined in equations (31a) to (31d) up to the fourth cumulant). Recall the expression for the mean fitness after selection given in equation (22a). By comparing this to the above expressions, notice that y plays the role of selection strength in the associated infinite population problem, so for an infinite population one could simply set $y = \beta$.

To calculate q_∞ we solve equation (34b) for y and then substitute this value into equation (34a). In general this must be done numerically, although the weak selection expansion gives a very good approximation in many cases. The third cumulant in equation (35b) will be negative for $K_1 > 0$ because of the negative entropy gradient and this will accelerate the increased correlation under selection.

4.4.2 Duplication Term

The duplication term Δq_d is defined in equation (32). As in the selection calculation presented in section 3.1, population members are independently averaged over a distribution with the correct cumulants to calculate the expectation value of this quantity. In general the expressions must be computed numerically, but the results can be expanded in $1/N$ for sufficiently weak selection (Rattray & Shapiro, 1996). In this case one finds,

$$\Delta q_d = \frac{e^{(\beta\sigma)^2}[1 - q_\infty(2\beta)]\rho(2\beta)}{N\rho^2(\beta)} + O\!\left(\frac{1}{N^2}\right), \tag{36}$$

where $q_\infty(y)$ is defined in equation (34a) and $\rho(\beta)$ is the characteristic function defined in equation (5). Notice that the factor involving the noise here is the same as in the cumulant result presented in equation (21). The effects of noise is therefore removed by the same population size increase as described in equation (23).

It is instructive to expand in β as this shows the contribution from each cumulant explicitly. To third order in β for three cumulants one finds,

$$\Delta q_d \simeq \frac{e^{(\beta\sigma)^2}}{N}\left(1 - q_\infty(2\beta)\right)\left(1 + K_2\beta^2 - K_3\beta^3 + O(\beta^4)\right). \tag{37}$$

Selection leads to a negative third cumulant (see equation (22c)), which in turn leads to an accelerated increase in correlation under further selection. Crossover reduces this effect by reducing the magnitude of the higher cumulants.

4.5 SIMULATIONS

The dynamics of the GA can be simulated by iterating the expressions in the preceding sections. In figure 1 the theoretical results are compared to simulation results from a GA averaged over 1000 samples for a typical choice of parameters. The trajectories are shown for the mean and variance of the fitness distribution. The zero noise case is compared to noisy one-max with $\sigma^2 = 6\kappa_2$ and $\sigma^2 = 12\kappa_2$, showing how increased noise leads to reduced performance. The theoretical results show excellent agreement. The noise was measured in terms of κ_2 because this provides the most natural units for measuring noise (for example, any breakdown in the theory might be expected to occur for a particular value of σ^2/κ_2). This may seem rather unnatural, although in many cases the noise will fall off as fitness increases. For example, this is the case in the binary perceptron problem which is considered in the next section. In view of this, a fixed noise level might be an equally artificial construction. These considerations are not of critical importance here, however, as the aim is to verify the theory and a more realistic situation is introduced in the next section.

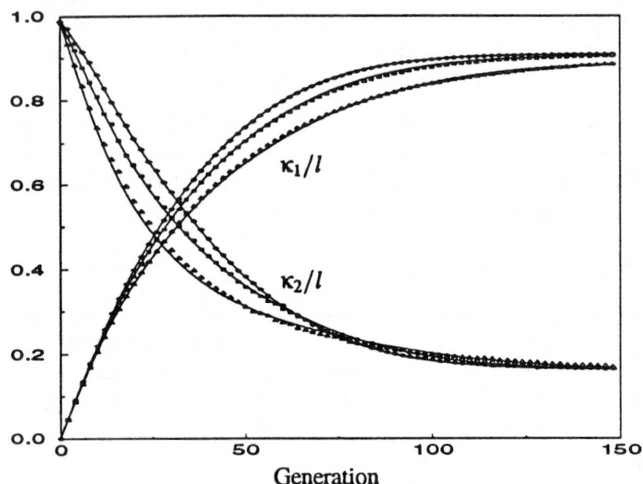

Figure 1: The theory for noisy one-max is compared to results averaged over 1000 runs of a GA. The mean (κ_1) and variance (κ_2) are shown, with solid lines showing theoretical predictions. The result for zero noise ($\Diamond$) is compared to results with additive Gaussian noise of strength $\sigma^2 = 6\kappa_2$ ($\square$) and $\sigma^2 = 12\kappa_2$ ($\triangle$). The other parameters were $l = 155$, $\beta_s = 0.3$, $p_m = 0.005$, $N = 100$ and bit-simulated crossover was used.

Notice that the strength of the noise is greater than the population's standard deviation in this example, which emphasizes how robust the GA is even with high levels of noise. For very high levels of noise the theory breaks down, probably because the weak selection, low noise approximation is required to calculate the duplication contribution to the correlation after selection. There may well be a better approximation for this term, although the approximation used here seems to be accurate for reasonable levels of noise. It may also be the case that when noise levels are high the dynamics do not average well, since there are large fluctuations from mean behaviour. In this case it might be necessary to follow an ensemble of populations, as described in (Prügel-Bennett, 1996).

5 GENERALIZATION IN THE BINARY PERCEPTRON

One of the key questions in learning theory is when and how one might generalize to learn a rule from a set of training examples. A simple example of this is the case where a perceptron with binary weights is trained on patterns generated from a teacher perceptron, also with binary weights. The statistical mechanics formalism was applied to this problem in (Rattray & Shapiro, 1996) and here we review these results in order to show how this work may be of relevance to problems from machine learning.

The perceptron has weights $S_i \in \{-1, 1\}$ and maps a binary vector with components $\zeta_i^\mu \in \{-1, 1\}$ onto a binary output,

$$O^\mu = \mathrm{sgn}\left(\sum_{i=1}^{l} S_i \zeta_i^\mu\right); \qquad \mathrm{sgn}(x) = \left\{ \begin{array}{ll} 1 & x \geq 0 \\ -1 & x < 0. \end{array} \right. \tag{38}$$

Let T_i be the weights of the teacher perceptron and S_i be the weights of the student. The stability of a pattern is a measure of how well it is stored by the perceptron and the stability of pattern μ for the teacher and student are Λ_t^μ and Λ_s^μ respectively,

$$\Lambda_t^\mu = \frac{1}{\sqrt{l}} \sum_{i=1}^{l} T_i \zeta_i^\mu \qquad \Lambda_s^\mu = \frac{1}{\sqrt{l}} \sum_{i=1}^{l} S_i \zeta_i^\mu. \tag{39}$$

The training error will be defined as the number of patterns the pupil misclassifies,

$$E = \sum_{\mu=1}^{\lambda l} \Theta(-\Lambda_t^\mu \Lambda_s^\mu); \qquad \Theta(x) = \left\{ \begin{array}{ll} 1 & x \geq 0 \\ 0 & x < 0, \end{array} \right. \tag{40}$$

where λl is the number of training patterns presented in a batch. To simplify the analysis a new batch of training examples is presented each time the training error is calculated.

The GA processes a population of student weight vectors and the training energy acts as a negative fitness (this is the measured, noisy fitness). Define the ideal fitness f to be the overlap between the weight vectors of the teacher and the student. We choose $T_i = 1$ at every site without loss of generality, in which case the overlap associated with population member α is f_α and is defined,

$$f_\alpha = \frac{1}{l} \sum_{i=1}^{l} S_i^\alpha. \tag{41}$$

This is simply the one-max fitness measure defined in equation (24), normalized to be of order unity (the nth cumulant is now typically of $O(l^{1-n})$ rather than $O(l)$). Thus, this problem is equivalent to a noisy version of one-max and the only difference is in the conditional probability distribution relating training error to the overlap between teacher and student. This can be determined and if the size of each batch is $O(l)$ then $p(E|f)$ is well approximated by a Gaussian distribution (Rattray & Shapiro, 1996),

$$p(E|f) = \frac{1}{\sqrt{2\pi\sigma^2}} \exp\left(\frac{-(E - E_g(f))^2}{2\sigma^2}\right), \tag{42}$$

where the mean and variance are,

$$E_g(f) = \frac{\lambda l}{\pi} \cos^{-1}(f) \tag{43a}$$

$$\sigma^2(f) = E_g(f)\left(1 - \frac{E_g(f)}{\lambda l}\right). \tag{43b}$$

Here, $E_g(f)$ is the generalization error, which is the probability of misclassifying a randomly chosen training example multiplied by the batch size (errors are chosen proportional to l here). The variance expresses the fact that there is noise in the training error (negative fitness) evaluation due to the finite size of the training set.

5.1 SELECTION

If the training error is considered to be a negative fitness ($E = -F$) then equation (17) generates the cumulants for the overlap distribution after selection. As before, the integrals have to be computed numerically. Notice that the mean and variance of $p(E|f)$ are non-linear functions of the overlap f, so this problem is not exactly equivalent to the noisy one-max problem which was considered in section 4.

For weak selection and large l it is possible to apply the weak selection expansion which was introduced in section 3.3. Since the variance of overlaps within the population is $O(1/l)$ one can expand the mean of $p(E|f)$ around the mean of the population in this limit ($f \simeq K_1$). It is also assumed that the variance of $p(E|f)$ is well approximated by its leading term in this limit. Under these simplifications one finds,

$$E_g(f) \;\simeq\; \frac{\lambda l}{\pi}\left(\cos^{-1}(K_1) - \frac{(f - K_1)}{\sqrt{1 - K_1^2}}\right) \tag{44a}$$

$$\sigma^2 \;\simeq\; \frac{\lambda l}{\pi}\cos^{-1}(K_1)\left(1 - \frac{1}{\pi}\cos^{-1}(K_1)\right). \tag{44b}$$

Now the mean of $p(E|f)$ is a linear function of f and the problem is very similar to selection corrupted by Gaussian noise. The cumulants after selection are found to be,

$$K_n^s = \lim_{\gamma \to 0}\frac{\partial^n}{\partial \gamma^n}\left[\sum_{i=1}^{\infty}\frac{(\gamma + k\beta)^i K_i}{i!} - \frac{e^{(\beta\sigma)^2}}{2N}\exp\left(\sum_{i=1}^{\infty}\frac{(2^i - 2)(\gamma + k\beta)^i K_i}{i!}\right)\right], \tag{45}$$

where

$$k = \frac{\lambda l}{\pi\sqrt{1 - K_1^2}}. \tag{46}$$

This is equivalent to selecting on f directly (see equation (21)) where $k\beta$ is the effective selection strength and σ/k is the effective standard deviation of the noise. The correlation result can similarly be calculated by generalizing the noisy one-max result in section 4.4 and one finds that the results are equivalent under the same effective selection strength and noise. A more thorough discussion of these results is given in (Rattray & Shapiro, 1996).

5.2 RESIZING THE POPULATION

The noise introduced by the finite sized training set increases the magnitude of the detrimental finite population terms in selection. In the limit of weak selection and large problem size discussed in the preceding section, the effects of noise can be removed by increasing the population size according to equation (23). This maps the trajectory of the finite training set GA onto the trajectory of the GA in the zero noise, infinite training set situation. This expression is valid if the effective selection strength $k\beta$ is independent of batch size (which determines the noise strength). For this to be the case β must be chosen proportional to $1/\lambda$, which is the most natural scaling in any case because the training error is proportional to λ. It is then convenient to rewrite equation (23),

$$N = N_0 \exp\left(\frac{\lambda_o}{\lambda}\right), \tag{47}$$

where,

$$\lambda_o = \lambda(\beta\sigma)^2 = \frac{(\lambda\beta)^2 l}{\pi} \cos^{-1}(K_1) \left(1 - \frac{1}{\pi}\cos^{-1}(K_1)\right). \tag{48}$$

Here, λ_o is independent of λ because of the β scaling described above. Choosing N according to this expression removes the effects of noise due to the finite batch size and maps the dynamical trajectory onto the infinite training set dynamics (where $E = E_g(f)$) for a GA with population size N_0. Typically β is of order $1/\sqrt{l}$ and this population resizing will not blow up with increases in problem size (for fixed λ). This is consistent with the result in (Baum $et\ al$, 1995), although they provide a rigorous proof for the scaling of their algorithm.

Both selection strength and noise variance will change over time, and it would therefore be necessary to change the population size each generation in order to apply the above expression. However, this is problematic when the population size has to be increased, as this leads to an increased correlation[5]. In this case the dynamics will no longer exactly map onto the infinite training set situation.

Instead of varying the population size, one can fix the population size and vary the size of each training batch. In this case one finds,

$$\lambda = \frac{\lambda_o}{\log(N/N_0)}. \tag{49}$$

Figure 2 shows how choosing the batch size each generation according to this expression leads to the dynamics converging onto the infinite training set trajectory of a GA with a smaller population. The infinite training set result for the largest population size is also shown, as this gives some measure of the potential variability of trajectories available under different batch sizing schemes. Any deviation from the weak selection, large l limit is not apparent here.

In this work the effective selection strength was scaled inversely to the standard deviation of overlaps ($\beta = \beta_s/k\sqrt{\kappa_2}$). This is a rather artificial choice, as it requires information about overlap statistics which would not be known in practice. However, the population resizing in equation (47) and the corresponding batch sizing expression in equation (49) are valid given any fixed schedule for determining selection strength. The choice of selection scaling used here is equivalent (on average) to an appropriate schedule for the infinite training batch problem.

5.3 OPTIMAL BATCH SIZE

In the previous section it was shown how population size can be increased in order to remove the effects of noise associated with a finite training batch. Fitzpatrick and Grefenstette also identified the existence of such a tradeoff between population size and batch size, and they suggest that there is often an optimal choice of batch size (or measurement accuracy) (Fitzpatrick & Grefenstette, 1988). If the population resizing in equation (47) is used, then it is possible to identify such an optimal batch size, which minimizes the computational cost of training error evaluations. This choice of batch size will also minimize the total number of training examples presented when independent batches are used.

---

[5]This is a problem for a real GA which produces a finite population after selection. The theoretical model described in section 3 does not have this problem, as the population size is infinite after selection. In a real GA one might overcome this by creating a large but finite population after selection, some members of which could be discarded before the next round of selection.

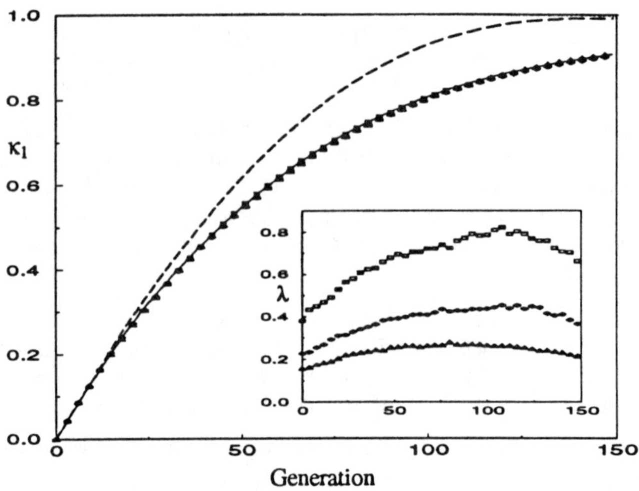

Figure 2: The mean overlap between teacher and student within the population is shown each generation, averaged over 100 runs of a GA training a binary perceptron to generalize from examples produced by a teacher perceptron. Training batch sizes were chosen according to equation (49), leading to trajectories converging onto the infinite training set result where $E = E_g(f)$. The solid curve is for the infinite training set result with $N_0 = 60$ and finite training set results are for $N = 90$ ($\square$), 120($\diamond$) and 163($\triangle$). The inset shows the mean choice of batch parameter (λ) each generation. The dashed line is the infinite training set result for $N = 163$, showing that there is significant potential variability of trajectories under different batch sizing schemes. The other parameters were $l = 279$, $\beta_s = 0.25$ and $p_\mathrm{m} = 0.001$.

It is assumed that computation is mainly due to error evaluation and that other overheads can be neglected. There are N error evaluations each generation with computation time for each scaling as λ. If the population size each generation is chosen by equation (47), then the computation time τ_c is related to batch size by,

$$\tau_c(\lambda) \propto \lambda \exp\left(\frac{\lambda_o}{\lambda}\right). \tag{50}$$

The optimal choice of λ is given by the minimum of τ_c, which is at λ_o (defined in equation (48)). Choosing this batch size leads to the population size being constant over the whole GA run and for optimal efficiency one should choose,

$$N = N_0 e^l \simeq 2.73 N_0 \tag{51a}$$
$$\lambda = \lambda_o, \tag{51b}$$

where N_0 is the population size used for the zero noise, infinite training set GA with the same dynamical trajectory. Notice that it is not necessary to determine N_0 in order to choose the size of each batch, since λ_o is not a function of N_0 (see equation (48)). One of the runs in figure 2 is for this choice of N and λ, showing close agreement to the infinite training set result ($N = 163 \simeq N_0 e$).

Unfortunately, the optimal batch size is a function of the mean overlap within the population, which would not be known in general (although it could be estimated from training error statistics). However, the initial optimal batch size provides an upper bound, since the variance of noise decreases as the mean overlap increases (see equation (44b)). Setting $K_1 = 0$ in equation (48) provides this bound,

$$\lambda_o \leq \tfrac{1}{4}(\lambda\beta)^2 l. \tag{52}$$

Recall that β is proportional to $1/\lambda$, so that the right hand side of this expression is independent of λ. This is a somewhat intuitive result, as it shows how more effort should be expended in determining fitness (through increasing the batch size) when the resulting decisions are more critical (through stronger selection). The selection strength β is typically of order $1/\sqrt{l}$ so that the optimum batch size is typically of order l (recall that the batch size is λl).

5.4 SIMULATIONS

The dynamics can be modelled by combining the selection results from section 5.1 with the expressions for mutation and crossover derived in section 4. Figures 3 and 4 show the trajectories of the mean and variance of the overlap distribution as well as the maximum overlap, averaged over 1000 runs of a GA for a typical choice of search parameters. The infinite training batch result, where $E = E_g(f)$, is compared to results for two fixed batch sizes, showing how performance degrades as the batch size is reduced. The theoretical curves show excellent agreement to simulation results. The theoretical estimate for the maximum overlap was obtained by assuming population members are randomly sampled from a population with the correct cumulants (Prügel-Bennett & Shapiro, 1995).

There is a slight systematic error in the curves for the smallest batch size and as the batch size is reduced further the theory breaks down. This is probably because a weak selection, low noise approximation was required to calculate the duplication contribution to the correlation after selection, as was also the case for the noisy one-max problem. It is also possible that the Gaussian approximation for $p(E|f)$ breaks down for small λ, in which case it would be necessary to expand the noise in terms of more cumulants. Results for the higher cumulants also agree with high significance, as shown in (Rattray & Shapiro, 1996).

6 CONCLUSION

A theory which describes selection on a finite population under a general stochastic fitness measure has been applied to two related problems, showing excellent predictive power. The problems considered were the one-max problem corrupted by Gaussian noise and a simple learning problem, generalization by a perceptron with binary weights. This work significantly extends the scope of a statistical mechanics formalism for describing the averaged dynamics of the GA and shows how important it is to correctly account for finite population effects.

In the limit of weak Boltzmann selection, the expressions describing the effect of selection on each fitness cumulant can be expressed analytically and we find that an increased population size removes the effects of noise in this limit. This may have important implications in learning theory, where there is often noise in fitness evaluation due to incomplete training data. Indeed, it is shown how this population sizing can be used to determine the optimal batch size in the binary perceptron problem, which minimizes computation time, as well as the total number of training examples required when independent batches are used.

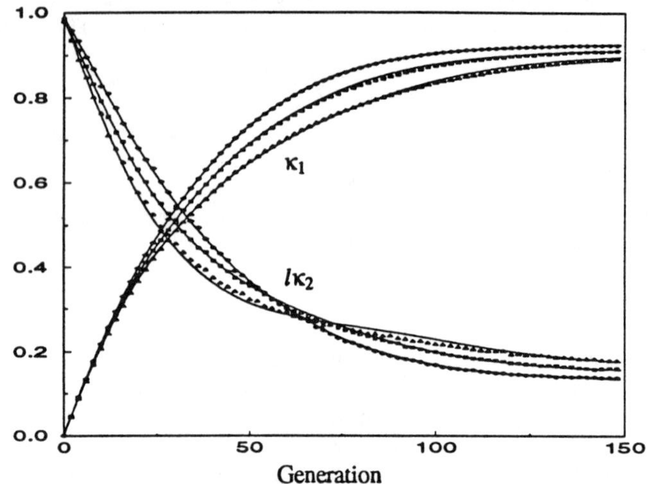

Figure 3: The theory is compared to averaged results from a GA training a binary perceptron to generalize from examples produced by a teacher perceptron. The mean and variance of the overlap distribution are shown averaged over 1000 runs, with solid lines showing theoretical predictions. The infinite training set result ($\Diamond$) is compared to results for a finite training set with $\lambda = 0.65$ ($\square$) and $\lambda = 0.39$ ($\triangle$). The other parameters were $l = 155$, $\beta_s = 0.3$, $p_m = 0.005$, $N = 80$ and bit-simulated crossover was used. Adapted from (Rattray & Shapiro, 1996).

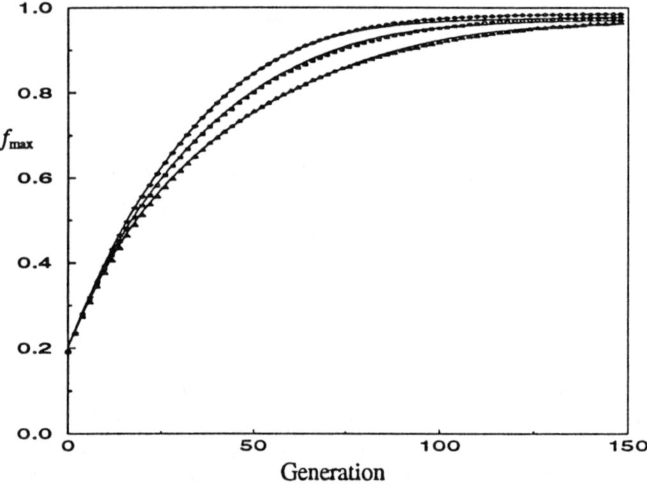

Figure 4: The maximum overlap between teacher and pupil is shown each generation, averaged over the same simulations as the results presented in figure 3. The solid lines show the theoretical predictions and symbols are as in figure 3.

Acknowledgements

We would like to thank Adam Prügel-Bennett for many helpful discussions and for providing some of the numerical code used here. We would also like to thank the anonymous reviewers for making a number of useful suggestions. MR was supported by an EPSRC award (ref. 93315524).

MAXIMUM ENTROPY DISTRIBUTION

After bit-simulated crossover the population is assumed to be at maximum entropy with constraints on the mean fitness and correlation within the population. This is a special case of the result derived in (Prügel-Bennett & Shapiro, 1995) for the paramagnet and this discussion follows theirs closely.

Let τ_i be the mean allele at site i within the population,

$$\tau_i = \langle S_i^\alpha \rangle_\alpha = \frac{1}{N} \sum_{\alpha=1}^{N} S_i^\alpha. \tag{53}$$

To calculate the distribution of this quantity over sites one imposes constraints on the mean overlap and correlation with Lagrange multipliers x and z,

$$zNK_1 \;=\; z \sum_{\alpha=1}^{N} \sum_{i=1}^{l} S_i^\alpha = zN \sum_{i=1}^{l} \tau_i \tag{54a}$$

$$\tfrac{1}{2}(xN)^2 q \;=\; \frac{x^2}{2l} \sum_{\alpha=1}^{N} \sum_{\beta=1}^{N} \sum_{i=1}^{l} S_i^\alpha S_i^\beta = \frac{(xN)^2}{2l} \sum_{i=1}^{l} \tau_i^2. \tag{54b}$$

The correlation expression is for large N and finite population corrections can be included retrospectively.

Without constraints, the fraction of allele configurations which are compatible with mean allele τ_i is given by a binomial coefficient,

$$\Omega(\tau_i) = \frac{1}{2^N} \binom{N}{N(1+\tau_i)/2}. \tag{55}$$

One can then define an entropy,

$$S(\tau_i) = \log[\Omega(\tau_i)] \sim -\frac{N}{2} \log(1 - \tau_i^2) + \frac{N\tau_i}{2} \log\left(\frac{1-\tau_i}{1+\tau_i}\right), \tag{56}$$

where Stirling's approximation has been used. The probability distribution for allele configurations decouples at each site,

$$p(\{\tau_i\}) = \prod_{i=1}^{l} p(\tau_i) = \prod_{i=1}^{l} \exp[S(\tau_i) + zN\tau_i + (xN\tau_i)^2/2]. \tag{57}$$

A Gaussian integral removes the square in the exponent,

$$p(\tau_i) = \int \frac{d\eta_i}{\sqrt{2\pi}} \exp\left(\frac{-\eta_i^2}{2} + NG(\tau_i, \eta_i)\right); \quad G(\tau_i, \eta_i) = S(\tau_i)/N + z\tau_i + x\eta_i\tau_i. \tag{58}$$

The maximal value of G with respect to τ_i gives the maximum entropy distribution for τ_i at each site,

$$\tau_i = \tanh(z + x\eta_i), \tag{59}$$

where η_i is drawn from a Gaussian with zero mean and unit variance. The constraints can be used to obtain values for the Lagrange multipliers,

$$K_1 = \sum_{i=1}^{l} \overline{\tanh(z + x\eta_i)} \qquad q = \frac{1}{l}\sum_{i=1}^{l} \overline{\tanh^2(z + x\eta_i)}. \tag{60}$$

Bars denote averages over the Gaussian noise which in general must be done numerically (Gauss-Hermite quadrature was used here (Press *et al*, 1992)).

The third and fourth order terms in equations (31c) and (31d) can be found once the Lagrange multipliers have been determined,

$$\sum_{i=1}^{l} \langle S_i^\alpha \rangle_\alpha^3 = l\,\overline{\tanh^3(z + x\eta)} \qquad \sum_{i=1}^{l} \langle S_i^\alpha \rangle_\alpha^4 = l\,\overline{\tanh^4(z + x\eta)}. \tag{61}$$

Again, bars denote averages over the Gaussian noise.

References

J. E. Baker (1987) "Reducing Bias and Inefficiency in the Selection Algorithm," Proc. of the 2nd Int. Conf. on Genetic Algorithms, ed J. J. Grefenstette (Hillsdale, NJ; Lawrence Erlbaum) p 14-21.

E. B. Baum, D. Boneh and C. Garret (1995) "On Genetic Algorithms," in COLT '95: Proc. of the 8th Annual Conf. on Computational Learning Theory (New York; Assoc. for Computing Machinery Inc.) p 230–239.

T. Blickle, L. Thiele (1995) "A Comparison of Selection Schemes used in Genetic Algorithms," Computer Engineering and Communication Network Lab, Swiss Federal Institute of Technology, Gloriastrasse 35, 8092 Zurich, Switzerland TIK-Report Nr.11 Version 2.

M. De la Maza, B. Tidor (1991) "Increased Flexibility in Genetic Algorithms: The Use of Variable Boltzmann Selective Pressure to Control Propagation," Proc. of the ORSA CSTS Conference - Computer Science and Operations Research: New Developments in their Interfaces, p 425–440.

B. Derrida (1981) "Random-energy Model: An Exactly Solvable Model of Disordered Systems," Phys. Rev. **B 24**, 2613–2625.

W. J. Ewens (1979) "Mathematical Population Genetics," (Berlin; Springer-Verlag).

J. M. Fitzpatrick, J. J. Grefenstette (1988) "Genetic Algorithms in Noisy Environments," Machine Learning **3**, 101–120.

D. E. Goldberg (1989) "Genetic Algorithms in Search, Optimization and Machine Learning," (Reading, MA; Addison-Wesley).

D. E. Goldberg, K. Deb, J. H. Clark (1992) "Genetic Algorithms, Noise, and the Sizing of Populations," Complex Systems **6**, 333-362.

J. H. Holland (1975) "Adaptation in Natural and Artificial Systems," (Ann Arbor; The University of Michigan Press).

B. L. Miller, D. E. Goldberg (1995) "Genetic Algorithms, Selection Schemes and the Varying Effects of Noise," Dept. of General Engineering, University of Illinois at Urbana-Champaign, 117 Transportation Building, Urbana, IL 61801. (IlliGAL Report No. 95009).

H. Mühlenbein, D Schlierkamp-Voosen (1995) "Analysis of Selection, Mutation and Recombination in Genetic Algorithms," Lecture Notes in Computer Science **899**, 188-214.

W. H. Press, B. P. Flannery, S. A. Teukolsky, W. T. Vetterling (1992) "Numerical Recipes in C : The Art of Scientific Computing," 2nd ed. (Cambridge; Cambridge University Press).

A. Prügel-Bennett, J. L. Shapiro (1994) "An Analysis of Genetic Algorithms using Statistical Mechanics," Phys. Rev. Lett. **72**(9), 1305.

A. Prügel-Bennett, J. L. Shapiro (1995) "The Dynamics of a Genetic Algorithm for Simple Random Ising Systems," Computer Science Dept., University of Manchester, Oxford Road, Manchester M13 9PL, U.K. (to appear in Physica D).

A. Prügel-Bennett (1996) "Modelling Evolving Populations," NORDITA, Blegdamsvej 17, DK-2100 Copenhagen, Denmark, (submitted to J. Theor. Biol.).

L. M. Rattray (1995) "The Dynamics of a Genetic Algorithm under Stabilizing Selection," Complex Systems 9(3), 213–234.

L. M. Rattray (1996) "Modelling the Dynamics of Genetic Algorithms using Statistical Mechanics," Computer Science Dept., University of Manchester, Oxford Road, Manchester M13 9PL, UK (PhD. Thesis - In Preperation).

L. M. Rattray , J. L. Shapiro (1996) "The Dynamics of a Genetic Algorithm for a Simple Learning Problem," Computer Science Dept., University of Manchester, Oxford Road, Manchester M13 9PL, UK (to appear in J. Phys. A).

J. L. Shapiro, A. Prügel-Bennett, L. M. Rattray (1994) "A Statistical Mechanical Formulation of the Dynamics of Genetic Algorithms," Lecture Notes in Computer Science **865**, 17–27.

M. Srinivas, L. M. Patnaik (1995) "Binomially Distributed Populations for Modelling GAs," Proc. of the 5th Int. Conf. on Ganetic Algorithms, ed S. Forrest (San Mateo, CA; Morgan Kaufmann) p 138–145.

A. Stuart, J. K. Ord (1987) "Kendall's Advanced Theory of Statistics, Vol 1. Distribution Theory," 5th ed. (New York; Oxford University Press).

G. Syswerda (1993) "Simulated Crossover in Genetic Algorithms," in Foundations of Genetic Algorithms 2, (San Mateo, CA; Morgan Kaufmann).

D. Thierens, D. Goldberg (1995) "Convergence Models of Genetic Algorithm Selection Schemes," Parallel Problem Solving from Nature III (in Lecture Notes in Computer Science 866), 119–129.

M. D. Vose, A. H. Wright (1994) "Simple Genetic Algorithms with Linear Fitness," Evol. Comp. **2**, 347–368.

Probing Genetic Algorithm Performance
of Fitness Landscapes

Stefan Bornholdt
Institut für Theoretische Physik, Universität Kiel
Leibnizstr. 15, D-24098 Kiel, Germany
bornholdt@theo-physik.uni-kiel.de

Abstract

Fitness correlations on optimization landscapes have been proposed as performance measures of optimization algorithms. What do fitness correlations tell about genetic algorithm performance? In this paper, they are being related to dynamical models of genetic algorithms. As dynamical model a statistical mechanics approach is used based on an expansion in cumulants of the fitness distribution. Statistical measures of parent-children fitness correlation are defined, and subsequently employed to determine the model dynamics.

1   Introduction

Given an optimization problem, what is the best optimization algorithm to apply? In general, the performance of an algorithm depends on the underlying problem (Wolpert & Macready 1995). However, even for a given problem it is difficult to predict the performance of an optimization procedure.

Empirically, it has been found that fitness correlations are useful performance measures of genetic algorithms (Manderick et. al. 1991). They characterize properties of an optimization landscape in the presence of the move set of a given algorithm (Stadler 1995). Intuitively, one expects fitness correlations between parents and children to be a driving force in genetic optimization. Designing clever genetic representation schemes often means to increase the parent-children fitness correlation. In biological systems this correlation is often found to be very large.

Theoretically, the basis of genetic algorithm performance is less well understood. Various theoretical approaches, e.g., on the basis of schemata or the so-called building block hypothesis (Goldberg 1989, Mitchell et. al. 1992), feel the difficulty that lies in the dynamical nature of an evolving system. Other studies explicitly model the population dynamics of a genetic algorithm in terms of fitness properties of the population (Baum et. al. 1995, Grefenstette 1995, Prügel-Bennett & Shapiro 1994). In the following the model of Prügel-Bennett & Shapiro (1994) for finite populations will be used.

In the following, fitness correlation measures will be combined with a dynamical model of genetic algorithms in order to understand the dynamical implications of parent-children correlations. It further allows for the question whether a specific correlation measure is sufficient to describe the genetic algorithm dynamics, in which case one could run these models on measured parameters of a given problem. The vision behind this approach is to work towards a statistical probe for fitness landscapes which assists the choice of a suited optimization algorithm for a given problem.

The dynamical model considered here is motivated by statistical mechanics. The usual approach to modeling physical systems with a large number of degrees of freedom is to find a few macroscopic variables that describe the average behavior of a system (e.g., temperature for a gas of many atoms). In equilibrium systems, there are canonical procedures to describe these variables. In systems far from equilibrium, as are genetic algorithms, one can sometimes identify distributions that tend to become stationary under the dynamics. In the model of Prügel-Bennett & Shapiro (1994) the fitness distribution of the population is used as the characteristic evolving quantity. In order to get a small number of system variables, the fitness distribution is expanded in cumulants around a Gaussian distribution. When modeling the average dynamics of genetic algorithms one has to keep in mind that it does not only depend on the fitness properties of the population. Although the selection process is completely determined by the fitnesses alone, mutation and crossover effects also depend on structural properties of how they operate on the genotypes. In order to describe the dynamics in terms of a fitness distribution, these structural effects have to be averaged over and re-expressed in terms of fitnesses. In Prügel-Bennett & Shapiro (1995) this is done via a maximum entropy assumption. Here, the same type of cumulant dynamics is assumed, however, the effects of mutation and crossover are determined from statistical measures of fitness landscapes. Where necessary, a structural ("genotypic") variable is included, namely the convergence of the strings in the population. Empirically, the inclusion of a genotypic variable in the definition of fitness correlation measures proved to be useful in genetic algorithm evaluation (Jones & Forrest 1995). However, the genetic correlation used here is theoretically derived to include convergence effects in the population.

Before defining parent-children correlation measures and linking them to dynamics, an outline of the dynamical model will be given.

2   The dynamical model

The dynamics of the model is described in terms of the fitness distribution $\rho(f)$ of the population which is expressed as an expansion in cumulants. The cumulants κ_n of a distribution $\rho(f)$ are defined through

$$\ln \int_{-\infty}^{\infty} \exp(\beta f)\, \rho(f)\, df = \sum_{n=1}^{\infty} \frac{\kappa_n \beta^n}{n!} \tag{1}$$

such that

$$\kappa_n = \frac{\partial^n}{\partial \beta^n} \left[\ln \int_{-\infty}^{\infty} \exp(\beta f)\rho(f)df \right] \Bigg|_{\beta=0} \tag{2}$$

The first four cumulants of a fitness distribution $\rho(f)$ are then

$$\begin{aligned}
\kappa_1 &= \langle f \rangle \\
\kappa_2 &= \langle f^2 \rangle - \kappa_1^2 \\
\kappa_3 &= \langle (f - \kappa_1)^3 \rangle \\
\kappa_4 &= \langle (f - \kappa_1)^4 \rangle - 3\kappa_2^2.
\end{aligned} \tag{3}$$

They represent the mean, variance, skew, and curtosis of the fitness distribution. To give an intuitive picture, the first two cumulants roughly capture the infinite population size limit of the model. The higher cumulants, skew and curtosis, are important to describe the dynamics of a finite population where, e.g., selection lets the fitness distribution quickly become skewed and thus deviate from a Gaussian. An evolving population can, at each time step, be approximated by a set of these variables. Its dynamics can then be viewed in terms of the evolution of the cumulants. In the following, the dynamics of an evolving population will be modeled using a truncated expansion in the first four cumulants. The different operations of a genetic algorithm, selection, mutation, and crossover, interact in different ways with this representation.

Consider first the - from this viewpoint - simplest operator: selection. Its dynamics is solely determined by the fitness distribution of the population. Here, Boltzmann selection is considered in a population of P strings with fitnesses f_α and $\alpha = 1, \ldots, P$. A member with fitness f_α is chosen from the population with the probability

$$p_\alpha = \frac{e^{\beta f_\alpha}}{Z}, \quad Z = \sum_{\alpha=1}^{P} e^{\beta f_\alpha} \tag{4}$$

where β parametrizes the strength of selection. After selection, the cumulants are given by

$$\kappa_n^s = \frac{\partial^n}{\partial \beta^n} < \log Z >_\rho \tag{5}$$

where the average is taken over all possible populations with individual fitnesses such that $\rho(f)$ is satisfied. This expression can be solved similarly to the solution of the random energy model (Derrida 1984), as shown in Prügel-Bennett & Shapiro (1995). One obtains the cumulants after selection as functions of the cumulants before selection, either by means of numerical integrals or, in the limit of small selection (small β), as

$$\begin{aligned}
\kappa_1^s &= \kappa_1 + \beta\left(1 - \frac{1}{P}\right)\kappa_2 + \frac{\beta^2}{2}\left(1 - \frac{3}{P}\right)\kappa_3 + \frac{\beta^3}{6}\left[\left(1 - \frac{7}{P}\right)\kappa_4 - \frac{6}{P}\kappa_2^2\right] + \ldots \\
\kappa_2^s &= \left(1 - \frac{1}{P}\right)\kappa_2 + \beta\left(1 - \frac{3}{P}\right)\kappa_3 + \frac{\beta^2}{2}\left[\left(1 - \frac{7}{P}\right)\kappa_4 - \frac{6}{P}\kappa_2^2\right] + \ldots \\
\kappa_3^s &= \left(1 - \frac{3}{P}\right)\kappa_3 + \beta\left[\left(1 - \frac{7}{P}\right)\kappa_4 - \frac{6}{P}\kappa_2^2\right] + \ldots \\
\kappa_4^s &= \left[\left(1 - \frac{7}{P}\right)\kappa_4 - \frac{6}{P}\kappa_2^2\right] + \ldots .
\end{aligned} \tag{6}$$

When truncating the expansion after the fourth cumulant, a closed expression is obtained which can be iterated to give the evolution of the population under selection. Furthermore, using the rescaled selection parameter

$$\beta = \beta_s \sqrt{\frac{2\ln P}{\kappa_2}} \tag{7}$$

with fixed β_s makes selection independent of absolute fitness values. The cumulants after selection have been derived under the assumption as in Prügel-Bennett & Shapiro (1995) of drawing the new population from a continuous fitness distribution. Only the dominant finite-population-effect is kept which comes from the stochastic sampling of the new population in the selection step.

3 Dynamics from correlation measures

One can now express the effects of mutation via cumulants in the same manner. The average cumulants after mutation κ_n^m can be obtained by averaging over fitness values and mutation events of random mutants f^m. For the first two this is

$$\begin{aligned}
\kappa_1^m &= \left\langle \langle f^m \rangle_{\mathcal{P}} \right\rangle_{mut} \\
\kappa_2^m &= \left\langle \langle (f^m)^2 \rangle_{\mathcal{P}} - \langle f^m \rangle_{\mathcal{P}}^2 \right\rangle_{mut}.
\end{aligned} \tag{8}$$

where $\langle \ldots \rangle_{\mathcal{P}}$ denotes the average over the population and $\langle \ldots \rangle_{mut}$ the average over all possible mutation events. Let us neglect finite-population-effects in the mutation step which are much smaller than the one considered for selection. Then, for all following purposes, the members of the population can be considered as independent and the population average simplifies to

$$\langle f \rangle_{\mathcal{P}} = \left(\prod_{\alpha=1}^{P} \int_{-\infty}^{\infty} \rho(f_\alpha)\, df_\alpha \right) \frac{1}{P} \sum_{\alpha=1}^{P} f_\alpha = \int_{-\infty}^{\infty} f\, \rho(f)\, df \tag{9}$$

and similar expressions for higher terms. Evaluating the mutation cumulants, one finds that they do not always depend on the pure cumulants before selection. In general, the dynamics also depends on properties of the genetic coding, since mutation directly acts on the genome. The same is true for crossover. If the fitness distribution is all one knows about a population, one has to make additional assumptions at this point. In the original model (Prügel-Bennett & Shapiro 1994), it is postulated that all structural quantities occurring in the calculation assume their most likely values, given the known fitness distribution. This requires detailed knowledge about the fitness function and an involved averaging step. Here, in contrast, one derives the mutation cumulants from a model for a "microscopic" mutation event based on the assumption that a main driving force of population dynamics is the parent-child fitness correlation. The input of the model is the fitness correlation of mutation applied to the landscape which can be calculated for simple functions or measured from more complex fitness landscapes. Effects of the mutation procedure as well as properties of the genetic encoding are contained in these parameters.

In the following, let us derive the statistics of an evolving population from the micro-statistics of single mutation and crossover events applied to a specific fitness landscape.

Applying mutation to a member α of the population with initial fitness f_α, the resulting member will in general have a different fitness value f_α^m. For example, taking a member coding for a very short Traveling Salesman Tour, its child is likely to be a much longer tour unless encoding and mutation operation are well chosen. In the first case, the child will not do much better that a random tour, while in the latter case its fitness will be close to the parent's fitness. The case of maximum correlation $f_\alpha^m = f_\alpha$ is where mutation does not affect the fitness of the child at all. It has a post-mutation probability distribution $\rho(f_\alpha^m | f_\alpha) = \delta(f_\alpha^m - f_\alpha)$. For the other extreme, where mutation equals a random change in fitness, the conditional probability density $\rho(f_\alpha^m | f_\alpha)$ is given by the fitness distribution of a *random* population $\rho^0(f_\alpha^m)$. Let us parametrize the possible correlations in the range of these two extremes by approximating the fitness distribution of the child as

$$\rho(f_\alpha^m | f_\alpha) = m \, \delta(f_\alpha^m - f_\alpha) + (1 - m) \, \rho^0(f_\alpha^m) \tag{10}$$

with

$$\rho^0(f) = \frac{1}{\sqrt{2\pi\kappa_2^0}} \, exp\left(-\frac{(f - \kappa_1^0)^2}{2\kappa_2^0}\right). \tag{11}$$

Here, κ_1^0 and κ_2^0 are the cumulants of the initial distribution. In this way, the degree of correlation between parent and child under mutation is parametrized by m. The choice of the two distributions is natural since in general ρ^0 is the fixpoint distribution of the mutation operator. In the case of a single mutation event one can interpret m as the probability for the mutant to be of the high correlation type and similarly $(1 - m)$ as the probability to be a weakly correlated mutant. For this model, the total fitness distribution of the children population is given by

$$\rho_m(f_\alpha^m) - \int_{-\infty}^{\infty} \rho(f_\alpha^m | f) \, \rho(f) \, df \tag{12}$$

whose first four cumulants are

$$\begin{aligned}
\kappa_1^m &= m \, \kappa_1 + (1 - m) \, \kappa_1^0 \\
\kappa_2^m &= m \, \kappa_2 + (1 - m) \, \kappa_2^0 + m(1 - m) \, (\kappa_1 - \kappa_1^0)^2 \\
\kappa_3^m &= m \, \left(\kappa_3 + 3\kappa_1\kappa_2 + \kappa_1^3\right) + (1 - m) \, \left(3\kappa_1^0\kappa_2^0 + (\kappa_1^0)^3\right) - 3\kappa_1^m\kappa_2^m - (\kappa_1^m)^3 \\
\kappa_4^m &= m \, \left(\kappa_4 + 4\kappa_1\kappa_3 + 3\kappa_2^2 + 6\kappa_2\kappa_1^2 + \kappa_1^4\right) + (1 - m) \, \left(3(\kappa_2^0)^2 + 6\kappa_2^0(\kappa_1^0)^2 + (\kappa_1^0)^4\right) \\
&\quad - 4\kappa_3^m\kappa_1^m - 3(\kappa_2^m)^2 - 6\kappa_2^m(\kappa_1^m)^2 - (\kappa_1^m)^4.
\end{aligned} \tag{13}$$

This set of four equations defines a closed expression for the fitness distribution of the population after mutation as a function of the distribution prior to mutation. It will serve as an iteration step in describing the complete dynamics.

A similar formulation can be set up for crossover. In that case, one has to consider two parents for an individual crossover event yielding two possible children. The basic parameters that are used to define an event are the fitnesses of the parents f_α and f_β, those of the two children f_α^c and f_β^c, as well as the parameters of the fitness distribution of a random population defined through κ_1^0 and κ_2^0. Applying crossover, the resulting offspring will in general have different fitness values f_α^c and f_β^c. Again using the above example, taking two parents each coding a short Traveling Salesman Tour, their child will most probably encode a much longer tour than either of the parents unless the encoding and crossover operation are very special. In the first case, the child will perform similar to a random tour, while in the second case its fitness will resemble the parents. These different regimes are parametrized by a correlation coefficient c as follows. A neutral crossover event, where the fitness of a child equals the fitness of one of its parents, is characterized by a conditional probability density with $\rho(f_\alpha^c|f_\alpha, f_\beta) = \delta(f_\alpha^c - f_\alpha)$ and a maximum correlation parameter $c = 1$ (corresponding to m in the case of mutation). In the opposite case, one has $\rho(f_\alpha^c|f_\alpha, f_\beta) = \rho^0(f_\alpha^c)$ if there is no correlation at all ($c = 0$). In analogy to the mutation case, the probability distribution of an individual crossover event is written as

$$\rho(f_\alpha^c|f_\alpha, f_\beta) = \frac{c}{2} \left[\delta(f_\alpha^c - f_\alpha) + \delta(f_\alpha^c - f_\beta)\right] + (1 - c)\, \rho^0(f_\alpha^c). \tag{14}$$

Again, it can be interpreted in terms of probability densities governing single crossover events. Clearly, more complicated models with a larger number of degrees of freedom are possible (and may be more powerful). In particular, events of intermediate correlation could be included. The correlation between a child and its two parents may even be asymmetric. However, here let us concentrate on this simple model with one free parameter c. When deriving statistical quantities from this distribution by averaging over both parents, the result is symmetric in f_α and f_β. The total distribution of the children fitnesses

$$\rho_c(f_\alpha^c) = \int\limits_{-\infty}^{\infty} \int\limits_{-\infty}^{\infty} \rho(f_\alpha^c|f, g)\, \rho(g)\, \rho(f)\, dg\, df \tag{15}$$

is given by cumulants defined exactly as in the case of mutation (13) with c replacing m.

In practical cases, when only some fraction of the members underlies the genetic operators during each step, diluted equations have to be defined. They have to include the probabilities p_m for mutation and p_c for crossover to happen to each member during one time step. The true probability distribution ρ_{p_m} after mutation then includes a part of the unaltered population

$$\rho_{p_m}(f) \quad = \quad p_m\, \rho_m(f) + (1 - p_m)\, \rho(f). \tag{16}$$

The cumulants for this distribution are

$$\begin{aligned}
\kappa_1^{p_m} &= p_m\, \kappa_1^m + (1 - p_m)\, \kappa_1 \\
\kappa_2^{p_m} &= p_m\, \kappa_2^m + p_m(1 - p_m)\, (\kappa_1^m - \kappa_1)^2 + (1 - p_m)\, \kappa_2 \\
\kappa_3^{p_m} &= p_m\, \kappa_3^m + (1 - p_m)\, \kappa_3 + 3\, p_m(1 - p_m)\, (\kappa_1^m - \kappa_1)(\kappa_2^m - \kappa_2) \\
&\quad + p_m(1 - p_m)(1 - 2p_m)\, (\kappa_1^m - \kappa_1)^3 \\
\kappa_4^{p_m} &= -6\, \left(p_m\, \kappa_1^m + (1 - p_m)\, \kappa_1\right)^4 \\
&\quad +12\, \left(p_m\, \kappa_1^m + (1 - p_m)\, \kappa_1\right)^2 \left(p_m\, \left((\kappa_1^m)^2 + \kappa_2^m\right) + (1 - p_m)\, \left(\kappa_1^2 + \kappa_2\right)\right) \\
&\quad -3\, \left(p_m\, \left((\kappa_1^m)^2 + \kappa_2^m\right) + (1 - p_m)\, \left(\kappa_1^2 + \kappa_2\right)\right)^2 \\
&\quad -4\, \left(p_m\, \kappa_1^m + (1 - p_m)\, \kappa_1\right) \left(p_m\, \left((\kappa_1^m)^3 + 3\kappa_1^m\kappa_2^m + \kappa_3^m\right)\right. \\
&\quad \left. +(1 - p_m)\, \left(\kappa_1^3 + 3\kappa_1\kappa_2 + \kappa_3\right)\right) \\
&\quad +p_m\, \left((\kappa_1^m)^4 + 6(\kappa_1^m)^2\kappa_2^m + 3(\kappa_2^m)^2 + 4\kappa_3^m\kappa_1^m + \kappa_4^m\right) \\
&\quad +(1 - p_m)\, \left((\kappa_1)^4 + 6(\kappa_1)^2\kappa_2 + 3\kappa_2^2 + 4\kappa_3\kappa_1 + \kappa_4\right)
\end{aligned} \tag{17}$$

and similarly for crossover. Together with the sets of cumulants from selection κ_n^s, mutation κ_n^m, and crossover κ_n^c, they define the iteration step of one "generation", where the operations are applied in this order.

4 Measuring correlations

In order to apply the evolution equations obtained so far to a given fitness landscape, one has to determine the model parameters m and c for mutation and crossover on that landscape. Here, some suitable statistical quantities are defined to *measure* them for a given function. With the distribution (10) in mind let us define the parent-children fitness correlation coefficient c^m by

$$c^m = \langle f_\alpha f_\alpha^m \rangle_{\alpha,mut} - \langle f_\alpha \rangle_\alpha \langle f_\alpha^m \rangle_{\alpha,mut} . \tag{18}$$

Averaging over parent fitnesses and all possible mutations involves the distribution $\rho(f_\alpha, f_\alpha^m) = \rho(f_\alpha^m | f_\alpha)\rho(f_\alpha)$ and one obtains

$$c^m = m\,\kappa_2 \tag{19}$$

which makes m measurable via the correlation c_m.

In order to approximate the effect of crossover by this formalism, one can use a measured crossover coefficient c. This can be done in the same way by sampling crossover events on random representatives of a landscape. One can define the following two correlation measures for a crossover event with parents f_α and f_β and children f_α^c and f_β^c:

$$\begin{aligned} c^c &= \langle f_\alpha f_\alpha^c \rangle_{\alpha,\beta,cross} - \langle f_\alpha \rangle_\alpha \langle f_\alpha^c \rangle_{\alpha,\beta,cross} \\ c^x &= \langle f_\beta f_\alpha^c \rangle_{\alpha,\beta,cross} - \langle f_\beta \rangle_\beta \langle f_\alpha^c \rangle_{\alpha,\beta,cross} . \end{aligned} \tag{20}$$

The averaging over the distribution $\rho(f_\alpha^c, f, g) = \rho(f_\alpha^c | f, g)\rho(f)\rho(g)$ yields the coefficients

$$c^c = c^x = \frac{c\,\kappa_2}{2} \tag{21}$$

and the crossover parameter c is given by the symmetrized measure

$$c = \frac{c^c + c^x}{\kappa_2}. \tag{22}$$

5 Fitness correlation and population dynamics

Now everything is prepared to test how well the above assumptions hold. Before actually running simulations with the iterated equations, it is instructive to look at two analytically tractable models in this formalism. The first problem is the simplest additive fitness, a random field paramagnet

$$f_\alpha = \sum_{i=1}^{N} J_i\, S_i^\alpha \tag{23}$$

with random couplings J_i taken from a Gaussian distribution with mean 0 and variance 1. The N sites S_i^α with $i = 1, \dots, N$ and $S_i^\alpha = \pm 1$ form the genetic string of the member α of the population. The second function will be the NK-model fitness (Kauffman & Weinberger 1989)

$$f_\alpha = \sum_{i=1}^{N} E_i(S_i^\alpha; S_{i_1}^\alpha, \ldots, S_{i_K}^\alpha) \tag{24}$$

with 2^{K+1} random energy values E_i drawn from a uniform distribution over the interval $[0, 1]$ and randomly chosen sites i_1 to i_K, both for each i. For these functions, let us derive the correlation constants under mutation and crossover.

For the paramagnet, the fitness of a mutated member can be written as

$$f_\alpha^m = \sum_{i=1}^{N} J_i \, S_i^\alpha \sigma_i^\alpha \tag{25}$$

where mutation has been introduced by a random variable $\sigma_i^\alpha = -1$ with probability γ and $\sigma_i^\alpha = 1$ with probability $1 - \gamma$. Inserting this into (18) and calculating the averages for an arbitrary, finite population one obtains

$$m = 1 - 2\gamma. \tag{26}$$

Thus, in this case of a purely additive fitness function, m only depends on the Bit mutation rate γ. Influences of the population size P and convergence effects in the course of evolution drop out due to the special form of the function. In this case, one expects the fitness correlation of a landscape, expressed in terms of m, to be a reasonable measure for the expected evolution of a population. In similar fashion, the crossover correlation can be derived. Write the fitness of a child produced by crossover as

$$f_\alpha^c = \sum_{i=1}^{N} J_i \left[S_i^\beta \xi_i^\alpha + S_i^\alpha (1 - \xi_i^\alpha) \right]. \tag{27}$$

Here, a random variable for each site describes uniform crossover where $\xi_i^\alpha = 1$ with probability a and $\xi_i^\alpha = 0$ with probability $1 - a$. Inserting this into (20), the averaging over all possible crossover events can be done

$$\begin{aligned}
c^c + c^z &= \frac{1}{P(P-1)} \sum_{\alpha=1}^{P} \sum_{\beta=1; \beta \neq \alpha}^{P} (f_\alpha + f_\beta)\left[(1-a)f_\alpha + a\, f_\beta\right] \\
&\quad - \frac{2}{P} \sum_{\gamma=1}^{P} f_\gamma \frac{1}{P(P-1)} \sum_{\alpha=1}^{P} \sum_{\beta=1; \beta \neq \alpha}^{P} \left[(1-a)f_\alpha + a\, f_\beta\right]
\end{aligned} \tag{28}$$

and with (22) one obtains for the crossover correlation

$$c = 1 - \frac{1}{P-1}. \tag{29}$$

The dependence on the population size P follows from drawing the two parents from a finite population. Since the model describes average fitness properties of the population and the fitness function is purely additive, it is not surprising that crossover averages away here (apart from the sampling effect in finite populations). Thus, for the additive fitness, both, m and c do not depend on fitness or convergence properties of the population.

How does this compare to a fitness function with many local minima? Let us choose the NK-model fitness function (24) and derive the correlation coefficients in the same manner. The fitness of a mutated string is obtained by writing down (24) with each site S_i^α multiplied by a random $\sigma = \pm 1$. The energy of a single E_i changes to an unpredictable value if at least one of the sites is changed and remains constant otherwise. The average fitness of a string after mutation can then be approximated by

$$\langle f_\alpha^m \rangle_{mut} = \sum_{i=1}^{N} \left(E_i(\vec{S}^\alpha)\,(1-\gamma)^{K+1} + \frac{1}{2}\left[1-(1-\gamma)^{K+1}\right] \right) \tag{30}$$

where $\vec{S}^\alpha$ is the Bit string configuration before mutation. In the same way one evaluates (18) and obtains

$$m = (1-\gamma)^{K+1}. \tag{31}$$

Again, this coefficient is independent of fitness properties of the population. In order to include crossover, let us write the fitness of a child averaged over all possible crossover events as

$$
\begin{aligned}
\langle f_\alpha^c \rangle_{cross} = {} & \sum_{n=0}^{K+1} \binom{K+1}{n} a^n\,(1-a)^{K+1-n} \sum_{i=1}^{N} \left\{ \frac{1}{2}\left[E_i(\vec{S}^\alpha) + E_i(\vec{S}^\beta)\right] q^{K+1} \right. \\
& + E_i(\vec{S}^\alpha)\,q^n\left(1-q^{K+1-n}\right) + E_i(\vec{S}^\beta)\,q^{K+1-n}\left(1-q^n\right) \\
& + \left. \frac{1}{2}\left(1-q^n\right)\left(1-q^{K+1-n}\right) \right\}.
\end{aligned}
\tag{32}
$$

Here, n denotes the number of sites swapped between the arguments of one corresponding energy term E_i of the parents. The sum is followed by the probability of exactly n swapped sites in a set of $K+1$ sites relevant for each energy term. The last term is the average energy of the child, where q is the average probability that two random sites S_i^α and S_i^β are equal in the population. Writing the remaining terms of (20) in the same spirit and averaging over the two parents in a finite population one obtains

$$c = \left(1 - \frac{1}{P-1}\right)\left[(1+a(q-1))^{K+1} + (q-a(q-1))^{K+1} - q^{K+1}\right]. \tag{33}$$

For symmetric crossover with $a = 0.5$ used here, and for an initial average correlation $q = 0.5$ one observes that c sharply decreases with increasing complexity (increasing K) of the landscape. On the other hand, via q it depends on the degree of correlation in the population and will approach unity for a converging population. In this case, c, if measured from an isolated fitness function, is a rather indirect measure of the population dynamics under crossover and has to be corrected for convergence effects in the population.

6 Numerical studies

In the following, numerical evidence is given for the dynamics of the discussed test problems under a genetic algorithm and compared to the above model. The simulation results are averaged over 10000 runs of a genetic algorithm with population size $P = 50$ and selection strength $\beta_s = 0.01$ (with a newly selected random fitness function for each run). The size of the genetic string is $N = 128$ sites and the mutation probability for each site is $\gamma = 1/2N$.

In Fig. 1, the iterated cumulant expansion is compared to the dynamics of a genetic algorithm for the random field paramagnet with selection and mutation ($p_m = 1, p_c = 0$). The solid curves show mean and variance of the genetic algorithm fitness distribution.

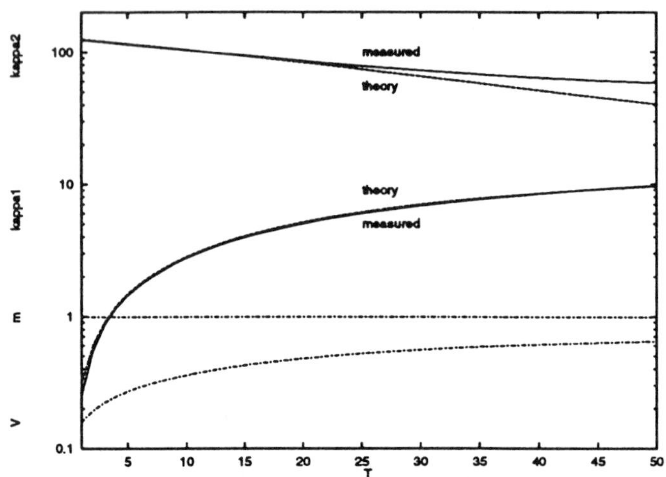

Figure 1: Measured and predicted evolution of κ_1 and κ_2 for a paramagnet fitness under selection and mutation. Below, the average fitness correlation m and the average convergence V of the population are shown during the course of evolution.

The evolution of mean and variance of the fitness is well approximated by the theoretical approach. The theoretical curves are based on $m = 0.9922$ measured from 10^6 test points. Thus, this is a prediction based on measurements. The measured value of the average fitness correlation m coincides with (26). On the bottom, m as measured over the course of evolution of the genetic algorithm runs is shown and proves to be invariant, in agreement with the theoretical expectation. The remaining curve shows the degree of convergence V in the population defined by

$$V = \frac{1}{N} \sum_{i=1}^{N} \left| \frac{1}{P} \sum_{\alpha=1}^{P} S_i^\alpha \right|. \tag{34}$$

It considerably changes over time without affecting the fitness correlation m. The chosen initial values for the iteration of the cumulants are those of a Gaussian with variance $\kappa_2^0 = 128$. Including corrections for finite string length N does not change the basic picture here. Note that continuous distributions are used for the modeling of mutation and crossover. Therefore one has to use the infinite population size limit values for the initial cumulants and correlation coefficients.

Adding crossover to the previous simulation ($p_c = 1, p_m = 1$), the modeling based on parent-children fitness correlations is shown in Fig. 2. Crossover has been defined to be uniform, where each site is swapped with probability $a = 0.5$ between the parents and both resulting

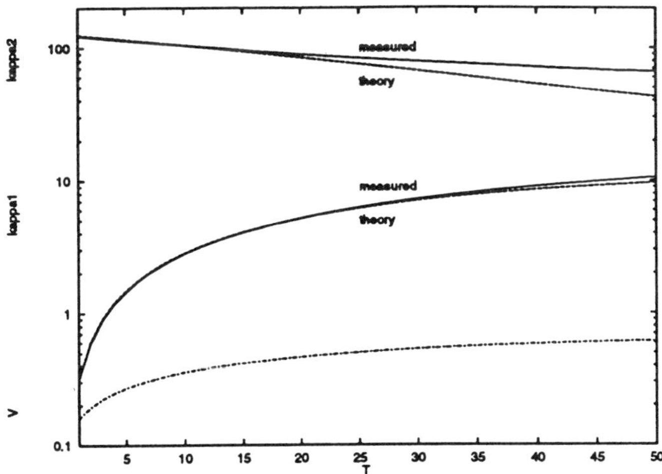

Figure 2: Measured and predicted evolution of κ_1 and κ_2 for the paramagnet fitness under selection, mutation, and crossover. Below, again the measured average convergence V.

children are taken. Here, the model uses the theoretical value of $c = 1$ while the remaining parameters of the simulations and the model are chosen as above. Note, that the maximum number of generations used in the model is limited by the accuracy of the expansion in cumulants.

In Fig. 3, the evolution of the NK-model fitness distribution for selection and mutation is shown. Here, the solid curves show the mean and variance of the measured genetic algorithm fitness distribution. The initial cumulants are chosen as above to match a Gaussian, here with the average initial values of the NK-landscape $\kappa_1^0 = 64$ and $\kappa_2^0 = 10.67$. The correlation is $m = 0.9656$ from a measurement of 10^6 test points of random functions and coincides with (31). All other parameters are chosen as in the previous case. For the plot, κ_1 is depicted as $\kappa_1 - \kappa_1^0$.

Finally, in Fig. 4 the evolution of the NK-model fitness distribution for selection and crossover is shown using a selection strength $\beta_s = 0.02$ (again, $\kappa_1 - \kappa_1^0$ is plotted). Here, the naive approach of using the theoretical prediction for the initial crossover parent-children fitness correlation c as a (constant) measure for the genetic algorithm dynamics fails (lower dot-dashed curve). As seen above, the convergence of the genotypes in the population enters in the dynamic equations. A better estimate is obtained using a time varying correlation $c(t)$. Since the convergence properties of the population are not described by the above model, the measured average convergence V over time is used which is available from the genetic algorithm runs that produced the solid curves. From this, $c(t)$ can be estimated via (33) which leads to an improved model. However, this can at most be considered a rough estimate. The correlation has to be included as a full dynamical variable for an accurate treatment.

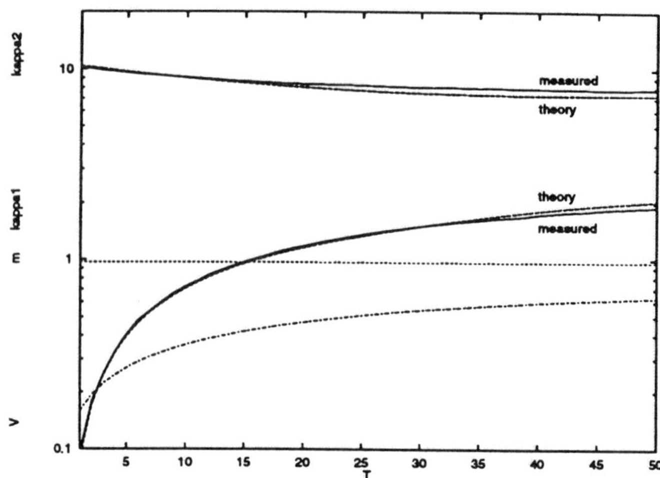

Figure 3: Measured and predicted evolution of $\kappa_1 - \kappa_1^0$ and κ_2 for the NK-model fitness under selection and mutation. Below, the fitness correlation m and the average convergence V of the population.

7 Summary

In this paper a theoretical understanding is obtained of the common intuition that the fitness correlation between parents and children is a measure for the convergence properties of genetic algorithms. On the basis of such correlation measures, a model for a microscopic mutation and crossover event has been postulated. This model is used as an input for a dynamical formalism of genetic algorithms based on statistical mechanics (Prügel-Bennett & Shapiro 1994). For two test functions, an additive, random field paramagnet fitness and the NK-model fitness, the correlation measures have been derived which determine the model dynamics. It has been found that in the case of the purely additive fitness function, the correlation measures do not depend on fitness or convergence properties of the population. In this case, the fitness correlations of a landscape showed to be measures of the expected evolution of a population under mutation as well as crossover. The same is true for the NK-model under mutation and selection. For crossover, however, the NK-model fitness correlation depends on the degree of convergence in the population and thus on the course of evolution. In that case, the correlation measure has to be corrected for convergence effects.

A second goal was to link fitness correlation measures, which are often used as empirical measures for genetic algorithm performance, to dynamical models of genetic algorithms. For the above functions one can thus obtain statistically measured predictions for genetic algorithm performance, which, under the caution of the above results, may be a useful approach for other fitness landscapes.

Possible extensions include multiple variables, pheno- or genotypic, where these one-dimensional models are too crude. In general, for each time step, the dynamical model employed here has to predict four cumulants after the genetic operation as a function of

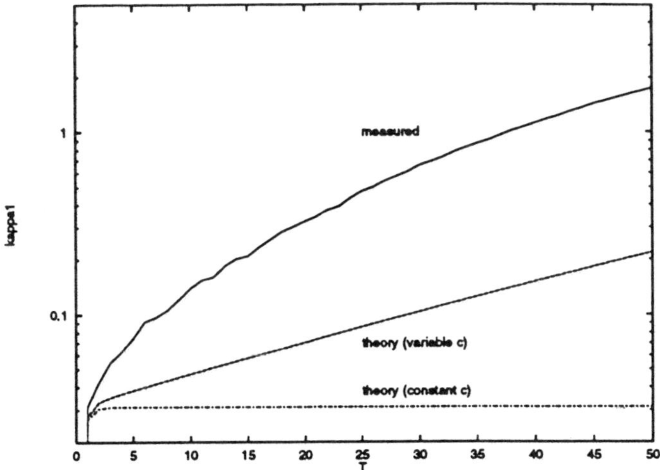

Figure 4: Measured and predicted evolution of $\kappa_1 - \kappa_1^0$ for the NK-model fitness under selection and crossover. Below, the horizontal line is the model according to the (wrong) assumption of a constant fitness correlation c, the middle curve uses a time varying $c(t)$ corrected according to (33) based on q measured during the genetic algorithm simulations.

four variables before. For the functions studied here, however, a working one-parameter approximation to this problem has been defined.

References

D.H. Wolpert and W.G. Macready. (1995) No free-lunch theorems for search. Santa Fe Institute working paper 95-02-010.

B. Manderick, M. de Weger, and P. Spiessens. (1991) The genetic algorithm and the structure of the fitness landscape. In R.K. Belew and L.B. Booker (eds.), *Proceedings of the Fourth International Conference on Genetic Algorithms*. San Mateo, CA: Morgan Kaufmann.

P.F. Stadler. (1995) Towards a theory of landscapes. In R. Lopez-Pena et. al. (eds.), *Complex systems and binary networks*. Berlin: Springer Verlag.

D.E. Goldberg. (1989) Genetic algorithms and Walsh functions. *Complex Systems* 3:129-171.

M. Mitchell, S. Forrest, and J.H. Holland. (1992) The royal road for genetic algorithms: Fitness landscapes and GA performance. In *Proceedings of the First European Conference on Artificial Life*. Cambridge, MA: MIT Press.

E. B. Baum, D. Boneh, and C. Garrett. (1995) On genetic algorithms. In *Proceedings of the 8th Annual Conference on Computational Learning Theory*. New York: ACM Press.

J. J. Grefenstette. (1995) Predictive models using fitness distributions of genetic operators. In D. Whitley (ed.), *Foundations of Genetic Algorithms 3*. San Mateo CA: Morgan

Kaufmann.

A. Prügel-Bennett and J.L. Shapiro. (1994) An analysis of genetic algorithms using statistical mechanics, *Physical Review Letters* **72**:1305.

A. Prügel-Bennett and J.L. Shapiro. (1995) The dynamics of a genetic algorithm for simple random Ising systems. University of Manchester preprint and to be published in *Physica D*.

T. Jones and S. Forrest. (1995) Fitness distance correlation as a measure of problem difficulty for genetic algorithms. In L.J. Eshelman (ed.), *Proceedings of the Sixth International Conference on Genetic Algorithms*. San Mateo CA: Morgan Kauffmann.

B. Derrida. (1984) Random-energy model: An exactly solvable model of disordered systems. *Physical Review* **B 24**:2613.

S. Kauffman and E. Weinberger. (1989) The N-k model of rugged fitness landscapes and its application to maturation of the immune response. *Journal of Theoretical Biology* **141**:211.

Replicators, Majorization and Genetic Algorithms: New Models and Analytical tools

Anil Menon[†]   Kishan Mehrotra[†]   Chilukuri K. Mohan[†]   Sanjay Ranka[*]

Abstract

This paper advocates the use of replicator selection models and quadratic crossover models for the analysis of evolutionary algorithms. We establish two sets of results. The first is a global optimization theorem for replicator systems that allows replicator fitnesses to vary, depending on the replicator proportions. The second set of results establishes a strong connection between evolutionary algorithms and majorization theory, using replicator models as a bridge. Specifically, we establish sufficient conditions for replicator selection and crossover models to implement the majorization ordering. The connection with majorization theory suggests new selection and crossover operators, new convergence results and significant theoretical gains such as generalization of previous results on quadratic dynamical systems. Quantities such as relative entropy are known to increase in quadratic crossover models; majorization results are used to derive bounds on the increase.

1   Introduction

It has long been observed that diversity is the engine that drives evolutionary systems (Hutchinson 1965). However, the nature of this engine is ill-understood, and current theory provides neither a proscriptive (what cannot be done), prescriptive (what should be done) nor prospective (what may be done) view on the scope of evolutionary algorithms. This lack of understanding has hampered applications as well as analyses. In response to this issue, several models have been proposed including Markov models (Nix and Vose 1992), functional analysis (Vose 1993), schema analysis (Holland 1975), and models based on mathematical

[†]Dept. of Electrical Engineering and Computer Science, 2–120 Center for Science and Technology, Syracuse University, Syracuse NY 13244-4100, Phone: (315) 443-2368, FAX: (315) 443-1122, {armenon,kishan,mohan}@top.cis.syr.edu. Address all queries to second author.
[*]Dept. of Computer Science, CSE Bldg. #301, University of Florida, Gainesville, FL 32611, Phone: (352) 392-1526, ranka@cis.ufl.edu.

genetics (Altenberg 1994). A fundamental difficulty is deciding upon the right level of abstraction: how much detail needs to be incorporated to render a model useful, and how much needs to be thrown away to make it tractable? We propose *replicator models* as a solution to this problem, since they offer a level of abstraction that makes them ideal for analyzing the behavior of evolutionary algorithms.

Replicator models are first order non-linear differential systems capable of modeling the effects of selection as well as crossover. The study of the simple pendulum was pivotal in understanding dynamic physical systems; analogously, replicators hold the promise of serving as the "pendulum" of evolutionary algorithms. Our optimism regarding replicator models is based on the following considerations.

1. In many respects, a replicator model is the *simplest* complex system of equations capturing the dynamics of a group of competing and co-operating units. Examples include certain neural networks (Cohen and Grossberg 1993), socio-biological models (Schuster, Sigmund, Hofbauer, and Wolff 1981), prebiotic models (Eigen and Schuster 1979), Lotka-Volterra systems (Peschel and Mende 1986; Akin 1987), bimatrix game theory (Hofbauer, Schuster, and Sigmund 1982), and immune networks (Stadler, Schuster, and Perelson 1994).

2. Finding the stable solutions of the replicator selection equations (without crossover terms) can be shown to be equivalent to solving the non-linear complementarity problem fundamental in mathematical programming (Menon, Mehrotra, Mohan, and Ranka 1995). Besides the practical benefits of this association (for example, sophisticated techniques such as interior-point methods become applicable), the connections between classical approaches and the newer evolutionary techniques become explicit.

3. Replicator systems have strong roots in common with mathematical genetics as well as genetic algorithm theory. There is a significant body of work that deals with the analyses of replicator models (Akin 1987; Hofbauer and Sigmund 1988).

4. The replicator model does not require that the fitnesses of the replicators (chromosomes) be constant. Density dependent fitnesses are useful in several contexts (Menon, Mehrotra, Mohan, and Ranka 1995; Mühlenbein, Georges-Schleuter, and Krämer 1988; Voigt 1986).

To illustrate the power of the replicator approach, we focus our efforts on two aspects of replicator models:

1. *What are the optimizing properties of replicator models?*

   This problem is important because evolutionary algorithms continue to be used as generic optimization tools. In optimization applications, selection often receives much less attention than crossover (in genetic algorithms) or directed mutation (in evolutionary strategies). An understanding of selection operators becomes especially important if fitnesses are allowed to vary with time. We show that:

   (a) The conditions for replicator models to be gradient systems are closely related to Hajek's convergence conditions for simulated annealing.

(b) Global optimization is possible *via* selection pressure alone. The catch is that one may need to transform variables, and increase the dimensionality of the problem space.

(c) Sufficient conditions can be established so that the average fitness of the population increases over time.

These results are significant in that they establish strategic connections with other areas, tools and applications; the first result with reversible, ergodic Markov processes, the second with approximation theory, and the third with classical convex analysis.

2. *What is the relationship between "diversity" and operators in evolutionary algorithms?*

At the heart of all evolutionary algorithms is the fundamental issue of how diversity is to be managed. Selection operators generally reduce population diversity, while crossover operators generally increase it, a yin-yang combination sometimes expressed as "exploitation" vs. "exploration." Arguably, it is this heuristic that distinguishes genetic algorithms from other optimization methods. While some classical techniques (notably, pattern search techniques) do incorporate this heuristic, evolutionary algorithms were perhaps the first to take it really seriously. It may be the case that specific selection and crossover operators perform "better" than others on specific problem spaces. But we also expect that there are some general, fundamental properties relating to this "exploitation-exploration" heuristic, properties that can be understood independent of individual operators and their idiosyncrasies. Since most early models for genetic algorithms were based on differential systems, previous efforts to study this "exploitation-exploration" heuristic were based on the dynamics of differential systems.

In this paper, we use the concept of *majorization* to introduce what is essentially an *algebraic*, rather than a dynamical approach to this problem. Majorization is a preordering on vectors in n-dimensional real space, fundamental to the study of inequalities. If it is known that one vector majorizes another, then it automatically establishes a set of functional inequalities between them.

We show that the selection operator may be identified with majorization in one direction, and the crossover operator with the other direction, under some conditions. This identification has many consequences: the availability of the powerful convergence theory of doubly stochastic inhomogeneous Markov processes, a deep connection with probabilistic greedy approaches, the possibility of new selection and crossover operators, and the unification of selection and crossover under a single theoretical concept. These issues will be discussed in more detail in later sections.

Notation: $\mathbb{N}$ denotes the set of natural numbers, $\mathbb{R}^n$ the n-dimensional real space, and $\mathbb{R}^n_+$ the positive n-dimensional real space. The unit n-dimensional simplex is defined by $S^n = \{(p_1, \ldots, p_n) : 0 \le p_i \le 1, \sum_i p_i = 1\}$. S^n_+ is the set of positive vectors in S^n. The transpose of a vector x is indicated by x^t. Vectors containing all zeroes and all ones are denoted by $\mathbf{0}$ and $\mathbf{1}$ respectively. $A = (a_{i,j})_{n \times m}$ indicates a real matrix with n rows and m columns. I denotes an identity matrix. For any $x = (x_1, \ldots, x_n) \in \mathbb{R}^n$, $x_{[1]} \ge x_{[2]} \ge \cdots \ge x_{[n]}$ denote the components of x in non-increasing order. The symbol ϵ is used to denote a small positive real number.

<u>Note</u>: In this paper, all new results are called "Theorems," while the term "Proposition" is used to refer to results cited from external sources.

Section 2 presents replicator selection models, and establishes a connection with ergodic, reversible Markov processes. Section 3 demonstrates a global optimization result for replicator systems. Section 4 shows that the average fitness of a replicator system is monotonically non-decreasing. Section 5 shows that replicator models can be extracted from majorization orderings, and *vice versa* under some conditions. Replicator crossover models are considered in Section 6, obtaining conditions under which a majorization ordering is implied. Section 7 discusses the advantages of examining evolutionary algorithms using the majorization approach. The last section summarizes the results obtained in this paper.

2 Replicator selection models

The selection operator, in conjunction with crossover and mutation operators, forms the basis of many different evolution-based methodologies, and has been the focus of several important studies (Bäck and Schwefel 1993; Bäck 1994; Thierens and Goldberg 1994). Selection-based methodologies have been proposed as early as the mid 1980's (Voigt 1986; Mühlenbein, Georges-Schleuter, and Krämer 1988), and also studied more recently (Voigt, Mühlenbein, and Schwefel 1990; Voigt 1989). Replicator models are especially well suited for the study of such methodologies.

A *replicator* is a fundamental unit in evolutionary processes, analogous to an individual in a population (Dawkins 1982). Each (ith) replicator is associated with a time-varying *fitness* $f_i(t)$, generally chosen to be a non-negative real number, and a non-negative time-varying *proportion* $p_i(t)$ indicating the percentage of the population identical to this replicator. The proportions of replicators in a population change as a result of their mutual interactions, and their relative fitnesses. Replicator fitnesses are allowed to be functions of the replicator proportions as well as time. Their dynamics are described by a system of first order nonlinear difference or differential equations known as the *replicator equations*. The simplest replicator selection equations are defined as follows, where $\sum_j p_j(t) = 1$ and $\bar{f}(t)$ denotes the *average fitness* of the replicator population at time t.

Discrete replicator selection equations: For $i = 1 \ldots n$,

$$p_i(t + 1) = p_i(t) \frac{f_i(t)}{\sum_{j=1}^{n} p_j(t) f_j(t)} = p_i(t) f_i(t)/\bar{f}(t).$$

Continuous replicator selection equations: For $i = 1 \ldots n$,

$$\frac{dp_i}{dt} = p_i(t) (f_i(t) - \bar{f}(t)). \tag{1}$$

There are four ways in which replicator selection models pertain to selection in genetic algorithms.

Case 1: The first and simplest case is that of a population of chromosomes with constant fitnesses subject to proportional selection. This corresponds to the replicator selection model, with chromosomes playing the role of replicators.

Case 2: The second situation arises when selection operators (besides proportional selection) can be modeled indirectly as proportional selection on chromosomes with time-dependent fitness functions. A case in point is ranking selection, where selection is done on the basis of the current ranks of the chromosomes. In other words, even if selection is not proportional, it may be possible to treat it as a proportional selection operator by a redefinition of fitness functions.

Case 3: If the selection operator in question can be modeled as a system of differential equations, then there is a good chance that the system can be reduced to a replicator selection system through variable transformation (Peschel and Mende 1986).

Case 4: An important property of replicator systems is that the dynamics of aggregates of replicators can also be expressed as a replicator system. To see this, classify the replicators into mutually exclusive and exhaustive groups $S_1, S_2, \ldots, S_k$. Then f_{S_i}, the fitness of ith group S_i is given by

$$f_{S_i} = \frac{\sum_{\alpha \in S_i} p_\alpha f_\alpha}{\sum_{\beta \in S_i} p_\beta} = \frac{\sum_{\alpha \in S_i} p_\alpha f_\alpha}{p_{S_i}}, \tag{2}$$

where p_{S_i} is the proportion of replicators in group S_i. Combining equations (1) and (2), we obtain,

$$\frac{dp_{S_i}}{dt} = p_{S_i}(t)\,(f_{S_i}(t) - \bar{f}(t)), \quad i = 1, \ldots, k. \tag{3}$$

As expected, aggregation does not change the average fitness of the population. Clearly, the system in Equation (3) is also a replicator selection system (this statement applies to discrete replicator selection models as well). Aggregation in replicators corresponds to the concept of schemas in genetic algorithms. Observe that since the proportions of the constituent members in any schema change with time, schema fitnesses are not constant. In a population of chromosomes subject to proportional selection, selection of schemas is also modeled by a replicator selection system. This fact allows us to significantly clarify the content and scope of the Schema theorem.

We shall often assume conditions such as continuity and the existence of first partials. For example, if the partial of a function is introduced without further comment, it is to be understood that its existence has been assumed. In the following, we consider the case of continuous replicator equations. Similar results can be obtained using difference equations rather than differential equations; we do not anticipate major changes to the theorems.

2.1 Gradient Ascent

The first application of replicator theory to genetic algorithms is to establish conditions for it to behave like a gradient system, with non-decreasing average fitness.

It is possible to avoid the assumption that crossover effects and mutation are small. To see this, choose the S_i's in Equation (3) to be a *primary schema partition*, i.e., a collection of all schemas that have fixed bits in the same positions (e.g. 00 * *, 01 * *, 10 * * and 11 * *). For such schemas with the same defining lengths and orders, the mutation and crossover terms in the Schema theorem are irrelevant[1]. Clearly, the Schema theorem is a

---

[1]From the Schema theorem $p_{S_i}(t+1) \geq p_{S_i}(t)\,\frac{f_{S_i}(t)}{\bar{f}(t)}\,[1 - p_x\,\frac{l(S_i)}{l(S_i)-1} - o(S_i)\,p_m]$, where

theorem about selection rather than crossover or mutation. Yet, it asserts very little even in this restricted context, because the monotonicity of the average fitness only follows from the assumption that the chromosome fitnesses do not change over time. One direction in which the Schema theorem can be extended is to model the crossover and selection effects more accurately (Thierens and Goldberg 1994). Another direction is to see what can be done for dynamically varying (for example, density dependent) fitnesses. We consider this problem, and show how a powerful result from replicator theory can be brought to bear on this question.

A dynamical system of the form,

$$\frac{dx_i}{dt} = g_i(x_1, \ldots, x_n), \quad i = 1, \ldots, n \tag{4}$$

is said to be a gradient dynamical system when it can be written in the form,

$$\frac{dx_i}{dt} = g_i(x_1, \ldots, x_n) = \nabla_\alpha E \tag{5}$$

where E and the g_i's are real valued functions, and $\nabla_\alpha E$ is the gradient of E with respect to some metric α. It is possible for a dynamical system to be a gradient system with respect to one metric but not with respect to another metric.

The Shahshahani metric is defined at $p \in S^n_+$ by $<x, y>_p = \sum_i^n (x_i y_i)/p_i$, for x and y in $\mathbb{R}^n$. This metric depends on *where* it is evaluated and the associated space is therefore Riemannian, rather than Euclidean[2]. Proposition 2.1 gives necessary and sufficient conditions for the selection equations to constitute a gradient system in Shahshahani space, with the existence of a function $E : S^n_+ \to \mathbb{R}$, such that dp_i/dt equals the i-th component of the Shahshahani gradient of E, defined as $(\nabla_s E)_i = p_i(\partial E/\partial p_i)$ (Hofbauer and Sigmund 1988, pp. 236-240).

Proposition 2.1 : (Selection Theorem)(Hofbauer and Sigmund 1988, pp. 242-243) If the selection equations constitute a gradient system in Shahshahani space then,

$$\frac{\partial f_i}{\partial p_j} + \frac{\partial f_j}{\partial p_k} + \frac{\partial f_k}{\partial p_i} = \frac{\partial f_i}{\partial p_k} + \frac{\partial f_k}{\partial p_j} + \frac{\partial f_j}{\partial p_i} \tag{6}$$

for all $p_i, p_j, p_k > 0$ such that i, j, k are distinct. Conversely, if the fitness functions f_i are such that Equation (6) is satisfied, then there exist functions $E, F : S^n_+ \to \mathbb{R}_+$ such that

$$f_i = \partial E/\partial p_i + F(p_1, \cdots, p_n),$$

and

$$dp_i/dt = (\nabla_s E)_i. \blacksquare$$

$S_1, \ldots, S_k$ are the primary schemas, ρ_x and ρ_m are the crossover and mutation rates, and $l(S_i)$ and $o(S_i)$ are the defining length and order of the schema respectively. The bracketed term is the same for schemas in a primary partition, and hence irrelevant in discussing their dynamics, as follows from a result of Hofbauer and Sigmund mentioned in the next section.

[2]In recent years, it has become increasingly clear that non-Euclidean geometries play a fundamental role in the study of mathematical genetics. See Ewens's development for an elegant generalization of the Shahshahani metric (Ewens 1992).

Proposition 2.1 asserts that the replicator selection system is under certain conditions a gradient system with respect to the Shahshahani metric, and has several useful applications. First, because it asserts that E is (locally) maximized, it is useful for optimization problems (Menon, Mehrotra, Mohan, and Ranka 1995; Mühlenbein, Georges-Schleuter, and Krämer 1988; Voigt 1986). Second, we have as a corollary that a population of chromosomes with constant fitnesses and subject to proportional selection *alone* will act like a gradient system. Third, the result can also handle the case when chromosome fitnesses are not constant. Fourth, the cyclic symmetry condition has an intriguing connection with Hajek's convergence conditions for annealing, as shown below.

Theorem 2.1 Let $f_i(t)$ denote the non-negative fitness of the ith replicator, for $i = 1, \dots, n$. For each instant $t \geq 0$, define the $n \times n$ stochastic matrix $Q(t) = [q_{i,j}(t)]$, where

$$q_{i,j}(t) = \frac{\exp(\frac{\partial f_i}{\partial p_j})}{\sum_{l=1}^{n} \exp(\frac{\partial f_i}{\partial p_l})} > 0. \tag{7}$$

Then, the replicator selection system constitutes a gradient ascent system with respect to the Shahshahani metric, iff each chain induced by the matrix $Q(t)$ is reversible and ergodic at each time instant $t \geq 0$.

Proof: By definition, each $q_{i,j}(t) > 0$ and $\sum_{j=1}^{n} q_{i,j}(t) = 1$, hence $Q(t)$ is a stochastic matrix. In terms of the components of $Q(t)$, Equation (6) may be expressed as:

$$q_{i,j}(t)\, q_{j,k}(t)\, q_{k,i}(t) \;=\; q_{i,k}(t)\, q_{k,j}(t)\, q_{j,i}(t). \tag{8}$$

Let $t = t_0$. If a stochastic matrix $Q(t_0) = [q_{i,j}(t_0)]$ has all positive entries and satisfies Equation (8), then the Markov chain induced by $Q(t_0)$ is reversible and ergodic (Kemeny and Snell 1960, pp. 111). ∎

The Markov chain induced by $Q(t)$ is analogous to an annealing chain. In fact the reversibility and ergodicity conditions for convergence constitute half of Hajek's celebrated conditions for convergence of simulated annealing (Hajek 1986). Further correspondence between the simulated annealing methodology and the replicator approach is obtained by appropriately defining the fitness functions $f_i(t)$, and imposing monotonicity conditions on the partial derivatives $\partial f_i / \partial p_j$, analogous to Hajek's monotonicity conditions on temperature (Hajek 1986). Hence, the global optimization property of simulated annealing suggests that global optimization is feasible by the manipulation of selection pressure alone, provided every replicator type has at least one instance in the population.

Requiring non-zero replicator proportions does not make the problem of global optimization trivial. The fitness distributions of the replicators are allowed to vary, and are not fixed, as in continuous models of genetic algorithms (Qi and Palmieri 1994; Vose 1993). Given an objective function E, and an initial $p \in S_+^n$, Theorem 2.1 suggests that by imposing monotonicity conditions on the partials of the fitness functions (perhaps by introducing a "temperature" parameter) it is possible to do global optimization in a gradient replicator selection system.

The importance of Theorem 2.1 lies partly in the fact that it connects the rather mysterious cyclic symmetry convergence condition in Equation (6), to the more familiar reversibility and ergodicity properties of Markov processes. Another reason is that it gives a novel connection with annealing, identifying selection as the main link (rather than directed mutation or constructing special crossover operators).

The next section presents a completely different approach; a global optimization property of replicator models is established with the help of an extension of Kolmogorov's approximation theorem.

3 Global Optimization

In this section, we prove a global optimization property of replicator systems, exploiting Kurkova's version of Kolmogorov's well-known approximation theorem and the following result related to Ewens's extension of Fisher's fundamental theorem (Ewens 1969).

Proposition 3.1 (Ewens's Theorem)[3] Consider a replicator system of the form

$$\frac{dp_i}{dt} = p_i(t)(f_i(p_i) - \bar{f}(p)), \tag{9}$$

where $f_i(p_i) \geq 0$, the ith replicator's fitness, is a non-decreasing function of p_i alone, and $\bar{f}(p) = \sum_i p_i f_i$. Then, there is a unique, globally attracting stable point p^* for the above system. In particular, $\bar{f}(p^*) \geq \bar{f}(p)$ for all $p \in \mathbb{S}^n_+$.

Ewens's theorem shows that if the fitness of the ith replicator depends monotonically on the ith proportion alone, then global optimization of the average fitness is a necessary consequence. In general however, fitnesses are complicated non-linear multivariate functions of proportions. This problem is resolved by using the Kurkova-Funahashi theorem, a variation of Kolmogorov's celebrated representation theorem (Kurkova 1992; Funahashi 1989), and is stated below.

Proposition 3.2 (Kurkova 1992; Funahashi 1989) Let $n \in \mathbb{N}$, and let $\sigma : \mathbb{R} \to [0,1]$ be any sigmoidal function[4]. Let $S(\sigma)$ denote the set of all finite linear combinations of affine transformations of $\mathbb{R}$ with $\sigma(\cdot)$, of the form $\sum_{i=1}^{k} a_i \sigma(b_i x + c_i)$ for some scalars a_i, b_i and c_i. Let $F : [0,1]^n \to \mathbb{R}$ and $\epsilon > 0$. Then, there exist $k \in \mathbb{N}$ and functions $\phi_i, \psi_{j,i} \in S(\sigma)$ such that for every $q \in [0,1]^n$,

$$\left| F(q_1, \ldots, q_n) - \sum_{i=1}^{k} \phi_i\left(\sum_{j=1}^{n} \psi_{j,i}(q_j)\right) \right| < \epsilon.$$

Many smooth sigmoidal functions, such as the hyperbolic tangent, are also monotonically increasing functions. For this class of sigmoids, we obtain the following theorem by combining Proposition 3.1 with Proposition 3.2.

Theorem 3.1 (Global Optimization) Let $F : [0,1]^n \to \mathbb{R}$ have a single global maximum, and $\epsilon > 0$. Then there exist N functions $\phi_i \in S(\sigma)$, and a transformation from the n

---

[3]Our proof, omitted here for reasons of space and paper focus, utilizes the Cohen-Grossberg theorem, suggesting how Proposition 3.1 may be extended to slightly more general dynamical systems (Casti 1988, pp. 333-334).

[4]Recall that a function $\sigma : \mathbb{R} \to [0,1]$ is *sigmoidal* if $\lim_{t \to \infty} \sigma(t) = 1$ and $\lim_{t \to -\infty} \sigma(t) = 0$, and $\sigma(t) > \sigma(t')$ iff $t > t'$.

variables q_i to N bounded variables $z_1, z_2, \ldots, z_N$, for some $N \geq n$, such that for every $q \in [0,1]^n$,

$$\left| F(q_1, \ldots, q_n) - \sum_{i=1}^{N} \phi_i(z_i) \right| < \epsilon. \tag{10}$$

Furthermore, two real constants K^+, K^- can be chosen, determining the replicator system in Equations 11,12,13, such that:

1. the average fitness $\bar{f}$ converges to the global maximum of the function F arbitrarily closely, and

2. each replicator's fitness $f_i(z, p) \geq 0$ (for $i = 1, \ldots, n$).

The replicator system is defined by

$$dp_i/dt = p_i\,(f_i(z, p_i) - \bar{f}(z, p)), \tag{11}$$

where

$$p_i = \frac{\exp(z_i)}{\sum_{j=1}^{N} \exp(z_j)}, \tag{12}$$

$$f_i(z, p) = \begin{cases} (\phi_i(z_i) + K^+)/p_i & \text{if } (\partial\phi_i(z_i))/\partial z_i \geq 0 \\ (\phi_i(z_i) + K^-)/p_i & \text{if } (\partial\phi_i(z_i))/\partial z_i < 0. \end{cases} \tag{13}$$

Proof: Proposition 3.2 implies that there exist bounded variables z_i and functions $\phi_i(z_i)$ that approximate F in the sense of Equation (10). Using Equation (12), we obtain

$$\frac{dp_i}{dt} = p_i\left(\frac{dz_i}{dt} - \sum_{j=1}^{N} p_j \frac{dz_j}{dt}\right), \tag{14}$$

for $i = 1, \ldots, N$. Thus, to establish the correspondence with the replicator system defined by Equation (11), we must have

$$\frac{dz_i}{dt} = f_i(z) \tag{15}$$

$$= \begin{cases} (\phi_i(z_i) + K^+)/p_i & \text{if } (\partial\phi_i(z_i))/\partial z_i \geq 0 \\ (\phi_i(z_i) + K^-)/p_i & \text{if } (\partial\phi_i(z_i))/\partial z_i < 0 \end{cases} \tag{16}$$

for $i = 1, \ldots, N$. Since $\phi_i(z_i) = a_i\sigma_i(z_i) + b_i$, we obtain

$$\frac{\partial\phi_i(z_i)}{\partial z_i} = a_i \frac{\sigma_i(z_i)}{\partial z_i}. \tag{17}$$

The sign of $\partial\phi_i(z_i)/\partial z_i$ is completely determined by the sign of the coefficient a_i, since $\sigma(z_i)$ is a sigmoid function. Define the two index sets, $S^+ = \{i : a_i \geq 0\}$ and $S^- = \{i : a_i < 0\}$. With this new notation, and substituting for p_i, we rewrite Equation (16) as:

$$\frac{dz_i}{dt} = \begin{cases} (\sum_{j=1}^{N} \exp(z_j))(\phi_i(z_i) + K^+)(\exp(z_i))^{-1} & \text{if } i \in S^+ \\ (\sum_{j=1}^{N} \exp(z_j))(\phi_i(z_i) + K^-)(\exp(z_i))^{-1} & \text{if } i \in S^-. \end{cases}$$

If this system is globally asymptotically stable, then so is the system (14), by definition of each p_i. On the other hand, invoking the arguments of Hofbauer and Sigmund[5] (Hofbauer and Sigmund 1988, pp. 92), global asymptotic stability of the system (16) is implied by that of the following system:

$$\frac{dz_i}{dt} = \begin{cases} \exp(-z_i)\,(\phi_i(z_i) + K^+) & \text{if } i \in S^+ \\ \exp(-z_i)\,(\phi_i(z_i) + K^-) & \text{if } i \in S^- \end{cases} \tag{18}$$

System (18) is globally asymptotically stable, as a consequence of the Cohen-Grossberg theorem (Cohen and Grossberg 1993).

Using arguments almost identical to those used to prove Ewens's theorem, we can show that there is a *unique* fixed point towards which the replicator system evolves. This point is determined by the values of the coefficients (a_i and b_i) that determine the functions ϕ_i, for $i = 1, \ldots, N$.

The average fitness is given by:

$$\bar{f} = \sum_{j=1}^{N} p_j f_j \tag{19}$$

$$= \sum_{j \in S^+} (\phi_i(z_i) + K^+) + \sum_{j \in S^-} (\phi_i(z_i) + K^-) \tag{20}$$

$$= \sum_{i=1}^{N} \phi_i(z_i) + \text{constant.} \tag{21}$$

Thus, maximizing $\bar{f}$ is equivalent to maximizing the right hand side of Equation (21) and hence F. We now prove that average fitness is non-decreasing with time. We find that

$$\frac{d\bar{f}}{dt} = \sum_{j \in S^+} \frac{\partial \phi_i(z_i)}{\partial z_i}\frac{dz_i}{dt} + \sum_{j \in S^-} \frac{\partial \phi_i(z_i)}{\partial z_i}\frac{dz_i}{dt} \tag{22}$$

$$= \sum_{j \in S^+} a_i \frac{\partial \sigma(z_i)}{\partial z_i}\frac{\phi_i(z_i) + K^+}{p_i} + \sum_{j \in S^-} a_i \frac{\partial \sigma(z_i)}{\partial z_i}\frac{\phi_i(z_i) + K^-}{p_i}. \tag{23}$$

In Equation (23), we can choose K^+ and K^- so that $d\bar{f}/dt > 0$. Thus the dynamics of the replicator system is such that the average fitness increases monotonically. Since the variables z_i are bounded, and E has a finite global maximum, $\bar{f}$ converges to it. By an appropriate choice of coefficients of the functions ϕ_i, we can make the average fitness approximate F as closely as we desire. ∎

Remark 3.1 The definition of the p_i as ratios of exponential functions (Equation (12)) ensures that for all i, $p_i > 0$. This is equivalent to the "infinite population" assumption.

Theorem 3.1 asserts that for a very wide class of functions, there exist transformations to a new set of variables such that replicator dynamics suffice to find a vector (in the new space)

---

[5]Hofbauer and Sigmund observed that if two dynamical systems differ only by a positive factor W, i.e., $dx_i/dt = g_i(x)$, and $dx_i/dt = W(x)\,g_i(x)$ where $W(x) > 0$ and independent of i, then the two systems have the same orbits, i.e., the vector fields associated with both systems differ only in their magnitudes; their directions are the same.

at which the function is globally maximized. But the replicator selection equations are *not* structurally stable with respect to this class of transformations. Hence, the system in variables x may have different stability properties than the system in the transformed variables z. The theorem asserts that global maximization is possible *if* such a transformation can be found. Unfortunately there is no indication as to how such transformations are to be found, and it is not possible to determine it *a priori*. It is possible that constructive results from approximation theory may be helpful in such attempts.

We emphasize that our use of Kolmogorov's theorem allows us to address the notion of "epistasis" invoked in attempts to understand genetic algorithms. In the current context, epistasis translates to the interdependencies between replicators reflected in the multivariate fitness functions associated with each replicator, making a global optimization result difficult to obtain. Ewens's theorem applies when there is minimal epistasis: the fitness function is a monotonic, single variable function of a single replicator proportion. Kolmogorov's theorem may be interpreted as giving the zero-epistasis representation of a fitness function. In the variables of this new representation, global optimization is indeed possible. It is hoped that this application of Kolmogorov's theorem will be as important for the theory of evolutionary algorithms as similar results have been in neural network theory (Kurkova 1992; Hecht-Nielsen 1987).

4 Average Fitness Dynamics

In solving optimization problems with evolutionary algorithms, it is necessary to distinguish between two functions: the average fitness of the population, and the objective function to be maximized. The increase of one quantity does not necessarily imply the increase of the other. Everything depends on how the replicator fitnesses have been defined. In standard models of genetic algorithms, fitnesses are constant, and we have a trivial consequence that the average fitness is non-decreasing. In general, this is not true of dynamically varying fitness functions, of which density dependent fitnesses are an example (Akin 1983). In this section, we show that if the fitnesses are defined as partial derivatives of a function E to be maximized, then the average fitness $\bar{f}$ is non-decreasing along the trajectories of the selection replicator equations. The aim of this section is to exhibit the specific conditions under which both the average fitness and the objective function are non-decreasing.

Theorem 4.1 Let $E : \mathbb{S}^n_+ \to \mathbb{R}_+$ denote the function to be maximized, with a non-zero Hessian, and with continuous first and second order partial derivatives in $\mathbb{S}^n_+$. If the fitnesses are non-negative and given by $f_i = \partial E / \partial p_i$, then both E and the average fitness $\bar{f} = \sum_i p_i f_i$ are non-decreasing along the trajectories of the discrete replicator selection equation.

Proof: From the definition of the fitnesses and Proposition 2.1, it can be seen that E is non-decreasing along the trajectories of the replicator selection equation, i.e.,

$$\frac{dE}{dt} \geq 0. \tag{24}$$

Since the Hessian of E is non-zero, Donkin's theorem (Gantmacher 1970, pp. 74-75) implies that there exists a function $G = G(f_1, \ldots, f_n)$ such that $p_i = \partial G / \partial f_i$ and

$$G = \sum_{i=1}^{n} p_i f_i - E = \overline{f} - E.$$

To show that the average fitness is non-decreasing, under replicator dynamics and stated conditions, it suffices to show that $d\overline{f}/dt \geq 0$, i.e.,

$$d\overline{f}/dt = d(G + E)/dt \geq 0.$$

Then from Equation (24), it suffices to show that $dG/dt \geq 0$ in S_+^n.

$$
\begin{aligned}
\frac{dG}{dt} &= \sum_{k=1}^{n} \frac{\partial G}{\partial f_k} \frac{df_k}{dt} = \sum_{k=1}^{n} p_k \left\{ \sum_{j=1}^{n} \frac{\partial f_k}{\partial p_j} \frac{dp_j}{dt} \right\} \\
&= \sum_{k,j} \frac{\partial f_k}{\partial p_j} p_j p_k (f_j - \overline{f}).
\end{aligned}
$$

Using the abbreviation $\alpha_{k,j} = \partial f_k / \partial p_j$, we obtain

$$
\frac{dG}{dt} = \left(\sum_{k,j} \alpha_{k,j} p_k (p_j f_j / \overline{f}) - \sum_{k,j} \alpha_{k,j} p_k p_j \right) \overline{f}.
$$

Since $\overline{f} \geq 0$, we conclude that $dG/dt \geq 0$ if

$$
\sum_{k,j} \alpha_{k,j} p_k (p_j f_j / \overline{f}) \geq \sum_{k,j} \alpha_{k,j} p_k p_j. \tag{25}
$$

The continuity and existence of the first and second partials of E and the fact that $f_k = \frac{\partial E}{\partial p_k}$ implies that $\alpha_{k,j} = \alpha_{j,k}$. Then from a result due to (Losert and Akin 1983), it follows that Equation (25) is true.

We have thus proved that $dG/dt \geq 0$, and hence $d\overline{f}/dt \geq 0$. ∎

The importance of Theorem 4.1 is two-fold. First, it provides a guideline for using replicators for optimization purposes, e.g., graph partitioning (Menon, Mehrotra, Mohan, and Ranka 1995).

Second, the proof of the theorem introduced the function G, defined as the difference of the average fitness and the objective function E. G is closely related to the notion of the Legendre transform of a function (Duffin, Peterson, and Zener 1967). The graphs of E, G and $\overline{f}$ are n-dimensional surfaces that change over time. The adaptive landscape envisioned by Wright was the "surface" of the average fitness function (Wright 1932). Theorem 4.1 suggests that *three* adaptive surfaces or landscapes (E, G and $\overline{f}$) can thus be associated with an optimization problem. In convex analysis, one often finds that much light can be cast on one function by studying its Legendre transform (Rockafellar 1970). If fitnesses are defined as partials of E, then fitness and proportions turn out to be conjugate variables (i.e., related *via* Donkin's theorem (Gantmacher 1970, pp. 74-75)), a fact of considerable importance in dynamical contexts. In the light of these remarks, much of the classical analysis of dynamical systems becomes relevant.

In the next few sections, we study the relationship between majorization preorderings and replicator models. We exhibit the conditions under which selection and crossover implement this ordering.

5 Selection: Majorization and Replicator models

The following definitions are fundamental to the rest of the paper.

Definition 5.1 If $x, y \in \mathbb{R}^n$, then x is said to *majorize* y, denoted $y \preceq x$ if the following conditions are satisfied (Marshall and Olkin 1979, pp. 7):

- $\sum_{i=1}^{k} y_{[i]} \geq \sum_{i=1}^{k} x_{[i]}$, for $k = 1, \ldots, n - 1$;
- $\sum_{i=1}^{n} y_{[i]} = \sum_{i=1}^{n} x_{[i]}$. ∎

It is important to note that $y \preceq x$ indicates that that the successive sums of the decreasingly *sorted* components of y are less than the corresponding sums of x. Thus if $y \preceq x$, then for all $n \times n$ permutation matrices P, $Py \preceq Px$.

Definition 5.2 A matrix $A = [a_{i,j}]_{n \times n}$ is said to be *doubly stochastic* if every row sum and every column sum equals 1. ∎

We will also have occasion to use the Hardy-Littlewood-Polya theorem, stated below.

Proposition 5.1 (Marshall and Olkin 1979, pp. 108, 4.B.1) The inequality $\sum_{i=1}^{n} g(y_i) \leq \sum_{i=1}^{n} g(x_i)$ holds for all continuous convex functions $g : \mathbb{R} \to \mathbb{R}$ iff $y \preceq x$.

We first show that a sequence of vectors that successively majorize each other can be easily cast as a replicator system. The following result is key in such demonstrations.

Proposition 5.2 (Chao and Wong 1992) If $x, y \in \mathbb{R}^n$, then $y \preceq x$ iff there exists a non-negative definite doubly stochastic matrix M such that $y = M x$.

Proposition 5.2 implies that if we have a sequence of vectors $x(0), x(1), \ldots, x(t), \ldots$ such that $x(t) \preceq x(t+1)$, then we have an equivalent inhomogeneous doubly stochastic Markov process given by

$$x(t) = M(t) x(t + 1) \tag{26}$$

where $M(t) = [m_{i,j}(t)]$ is a doubly stochastic matrix. There are several ways to associate a replicator system with the above process. For example, in Section 2 we associated a Markov process with a replicator system by defining transition probabilities $q_{i,j}$ based on the fitnesses of the replicators. The process can be carried out in reverse[6]. Theorem 5.1 pursues an alternate approach by considering the special case when the matrix M is non-singular and independent of time.

---

[6] Peschel and Mende have conducted detailed studies of the relationship between general linear iterative systems and replicator models (Peschel and Mende 1986).

Theorem 5.1 (Majorization $\Rightarrow$ Replicators) Let $x(t) \in \mathbb{R}^n$ be a sequence of vectors such that $x(t) = M\,x(t+1)$, where M is a doubly stochastic, non-singular, and time-invariant matrix. Assume that $x(0) \neq 0$, and each $x_i(0) \geq 0$. Then, corresponding to the sequence $\{x(t)\}$, there exists a replicator system whose proportions and fitnesses are related by a matrix $A = [a_{i,j}]_{n \times n}$ such that

$$f_i(t) = \sum_{j=1}^{n} \frac{a_{i,j}}{p_i(t)}\, p_j(t).$$

Proof: Since M is non-singular, we can define its "logarithm" A as follows:

$$\begin{aligned} A &= \ln(M), \\ &= \sum_{j=1}^{\infty} \frac{(-1)^{j+1}}{j}\,(M - I)^j, \end{aligned}$$

where I is the identity matrix. Hence, $x(t+1) = \exp(A)\,x(t)$, and we may treat $x(t)$ as the solution to the non-autonomous differential system

$$\frac{dx(t)}{dt} = A\,x(t) \tag{27}$$

with suitably defined boundary conditions. Change variables from x to p, where

$$p_i(t) = \frac{x_i(t)}{\sum_{j=1}^{n} x_j(t)} \tag{28}$$

Since each $x_i(0) \geq 0$ and M is a non-negative matrix, each $x_i(t) \geq 0$ and $p(t)$ is well defined. Hence we obtain Equation (1) on recasting Equation (27) in terms of the new variables $p_i(t)$ and using the fact that $x_i(t) \neq 0 \Rightarrow p_i(t) \neq 0$, along with a little algebra and elementary calculus. $\blacksquare$

The converse problem, that of associating a majorization sequence with a given replicator selection model, is more difficult. With the availability of an objectively determined fitness function, selection operators acquire a particularly simple characterization. Intuitively, the task of a selection operator is to ensure that:

> Replicators of higher fitness increase in their numbers, at the expense of replicators of lower fitness.

Suppose we call replicators with above average fitness, the "rich," and those with below average fitnesses, the "poor." Then, selection operators can be said to increase the proportions of the rich, *at the expense of the poor*. Now, since the richness of a replicator depends on its fitness, and if it could be guaranteed that fitnesses were not *inversely* related to proportions, then the rich would get richer, and the poor poorer. Traditional genetic algorithms constitute a special case in which fitnesses are assumed to be constant, an assumption that is not made in our arguments.

There is a class of linear transformations T, the Robin Hood transforms, that do the reverse: they decrease the proportion of a unit that is richer (in terms of some measure that can be

used to compare units) and increase the proportion of a poorer unit. The application of
a series of such transformations eventually equalizes proportions. A fundamental result of
majorization theory is that a vector y is majorized by x iff there is a series of Robin Hood
transforms $T_1, T_2, \ldots, T_k$ such that, $y = T_k T_{k-1} \ldots T_1 x$.

A single step of a selection operator acts like a "reverse" Robin Hood transform. If, as we
mentioned earlier, the changes in proportions are positively correlated with fitnesses, then a
series of such selection steps give rise to a majorization ordering on the proportion vectors
in each generation.

In view of its importance to what follows, we further exemplify this point. If at any time t,
$p_i(t) > p_j(t)$, and $f_i(t) \geq f_j(t)$ then selection operators maintain this inequality between
the proportions at $t + 1$, i.e., $p_i(t + 1) \geq p_j(t)$. Observe that there is no requirement
that selection operators maintain the inequality between the *fitnesses*. Because fitnesses are
(typically) objectively defined, one may have that $f_i(t + 1) \leq f_j(t + 1)$. This in turn may
imply that at $t + 2$, $p_i(t + 2) \leq p_j(t + 2)$. For example, with density dependent fitnesses,
it is possible to have oscillations, cycling and other unstable behavior in the proportion
changes of the replicators. On the other hand, by imposing some "regularity" conditions
on the fitness functions it is possible to derive results on the stable behavior of replicator
proportions. Theorem 5.2 is a result of this kind, and is based on the following definition
and proposition.

Definition 5.3 Two vectors a, b of equal length are said to be *similarly ordered* iff $(a_i -
a_j)(b_i - b_j) \geq 0$ for all i, j. ∎

Proposition 5.3 (Marshall and Olkin 1979, pp. 445, 16.A.2.a)
The inequality $\sum_{i=1}^{n} a_i x_i \leq \sum_{i=1}^{n} b_i x_i$ holds whenever $x_1 \leq x_2 \leq \quad \leq x_n$ iff $b \preceq a$.

Theorem 5.2 Consider the sequence $\{p(t)\}$, where $p(t) \in \mathbb{S}_n^+$, and obey the continuous
replicator selection dynamics. If the fitness functions $f_i(t)$ are such that $f(t)$ and $p(t)$ are
similarly ordered for all $t > 0$, then $p(t) \preceq p(t + 1)$.

Proof: Define $E(x) = \sum_{i=1}^{n} g(x_i)$, where g is any continuous, convex function whose first
derivative exists[7] in the interval $(0, 1)$. From Proposition 5.1, it suffices to show that $E(p)$
is monotonically non-decreasing under replicator dynamics, i.e., $E(p(t)) \leq E(p(t + 1))$ for
all t, i.e.,

$$\frac{dE(p(t))}{dt} = \sum_{i=1}^{n} g'(p_i(t)) \frac{dp_i}{dt} \geq 0,$$

where $g'(p_i(t))$ is the derivative of g evaluated at $p_i(t)$. Substituting for dp_i/dt from Equation (1), we must show that

$$\sum_{i=1}^{n} g'(p_i(t)) \, p_i(t)(f_i(t) - \bar{f}(t)) \geq 0.$$

Thus it suffices to show that

$$\sum_{i=1}^{n} g'(p_i(t)) \, p_i(t) f_i(t) \geq \sum_{i=1}^{n} g'(p_i(t)) \, p_i(t) \bar{f}(t). \tag{29}$$

---

[7]The assumption of differentiability is not essential, but it does simplify the proof.

Without loss of generality, assume $p_1(t) \leq p_2(t) \cdots \leq p_n(t)$. Since g is a convex function, this implies that $g'(p_1) \leq g'(p_2) \leq \cdots \leq g'(p_n)$ (Marshall and Olkin 1979, pp. 447, 16.B.3.b). Substituting $x_i = g'(p_i)$, $a_i = p_i \bar{f}(t)$, and $b_i = p_i(t) f_i(t)$ in Proposition 5.3, we see that Equation (29) will be true iff

$$\sum_{i=1}^{k} p_i(t) \bar{f}(t) \;\geq\; \sum_{i=1}^{k} p_i(t) f_i(t) \tag{30}$$

for $1 \leq k \leq n$, and

$$\sum_{i=1}^{n} p_i(t) \bar{f}(t) \;=\; \sum_{i=1}^{n} p_i(t) f_i(t). \tag{31}$$

Since $p(t) \in \mathbb{S}_n^+$, Equation (31) is satisfied by the definition of $\bar{f}(t)$. We complete the proof by showing that if $p(t)$ and $f(t)$ are similarly ordered, then the inequality (30) is satisfied. This holds since inequality (30) can be written as

$$\bar{f}(t) \geq \sum_{i=1}^{k} \frac{p_i(t)}{\sum_{j=1}^{k} p_j(t)} f_i(t),$$

which follows from Proposition 5.3, using the substitutions $x = f(t)$, $b = p(t)$, and

$$a = \left(\frac{p_1(t)}{\sum_{j=1}^{k} p_j(t)}, \ldots, \frac{p_k(t)}{\sum_{j=1}^{k} p_j(t)} \right). \quad \blacksquare$$

Definition 5.4 A function $F : \mathbb{R}^n \to \mathbb{R}$ is said to be *Schur-convex*, if $x, y \in \mathbb{R}^n$ and $y \preceq x$ implies that $F(y) \leq F(x)$.

It can be shown that if F is continuous, and has first partials, then F is Schur-convex iff F is symmetric, and

$$(x_i - x_j) \left(\frac{\partial F}{\partial x_i} - \frac{\partial F}{\partial x_j} \right) \geq 0. \tag{32}$$

Remark 5.1 If $p(t) \preceq p(t+1)$, then $F(p(t)) \leq F(p(t+1))$ for *all* Schur-convex functions $F : \mathbb{S}_+^n \to \mathbb{R}$. The construction of interesting Lyapunov functions for selection processes is greatly facilitated by this simple fact.

Remark 5.2 Theorem 5.2 assumes that the fitness vector $f(t)$ and proportion vector $p(t)$ are similarly ordered, an assumption that can be weakened. If the fitnesses are defined as partials of a Schur-convex function $E : \mathbb{S}_+^n \to \mathbb{R}$ so that $f_i(t) = \partial E / \partial p_i$, then $f(t)$ and $p(t)$ are similarly ordered for all t (this follows from Definition 5.4). This is an important case in which Theorem 5.2 applies.

In genetic algorithms with constant fitnesses, the theorem implies that if we begin with a uniformly distributed population , then the current proportion vector is majorized by that of the next generation. The non-uniform case can be dealt with (*via* "weighted" majorization) but we do not consider this problem here.

It is important to note the "direction" of majorization. The proportion vector at instant t (the present), is majorized by the proportion vector at instant $t + 1$ (the future). In the next section, we will show that under some conditions crossover operators reverse this situation. We model crossover operators in the traditional manner, viz., by quadratic dynamical models, and establish their relationship with majorization.

6 Crossover: Majorization and multiplicative models

This section continues our program of viewing evolutionary operators in the context of majorization theory. Replicator models have been extended to include the effects of crossover and mutation (in addition to selection). In this section, we focus attention on the relationship between crossover and majorization. It should be understood that we use crossover to refer to that process where replicators of two types (say k and l) interact to produce replicators of two other types (say i and j). In the context of genetic algorithms, a replicator of a certain type corresponds to a specific chromosome.

The model we adopt for crossover is the eponymous model developed by Moran on random collision arguments (Moran 1961). By considering the change in the proportion of the ith replicator, Moran obtained the following continuous model:

$$\frac{dp_i}{dt} = -p_i(t) + \sum_{j,k,l=1}^{n} \pi(i,j|k,l)\, p_k(t) p_l(t) \tag{33}$$

for each of the n replicators with proportions $p_1, \dots, p_n$. The interaction term $\pi(i,j|k,l)$ is a *non-negative* (possibly time-dependent) factor measuring the probability that replicators i and j are produced as offspring in a mating between replicator types k and l.

Equation (33) may be rewritten using matrix notation:

$$\frac{dp_i}{dt} = -p_i(t) + p^t A^{(i)} p, \tag{34}$$

where $A^{(i)} = [a^{(i)}_{k,l}]$, and $a^{(i)}_{k,l} = \sum_j \pi(i,j|k,l)$.

Equation (33) has a discrete counterpart:

$$p_i(t+1) = \sum_{j,k,l=1}^{n} \pi(i,j|k,l)\, p_k(t) p_l(t) \tag{35}$$

$$= p^t A^{(i)} p. \tag{36}$$

Equation (34) and Equation (36) are examples of "quadratic dynamical systems," long used to model crossover or random *mating* as a mixing process (Coppel 1966; Geiringer 1944; Jenks 1968; Kesten 1970; Moran 1961; Nishimura 1974; Streater 1984; Rabinovich, Sinclair, and Wigderson 1992).[8]

---

[8]Quadratic models have been popular since they are among the simplest models of crossover.

Moran's results assume that interaction coefficients satisfy three conditions:

<u>Normalization:</u>

$$\sum_{i,j} \pi(i,j|k,l) = 1 \qquad (37)$$

<u>Symmetry:</u>

$$\pi(i,j|k,l) = \pi(i,j|l,k) = \pi(j,i|k,l) \qquad (38)$$

<u>Bi-exchangeability:</u>

$$\pi(i,j|k,l) = \pi(k,l|i,j) \qquad (39)$$

These conditions on the interaction terms are quite reasonable. The first condition is necessarily true, and merely says that any mating must have a definite outcome. The second and third conditions are reasonable under the assumption of random mating of replicators (which is the ideal case in a population during the crossover phase). The third condition implies that any crossover operation can be "reversed," so that if replicators k and l mate to produce i and j with a certain probability, then replicators i and j can mate to produce k and l with the same probability.

Let $\hat{p}(t)$ be the vector with the following n^2 components:

$$(p_1(t)p_1(t), p_1(t)p_2(t), \ldots p_i(t)p_j(t), \ldots, p_n(t)p_n(t)) .$$

Theorem 6.1 (Crossover $\Rightarrow$ Majorization, I) Let $\hat{p}(t), p_i(t)$, and $\pi(i,j|k,l)$ be defined as above. If

$$p_i(t+1) = \sum_{j,k,l=1}^{n} \pi(i,j|k,l)\, p_k(t)p_l(t),$$

then $\hat{p}(t+1) \preceq \hat{p}(t)$.

Proof: Normalization together with bi-exchangeability implies that

$$\sum_{k,l} \pi(i,j|k,l) = 1. \qquad (40)$$

Let T be the $n^2 \times n^2$ matrix whose (ij, kl)th element is $\pi(i,j|k,l)$. From the given dynamics, and the definition of $\hat{p}(t)$, we have $\hat{p}(t+1) = T\hat{p}(t)$. From Equation (37) and Equation (40),

---

Although they must be fine-tuned to fit any given operator (Altenberg 1994), they capture the fundamental mixing action of various operators, which is perhaps more important than the finer details of each operator. A considerable amount of work has been done on quadratic models; the earliest experimental studies on these models pre-date Ulam and his Los Alamos colleagues (Ulam, Stein, and Menzel 1990). More recently, in the spirit of Ulam's original studies, the complexity of simulating quadratic systems was taken up by (Arora, Rabani, and Vazirani 1994) who have shown it to be PSPACE-complete. Rabinovich *et al.* recently introduced a model essentially identical to that of Moran's, and provided an interesting application of its dynamics to a combinatorial matching problem (Rabinovich, Sinclair, and Wigderson 1992).

T is doubly stochastic and inhomogeneous, and the theorem then follows from the definition of majorization. ∎

Analogous results can be obtained for the continuous case as well. Theorem 6.1 emphasizes the role of majorization, restating the dynamics of the above quadratic dynamical system in a space of dimensionality n^2.

Theorem 6.1 clarifies the relationship between mutation and crossover. In replicator theory, mutation is modeled by means of master equations (Hofbauer and Sigmund 1988, pp. 249–256). For such systems, the current proportion vector majorizes the future proportion vector, opposite to the direction we established for selection (Ruch and Mead 1976). Mutation, as modeled by master equations, is something of an "reverse" selection operator. Theorem 6.1 says that crossover too is a majorization operator acting in the same direction as mutation, but in a *higher dimensional* space. The majorization ordering is imposed not on p, but on $\hat{p}$. Analogous extensions should be possible for multi-parent crossover (with more than two parents), by considering even higher dimensional spaces, following Streater's approach (Streater 1984).

If no novelty is possible with selection operators, how is it possible with mutation and crossover? The answer lies in the *direction* of the majorization operator. In selection, the future majorizes the past; this implies that those with zero proportions can never increase. Majorization operators acting in this direction "concentrate" the distribution. In crossover and mutation, the present majorizes the future; majorization working in this direction "spread" out the distribution, introducing new replicators into the process.

Although Theorem 6.1 yields a useful result, it does not answer whether a majorization ordering can be defined directly on the proportion vectors. When does crossover act like a mutation operator? Alternatively, when is it possible for $p(t+1) \preceq p(t)$, just as $\hat{p}(t+1) \preceq \hat{p}(t)$? We first discuss why in general the answer is expected to be negative, and then define a sufficient condition under which an affirmative answer obtains.

From the theorem of Hardy, Littlewood and Polya (Proposition 5.1), we know that the inequality $\sum_{i=1}^{n} g(p_i(t+1)) \leq \sum_{i=1}^{n} g(p_i(t))$ holds for all continuous convex functions $g : \mathbb{R} \to \mathbb{R}$ iff $p(t+1) \preceq p(t)$. For the continuous crossover model (Equation (33)), Moran showed that if $\sum_{i=1}^{n} g(p_i(t+1)) \leq \sum_{i=1}^{n} g(p_i(t))$, then $g(x)$ had to be of the form

$$A + B\,x + C\,x\,\ln(x),$$

where A, B, C are some constants (Moran 1961). Moran's result appears to rule out the possibility that $p(t+1) \preceq p(t)$ during crossover. This is because, of all continuous concave functions of the form $\sum_{i=1}^{n} g(p_i)$, *only* variants of the Kullback-Leibler entropy function are non-decreasing with respect to time (Nishimura 1974). In particular, both the discrete and continuous crossover models show that Shannon's entropy (a special case of the Kullback-Leibler entropy) is non-decreasing during crossover, i.e., $H(p(t+1)) \geq H(p(t))$ where $H(p(t)) = -\sum_{i=1}^{n} p_i(t) \ln p_i(t)$.

Cross-exchangeability: Moran's result is applicable provided the interaction coefficients $\pi(i,j|k,l)$ satisfy the conditions of normalization, symmetry and bi-exchangeability. We can extend the results of Moran and Nishimura by imposing an alternative condition on the proportions $\pi(i,j|k,l)$. The new condition, which we call *cross-exchangeability*, requires that

$$\pi(i,j|k,l) \;=\; \pi(i,k|j,l). \tag{41}$$

Cross-exchangeability implies that if k and l can be used to generate i and j, then j and l can be used to generate i and k. This condition does not always hold (e.g., for one point crossover of $0 - 1$ chromosomes), but is plausible for permutation-based representations. With the assumption of cross-exchangeability, we obtain the following result.

Theorem 6.2 (Crossover $\Rightarrow$ Majorization, II) Let $p(t)$ represents the distribution of a population of replicators at time t, and let $p(t + 1)$ be given by Equation (33) or Equation (35). If the interaction coefficients are symmetric and cross-exchangeable, then

$$p(t + 1) \preceq p(t)$$

Proof: We consider the continuous case (Equation (33)); the discrete case is obtained in a similar manner. Define $E(x) = \sum_{i=1}^{n} g(x_i)$, where $g : \mathbb{R} \to \mathbb{R}$ is any continuous, convex function whose first derivative exists in the interval $(0, 1)$. From Proposition 5.1, it suffices to show that $E(p(t))$ is non-increasing under the given dynamics, i.e.,

$$\frac{dE(p(t))}{dt} = \sum_{i=1}^{n} g'(p_i(t)) \frac{dp_i}{dt} \leq 0,$$

where $g'(p_i(t))$ is the derivative of g evaluated at $p_i(t)$. Substituting from Equation (34), we must show that

$$\sum_{i=1}^{n} g'(p_i(t)) \left(-p_i(t) + p^t A^{(i)} p \right) \leq 0, \tag{42}$$

which is equivalent to showing that

$$p^t \left[\sum_{i=1}^{n} g'(\overline{p}_i(t)) A^{(i)} \right] p \leq \sum_{i=1}^{n} g'(p_i(t)) p_i(t). \tag{43}$$

Introduce the matrix $C = [c_{i,k}]$ where, $c_{i,k} = \sum_{l=1}^{n} a_{k,l}^{(i)} p_l = \sum_{l,j=1}^{n} \pi(i,j|k,l) p_l$. Matrix C is doubly stochastic, because

$$\sum_{k=1}^{n} c_{i,k} = \sum_{k=1}^{n} \sum_{l=1}^{n} \sum_{j=1}^{n} \pi(i,j|k,l) p_l,$$

$$= \sum_{l=1}^{n} p_l \sum_{k=1}^{n} \sum_{j=1}^{n} \pi(k,j|i,l),$$

$$\text{(by symmetry and cross-exchangeability)}$$

$$= \sum_{l=1}^{n} p_l \quad \text{(by normalization)}$$

$$= 1,$$

and, following similar arguments,

$$\sum_{i=1}^{n} c_{i,k} = \sum_{i=1}^{n} \sum_{l=1}^{n} \sum_{j=1}^{n} \pi(i,j|k,l) p_l = 1.$$

In terms of the matrix C, inequality (43) may be rewritten as

$$p^t Cg' \le p^t g'. \tag{44}$$

Since C is doubly stochastic and g is convex, inequality (44) follows from Gouzé's result (Gouzé 1990)[9]. Hence $p(t+1) \preceq p(t)$. ∎

Remark 6.1 The condition of cross-exchangeability is sufficient but not necessary; the proof of Theorem 6.2 depends on C being doubly stochastic, i.e., $\sum_{j,k=1}^{n} \pi(i,j|k,l) = 1$.

Remark 6.2 Consider the process $p(0), p(1), p(2), \ldots, p(t) \ldots$, where $p(t+1) = M(t) p(t)$, and $M(t)$ is a doubly stochastic matrix. Analysis of this Markov process is trivial when M is constant (i.e., the process is homogeneous). For the more interesting non-homogeneous case, Maksimov's celebrated theorem gives necessary and sufficient conditions for the process to be convergent (Maksimov 1970).

From Theorem 6.2, it follows that $F(p(t+1)) \le F(p(t))$ for any Schur-convex function F, such as entropy. This inequality can be sharpened. The following definitions are needed.

Definition 6.1 (Relative ϕ entropy) (Cohen, Derriennic, and Zbaganu 1993) Let ϕ be a real valued function on $(0, \infty) \times (0, \infty)$ that is (i) homogeneous, (ii) jointly convex in its arguments, and (iii) $\phi(1,1) = 0$. For any two finite-dimensional positive vectors x and y, their relative ϕ-entropy is defined by $H_\phi(x, y) = \sum_i \phi(x_i\, y_i)$.

Definition 6.2 (Dobrushin's coefficient) (Cohen, Derriennic, and Zbaganu 1993) For any column stochastic $m \times n$ matrix A, Dobrushin's coefficient of ergodicity is defined by

$$\alpha(A) = \min_{j,k} \sum_{i=1}^{m} \min(a_{i,j}, a_{i,k}).$$

Its complement $\bar{\alpha}(A) = 1 - \alpha(A)$.

Theorem 6.3 (Quantitative majorization) Let the process $p(0), p(1) \ldots$, be such that for each t, $p(t+1) = M(t) p(t)$, where $M(t)$ is a doubly stochastic matrix. If $p(0) \in S_+^n$, then

$$H_\phi(M(t)p(t),\, 1) \le \bar{\alpha}(M(t))\, H_\phi(p(t+1),\, 1)$$

for every relative entropy function H_ϕ, where 1 is the vector of all ones.

Proof: (Cohen, Derriennic, and Zbaganu 1993) proved that if A is a non-negative, column-stochastic, matrix with at least one positive element in each row, and $p, q \in S_+^n$, then $H_\phi(Ap, Aq) \le \bar{\alpha}(A) H_\phi(p, q)$.

Since $M(t)$ is doubly stochastic, it satisfies the conditions of their result. Our theorem follows, on observing that $M(t)1 = 1$, and setting $q = 1$, $A = M(t)$ in the result of Cohen et al. ∎

The importance of this result stems from the property that the definition of relative entropy (Cohen, Derriennic, and Zbaganu 1993) encompasses the Kullback-Leibler measure, Pearson's χ^2-statistic, L_1 norms, and the G^2 likelihood ratio statistic from the theory of contingency tables.

7 Discussion

The processes of selection and crossover are to some extent antagonistic (Layzer 1978). For example, selection tends to increase average sample fitness and lower sample variance, whereas crossover tends to increase variance and lower average fitness. In this sense, *any* operator T such that $p(t+1) = T(p(t))$, and $p(t+1) \preceq p(t)$ can be considered a "crossover" operator. Similarly, any operator T such that $\hat{p}(t+1) = T(\hat{p}(t))$, and $p(t) \preceq p(t+1)$ can be considered a selection operator. As mentioned earlier, mutation effects are usually modeled as a set of master equation terms (Hofbauer and Sigmund 1988, pp. 249-256). For master equation systems (with constant transition rates), Ruch and Mead have shown that a majorization relation holds (Ruch and Mead 1976). The approach from majorization thus unites selection, crossover and mutation under the same rubric, differing only in directionality and dimensionality. A few other implications are discussed below.

Given a vector $p(t)$, there exist many order-preserving transformations (Marshall and Olkin 1979, pp. 54-158) that generate a vector $p(t+1)$ such that $p(t) \preceq p(t+1)$. Results in the preceding sections show that replicator systems and the majorization preordering are roughly interchangeable concepts, subject to regularity conditions. Together, these facts suggest a new approach: rather than trying to obtain conditions under which majorization is "replicator-like" and *vice versa*, we may instead begin by treating vector majorization as a new selection/crossover operator. For example, instead of using a selection method such as proportional selection, a suitable order-preserving operator can be applied to the current distribution to obtain the next one. There are several advantages to this approach:

1. There are a large number of order-preserving transformations to choose from, of which some will be more convenient than others for a given problem. One is not tied to any particular transformation.

2. Both maximization as well as minimization are captured by the same process, since
$p(t) \preceq p(t+1) \Rightarrow F(p(t)) \leq F(p(t+1))$, and $p(t+1) \preceq p(t) \Rightarrow F(p(t)) \geq F(p(t+1))$.

3. Order-preserving transformations are mapped precisely onto the class of inhomogeneous doubly stochastic matrices. More precisely, if $p(t+1) = T(p(t))$ for some order-preserving function T, and if $p(t+1) \preceq p(t)$, then there exists some doubly stochastic matrix $A(t)$ such that $p(t+1) = A(t)p(t)$. Thus, the repeated application of such transformations is equivalent to an inhomogeneous doubly stochastic Markov process. The asymptotic behavior of such processes is thoroughly understood (Maksimov 1970). In the context of genetic algorithms, most replicators (chromosomes) will not be represented in the current population (i.e., their proportions are zero), and this sparsity is computationally helpful.

4. There are stochastic optimization techniques (e.g., simulated annealing) which are also based on inhomogeneous Markov processes (though not necessarily doubly stochastic). Many of the theoretical results for such optimization techniques are also pertinent for

selection. There have been several attempts to link annealing with the evolutionary methodology; the connection *via* majorization and doubly stochastic matrices appears particularly natural and useful.

Above all, majorization is a *tool* for studying diversity. Almost all the diversity and income inequality functions devised over the last 100 years in evolution and economics are Schur-convex functions. In the study of evolutionary algorithms, the viewpoint of majorization theory gives a central place to the creation and destruction of inequalities between units in the population.

To summarize, we have given a global optimization result for replicator systems. We have examined the role of selection and crossover from the perspective of majorization theory and replicator models. We have shown that majorization implies an underlying replicator dynamics, and given sufficient conditions for the converse. Majorization may also be seen as a powerful new selection/crossover operator, with advantages from several viewpoints, including versatility and analytical tractability. We have given a new perspective to the analysis of evolutionary algorithms, and hope that future work using this approach will improve understanding of the capabilities and limitations of evolutionary algorithms.

References

Akin, E. (1983). Cycling in simple genetic systems. *J. Math. Biology 13*, 305–324.

Akin, E. (1987). The differential geometry of populations genetics and evolutionary games. In S. Lessard (Ed.), *Mathematical and Statistical Developments of Evolutionary Theory*, pp. 1 03. NATO ASI Series, Vol. 229.

Altenberg, L. (1994). The Schema theorem and Price's theorem. In D. Whitley and M. Vose (Eds.), *Foundation of Genetic Algorithms*, Volume 3, pp. 23–50. Morgan Kaufmann, San Mateo, CA.

Arora, S., Y. Rabani, and U. Vazirani (1994). Simulating quadratic dynamical systems is PSPACE-complete (preliminary version). In *Proc Twenty-Sixth Annual ACM Symposium on Theory of Computing*, Montreal, Quebec, Canada, pp. 459–467.

Bäck, T. (1994). Selective pressure in evolutionary algorithms. In *Proceedings of the First IEEE Conference on Evolutionary Computation*, pp. 57–62. IEEE Press.

Bäck, T. and H.-P. Schwefel (1993). An overview of evolutionary algorithms for parameter optimization. *Evolutionary Computation 1*(1), 1–23.

Casti, J. (1988). *Alternate Realities: Mathematical Models of Nature and Man*. New York: Wiley-Interscience.

Chao, K.-M. and C. S. Wong (1992). Application of M-matrices to majorization. *Linear Algebra and its Applications 169*, 31–40.

Cohen, J. E., Y. Derriennic, and G. H. Zbaganu (1993). Majorization, monotonicity of relative entropy, and stochastic matrices. In H. Cohn (Ed.), *Doeblin and Modern Probability*, pp. 251–259. Providence, R.I.: American Mathematical Society.

Cohen, M. and S. Grossberg (1993). Absolute stability of global pattern formation and parallel memory storage by competitive neural networks. *IEEE Trans. Systems, Man, and Cybernetics 13*(5), 70–81.

Coppel, W. A. (1966). A survey of quadratic systems. *Journal of Differential Equations 2*, 293–304.

Dawkins, R. (1982). *The Extended Phenotype.* San Francisco, CA: Oxford and Freeman.

Duffin, R., E. Peterson, and C. Zener (1967). *Geometric programming: theory and application.* New York: Wiley.

Eigen, M. and P. Schuster (1979). *The Hypercycle: A Principle of Natural Selection.* Berlin, Germany: Springer-Verlag.

Ewens, W. J. (1969). A generalized fundamental theorem of natural selection. *Genetics 63*, 531–537.

Ewens, W. J. (1992). An optimizing principle of natural selection in evolutionary population genetics. *Theoretical Population Biology 42*, 333–346.

Funahashi, K. (1989). On the approximate realization of continuous mappings by neural networks. *Neural Networks 2*(3), 183–192.

Gantmacher, F. (1970). *Lectures in Analytical Mechanics.* Moscow: MIR Publishers. Translated from the Russian by George Yankovsky.

Geiringer, H. (1944). On the probability theory of linkage in Mendelian heredity. *The Annals of Math. Statistics 15*, 25–57.

Gouzé, J.-L. (1990). An inequality involving nonnegative matrices and increasing functions. Technical Report No. 1330, INRIA, BP 109, Sophia-Antipolis, 06561 Valbonne Cedex, France.

Hajek, B. (1986). Optimization by simulated annealing: a necessary and sufficient condition for convergence. In J. Van Ryzin (Ed.), *Adaptive Statistical Procedures and Related Topics: proceedings of a symposium in honor of Herbert Robbins*, pp. 417–427. Institute of Mathematical Statistics.

Hecht-Nielsen, R. (1987). Kolmogorov's mapping neural network existence theorem. In *IEEE Intl. Conf. on Neural Networks*, San Diego, California, pp. 11–14.

Hofbauer, J., P. Schuster, and K. Sigmund (1982). Competition and cooperation in catalytic self-replication. *Biol. Cybernetics 43*, 51–57.

Hofbauer, J. and K. Sigmund (1988). *The Theory of Evolution and Dynamical Systems.* Cambridge: Cambridge University Press.

Holland, J. H. (1975). *Adaptation in Natural and Artificial Systems.* Ann Arbor: Univ. of Michigan Press.

Hutchinson, G. E. (1965). Homage to Santa Rosalia, or why are there so many kinds of animals. In E. J. Kormondy (Ed.), *Readings in Ecology*, pp. 204–208. Englewood Cliffs, New Jersey: Prentice-Hall, Inc.

Jenks, D. R. (1968). Homogeneous multidimensional differential systems for mathematical models. *J. of Diferential Equations 4*, 549–565.

Kemeny, J. G. and J. L. Snell (1960). *Finite Markov chains.* Princeton, N. J.: Van Nostrand.

Kesten, H. (1970). Quadratic transformations -I. *Adavnces in Applied Probability 2*, 1–82.

Kurkova, V. (1992). Kolomogorov's theorem and multilayer neural networks. *Neural Networks 5*, 501–506.

Layzer, D. (1978). A macroscopic theory of population genetics. *J. of Theor. Biology 73*, 769–788.

Losert, V. and E. Akin (1983). Dynamics of games and genes: Discrete versus continuous time. *J. Math. Biology 17*, 241–251.

Maksimov, V. M. (1970). Convergence of non-homogeneous bistochastic Markov chains. *Theory of Probability and its Applications XV*(4), 604–618.

Marshall, A. W. and I. Olkin (1979). *Inequalities: Theory of majorization and its Applications*. New York: Academic Press.

Menon, A., K. Mehrotra, C. Mohan, and S. Ranka (1995). Optimization using replicators. In *Proceedings of the Sixth International Conference on Genetic Algorithms*, San Mateo, California, pp. 209–216. Morgan Kaufman.

Moran, P. A. P. (1961). Enropy, Markov processes and Boltzmann's H-theorem. *Proc. Cambridge Phil. Soc. 57*, 833–842.

Mühlenbein, H., M. Georges-Schleuter, and O. Krämer (1988). Evolution algorithms in combinatorial optimization. *Parallel Computing 7*, 65–85.

Nishimura, S. (1974). Random collision processes and their limiting distribution using the discrimination information. *J. of Applied Probability 11*, 266–280.

Nix, E. A. and D. M. Vose (1992). Modeling genetic algorithms with Markov chains. *Annals of Math. and Artificial Intelligence 5*, 79–88.

Peschel, M. and W. Mende (1986). *The Predator-Prey Model : Do We Live in a Volterra World?* New York: Springer.

Qi, X. and F. Palmieri (1994). Theoretical analysis of evolutionary algorithms with an infinite population size in continuous space — Part I: Basic properties of selection and mutation. *IEEE Trans. on Neural Nets 5*(1), 102–119.

Rabinovich, Y., A. Sinclair, and A. Wigderson (1992). Quadratic dynamical systems (preliminary version). In *Proc. 33rd Annual Symp. Foundations of Computer Science*, Pittsburgh, pp. 304–313.

Rockafellar, R. T. (1970). *Convex analysis*. Princeton: Princeton University.

Ruch, E. and A. Mead (1976). The principal of mixing character and some of its consequences. *Theoretica Chim. Acta 41*, 95–117.

Schuster, P., K. Sigmund, J. Hofbauer, and R. Wolff (1981). Self regulation of behavior in animal societies, part I: Symmetric contests. *Biological Cybernetics 40*, 1–8.

Stadler, P. F., P. Schuster, and A. S. Perelson (1994). Immune networks modeled by replicator equations. *J. Math. Biology 33*, 111–137.

Streater, R. F. (1984). Convergence of the iterated Boltzmann map. *Publ. of the Research Institute for Mathematical Sciences, Kyoto Univ. 20*, 913–927.

Thierens, D. and D. E. Goldberg (1994). Convergence models of genetic algorithm selection schemes. In Y. Davidor, H.-P. Schwefel, and R. Männer (Eds.), *Parallel Problem Solving from Nature — PPSN III, International Conference on Evolutionary Computation*, pp. 119–129. Berlin: Springer.

Ulam, S. M., P. R. Stein, and M. T. Menzel (1990). Quadratic transformations, Part I. In A. R. Bednarek and F. Ulam (Eds.), *Analogies between analogies: the mathematical reports of S. M. Ulam and his Los Alamos collaborators*, pp. 189–290. Univ. of California Press.

Voigt, H.-M. (1986). *Pattern formation by natural selection with applications to decision support*. Lecture notes in Economics, 273. Berlin: Springer-Verlag.

Voigt, H.-M. (1989). *Evolution and Optimization: An Introduction to Solving Complex Problems by Replicator Networks*. Berlin: Akademie-Verlag.

Voigt, H.-M., H. Mühlenbein, and H.-P. Schwefel (1990). *Evolution and Optimization '89. Selected Papers on Evolution Theory, Combinatorial Optimization, and Related Topics*. Berlin: Akademie-Verlag.

Vose, M. (1993). Modeling simple genetic algorithms. In D. Whitley (Ed.), *Foundation of Genetic Algorithms*, pp. 63–73. Morgan Kaufmann, San Mateo, CA.

Wright, S. (1932). The roles of mutation, inbreeding, crossbreeding, and selection in evolution. *Proc. of the Sixth Intl. Congress on Genetics 1*, 356–366.

Nonlinearity, Hyperplane Ranking and the Simple Genetic Algorithm

R. B. Heckendorn, D. Whitley, and S. Rana
Department of Computer Science
Colorado State University
Fort Collins, Colorado 80523 USA
{heckendo,whitley,rana}@cs.colostate.edu

Abstract

Several metrics are used in empirical studies to explore the mechanisms of convergence of genetic algorithms. The ϕ metric is designed to measure the consistency of an arbitrary ranking of hyperplanes in a partition with respect to a target string. Walsh coefficients can be calculated for small functions in order to characterize sources of linear and nonlinear interactions. A simple deception measure is also developed to look closely at the effects of increasing nonlinearity of functions. Correlations between the ϕ metric and deception measure are discussed and relationships between ϕ and convergence behavior of a simple genetic algorithm are studied over large sets of functions with varying degrees of nonlinearity.

1 Introduction

A recurring theme in Holland's 1975 book is that genetic algorithms process schemata. One of the ways they do that is by ranking schemata in the population according to their usefulness. Whitley et al. [4] developed a metric ϕ which can be used to measure the consistency of an ordered set of hyperplanes in a partition with respect to a specified target string. This metric makes it possible to measure the consistency of the ranking of hyperplanes in all partitions of the search space with respect to a target string when the hyperplanes are 1) sorted with respect to their static average fitness and 2) sorted by proportional representation in the population of an actual genetic algorithm.

Whitley et al. [4] show that during the first few generations of a genetic algorithm the dynamic ranking of the hyperplanes in any partition, measured in terms of their proportional representation in the population, is highly correlated with the average hyperplane fitness measured over all strings in each hyperplane. Furthermore, as the number of generations of the genetic algorithm increases, schemata in a population are not dynamically ranked according to their observed fitness; rather, empirical results suggested that the proportional representation of schemata in the population rank schemata with respect to their consistency with the string or set of strings that come to dominate the population.

This work provided indirect evidence that genetic algorithms use information about numerous partitions implicitly and in parallel. However, the degree to which a genetic algorithm is able to ultimately exploit this information is limited by the degree of consistency in the ranking that inherently exists in the function.

In this paper we extend the work of Whitley et al. by presenting evidence to support the hypothesis that the degree of nonlinearity of a function has a direct impact on the degree to which a function displays a consistent static ranking and deception. To this end we introduce the ϕ *spectrum* metric. This is a measure of ϕ with respect to all points in the search space using the static ranking of hyperplanes based on the fitness function.

Instead of using randomly generated functions (as Whitley et al. [4]), we look at functions with differing degrees of nonlinearity created using Walsh coefficients [1, 2] and measure the distribution of the nonlinearity with a new measure called the *Walsh sum*.

With these analysis tools we go on to show that the static metric, ϕ_{sum}, is a strong indicator of dynamical convergence behavior. In particular we show how the ϕ *spectrum* indicates which strings are most likely to survive in the population of a simple genetic algorithm. In fact, on average, the ϕ_{sum} of a function computed with respect to the point of convergence tends to be higher than the ϕ_{sum} associated with the global optimum.

2 Measures of Order

2.1 Basic Notation

Let L be the length of the binary strings which we are processing. A string of all 1's will be denoted by $\vec{1}$. A schema is one of the 3^L strings of 0's, 1's and *'s where a 0 or 1 occupy each **fixed bit position** and the *'s represent either a 0 or a 1 in the **variable bit positions**. A schema represents a **hyperplane** which is a set of strings with the same, possibly null, set of fixed bit positions. A schema with C fixed bit positions represents a hyperplane of order C containing 2^{L-C} strings. A **partition** is a set of competing hyperplanes specified by a string with bits b in positions of competition and *'s in all other positions. A partition with C b's and $(L - C)$ *'s is of **order** C and defines a set of 2^C hyperplanes.

A **ranking** of a partition is an ordering of all hyperplanes in the partition by a **ranking function** R. An **evaluation function**, $f(x)$, is a function that returns the fitness of a string x. A ranking function is often an extension of an evaluation function to include not just strings but hyperplanes, where the fitness returned for a hyperplane is the average of the fitnesses of all the strings in that hyperplane and is denoted by μ.

Hyperplanes in a partition can, for example, be ranked in terms of their average fitness μ. This is called a **static ranking**, since it doesn't change during the evolution of population in a genetic algorithm. Hyperplanes in a partition can also be ranked in terms of their proportional representation in a population at time t, denoted by $P(\xi, t)$ for hyperplane ξ. This is a **dynamic ranking** since it changes from one generation to the next.

2.2 Consistency

Using the ranking function $R = \mu$, all hyperplanes within a particular partition can be ranked according to their average fitness. This partition is said to have a **consistent static ranking** if there exists a **target string**, τ, such that when all the hyperplanes in the partition are sorted with respect to their average fitness, μ, each hyperplane closer in Hamming distance to the target string will have a greater fitness than any hyperplane farther away. Note that the target string can be any string in the space. For example, let ranking function $R(\xi) = \mu_\xi$, be the average fitness of the strings in hyperplane ξ. Assume the target string is $\vec{1}$. Consider the following fitness relationships for the partitions $bb**$ and $*bb*$ which have a consistent static ranking:

$$\mu_{11**} > \{\mu_{10**}, \mu_{01**}\} > \mu_{00**} \quad \text{and} \quad \mu_{*11*} > \{\mu_{*10*}, \mu_{*01*}\} > \mu_{*00*}$$

Notice that a given partition may support several choices for the target string. For example, the second partition could fully support 0110 as the optimal string as well as 1111. However, the first partition can't fully support 0110 since the fitness of $11**$ is better than $01**$.

Given the definition of consistency for a partition, we can use that definition to define consistency for a function. We say that a **function has a consistent static ranking** if all partitions can be consistently statically ranked with respect to the *same* target string. For example, if a fitness function for a string counts the number of 1 bits in the string, the maximum μ is at the string $\vec{1}$. Each partition is consistently ranked with respect to the same target string, $\vec{1}$. Therefore, the function is consistently statically ranked.

When functions are consistent, however, it is easily proved that they can only be consistent about the global optimum.

Theorem 1 *Functions can only be consistently ranked when the target string is the global optimum.*

Proof: Assume to the contrary that there exists a target string τ not equal to the global optimum. Since the function is consistent, all partitions are consistent with respect to the same target string τ. In particular the partition of all hyperplanes is consistent with respect to τ. This implies that τ is the global optimum which contradicts our assumption. Therefore the theorem is proven.**QED**

It can also be similarly proven that order $N-1$ hyperplanes can also only be consistent with the global optimum. More often than not, nonlinear functions are not consistent. A common conflict occurs when two partitions share fixed bit positions but the hyperplanes may be ranked such that the highest ranked hyperplane in one partition contains conflicting bits with the highest ranked hyperplane in the other partition. The following is an example of two partitions having an inconsistent static ranking no matter what target string is chosen:

$$\mu_{11**} > \{\mu_{10**}, \mu_{01**}\} > \mu_{00**} \quad \text{and} \quad \mu_{*00*} > \{\mu_{*10*}, \mu_{*01*}\} > \mu_{*11*}$$

If genetic algorithms are sampling hyperplanes according to their relative fitness then this inconsistent static ranking should have an impact on the performance of the genetic algorithm and its dynamical behavior. Note that if a simple genetic algorithm is applied to the example function above, as the population converges, the second bit position cannot be both a 1 and a 0; one or the other must come to dominate the population.

Let $P(\xi, t)$ denote the proportional representation of hyperplane ξ at generation t in a genetic algorithm. If a function has a consistent static ranking then this should have implications for a dynamic measurements based on $P(\xi, t)$. The orderings

$$P(11{*}{*}, t) > P(00{*}{*}, t) \quad \text{and} \quad P({*}00{*}, t) > P({*}11{*}, t)$$

cannot both be true as the population reaches convergence. However, the orderings

$$P(11{*}{*}, t) > P(00{*}{*}, t) \quad \text{and} \quad P({*}11{*}, t) > P({*}00{*}, t)$$

can both be true as the population reaches convergence. If static hyperplane relationships impact dynamical sampling of the hyperplanes, then a consistency metric should be a useful tool for characterizing functions and how they are processed by a simple genetic algorithm.

To support the comparison of the dynamic ranking of hyperplanes with static ranking, we say that a **partition** has a **consistent dynamic ranking** at time t if there exists a target string, such that when all the hyperplanes in the partition are sorted with respect to their proportional representation, $R(\xi) = P(\xi, t)$, each hyperplane closer in Hamming distance to the target string will have a greater representation than any hyperplane farther away. It is clear that a consistent dynamic ranking of a function is defined similarly to its static analog but with R being a dynamic measure.

2.3 Degree of Consistency for a Partition and the ϕ Metric

The notion of consistency is really a binary valued variable – either a partition or function is consistent or it is not. However, it is useful to quantify the amount of consistency inherent in a partition or function. This section describes the ϕ metric (as proposed by Whitley et. al. [4]) which can be used to measure the *degree of consistency* of a partition. The next section will expand the definition of ϕ to define the *degree of consistency* for a function.

The degree of consistency for an order k partition π containing hyperplanes $\xi_1, \xi_2, \ldots \xi_{2^k}$ is defined as follows[1]

$$\phi(R, \pi, \tau) = \sum_{i=1}^{2^k} \sum_{j=1}^{2^k} [\text{Pred}(R(\xi_i) > R(\xi_j)) \; \text{Pred}(M(\xi_i, \tau) > M(\xi_j, \tau))] \; (M(\xi_i, \tau) - M(\xi_j, \tau))$$

where R is a ranking function of a hyperplane, π is a k order partition, τ is a target string[2] and $\text{Pred}(expression)$ returns a 1 if the expression is true and 0 if it is false. $M(\xi, \tau)$ is a match count function that measures the number of bits that match between the target string τ and hyperplane ξ in the fixed bit positions. For example, $M({*}1100{*}, 110100) = 2$. M can be thought of as an inverse Hamming distance function. In using ϕ we often assume $\tau = \vec{1}$. In these cases we denote $M(\xi, \vec{1})$ as $M(\xi)$ and $\phi(R, \pi, \vec{1})$ as $\phi(R, \pi)$.

The metric ϕ can be thought of as a summation of the difference between the match counts of all ordered pairs of hyperplanes in which the ordering of the pair by match count and by ranking agree in one direction. In short the two predicates decide if the weighting factor

---

[1]This definition is functionally the same as in Whitley et al. but expressed differently to more clearly show the conditions under which the value of ϕ is increased.

[2]The function to which this is applied is left out of the argument list to reduce the notational load.

determined by the difference of the match counts should be added to the grand total or not. We don't add in the difference of match count functions in the other direction, namely,

$$\text{Pred}(R(\xi_i) < R(\xi_j))\ \text{Pred}(M(\xi_i, \tau) < M(\xi_j, \tau))$$

since this would be a duplicate of the case where hyperplanes i and j are interchanged[3].

The resulting ϕ function has its largest value for a partition when a sort of all of the hyperplanes in the partition by increasing R results in the hyperplanes being sorted by increasing M. Thus the function has a larger value when the hyperplanes in π are more consistently ranked. ϕ is zero when the sort by ranking function results in the hyperplanes being sorted by decreasing M.

For the specific case of $R = \mu$ (denoted R_{stat}), we say ϕ measures the **degree of static ranking** for a partition. When $R = P(\xi, t)$ from a genetic algorithm population (denoted R_{dyn}), we say ϕ measures the **degree of dynamic ranking** for a partition at time t.

The maximum possible ϕ value for a partition π of order k can be computed [4] as:

$$\phi^{max}(\pi) = \sum_{q=1}^{k} \binom{k}{q} \sum_{i=0}^{q-1} \binom{k}{i}(q - i) \quad \text{where} \quad k = order(\pi)$$

Notice that ϕ^{max} does not take τ or R as arguments since the target string and ranking function are irrelevant to computation of the maximum possible ϕ. ϕ^{max} allows ϕ to be normalized by dividing each count so that the resulting measure for each partition is between 0 and 1.

$$\widehat{\phi}(R, \pi, \tau) = \phi(R, \pi, \tau)/\phi^{max}(\pi) \qquad \in [0, 1]$$

Table 1 shows an example computation of $\phi(R, \pi)$ for two different ranking functions R_1 and R_2 and the partition $\pi = bbb***$. The definition of the ranking functions are not specified, but their values are given in the table. The table is sorted by R from greatest to least to aid hand verification of the results at the bottom of the table.

R_2 provides a good example of the computation of ϕ. The two sums in the formula for ϕ examine all possible ordered pairs. If we take the first two hyperplanes for example. We evaluate the product of the two predicates as:

$$\text{Pred}(R(111***) > R(100***))\ \text{Pred}(M(111***, \vec{1}) > M(100***, \vec{1}))$$

which becomes the product $\text{Pred}(21.0 > 13.0)\ \text{Pred}(3 > 1)$. Since both predicates are true their product returns 1. This is multiplied by

$$(M(111***, \vec{1}) - M(100***, \vec{1}))$$

giving a value of 2 which is added to the sum. The other terms are similarly computed to produce the final calculation, $\phi(R_2, \pi) = 20$, which is normalized using $\phi_{max} = 30$ to yield $\widehat{\phi}(R_2, \pi) = 0.66\overline{6}$.

$\phi(R, \pi, \tau)$ exhibits an interesting property for $R = R_{dyn}$ in a simple genetic algorithm with no mutation. As the population converges, a single individual eventually becomes the only

---

[3]In an actual implementation there is much room for taking advantage of symmetry and other tricks to improve the performance of this calculation.

ξ_i	$R_1(\xi_i)$	$M(\xi_i)$	ξ_i	$R_2(\xi_i)$	$M(\xi_i)$
111***	19.0	3	111***	21.0	3
110***	17.0	2	100***	13.0	1
101***	13.0	2	010***	8.0	1
011***	11.0	2	101***	5.0	2
001***	7.0	1	001***	3.0	1
010***	5.0	1	011***	2.0	2
100***	3.0	1	000***	1.0	0
000***	2.0	0	110***	1.0	2
$\phi(R_1,\pi) = 30$			$\phi(R_2,\pi) = 20$		
$\widehat{\phi}(R_1,\pi) = 1.0$			$\widehat{\phi}(R_2,\pi) = 0.66\overline{6}$		

Table 1: Computations of ϕ for two Example Rankings.

the member of the population. This means that $Pred(R(\xi_i) > R(\xi_j))$ is true for only one value of i in each partition while the remaining hyperplanes are *tied*. Ties occur quite often using R_{dyn} but rarely using R_{stat}. The method for handling ties is to rank the tied hyperplanes in reverse order in terms of Hamming distance from τ. This is done so that ties contribute nothing to the value of ϕ. As a population converges, the increasing number of ties for the dynamic ranking results in a decrease in the attainable value of ϕ. For this reason our experiments limited the observation of ϕ to the first 20 generations.

2.4 Degree of Consistency for a Function and the ϕ_{sum} Metric

As stated earlier, functions are usually not consistent. For this reason, a measure of the degree of consistency of a function can be defined. We define the **degree of consistency** for a function with respect to a target string τ as:

$$\phi_{sum}(R,\tau) = \sum_{\pi \in P} \widehat{\phi}(R,\pi,\tau), \qquad R = R_{stat}$$

where P is the set of all partitions. Thus, ϕ_{sum} is measured over 2^L partitions and ranges from 0 to $2^L - 1$. The maximum degree of consistency, $2^L - 1$, occurs only when a function is consistent.

2.5 The Deception Count Metric

Discussions of deception typically indicate whether functions are not deceptive, partially deceptive or fully deceptive. Deception occurs when a hyperplane with the best average fitness in a partition does not contain the global optimum. We introduce the notion of a **deception count** to measure the *number* of partitions that are deceptive with respect to a given target string. Note that ϕ_{sum} and the deception count are closely related, but the deception count is a coarser measure. Formally, the deception count is defined as:

$$\mathcal{D}(R,\tau) = \sum_{\pi \in P} \text{NotOpt}(R,\pi,\tau)$$

where NotOpt is a function that returns 1 if the hyperplane with the highest average fitness in partition π does not contain the target string τ and 0 otherwise. This function ranges in value from 0, for functions that at least have τ in the highest ranked hyperplane in every partition, to $2^L - 1$, for the case when τ appears in none of the highest ranked hyperplanes. Again, $\mathcal{D}(R, \vec{1})$ can be simplified to $\mathcal{D}(R)$ since all functions can be rotated such that the optimum occurs at $\vec{1}$.

2.6   Orders of Interaction and the Walsh Sum Metric

Nonlinearity is one of the major factors that makes search difficult. One way to look at the amount of interaction between alleles is to examine the Walsh coefficients of the function. For an L bit function there are 2^L values in the domain of the function. There are also 2^L Walsh coefficients, denoted by w_i, needed to represent the function.

For our experiments we wished to generate functions with limited nonlinearity. For this reason we created a condensed measure of the degree of interaction. Unlike the Walsh coefficients, which allow for the complete reconstruction of the function, the Walsh sums preserve only the orders of interactions. Let the **Walsh sum**, denoted by W_b, be the sum of the absolute value of the coefficients for Walsh functions with exactly b bits set to 1. This is said to be the **order** b Walsh sum. For example $W_0 = |w_0|$, where w_0 is the only Walsh coefficient with no 1 bits, and $W_1 = |w_1| + |w_2| + |w_4| + \ldots$, where each w_i has only one 1 bit set. W_2 is the sum over the $\binom{L}{2}$ Walsh coefficients for the pairwise interactions between bits, etc. This means that for an L bit function there are $L + 1$ Walsh sums.

The **order** of a function, $\Omega(f)$, is defined as the largest i such that $W_i \neq 0$. So, for example, if $\Omega(f) = 1$ then the function is bitwise linearly independent and there are no pairwise or higher order interactions.

3   Experimental Design

3.1   Generating Test Functions

Our goal was to examine the behavior of a simple genetic algorithm on functions with controlled nonlinearity. We wanted to ensure a good diversity of functions along two measures: internal consistency as measured by ϕ_{sum} and limited order of interactions as measured by Ω. We generated 6 sets of 100 8 bit test functions with $\Omega(f)$ equal to 1 through 6.

The process of generating each test function began by randomly generating the Walsh coefficients for the function in the range $[-1, 1]$. This created a set of 2^8 Walsh coefficients for each 8 bit function. If the index of the Walsh coefficient had a number of 1's greater than the intended Ω for the function then the coefficient was set to 0 to limit the degree of interaction.

For any given $\Omega(f)$, a scaling factor was devised so that the W_i would decay linearly starting at $W_0 = 1.0$ decaying to $W_{(\Omega+1)} = 0$. These factors were applied to the Walsh coefficients. Our intent was to let the Walsh sums at higher orders, and hence the nonlinearity at higher orders, decay smoothly to zero. We conjecture that many naturally occurring optimization problems may exhibit some sort of bounded nonlinearity. A second feature of the scaling factor was that it fixed the value of Walsh sums at a constant from one function to the next so that fluctuations in interaction levels are not a variable in our experiments.

b	W_b	RawSum	NumCoefs	%Nonzero
0	1	1	1	100.00
1	0.8333	-0.7458	8	100.00
2	0.6667	0.04343	28	100.00
3	0.5	-0.1441	56	100.00
4	0.3333	-0.01136	70	100.00
5	0.1667	-0.02983	56	100.00
6	0	6.787e-17	0	0.00
7	0	-1.691e-17	0	0.00
8	0	-6.939e-18	0	0.00

Table 2: Table of Walsh Sums for a Function from our Experiments with $\Omega = 5$.

From the Walsh coefficients a complete function table of 2^8 elements was generated[4] that mapped the function domain to its range. The function was then rotated in the domain space so that the maximum was at $\vec{1}$. This has no effect on the Walsh sums [work in progress] or on the value of ϕ_{sum}, since a rotation does not disturb the Hamming distance or the sets of hyperplane pairs that satisfy the predicates in the formula for ϕ.

The particular infinite population model for a genetic algorithm that we used for our experiments required that the values of the functions be nonnegative everywhere. The generated functions that had negative minimums were translated by subtracting the value of the minimum, $f(min)$, from each element in the function table. This translation is often done when using genetic algorithms and has no effect on the value of ϕ_{sum}. The value of W_0 will now be $W_0 - f(min)$ and all other W_i will remain constant. The results we present for the translated set of functions will be the same for the untranslated functions.

Table 2 is an example of a Walsh sum table for a function with $\Omega = 5$ that we used in our experiments. In the first column is the order of the Walsh sum, b. The second is the Walsh sum W_b. The third is the sum of the Walsh coefficients of order b without taking the absolute value. The last two columns are the count of the number of Walsh coefficients of order b that are nonzero and what percentage this count is of the total possible Walsh coefficients of order b. Notice in column 3 that Walsh sums of order greater than 5 are essentially zero (within round off error). Also note the linear decay of the Walsh sums.

3.2   Deception, ϕ and the Walsh Sums

The amount of deception underlying any function will affect genetic algorithm behavior. As the genetic algorithm processes hyperplanes, it will allocate a higher proportional representation to hyperplanes with higher average fitnesses. If the underlying function is deceptive, the hyperplanes with higher average fitnesses may be driving the genetic algorithm away from the global optimum. In terms of partitions and hyperplanes, deception can be defined as occurring when the highest ranked hyperplane is not the hyperplane in which the global optimum occurs.

A simple deception count can illustrate the complexity differences that occur as the nonlinearity of functions, as measured by Ω, is increased. The graphs in Figure 1 show the *average*

---

[4]This was done using the fast Walsh transform of Cooley and Tukey which is explained in [1].

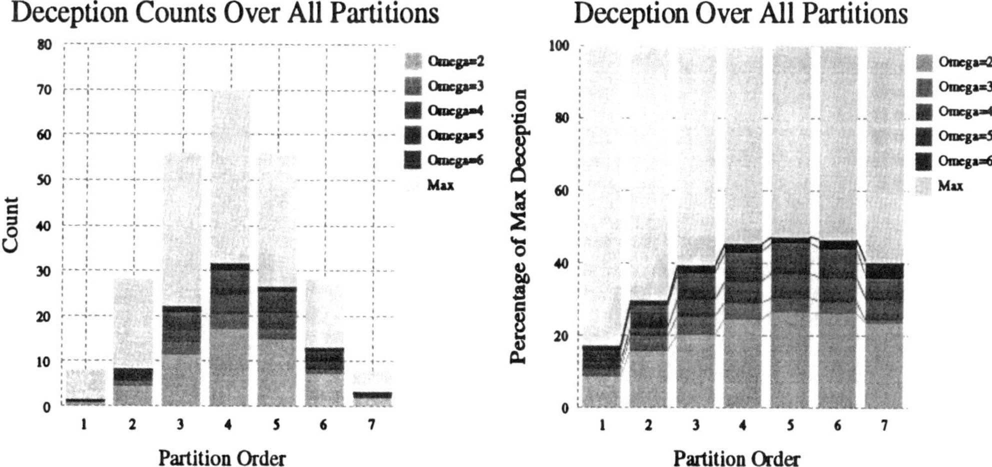

Figure 1: Sum of Deception Counts versus the Different Orders of Functions

deception count $\mathcal{D}(R_{stat}, \tau_{opt})$ about the optimum string τ_{opt} for the sets of 100 functions of each order 2 through 6 broken down by the orders of the partitions at which the deception occurs. The bars in the graphs are overlapping so that the value for each Ω is the full height of the bar from the base of the graph. The deception count is bounded by the maximum number of partitions possible for each given partition order $\binom{L}{n}$ where L is the length of the string and n is the order of the partition. The maximum for each of the partition orders is included in the graphs and is denoted by **Max**. Note that number of partitions at the various orders (and hence Max) is binomially distributed. The histogram on the left shows the increase in deception across all partition orders as the amount of nonlinearity in the functions increases. The graph on the right shows the same numbers but as a percentage of possible partitions that could be deceptive. Clearly, there is more deception occurring in higher order partitions than in lower order partitions. Functions of order 1 were not plotted since they display no deception.

The ϕ metric relates to deception in that it measures how *consistent* the ranked hyperplanes belonging to a partition are with respect to a target string (in this case, the target string is the global optimum). When deception occurs in a given partition, the ϕ for that partition will be very low indicating that the ranking of the hyperplanes in that partition are not consistent with the global optimum. In other words, as the deception increases, the ϕ decreases. The deception counts are strongly negatively correlated with the ϕ values for all 600 functions (the Pearson's r correlation varied from -0.9 to -0.85 across all six sets of test functions). Therefore, in terms of ϕ, the ϕ_{sum} will become smaller as Ω is increased indicating less *consistency* between the ranked hyperplanes and the global optimum as nonlinearity increases.

3.3 A Model of the Genetic Algorithm

The dynamic analysis was done using an executable infinite population model of a simple genetic algorithm with 1-point crossover [3, 5] to model the expected trajectory of the search. An infinite population model was chosen because it is less susceptible to truncation

Ω	Gen 1	Gen 5	Gen 10	Gen 20
1	0.9994	0.9984	0.9975	0.9223
2	0.9985	0.9748	0.9339	0.8639
3	0.9990	0.9791	0.9417	0.8622
4	0.9993	0.9870	0.9641	0.8954
5	0.9994	0.9731	0.9320	0.8525
6	0.9991	0.9747	0.9281	0.8454

Table 3: Pearson's r correlation between Static and Dynamic Ranks for functions with $\Omega = 1$ through 6 (sets of 100 functions per Ω).

effects caused by having a fixed number of individuals. Since there is no sampling taking place, the infinite population model also offers a benefit in eliminating the need for multiple trials as would be required if a finite population were used. The crossover rate was set at 0.6 and there was no mutation[5]. Initially each string had an equal representation in the population. At the end of each generation t the proportional representation of each individual was collected, allowing us to compute $\phi_{sum}(R_{dyn}(t))$ for each generation, where the dynamic ranking function $R_{dyn}(t)$ is based on $P(\xi, t)$.

In the next section we will examine how static and dynamic ranking are related and how static ranking is a strong indicator of the survivability of a string in a population and of the point of convergence for a genetic algorithm. We then compare performance of both an infinite population model and sample runs of a finite population simple genetic algorithms using various static measures of the function being optimized.

4   Results

4.1   Static versus Dynamic Ranking

Our initial experiment examines the relationship between static and dynamic ranking. In Whitley et. al. [4], it was shown that the correlation between static and dynamic ranking is highest at earlier generations. We also present similar results here; however, our results are broken out by orders of interaction using 6 sets of functions with Ω equal to 1 through 6. Figure 2 shows the static ranking ($\phi_{sum}(R_{stat})$) plotted against the dynamic ranking ($\phi_{sum}(R_{dyn}(t))$) at generations 0, 1, 10 and 20. Results were generated for sets of 100 functions for each of the 6 Ω's; however, only the first 20 of the 100 functions for each Ω were used to simplify the plots. Each of the 120 points on the graph corresponds to a single function. At generation 0, there is no dynamic ranking; that is, all hyperplane of order π tie with an equal representation. Therefore, all functions have the same $\phi_{sum}(R_{dyn}(0))$. At generation 1, however, $\phi_{sum}(R_{stat})$ and $\phi_{sum}(R_{dyn}(1))$ are very strongly correlated which is in part due to the fact that the genetic algorithm uniformly samples the space only at the first generation. As the genetic algorithm continues execution, the correlation between the static and dynamic ranks decreases as can be seen in the two lower plots corresponding to generations 10 and 20.

---

[5]We will study the effects of mutation in future work.

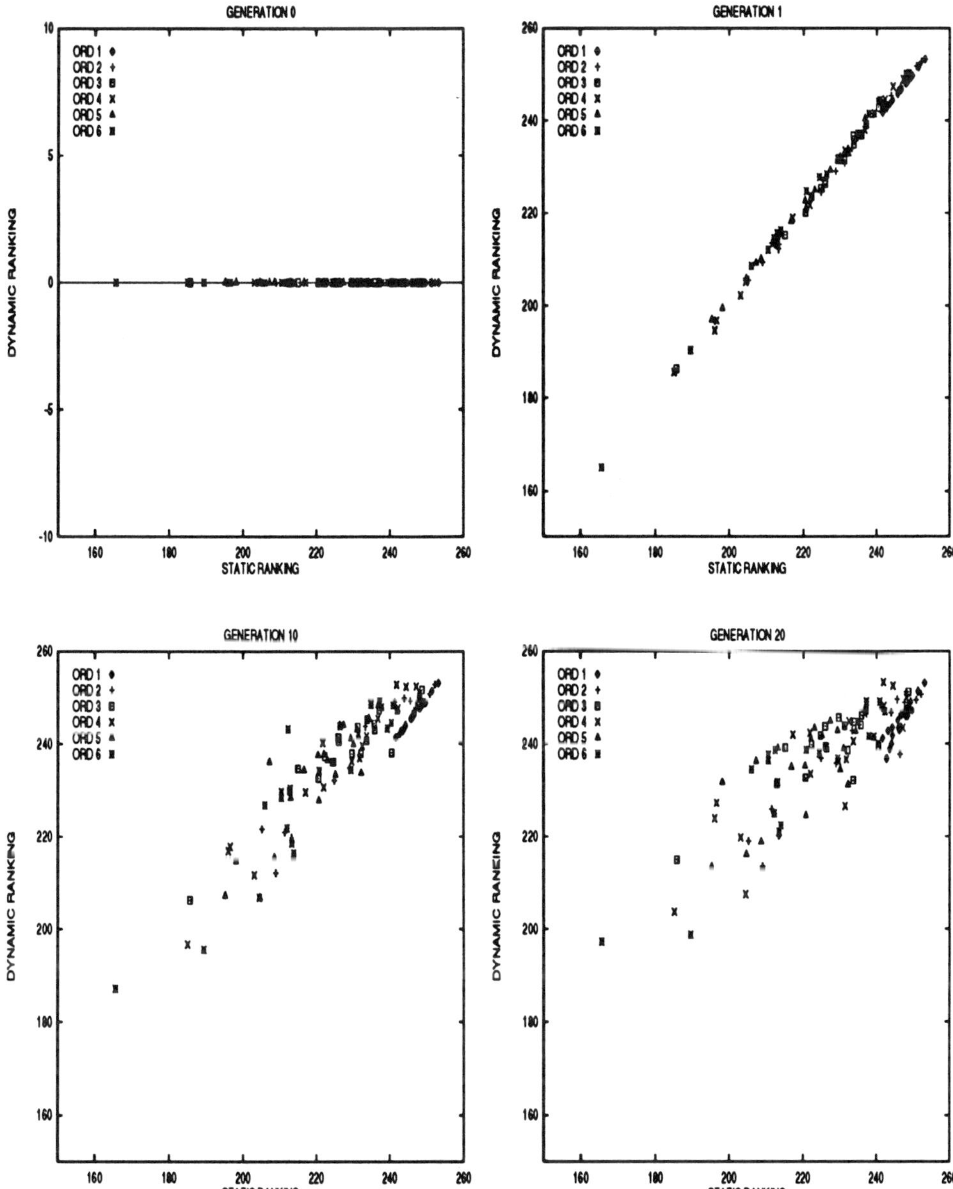

Figure 2: Static Ranking versus Dynamic Ranking for Generations 0, 1, 10 and 20.

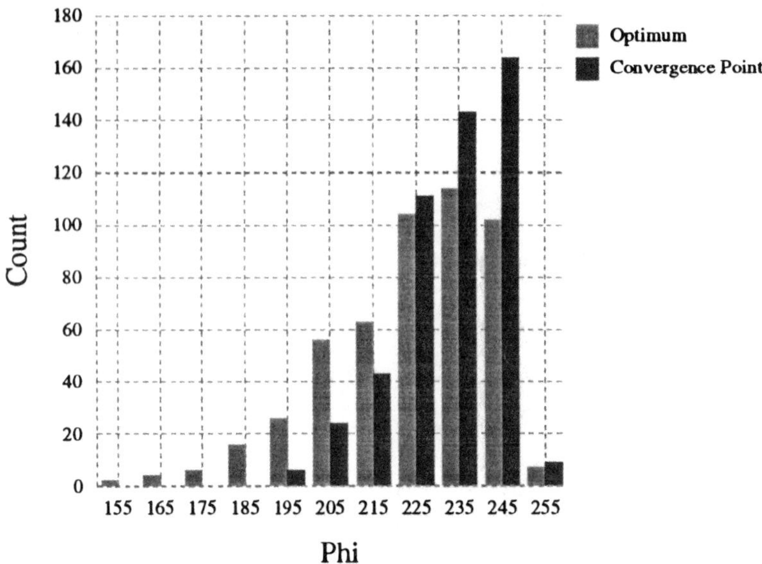

Figure 3: Count of the Number of Occurrences Grouped by Static Ranking About the Global Optimum and Point of Convergence.

Table 3 illustrates that the correlation between static and dynamic ranks also changes as we move from lower to higher orders of nonlinearity. The table was generated using the full set of 100 functions per Ω. Given the correlation can range from 1 to -1 (1 being perfectly correlated and -1 begin perfectly negatively correlated), it is clear that the static and dynamic ranks are still strongly correlated at the 20th generation. However, the trend moving from lower to higher orders of nonlinearity is that the correlation between the static and dynamic ranks decreases. We believe this behavior is due to the decreasing *consistency* in functions as Ω is increased.

4.2 Static Ranking and Point of Convergence

We have illustrated that the static ranking is strongly correlated with the dynamic ranking using functions with varying degrees of nonlinearity. However, this does not answer the question of whether or not the static ranking can be used to predict the convergence behavior of a simple genetic algorithm. Since ϕ can be computed about arbitrary points in the search space, we compare ϕ at (i.e., with respect to) the global optimum, $\phi_{sum}(R_{stat}, \tau_{opt})$ and ϕ at the point of convergence τ_C, $\phi_{sum}(R_{stat}, \tau_C)$. Using the set of 600 functions with varying Ω's, we found that in 93% of the cases where the point of convergence was some string other than the global optimum, $\phi_{sum}(R_{stat}, \tau_C)$ was higher than $\phi_{sum}(R_{stat}, \tau_{opt})$.

The histogram in Figure 3 compares the distribution of $\phi_{sum}(R_{stat})$ using the infinite population model with respect to both the global optimum and the point of convergence. Despite the fact that the global optimum was also the point of convergence in 70% of the cases, the

Ω	Average ϕ_{sum} for Convergence Point		Average ϕ_{sum} for Optimum Point	
	Mean	Std Dev	Mean	Std Dev
1	246.27	3.14	246.27	3.14
2	238.92	9.43	235.06	11.79
3	233.92	11.48	229.57	15.16
4	234.03	11.48	224.13	18.27
5	229.34	12.21	217.46	17.35
6	227.40	13.23	213.84	20.09

Table 4: Average ϕ_{sum} for Each Ω Tested.

graph clearly shows a larger $\phi_{sum}(R_{stat})$ value associated with the point of convergence than with the global optimum.

The results from the histogram can be partitioned based on the varying Ω's. Table 4 shows the average ϕ_{sum} for both the convergence point and the optimum. For **convergence point** we used the string in the population with the highest proportional representation at the end of generation 20. It is easy to see that, **on average**, for the sample functions ϕ_{sum} of the converged point is greater than or equal to the ϕ_{sum} for the optimum. The means are equal for the order 1 functions since all bitwise linearly independent functions always converge to the optimum. Note that the means of the ϕ_{sum}'s decrease as the Ω increases. This can be explained using the earlier observation that as the degree of nonlinearity is increased functions become less *consistent*. When functions become less *consistent*, the mean ϕ_{sum} for those function will be lower than that of functions that are more *consistent*. Also note the standard deviation of the ϕ_{sum} increases as the Ω increases. The increased degrees of freedom afforded functions with higher degrees of nonlinearity creates a more diverse set of functions yielding a wider possible range of attainable ϕ_{sum}'s.

Table 5 shows for each set of functions, $\Omega = 1$ through 6, the number of times the infinite population model genetic algorithm converged to a point at a given Hamming distance after 20 generations. For instance, of the 100 fourth order functions tested, 11 converged to a point 2 bits away from the optimum point. A Hamming distance of zero, of course, indicates that functions converged to the optimum. Two observations should be made from these results. First, as Ω increases, the genetic algorithm becomes less likely to converge to the global optimum. Second, as Ω increases, the Hamming distance between the point of convergence and the global optimum increases.

4.3 The ϕ Spectrum

Comparing the convergence point and the global optimum illustrates that ϕ generally results in higher values for the convergence point than the global optimum. However, in order to determine how accurate the ϕ metric is at predicting the convergence point, the ϕ_{sum} at the convergence point needs to be compared to ϕ_{sum} at all other points in the space. We define the ϕ spectrum to be a vector in which each element is associated with one of the 2^L possible strings in the population. The value of each element is $\phi_{sum}(R, \tau)$ computed using the string associated with that element as the target string τ. Each element in the vector therefore represents the degree to which that string could be "supported" as a potential

Ω	Hamming Dist.					% Converged to Nonoptimum
	0	1	2	3	4	
1	100	0	0	0	0	0%
2	78	18	4	0	0	22%
3	78	19	2	1	0	22%
4	60	28	11	1	0	40%
5	56	26	15	2	1	44%
6	52	31	9	7	1	48%

Table 5: Hamming Distance from the Optimum for $\Omega = 1$ through 6.

solution by ranking R. With ϕ *spectrum* and $R = R_{stat}$, we get a much broader view of the biases that exist in the ranking information inherent in the function than with the ϕ_{sum} relative to a single target string.

The scatter-plot in Figure 4 illustrates a strong relationship between the ϕ *spectrum* and the proportional representation of strings in a simple genetic algorithm at generation 20. The points in the graphs represent each possible string τ in the search space. On the x-axis is the $\phi_{sum}(R_{stat}, \tau)$. On the y-axis is $P(\tau, 20)$, i.e. the string's proportional representation in the infinite population at generation 20. The graph shows that the strings with highest proportional representation in the population are also those strings that have the highest $\phi_{sum}(R_{stat}, \tau)$. It also drives home the point that strings with even moderate $\phi_{sum}(R_{stat}, \tau)$ values have little chance of competing for representation in the population. These graphs universally represent the behavior found for all the functions tested regardless of their order.

When we computed the ϕ *spectrum* for all 600 functions, we observed that the point of convergence did not always produce the highest $\phi_{sum}(R_{stat}, \tau)$ measures in the ϕ *spectrum*, but the point of convergence was always among the highest values in the ϕ *spectrum*. Bitwise linear functions with $\Omega = 1$ always had the convergence point (the global optimum) ranked highest in the ϕ *spectrum* and were not included in any analysis. Figure 5 shows where the convergence point ranked in the ϕ *spectrum* for the functions with $\Omega = 2$ through 6. For example, over 50 of the order 2 functions had their convergence points ranked highest in the ϕ *spectrum*. Unlike previous bar graphs, the bars are additive rather than overlapping in order to have the total height of the bar represent the total count for all 500 functions. What is clear from the graph is that the convergence points usually rank very high in the ϕ *spectrum* over all functions. In fact, 89.4% of the convergence points fell into the top 5 positions in the ϕ *spectrum*. This experiment suggests that the static metric, $\phi_{sum}(R_{stat}, \tau)$, is a strong indicator of dynamical convergence behavior.

4.4 Infinite Population versus Finite Population

The infinite population model of the simple genetic algorithm is a useful tool for studying the various metrics described here because it simplifies the problem of modeling the genetic algorithm. However, we contend that ϕ will have similar performance prediction capabilities for a finite population simple genetic algorithm as it has for the infinite population model. In Figure 6 we compare the results of the infinite population model and a finite population simple genetic algorithm run on the same functions. In both cases, the probability of crossover is 0.6, no mutation is used and they were both run to 20 generations. The left

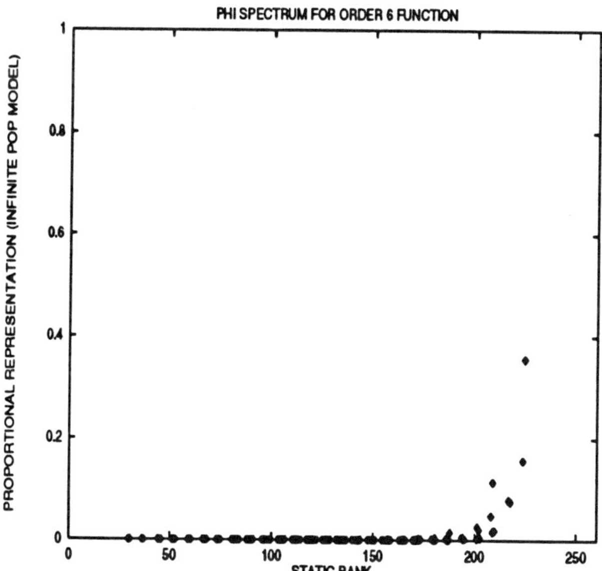

Figure 4: Static Ranking Versus Proportional Representation for all Points in the Search Space for an $\Omega = 6$ Function at Generation 20.

column is the plot of the infinite population model run on one randomly chosen function in each of two orders: $\Omega = 2$ and $\Omega = 6$. The right column corresponds to 5 runs of a finite population simple genetic algorithm with a population of 50 using the same functions used by the infinite population model. The graphs show $P(\tau, 20)$ versus $\phi_{sum}(R_{stat}, \tau)$. Note that the behavior of the finite population examples is not radically different from the infinite population model for the case where the population size was less than 20% of the total possible number of strings. This indicates that the an extrapolation from our infinite population model to moderate finite populations is not unreasonable.

5 Conclusions

The purpose of this paper has been to relate increased nonlinearity with hyperplane ranking and ultimately with the convergence of a simple genetic algorithm. To achieve this goal, we first required a new function generation technique so that functions with a controlled amount of nonlinearity could be generated. Using Walsh coefficients and Walsh Sums enabled us to generate large sets of functions with fixed degrees of nonlinearity.

The majority of this paper is dedicated to studying the ϕ metric in order to analyze the relationships between hyperplanes with the underlying belief that those relationships will affect the convergence behavior of the simple genetic algorithm. To this end, we refine the notion of consistency as introduced by Whitley et. al. [4]. We relate consistency and the ϕ metric with deception and illustrate that increasing nonlinearity results in more deception and a lower ϕ, and thus a lower degree of consistency. We empirically show that the static ϕ is strongly correlated with the dynamic ϕ which illustrates that there is a relationship

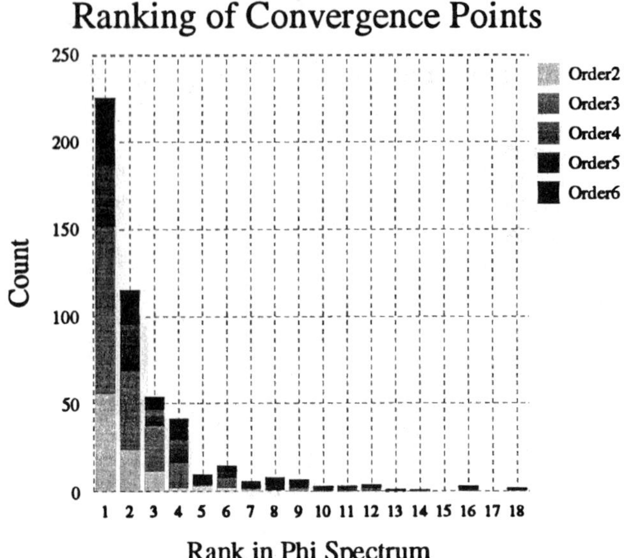

Figure 5: Cumulative Counts Grouped by Ranking in the ϕ *Spectrum* of the Convergence Point.

between average hyperplane fitness and proportional representation of a hyperplane in the execution of a simple genetic algorithm.

The most compelling results we show are using the ϕ spectrum. These results show that the degree of consistency is (more often than not) higher for the point of convergence in the simple genetic algorithm than for the global optimum. Upon closer examination, the vast majority of the convergence points were found to occur in the top five positions in the ϕ spectrum across 600 functions. These results indicate that the ϕ metric can be a strong indicator of dynamical convergence behavior for a simple genetic algorithm. We are extending this work to include mutation in both the infinite population model and the finite population simple genetic algorithm.

This research was supported by NSF grant IRI-9503366 and by the Colorado Advanced Software Institute (CASI). Soraya Rana was supported by a National Physical Science Consortium Fellowship.

References

[1] David Goldberg. Genetic Algorithms and Walsh Functions: Part I, A Gentle Introduction. *Complex Systems*, 3:129–152, 1989.

[2] Collin Reeves and Christine Wright. An Experimental Design Perspective on Genetic Algorithms. In D. Whitley and M. Vose, editors, *FOGA - 3*, pages 7–22. Morgan Kaufmann, 1995.

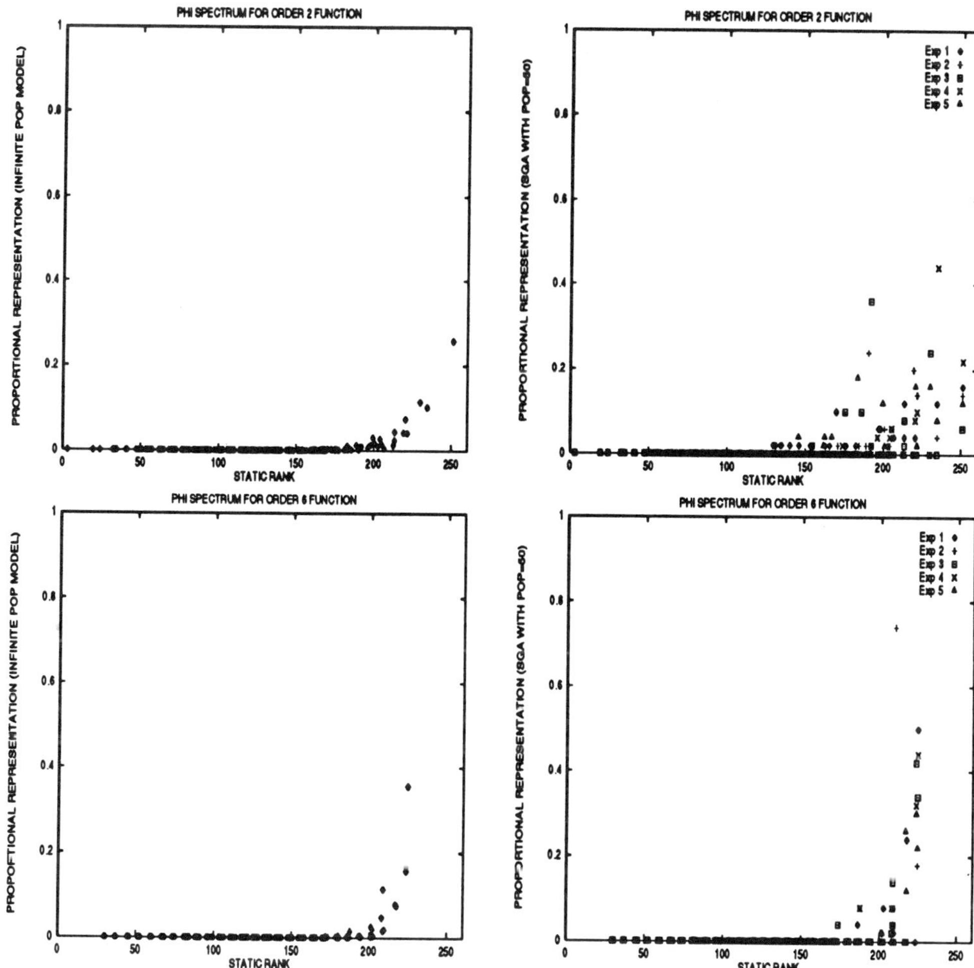

Figure 6: A Comparison of Convergence in Infinite and Finite Populations at Generation 20.

[3] M. Vose and G. Liepins. Punctuated Equilibria in Genetic Search. *Complex Systems*, 5:31.44, 1991.

[4] Darrell Whitley, Keith Mathias, and Larry Pyeatt. Hyperplane Ranking in Simple Genetic Algorithms. In L. Eshelman, editor, *Proc. of the 6th Int'l. Conf. on GAs*. Morgan Kaufmann, 1995.

[5] L. Darrell Whitley. An Executable Model of the Simple Genetic Algorithm. In L. Darrell Whitley, editor, *FOGA - 2*, pages 45–62. Morgan Kaufmann, 1993.

APPENDIX

A   Theorems and Observations about Linear Functions

We now present several theorems and observations relating the ϕ metric to bitwise linear functions. We assume functions are rotated with the optimum at $\vec{1}$.

Whitley et al. [4] have previously proven the following theorem.

Theorem 2 *Given a bitwise linear function F, F has a consistent static ranking (has maximum ϕ in every hyperplane partition) if and only if the set of all strings in the search space have a consistent static ranking.*

Note that nonlinear functions, such as linearly dominated functions, may also have a consistent static ranking.

Theorem 3 *For a static ranking function R based on a bitwise linear evaluation function F with a unique optimum at $\vec{1}$, sort the bitwise weight coefficients ω_i in descending order and index the sorted set from from L to 1. The smallest possible ϕ_{sum} occurs for linear functions that have weights where $\omega_L > \sum_{i=1}^{L-1} \omega_i$, $\omega_{L-1} > \sum_{i=1}^{L-2} \omega_i$ and in general, $\omega_j > \sum_{i=1}^{j-1} \omega_i$.*

Proof: Since the function is linear, the actual position of the various bits is irrelevant. Without loss of generality we pick a prototype case that induces this particular ranking, then discuss the ϕ metric and partitions for linear functions having minimal ϕ values with respect to this prototype case. Such a function is the standard binary function that maps binary strings to integers; we will denote the resulting ranking by R_B.

The proof is inductive. The proof is constructed to apply to a set of strings, but as will be shown it also applies to subsets representing hyperplanes.

For strings of length 1, 2 and 3 one can show by exhaustive enumeration that R_B results in the minimal ϕ compared to all other ordering that are consistent with linear functions.

Assume R_B represents the ranking that results in the lowest possible ϕ for sets of strings of length L or less. We show that the R_B ranking then results in the lowest ϕ for a linear function over a set of strings of length L+1. Take the set of strings at length L sorted according to R_B. Construct the $L + 1$ ordering of binary strings by making two copies of the set of the strings of length L. Construct set C1 by appending a 1 to the beginning of the strings in the first copy of the set, and construct set C2 by appending a 0 to the second copy. Since the function is linear, the rankings among members of the sets C1 and C2 must be the same as the rankings of the original set of strings of length L. To conclude the proof, we must now show that all members of C1 must be ranked higher than all members of C2 in order to minimize ϕ. This corresponds to showing that the weight ω_{L+1} associated with the new bit must larger than the sum over all the other bits.

When comparing members of C1 and C2 note that for any binary string X of length L, the string 1X must be ranked before any string of the form 0X in the overall ranking, since the contribution of bits for substring X is identical for linear functions. We now show that $\omega_{L+1} > \sum_{i=1}^{L-1} \omega_i$ is necessary to minimize ϕ; it is also sufficient since it produces a total ordering over the set of strings.

The lowest ranked string in C1 is 10^L and the highest ranked string in C0 is 01^L. Assume the weight associated with the new bit is not greater than the sum of the other weights; then the ranking of 10^L drops below 01^L which increases ϕ.

Similarly, and in general, one can prove inductively that for sets C1 and C2, there are more 1 bits in the top K strings than in the bottom $2^L - K$ strings when C1 and C0 are sorted best to worst by evaluation (we assume $K < 2^L$ since no string can drop below 00^L in rank). Thus, any string of length L+1 that starts with a 1 that moved down in rank below strings that start with 0 increases ϕ since 1X cannot move below 0X and moving strings with more 1 bits to higher ranked positions makes the overall ranking more consistent with the target $\vec{1}$ and increases ϕ.

Ignoring bit position without loss of generality, any ranking other than one consistent with R_B results in an increase in ϕ, given that the function is linear. Thus, the ranking represented by R_B results in the lowest possible ϕ for a linear function over the partition composed of strings.

Finally, we use the following theorem to show that if the the set of all strings has a minimal ϕ, every partition of a linear function also has a minimal ϕ. **QED**

Theorem 4 *Given a linear function F with the lowest possible ϕ over the set of all strings, each partition of the space has the lowest possible ϕ compared to the possible ϕ value for the same partition over all possible linear functions.*

Proof: Since the functions are linear, each partition of order-k can be treated as a linear function with string length k since the values contributed by each bit are independent. We convert each hyperplane ξ in partition π into a string, Z_ξ, by *discarding* $*$ symbols in ξ. Given the pattern established for characterizing the lowest possible ϕ value for a linear function over a set of strings, it follows that when the k relevant bits are still sorted in descending order and after reindexing the remaining bits that $w_j > \sum_{i=j}^{k} w_i$ still holds. Since every partition of order k can be converted into a linear function over strings of length k, it follows that the resulting ϕ must be minimal for that partition. **QED**

Minimal ϕ for Linear Functions

We now show how to compute the minimum possible ϕ value for each partition of a linear function whose maximum is at $\vec{1}$. We present the results without a proof, although we have verified the results empirically. Since any order-k partition of a linear function over L bits can be converted to a linear function over k bits, the result generalizes as a method to compute the worst case ϕ for all partitions.

First, we take advantage of the recursive structure of the bit patterns over the set of standard binary strings when sorted from largest to smallest. Figure 7 shows this pattern for bit strings of length 3 and shows how ϕ can be computed in a recursive fashion for this particular set of strings. The minimal ϕ for strings of length 1 is given by summing over the terms in the inner most box shown under the recursive ϕ (i.e., $\phi = 1$). The minimal ϕ for strings of length 2 is given by summing over the terms in the middle box ($\phi = 3 + 1 + 1 + 1 = 6$). Finally, the minimal ϕ for strings of length 3 is given by summing over all the terms in the outer-most box. Note these boxes follow the recursive structure of the binary encoding as shown. Thus, the recursive ϕ at length L+1 first duplicates the recursive *phi* at length L,

	Phi			Recursive Phi		
111	12	1 1 1		1	3	8
110	5	1 1 0		0	1	4
101	5	1 0 1		1		4
100	1	1 0 0		0		1
011	4	0 1 1		1	3	
010	1	0 1 0		0	1	
001	1	0 0 1		1		
000	0	0 0 0		0		

Figure 7: Recursive Phi.

then adds in additional terms. So how are these new terms computed?

The critical values can be reduced to the following nonrepeating matrix form, which is extended in this example to cases with string length 6. As will be shown, we can use the binomial distribution to get back the original repetition of values.

$$
\begin{array}{ccccccc}
1 & 3 & 8 & 20 & 48 & 112 & 256 \\
  & 1 & 4 & 12 & 32 & 80 & 192 \\
  &   & 1 & 5 & 17 & 49 & 129 \\
  &   &   & 1 & 6 & 23 & 72 \\
  &   &   &   & 1 & 7 & 30 \\
  &   &   &   &   & 1 & 8 \\
  &   &   &   &   &   & 1
\end{array}
$$

We will refer to this upper triangle matrix as the T-matrix. We will index T from 0 to $L-1$ (i.e., column index j corresponds to L-1). The diagonal of the matrix corresponds to the contribution associated with the recursive ϕ for strings of length 1 (or $0^{L-1}1$ compared to 0^L), thus:

$$t(i,j) = 1 \text{ when } i = j$$

The sum of the first row of the T-matrix corresponds to the contribution to ϕ associated with $\vec{1}$. Since $\vec{1}$ dominates every other string, it dominates $\frac{2^L L}{2}$ zeros which is also its contribution to ϕ. Thus, $\sum_{i=0}^{j} t(0,i) = \frac{2^L L}{2} = 2^{L-1}L$. Therefore the first (i.e., 0th) row of the matrix is given by:

$$t(0,j) = 2^j(j+1) - \sum_{i=0}^{j-1} t(0,i)$$

$$t(0,j) = 2^j(j+1) - (2^{j-1}j)$$

Empirically, we observe that for all $j > i, i > 0$ the matrix has the following properties:

$$t(i,j) = \sum_{k=0}^{j-1} t(i-1,k)$$

$$t(i,j) = \left[\sum_{k=0}^{j-2} t(i-1,k)\right] + t(i-1,j-1)$$

$$t(i,j-1) = \sum_{k=0}^{j-2} t(i-1,k)$$

$$t(i,j) = t(i,j-1) + t(i-1,j-1)$$

We can prove the correctness of this observation only for select rows of the T-matrix (those rows for which we can compute a closed form for the sum of the elements in that row), but we do not have a general proof. However, we have empirically verified the T-matrix.

Assuming the T-matrix is correct, let $F_\phi(k)$ be a recursive function that generates the minimal ϕ over a partition of strings of length k when strings are ranked using R_B.

$$F_\phi(k) = 2F_\phi(k) + \sum_{j=0}^{k-1} \binom{k-1}{j} t(i,j) \quad ; \qquad F_\phi(1) = 1$$

By induction, one can prove that

$$F_\phi(k) = \sum_{i=0}^{k} 2^{k-1-i} \left[\sum_{j=0}^{i} \binom{i}{j} t(i,j)\right].$$

Thus,

$$\phi_{sum} = \sum_{i=1}^{L} \binom{L}{i} \frac{F_\phi(i)}{Max(\phi(R,\pi),i)}$$

is the lower bound on the possible ϕ_{sum} value for a linear function of length L.

Convergence Controlled Variation

Larry J. Eshelman, Keith E. Mathias and J. David Schaffer
Philips Research Laboratories
Briarcliff Manor, NY 10510
lje/kem/ds1@philabs.research.philips.com

Abstract

We examine a class of algorithms that we refer to as Convergence Controlled Variation Algorithms (CCVAs). These algorithms use the degree of genotypic convergence in the population to control the variations produced. A genetic algorithm using crossover as its main operator may be considered a CCVA. Our main focus is to determine what advantages, if any, crossover has over other CCVA reproductive mechanisms, such as those used by BSC and PBIL. We compare CCVA's that operate on numeric, as well as symbolic, representations. We conclude that crossover's advantage lies with its ability to propagate the linkage inherent in the representation, but that this often has very little to do with recombination as commonly understood.

1   Introduction

Among stochastic sampling algorithms the singular distinction of evolutionary algorithms is the use of a population of trial solutions. One can further subdivide the evolutionary algorithms (EAs) on the basis of the way(s) the population is used. EAs exploit the population to achieve soft selection wherein a new trial solution does not have to be a strict improvement on its progenitor(s) in order to survive and have an opportunity to influence the future course of search. Non-evolutionary algorithms must resort to exogenous schemes to allow an "uphill" step such as fixed probabilities or cooling schedules. EAs are inherently self-tuning in that selection pressure increases as the population becomes more fit. EAs that use only mutation exploit only soft selection, while those that use crossover go on to exploit the population in an additional way: they use the diversity in the population to constrain the exploration. Forms of crossover that operate on pairs of binary strings have the important feature that allele values that are not present in the two parents cannot be introduced into the offspring. Thus, the allowable variations are constrained by how converged the population is. The use of diversity in the population to constrain the variations introduced into the offspring will be referred to here as *Convergence Controlled Variation* (CCV). CCV also makes the variation in future trials self-tuning; as the population converges, the variations become more and more focused. Although mutation based EAs can also be self-tuning (e.g., by carrying mutation-controlling parameters and allowing them to mutate as well [1, 10]), they do not make use of the information provided by the distribution of allele values in the population.

GAs that use forms of crossover other than symbol recombination[1] can also be viewed as CCV algorithms (CCVAs). For example, GAs that use a crossover operator that operates on numeric parameters by "blending" the values of the parent parameters would be considered CCVAs. This blending might be accomplished by averaging the parents' values or generating a random value bounded by the parents' parameter values. Although the generated allele value is not strictly present in either parent, the variations are still constrained by the distribution of the allele values in the population. As the population converges, the blending operation becomes more and more focused.

CCVAs are not limited to those that use *pair-wise* mating (i.e., crossover). For example, Syswerda's Bit-Simulated Crossover (BSC) algorithm [19] uses the distribution of the allele values in the population to produce a probability vector that is used to generate a string of ones and zeroes. Baluja's Population-Based Incremental Learning (PBIL) algorithm [2] goes one step further and maintains only a probability vector, using an update rule based on the fitness of the samples generated to modify the probability vector. Instead of the traditional pair-wise mating operator, these algorithms use a *pool-wise* mating operation, a kind of "ménage-à-N", where N is the population size. Thus, we will refer to these types of CCVAs as pool-wise algorithms.

What differences are to be expected from CCVAs using pair-wise and pool-wise mating? From the point of view of Holland's schema sampling theorem, a pair-wise CCVA is more likely to propagate higher order schemata from the parents to the offspring. This will be important in cases where there is linkage among the alleles, i.e., the fitness contributed by a higher order building block is not reflected by the sum of its parts. Although it might seem obvious that this settles matters, it is important to keep in mind that preserving linkage has a negative side as well: exploitation of spurious correlations, or hitchhiking [18]. So the question becomes when is preservation of linkage so important that it is worth paying the cost of hitchhiking? This is the question that we explore in this paper. We also show why many popular test functions are easy for pool-wise CCVAs, often doing better than pair-wise CCVAs.

---

[1]'Symbol recombination' refers to the swapping of allele values between mates. The only symbols considered in this paper are binary alleles.

2   Propagation of Linkage

There are several reasons why propagation might be considered important. First, if the GA replaces the parents by the children each generation, then the only way of preserving the good schemata is by propagating them to the offspring each generation. We have argued that preservation can be separated from propagation using a biased replacement strategy which only replaces the worst members of the parent population by better offspring [8].

A second reason for stressing propagation is that it is central to the building block hypothesis. Crossover, i.e., pair-wise mating, should be especially advantageous in those problems which have the following features [9]: (1) there are middle level building blocks that are highly epistatic and so cannot be built up incrementally from low level building blocks; (2) but these middle level building blocks are small enough that they can be found in the initial population; (3) and the higher level building blocks can be built up incrementally from these middle level building blocks.[2] In other words, crossover is good at solving problems composed of deceptive or misleading segments which can be discovered by chance and can be incrementally assembled.

If crossover's competitive advantage is limited to such problems, then it would seem that crossover's niche is fairly small. This would be consistent with recent experimental data indicating that pool-wise CCVAs are as good as, if not better than, pair-wise CCVAs for solving many of the popular test problems [2].

We believe we have identified a phenomenon that points to another advantage for pair-wise mating: the *maverick phenomenon*. Suppose a population has largely congregated in some region of the search space, but one individual (i.e., the maverick) lies outside this region. Let us further suppose that the maverick lies within a *better attraction basin* than the majority, but that the maverick has only *average fitness* as compared with the rest of the population. Although the discovery of a maverick individual in a better attraction basin is by no means guaranteed, it is instructive to note that the pool-wise method of producing offspring will tend to produce individuals that are distributed near the majority and would be less likely to explore the outlying region around the maverick. On the other hand, a CCVA using pair-wise mating will give the maverick a greater influence. Thus, the pair-wise mating CCVA is more likely to explore the region around the maverick individual, and therefore, more likely to discover the better attraction basin. Pool-wise mating gives the maverick a small influence (inversely proportional to the population size) on every offspring, while pair-wise mating gives the maverick a large influence on a small number of offspring (only his own). In other words, pair-wise mating is a weapon against the tyranny of the majority.

Consider the following example. Suppose the population size is 100, and that an individual of average fitness has some unique combination of allele values, say all ones in the first three positions. This individual will have a 0.01 probability (one out of 100) of being selected for mating. If uniform crossover is being used, with a 0.5 probability of swapping the values at each locus, and one offspring is being produced per mating, then the probability of the three allele values being propagated without disruption has a lower bound of 0.125 (0.5^3). This is assuming the worst case scenario that every other member in the population has all zeros in the first three positions (and ignoring the possibility of mating this individual with a copy of itself). Thus, the probability of propagating this schema is 0.00125 ($0.01 * 0.125$). On

---

[2]'Level' either refers to the defining length, if some form of segment based crossover is used (e.g., one point), or to the order, if some form of bit-wise crossover is used (e.g., uniform).

the other hand, if a pool-wise CCVA is being used, then the probability of propagating this schema is much lower. Since there is only one instance of this individual in the population, there is only one chance in 100 of propagating each allele and only 0.000001 (0.01^3) of propagating all three. Even if we don't assume the worst case, the likelihood of propagation will generally be lower for the pool-wise CCVA.

Bit-wise CCVAs re-distribute the allele values from the mating population to the child population without significantly affecting the extent to which the population is converged.[3] However, they differ in how they affect the distribution of the genotypes. One measure that we expect to reflect these differences is the variance (i.e., the sum of the squared Hamming distances of each individual from the population average profile string divided by the population size, *where the population average profile is defined as the binary string which reflects the allele value most frequently found at each locus*).

CCVAs can be implemented so that the allele frequency at each locus is identical for both the child population and mating populations. In the case of a pair-wise CCVA the method for doing this is well known: Two children are created from two parents. Since all allele values in the parents are passed to one or the other of the children, their frequency in the population will be strictly conserved. An analogous method for a pool-wise CCVA would be one in which the child population is created from the mating population by shuffling the allele values at each locus over the entire population.

One phenomenon we are interested in here is how the variance in the child population of genotypes is affected by the method of generating the children. Intuition suggests that a pool-wise method for generating offspring will tend to a normal distribution of offspring around the population profile string (i.e., the Hamming distance from the profile string). However, a pair-wise method will have a greater tendency to preserve any multi-modality in the distribution of the mating pool that derives from groups of individuals that share structural features (i.e., schemata). Such a distribution (e.g., bimodal) will tend to have higher variance than a normal distribution. On the other hand, if the mating pool has a normal distribution of genotypes, then there is no special structure for a pair-wise mating method to preserve and both methods of producing offspring should produce normal distributions with no significantly different variances. Thus, if the pair-wise method for producing offspring shows higher variance than the pool-wise method (other things being held equal), the presence of linkage is indicated which the pair-wise mating scheme is better able to propagate. On the other hand, if the distribution of the genotypes in the mating population has very small variance, then a pair-wise method might yield an offspring distribution with less variance than a pool-wise method.

To understand the relationship of linkage and population variance we implemented CCVAs using pair-wise and pool-wise methods.[4] For the pair-wise CCVA two offspring populations were produced at each generation using the same mating pool (Figure 1). One offspring population was produced using a pair-wise method and the other using a pool-wise method. However, search was continued by evaluating only the strings in the pair-wise offspring population and then choosing the best N individuals from the pair-wise offspring and parent populations, where N is the population size.

---

[3]The mating population is simply the members of the parent population, including multiple copies, that are selected for reproduction.

[4]Details of the pair-wise and pool-wise CCVAs are provided in Section 3.1.

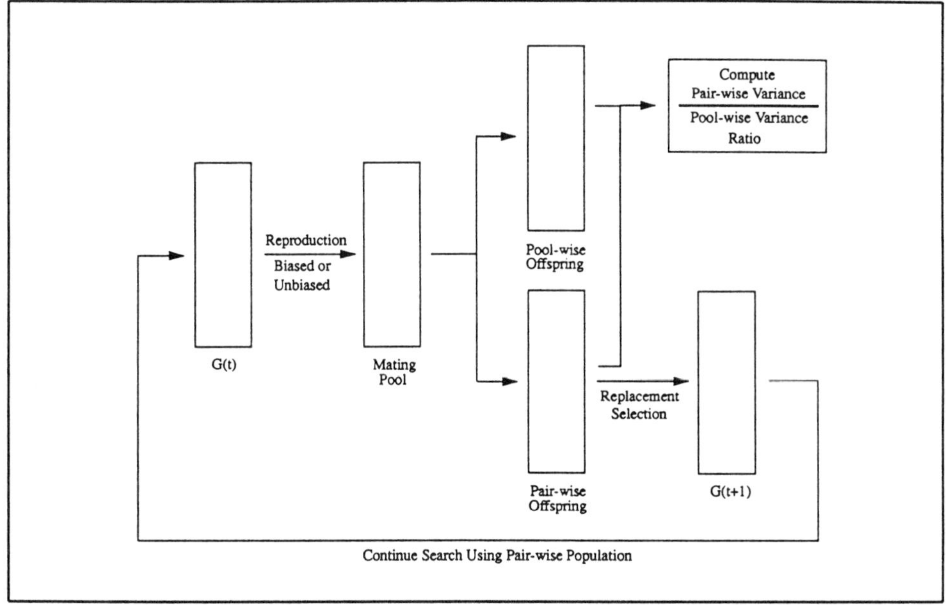

Figure 1: Variance Ratio Measurement Using a Pair-wise CCVA.

The production of offspring populations using both pair-wise and pool-wise methods provided the material for comparing the allele variance resulting from the two methods. The allele variance was computed for both the pair-wise and pool-wise offspring populations. Using the variances from the two offspring populations a ratio of the variance of the pair-wise offspring to the pool-wise offspring was computed. Since both offspring populations were produced from the same mating pool in every case, and the allele frequency remained constant for both the offspring population and mating pool, any differences in the ratios for these two algorithms, plotted over time, reflect the interaction of selection with the bias of each method of producing offspring.

This process was repeated using a pool-wise CCVA. The procedure for the pool-wise CCVA process was identical to that of the pair-wise CCVA in every respect except that only the offspring produced using the pool-wise methods were evaluated and used in the replacement selection process to determine the parent population for the next generation (Figure 2). The variance of each offspring population was computed in the same manner as described above, allowing computation of the same variance ratio without affecting the search.

Figure 3 shows variance ratio curves for four functions. Functions F1 and F2 are the first two functions in the DeJong test suite (see Section 3.2). The third function is a 100-bit onemax problem where the performance measure is the number of ones in the string. The fourth function is Liepins's and Vose's deceptive function consisting of 10, 5-bit fully deceptive segments [13]. Each plot shows two curves, one for the pool-wise CCVA and one for the pair-wise CCVA. It is important to keep in mind that although both algorithms produce two offspring populations each generation, each algorithm is controlled by the selection process

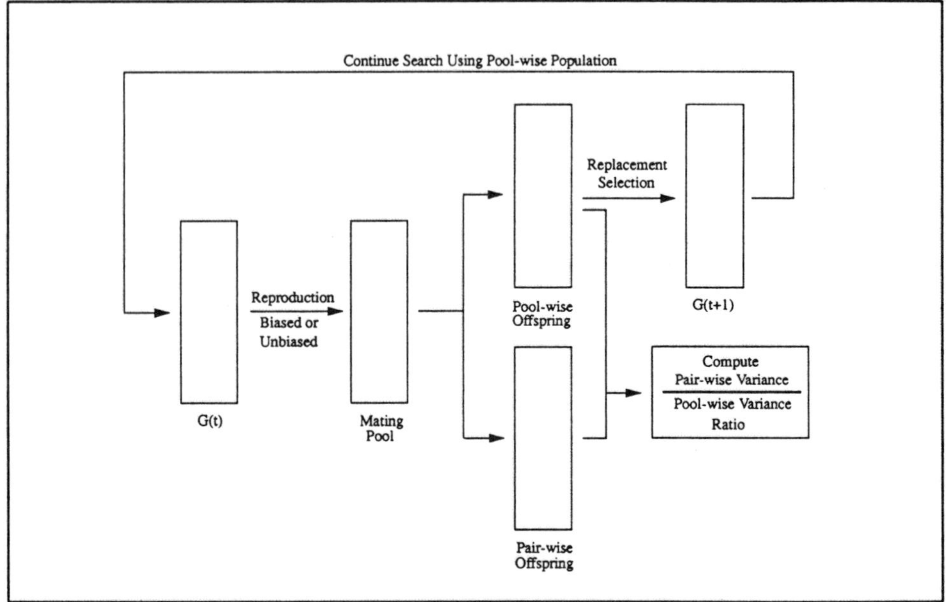

Figure 2: Variance Ratio Measurement Using a Pool-wise CCVA.

operating on the designated offspring group, i.e., the pair-wise CCVA uses only the pair-wise generated offspring, and the pool-wise CCVA uses only the pool-wise generated offspring.

We conjecture that if the function has strong linkage, relative to a given representation, then the variance for the pair-wise method of generating offspring will be greater than for the pool-wise method. Since the variance for the pool-wise method of generating offspring is used as the denominator in the ratios, this will be indicated by a ratio greater than 1.0. Furthermore, since the two curves are generated using different algorithms, they may be compared and may tell us something about the dynamics of the algorithms. In particular, we conjecture that a higher variance ratio for the pool-wise CCVA than the pair-wise CCVA indicates that the pair-wise method of generating offspring is more successful at propagating schemata. On the other hand, a lower variance ratio for the pool-wise CCVA than the pair-wise CCVA indicates that the pool-wise CCVA is not only failing to propagate schemata with high linkage, but also driving such structures out of the population.

Function F1 has weak linkage and as one would expect the variance ratios for both algorithms tend to wander horizontally around the value of 1. Figure 3 shows that there is no significant difference between the ratios for the two algorithms. On the other hand, F2 has much more linkage. And as expected, the ratios for the two algorithms exhibit different behavior. Both algorithms exhibit an increase in the variance ratios as search progresses but the variance ratio increases more for the pool-wise CCVA than the pair-wise CCVA. However, the differences do not appear significant until after generation 100.

The onemax problem is an exception to our generalization. One might expect that since it has even less epistasis than F1, that it would also move horizontally around 1. Instead the curves for both algorithms move from around 1.0 to about 0.7 as the populations converge.

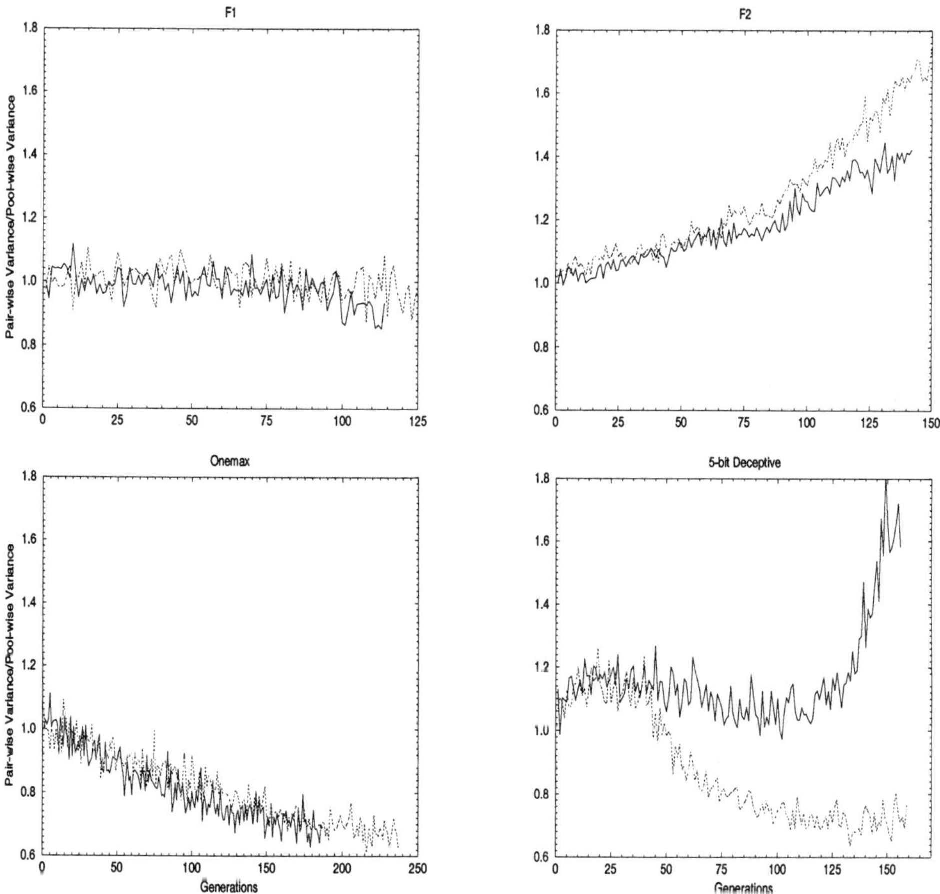

Figure 3: Pair-wise Variance to Pool-wise Variance ratios for the F1, F2, Onemax and 5-bit deceptive problems. Each plot shows the variance ratio for two algorithms: a pair-wise CCVA (solid line) and a pool-wise CCVA (dotted line). Each curve results from averaging 50 independent experiments; each experiment halts when the population converges.

This can be explained most easily by an extreme case. Suppose that for a population of 50 individuals and for strings of length 50 each string contains ones at all loci except one, and that this is a different locus for each individual. When any pair of individuals are crossed over the offspring can vary from the binary profile string of all ones by at most two bits. On the other hand, when pool-wise generation is used, the variations can be greater than two bits yielding significantly higher variance.

In light of the above, the plots for the deceptive function should not be surprising. The curve for the pool-wise algorithm after the first few generations is similar to that of the onemax problem. This is because the pool-wise algorithm is not able to preserve linkage and quickly drives the optimal segments out of the population. That is, the algorithm treats this problem as though it were a onemax problem, climbing the false peaks. The pair-wise algorithm, on the other hand, is able to sometimes retain one or two optimal segments which accounts for the higher variance ratio.

So far we have not said anything about performance. In the case of F1 and onemax, the pair-wise and pool-wise algorithms perform about the same. In the case of the other two functions, the pair-wise algorithm does significantly better. In the next section we compare the performance of pool-wise and pair-wise CCVAs in more detail, focusing on linkage and its relationship to both symbolic and numeric representations.

3 Methods

3.1 Four CCV Algorithms

To determine the contributions of pair-wise and pool-wise "mating" operators when using either symbolic-based or numeric-based representations, we tested four algorithms covering the four possible combinations. As our basic CCV algorithm (CCVA) we used CHC [6]. There are three reasons for this choice. First, it is an example of a pure CCVA: CHC does not use any mutation when generating offspring, but only crossover. When the population has converged it does a restart, using the best individual found so far as a seed for generating a new population. Second, we have found that the CHC algorithm is relatively insensitive to parameter settings. The "standard" parameter settings work fairly well on most problems, and thus there is less likelihood that the better algorithm only won because it had the advantage of better parameter settings. Third, we have found CHC to be a very effective function optimizer. In particular, we have tested CHC against a simple (or traditional) GA on a number of functions, and have found that CHC using its standard settings does better than a simple GA on most problems, especially the hard ones, even after tuning a simple GA for each problem [6, 14]. Furthermore, our CHC-based pool-wise CCVAs performed better than our implementations of BSC or PBIL on these problems.

Our four CHC-based algorithms had the following features in common:

- At each generation, a parent population of size 50 is used to generate an intermediate population of 50 individuals, which are randomly paired and used to generate 50 potential offspring. The intermediate population may be a biased sample of the parent population, with multiple copies of the better individuals, or an exact copy of the parent population, depending upon whether reproduction with emphasis (fitness biased) is used or not (unbiased).

- Potential offspring that are too similar are culled by an "incest prevention" mechanism and not evaluated. This is used to help maintain population diversity and to slow the genotypic convergence experienced in genetic search.

- Selection for replacement is elitist. The members of the parent and child populations are sorted and the worst members (if any) of the parent population are replaced by better members of the child population.

- There is no mutation during the "mating" cycles. Instead, when the population converges or no new offspring are being generated which are better than any members of the parent population, the best individual found is used as a template to reinitialize the population with one instance of the best individual inserted unchanged.

The **pair-wise symbolic-based CCVA** uses HUX [6] as its basic operator. HUX is a variant of uniform crossover which randomly swaps half of the differing bits in the two parents to produce two offspring. The **pair-wise, numeric-based CCVA** uses BLX

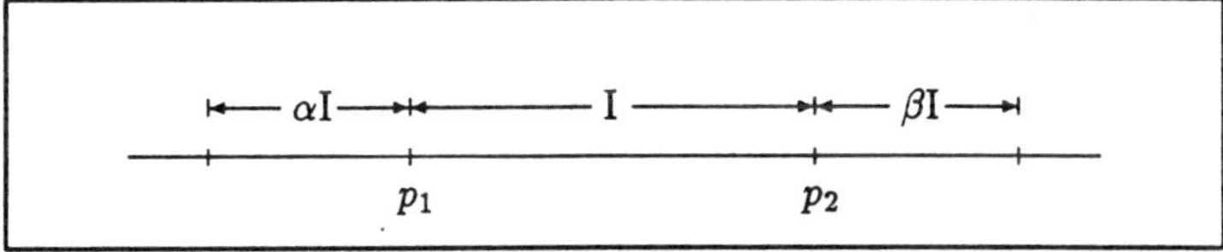

Figure 4: BLX Selection Interval.

(blend crossover) [7], as its basic operator. BLX blends the numeric parameters of the two parents by randomly choosing, for each parameter, a point on an interval defined by the values of the parents' parameters. If a particular parameter for the first parent has the value p1 and the second parent has a value of p2, then the value for the offspring's parameter is generated by randomly choosing a point within the *discretized* interval

$$[p1 - \alpha, p2 + \beta] :: (p1 < p2)$$

where α is a distance extending past the parameter value of the first parent and β is a distance extending past the parameter of the second parent (see also Figure 4). For the algorithms discussed in this paper, the values of α and β are defined as $0.5 * (|p2 - p1|)$ for the parameter of the parent whose fitness is the better of the two and 0.0 for the other.

So as not to introduce confounding differences into the algorithms we have tried to keep the algorithms as similar as possible. Thus, we have made the numeric-based CCVAs have the *same range and precision* as the symbolic-based CCVAs.

The pair-wise symbolic-based CCVA uses the Hamming distance between the two parents as a measure of similarity. Pairs of individuals whose Hamming distance is below an "incest" threshold are not allowed to produce offspring. This threshold is dynamically adjusted downward each generation in which no offspring are accepted into the parent population. When the incest threshold has fallen to zero, it is assumed that the algorithm has stopped making progress, and a restart is triggered with the incest threshold reset to the expected Hamming distance of any two members of the new population.

The pair-wise numeric-based CCVA also uses the Hamming distance between the two parents as a measure of similarity. The integer values of the two individuals' parameters are encoded into bit strings using binary reflected Gray coding [12] and the Hamming distance between the parents is measured. Although there may be other more direct ways of measuring similarity, we have found that this method works as well as, if not better than, any other method that we have tried.

The **pool-wise symbolic-based CCVA** uses the distribution of the alleles in the intermediate population to generate new individuals. For each locus, a '1' is generated with a probability equal to the fraction of the intermediate population that has a '1' at that locus. Incest prevention is applied to successive pairs of offspring since they have no parents in the usual sense. While it cannot be claimed that it is the same operation as used in the pair-wise algorithm, it does serve to maintain diversity and does improve the performance of this algorithm as well.

Ideally, a **pool-wise numeric-based CCVA** should model the distribution of the parameters in the intermediate population and then use this distribution to generate new individuals. There are several implementation drawbacks to this approach. First, it would be computationally quite expensive. Second, it would mean introducing a large number of new parameters which would require tuning. Furthermore, since our goal was to create an operator for generating new individuals that was as close as possible to the BLX operator, but was population-based, we took a different approach. An individual is generated as follows: for each parameter, two instances of the parameter are picked at random from the intermediate population, and a new parameter value is generated by using the BLX operator as is the case with the pair-wise algorithm. In particular, the interval is extended, as before, past the value of the better "parent". The major difference from the pair-wise CCVA is that each parameter of the new individual usually has a different pair of "parents." Instead of modeling the distribution of the parameter values of the intermediate population, we are re-sampling from this distribution, although the re-sampling is not necessarily unbiased.

Incest prevention for the pool-wise numeric-based algorithm is accomplished the same way as in the pool-wise symbolic algorithm. The Hamming distance between potential mates (after being Gray coded for this purpose) is measured and compared to a decreasing incest threshold. As before, we found that this dramatically improved performance for most functions.

Two additional differences among the algorithms need to be mentioned. Both symbolic-based algorithms used a restart mutation rate of 0.35, i.e., 49 new individuals were created by using the best individual as a template and flipping 35% of its bits. For the numeric-based algorithms, the 49 "mutated" individuals in the restart population were completely random. As with the symbolic-based algorithms, the restart population included one instance of the best individual found so far. Generally speaking we have found that the restart rate of 0.35 works better when using HUX than a random restart. However, the numeric-based algorithms have a stronger tendency to converge upon the elite individual, and so require a more vigorous randomization when restarting.

One additional factor was varied with these algorithms: whether the intermediate population was generated with or without a fitness bias. All algorithms were run both ways. While not a major part of our investigation, this factor did make a significant difference in the performance of some algorithms on some functions so we included it in our design.

3.2 The Test Problems

Functions contained in common EA test suites have been under attack for quite some time [4, 14, 21]. Whitley, et al. [20] illustrated the importance of understanding the various characteristics of test functions before using them for performance comparisons or algorithm analysis. With this in mind, the following test problems were chosen to explore the difference in the dynamics of the algorithms described in Section 3.1, not to make claims about the general superiority of particular algorithms.

The test functions used in the following analysis include four functions from the DeJong [5] test suite: F1, F2, F3, and F5. We also included two functions introduced by Schaffer, et al. [17]: F6 and F7. Functions F6 and F7 are known as the sine envelope sine wave and stretched-V sine wave respectively. A 20-parameter Rastrigin (F10), 10-parameter Schwefel (F11) and 10-parameter Griewank (F12) function [16] round out the test suite. This suite includes functions that are unimodal and multi-modal, continuous and discontinuous, and have large and small search spaces. The mathematical representation for these functions is shown in Table 1.

$$F1 : f(x_i \,|_{i=1,3}) = \sum_{i=1}^{3} x_i^2 \qquad\qquad x_i \in [-5.12, 5.11]$$

$$F2 : f(x_i \,|_{i=1,2}) = 100(x_1^2 - x_2)^2 + (1 - x_1)^2 \qquad\qquad x_i \in [-2.048, 2.047]$$

$$F3 : f(x_i \,|_{i=1,5}) = \sum_{i=1}^{5} \lfloor x_i \rfloor \qquad\qquad x_i \in [-5.12, 5.11]$$

$$F5 : f(x_i \,|_{i=1,2}) = \left[0.002 + \sum_{j=1}^{25} \frac{1}{j + \sum_{i=1}^{2}(x_i - a_{ij})^6} \right]^{-1} \qquad\qquad x_i \in [-65.536, 65.535]$$

$$F6 : f(x_i \,|_{i=1,2}) = 0.5 + \frac{sin^2 \sqrt{x_1^2 + x_2^2} - 0.5}{[1.0 + 0.001(x_1^2 + x_2^2)]^2} \qquad\qquad x_i \in [-100, 100]$$

$$F7 : f(x_i \,|_{i=1,2}) = (x_1^2 + x_2^2)^{0.25}[sin^2(50(x_1^2 + x_2^2)^{0.1}) + 1.0] \qquad\qquad x_i \in [-100, 100]$$

$$F10 : f(x_i \,|_{i=1,n}) = (n * 10) + \left[\sum_{i=1}^{n} (x_i^2 - 10cos(2\pi x_i)) \right] \qquad\qquad x_i \in [-5.12, 5.11], n = 20$$

$$F11 : f(x_i \,|_{i=1,10}) = \sum_{i=1}^{10} -x_i sin(\sqrt{|x_i|}) \qquad\qquad x_i \in [-512, 511]$$

$$F12 : f(x_i \,|_{i=1,10}) = 1 + \sum_{i=1}^{10} \frac{x_i^2}{4000} - \prod_{i=1}^{10}(cos(x_i/\sqrt{i})) \qquad\qquad x_i \subset [-512, 511]$$

Table 1. Test Functions.

F1, F3, F10 and F11 are known to be separable[5] at the numeric parameter level [20]. Functions F2, F6, F7, and F12 contain nonlinear parameter interactions, although for F12 the effect of the product term causing inter-parameter interactions decreases as the number of parameters increases.

4   Results

Tables 2 and 3 show the average number of function evaluations (with the standard error of the mean, SEM) necessary to find the optimum solution to each problem for the pair-wise and pool-wise algorithms. The number of function evaluations necessary to find the optimum solution were averaged over 30 independent experiments in all cases. All of the CCVAs consistently located the optimal solution for all functions except in two cases. The

---

[5]The separable problems used in this work consist of the summation of multiple instances of single parameter nonlinear sub-problems and thus, the parameters are independent of each other.

Func		Pool-wise CCVA		Pair-wise CCVA	
		Mean Evals	SEM	Mean Evals	SEM
f1	b	792	30	b	899	45
f2	b	12,429	960	b	8,691	769
f3	b	775	48	b	917	48
f5	b	1,164	66	b	1,283	71
f6	b	8,030	1,176	u	6,496	737
f7	u	3,297	203	u	3,743	321
f10	b	(27) 300,669	20,507	b	85,473	5,685
f11	u	16,790	2,993	u	10,022	863
f12	u	228,827	24,482	u	60,825	6,696

Table 2: CCVA Performances on Test Functions Using Bit-wise Representations.

pool-wise CCVA failed to consistently locate the optimal solution for F10 when a bit-wise representation was used after 500,000 evaluations and when using a numeric representation for F2 after 50,000 evaluations. These exceptions are annotated in Tables 2 and 4 using (x), where x indicates the number of experiments where the optimum was successfully located.

Table 2 shows the performance results for the pool-wise and pair-wise CCVAs using a bit-wise representation while Table 4 shows the performance results for the same CCVAs when a numeric representation is used. Both the numeric and Gray coded representations use the same discretization interval and range for the input parameters. For all bit-wise representations we used binary reflected Gray coding [12] because it preserves the adjacency of consecutive numeric values consistent with a numerically defined parameter optimization function [15, 20].

To avoid adding another dimension to the tables we have collapsed these results on the dimension of fitness-biased or unbiased selection. In each case we show the better result and flag it as 'b' (for fitness biased) or 'u' (for unbiased). From the perspective of the CCV framework we can identify some of the factors affecting these results. Biased selection can enhance the performance of CCVAs if the response surface is fairly easy to search or the reproduction operator preserves variance sufficiently so that strong selection pressure does not lead to fatal premature convergence. Biased selection can also enhance the performance of a pool-wise CCVA on highly epistatic problems by increasing the influence of a highly fit, outlying individual.

Table 3 shows that when using numeric representations, the pool-wise CCVAs perform better than the pair-wise CCVAs on all functions except F2. However, the results are quite different when using bit-encoded representations where the pool-wise CCVAs perform better on only functions F1, and F3. The performances are statistically indistinguishable on F5, F6 and F7, and pair-wise prevails on F2, F10, F11, and F12. We now examine the details in order to understand these patterns.

4.1 Numeric Representations

The fitness value in problems F1, F3, F10, and F11 is a summation of the same function applied to each parameter. The pool-wise CCVA using a numeric representation, which de-links all parameters, obviously should have no trouble in these cases. Therefore, its overall performance will depend only on the ability of its variation mechanism to solve one instance

Func		Pool-wise CCVA			Pair-wise CCVA	
		Mean Evals	SEM		Mean Evals	SEM
f1	u	624	11	u	659	10
f2	b	(11) 13,499	2,028	b	2,817	207
f3	u	1,737	100	u	2,663	218
f5	u	3,545	233	u	5,940	583
f6	b	9,390	1,051	u	13,045	1,407
f7	b	914	11	b	956	13
f10	u	24,046	1,138	u	47,693	2,744
f11	u	9,058	715	u	30,374	2,731
f12	b	20,275	1,517	u	38,296	3,999

Table 3: CCVA Performances on Test Functions Using Discretized Numeric Representations.

of the function. The results show this is not a problem, even for multi-peaked functions like Rastrigin (F10) and Schwefel (F11).

F6 and F7 are not only multi-peaked, but there is parameter linkage in the mathematical formulation (see Table 1). The pool-wise algorithm is more successful on these problems because the individuals which survive are clustered along the axes[6] where the parameters can be manipulated independently to solve the problem. Furthermore, since all valleys get progressively better as the central optimum is approached, the population variance strongly tends to span the optimum. This allows the CCVA mechanism to quickly discover the optimum (biased selection is not harmful). F5 is not symmetric, but does have the property that the location of the best region with respect to one parameter is independent of the other(s) — in this case it is a flat plane. The potential difficulties are the barriers dividing the distinct good regions, and the location of the optimum at one edge of the plane (not the center as in F6 and F7). The restart mechanism allows the algorithm to "creep to the edge" but it is less effective than exploiting the schemata available with bit-coding (the same pattern is evident for F3).

Although F12 has a nonlinear component which causes inter-parameter interactions, as the number of parameters increases the fitness of the function is dominated by the linear summation term as pointed out by Whitley, et al. [20]. Thus, it is not surprising that the pool-wise CCVA using a numeric representation performs better than the pair-wise CCVA on F12.

Tables 2 and 3 both show that the pair-wise CCVA exhibits a distinct advantage in solving the F2 test function over the pool-wise CCVA. In a continuous numeric representation F2 has a single optimum as illustrated by the contour plot and 3-dimensional rendering of the function in Figure 5. The superior performance of the pair-wise CCVA is a result of its ability to preserve inter-parameter linkage and negotiate the curved attraction basin which is located in a diagonal orientation to the axes (see Figure 5). Evidence for this observation is provided by the plots in Figure 6. The four plots in Figure 6 show the $x1$ and $x2$ parameters of the offspring being generated by the pair-wise CCVA (top two plots) and a pool-wise CCVA (bottom two plots), both using biased selection. In order to illustrate the progress of the algorithms over time the left hand plots show the offspring generated

---

[6]Although the individuals are initially distributed uniformly over the search space, because those points located close to an axis can be improved one parameter at a time, they have a higher probability of producing surviving offspring [7].

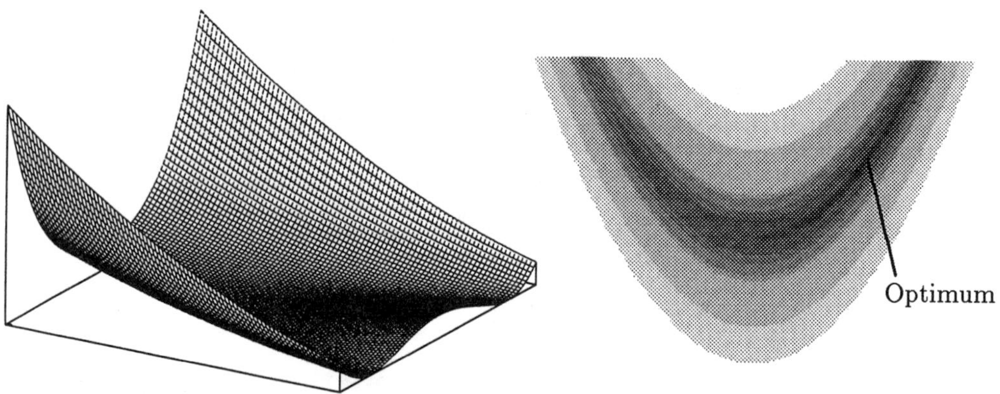

Figure 5: 3-Dimensional Rendering of Rosenbrock's Saddle and Corresponding Contour Plot. The 3-dimensional rendering has been rotated to enhance viewing.

over the first half of the search and the right hand plots show all offspring generated up to the first convergence.

The pair-wise CCVA exhibits a search pattern in which surviving offspring are initially concentrated in the attraction basin close to the origin. The pair-wise CCVA is able to exploit surviving *maverick* offspring that lie along the diagonal, generating new offspring in the proximity of the maverick. On the other hand, the pool-wise CCVA has more difficulty generating new offspring near the maverick. This is directly related to the de-linking of the parameters when producing offspring. To navigate in a trajectory diagonal to the axes requires changing both parameters in concert. Changing only one parameter at a time will often yield offspring with worse fitness values than their respective generators. Assuming a population of size 50, the probability of the maverick having any influence over an offspring is 1 in 50, the same as for the pair-wise CCVA. However, the probability of both parameters in the offspring being influenced by the maverick is 1 in 2500. This explains why the pool-wise plots show strong horizontal and vertical sampling behavior and the absence of the diagonal pattern which is observed in the pair-wise plots.

Even though the BLX operator in a pair-wise CCVA is better at creeping down the valley than in a pool-wise CCVA, it is not particularly good at it. The steep sides of the valley cause the majority of the offspring not to survive. The result is that selection pressure forces the population to quickly converge, and multiple restarts are required in order for the algorithm to progress down the valley. An EA more adept at creeping should do better, and indeed a very simple implementation of Fogel's evolutionary programming (EP) algorithm [10], which applies a Gaussian mutation to every parameter of every surviving parent and uses no restarts, solves F2 in about half the trials needed by the pair-wise CCVA.

4.2 Binary Representations

The independence of the numerical parameters seems to provide little predictive power on the performance of bit-coded CCVAs. Since they operate on sub-parameter schemata, this

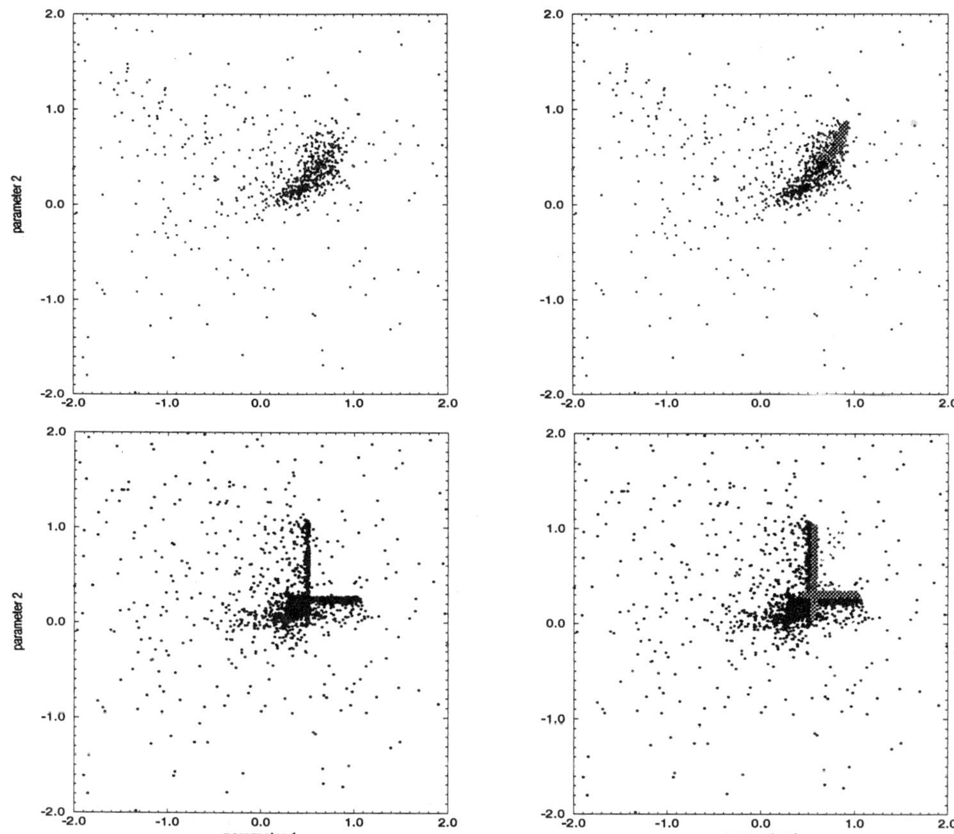

Figure 6: Distributions of generated offspring by pair-wise (top) and pool-wise (bottom) offspring parameter values on the F2 problem. The rightmost plots are at a later generation and are cumulative, with the gray areas representing the most recently generated offspring.

is not surprising, but it forces us to look elsewhere for factors that might predict algorithm behavior.

Functions F1, F3, F5 and F7 are known to be "hill-climbable" in their Gray coded representations [15]. This would indicate that the individual bits are generally independent, and we would conjecture that the Gray coded representation did not create any inner-parameter linkages, making the pool-wise CCVA more efficient than the pair-wise CCVA. As expected the pool-wise CCVA performs better than the pair-wise CCVA on these four functions.

While it has been shown that the F10, F11, and F12 functions have no significant inter-parameter linkage in their numeric representations and each of them can be solved using different forms of bit-wise stochastic hill climbers [15, 14], the results in Table 2 indicate that there is some form of linkage created when using a Gray coded representation. The pair-wise CCVA performs better on these functions than the pool-wise CCVA, although the linkage created by the Gray representation is not obvious in these cases. Analysis of the Schwefel function (F11) illustrates some of the complex dynamics that are created in binary coded search spaces which are not present when numeric representations are used.

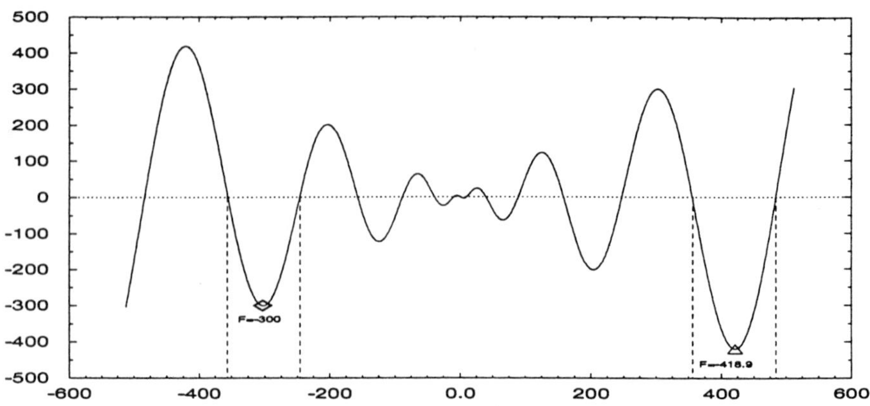

Figure 7: One Parameter Schwefel Function.

The Schwefel function (F11) is solved for the minimum solution using an integer unit of discretization with a range of -512 to 511 for each of 10 parameters. Figure 7 shows a one dimensional view of F11 annotating the numeric bounds of the extreme attraction basins and corresponding fitness values. Although the sub-optimum solution located at X=-325 is far away in numeric space from the optimum at X=421, the attraction basins in which these two points reside are very close in Gray coded Hamming space. Here, we will refer to the attraction basin containing the second best solution as the *sub-optimal attraction basin* and the attraction basin containing the global optimum as the *optimum attraction basin*.

String representations for each point in the sub-optimal attraction basin over the range [-355,-314] can be mapped sequentially to points in the optimum attraction basin over the range [413,454] by complementing two bits (at the same two loci in all cases). Each of the points in the optimum attraction basin has a better fitness value than the corresponding point in the sub-optimal attraction basin. For example, the Gray coded string 0010100001, representing the parameter -319, has a fitness of -266.514 while the string 1000100001, representing the parameter 449, has a fitness of -329.119. The bits that must be complemented to move from the points in the sub-optimal attraction basin to the optimal attraction basin are in positions 1 and 3 (numbering from left to right). In addition, a larger segment in the suboptimal attraction basin exists such that the complementing of the bits in the first, third and fourth positions corresponds to points in the optimal attraction basin with similar fitness improvement. This transformation is valid over the range [-356,-246] in the sub-optimal attraction basin which corresponds to the range [373,483] in the optimum attraction basin.

This discovery suggests that there is at worst only modest linkage in a single parameter version of F11. Further evidence for this is found in the performance of pool-wise (240 trials) and pair-wise (315 trials) algorithms on the single parameter problem (SEM about 15 for both). This result raises another question: if the parameters are independent (which we know) and pool-wise is better on a single parameter, how can pair-wise be better on a 10 parameter version? The answer lies in the restarts. Upon restarting, the population retains one copy of the best individual and 49 highly mutated siblings. Pool-wise mating cannot effectively propagate its accumulated good schemata. Of the 127 total restarts in the 30 experiments, only 52 (41%) of the restarts converged to improved values. However, pair-wise mating can propagate the accumulated schemata; 50 of the 61 restarts (82%) converged to improved values. The price of this propagation is the modest hitchhiking suggested by the single parameter performance. This example illustrates how difficult it is to make general predictions from simple cases. We may know what phenomena are occurring, but predicting performance requires quantitative estimates, not just qualitative.

Inter-parameter linkage is critical to solving the F2 test function when a numeric representation is used. Table 2 indicates that linkage is also critical in solving the binary representation of F2 as the pair-wise CCVA performs much better than the pool-wise CCVA. While the preservation of inter-parameter linkage is critical to solving the binary representation of the problem, there is another aspect to this problem which is even more interesting. By examining the population distributions, we see that the population quickly converges on the central region and then must creep down the valley. Creeping is rather inefficient for these algorithms. They must do repeated restarts as the steep valley walls cause selection pressure to rapidly reduce diversity. When we examine the best individuals at successive restarts we see what we call *bit churning*: the bits at many loci flip back and forth between zero and one at each improved convergence. The creeping behavior of the population necessary to make progress cannot be accomplished with building blocks.

The data in Tables 2 and 3 might suggest that the pair-wise CCVA using Gray coding and pool-wise CCVA using a numeric representation are the more competitive algorithms. The only functions for which one of these is not at least tied for the best performance are F3 (which is bit-climbable) and F2 (which is better solvable by EP and gradient methods). Such a conclusion would be premature as we show in the next section.

4.3 A Class of Highly Nonlinear Functions

Whitley, et al. [20] recommended that EA test suites include nonlinear problems where the nonlinearity does not deteriorate as the number of parameters is increased. Solving a set of linear equations is such a class of problems. The performance of EAs on this class has been studied by Bremermann [3] and Fogel and Atmar [11]. The problem can be stated as solving for the elements of a vector, X, given the matrix A and vector B in the expression: $AX = B$. Instances from this class can be generated randomly, and the extent of parameter linkage can be controlled by varying the probability of a non-zero term in A and the maximum distance from the diagonal of the non-zero terms. This class of problems can be scaled by changing the dimensions of the matrix A and vectors B and X.

Ten, 4-parameter and fifty, 10-parameter problems were created with no zero terms in A for maximum parameter interaction. For testing purposes the parameters were discretized in integer units over the range [-128,127] and the B vectors were computed such that the optimum for all problems was $X = 1$. Analysis of these functions reveals that all instances generated contained large numbers of local optima. Many of the best local optima have fitness values extremely competitive with, but located very far away from, the global optimum for both Gray coded binary and numeric representations.

Tables 4 and 5 present results for a small sampling of four and ten parameter problems on which we tested our four algorithms. These samples include the "easiest" and the "hardest" problems created and two additional problems representative of average difficulty.[7] Each

---

[7]The terms *easy*, *hard* and *average* are applied here with respect to the mean number of trials required to solve the problem or the number of times the optimal solution was found.

Prb.	Pool-wise CCV		Pair-wise CCV	
	Mean Evals	SEM	Mean Evals	SEM
1	2,017	175	1,176	90
2	13,288	1,574	3,424	320
3	18,009	2,178	9,477	960
4	138,899	21,631	90,486	14,073

Table 4: CCVA Performances on 4, Four-Parameter Linear System Functions Using Numeric Representations.

problem was tested 30 independent times resulting in an average number of trials to solve the problem and the standard error of the mean. Parameters for the initial population strings in these experiments were initialized randomly and uniformly. The evaluation function used is given by:

$$f = \sum_{i=1}^{n} \left[\left| \sum_{j=1}^{n} (a_{ij} * x_j) - b_i \right| \right]$$

where n is the number of parameters in the problem. The results in Tables 4 and 5 include data only for the CCVAs using a numeric representation. In no case did the average performance of either the pool-wise or pair-wise CCVA using a Gray coded representation approach that of the CCVAs using a numeric representation. Furthermore, in all cases the pair-wise CCVA performed significantly better than the pool-wise CCVA regardless of the representation used.

The difficulty of these functions varies dramatically with respect to the number of evaluations necessary to solve the problem. The hardest 10 parameter problem requires almost 15 times more function evaluations to solve than the easiest problem of the group and is by far the most difficult problem to solve for these algorithms with respect to number of function evaluations. The problem requiring the most function evaluations to solve in the set of 4 parameter problems requires two orders of magnitude more function evaluations than the easiest. However, for all test problems the pair-wise CCVA performed better than the pool-wise CCVA when using a numeric representation and the comparison was almost always statistically significant. This class of problems meets the criteria for scaling as expressed by Whitley, et al. [20] when comparing CCVA performances and provides a mechanism for controlling inter-parameter interactions in a predictable manner.

Prb.	Pool-wise CCV		Pair-wise CCV	
	Mean Evals	SEM	Mean Evals	SEM
1	32,002	2,690	22,008	1,166
2	(22) 263,930	34,196	(29) 190,995	24,739
3	(18) 277,239	38,054	(29) 179,732	24,957
4	(8) 402,164	33,437	(16) 340,816	32,696

Table 5: CCVA Performances on 4, Ten-Parameter Linear System Functions Using Numeric Representations.

5   Conclusions

The stress that GA theory has traditionally placed on propagation, as expressed in the schema theorem, is not misplaced. We have found that propagation is important and that pair-wise CCVAs are better at propagating schemata than pool-wise CCVAs. But the reason why propagation is important may be more mundane than usually supposed. Rather than as an expected outcome of recombination, CCVAs often *stumble* upon maverick individuals that are far from the population profile. Pair-wise CCVAs are better able to explore the neighborhood around the maverick individuals than pool-wise CCVAs, behaving more in the manner of a mutation-based algorithm or even a hill-climber. Thus, they are better able to discover superior points lying in the neighborhood of the mavericks. This is not to say that a mutation-based algorithm would necessarily be better. Perhaps the reason the maverick was discovered was because of the CCVA's vigorous exploration early in the search.

Sometimes, however, a CCVA is clearly not the best algorithm. When one looks at the variation-creation mechanism needed for highly linked problems like F2, one sees that vigorous bit churning is needed to creep along the attraction basin. *There simply are no consistently superior schemata in such a case.* Evolutionary algorithms more adept at creeping should do better. Indeed, we have observed that a simple implementation of evolutionary programming solves F2 in about half the trials needed by a pair-wise CCVA, and that good gradient methods are better still.

One of the reasons pool-wise CCVAs like PBIL [2] perform so well on many of the traditional test problems is that many of these problems not only have a low level of linkage among the numeric parameters, but also a low level of linkage among the bits that represent the parameters. We doubt, however, that this is a feature that accompanies most representations of real world optimization problems. Generally, we see that parameter independence strongly favors a pool-wise CCVA using numeric representations, but that this feature has less predictive power for CCVAs using binary strings.

To understand the proper niche for CCVAs using pair-wise mating, it is important to include test problems with a high degree of parameter linkage, such as the linear system functions. This class of problems has the additional important feature that the linkage is not attenuated or lost as the problems are scaled up. Our results for this class of problems provides evidence that the niche for crossover is significantly larger than we identified previously [9].

Finally, our results are consistent with previous empirical studies showing competitive or superior results using numeric representations for many problems. CCVAs operating on numeric representations focus their exploration in numerically adjacent regions of the search space and thus are able to exploit the property that better regions are often near good regions in functions with continuous variables.

References

[1] T. Bäck and H.P. Schwefel. An Overview of Evolutionary Algorithms for Parameter Optimization. *Evolutionary Computation*, 1:1–23, 1993.

[2] Shumeet Baluja. An Empirical Comparison of Seven Iterative and Evolutionary Function Optimization Heuristics Technical Report Nb. CMU-CS-95-193, School of Computer Science, Carnegie Mellon University, 1995.

[3] H.J. Bremermann. Optimization Through Evolution and Recombination. In Yovits, Jacobi, and Goldstein, editors, *Self-organizing Systems*, pages 93–106, 1962.

[4] Lawrence Davis. Bit-Climbing, Representational Bias, and Test Suite Design. In L. Booker and R. Belew, editors, *Proceedings of the Fourth International Conference on Genetic Algorithms*, pages 18–23. Morgan Kauffman, 1991.

[5] Ken DeJong. *An Analysis of the Behavior of a Class of Genetic Adaptive Systems*. PhD thesis, University of Michigan, Department of Computer and Communication Sciences, Ann Arbor, Michigan, 1975.

[6] Larry Eshelman. The CHC Adaptive Search Algorithm. How to Have Safe Search When Engaging in Nontraditional Genetic Recombination. In G. Rawlins, editor, *Foundations of Genetic Algorithms*, pages 265–283. Morgan Kaufmann, 1991.

[7] Larry Eshelman and J. David Schaffer. Real-Coded Genetic Algorithms and Interval-Schemata. In L. Darrell Whitley, editor, *Foundations of Genetic Algorithms - 2*, pages 187–202. Morgan Kaufmann, 1993.

[8] Larry Eshelman and J. David Schaffer. Productive Recombination and Propatating and Preserving Schemata. In D. Whitley and M. Vose, editors, *Foundations of Genetic Algorithms - 3*, pages 299–313. Morgan Kaufmann, 1995.

[9] Larry J. Eshelman and J. David Schaffer. Crossover's Niche. In Stephanie Forrest, editor, *Proceedings of the Fifth International Conference on Genetic Algorithms*, pages 9–14. Morgan Kauffman, 1993.

[10] David Fogel. *Evoluationary Computation: Towards a New Philosophy of Machine Intelligence*. IEEE Press, 1995.

[11] David B. Fogel and J. Ward Atmar. Comparing Genetic Operators with Gaussian Mutations in Simulated Evolutionary Processes Using Linear Systems. *Biological Cybernetics*, 63:111–114, 1990.

[12] E. N. Gilbert. Gray Codes and Paths on the n-Cube. *The Bell System Technical Journal*, pages 815–826, May 1958.

[13] G. Liepins and M. Vose. Representation Issues in Genetic Algorithms. *Journal of Experimental and Theoretical Artificial Intelligence*, 2:4–30, 1990.

[14] Keith E. Mathias and L. Darrell Whitley. Changing Representations During Search: A Comparative Study of Delta Coding. *Journal of Evolutionary Computation*, 2(3):249–278, 1994.

[15] Keith E. Mathias and L. Darrell Whitley. Transforming the Search Space with Gray Coding. In J. D. Schaffer, editor, *Proceedings of the IEEE International Conference on Evolutionary Computation*, pages 513–518. IEEE Service Center, 1994.

[16] H. Mühlenbein, M. Schomisch, and J. Born. The Parallel Genetic Algorithm as Function Optimizer. In L. Booker and R. Belew, editors, *Proceedings of the Fourth International Conference on Genetic Algorithms*, pages 271–278. Morgan Kauffman, 1991.

[17] J. David Schaffer, Richard A. Caruana, Larry J. Eshelman, and Rajarshi Das. A Study of Control Parameters Affecting Online Performance of Genetic Algorithms for Function Optimization. In J. D. Schaffer, editor, *Proceedings of the Third International Conference on Genetic Algorithms*, pages 51–60. Morgan Kauffman, 1989.

[18] J. David Schaffer, Larry Eshelman, and Daniel Offutt. Spurious Correlations and Premature Convergence in Genetic Algorithms. In G. Rawlins, editor, *Foundations of Genetic Algorithms*, pages 102–112. Morgan Kaufmann, 1991.

[19] G. Syswerda. Simulated Crossover in Genetic Algorithms. In L. Darrell Whitley, editor, *Foundations of Genetic Algorithms - 2*, pages 239–255. Morgan Kaufmann, 1993.

[20] Darrell Whitley, Keith Mathias, Soraya Rana, and John Dzubera. Building Better Test Functions. In L. Eshelman, editor, *Proceedings of the Sixth International Conference on Genetic Algorithms*. Morgan Kaufmann, 1995.

[21] Stewart W. Wilson. GA-Easy Does Not Imply Steepest-Ascent Optimizable. In L. Booker and R. Belew, editors, *Proceedings of the Fourth International Conference on Genetic Algorithms*, pages 85–89. Morgan Kauffman, 1991.

6 Appendix A - Linear Equation Matrices

Although Section 4.3 describes the methods used to randomly generate problem instances for systems of linear equations, Table 4 shows results for four specific instances of the problem using four parameters. The matrices for these problems are as follows:

1.
$$
\begin{vmatrix} 3 & 2 & 1 & 8 \\ 7 & 8 & 2 & 1 \\ 2 & 4 & 6 & 5 \\ 4 & 1 & 8 & 4 \end{vmatrix} \begin{vmatrix} 1 \\ 1 \\ 1 \\ 1 \end{vmatrix} = \begin{vmatrix} 14 \\ 18 \\ 17 \\ 17 \end{vmatrix}
$$

2.
$$
\begin{vmatrix} 9 & 2 & 1 & 5 \\ 4 & 7 & 4 & 3 \\ 2 & 8 & 6 & 8 \\ 7 & 8 & 7 & 9 \end{vmatrix} \begin{vmatrix} 1 \\ 1 \\ 1 \\ 1 \end{vmatrix} = \begin{vmatrix} 17 \\ 18 \\ 24 \\ 31 \end{vmatrix}
$$

3.
$$
\begin{vmatrix} 6 & 6 & 7 & 9 \\ 1 & 9 & 7 & 5 \\ 5 & 2 & 8 & 7 \\ 3 & 4 & 8 & 5 \end{vmatrix} \begin{vmatrix} 1 \\ 1 \\ 1 \\ 1 \end{vmatrix} = \begin{vmatrix} 28 \\ 22 \\ 22 \\ 20 \end{vmatrix}
$$

4.
$$
\begin{vmatrix} 2 & 2 & 9 & 5 \\ 2 & 4 & 7 & 3 \\ 2 & 1 & 8 & 5 \\ 3 & 9 & 9 & 2 \end{vmatrix} \begin{vmatrix} 1 \\ 1 \\ 1 \\ 1 \end{vmatrix} = \begin{vmatrix} 18 \\ 16 \\ 16 \\ 23 \end{vmatrix}
$$

The matrices for the ten parameter problem instances whose results are shown in Table 5 are:

1.
$$
\begin{vmatrix} 5 & 2 & 2 & 7 & 6 & 4 & 7 & 6 & 3 & 5 \\ 8 & 5 & 2 & 6 & 6 & 5 & 8 & 5 & 3 & 4 \\ 8 & 2 & 7 & 7 & 7 & 9 & 2 & 4 & 9 & 2 \\ 1 & 7 & 9 & 4 & 2 & 9 & 6 & 2 & 6 & 8 \\ 7 & 6 & 6 & 5 & 1 & 6 & 5 & 7 & 1 & 5 \\ 8 & 5 & 9 & 4 & 5 & 2 & 2 & 6 & 2 & 5 \\ 9 & 8 & 6 & 8 & 1 & 8 & 3 & 4 & 2 & 7 \\ 5 & 4 & 3 & 1 & 1 & 8 & 8 & 8 & 9 & 4 \\ 3 & 9 & 2 & 3 & 1 & 6 & 5 & 4 & 5 & 1 \\ 4 & 9 & 7 & 1 & 7 & 7 & 4 & 7 & 5 & 8 \end{vmatrix} \begin{vmatrix} 1 \\ 1 \\ 1 \\ 1 \\ 1 \\ 1 \\ 1 \\ 1 \\ 1 \\ 1 \end{vmatrix} = \begin{vmatrix} 47 \\ 52 \\ 57 \\ 54 \\ 49 \\ 48 \\ 56 \\ 51 \\ 39 \\ 59 \end{vmatrix}
$$

2.
$$
\begin{vmatrix}
3 & 8 & 7 & 1 & 8 & 6 & 8 & 1 & 4 & 3 \\
8 & 2 & 9 & 2 & 3 & 1 & 6 & 6 & 7 & 7 \\
7 & 4 & 7 & 7 & 2 & 6 & 7 & 2 & 1 & 4 \\
4 & 1 & 8 & 2 & 3 & 8 & 8 & 4 & 8 & 8 \\
1 & 9 & 5 & 1 & 2 & 4 & 1 & 7 & 5 & 9 \\
5 & 5 & 8 & 9 & 6 & 3 & 5 & 4 & 1 & 1 \\
5 & 3 & 9 & 8 & 1 & 9 & 2 & 9 & 7 & 3 \\
3 & 2 & 9 & 9 & 4 & 1 & 4 & 6 & 5 & 5 \\
6 & 5 & 8 & 3 & 5 & 5 & 6 & 4 & 7 & 9 \\
5 & 1 & 4 & 3 & 8 & 4 & 7 & 8 & 8 & 1
\end{vmatrix}
\begin{vmatrix} 1 \\ 1 \\ 1 \\ 1 \\ 1 \\ 1 \\ 1 \\ 1 \\ 1 \\ 1 \end{vmatrix}
=
\begin{vmatrix} 49 \\ 51 \\ 47 \\ 54 \\ 44 \\ 47 \\ 56 \\ 48 \\ 58 \\ 49 \end{vmatrix}
$$

3.
$$
\begin{vmatrix}
4 & 2 & 2 & 8 & 1 & 5 & 5 & 9 & 4 & 4 \\
7 & 3 & 6 & 3 & 7 & 5 & 8 & 6 & 4 & 6 \\
3 & 5 & 3 & 5 & 8 & 9 & 1 & 6 & 3 & 9 \\
9 & 7 & 7 & 2 & 7 & 8 & 1 & 9 & 7 & 4 \\
8 & 7 & 9 & 4 & 6 & 6 & 7 & 4 & 4 & 1 \\
3 & 6 & 9 & 8 & 1 & 3 & 7 & 3 & 3 & 6 \\
7 & 5 & 8 & 9 & 5 & 3 & 4 & 7 & 2 & 5 \\
2 & 1 & 4 & 2 & 3 & 7 & 7 & 4 & 1 & 1 \\
2 & 3 & 5 & 5 & 4 & 7 & 1 & 6 & 9 & 8 \\
5 & 9 & 1 & 8 & 4 & 1 & 1 & 3 & 9 & 4
\end{vmatrix}
\begin{vmatrix} 1 \\ 1 \\ 1 \\ 1 \\ 1 \\ 1 \\ 1 \\ 1 \\ 1 \\ 1 \end{vmatrix}
=
\begin{vmatrix} 44 \\ 55 \\ 52 \\ 61 \\ 56 \\ 49 \\ 55 \\ 32 \\ 50 \\ 45 \end{vmatrix}
$$

4.
$$
\begin{vmatrix}
5 & 4 & 5 & 2 & 9 & 5 & 4 & 2 & 3 & 1 \\
9 & 7 & 1 & 1 & 7 & 2 & 2 & 6 & 6 & 9 \\
3 & 1 & 8 & 6 & 9 & 7 & 4 & 2 & 1 & 6 \\
8 & 3 & 7 & 3 & 7 & 5 & 3 & 9 & 9 & 5 \\
9 & 5 & 1 & 6 & 3 & 4 & 2 & 3 & 3 & 9 \\
1 & 2 & 3 & 1 & 7 & 6 & 6 & 3 & 3 & 3 \\
1 & 5 & 7 & 8 & 1 & 4 & 7 & 8 & 4 & 8 \\
9 & 3 & 8 & 6 & 3 & 4 & 7 & 1 & 8 & 1 \\
8 & 2 & 8 & 5 & 3 & 8 & 7 & 2 & 7 & 5 \\
2 & 1 & 2 & 2 & 9 & 8 & 7 & 4 & 4 & 1
\end{vmatrix}
\begin{vmatrix} 1 \\ 1 \\ 1 \\ 1 \\ 1 \\ 1 \\ 1 \\ 1 \\ 1 \\ 1 \end{vmatrix}
=
\begin{vmatrix} 40 \\ 50 \\ 47 \\ 59 \\ 45 \\ 35 \\ 53 \\ 50 \\ 55 \\ 40 \end{vmatrix}
$$

Fitness Landscape Characterization by Variance of Decompositions

Akiko Aizawa
National Center for Science Information Systems
3-29-1 Otsuka, Bunkyo-ku
Tokyo 112, JAPAN

Abstract

In the present paper, we first present a new framework in which crossover operators are formalized as a combination of probabilistic linear decompositions and a randomized search. Then, as a means to theoretically analyze the behavior of different crossover operators for the infinite population case, we uniquely define crossover correlation using the variance between decompositions, i.e., after decomposing the solution space through a template of competing schemata, the variance between the decompositions, being expressed as variance coefficients, is used as a fundamental statistical measure. First, the employed linear decomposition hypothesis and variance coefficients are mathematically defined. Then, features and implications of utilizing such variance coefficients are presented by formulating relational equations describing the respective relationship between variance coefficients and Walsh coefficients, epistasis variance, and crossover correlation. An analysis of representative crossover operators is subsequently carried out using crossover correlation expressed as variance coefficients, after which we compare the coding effects of these crossover operators mathematically. Following this, a simulation is shown to evaluate analytical results in comparison with actual GA performance for the case in which the population size is large relative to the problem size.

1 Introduction

This paper addresses a classic problem in the study of genetic algorithms (GAs). That is, characterization of the solution space in terms of GA-hardness: the fundamental evaluative measure for elucidating the underlying mathematical structure of such solution space search algorithms.

With regard to what mathematical assumption makes the employment of GAs more effective than a crude random search, it is assumed that their performance correlates with predicting the fitness value of a binary string from component bits. Accordingly, this assumption has been taken as the basis of three well-known characterization methods, i.e., *Walsh function analysis, epistasis variance,* and *crossover correlation analysis.*

In Walsh function analysis, originally proposed for this purpose in [Bethke, 1981] and later re-introduced in [Goldberg, 1989-a,b], the solution space is transformed into the space of Walsh coefficients using Walsh functions as orthonormal bases. These functions intuitively define independent vectors, each of which represents different interdependencies between component bits, while the coefficients express the degree in which the interdependencies contribute to the overall fitness value. This analysis reveals all hidden dependencies in the solution space, yet it has drawbacks since computation time is intractable and only small-sized problems can be handled due to the solution space and Walsh-transformed space both having the same size. Moreover, while the analysis determines the strength of individual dependencies expressed as the absolute value of Walsh coefficients, it provides no information on the GA-hardness as a whole.

With regard to epistasis variance introduced in [Davidor, 1991], the degree of non-linearity in the solution space represents GA-hardness. Epistasis variance is therefore a single metric characterizing the solution space as a whole, yet in general, it does not correlate well with actual GA-hardness. Moreover, as the fitness function is modeled as a sum of independent bits and any dependencies between bits are interpreted as an unpredictable component, i.e., the epistasis, the method cannot capture the characteristics of GAs associated with non-linear optimization methods.

The third well-known method for expressing GA-hardness is crossover correlation analysis which was first introduced in [Manderic, 1991]. Correlation coefficients are termed here as crossover correlation in order to prevent confusion with the general statistics term. Under this approach, crossover correlation is used as a simple statistical measure for representing the correlation between the fitness of parents and the children obtained by applying a genetic operator. However, unlike Walsh coefficients and epistasis variance which analyze the given solution space independent of the respective genetic operator, crossover correlation associates GA-hardness with statistical observations obtained by applying a particular genetic operator. This method is easily applied to large-sized problems, yet its usefulness has only been empirically demonstrated., i.e., even for the case of an infinite population there exists no mathematical explanation as to why crossover correlation is a useful indicator of GA-hardness.

In the present paper, we first present a new framework in which crossover operators are formalized as a combination of probabilistic linear decompositions and a randomized search. Then, as a means to theoretically analyze the behavior of different crossover operators for the infinite population case, we uniquely define crossover correlation using the variance between decompositions, i.e., after decomposing the solution space through a template of competing schemata, the variance between the decompositions, being expressed as variance coefficients, is used as a fundamental statistical measure.

In Section 2, the employed linear decomposition hypothesis and variance coefficients are mathematically defined. Section 3 then presents features and implications of utilizing such variance coefficients by formulating relational equations describing the respective relationship between variance coefficients and Walsh coefficients, epistasis variance, and crossover correlation. An analysis of representative crossover operators is subsequently carried out in Section 4 using crossover correlation expressed as variance coefficients, after which we compare the coding effects of these crossover operators mathematically. Following this, Section 5 presents a simulation used to evaluate analytical results in comparison with actual GA performance for the case in which the population size is large relative to the problem size. Finally, we give conclusions in Section 6.

2 Linear Decomposition Hypotheses and Variance of Decompositions

2.1 Notation and Definitions

Let x be a binary string composed of L-elements $(x^{(1)} \cdots x^{(L)})$ in which $x^{(i)} \in \{0, 1\}$, while fitness function F is a mapping from the L-dimensional solution space $\mathcal{A} \, (= \{0, 1\}^L)$ to real numbers $\mathcal{R}$ expressed as

$$y = F(x), \quad x \in \mathcal{A}, \quad y \in \mathcal{R} \ , \tag{1}$$

where size of the solution space is $|\mathcal{A}| = 2^L$.

A decomposition π is also a L-dimensional binary string $(\pi^{(1)} \cdots \pi^{(L)})$ in which $\pi^{(i)} \in \{0, 1\}$. Using π, the solution space $\mathcal{A}$ is divided into disjunctive sub-spaces such that every x contained in a sub-space has the same value for positions $\pi^{(i)} = 1$. In GA terms, π represents a collection of schemata (hyperplanes) with '*' for positions $\pi^{(i)} = 0$ and '0' or '1' for positions $\pi^{(i)} = 1$. Notation '*' for $\pi^{(i)} = 0$ and '.' for $\pi^{(i)} = 1$ denotes a *free* and *fixed* bit, respectively. For example, $\pi =$ '0011' is '**..'.

The *order* of decomposition π is defined as the number of fixed positions in π, being denoted as $o(\pi)$. Also, N_π, and $N_{\bar{\pi}}$ are numbers determined as

$$N_\pi = 2^{o(\pi)} \qquad N_{\bar{\pi}} = 2^{L - o(\pi)} \ , \tag{2}$$

where $N_\pi \cdot N_{\bar{\pi}} = 2^L$. By definition, π divides the whole solution space $\mathcal{A}$ into N_π sub-spaces $\mathcal{A}(\pi) = \{\mathcal{A}_0^{(\pi)}, \cdots, \mathcal{A}_{N_\pi - 1}^{(\pi)}\}$ with size $N_{\bar{\pi}}$. For example, when $L = 4$, decomposition '**..' generates four sub-spaces '**00','**01','**10','**11' with four solutions each, such as $\{$'0000', '0100', '1000', '1100'$\}$ for '**00' (Figure 1).

Corresponding to the π values, there exist 2^L decompositions of the solution space. As a special case, when $\pi^{(i)} = 0$ for all i (i.e., $o(\pi) = 0$), π generates only one sub-space which is $\mathcal{A}$ itself. Also, when $\pi^{(i)} = 1$ for all i (i.e., $o(\pi) = L$), π generates 2^L sub-spaces respectively composed of a single string.

As basic statistical measures, we use $\mu_\mathcal{A}$ and $\sigma_\mathcal{A}^2$ as the the mean and variance of fitness values of all x included in $\mathcal{A}$, i.e.,

$$\mu_\mathcal{A} = \frac{1}{2^L} \sum_{x \in \mathcal{A}} F(x) \tag{3}$$

$$\sigma_\mathcal{A}^2 = \frac{1}{2^L} \sum_{x \in \mathcal{A}} (F(x) - \mu_\mathcal{A})^2$$

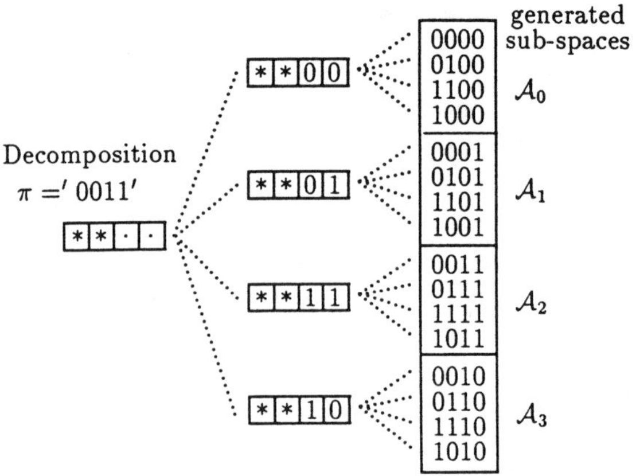

Figure 1: Decomposition of the solution space.

$$= \frac{1}{2^L} \sum_{x \in \mathcal{A}} F(x)^2 - \mu_{\mathcal{A}}{}^2 \ . \tag{4}$$

By considering a ($\in \mathcal{A}(\pi)$) to be a sub-space of $\mathcal{A}$ generated by π, the *fitness value* μ_a can be expressed as the average of the fitness values of all the strings included in a, i.e.,

$$\mu_a = \frac{1}{N_\pi} \sum_{x \in a} F(x) \ . \tag{5}$$

Accordingly, the *between variance* of decompositions $\sigma_B^2(\pi)$ is used to represent the variance of fitness values of all sub spaces $\mathcal{A}(\pi)$ generated by π, while the *within variance* of decompositions $\sigma_W^2(\pi)$ is used to represent the variance of fitness values of individual strings within a sub-space $\mathcal{A}_i^{(\pi)}$ averaged over $\mathcal{A}(\pi)$; where $\sigma_B^2(\pi)$ and $\sigma_W^2(\pi)$ are defined as follows [1].

Definition 1 *(Between and Within Variance of Decompositions)*

$$\sigma_B^2(\pi) = \frac{1}{N_\pi} \sum_{a \in \mathcal{A}(\pi)} (\mu_a - \mu_{\mathcal{A}})^2$$

$$= \frac{1}{N_\pi} \sum_{a \in \mathcal{A}(\pi)} \mu_a{}^2 - \mu_{\mathcal{A}}{}^2 \tag{6}$$

$$\sigma_W^2(\pi) = \frac{1}{N_\pi} \sum_{a \in \mathcal{A}(\pi)} \frac{1}{N_\pi} \sum_{x \in a} (F(x) - \mu_a)^2$$

$$= \frac{1}{2^L} \sum_{x \in \mathcal{A}} F(x)^2 - \frac{1}{N_\pi} \sum_{a \in \mathcal{A}(\pi)} \mu_a{}^2 \ . \tag{7}$$

---

[1] *Decomposition* as defined here corresponds to *relation* in [Kargupta and Goldberg, 1996] or *partition* in [Rudnick and Goldberg, 1991] and [Heckendorn, Whitley, and Rana, 1996], while *between variance* corresponds to *squared signal strength* in [Rudnick and Goldberg, 1991].

Thus, using Eqs. (4), (6), and (7), it can be easily shown that

$$\sigma_B^2(\boldsymbol{\pi}) + \sigma_W^2(\boldsymbol{\pi}) = \sigma_{\mathcal{A}}^2 \tag{8}$$

must hold.

Under Eq. (8), $0 \le \sigma_B^2(\boldsymbol{\pi}) \le \sigma_{\mathcal{A}}^2$ and $0 \le \sigma_W^2(\boldsymbol{\pi}) \le \sigma_{\mathcal{A}}^2$ for all $\boldsymbol{\pi}$. As special cases, when $\pi^{(i)} = 0$ for all i, $\sigma_B^2(\boldsymbol{\pi}) = 0$; and when $\pi^{(i)} = 1$ for all i, $\sigma_B^2(\boldsymbol{\pi}) = \sigma_{\mathcal{A}}^2$. Hereafter, we refer to $\sigma_B^2(\boldsymbol{\pi})$ as the *variance coefficient* of $\boldsymbol{\pi}$.

2.2 Formulation of the Linear Decomposition Hypothesis

Let $\Pi = \{\boldsymbol{\pi}_1, \cdots, \boldsymbol{\pi}_l\}$ $(1 \le l \le L)$ be a set of decompositions such that $o(\boldsymbol{\pi}_i) \ge 1$ and

$$\sum_{i=1}^{l} \boldsymbol{\pi}_i^{(k)} = 1 \qquad for \ \ \forall\, k = 1, \cdots, L \ . \tag{9}$$

In other words, $\boldsymbol{\pi}_1, \cdots \boldsymbol{\pi}_l$ are orthogonal vectors, and for each location only one $\boldsymbol{\pi}_1, \cdots, \boldsymbol{\pi}_l$ has the corresponding bit set to '1'.

For any solution $\boldsymbol{x}$, each $\boldsymbol{\pi}_i \in \Pi$ generates exactly one sub-space that includes $\boldsymbol{x}$, being denoted as sub-space $\boldsymbol{x}^{(\boldsymbol{\pi}_i)}$. For example, when $\Pi = \{\boldsymbol{\pi}_1, \boldsymbol{\pi}_2\}$ in which $\boldsymbol{\pi}_1 = \text{`..**'}$, $\boldsymbol{\pi}_2 = \text{`**..'}$, and $\boldsymbol{x} = \text{`1001'}$, the sub-spaces generated by $\boldsymbol{\pi}_1$ and $\boldsymbol{\pi}_2$ are $\boldsymbol{x}^{(\boldsymbol{\pi}_1)} = \text{`10**'}$ and $\boldsymbol{x}^{(\boldsymbol{\pi}_2)} = \text{`**01'}$, respectively.

A generalized formulation for the *Linear Decomposition Hypothesis* ($\mathcal{LDH}$) can now be defined as follows.

Definition 2 *(Linear Decomposition Hypothesis)*

$$F(\boldsymbol{x}) = c + \sum_{i=1}^{l} f_{(\boldsymbol{\pi}_i)}(\boldsymbol{x}^{(\boldsymbol{\pi}_i)}) + G(\boldsymbol{x}) \ , \tag{10}$$

where c and $f_{(\boldsymbol{\pi}_i)}$ are defined as

$$c \ = \ \mu_{\mathcal{A}} \tag{11}$$

$$f_{(\boldsymbol{\pi}_i)}(\boldsymbol{x}^{(\boldsymbol{\pi}_i)}) \ = \ \mu_{\boldsymbol{x}^{(\boldsymbol{\pi}_i)}} - \mu_{\mathcal{A}} \ , \tag{12}$$

while $G(\boldsymbol{x})$ expresses the contribution of the dependencies between sub-spaces generated by $\boldsymbol{\pi}_1, \cdots, \boldsymbol{\pi}_l$, i.e.,

$$G(\boldsymbol{x}) \ = \ F(\boldsymbol{x}) - c - \sum_{i=1}^{l} f_{(\boldsymbol{\pi}_i)}(\boldsymbol{x}^{(\boldsymbol{\pi}_i)})$$

$$= \ F(\boldsymbol{x}) - \mu_{\mathcal{A}} - \sum_{i=1}^{l} (\mu_{\boldsymbol{x}^{(\boldsymbol{\pi}_i)}} - \mu_{\mathcal{A}}) \ . \tag{13}$$

Averaging over the whole solution space $\mathcal{A}$ gives

$$E[f_{(\boldsymbol{\pi}_i)}(\boldsymbol{x}^{(\boldsymbol{\pi}_i)})] \ = \ 0 \tag{14}$$

$$E[f_{(\pi_i)}(\boldsymbol{x}^{(\pi_i)})^2] \;=\; \sigma_B^2(\pi_i) \tag{15}$$

$$E[G(\boldsymbol{x})] \;=\; 0 \tag{16}$$

$$E[G(\boldsymbol{x})^2] \;=\; \sigma_A^2 - \sum_{i=1}^{l} \sigma_B^2(\pi_i)\;. \tag{17}$$

2.3 Evaluation Criteria for the Linear Decomposition Hypothesis

There exist a number of possible equations in the form of Eq. (10) depending on the selection of the decomposition set Π. We consider that each selection represents a different *hypothesis* or *heuristic* in order to apply a probabilistic search technique.

Accordingly, the $\mathcal{LDH}$ in Eq. (10) allows considering l independent $(2^{k_1}, \cdots, 2^{k_l})$ -valued variables $(\boldsymbol{x}^{(\pi_1)}, \cdots, \boldsymbol{x}^{(\pi_l)})$ rather than L independent 2-valued variables $(x^{(1)}, \cdots, x^{(L)})$, while $f_{(\pi_i)}(\boldsymbol{x}^{(\pi_i)})$ is a mapping function expressing the contribution of those multi-valued variables to the overall fitness value. In other words, a hypothesis partitions the original problem into l independent sub-problems in which the structure of each sub-problem is completely unknown. Corresponding to each hypothesis selected, there subsequently exists a probabilistic search procedure, sometimes referred to as a partitioned random search [Tang, 1994], where each sub-problem is independently and randomly sampled, after which the best solution elements are combined. In the search, the function is viewed as a sum of l random variables with variance $\sigma_B^2(\pi_1), \ldots, \sigma_B^2(\pi_l)$. This approach has merit in that we can define an evaluation criteria that corresponds to the fitness of such a model.

More specifically, we define the evaluation criteria for a given $\mathcal{LDH}$ as the total ratio of linear (and thus predictable) components in the overall fitness value, which corresponds to the *coefficient of determination* in regression analysis. The linear components are expressed in the second term of Eq. (10), and from Eqs. (14)–(17), the evaluation criteria of the $\mathcal{LDH}$ can be simply defined as follows.

Definition 3 *(Evaluation Criteria of $\mathcal{LDH}$)*

$$cod(\Pi) \;=\; \frac{\displaystyle\sum_{\pi \in \Pi} \sigma_B^2(\pi)}{\sigma_A^2}\;, \tag{18}$$

where by definition $0 \leq cod(\Pi) \leq 1$ such that $cod(\Pi) = 1$ when sub-spaces $\boldsymbol{x}^{(\pi_1)}, \cdots, \boldsymbol{x}^{(\pi_l)}$ are independent, i.e., $G(\boldsymbol{x}) = 0$.

Based on Eq. (18), we now let π^* be a binary number of all '1's and $\overline{\pi^*}$ be the complement of $\overline{\pi}$. Thus, if $\Pi = \{\pi^*, \overline{\pi^*}\}$, then $f_{(\pi)}(\boldsymbol{x}^{(\pi^*)})$ is equivalent to $F(\boldsymbol{x})$ itself, $f_{(\overline{\pi^*})}(\boldsymbol{x}^{(\overline{\pi^*})}) = 0$, and $G(\boldsymbol{x}) = 0$. As such, the corresponding $\mathcal{LDH}$ makes no assumption on the structure of the solution space and considers $F(\boldsymbol{x})$ to be a random mapping from the whole solution space to $\mathcal{R}$. Finally, for any given F there exists an $\mathcal{LDH}$ such that $G(\boldsymbol{x}) = 0$ making $cod(\Pi) = 1$.

3 Variance Coefficients and Other Characterization Methods

3.1 Walsh Function Analysis

Let '$\prec$' be a precedence relationship of binary numbers, i.e., if $\pi_i \prec \pi_j$, $o(\pi_i) < o(\pi_j)$, and $\pi_i^{(k)} = 1$, then $\pi_j^{(k)} = 1$; and, by connecting the closest precedent-successor pairs via links, a *Hasse diagram expression of decompositions* is obtained as shown in Figure 2. Under this representation there are 2^L nodes and $L2^L$ links, with the nodes on the k-th level having k direct precedents, $(L - k)$ direct successors, a total of $2^{(L-k)}$ precedents, and a total of 2^k successors.

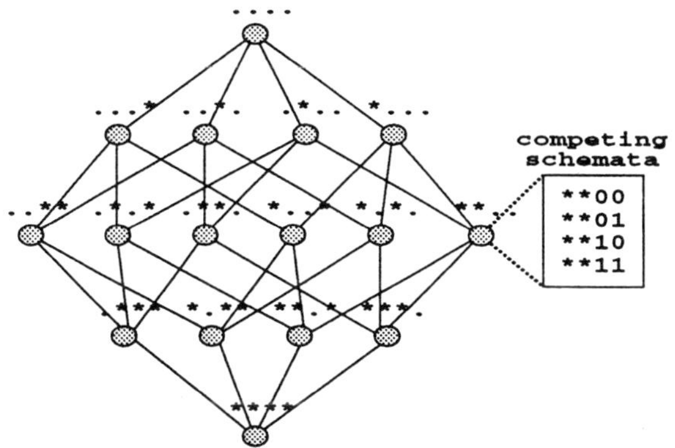

Figure 2: Hasse diagram expression of decompositions.

Here, we use ψ_i to represent a Walsh function in Paley order as defined in [Goldberg, 1989-a] and [Endo, 1993]. Walsh coefficients ω_i $(i = 0, \cdots, 2^L - 1)$ representing the strength of dependencies between 2^L different combinations of L bits can therefore be expressed as

$$\omega_i = \frac{1}{2^L} \sum_{x \in A} F(x)\psi_i(x) \ , \tag{19}$$

where ω_0 is defined as the average of the fitness values of all strings included in A, i.e.,

$$\omega_0 = \mu_A \ . \tag{20}$$

By applying the *Equation of Parseval*, i.e.,

$$\sum_{i=0}^{2^L-1} \mid \omega_i \mid^2 = \frac{1}{2^L} \sum_{x \in A} |F(x)|^2 \ , \tag{21}$$

an intrinsic relationship between Walsh coefficients and variance coefficients can be formulated as follows.

Formulation 1 *(Relationship between Walsh coefficients and variance coefficients)*

$$\sigma_B^2(\pi) = \sum_{j \preceq \pi} \omega_j^2 - \omega_0^2. \tag{22}$$

Figure 3 shows an example in which $L = 4$ and each node on the Hasse diagram is associated with decomposition π and a Walsh coefficient w_i whose suffix is the same as that of π when expressed in a binary form.

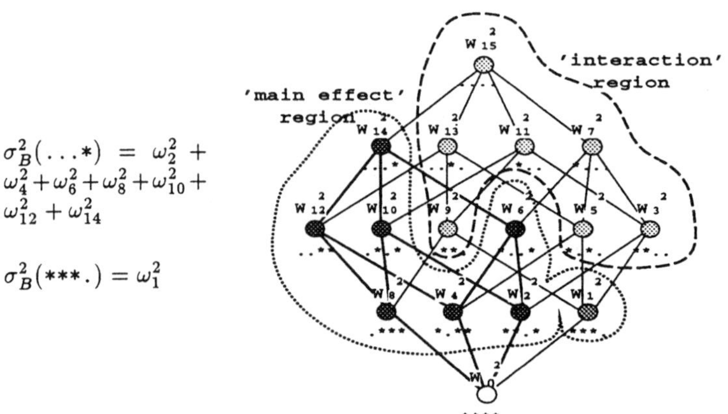

$$\sigma_B^2(\ldots*) = \omega_2^2 + \omega_4^2 + \omega_6^2 + \omega_8^2 + \omega_{10}^2 + \omega_{12}^2 + \omega_{14}^2$$

$$\sigma_B^2(***.) = \omega_1^2$$

Figure 3: Correspondence between Walsh coefficients and variance coefficients.

From Eq. (22), also derived in [Rudnick and Goldberg, 1991] as Eq. (3.11), the meaning of Walsh coefficients becomes apparent. That is, given a template of schemata such as '$\ldots*$', if the variance of fitness values of these competing schemata is calculated, then this value, called the variance coefficient of '$\ldots*$', equals the squared sum of the Walsh coefficients located below the schemata template on the Hasse diagram expression. Accordingly, the value of ω_0^2 needs special consideration, since as defined in Eq. (20), ω_0 is an average of all fitness values and the variance coefficients calculate the degree of deviation from ω_0.

It is also apparent that Walsh coefficients calculate the individual dependencies between bits independently while variance coefficients evaluate all the dependencies included in a particular combination of bits as a whole. For example, variance coefficient $\sigma_B^2('\ldots*')$ in Figure 3 represents the total strength of dependencies that exist between $\{1\}$, $\{2\}$, $\{3\}$, $\{1,2\}$, $\{2,3\}$, $\{3,1\}$, and $\{1,2,3\}$ -th bits.

In addition, an $\mathcal{LDH}$ given by a deccomposition set Π partitions the Hasse diagram into two disjunctive regions (Figure 3): 1) a lower region, termed as the *main effect region* in [Reeves and Wright, 1995], which includes all Walsh coefficients j such that $binary(j) \prec \pi \in \Pi$, being the dependencies evaluated by the $\mathcal{LDH}$; and 2) an upper region, termed as the *interaction region*, which includes any remaining j, being considered to be an error, i.e., a cause of GA-hardness by the $\mathcal{LDH}$.

3.2   Epistasis Variance

As proposed in [Davidor, 1991], epistasis variance is *"a simple static, a regression analysis predicting the function value from the bits, used as a mean to measure the amount of nonlinearity in a representation."*

Accordingly, there exists only one decomposition hypothesis, with the selection of Π being uniquely determined as $\Pi = \{u \mid u \in \{0,1\}^L, o(u) = 1\}$. That is, π_i's are simply L unit vectors $u_1, \cdots, u_L$ in which $u_i^{(k)} = 1$ if $k = i$ and $u_i^{(k)} = 0$ otherwise. Under this case, the $\mathcal{LDH}$ in Eq. (10) becomes

$$F(x) = c + \sum_{i=1}^{L} f_{(u_i)}(x^{(u_i)}) + G(x) \; , \tag{23}$$

and by substituting '$F(x)$' for '$v(S)$' in the original paper, '$E_i(a)$' for '$f_{(u_i)}(x^{(u_i)})$', and '$\overline{V}$' for 'μ_A', the *epistasis variance* σ_ε^2 can be expressed as follows.

Formulation 2 *(Relationship between epistasis variance and variance coefficients)*

$$\begin{aligned}
\sigma_\varepsilon^2 \; &\stackrel{\text{def}}{=} \; \frac{1}{2^L} \sum \left(v(S) - \sum E_i(a) - \overline{V} \right)^2 \\
&\quad - \; \sigma_A^2 - \sum_{i=1}^{L} \sigma_B^2(u_i) \\
&= \; \sigma_A^2 - \sum_{i=1}^{L} \omega_{2^{i-1}}{}^2 \\
&= \; \sigma_A^2 - \left(\omega_1^2 + \omega_2^2 + \omega_4^2 + \cdots + \omega_{2^{L-1}}{}^2 \right) \tag{24}
\end{aligned}$$

Under Eq. (24) It can be seen that σ_ε^2 only determines the contribution of a single bit to the overall fitness value, while any other interdependencies between bits are considered to be unexpected error.

The relationship between Walsh coefficients and epistasis variance is Eq. (24) was also derived in [Manela and Campbell, 1992] as *Theorem 1* and *2*, and in [Reeves and Wright, 1995] where the implication of epistasis variance was extensively discussed.

3.3   Crossover Correlation

Given a genetic operator *op*, the crossover correlation ρ_{op} is defined as

$$\rho_{op}(P, C) = \frac{Cov(P, C)}{\sigma(P)\sigma(C)} \; , \tag{25}$$

where P and C are random variables representing the fitnesses of the parents and children respectively, $\sigma(P)$ and $\sigma(C)$ are the standard deviation of P and C, and $Cov(P, C)$ is the covariance between P and C [Dzubera, 1995].

We present relational formulations expressing the relationship between crossover correlation and variance coefficients for various conditions in order to clarify the meaning of the crossover correlation mathematically. Such clarification is important from a practical standpoint because unlike Walsh coefficients, crossover correlation is based on fundamental statistical information and its value can be easily estimated even for large-sized problems.

We assume that a genetic operator *op* is *reflective*, i.e., the distributions of parents and children are identical, and that the selection of parents is completely random such that [2]

$$\sigma(P) = \sigma(C) = \sigma_{\mathcal{A}} \ . \tag{26}$$

Furthermore, *linkage equilibrium* is assumed, i.e., each bit is selected independently in the population, and $E[F_{(\pi_i)}(\boldsymbol{x}^{(\pi_i)})F_{(\pi_j)}(\boldsymbol{x}^{(\pi_j)})] = 0$ for parents and for children. If π_i is a combination of bits inherited from parent i when applying a genetic operator *op* to k-parents $\{1, 2, \cdots, k\}$, then, from the above assumptions, the following fundamental relationship is established for a particular decomposition set $\Pi = \{\pi_1, \pi_2, \cdots, \pi_k\}$:

$$Cov(P, C)|_{\Pi} = \sum_{\pi \in \Pi} \sigma_B^2(\pi) \ . \tag{27}$$

Note that Eq. (27) is conditioned by a particular decomposition set Π.

We assume crossover operators are generally formalized as a group of probabilistic searches in which one among other possible decomposition hypotheses is selected with certain probability, i.e., a crossover operator typically selects a crossover point randomly. In our terminology, this is equivalent to randomly selecting $\Pi = \{\pi_1, \pi_2, \cdots, \pi_k\}$.

If we now let $\mathcal{P}_{op}(\Pi)$ be the probability that Π is selected by *op*, then from Eq. (18), the crossover correlation is formulated as follows.

Formulation 3 *(Relationship between crossover correlation and variance coefficients)*

$$
\begin{aligned}
\rho_{op} &= \sum_{\Pi} \mathcal{P}_{op}(\Pi) \frac{Cov(P, C)|_{\Pi}}{\sigma(P)\sigma(C)} \\
&= \sum_{\pi \in \mathcal{A}} \mathcal{P}_{op}(\Pi) \frac{\displaystyle\sum_{\pi \in \Pi} \sigma_B^2(\pi)}{\sigma_{\mathcal{A}}^2} \ .
\end{aligned}
\tag{28}
$$

Crossover operators are generally expressed in Eq. (28) as a distribution of probabilities $\mathcal{P}_{op}(\Pi)$. We found this expression to be beneficial in eliminating ambiguity when referring to the definition of a crossover operator; for example, determining whether or not to to cut off at position 0 for 'a standard one-point crossover.' Note that although parents and children are uniformly distributed in the solution space under Eq. (26), the distribution of the crossover point, $\mathcal{P}_{op}(\Pi)$, may not necessarily be uniform. That is, providing $\mathcal{P}_{op}(\Pi)$ is time invariant, the distribution can be arbitrary in order to satisfy the reflectiveness condition.

By applying a number of simplifying assumptions, we use Eq. (28) to clarify the relationship between Walsh coefficients (static analysis of the solution space) and the crossover

---

[2] As originally defined in [Dzubera, 1995], P and C are the average fitness value of parents and children respectively, i.e., $\sigma(P) = \sigma(C) = \sigma_{\mathcal{A}}^2/(number\ of\ parents/children)$. The definition used here is for notational simplicity and does not affect the derivation of subsequent equations.

correlation (dynamic characterization of the search operator). In addition, the mathematical implication of using of the crossover correlation as a metric for search performance is shown.

4 Variance Coefficients and Crossover Operators

4.1 Formulation of Crossover Correlation for Crossover Operators

For standard crossover operators with two parents, only complementary decompositions $\pi_1(=\pi)$ and $\pi_2(=\overline{\pi})$ need be considered.

For uniform crossover, either of the parents' bits is taken for each location with probability 0.5 to generate a new child, giving 2^L different choices for π, in which all have the same probability $1/2^L$. Thus, averaging over all possible pairs of $(\pi, \overline{\pi})$ gives the expected value of the crossover correlation for uniform crossover ρ_u, being formulated as follows.

Formulation 4 *(Crossover correlation for uniform crossover)*

$$
\begin{aligned}
\rho_u &= \sum_{\pi \in \mathcal{A}} \frac{1}{2^L} \frac{\sigma_B^2(\pi) + \sigma_B^2(\overline{\pi})}{\sigma_{\mathcal{A}}^2} \\
&= 2 \sum_{i=1}^{2^L} \frac{\omega_i^2}{2^{o(i)}} ,
\end{aligned}
\tag{29}
$$

where $o(i)$ is the total number of '1's in i when represented in binary form.

In [Asoh and Mühlenbein, 1994], a formulation similar to Eq. (29) is proposed, where uniform crossover expresses the relationship between *genetic variance decomposition* and *heritability*, being equivalent to *variance coefficients* and *crossover correlation*, respectively. As they focused on population genetics, additional conditions were considered, e.g., $x^{(i)}$ is not restricted to binary alphabets and the occurrence probability of values of $x^{(i)}$ in a population is also considered. In their simulation study, the heritability is calculated using only lower-order dependencies in order to reduce computation time, which is applicable to our case as well.

For one-point crossover, an arbitrary position k $(1 \leq k \leq L)$ is randomly taken such that a child inherits either bits $x^{(i)}$ $(i < k)$ or $x^{(j)}$ $(j \geq k)$ from one parent and the rest from the other, giving $2L$ different choices for π, in which all have the same probability $1/2L$ (Figure 4(a)). Thus, if $\mathcal{A}_{1p}$ represents the possible $2L$ selections of π, then averaging over $\mathcal{A}_{1p}$ gives the expected value of the crossover correlation for one-point crossover ρ_{1p}, being formulated as follows.

Formulation 5 *(Crossover correlation for one-point crossover)*

$$
\rho_{1p} = \sum_{\pi \in \mathcal{A}_{1p}} \frac{1}{2L} \frac{\sigma_B^2(\pi) + \sigma_B^2(\overline{\pi})}{\sigma_{\mathcal{A}}^2} .
\tag{30}
$$

Under Eq. (30), only L decomposition hypotheses need be evaluated in order to calculate the theoretical value of ρ_{1p}.

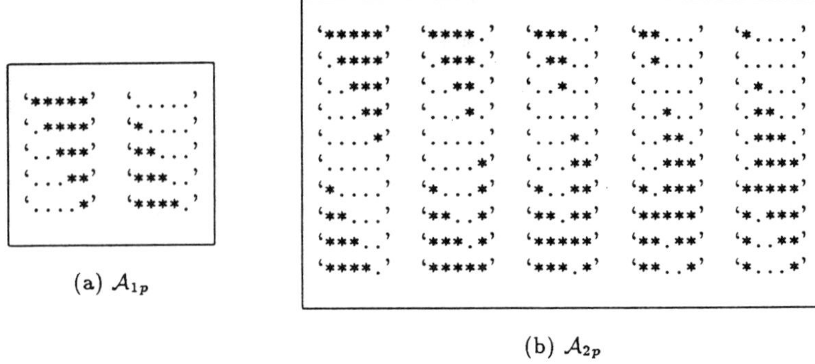

Figure 4: Selection of π for one-point crossover ($\mathcal{A}_{1p}$) and two-point crossover ($\mathcal{A}_{2p}$) for $L = 5$.

Two-point crossover is similarly represented, i.e., two arbitrary positions k_1 and k_2 ($1 \le k_1 \le L$, $1 \le k_2 \le L$) are randomly taken such that a child inherits either bits between k_1 and k_2 from one parent and the rest from the other, giving $2L^2$ different choices for π, in which all have the same probability $1/2L^2$ (Figure 4(b)). Thus, if $\mathcal{A}_{2p}$ represents the possible $2L^2$ selection of π, then averaging over $\mathcal{A}_{2p}$ gives the expected value of the crossover correlation for two-point crossover ρ_{2p}, being formulated as follows.

Formulation 6 *(Crossover correlation for two-point crossover)*

$$\rho_{2p} = \sum_{\pi \in \mathcal{A}_{2p}} \frac{1}{2L^2} \frac{\sigma_B^2(\pi) + \sigma_B^2(\overline{\pi})}{\sigma_A^2} .$$ (31)

4.2 Effect on Coding

The uniform crossover operator formulated in Eq. (29) evaluates all the decomposition hypotheses equally, whereas one-point and two-point crossovers in Eqs. (30) and (31) are biased such that they selectively evaluate the decomposition hypotheses which exploit knowledge about the structure of the search space. While this approach can increase the effectiveness of the latter operators, it also increases their sensitivity to the coding method.

Coding, as considered here, is represented as an arbitrary permutation of bits, i.e., $L!$ different codings exist for a string of length L. From this representation and Eqs. (29)–(31), the following properties can easily be shown to hold.

Property (1) *The crossover correlation of uniform crossover is invariant to the coding method.*

Proof. If we let Γ denote all possible permutations of composing bits and $\gamma \in \Gamma$, then as shown in Eq. (29), for $\forall \gamma \in \Gamma$ the value of ρ_u for any given γ (denoted as $\rho_u|_\gamma$) is obviously constant and must equal $2 \sum_{i=1}^{2^L} \left(\omega_i^2 / 2^{o(i)} \right)$.

Property (2) *If the crossover correlation of one-point and two-point crossovers are averaged over all possible permutations, then they have the same mean although the former has a greater deviation.*

Proof. Let n_k be the number of decomposition sets Π with orders $(k, L - k)$. For example, in case of one-point crossover, $n_k = |\{\pi | \pi \in \mathcal{A}_{1p}, o(\pi) = k\}|$. Note that for one-point and two-point crossovers, $\mathcal{P}_{op}(\pi, \overline{\pi})$ is constant for all selected pairs and thus only depends on the cardinality of the decomposition set. Averaging over all possible permutations gives, the expected value of ρ_{op}, or $\overline{\rho_{op}}$ as

$$\overline{\rho_{op}} = \frac{1}{|\Gamma|} \sum_{\gamma \in \Gamma} \rho_{op}|_{\gamma}$$

$$= 2 \sum_{\pi \in \mathcal{A}} \frac{1}{{}_nC_{o(\pi)}} \frac{n_{o(\pi)}}{\sum_{k=0}^{L} n_k} \sigma_B^2(\pi) . \tag{32}$$

For one-point crossover, $n_k = 1$ for $k = 0, L$ and $n_k = 2$ otherwise, with $\sum_{k=0}^{L} n_k = 2L$; while for two-point crossover, $n_k = L$ for $k = 0, L$ and $n_k = 2L$ otherwise, with $\sum_{k=0}^{L} n_k = 2L^2$. From Eq. (32), it immediately follows $\overline{\rho_{1p}} \equiv \overline{\rho_{2p}}$. Intuitively speaking, this can be explained as follows: Averaging results in only the ratio of the number of decompositions selected from each level affecting performance. And, from the definition of $\mathcal{A}_{1p}$ and $\mathcal{A}_{2p}$, both crossover operators have the same ratio.

Using test function 4_DPND with $L = 8$ (described in **5.1**), we calculate crossover correlation of each crossover operator for all possible permutations ($8! = 40320$). Table 1 summarizes the mean, deviation, minimum, and maximum values, where the resultant means are equal to corresponding values determined from Eqs. (29) and (32); thereby confirming Properties (1) and (2).

Table 1: Coding effects with on crossover correlation with formulated crossover operators.

Crossover operator	Mean value	Deviation value	Minmum value	Maximum value
Uniform	0.540	0.000	0.540	0.540
One-point	0.654	0.047	0.560	0.829
Two-point	0.654	0.028	0.614	0.733

From our overall standpoint , the problem of GA implementation, namely, designing a coding method and selecting an appropriate crossover operator, is interpreted as a problem of identifying promising decomposition hypotheses, or $\mathcal{P}_{op}(\Pi)$, which makes the probabilistic search more accurate.

Our assumption that variance coefficients are known and available without sampling should be noted to result in an evaluation criteria, i.e., $cod(\Pi)$, which does not consider GA performance based on computation time (by computation time, we refer both the population size and the generation size), instead, being solely based on the accuracy of the search. In other words, GA performance relative to the population and generation sizes is not considered here.

In reality though, such an operator is far from being the best among other more practical crossover operators; hence, in a problem with finite population, the sampling effect must be accounted for if crossover correlation is to be applied to study GA performance. This, however, we leave for future work.

5 Simulation Analysis

5.1 Analysis of Test Functions

We first analyze test functions EQ_IND, 4_DPND(1,5), 4_DPND(3,7), and RANDOM in which $L = 8$ and such that the size of the solution space is $2^8 = 256$.

These four test functions are described as follows: 1) EQ_IND is composed of eight independent bits that are equally weighted, with the fitness value being equal to the number of 1's in the string, 2) 4_DPND(1,5) is composed of two 4-bit sub-strings at positions 1,2,3,4 and 5,6,7,8, with the weights allocated for each 2^4 values of the sub-strings being selected independently and as its mapping function we apply the 4th-order deceptive problem developed in [Whitley, 1991], 3) 4_DPND(3,7) is similar to 4_DPND(1,5) but with two 4-bit sub-strings at positions 1,2,7,8 and 3,4,5,6 (bit-rotated), and 4) RANDOM is a function in which weights allocated for 2^8 values are uniformly distributed between 0 and 1. These functions are fully defined in the **Appendix**.

Figure 5(a)−(c) shows distributions of the variance coefficients ($\sigma_B^2(\boldsymbol{\pi})$) versus the order of the decompositions ($o(\boldsymbol{\pi})$) for EQ_IND, 4_DPND(1,5)/(3,7), and RANDOM, respectively. Note that the variance of EQ_IND is proportional to the order of decompositions; a behavior occurring because transformation into the Walsh domain gives Walsh coefficients that are equal and non-zero for the first-order decompositions and zero for higher-order ones. Thus, variance in Eq. (22) becomes proportional to the number of the first-order Walsh coefficients included in $\sigma_B^2(\boldsymbol{\pi})$, i.e., the number of level 1 nodes existing below $\boldsymbol{\pi}$ in the associated Hasse diagram expression is equal to the number of 1's in $\boldsymbol{\pi}$. In the resultant distribution obtained for RANDOM, the Walsh coefficients are equally distributed in the Walsh-transformed domain, which leads to the variance being approximately proportional to the number of Walsh coefficients included, i.e., $2^{o(\boldsymbol{\pi})} - 1$. Functions 4_DPND(1,5) and 4_DPND(3,7) have the same distribution since the only difference between them is the location of composing bits. Variance coefficients of 4_DPND appear to be distributed somewhat in-between those of EQ_IND and RANDOM, which indicates this function is not completely random due to the existence of higher-order dependencies.

Corresponding results for evaluation criteria $cod(\boldsymbol{\pi}, \overline{\boldsymbol{\pi}})$ are shown in Figure 5(d)−(f), where the distributions of evaluation values are symmetric with respect to $o(\boldsymbol{\pi}) = L/2$ due to $cod(\boldsymbol{\pi}, \overline{\boldsymbol{\pi}}) = cod(\overline{\boldsymbol{\pi}}, \boldsymbol{\pi})$ by definition. The resultant distribution for EQ_IND shows a constant $cod(\boldsymbol{\pi}, \overline{\boldsymbol{\pi}})$ of 1.0, which indicates this function is always linearly separable by $(\boldsymbol{\pi}, \overline{\boldsymbol{\pi}})$ regardless of the selected decomposition set II. 4_DPND is also linearly separable, but only for decomposition pairs $(o(\boldsymbol{\pi}), o(\overline{\boldsymbol{\pi}})) = (4, 4)$ and $(0, 8)$. RANDOM shows a distribution in which dependencies exist for all possible decomposition pairs except for $(o(\boldsymbol{\pi}), o(\overline{\boldsymbol{\pi}})) = (0, 8)$, i.e., decomposition of the original function itself.

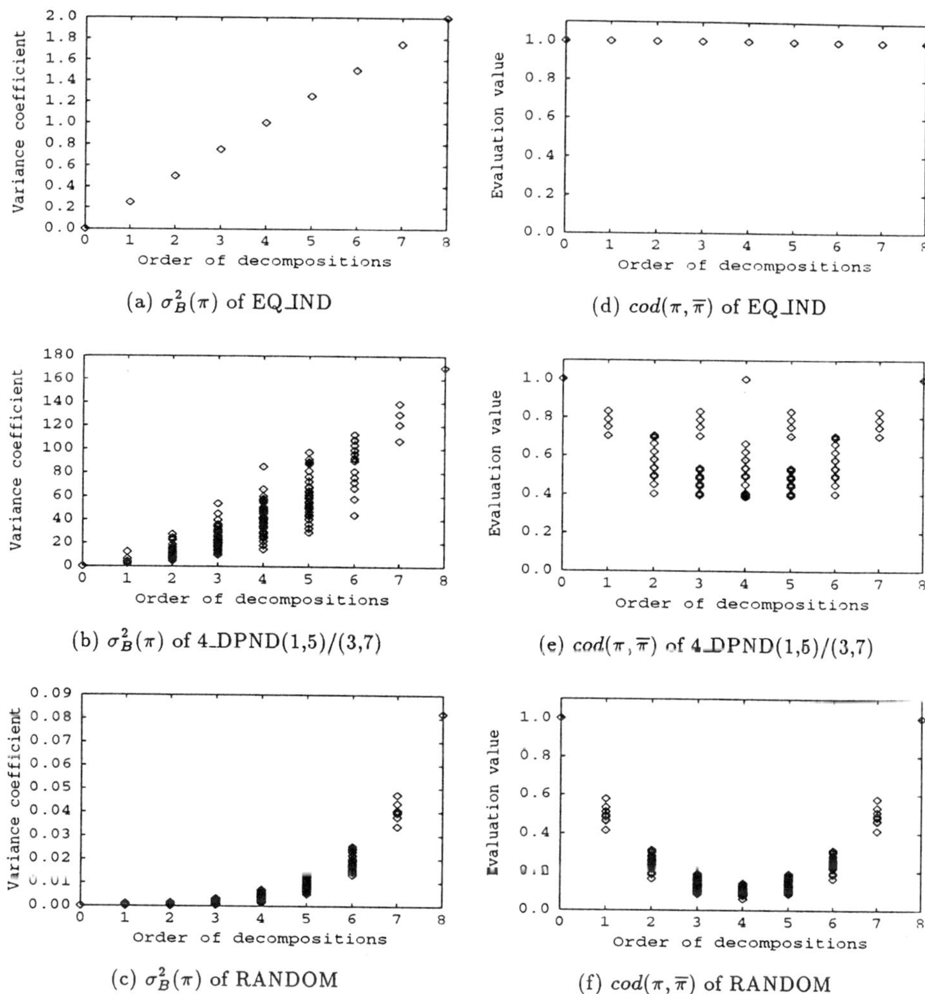

Figure 5: Distribution of variance coefficients $\sigma_B^2(\pi)$ and evaluation criteria $cod(\pi,\overline{\pi})$ values versus the order of decompositions $(o(\pi))$.

5.2 Analysis of Crossover Operators

We used the same four test functions to analyze the theoretical and observed values of crossover correlation for the uniform, one-point, and two-point crossover operators (ρ_u, ρ_{1p}, and ρ_{2p}).

Table 2 summarizes the results, where theoretical values were calculated using Eqs. (29), (30), and (31), respectively, while observed values were obtained by applying the operators to to randomly generated parents. The overall good agreement confirms validity of the employed formulations for these crossover operators. Also shown for comparison are values of the ratio of *genetic variance* ρ_g [Manela and Campbell, 1992], which is defined as $\rho_g = (\sigma_A^2 - \sigma_\varepsilon^2)/\sigma_A^2$ in which epistsis variance σ_ε^2 as is determined by from Eq. (24). All crossover operators have a value of 1.0 for EQ_IND as it only contains first-order dependencies. Note that ρ_g is much smaller than the corresponding crossover correlation values, which indicates these functions contain higher-order (greater than the first-order) dependencies. The fact that ρ_{1p} shows different values for 4_DPND(1,5) and 4_DPND(3,7) indicates one-point crossover is location dependent. In addition, although ρ_{2p} shows the same values in this example, two-point crossover is only rotation invariant and not permutation invariant as shown in Table 1; and RANDOM shows the smallest crossover correlation since it has the largest number of higher-order dependencies.

Table 2: Theoretical and observed values of crossover correlation applied to analyze various test functions. †

Test function	Crossover correlation			Ratio of Genetic variance ρ_g
	uniform crossover ρ_u	one-point crossover ρ_{1p}	two-point crossover ρ_{2p}	
EQ_IND	1.000 (1.000)	1.000 (1.000)	1.000 (1.000)	1.000 —
4_DPND(1,5)	0.540 (0.545)	0.809 (0.809)	0.713 (0.712)	0.291 —
4_DPND(3,7)	0.540 (0.543)	0.662 (0.664)	0.713 (0.709)	0.291 —
RANDOM	0.175 (0.178)	0.368 (0.375)	0.355 (0.352)	0.018 —

† Values in parentheses indicate observed crossover correlation.

Performance of crossover operators was also analyzed via a simulation analysis in which an actual GA was applied. The following parameters where selected as simulation conditions: crossover rate, 0.6; mutation rate, 0.01; population size, 40; and generation size, 20. The selected GA is generational, though elitist strategy is adopted so that the best individual always survives into the next generation. After 500 runs in which the initial population was randomly generated, the fitness of the best individual in the last generation was averaged as the final performance measure. Because we assumed infinite population in our formulation, the simulation was carried out using a sufficiently large population and generation sizes relative to the problem size. We also determined the optimal solution and the best performance obtained by a bitwise comparison.

Table 3 summarizes resultant values of the crossover operators, bitwise comparison, and optimal solution for the employed test functions. EQ_IND is a GA-easy problem, and all crossover operators are optimal, while those for RANDOM are also the same and almost exactly optimal. In the analysis of 4_DPND(1,5) and 4_DPND(3,7), as the GAs converge to either to the optimal (all '1' for the 4-bit sub-string) or the sub-optimal (all '0') values, performance is directly reflected by the ratio of optimal to sub-optimal points. That is, a value of 60.00 indicates that both sub-strings are optimal, 58.00 that one is optimal, and 56.00 that both are sub-optimal. Note that crossover operators clearly show superior performance compared to bitwise comparison. Also, one-point crossover shows the best performance for 4_DPND(1,5), while also being the only operator to show any significant difference in performance of the GA when applied to bit-rotated function 4_DPND(3,7). These results are consistent with corresponding theoretical values of crossover correlation shown in Table 2.

Table 3: Summary of results indicative of performance of crossover operators.

Test function	Uniform crossover	One-point crossover	Two-point crossover	Bitwise comparison	Optimal solution
EQ_IND	8.00	8.00	8.00	8.00	8.00
4_DPND(1,5)	58.23	58.74	58.48	56.00	60.00
4_DPND(3,7)	58.30	58.25	58.49	56.00	60.00
RANDOM	5.08	5.08	5.08	4.12	5.09

5.3 Analysis of Effect on Coding

The coding effects of each crossover operator were examined by a simulation in which GA performance was analyzed using 4_DPND with $L = 8$ and 32. For each run, the string is randomly permuted and values of crossover correlation and GA performance are determined.

In the simulation with $L = 8$, GA performance was averaged over 100 runs using the same GA parameters selected for the preceding simulation. Figure 6(a)–(c) shows the results, where every 1000 plotted points corresponds to a different permutation. Note that crossover correlation for uniform crossover shows a constant value equal to the theoretical value, and that the one-point crossover shows the most deviation in crossover correlation and in GA performance.

With $L = 32$, the 4_DPND function is composed of eight 4-order deceptive sub-strings and has an optimal value of 240. Due to the increase in problem size, the selected population and generation sizes were both increased to 100 while other GA parameters were kept the same. Also, because an exact value of crossover correlation is not possible due to the infeasibility of calculating the Walsh coefficients, it is determined using 10000 randomly generated parent pairs. Figure 6(d)–(f) shows the simulation results where in contrast to uniform crossover with $L = 8$, the crossover correlation does not show a constant value due to the use of randomly generated pairs. On the other hand, one-point crossover still shows the most deviation in both crossover correlation and GA performance, while the average performance in one-point and two-point crossovers is similar.

Table 4 summarizes simulation results using the mean and deviation of crossover correlation (ρ_{op}-mean/-dev) and observed GA performance (GA-mean/-dev). Also shown is the correlation between ρ_{op} and GA performance. Of interest, although ρ_{op}-mean and ρ_{op}-dev were estimated for $L = 8$ using only 1,000 out of 40,320 points, they show good agreement with theoretical values in Table 1. In addition, the resultant values of ρ_{op}-dev and GA-dev for one-point and two-point crossover are consistent with Properties (1) and (2) in **4.2**. Moreover, as Properties (1) and (2) are maintained with $L = 32$, this demonstrates the effectiveness of crossover correlation in cases when it is infeasible to calculate Walsh coefficients. When considering these results in conjunction with the good values of $\rho_{op} - GA\text{-}perf$ correlation, this supports the use of crossover correlation as an indicator of GA-hardness when the population size is large enough.

Table 4: Simulation results indicating the effectiveness of crossover correlation as shown by correlation between ρ_{op} and GA performance for the 4_DPND test function.

Test function	Crossover operator	ρ_{op}-mean	ρ_{op}-dev	GA-mean	GA-dev	ρ_{op}:GA-perf correlation
4_DPND $L = 8$	Uniform	0.540	0.000	58.37	0.10	0.00
	One-point	0.654	0.044	58.28	0.17	0.77
	Two-point	0.654	0.026	58.34	0.15	0.70
4_DPND $L = 32$	Uniform	0.540	0.003	226.84	0.16	0.03
	One-point	0.684	0.029	228.14	0.25	0.69
	Two-point	0.684	0.020	228.08	0.23	0.61

6   Conclusions

This paper formalizes crossover operators as a combination of probabilistic linear decompositions and randomized search, and addresses the issues in fitness landscape characterization in terms of GA-hardness.

In the paper, we only focus on the analytical aspect of the issue. Researches such as [Reeves and Wright, 1995] [Tang, 1994] [Peck and Dhawan, 1995] have similar views but take different approaches; They actually define new probabilistic search methods, for example, *adaptive partitioned random search* or *sequential elimination of levels*, that are more statistics oriented. These methods adopt strict statistical inference in order to identify the optimal strategy dynamically based on the statistical information obtained during the search. Thus, we can expect such methods to be more *robust* than GAs since the latter require certain knowledge for effectively implementing them in actual problems. At the same time, the former methods consume far more computation time for the statistical calculation.

Our view of this problem is that a genetic algorithm avoids the complex statistical inference by simply picking up the next search action (i.e. a decomposition hypothesis) from a predetermined hypotheses set. Though the performance inevitably depends on the selection of the genetic operator and the design of the coding method, the mechanism makes GAs easier and even more effective when these algorithms successfully exploit the knowledge of the solution space structure that is expressed implicitly as a possible hypotheses set.

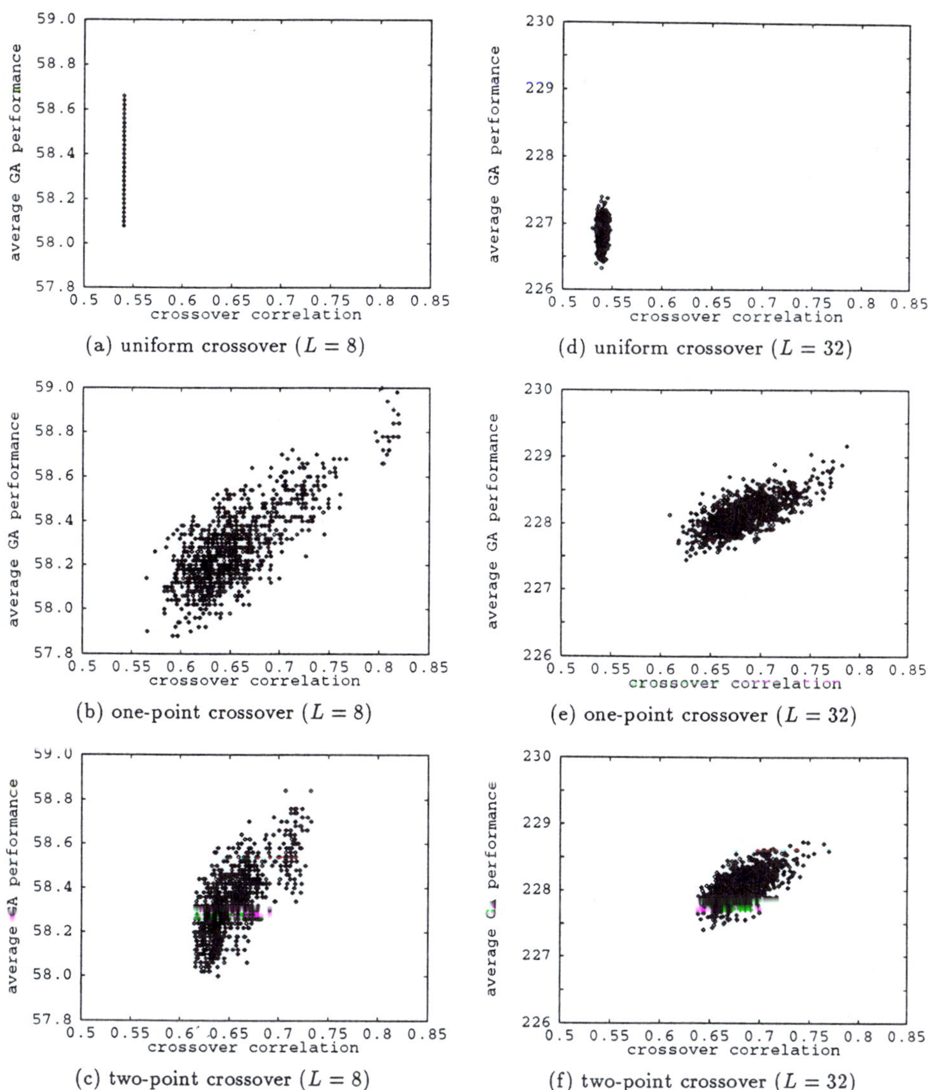

Figure 6: Simulation results showing coding effects on crossover correlation applied to the 4_DPND test function.

References

[Aizawa, 1996] Aizawa, A.: Characterization of the Solution Space by Variance of Decompositions, Workshop Notes on Parallel Processing for Artificial Intelligence, 9, Japanese Society for Artificial Intelligence (1996).

[Asoh and Mühlenbein, 1994] Asoh, H. and Mühlenbein, H.: Estimating the Heritability by Decomposing the Genetic Variance, *Parallel Problem Solving from Nature, 3*, pp. 98 - 107, 1994.

[Bethke, 1981] Bethke, A. D.: Genetic Algorithms as function optimizers, Doctorial dissertation, University of Michigan, 1981.

[Davidor, 1991] Davidor, Y.: Epistasis Variance: A Viewpoint on GA-hardness, *Foundations of Genetic Algorithms*, 23-35 (1991).

[Dzubera, 1995] Dzubera, J. and Whitley, D.: Advanced Correlation Analysis of Operators for the Traveling Salesman Problem, *Parallel Problem Solving from Nature, 3*, (1995).

[Endo, 1993] Endo, Y.: Walsh Analysis (*in Japanese*), Tokyo Denki University Press (1993).

[Goldberg, 1989-a] Goldberg, D. E.: Genetic Algorithms and Walsh Functions: Part I, A Gentle Introduction, in *Complex Systems*, 3, 129-152 (1989).

[Goldberg, 1989-b] Goldberg, D. E.: Genetic Algorithms and Walsh Functions: Part II, Deception and Its Analysis, in *Complex Systems*, 3, 153-171 (1989).

[Heckendorn, Whitley, and Rana, 1996] Heckendorn, R. B., Whitley, D. and Rana, S.: Nonlinearity, Walsh Coefficients, Hyperplane Ranking and the Simple Genetic Algorithm, *Foundations of Genetic Algorithms IV* (1996).

[Kargupta and Goldberg, 1996] Kargupta, H. and Goldberg, D. E.: SEARCH, Blackbox Optimization, and Sample Complexity, *Foundations of Genetic Algorithms IV* (1996).

[Manderic, 1991] Manderic, B, DeWeger, M. and Spiessens, P.: The Genetic Algorithm and the Structure of the Fitness Landscape, *proceedings of the 4-th International Conference on Genetic Algorithms*, 143-150 (1991).

[Manela and Campbell, 1992] Manela, M. and Campbell, J. A.: Harmonic Analysis, Epistasis and Genetic Algorithms, *Parallel Problem Solving from Nature, 2*, 57-64 (1992).

[Peck and Dhawan, 1995] Peck, C. C. and Dhawan, A. P.: Genetic Algorithms as Global Random Search Methods: An Alternative Perspective, Evolutionary Computation 3(1), pp. 39 - 80 (1995).

[Reeves and Wright, 1995] Reeves, C. R. and Wright C. C.: Epistasis in Genetic Algorithms: An Experimental Design Perspective, Proceedings of the 6-th International Conference on Genetic Algorithms, pp. 217 - 224 (1995).

[Reeves and Wright, 1995] Reeves, C. R. and Wright C. C.: Genetic Algorithms and Statistical Methods: A Comparison, Genetic Algorithms In Engineering Systems: Innovations and Applications, IEE Conference Publication, No. 414, pp. 137 - 140 (1995).

[Rudnick and Goldberg, 1991] Rudnick M. and Goldberg, D. E.: Signal, Noise, and Genetic Algorithms, in *IlliGAL Report*, No. 91005 (1991).

[Tang, 1994] Tang, Z. B.: Adaptive Partitioned Random Search to Global Optimization, IEEE Transactions on Automatic Control, Vol. 39, No. 11, pp. 2235 - 2244 (Nov. 1994).

[Whitley, 1991] Whitley, L. D.: Fundamental Principles of Deception in Genetic Search, *Foundations of Genetic Algorithms*, pp. 221 - 241 (1991).

Appendix

Definition of employed test functions

(1) EQ_IND

$$F_{EQ\_IND}(x) = \sum_{i=1}^{L} f(x^{(i)}), \qquad where \quad f(x^{(i)}) = \left\{ \begin{array}{ll} 1 & x^{(i)} = 1 \\ 0 & x^{(i)} = 0 \end{array} \right. .$$

(2) 4_DPND

$$F_{4\_DPND(1.5)}(x) = f(x^{(1234)}) + f(x^{(5678)})$$

$$F_{4\_DPND(3.7)}(x) = f(x^{(3456)}) + f(x^{(7812)}), \qquad where$$

$f(1111)=30$	$f(0100)=22$	$f(0110)=14$	$f(1110)=6$
$f(0000)=28$	$f(1000)=20$	$f(1001)=12$	$f(1101)=4$
$f(0001)=26$	$f(0011)=18$	$f(0101)=10$	$f(1011)=2$
$f(0010)=24$	$f(0101)=16$	$f(1100)=8$	$f(0111)=0$

(3) RANDOM

$$F_{RANDOM}(x) = f(x), \qquad where$$

$f(00000000)=0.841$	$f(00000001)=0.353$	$f(00000010)=0.447$	$f(00000011)=0.319$	$f(00000100)=0.886$
$f(00000101)=0.016$	$f(00000110)=0.584$	$f(00000111)=0.159$	$f(00001000)=0.384$	$f(00001001)=0.691$
$f(00001010)=0.059$	$f(00001011)=0.900$	$f(00001100)=0.164$	$f(00001101)=0.159$	$f(00001110)=0.533$
$f(00001111)=0.604$	$f(00010000)=0.583$	$f(00010001)=0.270$	$f(00010010)=0.391$	$f(00010011)=0.293$
$f(00010100)=0.742$	$f(00010101)=0.298$	$f(00010110)=0.075$	$f(00010111)=0.405$	$f(00011000)=0.857$
$f(00011001)=0.942$	$f(00011010)=0.663$	$f(00011011)=0.847$	$f(00011100)=0.003$	$f(00011101)=0.462$
$f(00011110)=0.533$	$f(00011111)=0.788$	$f(00100000)=0.266$	$f(00100001)=0.983$	$f(00100010)=0.307$
$f(00100011)=0.601$	$f(00100100)=0.609$	$f(00100101)=0.212$	$f(00100110)=0.886$	$f(00100111)=0.305$
$f(00101000)=0.152$	$f(00101001)=0.338$	$f(00101010)=0.388$	$f(00101011)=0.644$	$f(00101100)=0.754$
$f(00101101)=0.604$	$f(00101111)=0.532$	$f(00101111)=0.459$	$f(00110000)=0.652$	$f(00110001)=0.327$
$f(00110010)=0.946$	$f(00110011)=0.368$	$f(00110100)=0.944$	$f(00110101)=0.007$	$f(00110110)=0.517$
$f(00110111)=0.273$	$f(00111000)=0.024$	$f(00111001)=0.592$	$f(00111010)=0.205$	$f(00111011)=0.878$
$f(00111100)=0.059$	$f(00111101)=0.261$	$f(00111110)=0.303$	$f(00111111)=0.891$	$f(01000000)=0.498$
$f(01000001)=0.710$	$f(01000010)=0.286$	$f(01000011)=0.865$	$f(01000100)=0.675$	$f(01000101)=0.450$
$f(01000110)=0.960$	$f(01000111)=0.775$	$f(01001000)=0.377$	$f(01001001)=0.229$	$f(01001010)=0.354$
$f(01001011)=0.300$	$f(01001100)=0.670$	$f(01001101)=0.719$	$f(01001110)=0.566$	$f(01001111)=0.825$
$f(01010000)=0.391$	$f(01010001)=0.819$	$f(01010010)=0.844$	$f(01010011)=0.180$	$f(01010100)=0.943$
$f(01010101)=0.425$	$f(01010110)=0.521$	$f(01010111)=0.066$	$f(01011000)=0.913$	$f(01011001)=0.883$
$f(01011010)=0.761$	$f(01011011)=0.399$	$f(01011100)=0.688$	$f(01011101)=0.761$	$f(01011110)=0.405$
$f(01011111)=0.125$	$f(01100000)=0.485$	$f(01100001)=0.223$	$f(01100010)=0.873$	$f(01100011)=0.529$
$f(01100100)=0.001$	$f(01100101)=0.861$	$f(01100110)=0.010$	$f(01100111)=0.815$	$f(01101000)=0.243$
$f(01101001)=0.315$	$f(01101010)=0.966$	$f(01101011)=0.936$	$f(01101100)=0.809$	$f(01101101)=0.492$
$f(01101110)=0.220$	$f(01101111)=0.576$	$f(01110000)=0.289$	$f(01110001)=0.321$	$f(01110010)=0.261$
$f(01110011)=0.174$	$f(01110100)=0.002$	$f(01110101)=0.045$	$f(01110110)=0.241$	$f(01110111)=0.415$
$f(01111000)=0.702$	$f(01111001)=0.222$	$f(01111010)=0.504$	$f(01111011)=0.067$	$f(01111100)=0.393$
$f(01111101)=0.479$	$f(01111110)=0.218$	$f(01111111)=0.220$	$f(10000000)=0.916$	$f(10000001)=0.350$
$f(10000010)=0.193$	$f(10000011)=0.211$	$f(10000100)=0.634$	$f(10000101)=0.054$	$f(10000110)=0.783$
$f(10000111)=0.031$	$f(10001000)=0.444$	$f(10001001)=0.176$	$f(10001010)=0.932$	$f(10001011)=0.910$
$f(10001100)=0.473$	$f(10001101)=0.872$	$f(10001110)=0.696$	$f(10001111)=0.930$	$f(10010000)=0.455$
$f(10010001)=0.399$	$f(10010010)=0.893$	$f(10010011)=0.694$	$f(10010100)=0.839$	$f(10010101)=0.740$
$f(10010110)=0.651$	$f(10010111)=0.678$	$f(10011001)=0.577$	$f(10011001)=0.273$	$f(10011010)=0.935$
$f(10011011)=0.662$	$f(10011100)=0.047$	$f(10011101)=0.373$	$f(10011111)=0.618$	$f(10011111)=0.149$
$f(10100000)=0.377$	$f(10100001)=0.645$	$f(10100010)=0.026$	$f(10100011)=0.841$	$f(10100100)=0.077$
$f(10100101)=0.743$	$f(10100110)=0.256$	$f(10100111)=0.902$	$f(10101000)=0.378$	$f(10101001)=0.320$
$f(10101010)=0.211$	$f(10101011)=0.648$	$f(10101100)=0.251$	$f(10101101)=0.229$	$f(10101110)=0.251$
$f(10101111)=0.943$	$f(10110000)=0.137$	$f(10110001)=0.270$	$f(10110010)=0.549$	$f(10110011)=0.324$
$f(10110100)=0.865$	$f(10110101)=0.297$	$f(10110110)=0.680$	$f(10110111)=0.833$	$f(10111000)=0.876$
$f(10111001)=0.650$	$f(10111010)=0.073$	$f(10111011)=0.898$	$f(10111100)=0.254$	$f(10111101)=0.611$
$f(10111110)=0.842$	$f(10111111)=0.832$	$f(11000000)=0.373$	$f(11000001)=0.757$	$f(11000010)=0.109$
$f(11000011)=0.851$	$f(11000100)=0.559$	$f(11000101)=0.858$	$f(11000110)=0.343$	$f(11000111)=0.692$
$f(11001000)=0.345$	$f(11001001)=0.804$	$f(11001010)=0.050$	$f(11001011)=0.122$	$f(11001100)=0.982$
$f(11001101)=0.055$	$f(11001110)=0.615$	$f(11001111)=0.038$	$f(11010000)=0.377$	$f(11010001)=0.526$
$f(11010010)=0.282$	$f(11010011)=0.560$	$f(11010100)=0.607$	$f(11010101)=0.816$	$f(11010110)=0.447$
$f(11010111)=0.027$	$f(11011000)=0.472$	$f(11011001)=0.285$	$f(11011010)=0.293$	$f(11011011)=0.196$
$f(11011100)=0.018$	$f(11011101)=0.830$	$f(11011110)=0.573$	$f(11011111)=0.105$	$f(11100000)=0.733$
$f(11100001)=0.119$	$f(11100010)=0.224$	$f(11100011)=0.947$	$f(11100100)=0.739$	$f(11100101)=0.821$
$f(11100110)=0.826$	$f(11100111)=0.251$	$f(11101000)=0.257$	$f(11101001)=0.338$	$f(11101010)=0.388$
$f(11101011)=0.527$	$f(11101100)=0.266$	$f(11101101)=0.401$	$f(11101110)=0.871$	$f(11101111)=0.046$
$f(11110000)=0.295$	$f(11110001)=0.394$	$f(11110010)=0.560$	$f(11110011)=0.311$	$f(11110100)=0.823$
$f(11110101)=0.475$	$f(11110110)=0.091$	$f(11110111)=0.262$	$f(11111000)=0.917$	$f(11111001)=0.978$
$f(11111010)=0.332$	$f(11111011)=0.902$	$f(11111100)=0.241$	$f(11111101)=0.373$	$f(11111110)=0.752$
$f(11111111)=0.752$				

Learning Linkage

Georges R. Harik
Dept. of Electrical Engineering and Computer Science
University of Michigan at Ann Arbor
harikg@eecs.umich.edu

David E. Goldberg
Dept. of General Engineering
University of Illinois at Urbana Champaign
deg@uiuc.edu

Abstract

The topic of linkage has, with a few notable exceptions, been largely ignored. Recent studies have shown this approach to be a profound mistake— that GAs ignoring linkage do so at their own computational peril. Inversion, the operator usually called upon to solve this problem, has proven too slow *vis a vis* the forces of selection. Inversion is a mutation-like operator that acts on chromosomal structures. Where the evolution of linkage by mutation is too slow and has failed, it remains possible that evolution by pairwise recombination or crossover can be successful. This paper shows that tight linkage can be evolved within the environment of a new crossover operator. However, this linkage learning is evidenced only under specific conditions if the force of selection is not slowed.

1 Introduction

Early studies focused on the concepts of building blocks and linkage as central to understanding the GA (Holland, 1975). Since then, the topic of building blocks has been heavily explored while the topic of linkage has, with a few notable exceptions, been largely ignored (Goldberg, Korb, & Deb, 1989). Recent studies (Thierens & Goldberg, 1993) have shown this approach to be a profound mistake— that GAs ignoring linkage do so at their own computational peril.

It has long been thought that having tight linkage should be evolutionarily advantageous (Holland, 1975). It has further been assumed that any operator a working on the structural representation of chromosomes would eventually evolve tightly linked representations and allow for the solving of difficult problems. Unfortunately for inversion, the most commonly used of such operators, eventually doesn't come soon enough (Goldberg & Bridges, 1990).

The forces of selection are much too fast for inversion to accomplish its goals before the GA converges. Inversion is a mutation like operator that acts on chromosomal structures. Where evolution by mutation is too slow and has failed, it remains possible that evolution by pairwise recombination or crossover can be successful.

The purpose of this paper is to explore the theoretical basis for the assumption that tight linkage can be evolved within the environment of a new crossover operator.

We begin by defining and analyzing a measure of linkage. We proceed with the definition of a linkage-friendly crossover operator. We conclude with a theoretical and empirical investigation of this new operator and its interaction with our measure of linkage.

2 A Measure Of Linkage

To rigorously show the evolution of "tight linkage", we must be able to quantify a building block's linkage within a chromosome. Previous studies have used the building block's defining length as such a measure. This definition is appropriate under one-point crossover but irrelevant or imprecise under other crossover operators such as uniform and two-point crossover.

We take as a more general definition of a building block's linkage the probability that that building block is conserved under whichever crossover operator is used. Our proposed crossover operator will be similar to two-point crossover and so we use that crossover operator to define our measure of linkage.

We proceed now to a more concrete definition of linkage under our chosen crossover operator and to a calculation of the expected linkage of a randomly constructed order-k building block.

2.1 Calculating Linkage

We consider the case of a single building block embedded within an infinite sized chromosome. This both provides a limiting case for large problems as well as a model that is easily approachable in small problems with the addition of functionally neutral introns (Levenick, 1991).

This model has an elegant mathematical interpretation. Two-point crossover treats the chromosome as if it were connected end-to-end in a circle. When the number of genes defining a chromosome is small, the chromosome is akin to a necklace of beads or genes. As the amount of genetic material in the chromosome approaches infinity, the thickness of each of the above beads decreases to nothing. At the limit, a building block's genes become equivalent to a set of points on the chromosomal circle.

This model allows a simple expression for the preceding definition of linkage. Consider the chromosomal circle in question to be of circumference 1. An order-k building block is then represented as k points on the circle. We label the successive distances between

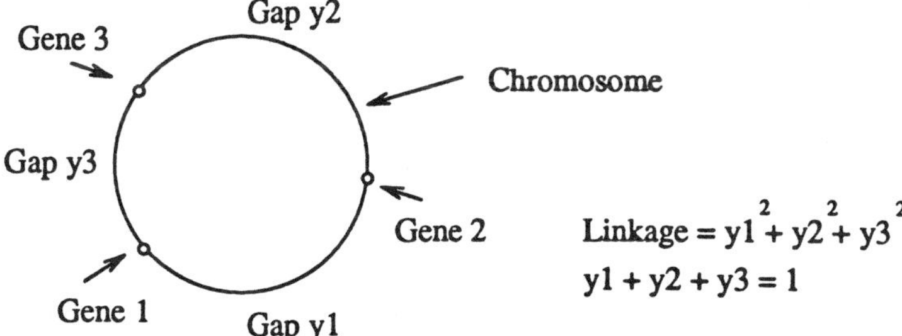

Figure 1: A three gene building block with its intergene gaps and linkage constraints.

adjacent points on the circle y_1 through y_k. This building block is preserved under two-point crossover precisely when both crossover points lie within the same gap between adjacent genes. Given that the crossover points are distributed randomly and uniformly over the circle, the probability of both crossover points falling within the same gap equals $\sum y_i^2$. Figure 1 demonstrates this model and its interpretation of linkage.

2.2 Random Linkage

We turn our attention now towards defining the ranges that bound our definition of linkage. We assume an order k building block. The maximum linkage attainable by this building block is 1. This case occurs when the points defining the building block are almost overlapping. Minimum linkage is attained when those points are maximally separated along the circle. In this case each of the successive gaps has length $1/k$ and the linkage equals $k(1/k^2) = 1/k$.

To calculate the starting point for any linkage learning algorithm, we calculate the expected linkage of a randomly created order k building block. Under two-point crossover, the fraction of the chromosome chosen for crossover is of random length and uniformly distributed over $[0, 1]$. If a fraction of the chromosome equal to p is chosen to be transferred during crossover, the probability that a random building block resides wholly in that portion or in the other portion of the chromosome (and thus is preserved) is $p^k + (1 - p)^k$. We calculate the expectation of this probability:

$$E(p^k + (1 - p)^k) = \int_0^1 p^k + (1 - p)^k\, dp = 2 \int_0^1 p^k\, dp = 2/(k + 1)$$

This value is termed the "random" linkage of an order-k building block and is the starting point for any linkage learning algorithm.

3 The Exchange Crossover Operator

The ability to evolve linkage requires a dynamic representation of gene positions. Genes and their alleles can be coded as (position,value) pairs, allowing them to reside anywhere in the chromosome. In this section, we propose and study a new crossover-like operator that manipulates such chromosomal structures. The defined operator is similar to two-point crossover.

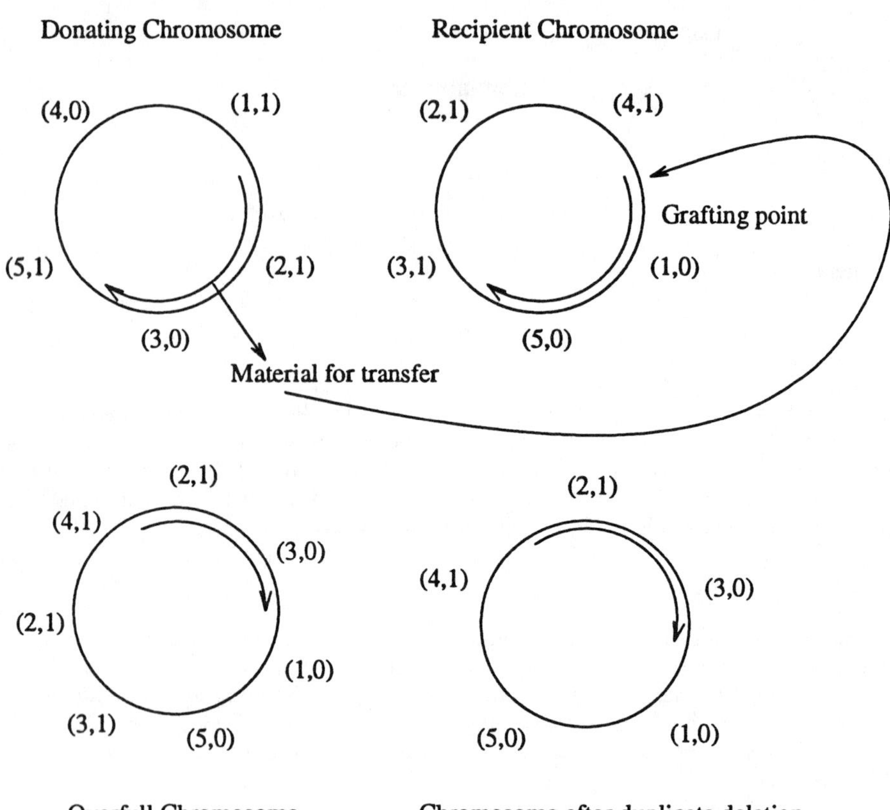

Figure 2: 5-gene chromosomes in the 4 steps of an exchange.

The "Exchange" operator is defined on pairs of chromosomes structured as above. One chromosome is designated the donor and the other the recipient. The operator selects a random segment of genetic material from the donor and grafts it onto the recipient at a random location. The recipient chromosome then becomes overfull in that it will contain multiple copies of various genes. The duplicates already present in the recipient are deleted leaving the resulting chromosome with at most one allele per gene. The structural form of the genes transferred from the donor remain intact in the recipient. The genes not deleted in the recipient are brought closer together.

The exchange operator considers both the donor and recipient to be connected circular chromosomes so as to avoid end effects. Both chromosomes are assumed to have an implicit orientation and genetic material is always chosen and grafted in the same orientation. This operator is directional in that it has different effects on the donor and recipient chromosomes. This asymmetry can be remedied by having the two chromosomes involved in an exchange alternately play both roles and produce two offspring.

Figure 2 shows the various steps involved in the exchange of the chromosome (4,0) (1,1)

(2,1) (3,0) (5,1) onto the chromosome (2,1) (4,1) (1,0) (5,0) (3,1). First a random segment of genetic material, (2,1) (3,0), is chosen from the donor chromosome. Second, a grafting point, right after (4,1), is chosen in the recipient chromosome. Third, the donated material is injected at the grafting point forming the overfull chromosome (2,1) (3,0) (1,0) (5,0) (3,1) (2,1) (4,1). Last, the excess genes in the recipient are deleted forming the complete individual (2,1) (3,0) (1,0) (5,0) (4,1). In this way, two chromosomes with completely different structure are recombined to form a new individual with a full gene complement.

4   The Evolution Of Linkage

We now investigate the interaction between our defined model of linkage and the exchange operator. We focus on a single fully deceptive building block within a larger problem. We choose the class of deceptive building blocks because they are known to be problematic for GAs not using linkage information, and thus present a natural testbed for any linkage learning algorithm (Thierens & Goldberg, 1993).

Since the exchange operator is directional, we separate our analysis into two distinct mechanisms. The first mechanism occurs when a chromosome containing the optimal building block is the donor of genetic material; the second occurs when it is the recipient of genetic material. In the following analysis, we consider the effect that both of these mechanisms have on the distribution of linkages of the optimal building block in the population. We find that the first mechanism introduces a linkage "skew" whereby the density function skews higher linkage values in an effect identical to fitness-proportionate selection. We also find that the second mechanism introduces a linkage "shift" whereby the entire density function is shifted and compressed towards higher linkages.

Our analysis assumes that during the GA's operation, the population converges to a mix of only deceptive and optimal building blocks and that the optimal building block occupies only a small proportion of that population. We will revisit the validity of this assumption in a later section.

4.1   Linkage Skew

Let L_t be the density function of the optimal building block's linkages at generation t. We explore the evolution of L in one generation, considering only the first mechanism, where the optimal building block is in the donor. Since by assumption the optimal building block occupies a small proportion of the population, we pay attention only to exchanges involving the optimal building block as a donor and the deceptive building block as a recipient.

The optimal building block either survives or is disrupted by the exchange operation. The survival rate of an optimal building block when exchanging onto a deceptive building block is $l/2$, where l is the building block's linkage. This is the chance that the building block is not interrupted by the crossover (l) and that it is copied whole instead of entirely ignored($1/2$). Therefore, to a constant factor, at each point l inside the linkage domain, $L_{t+1}(l) = ClL_t(l)$. The constant factor is determined by $\int_0^1 L_{t+1}(l)dl = 1$. Since $\int_0^1 lL_t(l)dl = E(L_t)$, $C = 1/E(L_t)$. Therefore $L_{t+1}(l) = lL_t(l)/E(L_t)$.

In short, the building blocks in question have differential survival rates under crossover and these rates are based on the building blocks' linkages. The equations that describe this situation precisely mirror those of fitness-proportionate selection, with the linkage of a building block here playing the role of its fitness score.

4.2 Linkage Shift

Again, let L_t be the density function of the optimal building block's linkages at generation t. We explore the evolution of L during one generation, considering only the second mechanism, where the optimal building block is in the recipient. We thus pay attention only to exchanges involving the optimal building block as the recipient and the deceptive building block as the donor of genetic material.

If any of the genes constituting the deceptive building block are copied onto the individual carrying the optimal building block, they will disrupt that building block. Even if an optimal building block is not disrupted, its linkage will be changed by the influx of new material and the corresponding deletion of this material from the original chromosome. We explore now the expected effect that the exchange operation has on an optimal building block with linkage value l given that it survives the exchange operation intact.

We assume that the gene distribution in the individual containing the deceptive building block is random. This assumption seems reasonable as the deceptive building block does not need tight linkage to be converged to. This assumption has been verified by experiment. Let y_i be the gap lengths in the individual containing the optimal building blocks and let l be the building block's linkage. The optimal individual will receive genetic material from the deceptive individual at a random location. We begin by measuring the effect this crossover has on the linkage of this individual if that location falls within the gap of length y_1 and if the optimal building block survives the crossover intact.

Let ϵ be the length of genetic material transferred in the exchange again considering the chromosome to be a circle of circumference 1. Since we are only interested in the effects on building blocks that survive this transfer, this material will be assumed to contain none of the genes defining the building block we are interested in. The original genes corresponding to the transferred material must be deleted from the original individual for there to be no gene duplication. Therefore, the newly formed individual will have gap lengths y_i' that differ from the original gap lengths. The gap into which the genetic material is injected will expand while the remaining gaps all contract.

The expected change in the y_i's is as follows:

$$y_1' = y_1 + (1 - y_1)\epsilon$$
$$y_j' = y_j(1 - \epsilon), j \neq 1$$

We calculate the difference between the new linkage, $\sum y_i'^2$, and the old linkage, $\sum y_i^2$, by separately calculating the various coefficients of the powers of ϵ.

$$CF_{\epsilon^0}(\Delta l) = y_1^2 + \sum_{j \neq 1} y_j^2 - \sum_i y_i^2 = 0$$
$$CF_{\epsilon^1}(\Delta l) = 2y_1(1 - y_1) - 2\sum_{j \neq 1} y_j^2 = 2y_1 - 2l$$
$$CF_{\epsilon^2}(\Delta l) = (1 - y_1)^2 + \sum_{j \neq 1} y_j^2 = 1 - 2y_1 + y_1^2 + \sum_{j \neq 1} y_j^2 = 1 - 2y_1 + l$$
$$\Rightarrow \Delta l = 2(y_1 - l)\epsilon + (1 - 2y_1 + l)\epsilon^2$$

We now extend our calculation to a probabilistic choice of the gap into which genetic material is injected. The ith gap is chosen as the recipient of a transfer with probability y_i. Multiplying the expected difference by the probability of choosing a particular gap and summing over all gaps, we get:

$$\Delta l = \sum_i [y_i (2(y_i - l)\epsilon + (1 - 2y_i + l)\epsilon^2)] =$$
$$\sum_i [(2y_i^2 - 2ly_i)\epsilon + (y_i - 2y_i^2 + y_i l)\epsilon^2] =$$
$$(2l - 2l)\epsilon + (1 - 2l + l)\epsilon^2 = (1 - l)\epsilon^2$$

We further extend our calculation to a probabilistic choice of the size of the material transferred, ϵ. The material chosen from the individual with the deceptive building block is assumed not to contain any of the building block's defining genes. The length of the segment originally chosen for exchange is uniform over $[0, 1]$. The segments that we consider in this analysis are those that do not contain any of the building block's genes in their material. A segment of length ϵ has a probability $(1 - \epsilon)^k$ of not containing any of the chosen building block's genes. Therefore, ϵ has a probability density at each point proportional to $(1 - \epsilon)^k$. The constant of proportionality is readily calculated as $(k + 1)$. We calculate the expected value of ϵ^2 and thus $(1 - l)\epsilon^2$:

$$E(\epsilon^2) = \int_0^1 \epsilon^2 (1 - \epsilon)^k (k + 1)dk, \text{ by symmetry } =$$
$$(k + 1) \int_0^1 \epsilon^k (1 - \epsilon)^2 dk = (k + 1) \int_0^1 \epsilon^k - 2\epsilon^{k+1} + \epsilon^{k+2}dk =$$
$$(k + 1)(1/(k + 1) - 2/(k + 2) + 1/(k + 3)) = 2/(k + 2)(k + 3)$$

Therefore $\Delta l = (1 - l)[2/(k + 2)(k + 3)]$ and thus $l(t + 1) = l(t) + (1 - l(t))[2/(k + 2)(k + 3)]$ is the simple recurrence describing the expectation of what happens to the linkage of any building block surviving an exchange under the second mechanism.

We now note that the probability of survival under this mechanism does not depend on the actual linkage of the optimal building block itself but only on whether the individual gets lucky and survives a crossover from a randomly ordered individual. Therefore, no "skew" occurs as in the first mechanism. What does happen however, is that the linkage density and correspondingly the average linkage for optimal building blocks surviving crossover "shifts" over to a higher linkage according to the above difference equation in each generation.

4.3 Experiments

We have dissected the proposed crossover into two mechanisms. We now experimentally verify the pair of theories proposed above. We design two sets of experiments that induce the assumptions made in the above analysis and attempt to verify our conclusions.

4.3.1 Linkage Skew

For a fully deceptive building block we use a 4-bit trap function with a deceptive to optimal fitness ratio of 0.6 (Deb & Goldberg, 1993). In order to approach the infinite chromosome model, we embed this building block within a chromosome of 150 genes, the other 146 of which are nonfunctional. We initialize the population with 6400 chromosomes all containing the optimal building block but with random orderings.

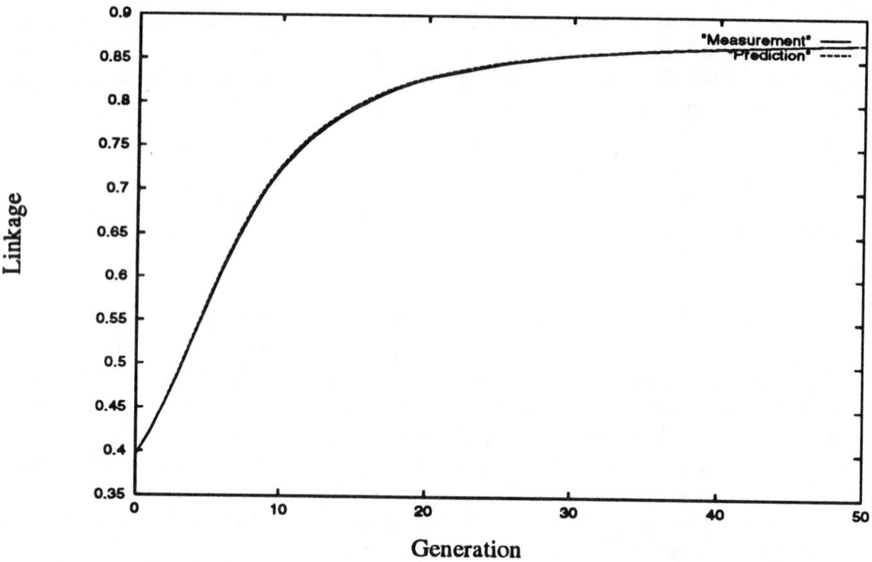

Figure 3: Predicted versus measured linkage averages under mechanism 1, using a 4-bit trap function and large rate of selection. The prediction, from one generation to the next, follows $l(t+1) = l(t) + \sigma^2(t)/l(t)$.

One generation of our simulation involves crossing this population with artificially generated individuals containing randomly ordered deceptive building blocks. We consider only one of the two children of the exchange - where the donor contains the optimal building block - as we are investigating the first mechanism only. Finally, only the optimal building blocks surviving the crossover are used to repopulate the next generation of 6400 chromosomes. This is because we are interested solely in the density function of the linkages of the optimal building block. Conceptually, our population here would in an actual GA represent the subpopulation consisting only of representatives of the optimal building block.

We run this simulation 50 generations and repeat it 30 times measuring at each step the population linkage's average and standard deviation.

We made the claim that the density of the linkages of the optimal building block under this mechanism operated identically to fitness-proportionate selection with the building block's linkage playing the role of its fitness. Fitness-proportionate selection abides by a simple recurrence from generation to generation. The expected increase in the average fitness in one generation equals the ratio of the variance to the average fitness at that generation.

To evaluate our hypothesis, we compare a plot of the average linkages of our experiments over the 50 generations versus a constructed variable l. This constructed variable begins at the random linkage of $2/(k+1)$ (0.4 here) and follows by $l(t+1) = l(t) + \sigma^2(t)/l(t)$ as is dictated by the equations of fitness-proportionate selection. As we see in Figure 3, these two plots are identical and our hypothesis is reflected in this experiment.

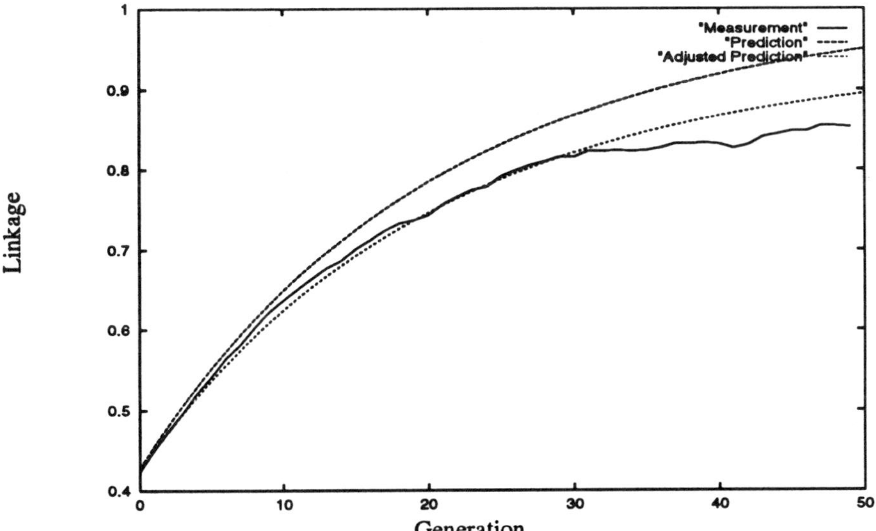

Figure 4: Predicted versus measured linkage averages under mechanism 2, using a 4-bit trap function and large rate of selection. The prediction follows $l(t + 1) = l(t) + (1 - l(t))/21$.

4.3.2 Linkage Shift

We repeat the above set of experiments for the second mechanism. This time, we restrict ourselves to using the deceptive building block as the donor and the optimal building block as the recipient. Based on our calculations above, our constructed variable in this case begins at 0.4 and follows the recurrence $l(t + 1) = l(t) + (1 - l(t))/21$.

Figure 4 shows that the original model is approximately correct. Any discrepancy between theory and experiment probably arises from the discretization of a continuous model. We adjust the model for the fact that a building block's linkage in our experiment has an approximate maximum linkage of $(146/150)^2 = 0.947$. We formulate an adjusted recurrence relation $l(t + 1) = l(t) + (0.947 - l(t)) * 1/21$. This adjusted model agrees quite well with our experiments and we are given good reason to believe that the model is accurate.

5   The Role Of Selection

So far, we have discussed the evolution of linkage in terms of the actions of the exchange operator's effects. Our discussion thusfar involves no role for the mechanism of selection in this evolution. When all is said and done, evolution is driven by the survival of the fittest and in GAs this means selection. It turns out that the effect of selection is necessary for the satisfaction of the first of our assumptions as well as the preservation of the optimal building block within a finite population.

Our first assumption was that the population converges to a mix of individuals containing only optimal and deceptive building blocks at some point during its evolution. It is unlikely that an initial distribution of chromosomes will consist solely of these two types of individuals. However, in a deceptive problem, and under the action of selection, the population does eventually migrate to a mix largely composed of deceptive and optimal building blocks and our assumption is satisfied.

Additionally, our distributional analysis does not consider overall rates of building block survival under the proposed crossover operator. Each generation of exchange eliminates a sizable fraction of the optimal building blocks in the population. In finite populations, selection is needed to counterbalance this loss of optimal individuals.

We now explore how far the predicted linkage-learning can take us in a real and uncontrolled setting including the effects of selection.

6   Uncontrolled Testing Of Linkage Learning

We remove all artificial constructs from our experiments and instead focus on running the GA the way a practitioner might. We look for traces of the proposed linkage-learning and make some conclusions as to the usefulness of the algorithm suggested by the exchange operator.

We focus on learning the linkage of a 3-bit deceptive subproblem embedded within a larger coding string of 100 bits the remainder of which are nonfunctional. We use a trap function with a deceptive to optimal fitness ratio of 0.6. In contrast with the previous experiments, we now have to choose a level of selection for this experiment.

The survival rate for optimal building blocks at an average linkage of l when crossing with deceptive building blocks is approximately $l/2 + 1/(k+1)$. The first and second terms here originate respectively from the first and second mechanisms. With a k of 3 the minimum attainable linkage is $1/4$ and the survival rate thus has a minimum of $1/2$. We therefore theorize that a selection rate of 2 should be enough to guarantee convergence to the optimal building block in this case. On the other hand, when a building block has tight linkage, its survival rate into the next population is $1/2 + 1/4 = 3/4$. Therefore we theorize that a selection rate of $4/3$ is near the minimum level of selection that can be used while still expecting convergence to the global optimum.

We run the GA through alternating stages of selection and exchange. We observe the population for 75 generations, which turns out to be long enough for all our runs to reach convergence. We vary the selection rate from 2.0 down to 1.2 by increments of 0.1. Fractional selection rates are implemented by a probabilistic choice of tournament size. That is, a selection rate of 1.3 implies a 30% chance of a tournament size of 2 and a 70% chance of a tournament size of 1. At each level of selection, we repeat our experiment 20 times. We gather averages at each generation for both the number of optimal building blocks and the average linkage for those building blocks. The population sizes are chosen large enough to avoid stochastic effects.

Figure 5 shows the various convergence plots as the selection ranges from 2.0 to 1.2. As theorized, the selection rates from 1.3 on up all show a convergence to the global optimum. With a selection rate of 1.2, we see the opposite, the population converges to the deceptive attractor. As we had predicted, the main indicator of the way the population would swing is the struggle between the conservative forces of selection and the destructive forces of crossover.

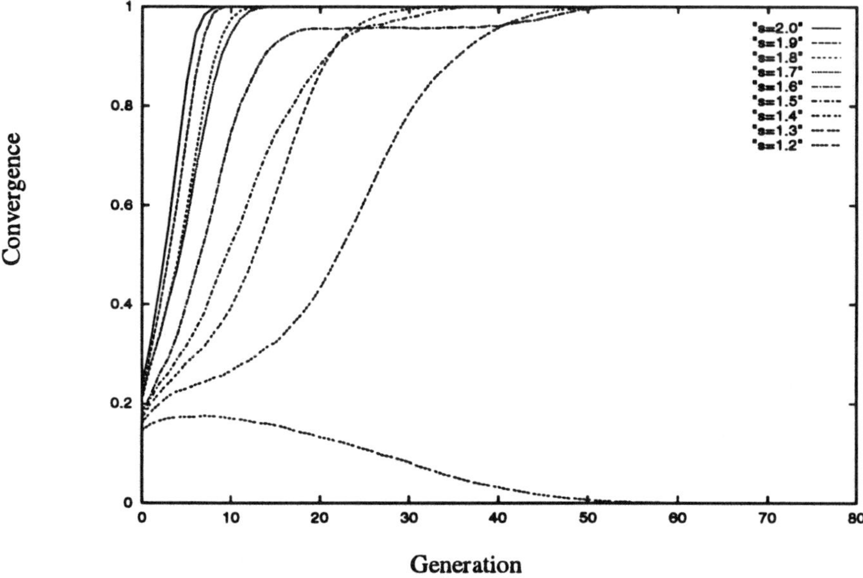

Figure 5: Uncontrolled convergence under various rates of selection. Here convergence measures the proportion of the population containing the optimal building block.

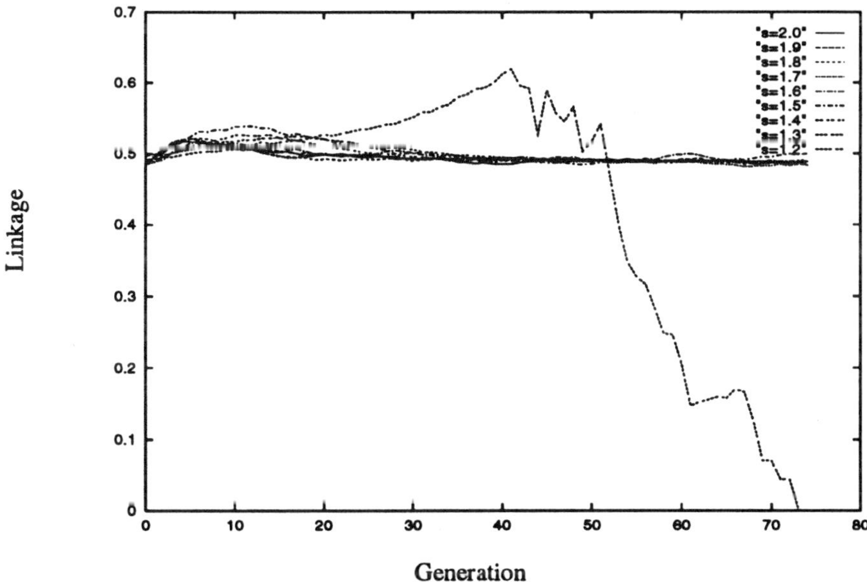

Figure 6: Uncontrolled linkage-learning under various rates of selection.

Figure 6 shows the average values for the linkages of the optimal building blocks at the various generations and levels of selection. We observe that the linkage-learning becomes more pronounced as the rate of selection decreases and is only really significant at a selection rate of 1.2. Unfortunately, at this level of selection, the population converges to the wrong building block.

This observation makes sense if we take a second to consider the framework in which linkage-learning occurs. Our theory becomes applicable only when a large fraction of the population has converged to the deceptive attractor and then remains applicable at the most until the population converges. The faster the selection rate, the less time the linkage evolution has to work under. Unfortunately, we can only slow down the selection rate so much before violating the schema theorem and leading convergence to an incorrect conclusion. Theoretically, investigating selection rates between 1.2 and 1.3 we might be able to precariously balance this process so as to lead to higher levels of linkage-learning. However, this method does not present us with a practical alternative because such a fine search for a selection rate then becomes it own intractable problem.

The level of linkage learned in these problems still seems quite a bit shy of what we we would have expected from our initial experimentation. This is most likely because our assumption of negligible optimal building block representation is violated in the real setting. We term this violation the "homogeneity effect" and in the next section, we study the destructive effects of this violation on our theory of the two linkage-learning mechanisms.

7 The Homogeneity Effect

In this section, we take a brief look at how the homogeneity effect changes the theory we had developed early on in this chapter. We will see that it has detrimental effects on both the first and second mechanisms of linkage learning. Because the homogeneity effect results in practice from having a non-negligible proportion of optimal individuals, it acts much like a negative feedback effect preventing linkage learning as convergence is takes place. One might think that linkage learning is not needed when the population converges to the right solution on the building block in question. However, in multiple building block problems, this effect will cause a building block to converge without first achieving tight linkage. This will cause other building blocks spuriously linked with the one that converged to converge incorrectly.

7.1 Linkage Skew

In the first mechanism, we showed a direct correlation under exchange between the survival probability under crossover of a building block and its linkage. We assumed that to survive, a building block must be copied whole from an optimal individual to a deceptive individual. This is not necessary if the receiving individual has a certain number of alleles that agree with the optimal building block. In that case, only the remaining genes need be copied over. In addition, the resulting building block's linkage need not be the same as that of the parent optimal building block since the positioning of the genes in the recipient parent is assumedly random. We now derive a more general expression for a building block's survival probability under the first mechanism.

Picture the optimal individual in Figure 7. As usual, let the y_i be the lengths of the intergene

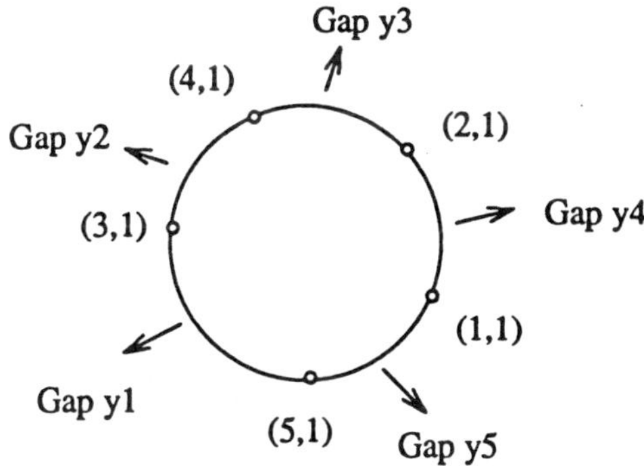

Figure 7: A sample 5-gene optimal building block

gaps and $l = \sum y_i^2$ be the optimal building block's linkage. Let p be the proportion of genes in the recipient individual that agree with the optimal building block. In our original calculations, $p = 0$ and the probability of survival equaled $l/2$. However, with a nonzero p, the two crossover points in the exchange can occur outside the same gap and still lead to a child with the optimal building block if the missing genes are picked up from the recipient individual.

Two crossover points, one in the gap of length y_1 and one in the gap of length y_2 (picking the outside segment for transfer) yield an optimal individual with probability p. This is the probability that the missing gene, $(3,1)$, is present in the recipient individual. Similarly, two crossover points in the gaps of length y_0 and y_2 (again picking the outside segment for transfer) yield an optimal individual with probability p^2— the probability that two genes are picked up from the recipient individual. Considering all indexes mod 5, the adjusted survival probability becomes:

$$l/2 + p\sum y_i y_{i+1} + p^2 \sum y_i y_{i+2} + p^3 \sum y_i y_{i+3} + p^4 \sum y_i y_{i+4} + p^5 l/2$$

We verify that when $p = 1$ the above formula equals $(\sum(y_i))^2 = 1$ as expected. We note that the above formula is not completely determined by a building block's linkage and is dependent on other functions of the intergene spacing. Calculations of the evolution of these functions could probably be made in a manner similar to those made on the linkage, and the homogeneity effect could be more closely modeled armed with such a theory. We do not proceed further along that line of inquiry as we have established what we had set out to do— to show that the mechanics of the first mechanism change under the homogeneity effect.

7.2 Linkage Shift

In the second mechanism we showed a tendency for crosses from the deceptive building block over onto the optimal building block to lead to a higher linkage in the building blocks that survive. We can come up with an approximation to the effect that a violation in our assumption has on our calculations. Recall that the probability of survival in this case was unrelated to the building block's level of linkage and equaled $1/(k+1)$ where k was the building block's order. Now, assuming that the donating building block has a proportion p of its genes in agreement with the optimal building block, then only the remaining $(1-p)k$ of the bits have to be excluded in the exchange for survival of the optimal building block. We calculate the proportion of non-destructive crossovers occurring under the original conditions to the total number of successful crossovers. We do this by comparing the original survival rate to the new survival rate:

> The original survival rate was $1/(k+1)$
> The new survival rate is $1/((1-p)k+1)$
> The ratio of the two rates is then $((1-p)k+1)/(k+1)$

As k becomes large, we conservatively approximate this proportion by $1-p$. Therefore a proportion equal to $1-p$ of the population is doing what we had expected it to do under the original calculations. On the other hand, the other p of the crossovers are injecting genetic material into the optimal building blocks at random positions throughout the coding string. We conservatively assume that this injection of random material causes the optimal building block to revert back to its random linkage value of $2/(k+1)$. Under these conditions, the new conservative difference equation for the average linkage value under the second mechanism becomes:

$$L(t+1) = p(2/(k+1)) + (1-p)(L(t) + (1-L(t)) * 2/(k+2)(k+3))$$

Even with a small p this difference equation is significantly slower than the one where $p = 0$. Furthermore, L is bounded under this equation at a value less than 1. To see this we set $L(t+1) = L(t)$ and solve for $L(t)$.

$$L = 2p/(k+1) + (1-p)(L + (1-L)2/(k+2)(k+3)) \Rightarrow$$
$$L-(1-p)L+L(1-p)(2/((k+2)(k+3))) = 2p/(k+1)+(1-p)(2/((k+2)(k+3))) \Rightarrow$$
$$L = (2p/(k+1) + (1-p)(2/((k+2)(k+3))))/(p+2(1-p)/((k+2)(k+3)))$$

For example, the maximum values attained for $p = 0, 0.1, 0.2$ and 0.3 and $k = 4$ are $0.58, 0.496$ and 0.46 respectively.

To confirm this analysis, we repeat the same kind of experiment we did when confirming our initial difference equation. Instead of using deceptive attractors as the originator of genetic material, this time we use building blocks containing a proportion p of their genes coinciding with the optimal building block. We look at a 4 bit trap function again with a deceptive to optimal fitness ratio of 0.6. We use a chromosome length of 150 and a population size of 200 optimal building blocks. Each generation, we perform an exchange on these building blocks with our constructed building block being the originator of the genetic material. We repeat this experiment 30 times to gather averages of the linkage levels for each of 50 generations and 3 different levels for p of .1, .2 and .3. Figure 8 shows the results of this experiment. As we see, our intuition is validated in that our model is reasonably accurate over the range of violations of our assumptions.

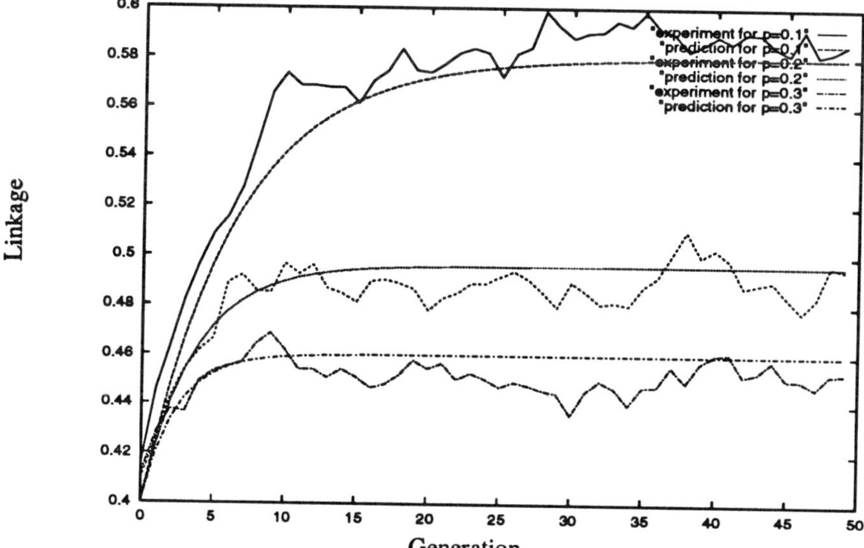

Figure 8: Here, we track how the evolution of linkage is hindered by various levels of the homogeniety effect.

8   Summary and Conclusion

In this paper, we have defined a new crossover operator capable of operating on structurally heterogeneous chromosomes, and analyzed a new measure of linkage appropriate for our defined operator. We have seen that under certain conditions the use of this operator demonstrates an advantage for and a tendency to drift towards tight linkage. We have also quantified and empirically verified the above advantage and drift.

The race between selection and linkage-learning still prevents this advantage from manifesting itself in an uncontrolled setting. What advantage, we can ask, does this hold over inversion which is also plagued by the same problem? First, the use of a crossover operator means that linkage can be learned concurrently over multiple building blocks. All the inversion-based schemes convert one parent to the form of the other before crossover — destroying any information contained in the second parent. Second, the time to solve the linkage problem using the exchange operator is around k^2 generations, with k being the order of the building block attempted. Since only the first mechanism identified in this paper comes into play using inversion, this time is likely faster than that of inversion alone; though these calculations have yet to be made.

Both of these reasons imply that the linkage-learning induced by this crossover operator is faster than that induced by inversion. Thus, we have less work to do in matching its time scale with that of selection. Indeed, the practical implementation of a working version of the exchange operator has recently become possible. This implementation hinges on changing an individual's representation to make it less susceptible to the homogeniety effect. This is done by requiring each individual to maintain both possible alleles for every gene position indefinitely. An additional step of probabilistic interpretation is then needed to form a

chromosome that can be acted on by a fitness function. Work in this area will be present
in a later paper.

Acknowledgements

This effort was sponsored by the Air Force Office of Scientific Research, Air Force Materi
Command, USAF, under grant numbers F4960-94-1-0103 and F49620-95-1-0338. The U
Government is authorised to reproduce and distribute reprints for Governmental purpo
notwithstanding any copyright notation thereon.

The views and conclusions contained herein are those of the authors and should not
interpreted as necessarily representing the official policies or endorsements, either express
or implied, of the Air Force Office of Scientific Research or the U.S. Government.

References

Deb, K., & Goldberg, D. E. (1993). Analyzing deception in trap functions. (pp. 93–10

Goldberg, D. E., & Bridges, C. L. (1990). An analysis of a reordering operator on a G
hard problem. *Biological Cybernetics*, *62*, 397–405. (Also TCGA Report No. 8800

Goldberg, D. E., Korb, B., & Deb, K. (1989). Messy genetic algorithms: Motivation, an
ysis, and first results. *Complex Systems*, *3*(5), 493–530. (Also TCGA Report 8900

Holland, J. H. (1975). *Adaptation in natural and artificial systems*. Ann Arbor: Univers
of Michigan Press.

Levenick, J. R. (1991). Inserting introns improves genetic algorithm success rate: Tak
a cue from biology. (pp. 123–127).

Thierens, D., & Goldberg, D. E. (1993). Mixing in genetic algorithms. In *Proceedings
the Fifth International Conference in Genetic Algorithms* (pp. 38–45).

On Searching α-ary Hypercubes and Related Graphs

Joseph Culberson
Department of Computing Science
University of Alberta
Edmonton, AB
T6G 2H1

Jonathan Lichtner
Department of Computing Science
University of Alberta
Edmonton, AB
T6G 2H1

Abstract

This paper develops two themes on landscapes in search algorithms. First it focuses on the notion of landscapes as being induced by operators and fitness functions together with a frequently overlooked influence, the way in which the operator is used within the algorithm. This latter influence is sometimes confused by the tendency to consider a landscape as representative of a search even when a different operator is introduced into the search. We make a finer distinction and show that even when the graph is strictly adhered to by the operators, functions can be found that exponentially differentiate between algorithms that use the neighbor generation in elitist, non-elitist, full neighbor search, and neighborhood sampling techniques. These results can be seen as a form of "no free lunch" in that to fully analyze an algorithm, no detail can be excluded from the analysis.

The second theme tries to abstract out salient properties of landscapes that are dependent on properties of graphs such as degree, diameter, and independent set structure. These properties limit the effects of adversaries in various ways. For this to make sense, we must give up the notion of universal problem solvers, and consider more restricted assumptions that better reflect our expectations of search on specific problem classes. This analysis is mostly restricted to operator graphs; that is, to graphs wherein the vertices represent sets of strings over fixed alphabets with edges joining sets that are linked by simple operations.

1 Introduction

1.1 Background

In recent work (Culberson, 1995; Gitchoff and Wagner, 1996; Jones, 1995; Stadler and Wagner,1996) there has been an attempt to understand genetic algorithms in terms of the landscapes induced by the operators on various functions. In this paper, we continue the work started in "Mutation-Crossover Isomorphisms and the Construction of Discriminating Functions" (Culberson, 1995) by considering the structure of the graphs induced by mutation and crossover operators and how we may extend this analysis to higher order alphabets. We also consider the limitations of such graphs and present a number of functions which sharply distinguish algorithms based on the way in which the the search is conducted.

The key to understanding this approach is to think of the search as generating new points that are close to previous points, where closeness is defined by the operators used to generate the new points. This is the only view the computational system can have of the search space, regardless of any external picture the user may have of the function. That is, at any point the algorithm can only see those neighbors provided by the operators.

Fitness landscapes have been influential in the theories of evolutionary biology (Provine, 1986). Genetic algorithms (GAs) (Holland, 1975) are stochastic search algorithms whose operations are based on simplified models of natural genetics. This leads naturally to attempts to apply the notions of landscape analysis to GAs (Horn and Goldberg, 1995), although much of the GA analysis has been independently developed. However, to be effective in the computational search setting, landscape analysis must be based on domains where the notion of neighborhood directly corresponds to the allowed changes in state experienced by the algorithm. Failure to do this can render the analysis meaningless. Wolpert and Macready (1996) make the point that unless the operators are chosen to correspond to the structure of the problem the user is trying to solve there is no reason to expect the efficiency of the search to differ from that of random search. Horn and Goldberg (1995) show that massive modality on the binary hypercube and other simple graphs is not necessarily an indicator of GA performance, and this is frequently because the GA is using operators that do not conform to those landscapes.

One difficulty is determining the right level of representation: one that is complete enough to accurately model the algorithm and problem, but not so detailed as to make analysis intractable. Typically, a landscape is constructed by considering the set of points in the domain, or that portion of the domain represented by a (necessarily) discrete and finite encoding. The points are joined by edges forming a graph, where the edges represent some connection between the set of points. For example, in a traditional genetic algorithm (TGA), the points may represent binary strings with edges joining two points if they differ in exactly one location. The graph formed in this case is the binary hypercube. A landscape is defined by adding fitness values to each of the points in the graph. The search is then perceived as moving on the graph, biased by the evaluations of the points.

There is a tendency to see the search as moving on a binary hypercube even when the methods used by the operators in the algorithm to generate new search points have little or nothing to do with the hypercube graph. A simple example is the use of multiple step operators, such as k-bit mutation. The graph associated with the k-bit operator is obtained by taking the k-closure of the hypercube; that is, by joining all pairs of vertices that are within distance k. This closure induces a landscape with quite different properties than the binary hypercube for many functions.

If we wish to model a crossover or other recombination operator then difficulties are increased because two (or more) points are now required to generate one (or more) new points. We may either construct a graph consisting of sets of points as in (Culberson, 1995; Jones, 1995) or create hyper-graphs (Gitchoff and Wagner, 1996). Crossover generates points by "moving" along edges of a graph induced on the set of points forming the Hamming closure of the two parents. If restricted to repeatedly mating and producing pairs of offspring, this space is isomorphic to a mutation space (Culberson, 1995) on the same number of points, but the strings are mapped to the points differently than in the standard hypercube. As a result the landscape induced by the assignment of fitness values to the strings will be quite different in general than that on the standard hypercube. So the binary hypercube is not necessarily a good graph for studying the behavior of a GA using crossover, *even when the GA is using a binary encoding.*

Another difficulty, frequently overlooked, arises because an operator may be used by an algorithm in a way that does not effectively exploit the properties of the operator, even when those properties correspond to the fitness function in useful ways. For example, it is argued in (Culberson, 1995) that TGAs do not use crossover as effectively as possible, and in particular TGAs use mutation much more effectively than they use crossover. Basically, for crossover to be effective there must be diversity, but proportional selection in a simple TGA quickly eliminates diversity from the population. Many papers (Spears, 1992) have appeared in a continuing debate on whether crossover or mutation is a better operator, but in our view that question is incomplete. The question ignores the fitness function subjecting it to the criticisms inherent in the NFL theorems (Wolpert and Macready, 1996), and more importantly it ignores the manner in which the operators are being employed in the algorithm.

A better question is "how effectively is the GA using the *potential* of the various operators supplied to it?" It seems obvious that this question cannot be answered unless we have some idea of the *potential* that an operator offers to an algorithm.

1.2 Introduction to Potential Based on Adversaries

In this paper, we explore the potential of an operator by examining the graphs associated with mutation and a simple form of crossover on string based representations over discrete α-ary alphabets. The effectiveness of such a graph is multifaceted, and depends on the assumptions made about the function space being searched and the algorithm using it. Even when the assumptions appear to be appropriate, there can be functions that cause difficulties for an algorithm based on how the search information is used. Part of our exploration is an extension of the work of Horn, Goldberg and Deb (1994). We show that details, such as whether or not elitism and stochastic neighbor sampling are in use, can make an exponential difference in efficiency. This is true even when the function is unimodal on the graph. Furthermore, the results are symmetric. That is, no matter which choice we make, functions can then be found that are unimodal and require exponential time, while taking only polynomial time under a different choice.

However, as far as possible, we also want to separate the potential of the graph from these other influences, under assumptions of the type "all else being equal." Under the No Free

Lunch assumptions (Wolpert and Macready, 1996) all graphs have equivalent potential in the sense that no (connected) graph provides a superior structure for any optimization algorithm if the performance of the algorithm is measured over all possible functions. If we are to make progress we will need to make assumptions that are more restrictive of the domain of discourse.

We will assume an adversarial model of search, in which an algorithm passes strings to an adversary (or the environment) and gets back an evaluation. Adversaries are allowed to make up their responses on-line; that is, as the queries are made. They are required to be consistent, both with previous responses and with the constraints imposed by the class of problems under consideration. In this way, it is possible to demonstrate the existence of functions that cause specific behavior of an algorithm, or to demonstrate fundamental limitations on all algorithms such as those imposed by the "No Free Lunch" theorems (Culberson 1996). In this paper, we mostly use adversaries informally to indicate that a function has been designed with full knowledge of an algorithm to make the algorithm behave in a particular way.

We informally describe several adversaries to help develop intuition. Formally distinguishing between vicious and friendly adversaries (as described below) would likely entail resolving the P versus NP question, since we would have to be able to provably distinguish hard from easy problems. Instead we will identify the adversaries by the functions they choose for a specific graph. Apart from the indifferent adversary, the adversaries are assumed to choose their functions with respect to the operator graphs that we are using.

An *indifferent* adversary generates a random value whenever a new string is encountered. This adversary is equivalent to the NFL (Culberson, 1996; Wolpert and Macready, 1996) assumption in that all functions are generated with equal probability. Against this adversary, all algorithms are equal, and so are all operator graphs. For this reason this adversary is quite uninteresting (except perhaps to those who still believe in universal problem solvers).

A *friendly* adversary tends to select from functions that are compatible with the graph induced by the operator and representation. Faced with a particular optimization problem, an engineer would prefer to choose an operator and representation which generates a landscape on the function that is easy for his algorithm to search. Making such a choice is effectively an act of faith in a friendly adversary. The algorithm using the operator must also be capable of making effective use of this friendly information. We will not let the adversary be too friendly, for example by making every point optimal.

A *vicious* adversary is one that chooses functions to minimize the potential effectiveness of a graph, or to maximize deception with respect to a certain graph. We would like to consider operators whose graphs maximize the potential with respect to a friendly adversary and minimize the damage of a vicious one.

A *mischievous* adversary will be used to bedevil algorithms with landscapes that are sometimes easy and sometimes hard, depending upon what mechanisms the algorithm is using with respect to the operator. For example, such landscapes can be used to make elitism good or bad, or random neighbor sampling better or worse than steepest ascent, all on the same operator graph. These adversaries are often more interesting than either the friendly or vicious ones, and certainly more so than the indifferent adversary.

We will present various measures of potential of several classes of graphs, including those induced by simple mutation applied repeatedly to a single string and by crossover on a small set of strings *acting as an individual*. We concentrate most of our analysis on α-ary hypercubes and related graphs. These crossover graphs appear to be related to more general crossover, at least in the binary case (Culberson, 1995; Gitchoff and Wagner, 1996). Culberson (1995) gave empirical evidence indicated that the discriminating functions which were hard for trivial one-point crossover search (i.e. on a pair of complementary strings) tended also to be harder for larger population searches relying on one-point crossover. Of course, contrary examples will also occur. We note that each crossover operation in a larger population takes one step on the crossover hypercube defined on the Hamming closure of the parents. This observation extends also to the larger alphabet crossovers we define in this paper.

1.3 Notation

In this section we introduce some graph theoretic notation, terminology related to deception and deceptive graphs and nomenclature for algorithms. We assume throughout this paper that we wish to optimize some discrete function over an n-element domain, and that we have an encoding mapping the domain using ℓ-character strings (strings of length ℓ) drawn from an α-ary alphabet and an evaluation function for these strings. Thus, $n = \alpha^\ell$. A *point* (or *vertex* or *node*) in the landscape will be a string or a set of strings.

We assume some *operator* (OP) that takes as input a point (that is a string or set of strings) and generates a new point. As a simplification, we assume that given a point x an operator(OP) is capable of generating a set of points $OP(x)$, each of which has the same cardinality as the parent point. We call the set of points which the operator is capable of generating the neighborhood of x. The operators considered in this paper will be symmetric, so if $x \in OP(y)$ then $y \in OP(x)$.

Such a system can be represented by an undirected graph $G = (V, E)$, with vertices V representing points, and edges E joining vertices representing neighbors. Since the operators we consider can be applied in equal fashion to all strings in the encoding, our graphs will be *symmetric*; that is, there will be an automorphism of the graph mapping any vertex x to any other vertex y. We define some graph notation:

Neighborhood
$$N(x) = \{y|(x,y) \in E\}$$

Note that $y \in N(x) \iff x \in N(y)$. We extend the neighborhood notation to sets of points X with $N(X)$ defined by[1]

$$N(X) = \{x|x \in N(y), y \in X\}$$

Degree The *degree* of a node x is
$$d(x) = |N(x)|$$

The symmetry of G implies $d(x) = d(y), \forall x, y \in V$. We can thus refer to the degree of a graph G.

---

[1]To be complete, we could distinguish between open and closed neighborhoods, but this will be unnecessary for this paper.

Path A *path* from x to y is a sequence of vertices joined by edges with end points x and y. The length of a path is the number of edges in it.

Distance The *distance*, $\text{dist}(x, y)$, is the length of a shortest path from x to y. The distance between two sets of points is

$$\text{dist}(X, Y) = \min_{x \in X, y \in Y} \text{dist}(x, y)$$

Diameter The *diameter* of a graph G is

$$D(G) = \max_{u, v \in V} \text{dist}(u, v)$$

In symmetric graphs, for every vertex u there is at least one vertex v at distance $D(G)$.

Degree-Diameter Product The degree-diameter product of a (symmetric) graph is

$$DP(G) = d \times D$$

The *expected* or average degree-distance cost measure of a graph is

$$AP(G) = \frac{\sum_{v \in V} d \times \text{dist}(v, x)}{n}$$

where x is some arbitrary fixed node. This is well defined for symmetric graphs, since as noted there is an automorphism mapping any vertex to any other in such graphs.

We assume without loss of generality that the search is for a maximum value of some function. For each $v \in V$, we assume $f(v) = \max_{s \in v} f(s)$; that is, the value of a point is the value of the best string in the set represented by the point. We define *deceptive regions* in terms of the graph and the evaluation function f. A trap region generalizes the common concept of a peak as a region that we cannot move out of except by moving from a point of higher value to a point of lesser value. See (Jones, 1995; Horn and Goldberg, 1995) for similar definitions.

Trap Region A subset $X \subseteq V$ in a graph G is a *trap region* when $\forall x \in X, \forall y \in N(x) \setminus X, f(y) < f(x)$.

Peak A trap region X is a *peak* if the induced subgraph $G[X]$ is connected and $\forall u, v \in X, f(u) = f(v)$. Note the implication that a peak is *maximal*; that is, if X is a peak then no proper superset of X is a peak. A trap region may contain multiple peaks, and in fact V is itself a (trivial) trap region.

False Peak A peak X is a *false peak* if there is some $y \in V \setminus X$ such that $f(y) > f(x), \forall x \in X$.

Region of Attraction We define a *region of attraction* of a peak X to be a maximal trap region containing X and no other peak. We leave as an exercise the proofs that the regions of attraction are unique, disjoint and that on any path joining two distinct peaks there is at least one vertex not in the region of attraction of either.

Distance Preserving Paths A path p on a graph G ... ce preserving($dpp(t)$) if for any two vertices k steps apart on the path, the d... G is at least $\min(k, t+1)$ (Reingold, Nievergelt, and Deo, 1977; Harary, Haye... 1988; Horn, Goldberg, and Deb, 1994; Horn, 1995; Horn and Goldberg,1995)... ave been used by Horn, Goldberg and Deb to develop interesting landscapes w... liar deceptiveness, and we extend this work in this paper.

We assume when an algorithm is at a point x it chooses some sam... et $S \subseteq N(x) \bigcup \{x\}$; that is, of the (closed) neighborhood of x. We provide some termi... r future reference. See (Mühlenbein, 1992) or page 18 of (Horn, 1995) for a number o... nt hill climbers.

Sampling Algorithm A *sampling algorithm* is one that randomly c... the sample S.

Stochastic Algorithm A *stochastic algorithm* randomly chooses the n... oint from the sample, usually biased by the values of the sampled points. Note tha... lgorithm can be stochastic, or sampling or both. Most versions of simulated annea... A) (Davis, 1987) are stochastic sampling algorithms.

Elitism If x is guaranteed to be in S then a non-stochastic algorithm is said ... e *elitist*. A *strongly elitist* algorithm requires that x is replaced by a new point only ... he new point is of strictly greater value than x. Frequently non-elitist algorithms are ... umed to explicitly exclude x from S (Horn 1995), and this will be our default assump... on.

NAHC The next ascent hill climber (Horn, 1995) flips bits in a cyclic sequence, moving to the first neighbor that improves in value. From that point the sequence is continued. Thus, it takes a deterministic sample of the neighbors, but the sample taken depends on how the algorithm arrived at the point x, and is truncated when the first improved neighbor is found. NAHC is strongly elitist since it only ascends.

SAHC A steepest ascent hill climber chooses $S = N(x)$ and moves to the best $y \in S$ if $f(y) > f(x)$, and so is strongly elitist.

BN A best neighbor (BN) algorithm chooses $S = N(x)$ and then chooses a $y \in S$ of maximal value without considering x, and so is strictly non-elitist.

Local Search Local search algorithms, a very general term, are usually non-elitist sampling algorithms, but the term frequently is used to include any of the above. Variations on TABU algorithms (Glover, 1989; Glover, 1990) are local search algorithms that maintain a list of recently visited points which are explicitly excluded from S.

Finally, to illustrate how the notation might be extended to population based searches, we consider a simple example of a steady state GA with special rules. We assume a fixed size population $\mathcal{P}$, and the points in our graph will represent populations. We assume two parents are chosen and mated using 1-point crossover producing two (symmetric) offspring, each of which then undergo 1-bit mutation. The two offspring then replace the two parents. The neighbors of a point are all populations that can be obtained from the current population by one mating. The size of the neighborhood of a point x, which is also the degree of vertex x, is

$$|N(x)| \leq \sum_{p_1, p_2 \in \mathcal{P}} (\text{dist}(p_1, p_2) + 1)\ell^2$$

$$\leq \binom{|\mathcal{P}|}{2}\ell^3$$

The number of po... $^{|-1}$). The diameter of the graph is $D \leq \ell|\mathcal{P}|/2$, since that allows
the 2^ℓ binary stri...roduce any set of strings from any other. The graph need not be
sufficient mutati... symmetric.

The reader ca... Nevertheless, once the graph is defined, the search can be viewed as a
and complex ... graph.
local search ...

1.4   Ove... and Motivation

In this s... we discuss and expand on some of the terminology of the previous section,
discuss ... underlying concepts and present an overview and motivation for the rest of
the pap...

The n... borhood of a point may be a superset of the actual points generated by an operator
when ... is used in a particular algorithm on a particular function. That is, an operator can
be u... to either generate all of the neighbors of a point in either fixed or random order, or
it c... generate some (possibly randomly distributed) subset. A *selection mechanism* will be
use to select the replacement point from the generated set using whatever (function biased)
criteria are appropriate. The selection mechanism may be interlaced with the generator, as
for example in NAHC. Under this assumption we can meaningfully talk about the average
number of neighbors generated before one with a particular value is achieved.

We are interested in the time cost of an algorithm. As estimates of this cost, we can count
the number of distinct strings evaluated, or the total number of strings generated, or the
number of points of the operator graph visited. These measures do not take into account
the time required to generate a string or to evaluate it. In particular, if an algorithm has
sufficient knowledge, then the time spent generating a string may be very large, while few
strings may be evaluated. However, such algorithms do not fit well with our adversarial
model of computation.

Counting only the distinct strings evaluated as in (Wolpert and Mcready, 1996) will not distinguish between algorithms that converge their search activity onto peaks from essentially
random ones. For example, an algorithm that spends a lot of time wandering around a large
deceptive region of attraction will not be distinguished from one that wanders around the
region once and then moves on. Remembering past points visited can affect the performance
of an algorithm and to distinguish this we count the total number of strings generated or
number of points visited or re-visited as our cost measure.

We want to explore how the characterisitics of the operator graph, the type of algorithm
being used, and the nature of the function with respect to the graph interact to affect
the cost of a search. For example, we expect that the size, number and distance between
regions of attraction of false peaks and the optimal peak will influence the efficiency of most
algorithms using an operator (Horn and Goldberg, 1995). The simplest false peak consists
of a single vertex, and the maximum number of peaks is trivially no more than the size
(number of vertices) of the maximum independent set in the graph. We briefly examine
deceptive possibilities based on regions of attraction in section 2.1.

Horn, *et al* (1994, 1995, 1995) invented what we might term a mischievous adversary by mapping values in increasing order along an exponentially long $dpp(1)$ on the binary hypercube. They demonstrated both empirically and theoretically that certain hill climbers, such as steepest ascent(SAHC), next ascent(NAHC), and fixed mutation rate(Mut), require exponential time to reach the global optimum on average. They also tested another algorithm called mutation with steepest ascent(Mut+SAHC) which solved the problem in linear time. This algorithm first does one single bit random mutation, then checks all neighbors and moves to the highest. Thus, it may take two steps in a single operation. In our terms, the graph would be the 2-bit binary mutation graph, $M_2(\ell)$. This clearly illustrates that features on one operator graph do not necessarily carry through to another.

In section 2.2 we present some results on the binary hypercube which distinguish algorithms based on how the operator is *used*, without allowing multi-step operations; that is, without changing the graph. We hope that this will clarify the intuitive distinctions we make between an operator's potential and how effectively it is used within a given circumstance, and how these differ from modifying an operator graph. The mishcievous adversary can achieve these distinctions even when the landscape is required to be unimodal. We use distance preserving paths. Distance preserving paths are also limited by the structure of the graph, and these limit the effectiveness of vicious or mischievous adversaries.

The main thrust of section 2 is to show that even when we restrict our algorithm to using a specific operator graph, the way in which it is used can significantly affect search results. We restrict the mischievous adversary to create unimodal functions. Without that restriction, we could make distinctions more easily and with even greater distinguishing costs. This shows that to fully analyze an algorithm, every detail must be considered.

The potential of a graph will be influenced by its degree and diameter since these influence the best, average, and worst case costs of moving across it. In general, the smaller that we can make each of these values, the cheaper it will be to explore the graph, assuming a friendly adversary. In particular, assuming a symmetric graph, and assuming an algorithm has no memory of past points visited, a simple uphill path using a steepest ascent hill climber will require DP evaluations to cross the graph. For simplicity, we normally ignore the cost of the last node which would require us to replace D by D + 1 in the definition of DP. If the algorithm remembers the last point visited, then d can be replaced by d − 1. These two considerations may be important if the diameter or degree are small, but usually will not change the nature of our results.

Since we usually start a search at a random point, it is also useful to consider the average work done on a friendly landscape. The expected work can be estimated by $AP(G)$. Again, for small degree and assuming algorithms with memory of the previously visited point, we may wish to subtract 1 from the degree. We would like to minimize DP and/or AP for a fixed n.

Despite the cautions related to section 2, in subsequent sections we do consider graphs in abstraction and in isolation from the rest of the program. The idea is to consider the potential of the graph to aid friendly adversaries, and divert vicious ones. Our approach is simply to evaluate the graphs with respect to size and number of independent sets, degree, diameter, DP, AP and the length of $dpp(t)$'s. But the reader should keep in mind that these are only indications and should not be used to make claims of universal superiority of one representation over another.

In section 3 we report on these measures for simple graphs, for hypercubes and for graphs induced by k-bit mutations. We illustrate how trade-offs between these measures may occur as the density (i.e. average degree) is increased.

In section 4 we extend this analysis to mutation graphs on larger alphabets, and observe that DP is minimized at $\alpha = 5$. Increasing α also reduces the maximum independent set size, and the maximal length of a $dpp(t)$. We extend the long paths construction of Horn, *et al* (1994) to graphs based on larger alphabets.

Culberson (1995) showed that the following mapping provides an isomophism between mutation on a single binary string x of length ℓ and crossover on a complementary pair of binary strings with length $\ell + 1$. The mapping is

$$
\begin{aligned}
\mathcal{I}(x) &= (a, \bar{a}) \\
a_i &= \left\{
\begin{array}{ll}
0 & \text{if } i = 1 \\
x_{i-1} \oplus a_{i-1} & 1 < i \leq \ell + 1
\end{array}
\right.
\end{aligned}
$$

where $\oplus$ is the *"exclusive or"* or *"sum mod 2"* function and x_i is an element of $\{0, 1\}$.

In section 5 we generalize this and show how a generalized crossover can mimic mutation for larger alphabets in different ways. Some of these are related to α-ary generalizations of the binary reflected Gray codes. Some result in codes that look at least superficially like DNA codes. In section 5.3 we "break" the isomorphisms in certain ways, and find graphs using binary codes which improve DP and AP over the simple binary hypercube or α-ary hypercube.

2   Adversaries and Search Graphs

In this section we explore the range of deception available on simple graphs. In section 2.2 we illustrate that even under the requirement of unimodal functions, any combination of algorithm features such as elitism and random sampling can have exponentially good or bad effects depending on the function. This should be sufficient warning that there is no universally superior algorithm, and warn against claims of the "weakness" or "strength" of specific selection methods when made independently of other considerations.

2.1   False Peaks and Deceptive Regions

We illustrate some of the ideas related to false peaks and trap regions in figure 1. In this figure, each dot or circle represents all the vertices at some fixed distance from an optimal point. The diagram on the left can be thought of as an abstraction of the "easy maximum modality functions" described in (Horn and Goldberg, 1995). In general, given any graph in which vertices at distance k are independent, a function creates such a landscape on the graph if the values alternate with distance from the optimal point as illustrated. A BN algorithm will find the optimal point on such a graph since, even when on a false peak, the neighbors are oriented towards the optimal point. However, an elitist algorithm will be trapped on a false peak with high probability.

On the right side of figure 1, peaks are separated from each other by larger surrounding regions of attraction. Bear in mind that each trap region in the schematic diagram may include several regions of attraction, since there may be multiple peaks at a given distance

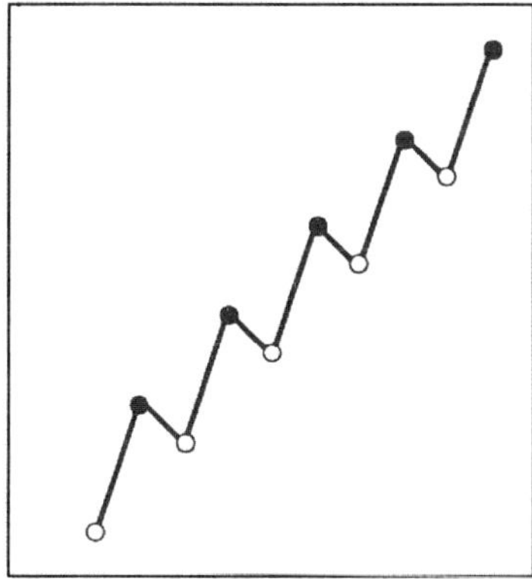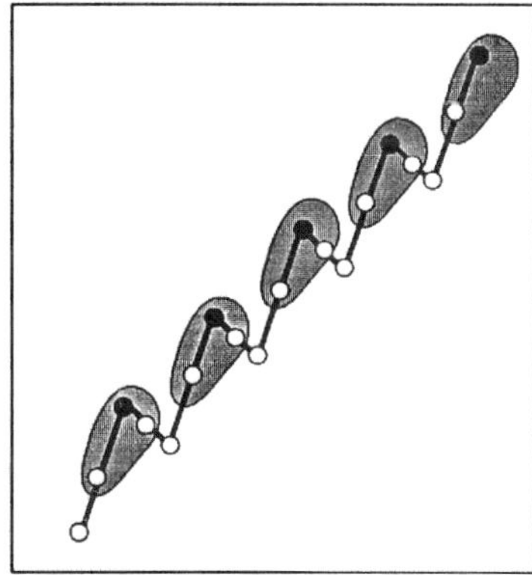

Figure 1: Massive Modality and Trap Regions

from the optimal point. Now BN will no longer find the optimal point in most cases. Even searches with a TABU list may fail, since there may be many peaks, paths and cycles in each trap region. It is tempting to think that a multiple population based search(e.g. a GA) could select points from different peaks, then through a process of extrapolation based on recombination could move upslope to the optimum point. However, for arbitrary graphs, or even hypercubes, it is difficult to determine a "direction" for extrapolation given two arbitrary points in the graph.

2.2 Mischievous Adversaries on the Hypercube

The first class of mischievous adversary functions is defined by performing a depth first search from the all zero string to strings with increasing numbers of ones while mapping values in decreasing order as we visit vertices. Figure 2 defines the function algorithmically.

Figure 3 illustrates this function on the 3-bit hypercube. The numbers in the figure are the function values. The heavy double lines illustrate the depth first tree used to define the function values. The arrows indicate paths of steepest ascent. The shaded region represents the leftmost path from bottom to top, which is also a steepest ascent path. The following can be observed from the diagram, and proven in general for arbitrary ℓ.

The function is unimodal on the hypercube. Let $U(x) \subseteq N(x)$ be the upper neighbors of vertex x; that is, those neighbors with one more zero bit than x, and $L(x)$ be the lower neighbors of x. For each x except the topmost, there is exactly one $y \in U(x)$ such that $f(y) > f(x)$; namely the parent of x in the depth first tree. $\forall z \in U(x) \setminus \{y\}$ we can see that $f(z) < f(w), \forall w \in L(x)$, since all lower neighbors of a vertex will be assigned a function value before the remaining (non-parent) upper neighbors and the values are assigned in decreasing order. In addition, for vertices not adjacent to a vertex in the leftmost path, the largest neighbor will be in $L(x)$. This last can be used to show that the longest steepest ascent path is of length $2\ell - 2$, since at most $\ell - 2$ downward moves can be made until a vertex or neighbor of the leftmost path is reached. In the figure, such a path starts from the vertex 011 with value 2.

```
v := 2ℓ; /* global next value to be assigned */
val[0...2ℓ − 1] := −1; /* function values as yet unassigned */

dfsval(x)
    val[x] := v;
    DEC(v);
    FOR i=1 TO ℓ DO
        IF the ith bit of x is 0 THEN
            y := x with the ith bit set to 1;
            IF val[y] == −1 THEN dfsval(y);
end;

dfsval(0); /* Initial call */
```

Figure 2: Recursive Algorithm Defining Class One Functions

On this landscape, a SAHC or BN will require at most $O(\ell^2)$ string evaluations, since they will follow a steepest path. An elitist sampling algorithm will also be efficient on average, since it will move rather efficiently towards the leftmost path, from which it can only move towards the goal.

However, a non-elitist sampling algorithm may take time exponential in ℓ on average to reach the goal. To see this, note that we expect such an algorithm to first move downward toward the leftmost path. Once on the leftmost path, the algorithm will move upward only if either the parent node from the depth first tree is in the sample, or all sample neighbors are from $U(x)$. Otherwise, without elitism, the algorithm will move downward and away from the goal.

As an example, for any x on the leftmost path such that $dist(\bar{0}, x) = k, 0 < k < \ell/2$, on a sampling algorithm with sample size s the probability that the parent node of x is in the sample is s/ℓ (making the assumption that the sampling technique does not allow repetitions). Note that $|L(x)| = \ell - k$ and $|U(x)| = k$. The probability that all s samples are from the remaining $U(x)$ is $\binom{k-1}{s}/\binom{\ell-1}{s}$, if $s < k$ and zero otherwise. Thus, the probability q of moving downward is at least

$$q \geq \left(1 - \frac{s}{\ell}\right)\left(1 - \frac{\binom{k-1}{s}}{\binom{\ell-1}{s}}\right)$$

$$> \frac{1}{2}, \text{ small } s \text{ and } k < \frac{\ell}{2}$$

For nodes at distance k not on the leftmost path, the probability of a downward move is at least q, since the only difference is that the parent node in these cases may have smaller value than some nodes in $L(x)$. Viewing the climb to the optimal as a random walk, and ignoring the time spent at $k > \ell/2$ by assuming a reflecting barrier at $\ell/2$, for fixed $q > 1/2$ the expected duration is $\Theta((q/(1 - q))^k)$ (see Ch. XIV] (Feller, 1968)). The probability q

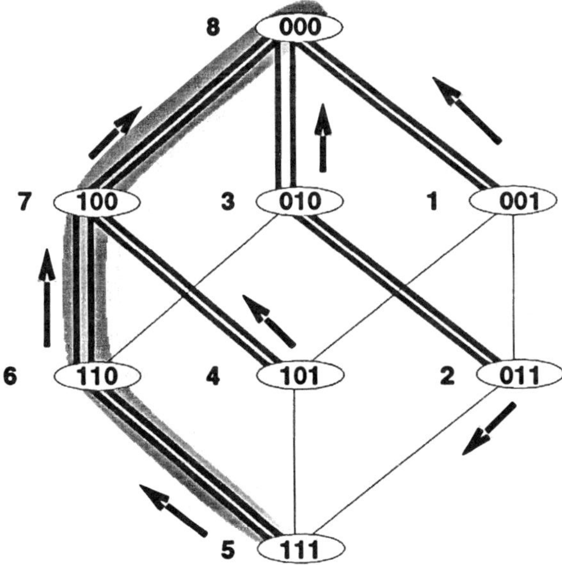

Figure 3: Class One Mischievous Adversary Example.

of a downward move increases as k is reduced or ℓ is increased. Since we expect initially $k \geq \ell/2$ with probability at least $1/2$, the expected time grows exponentially in ℓ.

Figure 4 shows some experimental results for an elitist and a non-elitist sampling program on this function for $\ell \in \{8, 12, 16, 20\}$. There were one hundred trials per point, and the average number of string evaluations required to find the optimum is plotted. These are sampling routines with the size of the sample S being $C\ell$, for $C \in \{0.2, 0.3, 0.4, 0.5\}$. The non-elitist sampling routine was terminated on the run with $\ell = 16$ and $C = 0.2$(the smallest sample size) and for $\ell = 20$ only $C = 0.4$ and 0.5 completed, due to excessive time. SAIIC only required a few more evaluations than the elitist sampling routine for each ℓ.

The second class of functions is based on a variation of the long path problem (Horn, Goldberg, and Deb, 1994), and is also unimodal. A *core path* is restricted to those strings which have either $\ell/2$ or $\ell/2+1$ 1-bits, where ℓ is even. It is constructed recursively, starting with a path of length 2 on 4-bit strings. This path is 0101, 1101, 1001. The recursion assumes a path of length k on an ℓ-cube, and constructs a path of length $2k + 2$ on an $\ell + 2$-cube. It takes two copies of the k-path, one in reverse order. To each string in the first copy prepend the characters 01 and to the other copy 10. Join the two paths by inserting the point formed by prepending 11 to the common substring at the end of one path and the beginning of the reverse path.

Induction shows that the core paths are of length $2^{\ell/2} - 2$, and that for $\ell = 2k$, the core path consists of vertices with only k or $k + 1$ 1-bits. Both end points have k 1-bits. In figure 5 the core path is the bold path running from left to right just below the shaded region.

Call one end of the core path the *low* end v_l. Continue the path from the other end by joining it to vertices in which the number of 1-bits are strictly decreasing by one, until the

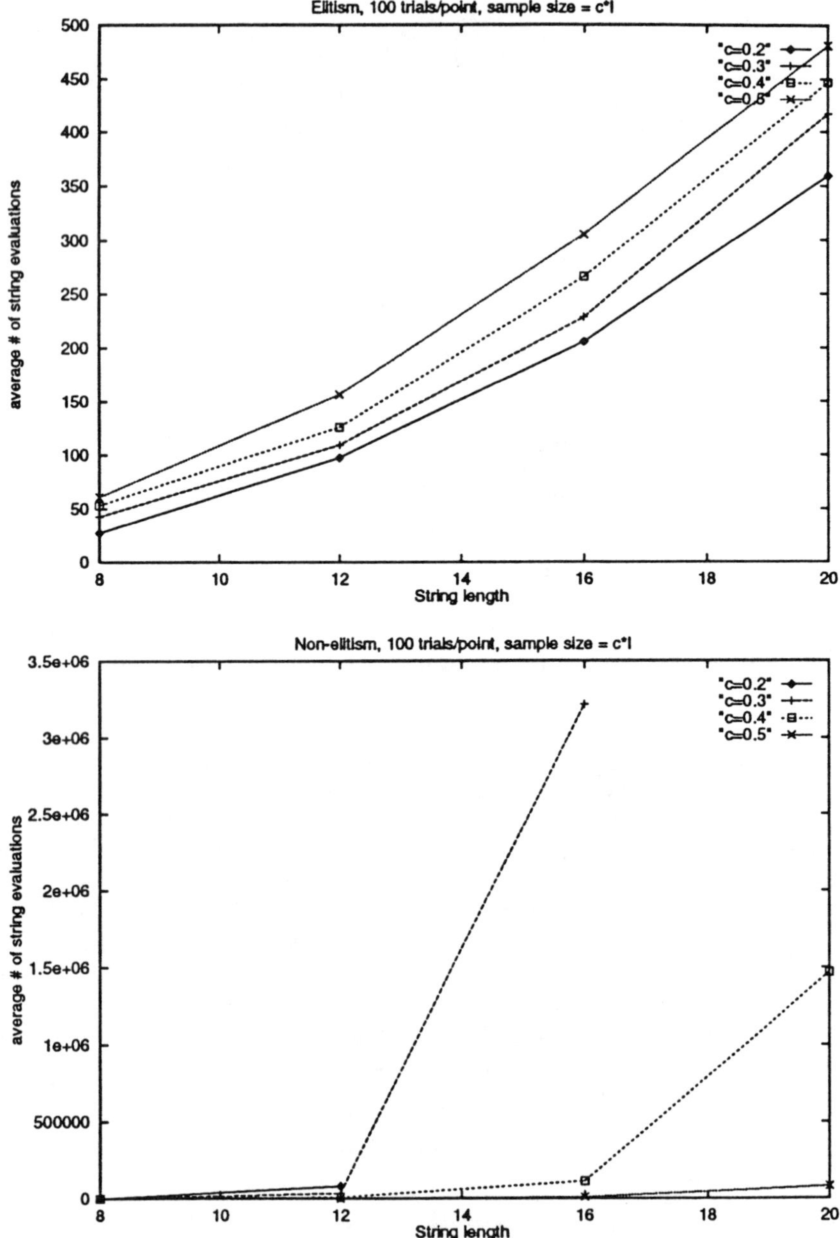

Figure 4: Elitist and non-elitist sampling on class one landscapes.

zero vector $\bar{0}$ is reached. Induction shows the path is $dpp(1)$. For example, the core path on $\ell = 6$ is

$$010101, \ 011101, \ 011001, \ 111001, \ 101001, \ 101101, \ 100101.$$

The continuation from the right end is $100100, \ 100000, \ 000000$.

The function definition is given by

$$f(x) = \ell^2 f_{path}(x) + f_{backgrd}(x)$$

where

$$f_{backgrd}(x) = \begin{cases} \ell(\ell - \mathrm{dist}(\bar{0}, x)), & \mathrm{dist}(\bar{0}, x) < \ell/2 \\ 0, & \mathrm{dist}(\bar{0}, x) = \ell/2 \\ \ell - \mathrm{dist}(v_l, x)), & \mathrm{dist}(\bar{0}, x) > \ell/2 \end{cases}$$

and

$$f_{path}(x) = \begin{cases} 0, & \text{if } x \text{ not on path} \\ \mathrm{dist}_{path}(v_l, x) + 1, & \text{otherwise} \end{cases}$$

where $\mathrm{dist}_{path}(v_l, x)$ is the distance along the path of x from v_l.

A schematic illustration of this landscape is given in figure 5. The long path stretches

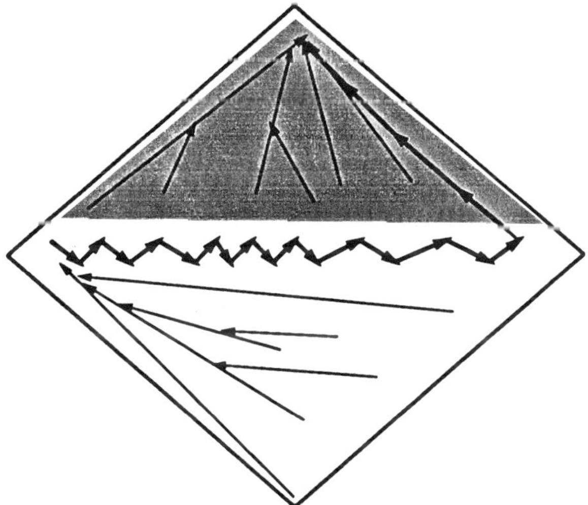

Figure 5: Schematic representation of a class two landscape

through the middle of the graph, while the "slope" above the path (shaded area) leads directly to the optimal point, and below the path the slope leads to the far end of the long path. An elitist sampling algorithm, SAHC, or BN will start in the lower half of the search space with probability approximately 1/2. They will then follow the slope to the end of the long path, and then take an exponential time to follow the path. A non-elitist sampling algorithm will also follow the slope towards the far end of the path, but because it can easily fall off the path, may move into the shaded region and then move quickly towards the goal.

This landscape reverses the effects of class one landscapes with respect to the various uses of the operator graph. Figure 6 shows some experimental results on the class two landscapes, confirming our claims.

A small modification to this landscape should also distinguish between a SAHC and an elitist sampling algorithm. Starting at v_l, traverse the core path. For each x with $k = \ell/2$ 1-bits, for each $y \in U(x)$ not yet assigned a value, let $f(y) = f(x) + 1$. Note that $f(y)$ is smaller than the next point on the path. For all vertices with $k < \ell/2 - 1$ 1-bits (those above the neighbors of the path points) increase the values to create a slope to the point $\bar{0}$. Now a SAHC or BN will be forced to follow along the path whenever they encounter it. But a sampling algorithm will be able to move off the path, even if it is strongly elitist.

3   Simple Graphs and Observations

We assume that the search starts at a randomly chosen point in the graph. Starting at a fixed point makes it too easy for the adversaries; a friendly adversary will place the maximum value at the starting point and a vicious one can make the starting point a false peak.

3.1   Cliques and Cycles

The first two example graphs are at the extremes of the degree-diameter trade-off, assuming connected graphs. These are the complete graph (or clique) and the simple cycle. The complete graph has degree $n - 1$ and diameter 1. It corresponds to random or complete enumeration search. It is not possible to choose any function with a single optimum such that this graph either assists or inhibits the search. If we generate the entire neighborhood, then we have generated the entire search space, and the graph has not helped us reduce the size of the search. If we randomly generate some subset, then after selecting the next point we are again faced with generating a subset from the entire space. Even if we remember previously generated subsets to avoid regenerating the same points, no algorithm can take advantage of any mapping of values onto the points to improve the search. A vicious adversary cannot select any function to make the search hard, and a friendly one cannot help us.

The clique has exactly one peak, and the longest distance preserving path consists of one edge. $DP = AP = n - 1$.

The cycle on the other hand has degree two and diameter $n/2$. It corresponds, for example, to a search operator where the neighbors are $N(x) = \{(x \pm 1) \bmod n\}$ with the first point x chosen at random. In this case, a friendly adversary can select functions that make the search easier for a hill climber than for a random search algorithm. For example, a single peak can be established, with values strictly decreasing with distance from the peak. If we assume that both neighbors of a node are generated, with selection of the higher valued node as the next point, then $n/2$ nodes would have to be generated on average to reach the maximum. An algorithm with memory of the previously visited point only needs to generate one neighbour (after the first point) and so can find the optimum in $n/4 + 1$ evaluations on average.

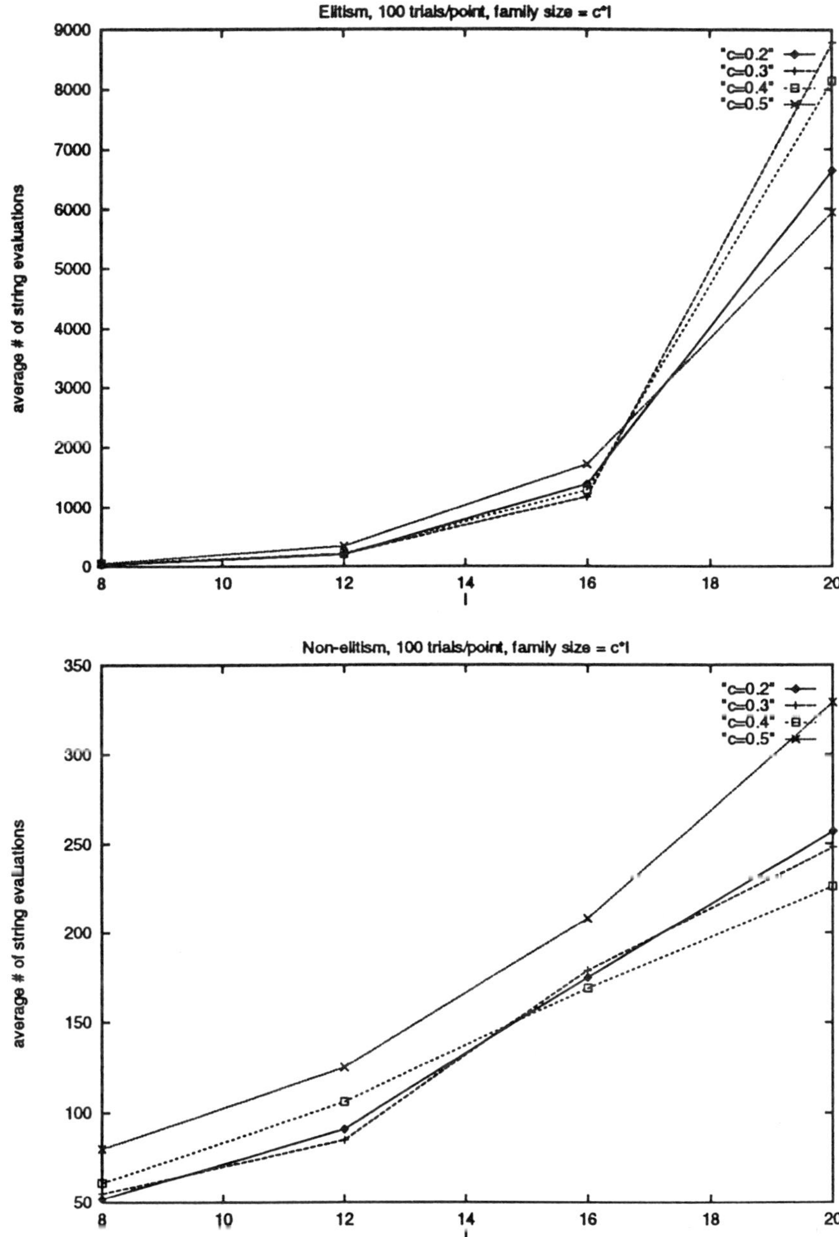

Figure 6: Elitist and non elitist sampling on class two landscapes.

The cycle has a maximum independent set of size $\lfloor n/2 \rfloor$ (every other vertex), and thus the same maximum number of peaks. Every path of length $k \le n/2$ is a k-distance preserving path, $dpp(k)$. $DP = n$ and $AP = n/2$.

3.2 Binary Hypercube

We denote the binary hypercube of dimension ℓ by $\mathcal{H}_M(\ell, 2)$. It has degree and diameter both ℓ, and thus $DP(\mathcal{H}_M(\ell, 2)) = \ell^2$. Here $\ell = \log_2 n$, and so this DP is a considerable improvement over cliques and cycles. $AP(\mathcal{H}_M(\ell, 2)) = \frac{\ell^2}{2}$, which can be easily obtained from the general result in section 4.

The maximum number of peaks is $n/2$ (Horn and Goldberg, 1995). An example is the set of nodes where the strings have even parity. No larger independent set can occur, since there is a Hamilton cycle (induced by the Gray code).

The longest distance preserving path (Horn, Goldberg, and Deb, 1994; Harary, Hayes, and Wu, 1988; Reingold, Nievergelt, and Deo, 1977) on the binary hypercube is exponential in ℓ. A construction is given in (Reingold, Nievergelt, and Deo, 1977) that on hypercubes of $n = 2^\ell$ vertices, produces $dpp(t)$ of length $(t+1)2^{a\ell}$ for some $a < 1$ ($a \approx 0.56$ for $t = 1$). It is known (Reingold, Nievergelt, and Deo, 1977) that

$$dpp(t) \le c\frac{2^\ell}{\ell^{\lfloor t/2 \rfloor}}$$

where c depends on t but not ℓ. Horn, *et al* (1994) mapped function values onto similar paths for $t = 1$ to produce a function that required exponentially long time on average to reach the optimum for a 1-bit mutation search, even though the function is unimodal on the hypercube.

3.3 k-bit Binary Mutation Graphs

Let $M_k(\ell)$ be the k-bit mutation graph on binary strings of length ℓ. We assume that from 1 to k bits may be flipped in any one operation, otherwise the graph may not be connected. This graph can be derived from the hypercube by joining all pairs x, y of vertices with $\text{dist}(x, y) \le k$. The diameter is reduced to $D(M_k(\ell)) = \lceil \ell/k \rceil$, while the degree is increased to $d = \sum_{i=1}^{k} \binom{\ell}{i}$. This last is $O(\ell^k)$ for fixed k.

The cost of crossing the graph is then

$$DP(M_k(\ell)) = \sum_{i=1}^{k} \binom{\ell}{i} \ell/k$$

which grows exponentially for small k. AP also grows exponentially in k.

We can create peaks by selecting for example all strings where the number of 1 bits is congruent to 0 mod $k + 1$. This yields

$$\text{Number of Peaks} = \sum_{i=0}^{\ell/(k+1)} \binom{\ell}{(k+1)i}$$

α	2	3	4	5	6	7
$DP/(\ln n)^2$	2.0814	1.6571	1.5610	1.5442	1.5574	1.5845
$AP/(\ln n)^2$	1.0407	1.1047	1.1708	1.2354	1.2979	1.3582

Table 1: Comparison of diameter-degree costs as α varies

In table 1 we compare the degree-diameter product normalized with respect to n. Since $\varepsilon_\alpha(n)$ is less than one, it is easy to see that these ratios are asymptotically accurate (as n becomes large with respect to α). Interestingly, table 1 shows that DP is minimized for an alphabet size of $\alpha = 5$ not 2, with 4 and 6 being close. Thus, under this measure we see that the binary hypercube is not optimal. The binary hypercube minimizes AP, although $\alpha = 3$ and 4 are close.

The largest independent set (and thus the maximum number of peaks) in $\mathcal{H}_M(\ell, \alpha)$ is $\alpha^{\ell-1} = n/\alpha$. To see there are no larger sets a simple induction using the recursive construction is sufficient. For $\ell = 1$, there can be only one independent vertex, as the graph is a clique. For the induction, if there is an independent set of size $\alpha^{\ell-1}$ in $\mathcal{H}_M(\ell, \alpha)$ then we can take at most one such set from each of the α copies in the recursive construction, which means that $\mathcal{H}_M(\ell + 1, \alpha)$ has at most α^ℓ vertices in an independent set. Conversely, in $\mathcal{H}_M(\ell, \alpha)$ there are $\alpha^{\ell-1}$ strings such that the sum of the elements equal 0 mod α, and it is easy to see that no two of these are adjacent in $\mathcal{H}_M(\ell, \alpha)$.

Long $dpp(t)$'s can be constructed by considering the subgraph induced by strings having only the characters 0 and 1. This induced subgraph is the binary hypercube, and so any long path on the binary hypercube can immediately be applied to $\mathcal{H}_M(\ell, \alpha)$. To see that the remaining characters do not provide shorter paths, notice that the distance between two vertices on the path is the number of positions in which the corresponding strings are different. Thus, the other characters have no impact.

Relative to the value of $n = \alpha^\ell$, these paths are exponentially shorter than those possible on the binary hypercube, although still exponential in ℓ. We do not know of any upper bounds on the longest possible paths such as exist for $\alpha = 2$. It seems clear the construction above is not optimal. For example, for $\alpha = 5$ we can build a (binary) $dpp(t)$ on 0 and 1 and another on the characters 3 and 4. We can then join these two paths without loss of the distance preserving property by replacing the 0's and 1's from one of the end points of the 01 path with 2's one at a time until a string of all 2's is completed. We then do the same from one of the end points of the 34 path. If the length of each binary $dpp(t)$ is k, then this path has length $2k + 2\ell$. Since k is exponential in ℓ, this is effectively twice as long as the binary paths. However, for a fixed n, the binary representation will use approximately 2.32 times as many characters as the 5-ary cube. Since the paths are exponential in ℓ, this implies that even this doubled path is far (exponentially) shorter than the equivalent binary cube would allow. For example, if we have paths of length approximately $2^{\ell/2}$ using Horn's construction (Horn, 1995) (or the one in section 2.2) then for the same $n = 2^\ell$ the doubling construction gives paths of length approximately $2^{(\ell/4.64)+1}$ on the 5-ary cube.

The construction generalizes to larger α. If $\alpha = 3m - 1$, then we get m binary paths of exponential length, and $m - 1$ connection paths of length 2ℓ. It may be possible to build even longer paths by lengthening the connection paths with a more complex construction, but it seems unlikely that we can obtain more than a fixed constant times the length of the binary subpaths in this manner. On the other hand, since as α increases the cube has more edges, smaller diameter and larger neighborhoods, it seems that we should not expect paths as long as those on the binary hypercube for the same n.

5 Graphs Related to Crossover-Mutation Isomorphisms

It was shown (Culberson, 1995) that the search space graph induced by one-point binary crossover on a pair of complementary binary strings of length ℓ is isomorphic to the search graph for one-bit mutation on a single binary string of length $\ell - 1$. This isomorphism can be generalized to arbitrary alphabets by applying any finite commutative group.

5.1 Generalized Isomorphism

For $\alpha > 2$ the crossover is not the usual two string operator used in GAs, but requires α strings. The requirement in (Culberson, 1995) that strings must be complementary is generalized to require that each alphabetic character must appear in each position $i, 1 \leq i \leq \ell$ in some string in the set. A crossover then chooses a cut point, and permutes the tails of the strings. Let $*$ be a finite commutative operator on an α-ary group with identity 0. We use the notation $< y >_i$ to indicate the string y' defined by $y'_j = y_j * i, 1 \leq j \leq \ell$. For a character Δ, a Δ crossover on a set of α strings $(y = < y >_0, < y >_1, \cdots, < y >_{\alpha-1})$ at position k is a new set of strings $(y' = < y' >_0, < y' >_1 \cdots < y' >_{\alpha-1})$ where $< y'_j >_i = < y_j >_i, 1 \leq j \leq k$ and $< y'_j >_i = < y_j >_{(i+\Delta)}, k < j \leq \ell$. We let $\mathcal{H}_X(\ell, \alpha, *)$ be the graph associated with the α-ary crossover operator, where two sets of strings are joined by an edge *iff* there is some Δ crossover that produces one set from the other. Since $*$ is a group operator, a Δ crossover is reversible by choosing the inverse of Δ.

For a string x, we define

$$
\begin{aligned}
\mathcal{V}(x) &= (y = < y >_0, < y >_1, \cdots, < y >_{\alpha-1}) \\
y_i &= \begin{cases} 0 & \text{if } i = 1 \\ x_{i-1} * y_{i-1} & 1 < i \leq \ell+1 \end{cases}
\end{aligned}
$$

If a mutation changes x_j to x'_j then under $*$ we define $\Delta = x_j^{-1} * x'_j$. Then,

Lemma 5.1 *The mapping $\mathcal{V}$ is an isomorphism from $\mathcal{H}_M(\ell, \alpha, *)$ to $\mathcal{H}_X(\ell, \alpha, *)$. That is, a mutation of Δ at k on an α-ary string is equivalent to one-point crossover at k of Δ crossover on the α strings generated by $\mathcal{V}$.*

Proof:

Assume (x,y) is an edge in $\mathcal{H}_M(\ell, \alpha, *)$. Then $x_k \neq y_k$ for some $1 \leq k \leq \ell$ and $x_i = y_i$ for all $i \neq k$. Further assume

$$
\begin{aligned}
\mathcal{V}(x) &= (a, < a >_1, \ldots, < a >_{\alpha-1}) \\
\mathcal{V}(y) &= (b, < b >_1, \ldots, < b >_{\alpha-1})
\end{aligned}
$$

Simple induction shows that

$$
b_i = a_i, \text{ for } 1 \leq i \leq k
$$

The longest induced path (distance preserving with $t = 1$) on these graphs is equivalent to the longest $dpp(k)$ on the hypercube and so is reduced exponentially with k, but is still exponential in ℓ for fixed k.

Increasing the mutation rate illustrates some of the trade-offs in degree versus diameter, but the hypercube yields better DP and AP costs by a significant amount.

4   Mutation Graphs for Larger Alphabets

We now consider mutation on strings taken over an α-ary alphabet, $\alpha \geq 2$, with default character set $0 \ldots \alpha - 1$. We assume that a one-character mutation operator is being used, which changes one character of the string to some other character. For strings of length ℓ we refer to the graph formed by the notation $\mathcal{H}_M(\ell, \alpha)$.

These graphs can be described recursively in terms of ℓ. $\mathcal{H}_M(1, \alpha)$ is a clique of size α. $\mathcal{H}_M(\ell, \alpha)$ for $\ell > 1$ can be constructed by making α copies of $\mathcal{H}_M(\ell - 1, \alpha)$ and labeling the vertices of the ith copy, $0 \leq i < \alpha$ by appending the character i to each of the string labels from $\mathcal{H}_M(\ell - 1, \alpha)$. Finally, all pairs of strings differing only in the last character are joined by an edge. This does not add any edge within a copy of the smaller hypercube, but forms α-cliques by joining corresponding vertices from each of the copies.

It is straight forward to derive the following characteristics of these cubes. The automorphism group $\Gamma(G)$ of a graph G is the group formed over the set of all automorphisms of the graph. The automorphism group of $\mathcal{H}_M(\ell, \alpha))$ can be constructed by noting that at each string location the values of the characters can be (independently) reassigned using any of the $\alpha!$ permutations, and the characters in the string can be reassigned in any of the $\ell!$ orders.

- $n = |V(\mathcal{H}_M(\ell, \alpha))| = \alpha^\ell$

- Automorphism Group Size $|\Gamma(\mathcal{H}_M(\ell, \alpha))| = (\alpha!)^\ell \ell!$

- Degree d $= (\alpha - 1)\ell = \frac{\alpha - 1}{\ln \alpha} \ln n$

- Diameter D $= \ell = \frac{\ln n}{\ln \alpha}$

- $DP(\mathcal{H}_M(\ell, \alpha)) = \frac{\alpha - 1}{(\ln \alpha)^2}(\ln n)^2$

- $AP(\mathcal{H}_M(\ell, \alpha)) = \frac{d}{\alpha^\ell} \sum_{i=0}^{\ell} i\binom{\ell}{i}(\alpha - 1)^i = \frac{(\alpha-1)^2}{\alpha(\ln \alpha)^2}(\ln n)^2$

These formulae are only accurate when n is a power of α. To encode a function on a domain of n elements where n is some fixed arbitrary integer, the length of the string changes depending upon which value of α is used. We are ignoring the problem specific issues in encoding. Encoding an n element domain requires a string of length

$$\ell = \left\lceil \frac{\ln n}{\ln \alpha} \right\rceil = \frac{\ln n}{\ln \alpha} + \varepsilon_\alpha(n)$$

where $\varepsilon_\alpha(n) < 1$ is a measure of the descretization error due to the fact that the number of characters in any alphabet must be an integer.

We will now show through induction that

$$b_{k+i} = < a_{k+i} >_{y_k * x_k^{-1}}, \text{ for } k+1 \le k+i \le \ell+1$$

Basis:

$$
\begin{aligned}
b_{k+1} &= a_k * y_k \\
&= y_k * x_k^{-1} * (a_k * x_k) \\
&= y_k * x_k^{-1} * a_{k+1} \\
&= < a_{k+1} >_{y_k * x_k^{-1}}
\end{aligned}
$$

Induction Hypothesis (IH): assume $b_{k+i} = < a_{k+i} >_{y_k * x_k^{-1}}$ for $k+1 \le k+i < \ell+1$. Then

$$
\begin{aligned}
b_{k+i+1} &= b_{k+i} * x_{k+i} \\
&= y_k * x_k^{-1} * a_{k+i} * x_{k+i} \\
&= y_k * x_k^{-1} * a_{k+i} * a_{k+i}^{-1} * a_{k+i+1} \\
&= y_k * x_k^{-1} * a_{k+i+1} \\
&= < a_{k+i+1} >_{y_k * x_k^{-1}}
\end{aligned}
$$

Therefore

$$
\begin{aligned}
b &= a_1 \cdots a_k < a_{k+1} \cdots a_{l+1} >_{y_k * x_k^{-1}} \\
<b>_1 &= < a_1 \cdots a_k >_1 < a_{k+1} \cdots a_{l+1} >_{y_k * x_k^{-1} * 1} \\
&\ \ \vdots \qquad \vdots \\
<b>_{\alpha-1} &= < a_1 \cdots a_k >_{\alpha-1} < a_{k+1} \cdots a_{l+1} >_{y_k * x_k^{-1} * (\alpha-1)}
\end{aligned}
$$

Note that $y_k * x_k^{-1}$ is just Δ. This shows that one-point mutation with Δ at position k is isomorphic to one-point crossover at k on a string of length $\ell+1$ with crossover of Δ (where each possible value of Δ specifies a unique crossover type).

∎

If the group operator is chosen to be addition modα, then the transformation is closely related to generalized α-ary cyclic Gray codes (Sharma and Khanna, 1978). We will look briefly at an example using $\alpha = 4$ in the next section.

5.2   An Example on $\alpha = 4$

Let the alphabet (with some presumption) be $\{A, T, C, G\}$ and let the operator $*$ be that of the Klein 4-group; i.e. identity A (representing 0) and $x * x = A$ for all x. The following table represents the Klein 4-group. Now consider the isomorphism for $\alpha = 4$ based on $*$ as defined by $\mathcal{V}$.

$$\mathcal{V}(x) = (< y >_A, < y >_T, < y >_C, < y >_G)$$

*	A	T	C	G
A	A	T	C	G
T	T	A	G	C
C	C	G	A	T
G	G	C	T	A

Table 2: The Klein 4-group.

where

$$< y_i >_A = \begin{cases} A, & i = 1 \\ x_{i-1} * y_{i-1}, & 1 < i \leq \ell + 1 \end{cases}$$

This isomorphism maps a single string to four pseudo-complementary strings, where A is always paired with T, and C with G. Two examples are:

	AC|CGA TG|GCT		AC|TAG TG|ATC
CATG →		CGTG →	
	CA|ATC GT|TAG		CA|GCT GT|CGA

Isomorphism examples induced by the Klein 4-group.

A mutation on a string x becomes a crossover under $\mathcal{V}(x)$. The above example shows the corresponding crossover when we mutate the A in the left hand illustration to a G on the right. We refer to this particular crossover operation as a "swap and twist" crossover, because it not only swaps the pair of tails, but twists them as well. The other crossovers (corresponding to other mutations) are either "twist" (i.e. the two tails are twisted but the pairs do not interact) or "swaps" in which the tails are swapped without twisting. We can characterize (without undue rigor) the crossover given by mutation. A mutation of the form $\{A \rightarrow A, T \rightarrow T, C \rightarrow C, G \rightarrow G\}$ causes no change; a mutation of the form $\{A \rightarrow T, T \rightarrow A, C \rightarrow G, G \rightarrow C\}$ causes each pair to twist but no exchange occurs between the pairs; a mutation of $\{A \rightarrow C, T \rightarrow G, C \rightarrow A, G \rightarrow T\}$ induces both pairs to cross with no twist; while a mutation of the form $\{A \rightarrow G, T \rightarrow C, C \rightarrow T, G \rightarrow A\}$ causes the pairs to cross and twist.

We remind the reader that the graph induced by the set of possible crossovers is isomorphic to the 4-ary hypercube. Also, the crossovers in our structures act within an individual. Some insight into the structure of the graph can be obtained by looking at the subgraphs induced by restricting the crossovers to one particular type. For example, consider the crossovers that induce no twists on strings of length $\ell + 1$. Now looking at the corresponding mutations, we see, given a particular starting string, only 2^ℓ strings can be generated and the structure is an ℓ-dimension binary hypercube. Since there are 4^ℓ possible strings of length ℓ, it follows that such a restriction produces a search space consisting of 2^ℓ binary hypercubes. The same structure would be obtained on restricting the crossover to either of the other two non-trivial cases.

5.3   Using Mutation on the Multi-string Representations

In this subsection, we consider the graphs obtained by allowing mutation on the multiple string representations.

For the binary case, mutation on a single string of length ℓ is isomorphic to crossover on two complementary strings of length $\ell + 1$ (Culberson, 1995). The bits in the single string correspond to transitions in the pair, with a 1 corresponding to either 01 or 10 (one occurs in each of the complementary strings) and 0 corresponds to either 00 or 11. Since both strings in the pair represent the same domain item, we assume that only one is evaluated from each pair generated. In fact, we only need to keep one string as a representative.

Since using crossover on this pair yields an isomorphic graph to $\mathcal{H}_M(\ell, 2)$, this search space has exactly the same characteristics as binary mutation. The landscapes induced by mapping function values will be different however, and this was used in (Culberson, 1995) to explore the differences between crossover and mutation.

Considering that a single string may be kept as a representative, we can also consider the graph induced by mutation on these strings. Mutation, which (necessarily) preserves complementarity, is equivalent to a pair of adjacent crossover operations on all except the end bits of the string, where it corresponds to a single crossover. By taking the inverse of the isomorphism we see that the graph is isomorphic to a mutation graph in which either two adjacent bits are flipped, or one of the end bits is flipped.

The graph that is generated can be visualized by considering the $\ell + 1$ binary hypercube. We use $\ell+1$ bit strings because each point consists of two complementary strings. Assuming $\ell + 1$ is even, draw the graph in a breadth first manner with all vertices labeled with strings having k one-bits at depth $k, 0 \le k \le \ell$. The new graph is then obtained by folding the bottom half of the hypercube onto the top half and adding the appropriate edges. For odd length strings, the center row folds onto itself. An example for $\ell = 4$ is shown in figure 7.

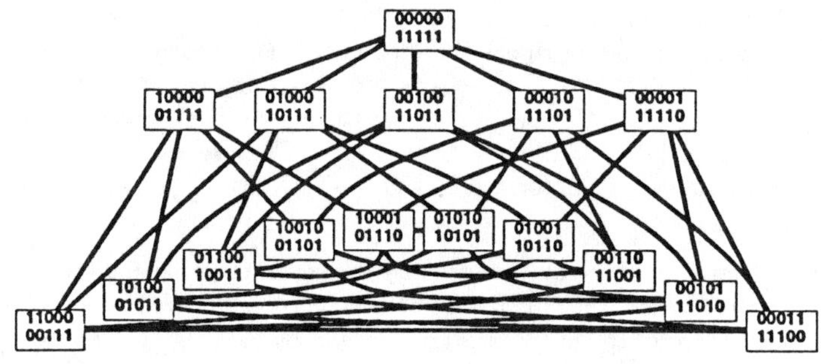

Figure 7: Mutation on the binary complementary pair

Since a string with k one-bits has as its complement one with $\ell + 1 - k$ one-bits, any string (or its representative) can be achieved from any other by flipping at most $\lceil (\ell + 1)/2 \rceil$ bits, and thus this is the diameter of the graph. The degree of the graph is $\ell + 1$, thus

$$DP = \left\lceil \frac{\ell+1}{2} \right\rceil (\ell+1) \approx \frac{(l+1)^2}{2}$$

For large ℓ, this effectively cuts the diameter-degree product in half as compared with the standard binary mutation cube.

To compute AP, the average traversal cost on these graphs, we first claim that the average distance between randomly chosen nodes is given by

$$E[\text{dist}] = \begin{cases} \frac{1}{2^\ell} \sum_{i=0}^{\ell/2} i\binom{\ell+1}{i} & \ell \text{ even} \\ \frac{1}{2^\ell} \left(\sum_{i=0}^{(\ell-1)/2} i\binom{\ell+1}{i} + \frac{(\ell+1)}{4}\binom{\ell+1}{(\ell+1)/2} \right) & \ell \text{ odd} \end{cases}$$

Multiplying this by the degree and computing for various ℓ, we find that for $\ell = 16$, $AP/(\ln n)^2$ is 0.9441, while for $\ell = 1001$ AP is 1.0164. (And it apparently converges very slowly to the hypercube average of 1.0407 at infinity).

With such success, it is natural to wonder whether iterating the isomorphism will yield further improvements. That is, if we apply the isomorphism to each of two complementary strings we will end up with a set of four strings of length $\ell + 2$. As an example, we show how a 5-bit string is transformed to four 7-bit strings. If we pair the top two strings of the two pairs on the right, we see that the characters in each position alternate between being the same and being complementary.

<table>
<tr><td rowspan="4">10010</td><td rowspan="4">→</td><td></td><td rowspan="4">→</td><td>0010111</td></tr>
<tr><td>011100</td><td>1101000</td></tr>
<tr><td>100011</td><td>0111101</td></tr>
<tr><td></td><td>1000010</td></tr>
</table>

However, for this expansion it can be shown that for every sequence of four bits, and the corresponding four set of strings, there are other sequences of four bits that will require two mutations to be reached. This implies that the diameter of these graphs is at least $(\ell+2)/2$ and thus the DP is approximately $(\ell+2)^2/2$. This is approximately the same as (slightly worse than) the one step expansion for large ℓ.

The other question that arises is whether a similar construction on larger alphabets will yield an improvement. For mutation on an α-ary isomorphic representation, the degree will be $(\alpha - 1)(\ell + 1)$. The diameter will be $\frac{(\alpha-1)}{\alpha}(\ell + 1) - \varepsilon_\alpha(\ell)$, where $\varepsilon_\alpha(\ell) < 1$. To see this, consider two sets of strings at maximum mutation distance. Let $y = y_1 \cdots y_{\ell+1}$ be the representative from the first set. Now each character y_i in y must also appear in the ith position of some string in the second set of strings. Since there are $\ell + 1$ positions, and only α strings, there must be some string(s) in the second set that agrees with y in $\left\lceil \frac{(\ell+1)}{\alpha} \right\rceil$ positions. The remaining positions will require one mutation each to convert the set of strings. (Recall that a mutation applies to all strings in this construction). Putting the degree and diameter together, we see that

$$DP \approx \frac{(\alpha - 1)^2}{\alpha} \left(\frac{\ln n}{\ln \alpha} + 1 \right)^2$$

This is asymptotically equivalent to AP on the α-ary hypercubes, which is minimized at $\alpha = 2$ (See table 1).

Using similar arguments, iterating the α-ary isomorphism k times yields degree $(\alpha-1)(\ell+k)$ and diameter approximately $(\ell+k)(\alpha-1)/\alpha$, since each character appears α^{k-1} times in each position in the α^k strings. Thus, larger alphabets do not gain us further advantage using this method.

6 Conclusions

We have shown that landscape analysis is a very tricky problem for complex search algorithms. Even when the algorithm is definitely restricted to making moves on the operator graph, functions can be derived that distinguish between elitist and non-elitist searches, full neighbor search and sampling techniques, with exponential differences in time in either direction. These distinctions can all hold even when the function is unimodal on the operator graph.

Under the assumption that we do have some knowledge of the functions, or that we wish to inhibit vicious or mischievous adversaries, we can see that different graphs may influence the effect of certain adversaries. We study some properties of graphs induced by operators on sets of strings and show that the binary hypercube, while better than many graphs, does not always minimize these costs.

However, we do not advocate the use of the comparative results of this paper as a basis for selecting operators in general situations unless the user can guarantee *all* the (implicit) assumptions underlying the results. In most situations it would be far more beneficial to select operators and algorithms based on knowledge of the function than to worry about the characteristics of the search graph developed here. The main objective of this paper is to raise questions concerning fundamental analysis, and not to present a design methodology.

As a final note the problem of minimizing DP is closely related to the problem of how large a graph can be constructed with given degree and diameter. This problem has a fairly long history (Dinneen and Hafner, 1994; Akers and Krishnamurthy, 1989). The only known bound is the Moore bound (Dinneen and Hafner, 1994) given by

$$n \leq \begin{cases} \frac{d(d-1)^{D}-2}{d-2}, & d > 2 \\ 2D + 1, & d = 2 \end{cases}$$

where n is the number of vertices. The binary hypercube of dimension ℓ produces a DP of ℓ^2 on a graph of $n = 2^\ell$ nodes, i.e. a cost quadratic in the logarithm of n. The absence of a better bound than the Moore bound suggests that it might be possible to do better. Graphs are known in which the diameter and degree both grow slower than logarithmically; for example, the pancake and star graphs defined in (Akers and Krishnamurthy, 1989).

Other considerations also apply. Many of the concerns that occupy designers of processor/communication interconnection networks (Akers and Krishnamurthy, 1989) are also of interest, for example, symmetry, connectivity and fault tolerance. Low connectivity would imply that a vicious adversary could inhibit passage from one part of the graph to another with a small trap region. A false peak can be seen as a kind of network fault.

But for GAs, we need to have graphs that result from easily encoded representations. The star and pancake graphs (Akers and Krishnamurthy, 1989) are on permutation induced graphs which might be useful for some problems such as travelling salesperson or graph coloring. But in general these graphs would be difficult to obtain using simple encodings for problems not inherently related to permutations. Further exploration of these graphs in this context is left for future research.

Acknowledgements

This work was supported by Natural Sciences and Engineering Research Council Grant No. OGP8053. The authors would also like to thank the anonymous referees.

References

S. B. Akers and B. Krishnamurthy (1989) A group-theoretic model for symmetric interconnection networks. *IEEE Transactions on Computers*, 38:555–566.

J. Culberson. (1994) Mutation-crossover isomorphisms and the construction of discriminating functions. *Evolutionary Computation*, 2(3):279–311.

J. Culberson. (1996) On the futility of blind search. Technical Report TR96–18, University of Alberta Department of Computing Science. ftp://ftp.cs.ualberta.ca/pub/TechReports/.

L. Davis, editor. (1987) *Genetic Algorithms and Simulated Annealing*. Research Notes in Artificial intelligence. Morgan Kaufmann.

M. Dinneen and P. Hafner. (1994) New results for the degree/diameter problem. *Networks*, 24:359–367.

W. Feller. (1968) *An Introduction to Probability Theory and Its Applications*, volume I. John Wiley & Sons, Inc., New York, New York.

P. Gitchoff and G. Wagner. (1996) Recombination induced hypergraphs: A new approach to mutation recombination isomorphism. *Complexity (In Press)*. Center for Computational Ecology preprint 33, Yale, http://peaplant.biology.yale.edu:8001/.

F. Glover. (1989) Tabu search–Part I. *ORSA Journal on Computing*, 1(3):190–206.

F. Glover. (1990) Tabu search–Part II. *ORSA Journal on Computing*, 2(1):4–32.

F. Harary, J. Hayes, and H. Wu. (1988) A survey of the theory of hypercube graphs. *Computers and Mathematics with Applications*, 15(4):277–289.

J. Holland. (1975) *Adaptation in Natural and Artificial Systems*. University of Michigan Press.

J. Horn, D. Goldberg, and K. Deb. (1994) Long path problems. In *Parallel Problem Solving from Nature—PPSN III, International Conf. on Evolutionary Computation, Proceedings*, volume 866 of *Lecture Notes in Computer Science*, pages 149–158. Springer-Verlag.

J. Horn. (1995) Genetic algorithms, problem difficulty and the modality of fitness landscapes. Master's thesis, University of Illinois, Urbana-Champaign.

J. Horn and D. Goldberg. (1995) Genetic algorithm difficulty and the modality of fitness landscapes. In L. Darrell Whitley and Michael D. Vose, editors, *Foundations of Genetic Algorithms 3*, pages 243–269. Morgan Kaufmann.

T. Jones. (1995) *Evolutionary Algorithms, Fitness Landscapes and Search*. PhD thesis, University of New Mexico, Albuquerque, NM.

H. Mühlenbein. (1992) How genetic algorithms really work i. mutation and hillclimbing. In R. Männer and B. Manderick, editors, *Parallel Problem Solving from Nature, 2*, pages 15–25.

W. Provine. (1986) *Sewall Wright and Evolutionary Biology*. University of Chicago Press, Chicago.

E. Reingold, J. Nievergelt, and N. Deo. (1977) *Combinatorial Algorithms: Theory and Practice*. Prentice-Hall, Inc.

B. Sharma and R. Khanna. (1978) On m-ary gray codes. *Information Sciences*, 15(1):31–43.

W. Spears. (1992) Crossover or mutation. In L. Darrell Whitley, editor, *Foundations of Genetic Algorithms 2*, pages 221–237. Morgan Kaufmann.

P. Stadler and G. Wagner. (1996) The algebraic theory of recombination spaces. Under Submission. Center for Computational Ecology preprint 44, Yale, http://peaplant.biology.yale.edu:8001/.

D. Wolpert and W. Macready. (1996) No free lunch theorems for search. Technical Report SFI-TR-95-02-010, The Santa Fe Institute, Santa Fe, New Mexico. ftp://ftp.santafe.edu/pub/wgm/.

SEARCH, Blackbox Optimization, And Sample Complexity

Hillol Kargupta [*]
Computational Science Methods Group
Los Alamos National Laboratory
Los Alamos, NM, USA.

David E. Goldberg
Department of General Engineering
University of Illinois at Urbana-Champaign
Urbana, IL, USA.

Abstract

The SEARCH (Search Envisioned As Relation & Class Hierarchizing) framework
developed elsewhere (Kargupta, 1995) offered an alternate perspective toward
blackbox optimization (BBO)—optimization in presence of little domain knowledge. The SEARCH framework investigated the conditions essential for transcending the limits of random enumerative search using a framework developed
in terms of relations, classes and partial ordering. This paper presents a summary
of some of the main results of that work. A closed form bound on the sample
complexity in terms of the cardinality of the relation space, class space, desired
quality of the solution and the reliability is presented. The two primary lessons of
this work are, a BBO (1) must search for appropriate relations and (2) can only
solve the so called class of order-k delineable problems in polynomial sample complexity. These results are applicable to any blackbox search algorithms, including
evolutionary optimization techniques.

1 Introduction

The SEARCH (Search Envisioned As Relation and Class Hierarchizing) framework introduced elsewhere (Kargupta, 1995) characterized blackbox optimization (BBO) in terms of
relation space, class space and construction of partial ordering in each of these spaces.
SEARCH is primarily motivated by the observation that searching for optimal solution in
a BBO is essentially an *inductive process* (Michalski, 1983) and in absence of any relation

---

The author can be reached at, P.O. Box 1663, XCM, Mail Stop F645, Los Alamos National
Laboratory, Los Alamos, NM 87545, USA. e-mail: hillol@lanl.gov

among the members of the search space, induction is no better than enumeration (Watanabe, 1969). SEARCH decomposed BBO into three spaces: (1) relation, (2) class, and (3) sample spaces. SEARCH also identified the importance of searching for appropriate relations in BBO. No BBO algorithm can efficiently solve a reasonably general class of problems unless it searches for relations. Kargupta (1995) also showed that the class of *order-k delineable* problems can be solved in SEARCH with sample complexity polynomial in problem size, desired quality and reliability of the solution. The objective of this work is not to re-establish the *need for bias* (Mitchell, 1980). SEARCH starts from this foundation. SEARCH first reminds us about the need to search for appropriate relations from the relation space defined by bias. This is quite relevant, given the fact that these days very few BBO algorithms, including evolutionary algorithms pay little attention to relation search. Very few evolutionary algorithms recognize the need for learning linkage (which is essentially the search for proper relations). There is hardly any work available on simulated annealing or tabu search that explicitly realizes the need for detecting proper relations from the given source of bias. SEARCH however takes another important step. It identifies the class of order-k delineable problems for a given algorithm, that can be efficiently solved.

Section 2 presents a brief review of the related works. Section 3 describes the main components of SEARCH. Section 4 discusses the different decision makings in SEARCH. The main analytical results for ordinal decision problem in class and relation spaces are presented in Section 5. Section 6 defines problem difficulty in SEARCH. This is followed by a description of the class of order-k delineable problems that can be solved in polynomial sample complexity in SEARCH. This is presented in Section 7. Section 8 discusses the similarities between SEARCH and computational learning theory. Section 9 offers a perspective of simulated annealing algorithm in the light of SEARCH. Section 10 notes some observations regarding genetic algorithms. Finally, Section 11 concludes this paper.

2 Background

Although optimization has been addressed in both theory and practice for several centuries, the fundamental approach for solving optimization problems has often followed a pattern: Given a very specific class of problems with some known properties, design an algorithm for solving this class. Unfortunately, because of the ever-growing list of different optimization problems, the process of designing new problem-specific algorithms is unlikely to terminate. Designing algorithms for solving blackbox problems—optimization problems with little knowledge available about the problem domain—offers an alternate approach. By assuming little knowledge (to be explained later) about the problem, algorithms designed using this approach aspire to solve a more general class of problems.

The purpose of this section is to introduce BBO and to review some earlier work. Section 2.1 introduces BBO and Section 2.2 reviews some existing works on BBO.

2.1 Blackbox optimization

Almost every discipline of engineering and science make use of optimization algorithms. As a result, a large number of optimization algorithms have been developed and applied to different problems. For example, smooth convex functions can be efficiently optimized using gradient search techniques (Papadimitriou & Steiglitz, 1982). The simplex algorithm (Dantzig, 1963) performs well for a large class of linear programming problems. Dynamic programming techniques (Dreyfus & Law, 1977) work well when the optimization problems are stage decomposable. Several analyses have been done for local and global optimization of real functions that are Lipschitz continuous with a known Lipschitz constant (Törn & Žilinskas, 1989; Vavasis, 1991). These approaches require characterization of the given problem in terms of known problem classes. Although such approaches may work for some problems with known categories (e.g. traveling salesman problem, graph coloring problem), a large body of engineering optimization problems are hard to characterize in terms of properties like convexity, Lipschitz continuity. For example, finding the Lipschitz constant of an optimization problem may be as hard as finding a reasonable solution. No wonder, such approaches to characterize problem class are hardly used in practice.

The growing demand for algorithms to solve new classes of difficult optimization problems and the never-ending process of designing algorithms that work for a restricted class of problems suggest the need for an alternate approach. The applicability of the previously mentioned optimization algorithms is very restricted, because these algorithms make assumptions about the properties of the objective functions that are often too restrictive. Therefore, one step toward designing optimization algorithms that work for a large class of problems is to reduce *quantitative assumptions* about the objective function. Since these algorithms make little assumption about the objective function, they should be able to solve problems using as little domain knowledge as possible. These problems would fall into the general class of blackbox optimization problems. In this model of optimization, the objective function is often available as a black box, i.e., for a given x in the feasible domain, it returns the function value $\Phi(x)$. No local or global information about the function is assumed. Let us denote the finite input and the output spaces by $\mathcal{X}$ and $\mathcal{Y}$, respectively. The general blackbox optimization problem can be formally defined as follows. Given a blackbox that somehow computes $\Phi(x)$ for an input x,

$$\Phi : \mathcal{X} \to \mathcal{Y} \qquad (1)$$

The objective of a maximization problem is to find some $x^* \in \mathcal{X}$ such that $\Phi(x^*) \geq \Phi(x)$ for all $x \in \mathcal{X}$. Although, we consider the maximization version of a BBO, the analysis remains valid for minimization version of BBO too. In this paper we shall consider only unconstrained optimization problems. This definition of BBO demands the best solution in the search domain. However, in the coming sections, we relax this requirement in an ordinal sense using standard order statistics. The desire According to this definition, BBO does not require any knowledge about the problem. However, the reader may recall that earlier in this paper we defined BBO as "optimization in presence of little domain knowledge". In BBO the bias introduces the domain knowledge implicitly. This is often far weaker than assuming any quantitative property and that is why we qualify such use of domain knowledge by the word "little". These observations will be quantified in the coming sections. The following section presents a brief review of some previous studies related to the work presented in this section.

2.2 Brief review of previous work

By definition, a strict blackbox search algorithm must work without any prior information about the quantitative properties of the objective function. Although the field of global optimization has a rich volume of literature, many studies are severely restricted because of their assumptions about the properties of the objective function (Schoen, 1991), and therefore it can be questioned whether they can really be called BBO algorithms. The objective of this section is to present a brief account of some previously developed algorithms that make little use of domain information about the problem. First, we present a classification of BBO algorithms based on whether the algorithm is deterministic or non-deterministic. Next, we concentrate on the non-deterministic or stochastic methods. Finally, we present a brief description of some previous efforts to relate different BBO algorithms with one another and to understand them on common grounds.

Although there may be several ways to classify optimization algorithms from different points of view (Törn & Žilinskas, 1989), one natural candidate is classification based on the deterministic or non-deterministic nature of the search algorithm. Several earlier efforts (Archetti & Schoen, 1984; Dixon & Szegö, 1978; Gomulka, 1978) suggested classification of global optimization algorithms using this approach. BBO algorithms can be similarly classified as

- Deterministic approaches

- Stochastic approaches
    - blind random search methods
    - adaptive sampling search methods

Each of these approaches will be briefly described in the following.

Deterministic enumeration of members of the search space is one method. Unfortunately, for most of the interesting optimization problems, deterministic enumeration becomes practically impossible because of the growth in the search space.

On the other hand, the stochastic algorithms introduce some random elements into the algorithm and try to solve the problem by relaxing the guarantee of the deterministic enumerative search. This relaxed nature of stochastic search algorithms makes them more suitable for practical applications.

Blind random search (Schoen, 1991; Törn & Žilinskas, 1989) is probably the simplest class of algorithms within the family of stochastic BBO algorithms. The Monte Carlo and multi-start algorithms are examples of this kind of algorithm. The Monte Carlo algorithm generates random samples from the search space according to a fixed distribution. Multi-start methods make use of local search techniques in addition to the Monte Carlo sample generation process. Although algorithms of this class are simple in nature, they are likely to be suitable for the worst case when different regions of the search space cannot be qualified and when evaluating a particular member of the search space does not provide information about another member.

Adaptive sampling search techniques try to exploit the information gathered from samples taken from the search space. They try to qualify different regions of the search space in terms of the fitness values of their members and use that information to decide which region to explore next. Bayesian algorithms, clustering methods, simulated annealing (SA) and genetic algorithms (GAs) are examples of this class of algorithms. This paper mainly considers this class of algorithms.

Bayesian algorithms (Betrò, 1983) try to develop a statistical model of the objective function. These algorithms do not explicitly construct a function; instead, they use a random variable to minimize the expected deviation of the estimate from the real global optimum. The expected value of the random variable is set to the best estimate of the function and the variance of the random variable capture the uncertainty about this estimate. The problem of Bayesian algorithms are that they are often complicated and involve fairly cumbersome computations, such as computing the inverse of the covariance matrix (Törn & Žilinskas, 1989).

Clustering methods (Rinnooy Kan & Timmer, 1984; Törn & Žilinskas, 1989) use a Monte Carlo sample generation technique. Cluster analysis algorithms are used to identify local minima. This is followed by a local search for each local optimum. Clustering methods have been found useful for many global optimization problems (Hart, 1994; Törn & Žilinskas, 1989). However they are likely to perform poorly when the objective function is multimodal and there are many local optima (Hart, 1994).

Since the early 80s, the simulated annealing (SA) algorithms (Kirpatrick, Gelatt, & Vecchi, 1983) and their variants have been used for solving blackbox problems. The natural motivation behind SA is the statistical behavior of molecules during the crystallization process in annealing. SA considers one sample at a time and this sample represents the state of the algorithm. A neighborhood generator is used to generate new samples. SA makes use of a probabilistic comparison statistic (the Metropolis criterion) for deciding whether the new sample should be accepted as the state of the algorithm. The Metropolis criterion dynamically changes along with a parameter known as temperature. The temperature takes a high value in the beginning and gradually decreases according to a chosen cooling schedule. The acceptance probability is often very high in the beginning, when the temperature is high. The acceptance probability decreases as the temperature reduces. SA has a proof for asymptotic convergence to the optimal solution (Kirpatrick, Gelatt, & Vecchi, 1983). SA has been applied to a wide range of blackbox problems. Many of them reported very promising results. However, in the recent past several negative results have also come out (Dueck & Scheuer, 1988; Ferreira & Žerovnik, 1993).

Genetic algorithms (GAs) (De Jong, 1975; Goldberg, 1989; Holland, 1975), evolutionary programming (Fogel, Owens, & Walsh, 1966), and evolutionary strategies (Rechenberg, 1973) are also getting increasing attention for dealing with global optimization in blackbox problems. Design of the simple genetic algorithm (GA) is motivated by natural evolution. Unlike the SA, it emphasizes the role of representation and the interaction between the representation and perturbation operators. GAs use the representation to implicitly divide the search space into several non-overlapping classes often called schemata (Holland, 1975). Unlike SAs, GAs work from a population of samples, with each sample often represented as sequences. This population of sequences is used to evaluate different schemata. New samples are generated by crossover and mutation operators. Crossover also implicitly combines the better schemata while generating new samples. GAs have been successfully applied to different classes of problems (Goldberg, 1989). However, the simple GA suffers from several limitations. Although the simple GA realizes the role of representation that induces relations among members of the search space, the simple GA does not really search for appropriate relations. Moreover, the evaluation of schemata is also very noisy in the simple GA.

With all these different BBO algorithms in our arsenal, it is quite natural to ask whether they can be studied on common grounds using common principles. Several previous efforts have been made to address this question. Although Holland's (1975) framework for adaptive search was primarily motivated by evolutionary computation, the underlying concepts of search based on schema processing and decision making are fundamental issues that are equally relevant in the context of any other adaptive BBO algorithms. In fact, Holland's work (1975) is the root of the current paper. Davis (1987) made an effort to put literature on SAs and GAs under a common title. Unfortunately, this book did not make any direct effort to link them; rather, it simply discussed them separately. Sirag and Weisser (1987) combined several genetic operators into a unified thermodynamic operator and used it to solve traveling salesperson problems. However, this paper did not study the fundamental similarities and differences between SAs and GAs. Goldberg (1990) addressed this issue. He presented a common ground to understand the effects of the different operators of SAs and GAs. He also proposed the Boltzmann tournament selection operator, which attempts to achieve Boltzmann distribution over the population. Mahfoud and Goldberg (1992) introduced a parallel genetic version of simulated annealing called *parallel recombinative simulated annealing*. This algorithm attempted to harness the strengths of both SAs and GAs. Recently Rudolph (1994) developed a Markov chain formulation of SAs and GAs for analyzing their similarities and differences. Jones and Stuckman (1992) made an interesting effort to relate GAs with Bayesian approaches to global optimization. They noted the similarities and differences between these two approaches and concluded that they share many common grounds. They also developed hybrid algorithms that try to harness the strengths of both approaches. Recently Jones (1995) proposed a framework to study the correspondence between evolutionary algorithms and heuristic state space search of graph theory. In this approach the search domain of the objective function is viewed as a directed, labeled graph. Jones and Forrest (1995) also proposed the fitness–distance-correlation measure for quantifying search difficulty and applied this measure to several classes of objective functions. Wolpert and Macready (1995) proposed the so called NFL theorem that confirmed the fundamental lessons of Watanabe's (Watanabe, 1969) ugly duckling theorem. (Radcliffe & Surry, 1995) made a similar effort and emphasized the need for representational bias.

Very few of the previous efforts actually made a quantitative effort to study the computational capabilities and limitations of BBO. Even fewer among them provided any insight for designing new BBO algorithms. Little attention has been paid to the role of relations in BBO, which is essential for transcending the limits of random enumerative search. We still lack any common framework that describes these different algorithms in terms of the basic concepts of theory of computation. The SEARCH framework, makes an attempts to do that. The following section presents a brief description of SEARCH.

3 SEARCH: An Informal Picture

SEARCH presents an alternate picture of blackbox optimization in terms of relations and classes that can be constructed among the members of the search space. SEARCH is also a formal framework that helps us quantify different aspects of BBO, such as sample complexity, problem difficulty, and many more. In this section we briefly review the framework and present the main analytical results without presenting the rigorous derivations given elsewhere (Kargupta, 1995). Section 3.1 presents the fundamental motivation behind SEARCH. Section 3.2 presents an overview of SEARCH. A more detailed picture is presented in Section 3.3.

3.1 Motivation

Some existing BBO algorithms try to find the optimal solution by directly searching the original domain of optimization variables. Samples are often used to estimate the best

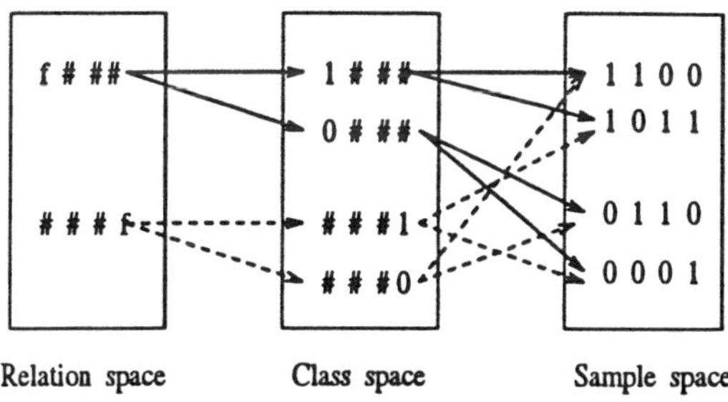

Figure 1: Decomposition of blackbox optimization in SEARCH. Note that SEARCH does not require the relations and classes to be equivalence relations and equivalence classes respectively. Equivalence relations and classes are used through out this paper only for the purpose of illustrations.

solution of the search space. In these approaches, a BBO algorithm always searches for a better solution compared to the current best solution. It takes one or more samples and then decides how to choose the next sample. Although the task is certainly non-trivial, the approach of finding the best solution by iteratively updating the best estimate has a fundamental problem. Sampling one particular point from the search domain does not necessarily tell us anything about another point. When a BBO algorithm makes a decision to sample another member from the domain, it is performing *induction*—the process of hypothesizing the premise from the consequences (Michalski, 1983). This is because we are first observing the objective function values for the members of the sample set and then trying to determine whether an unknown point should have a higher or lower objective function value. In other words, it is guessing; it is a proven fact that induction is no better than table-look-up when no relations exist between the members (Mitchell, 1980; Watanabe, 1969). If no prior relation is assumed between them, there is little reason to choose one member over others, and the blackbox search will be no better than enumerative search unless the algorithm assumes and exploits some relations among the members of the search domain.

If assuming and exploiting relations among the members of a search space is essential, then it will be wise to isolate this possibility, study it, and see how it can be used to the fullest. The SEARCH framework does that. Recall that SEARCH stands for *Search Envisioned As Relation and Class Hierarchizing*. Searching for better relations and better classes are the primary fronts emphasized in SEARCH. Relations classify the search space into different regions. Some relations classify the search space in such a way that it is relatively easier to detect the class containing the optimal solution. SEARCH tries to establish such relations among the members of the search space. Instead of directly searching for the best solution from the beginning, SEARCH tries to find these relations and then use them to locate the classes containing the optimal solution. The following section presents a brief overview of SEARCH.

3.2 Overview

The foundation of SEARCH is laid on a decomposition of the BBO into relation, class, and sample spaces. A relation is a set of ordered pairs. For example, in a set of cubes, some white and some black, the color of the cubes defines a relation that divide the set of cubes into two subsets—set of white cubes and set of black cubes. Consider a 4-bit binary sequence. There are 2^4 such binary sequences. This set can be divided into two classes using the equivalence relation[1] $f\#\#\#$, where f denotes position of equivalence; the $\#$ character matches with any binary value. This equivalence relation divides up the complete set into two equivalence classes, $1\#\#\#$ and $0\#\#\#$. The class $1\#\#\#$ contains all the sequences with 1 in the leftmost position and $0\#\#\#$ contains those with a 0 in that position. Note that SEARCH does not require the relations and classes to be equivalence relations and equivalence classes respectively. Equivalence relations and classes are used through out this paper only for the purpose of illustrations. Index of a relation is the number of classes defined by the relation. The order of a relation can be defined as the logarithm of its index. Order of a relation r will be denoted by $o(r)$. In a BBO problem, relations among the search space members are often introduced through different means, such as representation, operators, heuristics, and others. The above example of relations in binary sequence can be viewed as an example of relation in the sequence representation. In a sequence space of length ℓ, there are 2^ℓ such different equivalence relations. The search operators also define a set of relations by introducing a notion of neighborhood. For a given member in the search space, the search operator define a set of members that can be reached by one or several application of the operators. This introduces relations among the members. Heuristics identifies a subset of the search space as more promising than others often based on some domain specific knowledge. Clearly this can be a source of relations. Relations can sometimes be introduced in a more direct manner. For example, Perttunen and Stuckman (1990) proposed a Bayesian optimization algorithm that divides the search space into Delaunay triangles. This classification directly imposes a certain relation among the members of the search space. The same goes for interval optimization (Ratschek & Voller, 1991), where the domain is divided into many intervals and knowledge about the problem is used to compute the likelihood of success in those intervals. As we see, relations are introduced in any search problem either implicitly or explicitly. The role of relations in BBO is also very fundamental and important. Although, in a BBO, many relations can be introduced in different ways not all of the relations are appropriate from the optimization perspective. The objective of sampling based BBO is to detect regions of the domain that are most likely to contain the optimal solutions. In other words, a BBO algorithm tries to detect those classes defined by a relation which appear more promising. If a relation divides the search space in such a way that such detection is easier, then the relation is appropriate for that problem. We shall later formally define such relations as those which *properly delineates* the domain. Determining which relation is better requires first constructing a partial ordering among the classes defined by each of the relations. In a sampling based BBO all these decision making is done by taking a finite number of samples from the domain. Clearly, all the BBO algorithms often implicitly deal with the three distinct spaces: (1) relation space, (2) class space, and (3) sample space. SEARCH considers all of them explicitly in an effort to understand them rigorously. Figure 1 shows this fundamental decomposition in SEARCH. The major components of SEARCH can be listed as follows:

1. classification of the search space using a relation

2. sampling

---

[1] An equivalence relation is a relation that is reflexive, symmetric, and transitive.

Table 1: A function in 4-bit representation.

x	$\Phi(x)$
0000	2.5
0001	3
0010	1
0100	1
1000	1
0011	2
0101	2
1001	2
0110	0
1010	0
1100	0
0111	1
1011	1
1101	1
1110	3
1111	4

Table 2: Different class comparison statistics for the classes in $ff\#\#$.

Class	Average	Min	Max
11##	2.0	0	4.0
10##	1.0	0	2.0
01##	1.0	0	2.0
00##	2.125	1.0	3.0

3. evaluation, ordering, and selection of better classes

4. evaluation, ordering, and selection of better relations

5. resolution

Each component is discussed in more detail in the following paragraphs. To do so requires some notation that we shall use throughout the remainder of the section. A relation is denoted by r_i, where i is the index of the set of all relations, Ψ_r, under consideration of the algorithm. Let C_i be the collection of subsets, created by relation r_i. The set of relations S_r actually used by an algorithm to solve the given BBO is a subset of Ψ_r. Denote the members of C_i by $C_{1,i}, C_{2,i} \cdots C_{N_i,i}$, where the cardinality of the class C_i is $\|C_i\| = N_i$. Therefore, C_i is a collection of classes.

Once the relation is used to construct C_i the next step is to evaluate the classes in C_i. To do that we need samples from the domain of optimization. A perturbation operator $\mathcal{P}$ is defined as an operator that generates new samples. This operator can be either a random sample generator or a smarter one that exploits information from the relation, class, and

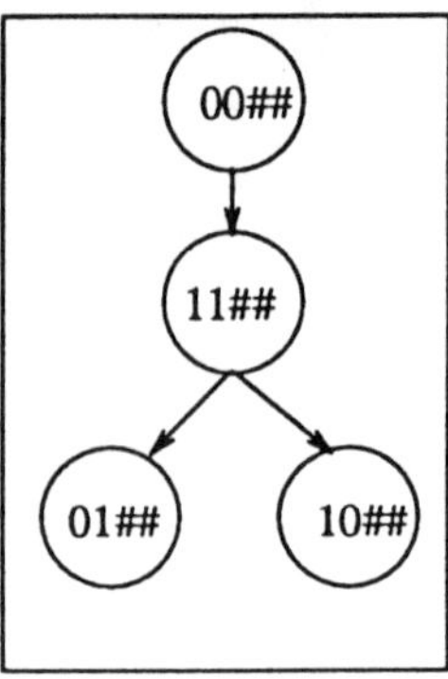
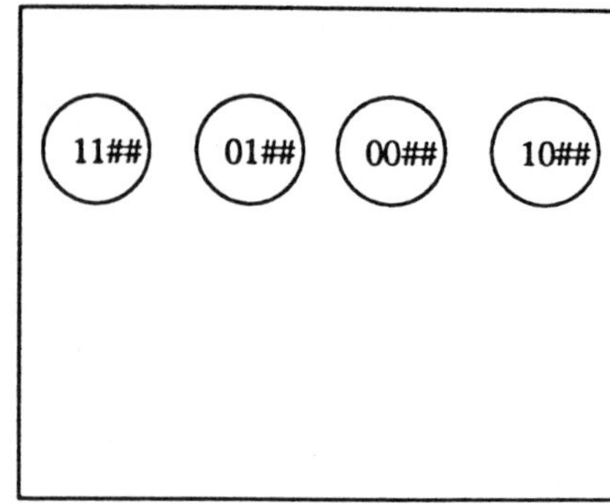

Figure 2: Ordering among classes for different class comparison statistics: *(left)* Comparison by average of objective function value. *(right)* $C_{2,i}$ is less than $C_{1,i}$ if the minimum objective function value of $C_{1,i}$ is greater than maximum value of $C_{2,i}$. Table 2 presents the corresponding statistic measures of the classes considered here. This figure illustrates that the ordering among the classes can change depending upon the choice of the particular statistic. Moreover, sometimes a linear order among classes may not be constructed.

sample memory.

The next step is to construct an ordering among the classes in C_i. To do so, we need a way to compare any pair of classes. A statistic $\mathcal{T}$ can be computed for each of the classes, and they may be compared on this basis. This statistic will be called a *class comparison statistic*. This class comparison statistic can be used for computing a tentative ranking among the classes in C_i. For certain choices of $\mathcal{T}$, some classes may not be compared with other classes. This means that sometimes a total order may not be constructed. Consider the example problem shown in Table 1. Table 2 shows different class comparison statistic value for the classes in $ff\#\#$. Figure 2 shows the ordering among the classes using those class comparison statistics. In general, a statistic $\mathcal{T}$ may be used to construct only a partial order on C_i. Let us denote this partially ordered collection by $C_{i[\ ]}$. Once the ordering is constructed, the next goal is to select some $1 \leq M_i \leq \|C_i\|$ top ranked classes from $C_{i[\ ]}$. M_i represents the total number of top ranked classes that will be selected for future considerations. The exact choice of M_i depends on the decision error probability in choosing an appropriate relation and ordering construction among the classes. For example, if sampling is insufficient, the ordering of classes cannot be relied upon with high confidence, and drastic elimination of classes may not be appropriate. Therefore, a relatively larger value of M_i may be used. These M_i classes constitute the updated version of the class search space.

Next, this ordering among the classes is used to evaluate the relation r_i itself. Different kinds of statistics can be used to compare relations with one another. we denote this relation comparison statistic by $\mathcal{T}_r$ and call it a *relation comparison statistic*. This statistic for relation r_i is now computed. The set of all relations currently under consideration is ordered based on this statistic. Note that, again, this ordering does not have to be a total ordering. The top M_r relations are kept for future consideration and the rest are discarded, in a manner very similar to what we did for the classes.

Not all the classes defined by a relation need to be considered. As more and more relations are evaluated, the information gathered may be used to prune out different classes before evaluating a new relation. Let r_0 be a relation that is logically equivalent to $r_1 \wedge r_2$, where r_1 and r_2 are two different relations; the sign $\wedge$ denotes logical AND operation. If either of r_1 or r_2 was earlier found to properly delineate the search space with certain value of M_i, then the information about the classes that are found to be bad earlier can be used to eliminate some classes in r_0 from further consideration. Blackbox algorithms often implement a resolution-like process to take advantage of any such possible decomposability. If the chosen relation r_i can be decomposed into a collection of different relations, denoted by $\cup_k r_k$, then resolution can eliminate bad classes using the information collected from possible earlier evaluations of some relations in $\cup_k r_k$.

Repeated iterations of the above steps result in gradual focusing into those regions of the search space which look better using the chosen class and relation comparison statistics. The set of all these relations $r_i, r_{i+1}, \ldots$ used to solve the problem is denoted by S_r. Whether or not the algorithm approaches the globally optimal solution, depends on success in finding proper relations, better classes, and sufficient sampling.

The following section presents a formal description of the different aspects of the SEARCH framework.

3.3 SEARCH: The detailed picture

The objective of this section is to present a more quantitative picture of SEARCH and formalize the earlier descriptions. The definition of a better relation requires defining what we mean by better classes. Therefore, the decision making in the class space is considered first, in Section 3.3.1. Section 3.3.2 considers the class selection process. This is followed by Section 3.3.3 that discusses the relation search. Finally, Section 3.3.4 presents the resolution process of SEARCH.

3.3.1 Classification and ordering of classes

This section considers the decision-making process among the classes. Classification of the search space requires defining relations. A relation can be defined using different sources, such as operators and representation. In this section we assume no specific source of relations and simply consider Ψ_r, a set of relations, as an abstract entity provided to the search process. However, we continue to give illustrative examples whenever required, using relations defined by sequence representation.

Let C_i be the collection of classes created by some relation r_i. Denote the members of C_i by $C_{1,i}, C_{2,i}, \ldots C_{N_i,i}$, where $\|C_i\| = N_i$. Once a relation r_i is used to define C_i, the collection of classes, each of its members needs to be evaluated first. Since we are interested in the relative "goodness" of the classes with an ultimate goal to pick up some and reject the rest, a statistic that compares any two classes can serve our purpose. If $\mathcal{T}$ is the class comparison statistic used to compare any two subsets $C_{j,i}$ and $C_{k,i}$, then given any two subsets, there must exist an algorithm Γ that returns the resulting order among the subsets when compared on the basis of $\mathcal{T}$. It may also be possible that the two classes cannot be compared based on Γ. The relation constructed among two ordered subsets of C_i is represented by $\leq_{\mathcal{T}}$. In other words, when $C_{j,i}$ and $C_{k,i}$ are compared to each other, then either $C_{j,i} \leq_{\mathcal{T}} C_{k,i}$ or $C_{k,i} \leq_{\mathcal{T}} C_{j,i}$, or they cannot be compared. When C_i is partially ordered on the basis of

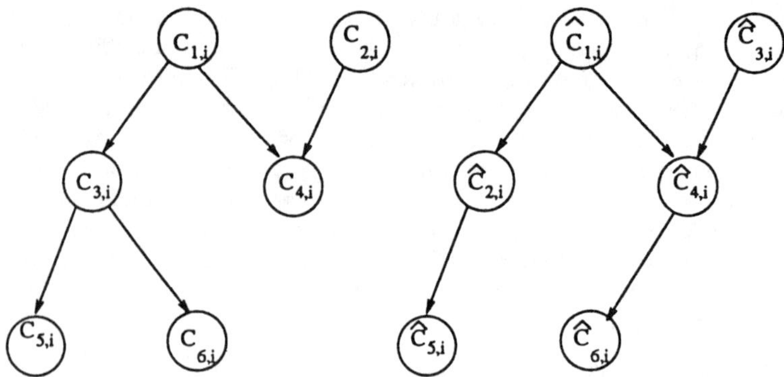

Figure 3: Hasse diagram representation of C_i *(left)* and $\hat{C}_i$ *(right)*.

$\leq_T$, it can be represented by a Hasse diagram. Figure 3 (left) illustrates this representation. In a Hasse diagram, the vertices are the members of a poset (partially ordered set); $C_{1,i}$ is drawn above $C_{2,i}$ if and only if $C_{1,i}, C_{2,i} \in C_i$ and $C_{2,i} \leq_T C_{1,i}$. We can say that $C_{1,i}$ covers $C_{2,i}$ if $C_{1,i}, C_{2,i} \in C_i$, $C_{2,i} \leq_T C_{1,i}$, and no element $C_{3,i} \in C_i$ satisfies $C_{2,i} \leq_T C_{3,i} \leq_T C_{1,i}$. The depth of a node, $C_{j,i}$ in a Hasse diagram is the minimum number of links that need to be traversed to reach $C_{j,i}$ from any node at the highest level. Note that this ordering depends on the chosen class comparison statistic.

In a sampling-based search, the partial-order construction process is based on a finite set of samples taken from each of the subsets, $C_{1,i}, C_{2,i}, \ldots C_{N_i,i}$. Let us denote the approximate descriptions of these classes using the sample sets by $C_{1,i}, C_{2,i}, \ldots C_{N_i,i}$ by $\hat{C}_{1,i}, \hat{C}_{2,i}, \ldots \hat{C}_{N_i,i}$. Let $C_{i[\,]}$ be the ordering of classes from relation i. Denote the class at rank b from the bottom of this ordering by $C_{[b],i}$. This means the top ranked class in this ordering is denoted by $C_{[N_i],i}$. he partial ordering constructed using the sample estimates may be different from the actual ordering. Figure 3 (right) shows that the partial ordering constructed from sample estimates may differ from the actual ordering.

3.3.2 Selection of better classes

Once the classes are partially ordered based on $\leq_T$, the next immediate objective is to select M_i "top" subsets. Since $C_{i[\,]}$ is a partial order, the notion of "top" needs to be properly defined. This is an implementation-specific issue. One possible way to define this may be based on the depth of a subset in the Hasse diagram. For the current purpose, we assume that there exists a subroutine $\text{TOP}(C_{i[\,]}, M_i)$ which returns the set of "top" M_i subsets from the collection $C_{i[\,]}$. Denote the particular subset that contains x^*—the globally optimal solution—by $C_{*,i}$. If we denote the ordered collection of sample sets $\hat{C}_{1,i}, \hat{C}_{2,i}, \ldots \hat{C}_{N_i,i}$ by $\hat{C}_{i[\,]}$, then we would like $\hat{C}_{*,i}$ to be one among the collection of classes returned by $\text{TOP}(\hat{C}_{i[\,]}, M_i)$. Unfortunately, this is very unlikely, unless $C_{*,i}$ itself is not within $\text{TOP}(C_{i[\,]}, M_i)$. This sets the stage for introducing the notion of inherently better or worse relations with respect to a given problem, a class comparison statistic, and memory size. This is considered in the following section.

3.3.3 Selection of appropriate relations: The delineation property

A relation is not appropriate with respect to the chosen class comparison statistic and the BBO problem if the class containing the optimal solution is not one among some top-ranked classes, ordered based on this statistic. If the class $C_{*,i}$ is not among the top M_i classes, the algorithm is not likely to succeed (neglecting any chance that may rank $\hat{C}_{*,i}$ higher than its actual ranking). Let us quantify this requirement of a relation to be appropriate by a function $DC(r_i, \mathcal{T}, M_i)$. This function returns a one if $C_{*,i} \in \text{TOP}(C_{i[\,]}, M_i)$; otherwise, it returns a zero. This will be denoted by $DC()$ in short (DC stands for Delineation Constraint), unless otherwise required.

Definition 1 (Proper delineation) : *For a given BBO problem, a relation r_i, a class comparison statistic $\mathcal{T}$, and a memory size, M_i, if $DC(r_i, \mathcal{T}, M_i) = 1$, we say that r_i properly delineates the search space.*

This *delineation constraint* plays an important role in SEARCH processes. It essentially qualifies or disqualifies a relation for a particular search problem. If a relation does not properly delineate the search space, there is very little chance that the class with the best solution will be detected. Therefore, for a given class comparison statistic, whether or not a relation is appropriate can be directly quantified based on this characteristic function. However, in reality the algorithm does not know this constraint. The algorithm has to decide whether or not a relation properly delineates the search space from the limited number of samples taken from the search space. Therefore, determining whether or not a relation properly delineates is again essentially a decision-making problem.

Given a finite set of samples from the search space, a class comparison statistic, $\mathcal{T}$, the memory size M_i, and a relation r_i, the goal is to determine whether a relation classifies the search space in such a way that $C_{*,i}$ is in $\text{TOP}(C_{i[\,]}, M_i)$. Since the problem is now reduced to a decision-making problem instead of the previous binary characteristic function, we can approach it using the same strategy that we took for selecting better classes. In other words, we can start comparing relations, estimate how well a relation would satisfy the delineation requirement compared to another relation, and choose the better relations. This problem is similar to the class selection problem; the only difference is that now we are trying to choose *better relations* instead of better classes. The first question is: How do we compare two relations? While comparing two classes, we needed a class comparison statistic, $\mathcal{T}$. The same thing can be done for relations. Let us denote a *relation comparison statistic* by $\mathcal{T}_r$. This statistic is used to compute an ordering among the relations. Denote this ordering relation by $\leq_{\mathcal{T}_r}$. The ordering among the relations in Ψ_r may not remain the same when relations are compared based on a limited number of samples. In other words, if $r_j \leq_{\mathcal{T}_r} r_i$, then it is not necessarily true that $\hat{r}_j \leq_{\mathcal{T}_r} \hat{r}_i$; we denote a relation r_i when compared based on limited sampling by $\hat{r}_i$. This process of relation selection involves decision making in absence of complete knowledge and it is therefore susceptible to decision errors. The following section describes the resolution process.

3.3.4 Resolution of classes

Resolution plays an important role in SEARCH. Resolution takes advantage of possible delineability of relations. Classification of the search space defined by a relation is moderated by the resolution process. If possible, resolution eliminates classes that are not necessary to consider by using the information gathered by previous evaluations of some other relations. Let r_j be a relation that properly delineates the search space with memory size M_j. Let r_i be the relation currently being evaluated, and r_i can be logically expressed as $r_j \wedge r_k$, where r_k is a relation. Resolution of C_i with respect to r_j eliminates those classes of C_i that need not be considered using our knowledge about r_j. This resolved set of classes in C_i can be formally defined as

$$\bigcup_{b=N_j,\ldots N_j-M_j} \bigcup_{a=1,\ldots N_i} C_{a,i} \bigcap C_{[b],j}$$

where the index b varies over the all M_j top ranked classes of relation r_j and index a denotes the different N_i classes in C_i. $C_{[b],j}$ is the rank b member of the ordered collection of classes in C_j and $C_{a,i}$ is the a member of the unordered collection of classes C_i. The following sections present a brief description of the analysis of the different decision problems in SEARCH.

4   Decision Making in SEARCH

The previous sections presented SEARCH from both informal and formal points of view. They also posed the class and relation selection processes as decision problems in absence of complete knowledge. In this section we analyze these two sources of decision error and combine them to develop an expression for the overall success probability.

Two kinds of decision errors may make the selection of better classes erroneous:

1. The relation used to define collection C_i is such that for the chosen $\mathcal{T}$, the subset $C_{*,i}$ is not in $\mathrm{TOP}(C_{i[\,]}, M_i)$. Therefore, despite how well the sampling is done, the selection process will always miss the subset containing x^*, unless $\hat{C}_{*,i}$ is ranked higher by sampling error. A search algorithm needs to determine whether or not a relation does this from a finite number of samples. Therefore, this could be a source of error. Let us call this error the *relation selection error*.

2. Even when $C_{*,i}$ is in $\mathrm{TOP}(C_{i[\,]}, M_i)$, sampling error can produce a different partial order structure for $\hat{C}_{1,i}, \hat{C}_{2,i}, \ldots \hat{C}_{N_i,i}$. As a result $\hat{C}_{*,i}$ may not be in $\mathrm{TOP}(\hat{C}_{i[\,]}, M_i)$. The sampling error may result in incorrect ordering of the classes and we call this the *class selection error.*

These two dimensions of decision error in BBO determine the success probability. The following sections analyze the success probabilities associated with each of these dimensions. Finally, they are combined to develop an expression for the overall success probability.

4.1   Relation selection success

If an algorithm does not properly delineate the search space, it is not likely to select the class containing the optimal solution. Since, in the absence of knowledge, there is no way to know whether a relation satisfies this requirement or not a priori, this can only be estimated based on the sampling information. Relations are ordered based on the measure $\mathcal{T}_r$, and $\|S_r\|$ top relations are selected. Since these top $\|S_r\|$ relations are just the estimated relations that satisfy the delineation constraint, there is the possibility of decision error. If r_i is actually in the top $\|S_r\|$ relations, then the probability that $\hat{r}_i$ will also be within the top $\|S_r\|$ relations depends on correct decision making in the comparison with at least $\Psi_r - \|S_r\|$ relations. Denote a relation which actually does not satisfy the delineation constraint by r_j. If the minimum probability that $\hat{r}_j \leq_{T_r} \hat{r}_i$ over all possible relations is denoted by, $Pr(\hat{r}_j \leq_{T_r} \hat{r}_i)_{min}$, the success probability that $\hat{r}_i$ will be one among the top $\|S_r\|$ relations is

$$Pr(CRS \mid r_i) \geq Pr(\hat{r}_j \leq_{T_r} \hat{r}_i)_{min}^{\|\Psi_r\|-\|S_r\|}, \tag{2}$$

where CRS stands for *correct relation selection*. The following section considers the decision making in class selection process.

4.2   Class selection success

Let us now consider the class selection problem. The probability that the best solution is in any of the selected subsets will be denoted by $Pr(CCS|r_i)$. CCS stands for *correct class selection* and conditional to r_i, reflects its association with relation r_i. Let $Pr(\hat{C}_{j,i} \leq_T \hat{C}_{\bullet,i})$ denote the success probability given that $C_{j,i} \leq_T C_{\bullet,i}$, and let $Pr(\hat{C}_{j,i} \leq_T \hat{C}_{\bullet,i})_{min}$ be the minimum value of $Pr(\hat{C}_{j,i} \leq_T \hat{C}_{\bullet,i})$ over every $\hat{C}_{j,i}$ which has a depth greater than that of $\hat{C}_{\bullet,i}$ and there is a link connecting it to $\hat{C}_{\bullet,i}$. Now noting that M_i top classes are selected,

$$Pr(CCS \mid r_i) \geq Pr(\hat{C}_{j,i} \leq_T \hat{C}_{\bullet,i})_{min}^{N_i-M_i}$$

This gives the success probability for a particular relation r_i.

4.3   Overall success

The overall success probability for all the considered relations in S_r then becomes

$$Pr(CS \mid \forall r_i \in S_r) = \prod_{\forall r_i \in S_r} Pr(CRS \mid r_i)Pr(CCS \mid r_i). \tag{3}$$

This equation captures the general idea that will be used in the following sections. As we see, at a higher level, the success of a blackbox search algorithm depends on

1. the success probability in finding relations that properly delineate the search space and

2. the success probability in detecting the class which actually contains the desired solution.

The following sections specialize the observations of this framework to a specific class comparison statistic and representation. First, we consider ordinal class and relation comparison statistic.

5   Ordinal Class and Relation Selection

Constructing a total order and selection of some M_i top subsets from that order have been studied using both parametric and non-parametric approaches (Gibbons, Sobel, & Olkin,

1977). If we are willing to make assumptions about the individual distributions of the members of C_i, nice statistics can be formulated to solve this selection problem. However, in the following discussion, we adopt a non-parametric, ordinal approach (David, 1981) that allows a distribution-free analysis of the relation and class comparison process. The purpose of this section is to derive bounds on the success probability and sample complexity for a quite general ordinal relation and class comparison statistics.

Section 5.1 considers an ordinal class comparison statistic and the SEARCH framework is specialized for this statistic. Section 5.2 further specializes SEARCH for an ordinal relation comparison statistic. Section 5.3 combines the decision making for both better classes and relations; it also bounds the overall success probability. Finally, Section 5.4 derives the overall sample complexity and discusses its properties.

5.1 Ordinal class selection

As we argued in the previous section, BBO can be viewed as a combined process of search for better relations and better classes defined by each of these relations. Let us first recall some definitions that will be used in this section. The i-th order statistic of a set of n elements is the i-th smallest element. For example, the minimum of a set of elements is the first order statistic ($i = 1$), and the maximum is the n-th order statistic ($i = n$). The cumulative distribution function (cdf) $F(x) = \sum_{x_j \leq x} f(x_j)$, where $f(x_j)$ is the probability density function. Let us now consider the class comparison process from an ordinal perspective. In order statistics any two classes will be compared based on their α quantile of the cdf. A quantile of order α can be defined as the number Φ_α, such that $F(\Phi_\alpha) = \alpha$, where $F(\Phi)$ is the cdf of Φ. This definition of quantile is not fully satisfactory when the cdf is discrete and the α quantile may not be unique. In such cases, however, we can define it as any convex combination of points in the closure of the set $\{\Phi : F(\Phi) = \alpha\}$. To convey the main idea without unnecessary cluttering of symbols, let us assume that the α quantile is unique. We should note that such quantile-based class comparison will always produce a total order on the collection C_i.

Consider the comparison between two classes $C_{j,i}$ and $C_{k,i}$. Assume that we take n samples from each of these classes. We shall denote n samples from the class $C_{j,i}$ by $\hat{C}_{1,j,i}, \hat{C}_{2,j,i}, \ldots \hat{C}_{n,j,i}$; the corresponding objective function values by $\Phi_{1,j,i}, \Phi_{2,j,i}, \ldots \Phi_{n,j,i}$. These n samples can be totally ordered on the basis of their objective function values as follows:

$$\hat{C}_{[1],j,i} \leq_* \hat{C}_{[2],j,i} \leq_* \cdots \leq_* \hat{C}_{[n],j,i}$$

where, $\hat{C}_{[\omega],j,i} \leq_* \hat{C}_{[\beta],j,i}$ if $\hat{\Phi}_{[\omega],j,i} \leq \hat{\Phi}_{[\beta],j,i}$. $\hat{\Phi}_{[k],j,i}$ denotes the k-th order statistic. The sample estimate of the α quantile for the class j is denoted by $y_{\alpha,j}$. Define an integer $\tau = \alpha(n+1)$; then, $y_{\alpha,j,i} = \hat{\Phi}_{[\tau],j,i}$. If $\alpha(n+1)$ is not an integer, we can set τ equal to the largest integer contained in $\alpha(n+1)$ and compute $y_{\alpha,j,i}$ as follows:

$$y_{\alpha,j} = [\tau + 1 - \alpha(n+1)]\hat{\Phi}_{[\tau],j,i} + [\alpha(n+1) - \tau]\hat{\Phi}_{[\tau+1],j,i}$$

This basically interpolates between two adjacent order statistics to approximate the point where the cdf is equal to α. Again, to keep things simpler, we assume that $\alpha(n+1)$ is an integer.

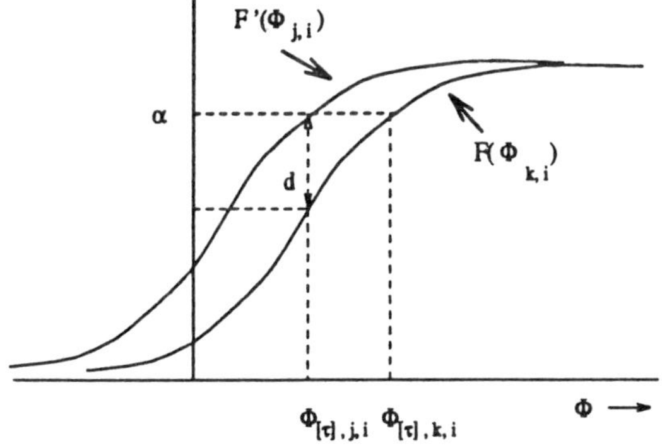

Figure 4: Fitness distribution function of two classes $C_{[j],i}$ and $C_{[k],i}$.

Figure 4 shows the cumulative distribution function F' and F of two arbitrary subsets $C_{j,i}$ and $C_{k,i}$, respectively. When these two classes are compared on the basis of the α quantile, then we say $C_{j,i} \leq_\alpha C_{k,i}$, since $\Phi_{[\tau],j,i} \leq \Phi_{[\tau],k,i}$; $\Phi_{[\tau],j,i}$ and $\Phi_{[\tau],k,i}$ are the solutions of $F'(\Phi_{j,i}) = \alpha$ and $F(\Phi_{k,i}) = \alpha$, respectively. Let us define

$$d = F(\Phi_{[\tau],k,i}) - F(\Phi_{[\tau],j,i}).$$

The variable d defines the *zone of indifference*, which is basically the difference in the percentile value of $\Phi_{[\tau],k,i}$ and that of $\Phi_{[\tau],j,i}$ computed from the same cdf F. Figure 4 clearly explains this definition.

It can be easily shown that for τ-th order statistics of set $C_{j,i}$ (David, 1981), $\Phi_{[\tau],j,i}$,

$$Pr(\hat{\Phi}_{[\tau],j,i} \leq c') = \sum_{w=\tau}^{n} \binom{n}{w}(F(c'))^w (1 - F(c'))^{n-w}. \tag{4}$$

The probability of correct selection among these two classes can be written as (Kargupta, 1995)

$$Pr(\hat{\Phi}_{[\tau],j,i} \leq_\alpha \hat{\Phi}_{[\tau],k,i}) \geq 1 - 2^{nH(\alpha)}(\alpha - d)^{\alpha n}. \tag{5}$$

where $H(\lambda)$ is the binary entropy function, $H(\lambda) = -\lambda \log_2 \lambda - (1 - \lambda) \log_2(1 - \lambda)$. $H(0) = H(1) = 0$ and $H(\lambda)$ takes the maximum value for $\lambda = 0.5$. For relation r_i, if we denote the cdf of the class containing the optimal solution x^* by $F(\Phi_{*,i})$, then define,

$$d'' = \min\{F(\Phi_{[\tau],*,i}) - F(\Phi_{[\tau],j,i}) | \forall j\},$$

the probability that the class $\hat{C}_{*,i}$ will be within the top M_i classes is

$$Pr(CCS \mid r_i) \geq [1 - 2^{nH(\alpha)}(\alpha - d'')^{\alpha n}]^{N_i - M_i}. \tag{6}$$

Given relation r_i that properly delineates the search space, Equation 6 can be used to compute the probability that $C_{*,i}$ will be within the top M_i classes. Before we proceed toward computing the overall correct selection probability, we need to consider the search in the relation space.

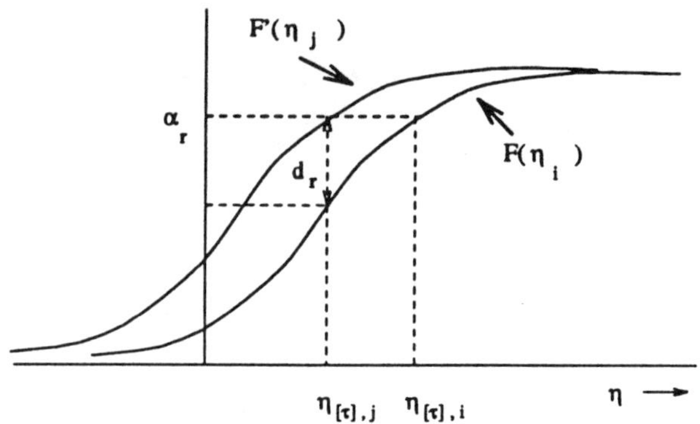

Figure 5: Cumulative distribution function of two relations r_i and r_j.

5.2 Ordinal relation selection

A relation is appropriate if it properly delineates the search space. Determining whether or not a relation satisfies this constraint with absolute certainty is not possible unless we completely enumerate the search space. Therefore, in reality, the characteristic function $DC()$ is replaced by an estimator that measures how likely a relation satisfies delineation constraint. Let us define a measure $\eta : \Psi_r \times 2^C \times 2^X \rightarrow \Re$. 2^C denotes the collection of classes and 2^X denotes the sample set. For a given relation r_i, the corresponding set of classes C_i, and a sample set S, this measure $\eta(r_i, C_i, S)$ returns a real value that corresponds to the chances of r_i to satisfy the delineation constraint (i.e. $C_{\bullet,i}$ is a member of $\text{TOP}(C_{i[\,]}, M_i)$). In short, $\eta(r_i, C_i, S)$ will be written as η_i. This measure will be used to order the equivalence relations $r_i, r_j \in \Psi_r$. Let us again adopt an ordinal approach to compare different relations, just as we did for selection of better classes. For any two relations r_i and r_j, the corresponding η_i and η_j can be treated as random variables. In the class space the random variable was defined to be the objective function value of the samples. Unlike that, here in the relation space the random variable is the measure η, which is defined over a collection of classes and a sample set. Since, for a given r_i, the computation of η_i depends on a tuple from $(2^C \times 2^X)$, a collection of n_r such tuples will generate a distribution of different values of η_i. Figure 5 shows the cdf of two competing relations r_i and r_j. Let us say that r_i satisfies the delineation constraint and r_j does not.

If we compare these two relations on the basis of some τ_r-th order statistic, the success probability is computed in exactly the same way that we just did for class comparisons. If α_r be the corresponding percentile,

$$Pr(\hat{r}_{[\tau_r],j} \leq_{\alpha_r} \hat{r}_{[\tau_r],i}) \geq 1 - 2^{n_r H(\alpha_r)}(\alpha_r - d_r')^{\alpha_r n_r} \tag{7}$$

where

$$d_r' = \min\{F(\eta_{[\tau_r],j}) - F(\eta_{[\tau_r],i}) | \forall j, \forall i\}$$

where F is the cdf of the relation comparison statistic of relation r_i. d_r' is essentially similar to d'', except that this is for relation comparison instead of the previous case of class comparison. In the most general case, a relation needs to be chosen out of all the possible relations in Ψ_r. However, in reality, it may be true that only a subset of Ψ_r is chosen at a time. In the following analyses we consider the general case, in which all relations in Ψ_r are under consideration. Let us assume that among these Ψ_r relations, the set $\Psi_g \subseteq \Psi_r$ contains all the relations that properly delineate the search space. If relation $r_i \in \Psi_g$, then the probability that r_i will be correctly identified is

$$Pr(CRS \mid r_i \in \Psi_g) \geq$$
$$[1 - 2^{n_r H(\alpha_r)}(\alpha_r - d'_r)^{\alpha_r n_r}]^{\|\Psi_r\| - \|\Psi_s\|}.$$

This is the success probability in choosing one good relation. If we need $S_r \subseteq \Psi_r$ relations to solve a problem, we can bound the overall success probability in the relation space as follows (Kargupta, 1995):

$$n_r > \frac{\log(1 - q_r^{1/(\|S_r\|(\|\Psi_r\| - \|\Psi_s\|))})}{-d_r^\bullet} \tag{8}$$

Inequality 8 can be further rearranged. Define the *delineation-ratio*,

$$\Omega = \frac{\|\Psi_g\|}{\|\Psi_r\|} \tag{9}$$

When this ratio is high, searching for appropriate relations is easier, since most of the members of the relation space are appropriate for properly classifying the search space. Using definition 9 and Inequality 8 we can write

$$n_r > \frac{\log(1 - q_r^{1/(\|S_r\| \, \|\Psi_r\|(1 - \Omega))})}{-d_r^\bullet}. \tag{10}$$

This bounds the overall computational complexity in the relation space. Inequality 10 can be further simplified using the approximation $\log(1 - x) \approx -x$ for $x << 1$,

$$n_r > \frac{q_r^{1/(\|S_r\| \, \|\Psi_r\|(1 - \Omega))}}{d_r^\bullet}. \tag{11}$$

This clearly shows that n_r increases as q_r increases and that n_r increases when $d_r^\bullet$ is reduced. Since $q_r \leq 1$, n_r decreases as Ω increases. As the number of relations needed to solve the problem, $\|S_r\|$, increases, n_r also increases. The collection of relations Ψ_r defines the complete search space for relations. The larger the number of relations in Ψ_r, the more computation is required for searching for appropriate relations.

The decision making in the relation and class spaces are combined in the following section.

5.3 Overall selection success

Let us now combine the search for better relation and better classes together and compute the overall success probability. Define

$$d' = \min\{F(\Phi_{[r],\bullet,i}) - F(\Phi_{[r],j,i})|\forall j, \forall i\}.$$

d' is basically the minimum possible value of d over all classes (index j) which are compared with class containing the optimal solution and all relations (index i) in S_r. Now let us consider the overall class selection success probability given by equation 3. Note that the relation $\leq_\alpha$ imposes a total order onto C_i. Define, $N_{\max}$ as the maximum possible value of N_i over all relations in S_r; Let $M_{\min}$ and q_r be the minimum value of memory size M_i and bound on success probability in choosing a relation respectively over all the relations in S_r. In formal notation,

$$N_{\max} = \max\{N_i | \forall r_i \in S_r\}$$
$$M_{\min} = \min\{M_i | \forall r_i \in S_r\}$$

If d^* is a constant such that $d' \geq d^*$, just like the previously defined d_r^*, then the overall success probability can be bounded as follows (Kargupta, 1995):

$$[(1 - 2^{nH(\alpha)}(\alpha - d^*)^{\alpha n})^{(N_{\max} - M_{\min})}]^{\|S_r\|} q_r \geq q$$

$$n > \frac{\log\left(1 - \left(\frac{q}{q_r}\right)^{\frac{1}{\|S_r\|(N_{\max} - M_{\min})}}\right)}{\alpha \log(\alpha - d^*)} \tag{12}$$

The denominator of Inequality 12 can be simplified to,

$$n > \frac{\log\left(1 - \left(\frac{q}{q_r}\right)^{\frac{1}{\|S_r\|(N_{\max} - M_{\min})}}\right)}{-d^*}. \tag{13}$$

This inequality bounds the number of samples needed from each class to achieve an overall success probability of q in the combined relation and class spaces; q_r gives the given level of success probability in choosing $\|S_r\|$ relations correctly. The cost of increasing the bound q_r can be realized using inequality 10.

5.4 Sample complexity

Evaluation of classes and relations require taking samples from the search space. The *sample complexity* of a BBO algorithm is the function $SC : \Re \times \Re \times \Re \times N \times N \times N \to N$ such that $SC(q, q_r, d^*, N_{\max}, \|S_r\|, M_{\min}$ is the maximum number of samples taken from the search space before producing a solution quality d^* with overall success probability of q and a success probability in the relation space of q_r. The maximum is taken over all execution of the algorithm on inputs $q, q_r, d^*, N_{\max}, \|S_r\|, M_{\min}$.

The closed-form bounds on the overall success probability derived in the previous section can be directly used to bound the overall sample complexity,

$$SC \leq \frac{N_{\max}\|S_r\| \log\left(1 - \left(\frac{q}{q_r}\right)^{\frac{1}{\|S_r\|(N_{\max} - M_{\min})}}\right)}{-d^*}. \tag{14}$$

This inequality gives the overall sample complexity when the probability to find the globally optimal solution is at least q. This expression can be further simplified using reasonable approximations to clearly explain its physical significance. Since $\left(\frac{q}{q_r}\right)^{\frac{1}{\|S_r\|(N_{\max} - M_{\min})}} \leq 1$ and $\log(1 - x) \approx -x$ for $x << 1$, we can approximate inequality 14 as follows:

$$SC \leq \frac{N_{\max}\|S_r\|}{d^*} \left(\frac{q}{q_r}\right)^{\frac{1}{\|S_r\|(N_{\max} - M_{\min})}}. \tag{15}$$

Inequality 15 presents a clear picture of the contributions of different parameters of the SEARCH framework into the sample complexity. Recall that q is the bound on the overall success probability in the relation and class spaces combined. Clearly, sample complexity SC grows polynomially with q. On the other hand, q_r is the minimum bound in the success probability in choosing all $\|S_r\|$ relations correctly. The cost of demanding higher success probability in the relation space shows up in inequality 10. However, as we increase our success probability in the relation space, the overall success probability in the combined relation and class spaces increases. The sample complexity should therefore decrease as success probability in the relation space increases. Inequality 15 clearly shows that SC decrease with increase in q_r. Note that the ratio $\left(\frac{q}{q_r}\right)^{\frac{1}{\|S_r\|(N_{\max}-M_{\min})}}$ approaches 1 in the limit as $\|S_r\|(N_{\max}-M_{\min})$ approaches infinity. Therefore, SC grows at most linearly with the maximum index value $N_{\max}$ and the cardinality of the set S_r. Recall that d^* defines the desired region of indifference; in other words, it defines a region in terms of percentile within which any solution will be acceptable. The sample complexity decreases as the d^* increases.

This bound on sample complexity establishes an insight introduced earlier in this section. In the beginning of Section 3, we argued that BBO can perform no better than random enumeration unless we try to exploit the relations among the members of the search space. Now that we have a closed-form bound on sample complexity, let us investigate the case when no relations are assumed among the members. Saying no relations are assumed essentially means that there exists only one relation in Ψ_r that basically divides the complete search space into a set of singleton classes. For our 4-bit problem representation, this could be the relation $ffff$. This relation divides the search space into 16 singleton classes, which is essentially the complete search space. From the definition of global optima, we know that such a relation always properly delineates the search space. Therefore, $S_r = 1$ and $q_r = 1$. The index of this relation is same as the cardinality of the search space. So, $N_{\max} = \|\mathcal{X}\|$, where $\|\mathcal{X}\|$ denotes the size of the search space $\mathcal{X}$. Substituting these in Inequality 15 we get

$$SC \leq \frac{\|\mathcal{X}\| q^{\frac{1}{\|\mathcal{X}\|-M_{\min}}}}{d^*}. \tag{16}$$

This inequality clearly tells us that the overall sample complexity becomes the size of the search space when we completely neglect all relations that put at least two members together in a class. The only advantage that we get comes from our relaxation in the desired solution quality (d^*) and the overall success probability (q). This confirms that although SEARCH provides one particular perspective of BBO, the importance on relations is fundamental, and it should be emphasized in all possible models of BBO that aspire to guide designing BBO algorithms that perform better than random enumerative search. No BBO algorithm can transcend the limit of random enumerative search without inducing relations among the members.

The following section defines problem difficulty in SEARCH.

6 Problem Difficulty

SEARCH presents an alternate perspective of problem difficulty in optimization. In this section we identify the main dimensions of problem difficulty in SEARCH and precisely define a characterization of difficult problems in SEARCH.

The expression for the sample complexity developed in the previous section immediately leads to identifying different facets of problem difficulty in SEARCH. As we saw from Inequality 14 the sample complexity grows linearly with the size of the set of relations considered to solve the problem, S_r. Often this size depends on the "size" of the problem; the word "size" defines a parameter ℓ that bounds the search domain. In a sequence representation with constant alphabet size, the length of the sequences needed to represent the search space may be an example of such a size parameter. This finally sets the stage for introducing problem difficulty in SEARCH.

Definition 2 (Problem difficulty in SEARCH) *Given an optimization function* Φ : $X \to \Re$ *and a set of relations* Ψ_r, *we call a problem difficult for an algorithm if the total number of samples needed to find the globally optimal solution grows exponentially with* ℓ, q, q_r, $1/d^*$, *and* $1/d_r^*$.

The size of the problem is represented by ℓ; q denotes the bound in the overall decision success probability in choosing the right classes; $1/d^*$ defines the quality of the desired solution.Both q and $1/d^*$ together can be viewed as representing the overall accuracy and the quality of the solution found; q_r is the bound in success probability in choosing the right relations, and $1/d_r^*$ represents the desired quality of the relations.

The above definition of problem difficulty in SEARCH can be interpreted as:

1. growth of the search space along problem dimension;

2. inadequate source of relations and decision making in relation space;

3. inaccurate decision making in choosing classes;

4. quality of the desired solution and relations.

This gives a general description of the SEARCH perspective of problem difficulty. The following section brings us closer to the ground by specializing the framework for sequence representation. We identify a class of problems in sequence representation that can be solved in polynomial sample complexity in SEARCH.

7 Sequence representation and the class of order-k delineable problems

Sequence representation is used in many evolutionary optimization algorithms. We therefore choose this for exploring the class of problems that can be efficiently solved.

A sequence representation can be defined as $I : X \to \Lambda^\ell$, where Λ is the alphabet set. This sequence representation induces a set of equivalence relations, $\Psi_r = \{f, \#\}^\ell$, where f indicates values that must match for equivalence and $\#$ is a wild character that matches any value. The cardinality of the set of all such equivalence relations $\|\Psi_r\| = 2^\ell$.

Definition 3 (Order k delineable problems) *Let us define a subset of* Ψ_r *containing every order-k relation as follows:* $\Psi_{\{o(r)\leq k\}} = \{r_i : o(r_i) \leq k \ \& \ r_i \in \Psi_r\}$, *where* $o(r)$

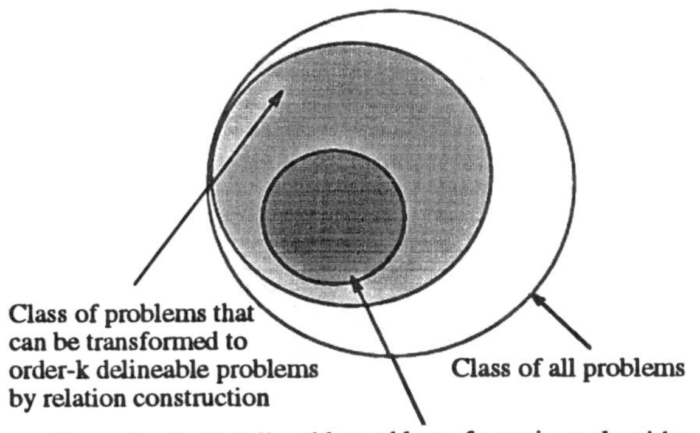

Figure 6: Optimization problems from the delineability perspective.

is the order of relation r. For a given class comparison statistic $\leq_{T_i}$, a problem is order-k delineable if there exists a subset $\Psi' \subseteq \Psi_{\{o(r) \leq k\}}$ and at least one member of Ψ' has an order equal to k, such that its every member r_i satisfies the delineation constraint with memory size M_i and the size of the intersection set,

$$\mathcal{G} = \bigcup_{a_1, a_2, \cdots a_k} \bigcap C_{[a_1], i} C_{[a_2], i} \cdots C_{[a_k], i},$$

is bounded by a polynomial of ℓ, $p(\ell)$. The indices $a_1, a_2, \ldots a_k$ can take any value in between 1 and M_i.

It has been shown elsewhere (Kargupta, 1995) that this class of problems can be solved in sample complexity polynomial in q, q_r, $1/d^*$, $1/d_r^*$, and the problem size ℓ. To achieve an overall success probability of q, the required sample complexity is,

$$SC \leq \|\Lambda\|^k k \frac{\log\left(1 - \left(\frac{q}{q_r}\right)^{\frac{1}{(\ell-k+1)(\|\Lambda\|^k - M_{min})}}\right)}{-d^*} + \rho(\ell). \tag{17}$$

When $q/q_r \ll 1$, this can be approximated as,

$$SC \leq \|\Lambda\|^k k \frac{\left(\frac{q}{q_r}\right)^{\frac{1}{(\ell-k+1)(\|\Lambda\|^k - M_{min})}}}{d^*} + \rho(\ell)$$

This basically says that the problems that can be solved using a polynomially bounded number of relations can be efficiently solved in SEARCH. Note that this class of problems is fundamentally defined in terms of relation space. Note that, a problem may be order-k-delineable in one relation space but fail to be for another relation space. Therefore when the relation space is already chosen by fixing the sequence representation, an optimization problem can be solved efficiently if it is order-k delineable in that relation space.

The notion of order-k delineability presents a picture of the general class of optimization problems from the perspective of an algorithm. In SEARCH, defining an optimization algorithm requires specifying the relation space, class comparison statistic, and the constant M

that defines how many "top" classes will be picked up. Therefore, by definition an algorithm in SEARCH specifies the class of order-k delineable problems. For a chosen class comparison statistic and M, the relation space restricts the class of order-k delineable problems for an algorithm. Changing the relation space by constructing new relations may convert a non-order-k delineable problem to an order-k delineable one. For some problems finding such transformation by constructing new relations may be possible in sample complexity, polynomial in problem size, reliability, and accuracy of the solution. Clearly, there may exist a class of non-order-k delineable problems, that can be transformed to order-k delineable problems in polynomial sample complexity. Figure 6 shows a schematic description of this classification of optimization problems.

It is important to note that, membership of a problem in the class of order-k delineable problems does not necessarily guarantee that the algorithm will solve that problem. It only says that the problem is " efficiently solvable" in the chosen relation space, class comparison statistic, and M. The algorithm needs to perform adequate sampling and make decisions with high confidence in the relation and class spaces in order to find the desired quality solution. Therefore, the first step of an algorithm should be to make sure it can solve its own order-k delineable class of problems. That will define the first milestone. The next step should be to introduce mechanism for new relation construction and investigate what kind of problems can be dynamically transformed to order-k delineable problems efficiently. Unfortunately, there hardly exists any algorithm that can adequately guarantee the capability of solving even its order-k delineable problems. More work is needed to develop optimization algorithms that follow the systematic decomposition of SEARCH.

The following section presents a comparative discussion between SEARCH and computational learning theory.

8 SEARCH and PAC Learning

Inducing relations should be an essential aspect of BBO. Although, induction is an essential aspect of BBO in SEARCH, BBO is not same as inductive learning. They differ in their respective scope. The goal of inductive learning is to find a set of plausibly correct hypothesis or relations. On the other hand BBO requires decision making in the class space and finally find a set of singleton classes, containing optimal or near-optimal solutions. The Probably Approximately Correct (PAC) learning theory (Haussler, 1989; Natarajan, 1991; Valiant, 1984) provides a framework to quantify the computation in inductive learning in a distribution-free, probabilistic, and approximate sense. SEARCH and PAC framework share some common characteristics, since they realize the need for detecting appropriate relations or hypotheses. However, they also differ in many fundamental aspects. The objective of this section is to point out the main similarities and differences between these two frameworks.

First, we present a brief review of some of the elementary concepts of PAC framework. Next, we discuss the similarities and the dissimilarities between SEARCH and PAC.

The PAC framework presents a computational theoretic perspective of inductive learning. This framework views inductive learning as a probabilistic process of learning hypothesis which sometimes may give incorrect results. This framework has now led to a separate field in itself with a large volume of literature, no effort will be made to cover all the results. A review of the recent progress in this area can be found elsewhere (Natarajan, 1991). In this section, we shall restrict ourself to cover some of the elementary results reported in the PAC literature which will suffice our main purpose—comparing PAC with SEARCH.

Theorem 1 (Blumer, Ehrenfeucht, Haussler, and Warmuth (1987)) : *Let H be a set of hypotheses over a universe U and let S be a set of m training examples drawn independently according to $P(u)$, $\epsilon, \delta > 0$. Then if $\hat{F} \in H$ is consistent with all training examples in S and*

$$m \geq \frac{1}{\epsilon} \left(\log \frac{1}{\delta} + \log \|H\| \right), \tag{18}$$

then the probability that $\hat{F}$ has error greater than ϵ is less than δ.

This inequality bounds the sample complexity in PAC. For a given hypothesis space H, acceptable error level ϵ, and failure probability δ, this inequality tells us the minimum number of samples needed to learn a hypothesis with error less than ϵ.

When we compare Inequalities 18 and 14, several observations can be made. First of all, note that both of these frameworks are probabilistic and approximate in nature. However, there are some fundamental differences between how these relaxations are introduced. The δ failure probability of PAC gives the overall bound on the chance to succeed. On the other hand, the success probability in SEARCH in introduced at the level of individual relation and class evaluation processes. Although both q and q_r are defined for bounding the overall success probabilities, the fundamental relaxations originate from the relaxed sampling during the relation evaluation process and the class comparison process.

The ϵ parameter of PAC presents a cardinal relaxation of the solution quality. In other words this relaxation parameter depends on the absolute values of the accuracy of the learned hypothesis. On the other hand, in the SEARCH framework, the relaxation is ordinal in nature, meaning the quality of the solution is determined by its ranking among all the members of the search space.

Both SEARCH and PAC adopt a distribution-free approach for computing the sample complexity. Another interesting similarity between these two can be observed by noting the role of Vapnik-Chervonenkis (VC) dimension in PAC framework. It has been shown elsewhere (Blumer, Haussler, & Warmuth, 1990) that a space of hypotheses H is PAC learnable if and only if it has a finite VC dimension. VC dimension is used as a measure to quantify the learnability of a hypothesis space. The SEARCH framework also has a counterpart of this measure—the delineation constraint. SEARCH requires a set of relations that can be defined over the search space, which must satisfy this constraint for a given class comparison statistic and memory size. If the number of relations satisfying this delineation requirement is too small compared to what is needed to the solve the BBO, success is very unlikely. The delineation-ratio provides a measure for that. When representation is used as the major source of relation, this requirement provides one way to quantify what it means to be an appropriate representation for BBO.

9   SEARCH And Simulated Annealing

Like many other algorithms, simulated annealing (SA) algorithm does not explicitly consider the relations. Therefore, the projection of SA into the SEARCH framework depends on our perspective toward SA as well. Since relations can be defined in many ways, when

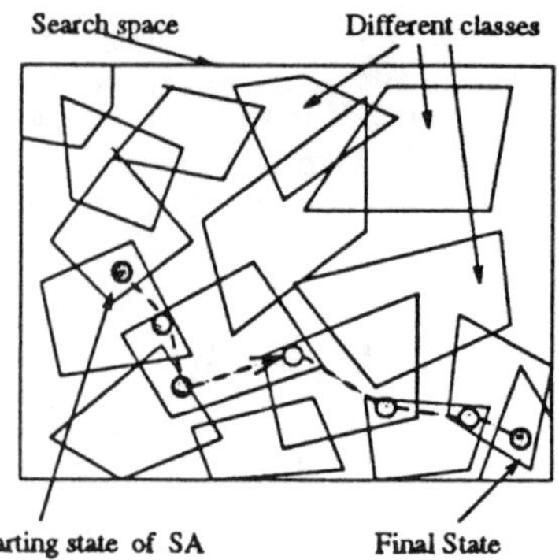

Figure 7: The SEARCH perspective of SA.

the relation space is not explicitly specified, identifying it leaves room for speculation. The original version of SA does not emphasize representation. Moreover, the random neighborhood generation operator does not pay enough consideration to the relations and classes defined by the chosen representation.

In this section, we therefore choose to view SA as a processor of relations and classes defined by the neighborhood generation operator. The following part of this section briefly discusses different counterparts of SEARCH in the SA.

- **Relation space:** A state x_i and the neighborhood generation operator ($\mathcal{P}$) are the two ingredients of the relations processed by the SA. For a given state x_i, the neighborhood generation operator defines a set of states that can be reached in certain number of steps (s) from x_i. This defines a relation among a certain subset of the search space. Therefore, a relation r_i in SA can be specified by the triple $(x_i, \mathcal{P}, s)$.

- **Class space:** The relation $(x_i, \mathcal{P}, s)$ divides the search space into two classes—(1) the set of states that can be reached from x by applying $\mathcal{P}$ for s number of times and (2) the rest of the search space. This defines the class space for a given relation. Let us denote the first class by $C_{1,i}$ and the second by $C_{2,i}$.

- **Sample space:** The SA processes only one sample at a time. The sample represents the state of the algorithm.

Searching for the optimal solution in SEARCH also requires different comparison statistics and resolution for combining the features of different classes from different relations. The following discussion points out their counterpart in SA.

- **Relation and class comparison statistics:** Since SA does not explicitly defines the relations and classes, only one statistic, defined by the *Metropolis criterion*, is used for serving both purposes. This comparison statistic varies as the *temperature* changes. The search for relation in SA can be viewed as the search for optimal cooling schedule. SA leaves this part to the user as a design issue. As we know, successful execution of

SA for different problems tunings for finding the optimal schedule, which reminds us the need for relation search in BBO.

- **Resolution:** Consider the two relations $(x_1, \mathcal{P}, s)$ and $(x_2, \mathcal{P}, s)$, where x_1 and x_2 are two arbitrary states from the search space. Let us denote the set of states that can be reached from x_1 and x_2 by applying $\mathcal{P}$ for s times by $C_{1,1}$ and $C_{1,2}$, respectively. Let x_i be the current state of SA and x_{i+1} be the next state. Now if x_1 and x_2 are such that the $x_i \in C_{1,1}$ and $x_{i+1} \in C_{1,2}$, then the next state, x_{i+1}, is basically a sample from the intersection set of the two classes $C_{1,1}$ and $C_{1,2}$. Generating samples from the intersection set of classes is essentially what resolution does.

The above discussion presents a perspective of SA in the light of SEARCH. Figure 7 pictorially depicts this perspective of SA. This figure schematically shows the trajectory of SA within the overlapping classes. As we mentioned earlier, this section presents only one possible way to define classes and relations in SA. Since SA does not explicitly define them, different possibilities may be speculated. The following section presents some observations about genetic algorithms in the light of SEARCH.

10 Genetic Algorithms: Some Observations

The relation between SEARCH and genetic algorithms should be quite obvious to readers, familiar with the GA literature. Notion of schemata, partitions ties quite well with the respective counterparts, classes and relations in SEARCH. Although, SEARCH is not restricted to sequence space and equivalence relations, the examples used in this paper are often borrowed from the traditional GA notion of schemata and partitions. In this section we offer some observations about GAs, that are not necessarily quite obvious.

10.1 Implicit definition of relation, class and sample spaces

In simple GA (SGA) the relation, class, and the sample spaces are defined together in a single population. As we noted earlier during the development of SEARCH, relation and class spaces require distinct decision makings and interference among them may cause decision error. The SGA uses a single selection operator for making decisions in each of these spaces. As a result decision making is very noisy in SGA. This is one among the major bottlenecks of the SGA.

10.2 Implicit parallelism

Parallel evaluation of multiple equivalence classes or schemata using the information provided by a single sample is called *implicit parallelism* (Holland, 1975). Implicit parallelism has always been a controversial issue in the GA literature. SEARCH offers some insight using its decomposition of BBO in terms of relation, class, and sample spaces.

Let us denote the set of relations Ψ_r, when ordered on the basis of the sequence, they are considered by the algorithm by $\gamma(\Psi_r)$; also define $\gamma(\Psi_r)_{<_o}$ as the set Ψ_r partially ordered based on the order of the relations, $o(r)$. Note that, $r_i <_o r_j$ if and only if $o(r_i) < o(r_j)$. The structure of $\gamma(\Psi_r)$, can be exploited to make the relation evaluation process efficient. In this section we show that when the poset $\gamma(\Psi_r)_{<_o}$ is not linearly ordered, relations can be evaluated in parallel at no additional sample evaluation. This observation offers a quantitative perspective toward the benefits of the so called *implicit parallelism*.

The perspective of the blackbox search as an exploration through $\gamma(\Psi_r)_{<_\bullet}$ opens up this interesting possibility. Parallel exploration along different branches in $\gamma(\Psi_r)_{<_\bullet}$ can be done at no additional cost compared to that along a single branch. *Such parallel evaluation is possible as long as $\gamma(\Psi_r)_{<_\bullet}$ is not a totally ordered set.* When $\gamma(\Psi_r)_{<_\bullet}$ is partially ordered, there will be relations of the same order. Therefore, all these relations of the same order can be evaluated using the same set of samples.

For example, the evaluation of $\#\#\#f, \#\#ff$ can be performed at no additional computational cost in terms of function evaluations when the relations $f\#\#\#, ff\#\#$ are already evaluated. Little attention will make it obvious. Both $f\#\#\#$ and $\#\#\#f$ divide the complete search space into two different ways. Similarly, the relation $ff\#\#$ divides the same search space in a different way than the one by $\#\#ff$ does. Clearly, the same set of samples used to evaluate classes $1\#\#\#$ and $0\#\#\#$ can be used for evaluating classes $\#\#\#1$ and $\#\#\#0$. No additional function evaluation is needed for a constant confidence requirement; the samples are just needed to be differently partitioned. In general, the sample set needed to evaluate a particular relation r_i of order o_i can be used for all other relations of the same order. This computational leverage can make an algorithm very efficient in solving the class of order k bounded, delineable problems. As stated earlier, these problems can be solved by evaluating a subset of all order k relations, whose intersection set is a singleton set. Since the globally optimal solution can be found by simply taking an intersection among the top ranked classes of this subset of all order k relations, the overall computational cost remains polynomial in the problem dimension and the success probabilities.

At this point one must take a moment to put this argument into proper perspective. Our definition of computational cost has been solely focused on the number of function evaluations, i.e., the number of distinct samples taken from the search space. According to this definition, parallel evaluations of several equivalence relations do not incur any additional cost. However, consideration of every different relation required partitioning the same set of samples in a different way, followed by the computation of the class comparison statistic. Although the sample complexity remains the same, the overall time complexity may increase.

Unfortunately, GAs pay a high price for implicit parallelism. The credit assignment in GA is at the string level. In other words, GAs do not have any mechanism to explicitly evaluate a class. GAs can only evaluate a set of classes at a time. This makes detecting a particular good class very difficult when it is accompanied by some instances of bad classes An example may make things more clear. Consider a three bit representation. Let us say the best solution is the string 111; the class $1\#\#$ is a good class whereas $\#0\#$ and $\#\#0$ are bad classes. Let us say the string 100 has a low objective function value. Since GAs do not have an explicit mechanism for evaluating all the order one equivalence classes $1\#\#$, $\#0\#$ and $\#\#0$, it may conclude that all three classes are bad. Evaluating the string 100 does not tell a GA anything about the specific classes. All it says that the intersection of the classes $1\#\#$, $\#0\#$ and $\#\#0$ is not a good class. Detection of good classes is therefore very noisy and often quite difficult to do correctly. The difficulty due to such noisy evaluation of classes is sometimes called *hitchhiking* (Forrest & Mitchell, 1993). Nevertheless, the benefits of implicit parallelism can be achieved at a much cheaper price if we pay careful attention to the distinct relation and class spaces.

10.3 Linkage: Search for relations

As we saw earlier, search for proper relations that satisfy the delineation requirement plays
an important role in the blackbox search.

The simple GA considers only a small fraction of equivalence relations defined by the representation. A simple GA with one-point crossover (De Jong, 1975) favors those relations in
which positions in sequence space defining equivalence are closer to each other and neglects
those relations that contain equivalence defining positions far apart. One-point crossover
also fails to generate samples for the intersection set of two equivalence classes in which
fixed bits are widely separated. For example, in a 20-bit problem, single-point crossover
is very unlikely to generate a sample from the intersection set of $1\#\#\cdots\#$ (first bit is
fixed) and $\#\cdots\#1$ (last bit is fixed). In biological jargon, this is called the *linkage problem*.
Unfortunately, this is a major bottleneck of SGA. Although Holland (1975) realized the
importance of solving this problem and suggested use of the *inversion* operator (Holland,
1975), it has been shown elsewhere (Goldberg & Lingle, 1985) that inversion is very slow
and unlikely to solve this problem efficiently. One-point crossover is not the only type to
suffer from this problem. Uniform crossover is another kind of crossover (Syswerda, 1989)
often used in the simple GA. In uniform crossover, the exchange of bit values among the
two parent strings takes place based on a randomly generated binary mask string. If the
value of this mask string at a particular locus is 1, the corresponding bits in the parent
strings get exchanged; otherwise they do not. Unlike one-point crossover, uniform crossover
does not have any preference bias toward the closely spaced partitions. Since the relation
space and the sample space are combined, random perturbation of the sample strings also
result in disrupting proper evaluations of the relations. Uniform crossover should also fail
to accomplish proper search in the relation space. In fact, this is exactly what Thierens
and Goldberg (1993) reported. Their analysis and experimental results showed that the
sample complexity grows exponentially with the problem size for solving bounded deceptive
problems (Thierens & Goldberg, 1993) using a simple GA with uniform crossover. This
discussion points out that the search in the relation space is very poor in the case of a simple GA with either one-point or uniform crossover. Unless GAs do a better job in linkage
learning, they will continue to search poorly in the relation space. It is important to note
that unlike many evolutionary algorithms, messy GAs (Deb, 1991; Goldberg, Korb, & Deb,
1989; Goldberg, Deb, Kargupta, & Harik, 1993; Kargupta, 1995) took the linkage learning
problem quite seriously and made important progress in the quest for BBO algorithms that
properly search for relations.

10.4 A note on biology

Adequate processing of relations and making good statistical decisions in the relation space
require storing information about good relations. If this is true, and if we believe natural
evolution to be a master piece of BBO algorithm, then there must be a place in the evolutionary information storage for keeping information about the good relations. This section
throws some observations in this area that may catch the imagination of the reader.

DNA is the carrier of genetic information in evolution. DNA is a sequence of nucleotide
bases. Functionally, DNA contains three kinds of base sequences:

1. genes, i.e. bases producing a certain protein;

2. functionally inactive bases;

3. control genes

Expression of genetic information takes place in every living cell during the process of *transcription* (construction of mRNA from DNA) and subsequent *translation* (production of protein from mRNA). Different control proteins produced by the control genes determine which set of bases gets transcribed resulting in the production of a particular protein. Although the same DNA is present in every cell of a living organism, different sets of genes get transcribed in different cells and this process is explicitly controlled by the control genes.

Traditionally genetic algorithms thrive on search operators like crossover. Events such as crossover are also strongly controlled by the proteins produced by the control genes. Recombination *nodules* are now known to control the crossover event site. These nodules are very large protein containing assemblies, which are again generated from the genes defined in the DNA.

These observations basically show that nature has a separate region in the DNA for storing information about better relations (among genes) and this information is primarily responsible for guiding the future directions of search. This clearly matches with the lessons of SEARCH. We believe that the field of evolutionary computation needs more emphasis on the intra-cellular flow of genetic information. Interested reader may find a detailed description of the biological implications of SEARCH elsewhere (Kargupta, 1996).

The following section concludes this paper.

11   Conclusions

This work made an attempt to take a small step toward systematic design of BBO algorithms. Some of main conclusions of this work are listed in the following:

1. A BBO algorithm should systematically quantify its bias. SEARCH offers that in terms of relation space and suggests the need for detecting appropriate relations.

2. A BBO algorithm can only solve those problems that can be solved considering those relations, with their order bounded by a constant. We choose to call it the class of order-k delineable problems.

3. Representation construction is a very popular topic these days. Unfortunately, most of the work on representation construction in BBO give little clue about the desired properties of the constructed representation. We need to quantify why a given representation is bad and what would make the constructed representation better. SEARCH offers one possible approach. SEARCH suggests that the goal of representation construction should be to convert a non-order-k delineable problem to an order-k delineable problem.

4. SEARCH suggests that the evolutionary computing community may be overlooking an important aspect of natural evolution—gene expression—the intra-cellular flow of information in evolution. The presence of operons, introns, and exons highly suggest the

clustering of functionally related genes. It is now widely acknowledged that the choice of crossover event site is not at all random; rather it is a precisely controlled event, catalyzed by different proteins. We suspect that nature pays much more careful attention to the processing of relations and classes than what we do today in evolutionary search algorithms.

Most of the work presented in this paper mainly addressed the intellectual desire for systematic design of better algorithms. However, the objective of this work is to reach out our everyday practice of BBO. Some progress have been made.

Patil (1996) incorporated the SEARCH framework in interval analysis and proposed an interval optimization algorithm. This work converted the notion of delineability using the interval algebra and implemented a check for bounded delineability for the given problem. Reader may want to note that interval optimization is not a BBO. It uses the interval representation of the analytic expression of the objective function.

The field of constrained optimization opens up a new door. SEARCH considers unconstrained optimization problem. Hanagandi and Kargupta (1996) extended SEARCH to handle constrained optimization problem. This work further decomposes the relation space in terms of relations for detecting optimal classes and relations for detecting feasible classes.

By definition, determining the delineability of a relation requires knowledge about the optimal solution. Unfortunately, we do not know that a priori. Even if we have the optimal solution, we may not be able to sure about its global optimality. A practical implementation of the lessons of SEARCH may originate from a different direction. Kargupta (1996) proposed the so called *gene expression messy GA* (GEMGA) that detects the locally optimal classes and uses relations to define plausibly better paths toward better solutions. This work offers a very distributed implementation of SEARCH, unlike the centralized framework developed here. Currently, the research on GEMGA is focusing on constructing order-k delineable problems from non-order-k delineable problems. Unlike traditional evolutionary algorithms, GEMGA uses a separate relation space (similar to the control genes), that stores the linkage information and controls the crossover and selection process.

Acknowledgment

This work was supported by AFSOR Grant F49620-94-1-0103 and the Illinois genetic Algorithm Laboratory. The first author also acknowledges the support from US. Department of Energy and the helpful comments from Jeffrey Horn and Georges Harik. Authors would also like to thank the reviewers.

References

Archetti, F., & Schoen, F. (1984). A survey on the global optimization problem: General theory and computational approaches. *Annals of Operations Research*, *1*(1), 87–110.

Betrò, B. (1983). A bayesian nonparametric approach to global optimization. In Stähly, P. (Ed.), *Methods of Operations Research* (pp. 45–47). Atenäum Verlag.

Blumer, A., Ehrenfeucht, A., Haussler, D., & Warmuth, M. K. (1987). Occam's razor. *Information Processing Letter*, *24*, 377–380.

Blumer, A., Haussler, D., & Warmuth, M. K. (1990). Learnability and the vapnik-chervonenkis dimension. *Journal of the Association for Computing Machinery*, *36*(4), 929–965.

Dantzig, G. B. (1963). *Linear programming and extensions.* New Jersey: Princeton University Press.

David, H. A. (1981). *Order statistics.* New York: John Wiley & Sons, Inc.

Davis, L. (Ed.) (1987). *Genetic algorithms and simulated annealing.* Los Altos, CA: Morgan Kaufmann.

De Jong, K. A. (1975). An analysis of the behavior of a class of genetic adaptive systems. *Dissertation Abstracts International*, *36*(10), 5140B. (University Microfilms No. 76-9381).

Deb, K. (1991). *Binary and floating-point function optimization using messy genetic algorithms* (IlliGAL Report No. 91004). Urbana: University of Illinois at Urbana-Champaign, Illinois Genetic Algorithms Laboratory.

Dixon, L. C. W., & Szegö, G. P. (1978). The global optimization problem: an introduction. In Dixon, L. C. W., & Szegö, G. P. (Eds.), *Towards global optimization 2* (pp. 1–15). Amsterdam: North-Holland.

Dreyfus, S. E., & Law, A. M. (1977). *The art and theory of dynamic programming.* New York: Academic Press.

Dueck, G., & Scheuer, T. (1988). *Threshold accepting–a general purpose optimization algorithm appearing superior to simulated annealing* (Technical Report No. 88.10.011). IBM Heidelberg Sci. Center.

Ferreira, A. G., & Žerovnik, J. (1993, 10/11). Bounding the probability of success of stochastic methods for global optimization. *Computers, Mathematics, Applications*, *25*, 1–8.

Fogel, L. J., Owens, A. J., & Walsh, M. J. (1966). *Artificial intelligence through simulated evolution.* New York: John Wiley.

Forrest, S. (Ed.) (1993). *Proceedings of the Fifth International Conference on Genetic Algorithms.* San Mateo, CA: Morgan Kaufmann.

Forrest, S., & Mitchell, M. (1993). Relative building-block fitness and the building-block hypothesis. In Whitley, L. D. (Ed.), *Foundations of Genetic Algorithms* (pp. 109–126). San Mateo, CA: Morgan Kaufmann.

Gibbons, J. D., Sobel, M., & Olkin, I. (1977). *Selecting and ordering populations: A new statistical methodology.* New York: John Wiley & Sons, Inc.

Goldberg, D. E. (1989). *Genetic algorithms in search, optimization, and machine learning.* New York: Addison-Wesley.

Goldberg, D. E. (1990). A note on Boltzmann tournament selection for genetic algorithms and population-oriented simulated annealing. *Complex Systems*, *4*(4), 445–460. (Also TCGA Report No. 90003).

Goldberg, D. E., Deb, K., Kargupta, H., & Harik, G. (1993). Rapid, accurate optimizaiton of difficult problems using fast messy genetic algorithms. See Forrest (1993), pp. 56–64.

Goldberg, D. E., Korb, B., & Deb, K. (1989). Messy genetic algorithms: Motivation, analysis, and first results. *Complex Systems*, *3*(5), 493–530. (Also TCGA Report 89003).

Goldberg, D. E., & Lingle, R. (1985). Alleles, loci, and the traveling salesman problem. In Grefenstette, J. J. (Ed.), *Proceedings of an International Conference on Genetic Algorithms and Their Applications* (pp. 154–159). Hillsdale, NJ: Lawrence Erlbaum Associates.

Gomulka, J. (1978). Deterministic vs probabilistic approaches to global optimization. In Dixon, L. C. W., & Szegö, G. P. (Eds.), *Towards global optimization* (pp. 19–29). Amsterdam: North-Holland.

Hanagandi, V., & Kargupta, H. (1996, February). *Constrained blackbox optimization: The SEARCH perspective.* To be presented in Institute for Operations Research and Management Sciences (INFORMS).

Hart, W. E. (1994). *Adaptive global optimization with local search.* Doctoral dissertation, Department of Computer Science, University of California, San Diego.

Haussler, D. (1989). Quantifying inductive bias: AI learning algorithms and Valiant's learning framework. *Artificial Intelligence, 2*(36), 177–222.

Holland, J. H. (1975). *Adaptation in natural and artificial systems.* Ann Arbor: University of Michigan Press.

Jones, D. R., & Stuckman, B. E. (1992). Genetic algorithms and the Bayesian approach to global optimization. *Proceedings of the 1992 International Fuzzy Systems and Intelligent Control Conference,* 217–235.

Jones, T. (1995). *Evolutionary algorithms, fitness landscapes and search.* Doctoral dissertation, Department of Computer Science, University of New Mexico, Albuquerque, NM.

Jones, T., & Forrest, S. (1995). Fitness distance correlation as a measure of problem difficulty for genetic algorithms. In Eshelman, L. (Ed.), *Proceedings of the Sixth International Conference on Genetic Algorithms* (pp. 184–192). San Mateo, CA: Morgan Kaufmann.

Kargupta, H. (1995, October). *SEARCH, Polynomial Complexity, and The Fast Messy Genetic Algorithm.* Doctoral dissertation, Department of Computer Science, University of Illinois at Urbana-Champaign, Urbana, IL 61801, USA. Also available as Illi-GAL Report 95008.

Kargupta, H. (1996, July). *Computational processes of evolution: The SEARCH perspective.* Presented in SIAM Annual Meeting, 1996 as the winner of the 1996 SIAM Annual Best Student Paper Prize.

Kirpatrick, S., Gelatt, C. D., & Vecchi, M. P. (1983). Optimization by simulated annealing. *Science, 220*(4598), 671–680.

Mahfoud, S. W., & Goldberg, D. E. (1992). A genetic algorithm for parallel simulated annealing. In Männer, R., & Manderick, B. (Eds.), *Parallel Problem Solving from Nature* (pp. 301–310). Amsterdam: Noth-Holland.

Michalski, R. S. (1983). Theory and methodology of inductive learning. In Michalski, R. S., Carbonell, J. G., & Mitchell, T. M. (Eds.), *Machine learning: An artificial intelligence approach* (pp. 323–348). Tioga Publishing Co.

Mitchell, T. M. (1980). *The need for biases in learning generalizations* (Rutgers Computer Science Tech. Rept. CBM-TR-117). Rutgers University.

Natarajan, B. K. (1991). *Machine learning, a theoretical approach.* San Mateo, CA: Morgan Kaufmann.

Papadimitriou, C. L., & Steiglitz, K. (1982). *Combinatorial optimization.* New Jersey: Prentice Hall.

Patil, R. (1996, October). *Verified global optimization using interval arithmatics.* Doctoral dissertation, Department of Computer Science, New Mexico State University, Las Cruces. USA.

Perttunen, C., & Stuckman, B. (1990). The rank transformation applied to a multi-univariate method of global optimization. *IEEE Transactions on System, Man, and Cybernetics, 20,* 1216–1220.

Radcliffe, N. J., & Surry, P. D. (1995). *Fundamental limitations on search algorithms.* To appear in Lecture notes of computer science.

Ratschek, H., & Voller, R. L. (1991). What can interval analysis do for global optimization? *Journal of Global Optimization, 1,* 111–130.

Rechenberg, I. (1973). Bionik, evolution und optimierung. *Naturwissenschaftliche Rundschau, 26,* 465–472.

Rinnooy Kan, A. H. G., & Timmer, G. T. (1984). Stochastic methods for global optimization. *American Journal of Mathematics and Management Sciences, 4*(1), 7–40.

Rudolph, G. (1994). Massively parallel simulated annealing and its relation to evolutionary algorithms. *Evolutionary Computation,* 361–383.

Schoen, F. (1991). Stochastic techniques for global optimization: A survey of recent advances. *Journal of Global Optimization, 1,* 207–228.

Sirag, D. J., & Weisser, D. J. (1987). Toward a unified thermodynamic genetic operator. In Grefenstette, J. J. (Ed.), *Proceedings of the Second International Conference on Genetic Algorithms* (pp. 116–122). Hillsdale, NJ: Lawrence Erlbaum Associates.

Syswerda, G. (1989). Uniform crossover in genetic algorithms. In Schaffer, J. D. (Ed.), *Proceedings of the Third International Conference on Genetic Algorithms* (pp. 2–9).

Thierens, D., & Goldberg, D. (1993). Mixing in genetic algorithms. See Forrest (1993), pp. 38–45.

Törn, A., & Žilinskas, A. (1989). *Global optimization.* Berlin: Springer-Verlag.

Valiant, L. G. (1984). A theory of the learnable. *Communications of the Association for Computing Machinery, 27*(11), 1134–1142.

Vavasis, S. A. (1991). *Nonlinear optimization: Complexity issues.* New York: Oxford University Press.

Watanabe, S. (1969). *Knowing and guessing - A formal and quantitative study.* New York: John Wiley & Sons, Inc.

Wolpert, D. H., & Macready, W. G. (1995). *No free lunch theorems for search* (Tech. Rep. No. SFI-TR-95-02-010). Santa Fe, NM: Santa Fe Institute.

A Stationary Point Convergence Theory
for Evolutionary Algorithms

William E. Hart*
Algorithms and Discrete Mathematics Department
Sandia National Laboratories
P. O. Box 5800
Albuquerque, NM 87185-1110
wehart@cs.sandia.gov

Abstract

This paper defines a class of evolutionary algorithms called evolutionary pattern search algorithms (EPSAs) and analyzes their convergence properties. This class of algorithms is closely related to evolutionary programming, evolution strategie and real-coded genetic algorithms. EPSAs are self-adapting evolutionary algorithms that modify the step size of the mutation operator in response to the success of previous optimization steps. The rule used to adapt the step size can be used to provide a stationary point convergence theory for EPSAs on any continuous function. This convergence theory is based on an extension of the convergence theory for generalized pattern search methods.

1 Introduction

This paper concerns the application of evolutionary search algorithms to solve an unconstrained minimization problem to find $x^* \in D$ such that

$$f(x^*) = \min_{x \in D} f(x),$$

where D is a compact subset of $\mathbf{R}^n$ and $f : D \to \mathbf{R}$. In particular, this paper concerns the convergence properties of a class of evolutionary algorithms (EAs) that is closely related to evolutionary programming (EP), evolutionary strategies (ES) and real-coded genetic

---

*http://www.cs.sandia.gov/~wehart/

algorithms (GAs), which use real-coded (floating-point) genes as opposed to binary-coded genes. The class of EAs that we analyze encompasses EP, ES and GAs to the extent that both mutation and crossover may be stochastically applied to generate new solutions.

In this paper we describe a convergence analysis for a class of EAs that adapt the mutation operator's step size to guarantee convergence to a stationary point of the objective function, where the gradient is zero, with probability one. Formally, the convergence theory guarantees that for a continuously differentiable function the sequence of best solutions found by these EAs, $\{x_k^*\}$, has the property that

$$\liminf_{k \to \infty} \| \nabla f(x_k^*) \| = 0,$$

where $\nabla f(x)$ is the gradient of $f(x)$ at x. This result can be extended to prove convergence on continuous nondifferentiable functions, where the limit points include points where the gradient does not exist or where the gradient is not continuous. This is a "global" convergence analysis since it guarantees convergence to a stationary point from almost any starting point.[1]

The EAs that we analyze are called evolutionary pattern search algorithms (EPSAs) because the convergence analysis for generalized pattern search methods [Torczon, 1993] is adapted to provide these convergence guarantees. Generalized pattern search methods are optimization algorithms that examine exploratory moves in search of solutions with lower functional values. In stochastic pattern search methods the exploratory moves may be stochastically selected. We generalize the convergence analysis for pattern search methods described by Torczon [Torczon, 1993] to stochastic pattern search methods. Then we demonstrate that EPSAs can be formulated as stochastic pattern search methods, which proves that EPSAs have a weak first-order stationary point convergence theory.

There are several reasons why a stationary point convergence theory for EAs is of interest. First, this analysis provides a rigorous justification for a method of adapting the step length of the mutation operator in an EA. While previous adaptive methods have been analyzed for specific classes of functions, our analysis demonstrates how the step length can be adapted to provide convergence for any continuous function. Second, stopping rules can be designed from this convergence theory that empirically terminate near a stationary point. Stopping rules based on weaker analyses like the Borel-Cantelli lemma would force EAs to terminate after a very large number of generations. Finally, this type of analysis offers the possibility of providing new bounds on the rate of convergence of EAs. Previous convergence analyses provide either weak bounds on the rate of convergence or convergence results for specific classes of functions (e.g., Bäck, Rudolph and Schwefel [Bäck et al., 1993]).

While EAs are typically described as methods for global optimization, this convergence analysis does not guarantee that the global optimum is found. However, experience with pattern search algorithms suggests that EPSAs can be successfully applied to global optimization problems. For example, Meza and Martinez [Meza and Martinez, 1994] have successfully applied a pattern search method, parallel directed search, to the global optimization of the conformational energy of a simple chain molecule. Their comparison of parallel directed search to GA and simulated annealing indicates that parallel directed search is equally effective at performing global optimization for this problem. In Hart [Hart, 1995] we describe

---

[1]This terminology is unfortunate in that convergence to a *global* minimizer of the function is *not* implied. However, "locally convergent" is reserved for another use in the optimization literature [Dennis and Schnabel, 1983].

preliminary experimental results for EPSAs that confirms that their ability to perform global optimization comparable to that of canonical EAs.

This paper is organized as follows. Section 2 provides some background on EP, ES and GAs, and reviews convergence theories for these EAs. Section 3 describes generalized pattern search methods and reviews their convergence properties. Section 4 defines generalized stochastic pattern search methods and describes a convergence theory for these algorithms. Section 5 presents a class of EAs and demonstrates that it fits within the framework of stochastic pattern search algorithms. Finally, we discuss some implications of these results.

2   Preliminaries

2.1   Definitions

Let $\mathbf{R}, \mathbf{Q}$ and $\mathbf{Z}$ denote the sets of real, rational and integer numbers, respectively. All norms will be Euclidean vector norms or the associated operator norm. We also define $L(x_0) = \{x \mid f(x) \leq f(x_0)\}$.

The pseudo-code in Figure 1 describes the steps executed in a canonical EA that encompasses EP, ES and real-coded GAs. We consider EAs that optimize a *fitness function* of the form $f : D \to \mathbf{R}$, D is a compact subset of $\mathbf{R}^n$. We assume that the function f is to be minimized. The *population* used by an EA consists of a N-tuple of vectors $x_i \in \mathbf{R}^n$. Each vector x_i, called an *individual* of the population, is a feasible solution to the problem, and the value $f(x_i)$ is said to be the *fitness* of the solution. Let $\{x_1^t, \ldots, x_N^t\}$ be the N individuals in a population at time t.

Select an initial population $\{x_1^0, \ldots, x_N^0\}$, $x_i^0 \in \mathbf{R}^n$
Determine the fitness of each individual
$x_0^* = \arg\min\{f(x_1^0), \ldots, f(x_N^0)\}$ and $y_0^* = f(x_0^*)$
Repeat $t = 1, 2, \ldots$
   Perform selection
   Perform crossover with probability χ
   Perform mutation with probability μ
   Determine the fitness of each individual
   $x_t^* = \arg\min\{x_{t-1}^*, f(x_1^t), \ldots, f(x_N^t)\}$ and $y_t^* = f(x_t^*)$
   Perform replacement
Until some stopping criterion is satisfied

Figure 1: **A Canonical Evolutionary Algorithm**

There are a number of details of EP, ES and real-coded GAs that distinguish them from these EAs, but this algorithmic framework captures the principle features of these algorithms. For further details of these algorithms see Fogel [Fogel, 1994, Fogel, 1995] for descriptions of EP, Bäck and Schwefel [Bäck and Schwefel, 1993] and Bäck, Hoffmeister and Schwefel [Bäck et al., 1991] for descriptions of ES, and Goldberg [Goldberg, 1989] and Davis [Davis, 1991] for descriptions of GAs. The principle feature distinguishing these EAs is the selection of operators used perform the evolutionary search. EP utilizes mutation to generate new solutions. ES and GAs utilize both mutation and crossover, although crossover is applied with relatively greater frequency in GAs.

The previous references provide a detailed description of each of the steps of EAs. In this paper, we distinguish between the process of selection and replacement. With high probability, the selection algorithm chooses the solutions from the current population that minimize $f(x_i^t) - f(x^*)$. The replacement algorithm determines which members of the previous population are replaced by the individuals generated by the genetic operators.

2.2 Convergence Analyses of Evolutionary Algorithms

In this section, we review literature related to the convergence of EP, ES and real-coded GAs. These methods have been successfully applied to the optimization problems with continuous objective functions over $\mathbf{R}^n$. Traditionally, researchers have used GAs with binary-coded genes that are decoded into real values to solve this problem [De Jong, 1975]. However, special manipulation of this encoding is often necessary to increase the efficiency of the algorithm [Schraudolph and Belew, 1992, Whitley et al., 1991]. Recent research on real-coded GAs suggests that they can be more efficient, provide increased precision, and allow for genetic operators that are more appropriate for a continuous domain [Eshelman and Schaffer, 1993, Janikow and Michalewicz, 1991, Wright, 1991].

Two different types of convergence analyses are commonly used to analyze EAs. First, authors have analyzed the convergence of the best solution in the population to the best solution in the sample space. Second, authors have analyzed the convergence of the entire population of solutions to the best solution in the sample space. We distinguish these types of convergence by calling them *point-wise* and *population-wise* convergence respectively.

Convergence analyses of real-coded GAs have naturally focused on the role of crossover, since crossover is typically the dominant mechanism of generating new solutions in GAs. Wright [Wright, 1991], Goldberg [Goldberg, 1990], Eshelman and Schaffer [Eshelman and Schaffer, 1993], and Qi and Palmeri [Qi and Palmieri, 1994a, Qi and Palmieri, 1994b] have examined population-wise convergence through analyses of how different types of real-coded GAs process schemata. Wright [Wright, 1991] defines connected schemata, which represent closed intervals along each dimension of the search domain. An analysis of these schemata shows that the schema theorem applies to real-coded GAs. Goldberg [Goldberg, 1990] uses one-dimensional slices of the search space to discuss the behavior of real-coded GAs that use standard, coordinate-wise crossover. He argues that a GA's convergence can be blocked when the population diversity is reduced such that crossover can only generate solutions in a finite number of basins of attraction that do not contain near-optimal solutions. A similar analysis by Qi and Palmeri [Qi and Palmieri, 1994b] analyzes the diversification role of coordinate-wise crossover of real-coded GAs with an infinite population size. Eshelman and Schaffer [Eshelman and Schaffer, 1993] discuss crossover operators for real-coded GAs that may circumvent these convergence problems by exploiting the gradualness of continuous functions. They define interval schemata, which are closely related to Wright's connected schemata, and provide a theoretic and empirical analysis of the failure modes of a particular crossover operator, the blend crossover operator.

Unfortunately, these types of schema analyses have not successfully provided provable convergence guarantees for real-coded GAs.[2] In fact, Rudolph's [Rudolph, 1994] analysis of

---

[2]Törn and Žilinskas [Törn and Žilinskas, 1989, page 78] and Rinnooy Kan [Rinnooy Kan, 1987]

binary-coded GAs makes it clear that "The schema theorem [Holland, 1976] does not imply that the Canonical GA will converge to the global optimum in static optimization problems."

Convergence analyses of EP, ES and real-coded GAs that focus on the role of mutation have been successful at providing provable convergence guarantees. Qi and Palmeri [Qi and Palmieri, 1994a] provide population-wise convergence results for real-coded GAs with an infinite population size. Their results show that the distribution of solutions generated by a real-coded GA with selection alone converges in distribution to the distribution concentrated at the optimum, and that the mean fitness of the populations of a real-coded GA with selection and mutation converges to the fitness of the optimal solution. For EP, ES and real-coded GAs with finite populations, a proof of point-wise convergence to solutions with near-optimal fitness can be shown using the Borel-Cantelli Lemma [Bäck et al., 1991, Bäck et al., 1993, Rudolph, 1994, Solis and Wets, 1981]. This proof requires that the mutation operator be applied with nonzero probability such that the joint distribution of possible new solutions has nonzero probability everywhere. Unfortunately, the assumptions used by these convergence proofs make them only of academic interest. Consequently, they are too too weak to provide practically relevant information about the rate of convergence of these methods.

These convergence results can be improved when examined specific classes of functions. Bäck, Rudolph and Schwefel [Bäck et al., 1993] have analyzed the rate of point-wise convergence of EP and ES in special contexts. They note that these methods have a geometrical convergence rate on strongly convex functions if the step size used by mutation is adapted. This result relies on a more general analysis by Rappl [Rappl, 1984, Rappl, 1989].

3 Generalized Pattern Search

3.1 Description

Pattern search methods are a class of direct search methods - methods that neither require nor explicitly approximate derivatives [Dennis and Torczon, 1994]. Torczon [Torczon, 1993] provides an abstract generalization of pattern search methods. This formulation of pattern search methods is used to establish a global first-order stationary point convergence theory that does not use the gradient or directional derivative to guarantee convergence.

Our definition of stochastic pattern search in Section 4 is only a slight generalization of the definition of pattern search provided by Torczon [Torczon, 1993]. Consequently we refer the reader to Torczon [Torczon, 1993] for complete details about the definition of pattern search methods. The pseudo-code in Figure 2 describes the main elements of a pattern search method. Pattern search methods use the exploratory moves algorithm to conduct a series of exploratory moves about the current iterate before identifying a new iterate. These moves can be viewed as a search about the current iterate for a trial point with a lower function value. Exploratory moves are generated by the exploratory moves algorithm using a *pattern matrix*. The pattern matrix is decomposed into a nonsingular basis matrix $B \in \mathbf{R}^{n \times n}$ and a generating matrix $C_k \in \mathbf{Z}^{n \times p}$, $p > 2n$; the subscript for C_k indicates that the generating matrix may vary with each iteration, but each possible C_k is constrained to include a subset of search directions with bounded length that span $\mathbf{R}^n$. Given a pattern

review the convergence guarantees typically used to define a convergence theory for stochastic algorithms.

matrix BC_k, there are p possible exploratory moves $\Delta_k BC_k$, where Δ_k is a step-length parameter. Conceptually, the generating matrix defines the directions that are searched, while the basis matrix rotates and scales the search directions to determine the coordinate system used during the search.

Let the initial solution $x_0 \in \mathbf{R}^n$ and step length Δ_0 be given
For $k = 0, 1, \ldots$
   Compute $f(x_k)$
   Determine a step s_k using an *exploratory moves algorithm*
   Compute $\rho_k = f(x_k) - f(x_k + s_k)$
   If $\rho_k > 0$ then $x_{k+1} = x_k + s_k$. Otherwise $x_{k+1} = x_k$.
   Update the *pattern matrix* and Δ_k

Figure 2: Pattern Search

If among the p possible exploratory moves there exists a move that provides a simple decrease in the function value, then the exploratory moves algorithm must return *some* step s_k that provides a simple decrease. If the exploratory moves algorithm fails to produce a trial step that gives a simple decrease, then the update algorithm reduces the step size by multiplying it by one of a finite set of rational values. If the exploratory moves algorithm does produce a trial step that gives a simple decrease, then the update algorithm either increases the step size (by multiplying it by a rational value) or preserves the current step size.

3.2 Convergence Analysis

Torczon [Torczon, 1993] shows that this notion of an exploratory moves algorithm can be used to prove weak first-order stationary point convergence by requiring only simple decrease on f. In particular, this proof of convergence does not explicitly require a notion of sufficient decrease on the iterates, like a fraction of Cauchy decrease or the Armijo-Goldstein-Wolfe conditions. In this section we review the major theorems in the convergence analysis of pattern search methods described in Torczon [Torczon, 1993]. This analysis is closely related to the analysis of multidimensional search [Torczon, 1989, Torczon, 1991].

The first theorem uses the simple decrease condition of the generalized pattern search algorithm, along with the algorithm for updating Δ_k, to describe the limiting behavior of Δ_k.

Theorem 1 ([Torczon, 1993], Theorem 3.3) *Assume that $L(x_0)$ is compact, then*

$$\liminf_{k \to +\infty} \Delta_k = 0$$

Torczon uses the following proposition to prove Theorem 2 by contradiction.

Proposition 1 ([Torczon, 1993], Proposition 3.4) *Assume that $L(x_0)$ is compact, that f is continuously differentiable on $L(x_0)$, and that $\liminf_{k \to +\infty} \| \nabla f(x_k) \| \neq 0$. Then there exists a constant $\Delta_{\mathrm{LB}} > 0$ such that for all k, $\Delta_k > \Delta_{\mathrm{LB}}$.*

Finally, the following theorem gives the result for weak first-order stationary point convergence for any generalized pattern search method.

Theorem 2 ([Torczon, 1993], Theorem 3.5) *Assume that $L(x_0)$ is compact and that $f : \mathbf{R}^n \to \mathbf{R}$ is continuously differentiable on $L(x_0)$. Then for the sequence of iterates $\{x_k\}$ produced by the generalized pattern search method (Figure 2),*

$$\liminf_{k \to +\infty} \| \nabla f(x_k) \| = 0.$$

This convergence guarantee is weak, since it only implies that the gradient is sampled often near a stationary point. Thus it is possible for $\limsup_{k \to +\infty} \| \nabla f(x_k) \| > 0$. However, the sequence of iterates generated by a pattern search method is monotone nonincreasing and bounded below, so $\lim_{k \to +\infty} f(x_k) = f(\bar{x}^*)$ for some stationary point $\bar{x}^*$. Furthermore, if f is strictly convex then we can prove the following corollary.

Corollary 1 *Assume that $L(x_0)$ is compact and that $f : \mathbf{R}^n \to \mathbf{R}$ is strictly convex and continuously differentiable on $L(x_0)$. Then for the sequence of iterates $\{x_k\}$ produced by the generalized pattern search method (Figure 2),*

$$\lim_{k \to +\infty} \| \nabla f(x_k) \| = 0.$$

Torczon [Torczon, 1993] further notes that this convergence analysis can be extended to handle most cases when the function f is nondifferentiable. This is reassuring since these methods are typically applied to nondifferentiable functions. Let X^* include the set of stationary points of the function f in $L(x_0)$, the set of all points in $L(x_0)$ where f is nondifferentiable, and the set of all points in $L(x_0)$ where the derivative of f exists but is not continuous. Theorem 2 can be extended to ensure convergence to a point in X^* as discussed in Torczon [Torczon, 1991].

4   Generalized Stochastic Pattern Search

Randomness can be introduced into pattern search methods in several different ways. A simple example would be to simply shuffle the order in which the exploratory moves algorithm considers the exploratory moves. Since each move will be considered once and since there are a bounded number of exploratory moves, this randomized exploratory moves algorithm is guaranteed to return a decreasing step if one exists. Consequently, the convergence theory for pattern search methods is immediately applicable to this class of stochastic pattern search methods.

In this section, we define a different class of stochastic pattern search methods in which the exploratory moves algorithm is only probablistically guaranteed to terminate. This class of algorithms allows the generating matrix C_k^h to vary with each iteration h of the exploratory moves algorithm, provided a subset of $2n$ columns of the form $[-M_k \; M_k]$ remains fixed during each call to the exploratory moves algorithm.[3]

---

[3]We use the notation $X = [YZ]$ to denote that the matrix X is partitioned into the matrices Y and Z.

Because the exploratory moves algorithm is only probablistically guaranteed to terminate, it is possible that an "unlucky" sequence of exploratory moves could fail to ever provide a simple decrease. To ensure that the exploratory moves algorithm terminates with high probability, the probability of selecting each of the $2n$ fixed columns must be greater than or equal to some constant greater than zero. When all $2n$ of the search directions defined by the fixed columns have been sampled, then the exploratory moves algorithm terminates. With these restrictions, the probability is zero that such an "unlucky" sequence occurs.

4.1 Description

This section introduces the abstraction of stochastic pattern search methods, which generalizes the abstract description of pattern search methods provided by Torczon [Torczon, 1993]. The definition of the pattern, the algorithm for generalized stochastic pattern search methods, and the update algorithm follow almost directly from Torczon's description. The definition of the exploratory moves algorithm generalizes Torczon's description to include stochastically selected exploratory moves.

The Pattern To define a pattern we need two components, a basis matrix and a generating matrix. A basis matrix can be any nonsingular matrix $B \in \mathbf{R}^{n \times n}$. A generating matrix is a matrix $C_k^h \in \mathbf{Z}^{n \times p}$, where $p > 2n$ and $h \geq 1$, where k is the iteration number of the stochastic pattern search algorithm. A generating matrix is partitioned into components

$$C_k^h = [M_k \ -M_k \ L_k^h] = [\Gamma_k \ L_k^h].$$

We call Γ_k the base generating matrix. We require that $M_k \in M \subset \mathbf{Z}^{n \times n}$, where M is a finite set of nonsingular matrices, and that $L_k^h \in \mathbf{Z}^{n \times (p-2n)}$ and contains a column of zeros.

A *pattern* is then defined by the columns of the matrix $P_k^h = BC_k^h$. Because both B and C_k^h have rank n, the columns of P_k^h span $\mathbf{R}^n$.

Given $\Delta_k \in \mathbf{R}$, $\Delta_k > 0$, we define a *trial step* s_k^h to be any vector of the form

$$s_k^h = \Delta_k B c_k^h,$$

where c_k^h denotes a column of C_k^h. Note that $B c_k^h$ determines the direction of the step, while Δ_k serves as a step length parameter. At iteration k, a *trial point* is any point of the form $x_k^h = x_k + s_k^h$, where x_k is the current iterate.

The Exploratory Moves Pattern search methods proceed by conducting a series of *exploratory moves* about the current iterate before identifying a new iterate. Stochastic pattern search methods differ from non-stochastic methods in that the exploratory moves algorithm is only probablistically guaranteed to terminate. Consequently, there is no fixed number of iterations of the stochastic exploratory moves algorithm; the algorithm terminates when a decreasing step has been found or after all $2n$ basic steps defined by M_k and $-M_k$ have been examined. In addition, the stochastic nature of the exploratory moves algorithm enables the generating matrix C_k^h to vary with each iteration h of the algorithm.

The following three conditions are placed on the exploratory moves s_k generated by an exploratory moves algorithm.[4] These three conditions constitute the **Hypothesis on Exploratory Moves.**

---

[4] If y is a vector and A is a matrix, then we define $y \in A$ to mean that y is a column of A.

1. $s_k = s_k^h \in \Delta_k P_k^h$, $h = 1, 2, \ldots$

2. If a simple decrease on the function value can be found among any of the $2n$ basic trial steps, then then $f(x_k + s_k) < f(x_k)$.

3. The exploratory moves algorithm terminates and returns $s_k = 0$ if each of the $2n$ *basic steps* defined by $\Delta_k B\Gamma_k$ have been examined without identifying a decreasing step. At each iteration of the exploratory moves algorithm, the probability of selecting each of the $2n$ basic steps is greater than or equal to a constant $\nu > 0$.

The addition of the last condition is the principal difference between this hypothesis on exploratory moves and the hypothesis on exploratory moves defined by Torczon [Torczon, 1993]. This condition uses the observation that Torczon's convergence theory relies solely on properties of the base matrix Γ_k. Since the trial steps in $\Delta_k BL_k^h$ are not critical to the convergence of the pattern search method, it is safe to terminate the exploratory moves algorithm after all of the basic steps have been examined. The requirement that the basic steps have probability greater or equal to ν is added to ensure that the sequence of calls to the exploratory moves algorithm terminates almost surely (i.e. with probability one).

The Updates Figure 3 defines the algorithm that updates the step size, Δ_k. This algorithm reduces the step size if the exploratory moves algorithm fails to produce a trial step that gives a simple decrease. If the exploratory moves algorithm does produce a trial step that gives a simple decrease, then this algorithm either increases the step size or preserves the current step size.

Given $\tau \in \mathbf{Q}$, let $\theta = \tau^{\omega_0}$ and $\lambda_i \in \Lambda = \{\tau^{\omega_1}, \ldots, \tau^{\omega_L}\}$, where $\tau > 1$ and $\{\omega_0, \omega_1, \ldots, \omega_L\} \subset \mathbf{Z}$, $L = |\Lambda| < \infty$, $\omega_0 < 0$, and $\omega_i \geq 0$, $i = 1, \ldots, L$.

If $\rho_k \leq 0$ then $\Delta_{k+1} = \theta \Delta_k$.
If $\rho_k > 0$ then $\Delta_{k+1} = \lambda_i \Delta_k$.

Figure 3· Updating Δ_k

The Generalized Stochastic Pattern Search Method Figure 4 defines the generalized stochastic pattern search method for unconstrained minimization. To define a stochastic pattern search method, it is necessary to specify the basis matrix B, the initial values of Γ_0 and L_0^0, the exploratory moves algorithm, and the algorithms for updating Γ_k, L_k^0 and Δ_k.

4.2   Convergence Theory

The following theorem extends the theoretical analysis in Torczon [Torczon, 1993] to provide a convergence theory for the stochastic pattern search methods.

Theorem 3 *Assume that $L(x_0)$ is compact and that $f \cdot \mathbf{R}^n \to \mathbf{R}$ is continuously differentiable on $L(x_0)$. Then for the sequence of iterates $\{x_k\}$ produced by the stochastic generalized pattern search method (Figure 4),*

$$P\left(\liminf_{k \to \infty} \|\nabla f(x_k)\| = 0\right) = 1.$$

Let $x_0 \in \mathbf{R}^n$ and $\Delta_0 > 0$ be given.
For $k = 0, 1, \ldots$
   Compute $f(x_k)$.
   Determine a step s_k using an exploratory moves algorithm.
   Compute $\rho_k = f(x_k) - f(x_k + s_k)$.
   If $\rho_k > 0$, then $x_{k+1} = x_k + s_k$. Otherwise $x_{k+1} = x_k$.
   Compute Γ_{k+1}, L^0_{k+1} and Δ_{k+1}.

Figure 4: **Generalized Stochastic Pattern Search**

Theorem 3 is proved in Appendix A. This analysis shows that the set of sequences of trial steps for which each exploratory move terminates has probability one. Using this fact, the major proofs used by Torczon [Torczon, 1993] to prove the convergence theory for generalized pattern search are generalized for stochastic pattern search methods. This generalization shows that each of the proof steps used to demonstrate the convergence of generalized pattern search is true for generalized stochastic pattern search with probability one. It follows that generalized stochastic pattern search methods converge with probability one. The extensions required to prove convergence for continuous but nondifferentiable functions are straightforward, so generalized stochastic pattern search methods converge to points in X^* on continuous nondifferentiable functions with probability one.

5 Evolutionary Pattern Search Algorithms

We now define a class of EAs that can be cast as stochastic pattern search methods. We refer to these EAs as evolutionary pattern search algorithms (EPSAs). Figure 5 shows the pseudo code describing EPSAs. The crossover operator generates individuals using coordinate-wise swaps, and the mutation operator adds a discrete random variable to a dimension of an individual, which may assume values $\{\pm\sigma_1, \ldots, \pm\sigma_m\}$, $\sigma_i \in \mathbf{Q}$. Let $\sigma_{min} = \min_{i=1,\ldots,m} |\sigma_i|$, and let ξ be the minimum nonzero probability that any of these values is generated. Let e_i be the standard unit vector in the i-th dimension. Let $\eta \in \{0,1\}^{2n}$ be a counter that indicates whether the $2n$ vectors $\pm\sigma_{min}e_i$ have been examined. The initial step length is $\Delta_0 = 1$, and the contraction factor is $\theta = 1/a$, $a \in \mathbf{Z}$.

The inner loop in EPSAs is used to highlight the relationship between EPSAs and generalized stochastic pattern search methods. Each iteration of the loop indexed by h corresponds to a set of moves of a stochastic pattern search algorithm with generating matrix C_k^h. Note, however, that this loop can easily be merged with the outer loop to provide a formulation of EPSAs that more closely resembles canonical EAs. The restriction on the replacement strategy ensures that the best individual found is kept for further processing. Together, these restrictions enable EPSAs to be viewed as a pattern search method with respect to the best individual in the each generation.

Table 1 illustrates the application of an EPSA to Rosenbrock's function, $f(x, y) = 100(x^2 - y)^2 + (1 - x)^2$. A population of size three is shown. For illustrative purposes, the crossover rate is zero, and every individual is mutated along a single dimension. The third column of the table shows the parent of each individual; individuals marked (1) are copied from the previous population by elitism. The fourth column shows the length of the mutation step,

```
1   Initialize the population of individuals {x_1^0, ..., x_N^0} such that x_i^0 ∈ Q^n
2   Compute the fitness of each individual and reorder such that x_1^t ≤ x_i^t, ∀i
3   Let t = 0 and η = {0}^2n
4   Repeat k = 0, 1, ...
5       Repeat h = 1, 2, ...
6           Perform selection with a policy which guarantees that the
                individual with the smallest fitness value is selected for processing
                at each generation with a probability of at least π > 0
7           Perform crossover with probability χ ∈ [0, 1)
8           Perform mutation with probability μ ∈ (0, 1] of mutating each dimension;
                mutation adds a vector of the form Δ_k ω, ω ∈ {0, ±σ_1, ..., ±σ_m}^n
9           If the mutation x_1^t + Δ_k σ_min e_i is generated, then η_i = 1
            Else, if the mutation x_1^t - Δ_k σ_min e_i is generated, then η_{i+n} = 1
10          Compute the fitness of each individual and reorder such that x_1^t ≤ x_i^t, ∀i
11          Perform replacement with an elitist replacement policy which guarantees that
                the individual with the smallest fitness value among the previous population
                and the newly generated individuals is included in the next generation.
12          t = t + 1; x_t^* = arg min{x_{t-1}^*, f(x_1^t), ..., f(x_N^t)} and y_t^* = f(x_t^*)
13      Until (y_t^* < y_{t-1}^*) or (∑_{i=1}^{2n} η_i = 2n)
14      If (∑_{i=1}^{2n} η_i = 2n) then Δ_{k+1} = θ Δ_k
15      η = {0}^2n
16  Until some stopping criterion is satisfied
```

Figure 5: Pseudo Code for EPSAs

Δ_k, and the fifth column shows the values in the η array, which records whether offsets from the best individual have been sampled. Table 1 illustrates the two cases in which η is cleared: (a) when an improving solution is found, and (b) when all offsets from the best individual have been sampled.

Note that EPSAs manipulate solutions that are vectors in Q^n. In principle, this distinguishes EPSAs from the canonical EAs, since these EAs manipulate vectors in R^n. However, any point in R^n can be approximated arbitrarily well by a point in Q^n, so this distinction does not affect the applicability of EPSAs.

In what follows we describe how the three central components of stochastic pattern search – updating step length, the generating matrix, and the exploratory moves algorithm – are implemented by EPSAs. This demonstrates that EPSAs can be described as stochastic pattern search methods. Consequently, from Theorem 3 we know that

$$P\left(\liminf_{t \to \infty} \|\nabla f(x_t^*)\| = 0\right) = 1.$$

Updating the Step Length   Step 14 of EPSAs performs the update to the step length Δ_k. This update is exactly as given in Figure 3. When the inner loop fails to generate a simple decrease on f, the step length is decreased by a multiple of θ. The settings that are defined by EPSAs are $\theta = 1/a$ and $\Lambda = \{1\}$. Thus $\tau = a$, $\omega_0 = -1$ and $\omega_1 = 0$.

Population	Fitness	Parent	Δ_k	η
(-0.024, -0.181)	4.338	-	1	0000
(-1.357, 0.197)	275.977	-		
(-2.024, -1.830)	3521.570	-		
(-0.024, -0.181)	4.338	(1)	1	0010
(-1.024, -0.181)	155.23	1*		
(-1.357, 1.197)	2882.570	2		
(-0.024, -0.181)	4.338	(1)	1	0110
(-0.024, 0.819)	68.063	1*		
(-1.024, -0.181)	155.233	1		
(-0.024, -0.181)	4.338	(1)	1	1110
(-0.024, -0.181)	4.338	2		
(0.976, -0.181)	128.455	1*		
(0.976, 0.819)	1.779	3	1	0000
(-0.024, -0.181)	4.338	(1)		
(-0.024, -1.181)	140.614	1		
(0.976, 0.819)	1.779	(1)	1	0101
(0.976, 1.819)	75.104	1*		
(0.976, -0.181)	128.455	1*		
(0.976, 0.819)	1.779	(1)	1	0111
(-0.024, 0.819)	68.063	1*		
(0.976, 2.819)	348.429	2		
(0.976, 0.819)	1.779	(1)	1	0111
(-0.024, 0.819)	68.063	1		
(0.976, 1.819)	75.104	1		
(0.976, 0.819)	1.779	(1)	1	0111
(-0.024, 0.819)	68.063	1		
(-0.024, 0.819)	68.063	1		
(0.976, 0.819)	1.779	(1)	1	0111
(0.976, -0.181)	128.455	1		
(-0.024, 1.819)	331.788	3		
(0.976, 0.819)	1.779	(1)	1	0111
(0.976, 0.819)	1.779	2		
(0.976, 1.819)	75.104	1		
(0.976, 0.819)	1.779	(1)	1	0111
(0.976, 1.819)	75.104	1		
(1.976, 1.819)	435.832	3		
(0.976, 0.819)	1.779	(1)	1	0111
(-0.024, 0.819)	68.063	1		
(0.976, -0.181)	128.455	1		
(0.976, 0.819)	1.779	(1)	0.5	0000
(-0.024, 0.819)	68.063	1		
(1.976, 0.819)	952.907	1*		

Table 1: An application of an EPSA to Rosenbrock's function.

The Matrices Pattern search methods are designed to generated test patterns from a single solution. To cast EPSAs within this framework, the individuals generated at each generation are viewed as patterns with respect to the best individual in the population. Figure 6 illustrates the pattern vectors generated by individuals created by crossover and mutation. Points A and B represent individuals created by mutation from the best individual, x_1. Point C represents an individual created by crossover from x_1 and x_i. Point D represents an individual created by mutation of x_i, and point E represents an individual created by crossover from x_1 and x_i followed by mutation. The arrows represent the pattern vectors, which are implicitly scaled by the basis matrix.

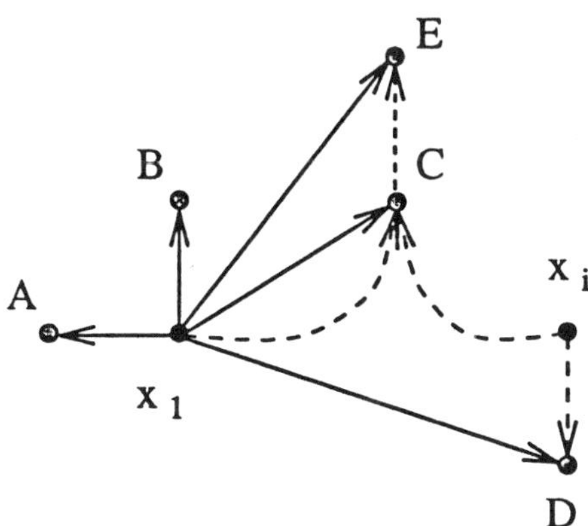

Figure 6: Illustration of pattern vectors that are offsets from the best individual, x_1. Solid arrows represent the vectors in the generating matrix and dashed arrows represent the genetic operations in an EPSA that generate new solutions.

The generating matrix C_k^h is constructed using all possible individuals that can be generated in the current generation t (as indexed by k and h). Let $f(x_1^t) \le f(x_j^t)$, $j = 2, \ldots, N$, for all t. Let $\mathrm{lcmd}(a_1/b_1, \ldots, a_r/b_r)$ equal the least common multiple of $\{b_1, \ldots, b_r\}$, $a_i, b_i \in \mathbf{Z}$. Then let $\gamma = \mathrm{lcmd}(x_1^0, \ldots, x_N^0, \sigma_1, \ldots, \sigma_m)$. The columns of C_k^h are generated by taking each individual $\hat{x}$ that can be generated by an EPSA at generation t and constructing the vector $\gamma(\hat{x} - x_1^t)/\Delta_k$. The basis matrix implicitly used by EPSAs is $B = \frac{1}{\gamma}I$, where I is the identity matrix, so the trial steps are

$$\Delta_k B c_k^h = \Delta_k B \gamma (\hat{x} - x_1^t)/\Delta_k = (\hat{x} - x_1^t). \tag{1}$$

Finally, note that the base generating matrix $\Gamma_k = \gamma \sigma_{min}[I \;\; -I]$ is a subset of C_k^h in all generations. Furthermore, the number of columns in C_k^h is bounded by the maximum number of individuals that can be generated by a finite population of size N.

It remains to prove that the patterns vectors c_k^h are in $\mathbf{Z}^n$.

Lemma 1 $C_k^h \in \mathbf{Z}^{n \times z}$ for some $z > 2n$ and for all $h = 0, 1, \ldots$ and $k = 0, 1, \ldots$.

Proof. Note that each of the pattern matrices C_k^h can be indexed by t. Each of the pattern vectors c_k^h has the form

$$\Delta_0 \gamma (\hat{x} - x_1^t)/\Delta_k = a^{r_k} \gamma (\hat{x} - x_1^t)$$

for some nonnegative integer r_k. If $\hat{x}$ is generated by both mutation and crossover, then

$$\hat{x} = \Delta_k \omega + (I_1 x_i^t + I_2 x_j^t)$$

where x_i^t and x_j^t are the parents used to generate $\hat{x}$, I_1 and I_2 are zero-one matrices that select the coordinates from x_i^t and x_j^t that are used in crossover, and ω is the vector that defines the mutation offset from the vector created by crossover. Thus a pattern vector c_k^h has the form

$$\gamma \omega + a^{r_k} \gamma (I_1 x_i^t + I_2 x_j^t - x_1^t).$$

We now proceed inductively. If $t = 0$, then $\gamma x_j^0 \in \mathbf{Z}^n$ from the definition of γ. Since $\gamma \omega \in \mathbf{Z}^n$ we have $c_k^h \in \mathbf{Z}^n$. This is true for all possible individuals that can be generated by the genetic operators, so $C_k^h \in \mathbf{Z}^{n \times z}$.

Now suppose that $C_k^h \in \mathbf{Z}^{n \times z}$ at step $t - 1$. Now an individual generated by crossover and mutation has the form

$$
\begin{aligned}
\hat{x} &= \Delta_k \omega + (I_1 x_i^t + I_2 x_j^t) \\
&= \Delta_k \omega + (I_1(\Delta_{k'} \omega' + (I_1' x_v^{t-1} + I_2' x_w^{t-1})) + I_2(\Delta_{k'} \omega'' + (I_1'' x_{v'}^{t-1} + I_2'' x_{w'}^{t-1})))
\end{aligned}
$$

The corresponding pattern vector c_k^h has the form

$$\gamma \omega + \gamma I_1 \frac{\Delta_{k'}}{\Delta_k} \omega' + a^{r_k} \gamma I_1 (I_1' x_v^{t-1} + I_2' x_w^{t-1}) + \gamma I_2 \frac{\Delta_{k'}}{\Delta_k} \omega'' + a^{r_k} \gamma I_2 (I_1'' x_{v'}^{t-1} + I_2'' x_{w'}^{t-1})$$

for some positive integer r_k. Each of the terms in this expression are in $\mathbf{Z}^n$. The first is integral from the definition of γ. The second and fourth terms are integral from the definition of γ and from the fact that $\Delta_{k'}/\Delta_k$ is either 1 or a. The third and fifth terms follow from our inductive assumption that $C_k^h \in \mathbf{Z}^{n \times z}$ at step $t - 1$. $\blacksquare$

Exploratory Moves The exploratory moves algorithm used by EPSAs is contained within the inner loop on steps 5 through 13. As required by the exploratory moves hypothesis, this loop only terminates if a solution is found that generates a simple increase, or if all $2n$ basic steps defined by $\Delta_k B \Gamma_k$ have been examined.

Equation 1 shows that all possible individuals that can be generated by EPSAs are captured in patterns in C_k^h. The base generating matrix represents the single-coordinate mutations for which mutation occurs with values σ_{min}. The restriction on the selection strategy ensures that each of these single-coordinate mutations can occur on x_1^t with probability greater than or equal to $\delta = \pi \xi (1 - \chi) \mu (1 - \mu)^{n-1} > 0$. Thus, the exploratory moves algorithm implicitly defined by EPSAs satisfies the hypothesis on exploratory moves.

6   Conclusions

The central contribution of this work is the development of a convergence theory for a class of EAs that guarantees convergence almost surely to a stationary point for any continuously differentiable function. This convergence result is qualitatively different from proofs of convergence to a global optimum. The difference stems from the fact that the problem of finding a solution x^* for which $f(x^*)$ is the global optimum is ill-conditioned [Törn and Žilinskas, 1989]. Consequently, these proofs of convergence to the global optimum only guarantee that the estimate of the fitness at the optimum, $\tilde{f}(x_t^*)$ converges to $f(x^*)$. Because the convergence theory for EPSAs only guarantees convergence to *some* stationary point $\bar{x}^*$, it can guarantee that the sequence of improving solutions x_t^* weakly converges to $\bar{x}^*$.

This convergence theory also provides a method of adapting the step length of the mutation operator. Previously, methods for adapting the mutation operator have been analyzed for specific classes of functions (e.g. see Rappl [Rappl, 1989]). However, the method of adapting the mutation operator used in EPSAs is the first such method that can be tied to the convergence to a stationary point for an EA on *any* continuously differentiable function (as well as convergence to certain nonstationary points on continuous functions).

It has long been recognized that pattern search methods do not enjoy fast local convergence properties [Torczon, 1993], so it is reasonable to expect that EPSAs converge slowly. Unfortunately, it has been difficult to establish convergence rates for EPSAs. The reason is that the convergence theory only requires a simple decrease in the objective function. In general, this is not sufficient to guarantee even a geometric rate of convergence, which is one of the weakest convergence rates typically analyzed. It may be possible to determine rates of convergence for EPSAs for specific classes of functions, like the strongly convex functions examined by Rappl [Rappl, 1984, Rappl, 1989].

Torczon [Torczon, 1993] describes a stronger convergence theory that guarantees that pattern search methods converge such that

$$\lim_{k \to +\infty} \| \nabla f(x_k)\| = 0.$$

We expect that convergence rates will be easier to determine for algorithms that satisfy the conditions of this convergence theory, since these conditions tie the decrease to the norm of the gradient. Among these restrictions is a bound on the norm of the pattern matrix C_t^h. For EAs, this implies that solutions would need to be culled from the population if they are too far away from the best solution in the population. We expect that this type of culling would limit the global search performed by EPSAs.

One potential advantage of this type of convergence theory is that it enables the definition of stopping rules that can be shown to empirically terminate the algorithm near a stationary point. Hart [Hart, 1995] describes stopping rules for EPSAs based on definitions of stopping rules commonly used for direct search methods. For example, EPSAs can be terminated when the step length falls below a given threshold (a commonly used stopping rule for pattern search algorithms). To my knowledge these are the first stopping rules for any class of EAs that reliably terminate close to a stationary point.

Acknowledgements

We thank John DeLaurentis, Virginia Torczon, Bruce Hendrickson and Juan Meza for their helpful discussions. I also thank several anonymous reviewers for their critical feedback. This work was supported by the Applied Mathematical Sciences program, U.S. Department of Energy, Office of Energy Research, and was performed at Sandia National Laboratories, operated for the U.S. Department of Energy under contract No. DE-AC04-94AL85000.

References

[Bäck et al., 1991] Bäck, T., Hoffmeister, F., and Schwefel, H.-P. (1991). A survey of evolution strategies. In Belew, R. K. and Booker, L. B., editors, *Proc. of the Fourth Intl. Conf. on Genetic Algorithms*, pages 2–9, San Mateo, CA. Morgan-Kaufmann.

[Bäck et al., 1993] Bäck, T., Rudolph, G., and Schwefel, H.-P. (1993). Evolutionary programming and evolution strategies: Similarities and differences. In *Proc. of Second Annual Conf. on Evolutionary Programming*, pages 11–22.

[Bäck and Schwefel, 1993] Bäck, T. and Schwefel, H.-P. (1993). An overview of evolutionary algorithms for parameter optimization. *Evolutionary Computation*, 1(1):1–23.

[Davis, 1991] Davis, L., editor (1991). *Handbook of Genetic Algorithms*. Van Nostrand Reinhold.

[De Jong, 1975] De Jong, K. A. (1975). *An Analysis of the Behavior of a Class of Genetic Adaptive Systems*. PhD thesis, University of Michigan, Ann Arbor.

[Dennis and Torczon, 1994] Dennis, J. E. and Torczon, V. J. (1994). Derivative-free pattern search methods for multidisciplinary design problems. In *The fifth AIAA/USAF/NASA/ISSMO Symposium on Multidisciplinary Analysis and Optimization*, pages 922–932.

[Dennis and Schnabel, 1983] Dennis, J. J. and Schnabel, R. B. (1983). *Numerical Methods for Unconstrained Optimization and Nonlinear Equations*. Prentice-Hall.

[Eshelman and Schaffer, 1993] Eshelman, L. J. and Schaffer, J. D. (1993). Real-coded genetic algorithms and interval schemata. In Whitley, L. D., editor, *Foundations of Genetic Algorithms 2*, pages 187–202. Morgan-Kauffmann, San Mateo, CA.

[Fogel, 1994] Fogel, D. B. (1994). An introduction to simulated evolutionary optimization. *IEEE Transactions on Neural Networks*, 5(1):3–14.

[Fogel, 1995] Fogel, D. B. (1995). *Evolutionary Computation*. IEEE Press, Piscataway, NJ.

[Goldberg, 1989] Goldberg, D. E. (1989). *Genetic Algorithms in Search, Optimization, and Machine Learning*. Addison-Wesley Publishing Co., Inc.

[Goldberg, 1990] Goldberg, D. E. (1990). The theory of virtual alphabets. In Schwefel, H.-P. and Männer, R., editors, *Parallel Problem Solving from Nature*, pages 13–22, New York. Springer-Verlag.

[Hart, 1995] Hart, W. E. (1995). Evolutionary pattern search algorithms. Technical Report 95-2293, Sandia National Labs.

[Holland, 1976] Holland, J. H. (1976). *Adaptation in Natural and Artificial Systems*. The University of Michigan Press.

[Janikow and Michalewicz, 1991] Janikow, C. Z. and Michalewicz, Z. (1991). An experimental comparison of binary and floating point representations in genetic algorithms. In Belew, R. K. and Booker, L. B., editors, *Proc. of the Fourth Intl. Conf. on Genetic Algorithms*, pages 31–36, San Mateo, CA. Morgan-Kaufmann.

[Meza and Martinez, 1994] Meza, J. and Martinez, M. L. (1994). Direct search methods for the molecular conformation problem. *Journal of Computational Chemistry*, 15(6):627–632.

[Qi and Palmieri, 1994a] Qi, X. and Palmieri, F. (1994a). Theoretical analysis of evolutionary algorithms with an infinite population size in continuous space part I: Basic properties of selection and mutation. *IEEE Trans. on Neural Networks*, 5(1):102–119.

[Qi and Palmieri, 1994b] Qi, X. and Palmieri, F. (1994b). Theoretical analysis of evolutionary algorithms with an infinite population size in continuous space part II: Analysis of the diversification role of crossover. *IEEE Trans. on Neural Networks*, 5(1):120–129.

[Rappl, 1984] Rappl, G. (1984). *Konvergenzraten von Random Search Verfahren zur globalen Optimierung*. PhD thesis, HSBw München, Germany.

[Rappl, 1989] Rappl, G. (1989). On linear convergence of a class of random search algorithms. *Zeitschrift f. angew. Math. Mech.*, 69(1):37–45.

[Rinnooy Kan, 1987] Rinnooy Kan, A. (1987). Probabilistic analysis of algorithms. *Annals of Discrete Mathematics*, 31:365–384.

[Rudolph, 1994] Rudolph, G. (1994). Convergence analysis of canonical genetic algorithms. *IEEE Transactions on Neural Networks*, 5(1):96–101.

[Schraudolph and Belew, 1992] Schraudolph, N. N. and Belew, R. K. (1992). Dynamic parameter encoding for genetic algorithms. *Machine Learning*, 9:9–21.

[Solis and Wets, 1981] Solis, F. and Wets, R.-B. (1981). Minimization by random search techniques. *Mathematical Operations Research*, 6:19–30.

[Torczon, 1989] Torczon, V. (1989). Multi-directional search: A direct search algorithm for parallel machines. Technical Report TR90-7, Rice University.

[Torczon, 1991] Torczon, V. (1991). On the convergence of the multidirectional search algorithm. *SIAM J. Optimization*, 1:123–145.

[Torczon, 1993] Torczon, V. (1993). On the convergence of pattern search methods. Technical Report TR93-10, Rice University. Revised Sept. 1994.

[Törn and Žilinskas, 1989] Törn, A. and Žilinskas, A. (1989). *Global Optimization*, volume 350 of *Lecture Notes in Computer Science*. Springer-Verlag.

[Whitley et al., 1991] Whitley, D., Mathias, K., and Fitzhorn, P. (1991). Delta coding: An iterative search strategy for genetic algorithms. In Belew, R. K. and Booker, L. B., editors, *Proc. of the Fourth Intl. Conf. on Genetic Algorithms*, pages 77–84, San Mateo, CA. Morgan-Kaufmann.

[Wright, 1991] Wright, A. H. (1991). Genetic algorithms for real parameter optimization. In Rawlins, G. J., editor, *Foundations of Genetic Algorithms*, pages 205–218. Morgan-Kauffmann, San Mateo, CA.

A   Convergence of Generalized Stochastic Pattern Search

This section extends the theoretical analysis in Torczon [Torczon, 1993] to provide convergence results for the stochastic pattern search methods. The following lemma shows that the set of sequences of trial steps for which each exploratory move terminates has probability one. This lemma enables us to apply the theoretical analysis for generalized pattern search methods to generalized stochastic pattern search methods with the confidence that the later will converge almost surely.

Lemma 2 *Let A be the set of sequences of moves for which each exploratory move terminates. Then $P(A) = 1$.*

Proof. Let $A_j \subset A$ be the set of sequences of moves for which the exploratory moves algorithm terminates in j or fewer steps. If a sequence of moves fails to terminate after j steps, then at least one of the $2n$ basic moves has not been examined. The probability of not sampling a particular basic move in j steps is no greater than $(1-\nu)^j$, so $P(A_j) \geq 1-(1-\nu)^j$. Now $A = \bigcup_{j=1}^{\infty} A_j$ and $A_j \subset A_{j+1}$. Consequently,

$$P(A) = \lim_{j \to \infty} P(A_j) \geq \lim_{j \to \infty} \left(1 - (1 - \nu)^j\right) = 1.$$

∎

Using Lemma 2, the following theorem describes the limiting behavior of Δ_k that occurs almost surely.

Theorem 4 *Assume that $L(x_0)$ is compact. Then $P\left(\liminf_{x \to \infty} \Delta_k = 0\right) = 1$.*

Proof. If each exploratory move terminates, then we can apply Theorem 1 to show that $\liminf_{x \to \infty} \Delta_k = 0$. From Lemma 2 we know that the set of sequences for which each exploratory move terminates has measure one, so $P\left(\liminf_{x \to \infty} \Delta_k = 0\right) = 1$. ∎

The following theorem uses the limiting behavior of Δ_k to extend the first-order stationary point convergence to stochastic pattern search methods. This is a global convergence theory since it is applicable for any initial point x_0 in the search domain, and not simply for an initial point that is sufficiently close to the stationary point.

Theorem 3 *Assume that $L(x_0)$ is compact and that $f : \mathbf{R}^n \to \mathbf{R}$ is continuously differentiable on $L(x_0)$. Then for the sequence of iterates $\{x_k\}$ produced by the stochastic generalized pattern search method (Figure 4),*

$$P\left(\liminf_{k \to \infty} \|\nabla f(x_k)\| = 0\right) = 1.$$

Proof. The proof is by contradiction. Suppose that $P\left(\liminf_{k \to \infty} \|\nabla f(x_k)\| = 0\right) < 1$. Then there exists a set of sequences of iterates $\{x_k\}$ with measure greater than zero for which $\liminf_{k \to \infty} \|\nabla f(x_k)\| \neq 0$. For these sequences, we know from Proposition 1 that there exists $\Delta_{LB} > 0$ such that $\Delta_k > \Delta_{LB}$. But this contradicts Theorem 4. ∎

Real Representations

Patrick D. Surry[a,b] **& Nicholas J. Radcliffe**[a,b]
{pds,njr}@quadstone.co.uk

[a]Quadstone Ltd, 16 Chester Street, Edinburgh, EH3 7RA, UK
[b]Department of Mathematics, University of Edinburgh, The Kings Buildings, EH9 3JZ, UK

Abstract

This paper introduces two new representations for real-parameter spaces—the Dedekind and Isodedekind representations. Point mutation and uniform crossover—in their generalised, representation-independent form—are shown, when instantiated with respect to these representations, to give rise to familiar operators for continuous domains, such as gaussian mutation, blend crossover and line recombination. Both the Dedekind and Isodedekind representations are highly non-orthogonal (admitting many illegal chromosomes), but, as is demonstrated, this causes no practical or theoretical problems. Moreover, these novel representations are shown to have sensible behaviour as the continuous limit is taken, while both "traditional" binary coding and Gray coding are shown to have pathological behaviour.

1 Introduction

Many optimisation problems are formulated as a search for vectors of real-valued parameters that form extrema of some function. A variety of both local and global techniques with varying degrees of specialisation have been proposed for tackling such problems. Evolutionary algorithms have also been regularly applied in these domains, a particular attraction being that they require only the ability to evaluate the function at any point. Indeed, evolution strategies have been primarily focussed on real-parameter optimisation, with theoretical results specialised to this domain. Traditional genetic algorithms, on the the other hand, are applied to such problems by mapping to a canonical representation space of binary strings for which simple operators are defined. Typical "practical" genetic algorithms specialise these operators by considering the phenotypic effects of the moves they generate in the search domain of real parameters.

In this paper, we demonstrate deep connections between the approaches favoured for continuous domains in evolution strategies and "pragmatic" genetic algorithms, and the operators developed in the "traditional binary" genetic algorithm school for combinatorial optimisation. This is achieved through exploiting a formal procedure for transferring algorithms and operators between arbitrary search domains. The general goal here is to forge a strong link between explicitly stated beliefs about which features of a search domain affect performance and the quality of the instantiated search algorithm. In particular, the aim is that good characterisations and beliefs lead to good search performance, but equally importantly that poor characterisations result in poor search.

We show that by explicitly designing representations that capture beliefs about the structure of the search domain of real parameters (such as the importance of locality and continuity), we can instantiate problem-independent algorithms built from generalised mutation and recombination operators. (In fact, precisely these algorithms have previously been instantiated in combinatorial optimisation domains; Surry & Radcliffe, 1996.) We find that when particular characterisations are employed, we derive commonly used operators such as blend crossover, line recombination and gaussian mutation from the generalised operators.

To facilitate this, we extend previous work on formal construction of representations in discrete (typically combinatorial) search problems to continuous domains. A sequence of representations forming increasingly accurate approximations to the continuous space is employed, and requirements for the limiting process are formulated. When conventional representations for real parameters are considered within this framework, previously suspected peculiarities in their behaviour are confirmed.

We proceed to develop two formal representations for real-parameter evolutionary optimisation based on a formal codification of beliefs about the nature and structure of continuous search domains. We have named the resulting representations the *Dedekind* and *Isodedekind* representations, for reasons that are explained later. We examine the limiting behaviour of these representations, and derive problem-specific forms of generic genetic operators introduced previously. These are seen serendipitously to reduce to 'sensible' operators already widely used for real optimisation.

Having constructed the new representations, we find ourselves able to apply identical (formal) genetic move operators, and therefore identical formal evolutionary *algorithms* with four different representations of real parameter spaces—"traditional" binary coding, Gray coding, Dedekind and Isodedekind. We observe striking qualitative differences in behaviour of these four representations for even the simplest objective functions (figure 1).

The primary purposes of this work are to illuminate deep connections between "evolution strategy style" and "genetic algorithm style" operators, to bridge a gap between discrete and continuous domains, and to expose the formal gene structure underpinning evolutionary approaches to continuous optimisation. It also, however, provides a study in the formal construction of representations and operators from explicit codifications of beliefs about the structure of search domains. In this connection, this work also demonstrates convincingly that the characterisation of a particular problem domain used to induce a representation need not be completely free of 'conflicting' beliefs. Although such characterisations can lead to highly *non-orthogonal* representations (in which the legal values for a given allele are dependent on the current values of others), this is not seen to be problematic in general—indeed the operators derived from such representations may be more powerful than those resulting from simpler ones.

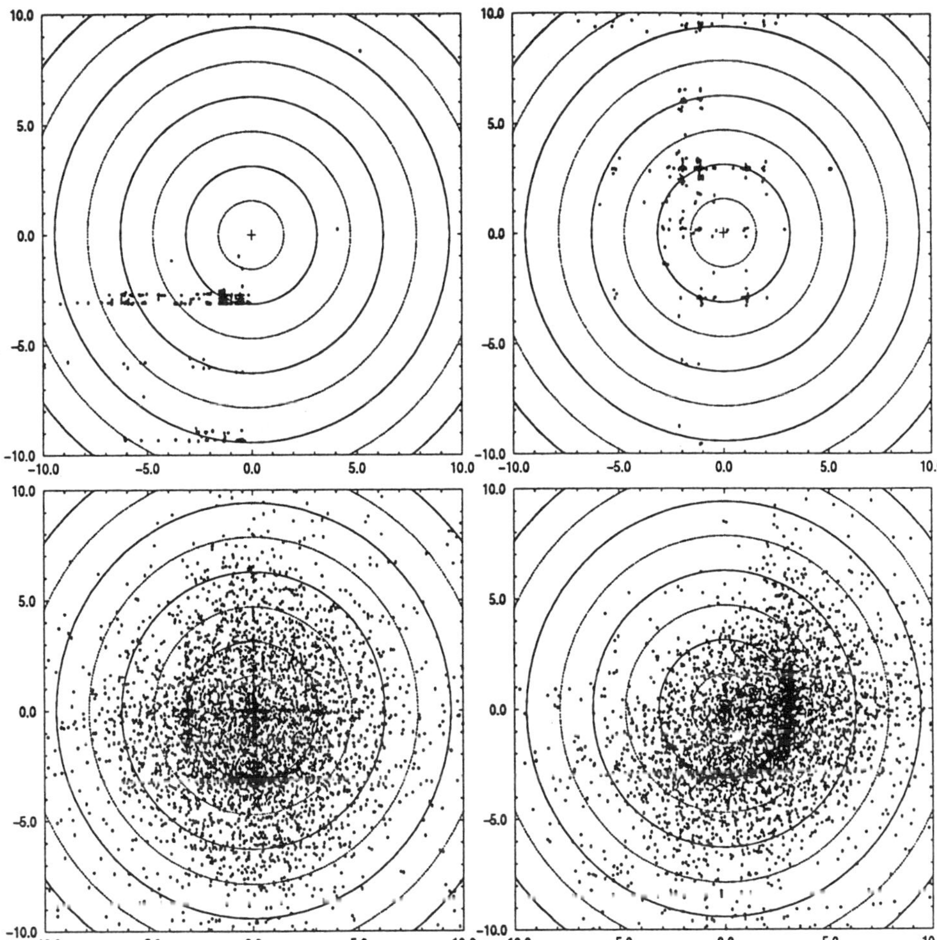

Figure 1: In the spirit of the work presented in Eshelman & Schaffer (1992), this figure illustrates the results of applying an identical formal algorithm instantiated with the four different real-parameter representations discussed herein to Schaffer's F6 function. The two-dimensional function is radially symmetric with global maximum at $(0, 0)$, local maxima on circles of radius $\pi, 2\pi, \ldots$, and local minima on circles of radius $\pi/2, 3\pi/2, \ldots$. The search domain is $[-100, 100] \times [-100, 100]$ of which the figures show the central region. Each figure shows all of the points sampled in one typical run of a fixed algorithm based on the R^3 and BMM operators (see appendix A). Each algorithm sampled approximately 9000 points in the central region during a run of 100 generations with population size 100. The binary representation (top-left) exhibits extremely poor coverage and an extremely striated sampling pattern based on the relative periodicity in the function and the representation. A Gray-coded representation (top-right) typically shows better coverage, as mutation is more effective, but the sampling pattern is clearly biased. The Dedekind representation (bottom-left) shows much better coverage, but since R^3 reduces to DLX-0 there is still a tendency to favour the axis directions, and an inward bias on the population. The algorithm based on the Isodedekind representation (bottom-right) still shows the inward population bias since R^3 reduces to line recombination, but the axial skew is removed.

2   Evolutionary real-parameter optimisation

Optimisation of functions defined over real parameters has a long history, so it is natural that the area has received significant attention from the evolutionary algorithms community. Several now converging schools of thought brought different points of view to the attack.

In the evolution-strategy paradigm (Rechenberg, 1973) and in the evolutionary-programming school (Fogel *et al.*, 1966), the vector of parameters is typically interpreted directly as a "genome", with "gene" values approximated by floating-point machine values. A variety of specialised recombination and mutation operators that directly manipulate these parameters have been employed, but to date their connection to operators used in other search domains has not been apparent. Work with evolution strategies (Baeck & Schwefel, 1993) stresses the importance of gaussian (creep) mutation (possibly with adapted width) as a search operator, based on the so-called *principle of strong causality*, by which small changes in parameter values are assumed to lead to small changes in the objective function. We will see later that by formalising this or other beliefs about the search domain, we can gain insight into what structures the resulting algorithms may be said to be "processing". Recombination methods including line recombination ($\vec{z} = \alpha\vec{x} + (1-\alpha)\vec{y}$), parameter-wise uniform crossover (also known as local-discrete recombination) and blend crossover (local-intermediate recombination) have been employed.

In the genetic-algorithm school, this "parameters-as-genes" approach has not been universally accepted. The common practice has been to represent and manipulate real parameters as fixed-length binary strings using either "traditional" integer coding (where bit strings are decoded as integers and linearly scaled to the appropriate parameter ranges) or "Gray coding" (in which consecutive integers are coded by bit strings that differ in only a single position). Such binary codings allow "standard" genetic operators such as N-point crossover and point mutation to be applied in real-parameter optimisation, albeit with the restriction that the discretisation must result in 2^k points per parameter, for some integer k. They also reflect continuing attachment by many to the dubious *principle of minimal alphabets* (Goldberg, 1989), which has been shown to be motivated by highly questionable theoretical observations (Radcliffe, 1991a; Vose & Liepins, 1991).

An increasing proportion of the genetic algorithms community, however, particularly those working on real-world applications, have pointed out the efficacy of working directly with the real parameters (e.g. Davis, 1991; Michalewicz, 1992). Using "standard" genetic operators in this case—viewing parameters as genes—is problematical as has been pointed out by Goldberg (1990), with the result that *ad hoc* operators have been generally been used, such as "creep mutation" (Davis, 1991) and blend crossover (Eshelman & Schaffer, 1992; generalised from the R^3 operator of Radcliffe, 1991a). Although practically useful, such approaches have lacked a formal basis (for instance, it is not clear what a gene is or how the genetic operators are formally defined), and operators are seen conceptually as acting directly in the search space rather than in a space of genotypes that represents it. In the coming sections we will show that both of the standard evolution-strategy style operators for reals and the standard genetic algorithm operators can be derived from common "representation-independent" template operators. The resulting equivalences are shown in table 1. Figure 2 shows graphically the (phenotypic) effect of the different recombination operators, and figure 3 illustrates the various mutation operators.

In addition to the need for satisfactory mathematical operator derivations, in the case of continuous domains there is a need for clearer understanding of the relationship between operators' effect in a discrete approximation space and in the underlying continuous space. In particular, it seems desirable that operators have well-defined behaviour as the grid spacing shrinks to zero, or at least that we

Evolution strategy term	Genetic algorithm term	Formal derivation
Local-discrete recombination	Uniform crossover	RAR, RTR+ Real
Local-intermediate recombination	BLX-0	RAR, R^3, RTR+ Dedekind
Line recombination	Line recombination	RAR, R^3, RTR+ Isodedekind
n/a	N-point crossover	$\sim$ GNX+ Real
Gaussian mutation	creep mutation	BMM+ Dedekind or Isodedekind
n/a	parameter-wise mutation	BMM+ Real
n/a	bit-wise point mutation	n/a

Table 1: The table summarises several of the operators commonly used in genetic algorithms and evolution strategies (often with different names). Although they may appear to be completely different from one another, they can all be derived as problem-specific forms of generalised problem-independent operators when particular representations are chosen. The "formal" operators RAR, RTR, R^3, GNX and BMM are described in appendix A, BLX-0 is blend crossover with parameter zero, and the Dedekind and Isodedekind representations are described in sections 5.3 and 5.4 respectively.

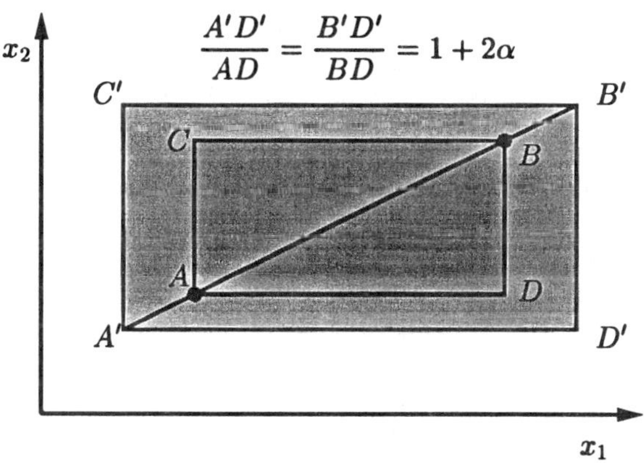

Figure 2: The figure illustrates some of the variety of crossover operators typically used in evolutionary optimisation of real parameters. Here, parents A and B, each a two-component vector, are crossed. Parameter-wise uniform crossover (termed discrete recombination in evolution strategies) generates A, B, C or D with equal probability. For the formal real representation, RAR, RTR, and R^3 are all equivalent to blend crossover with parameter 0 (BLX-0; termed intermediate recombination in evolution strategies), and generate a child uniformly from the rectangle $ACBD$. BLX-α ($\alpha > 0$) generates a child uniformly from the rectangle $A'C'B'D'$. Line recombination generates children uniformly on the line AB, and extended line recombination generates children uniformly on the line $A'B'$. Standard (N-point and uniform) operators with traditional binary codings generate non-localised children which is difficult to show schematically.

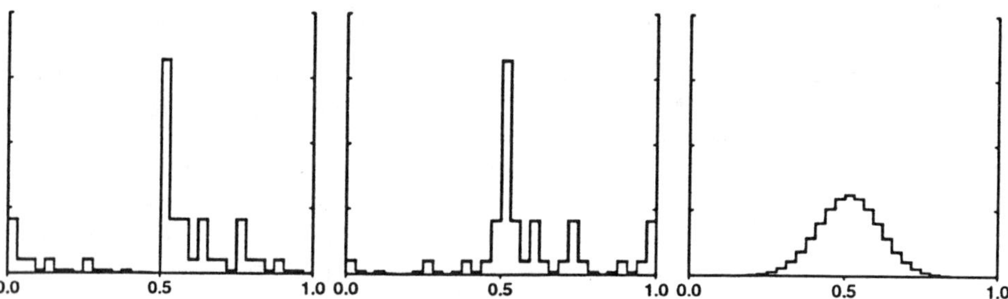

Figure 3: The figure illustrates the effects of instantiating the representation-independent mutation operator BMM (see appendix A) for traditional binary coding (left), Gray coding (center) and the Dedekind representation (right). For the first two representations, BMM reduces to standard point mutation, and in the last case to gaussian creep mutation. For each representation, the real interval [0, 1] has been discretised into 32 points, and the graphs show the probability distribution over possible offspring when the genome representing the point just right of 0.5 is mutated. The pathological distributions in the first two cases help explain some of the behaviour observed in figure 1.

understand what is happening if this is not the case. While gray coding has traditionally been put forward as a "smoother" binary representation for reals, the analysis here will show that it shares with "traditional" binary coding pathological limiting behaviour, while the Dedekind and Isodedekind representations have well-behaved natural continuous limits.

3 Representation in evolutionary search

Evolutionary algorithms are based on genetic operators that manipulate chromosomes. These chromosomes are *representatives* of the structures in the actual search domain, each of which has an associated quality measure. When considering the problem of how to represent a search domain in order to define evolutionary operators, most work has taken one of two approaches. In the first approach, a fixed "canonical" representation is used, and some mapping between the representation space and the search space is constructed. In the second approach, operators are designed specifically for each new search domain, and the problem of representation is largely ignored; conceptually the search operators work directly in the search space. Both of these approaches have significant drawbacks, and we propose an alternative methodology which captures the strengths of both while avoiding their weaknesses.

A canonical representation has the advantage that once operators (and hence algorithms) are defined, they can be applied to any new problem domain—all that is required is to define some mapping from, say, binary strings to the structures in the new search domain. Examples in which both genetic algorithms, which were first conceived for combinatorial problem domains, and evolution strategies, developed for continuous domains, have been coerced into other search domains are relatively commonplace. However, from the point of view of practical optimisation, this has a gigantic drawback. Recent work (Wolpert & Macready, 1995; Radcliffe & Surry, 1995) has confirmed what has been known intuitively for some time—there is no such thing as a free lunch! The representation of the search domain must capture, in some way, the structure of the objective function in order for there to be any possibility of out-performing enumeration. Simply transferring algorithms between problems using a fixed representation space, without explicitly considering the actual representation to be used, and how structure in the search space is preserved through it, is doomed to failure: no algorithm can be an effective black-box optimiser.

A problem-specific approach avoids these difficulties, as *ad hoc* operators can be defined to exploit known characteristics of the problem at hand, or "standard" operators can be modified by forcing them to make moves that appear "sensible" within the search space. However, this approach has the clear disadvantage that work is not easily transferable to new search domains.

The authors argue that a middle ground is preferable. A formalism has been developed that allows an appropriate representation for a given search domain to be generated directly from statements of belief about the search space. Universal "representation-independent" genetic operators can then be instantiated with respect to that representation. The theory is based on characterising beliefs about the structure of a domain of optimisation problems. This characterisation mathematically generates a representation space and growth function for any given instance of the problem. Once the representation has been chosen, problem-specific forms of any of the generalised genetic operators can be mathematically derived. This is important because many of the representations generated by explicitly characterising beliefs about the structure of the search problem turn out to be *non-orthogonal* (in which not all combinations of alleles are legal), meaning that "traditional" genetic operators can not be used. (Consider, for example, trying to use N-point crossover on two permutations: invalid solutions typically result). This framework enables the separation of algorithm and domain-knowledge to be made completely explicit. Representation-independent search algorithms (constructed with generalised move operators) can be precisely specified mathematically. For a given search domain, beliefs about its structure are mathematically formalised to construct a representation. This representation is then used to instantiate the generalised algorithm to derive a computationally effective, problem-specific search strategy.

It is worth noting that the significance of the choice of representation is *not* primarily the way in which real values are physically stored in a digital computer (which is ultimately always as bit patterns), but rather, the way in which it affects the moves effected in the search space by the chosen genetic operators. Representation, as discussed here, is simply a mathematical device for deriving domain-specific operators that incorporate our explicit beliefs about problem structure.

Forma analysis

The approach taken in this paper is based on *forma analysis* (Radcliffe, 1991a, 1991b, 1994), which is reviewed in appendix A for readers not already familiar with this material.

The basis of forma analysis is that formae (generalised schemata) capture beliefs about problem structure—in particular, that they group solutions of related performance—and that the objective function is to *some* degree separable over them (so that recombination and mutation can be effective). It is then possible to define "representation-independent" operators which manipulate the forma membership properties of solutions so as to respect our beliefs about the problem structure.

Although previous work has focused primarily on finite search domains, such as combinatorial problems like the traveling sales-rep problem (Radcliffe & Surry, 1994), neural network topology optimisation (Radcliffe, 1993), multi-objective pipeline optimisation (Surry et al., 1995) and so forth, some initial work was done on continuous domains (Radcliffe, 1991a, 1991b). In this paper we extend these ideas by considering a limiting sequence of discrete representations. These results are used to define two formal genetic representations for real-parameter optimisation, which are used to derive problem-specific forms of the generalised genetic operators.

Algorithms and search strategies

Once genetic operators have been defined independently of any particular representation or problem domain, it is possible to specify completely problem-independent algorithms—for example, not only can we prescribe the selection methodology, but also the exact recombination and mutation operators the algorithm will use. For any specific problem domain $\mathcal{D}$, we develop a representation using some characterisation χ of our beliefs about its structure, which is used to mathematically derive a problem-specific version of our algorithm. A well-defined mathematical procedure has been developed (Surry & Radcliffe, 1996) which, given a problem instance $I \in \mathcal{D}$ (over a search space $\mathcal{S}$), and a characterisation χ of $\mathcal{D}$, generates a representation space $\mathcal{C}_\chi$ and a growth function $g_\chi : \mathcal{C} \longrightarrow \mathcal{S}$ suitable for application of any of the representation-independent operators described in appendix A (see also figure 4).

4 Scaling properties of discretised representations

Previous work has focused on the representation of discrete spaces. However, we seek to extend our formalism to the case of continuous spaces such as the reals. It is clear that any implementation of a search algorithm using digital computers will be finite, so that we are forced to consider an *approximation* of some kind to the actual search space. It is the goal of this section to formalise the requirements that we might enforce in order to make this approximation meaningful.

First of all, we require that we can (in principle) generate a representation of the continuous search space to any desired level of accuracy. We then require that the actions of our search operators have sensible limiting behaviour as we arbitrarily increase the accuracy of our approximate search space.

Consider a problem domain $\mathcal{D}$ in which each instance I is defined on a continuous search space $\mathcal{S}$, typically a subset of $\mathbf{R}^m$. Suppose further that there is a distance metric, $d : \mathcal{S} \times \mathcal{S} \longrightarrow \mathbf{R}^+$ associated with $\mathcal{S}$. We wish to generate an approximate representation for any given problem instance in the domain, to any degree of accuracy. Let $n \in \mathbf{Z}^+$ indicate the degree of accuracy desired, as formalised below. We suppose that a characterisation, $\chi(I, n)$, is available, which is an automatic procedure for generating a finite representation space $\mathcal{C}_{\chi(I,n)}$ and growth function $g_{\chi(I,n)}$ (which we will abbreviate as $\mathcal{C}_n$ and g_n). The growth function maps chromosomes in the representation space into structures into a finite subset $\mathcal{S}_n$ of the search space, as illustrated in figure 4.

We first require that the approximation of $\mathcal{S}$ can be made arbitrarily good. Formally, we require that for any open subset of $\mathcal{S}$, there is some level of accuracy above which our approximation always represents some point in the subset:

$$\forall B \subseteq \mathcal{S} \ (B \text{ open}) \ \exists n_0 \in \mathbf{Z}^+ \ : \ n > n_0 \Longrightarrow \mathcal{S}_n \cap B \neq \varnothing,$$

where $\mathcal{S}_n = g_n(\mathcal{C}_n)$ is the subset of the search space currently represented.

Furthermore, we require that any search operators to be used exhibit reasonable limiting behaviour. Thus, as we change the degree of accuracy of our approximation, we desire that the action of the operators in the search space does not change radically with respect to the distance function defined on $\mathcal{S}$.

Any search operator, Ω, can be viewed as generating a child chromosome from one or more parent chromosomes and a control parameter selected uniformly from a control set (which provides "randomness"; see Radcliffe, 1994), thus

$$\Omega : \mathcal{C}^q \times \mathcal{K}_\Omega \longrightarrow \mathcal{C},$$

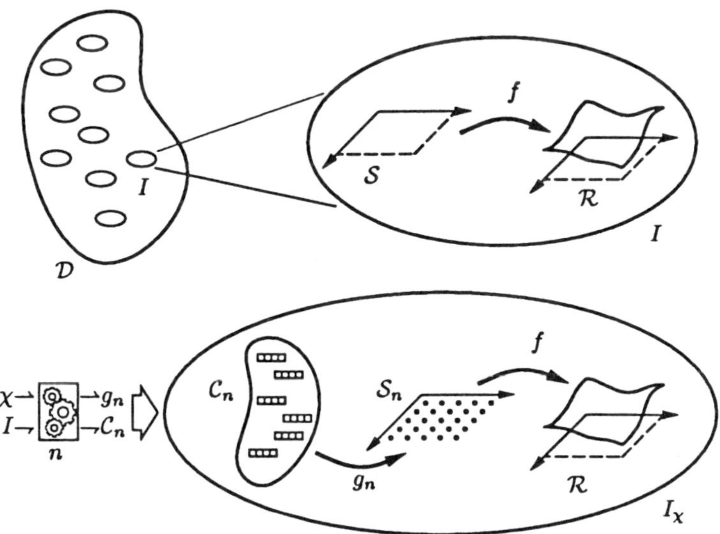

Figure 4: A *problem domain* $\mathcal{D}$ consists of a set of *problem instances*. Each instance I defines a *search space* S of candidate solutions, a *fitness function* f and a set of objective values $\mathcal{R}$. A *characterisation* χ of the domain specifies a set of equivalences among the solutions for any instance I, for any given accuracy n. These equivalences induce a *representation* made up of a *representation space* $\mathcal{C}_{\chi(I,n)}$ (of *chromosomes*) and a *growth function* $g_{\chi(I,n)}$ mapping chromosomes to a subset S_n of S. A chromosome x is a string of *alleles*, each of which indicates that x satisfies a particular equivalence on S. Algorithms can be completely specified by their action on the alleles of these generalised chromosomes, making them totally independent of the problem domain itself.

where $\mathcal{K}_\Omega$ is the set of possible control parameters (e.g. cross points, mutation masks, etc.), and q is the arity of the operator (so $q = 1$ for a mutation operator, $q = 2$ for a typical recombination operator, etc.). We can define an equivalent probabilistic form of Ω, which samples uniformly from the control set:

$$\tilde{\Omega}(x_1,\ldots,x_q) \triangleq \Omega(x_1,\ldots,x_q,\kappa) \; : \; \kappa \sim U(\mathcal{K}_\Omega).$$

In order to restrict the limiting behaviour of such an operator, we require that its action on chromosomes representing nearly the same point in the search space tends to be the same. Formally,

$$\forall \varepsilon > 0 \; \forall \{(a_i, x_i)\}_{i=1}^{q} \; (a_i \in S, x_i \in C) \; \forall B \subseteq S \; (B \text{ open}) \exists \delta, p_0 > 0 \; \exists n_0 \in \mathbb{Z}^+ \; :$$
$$n > n_0, \; \max_{1 \le i \le q} d(g_n(x_i), a_i) < \delta \implies |P(g_n(\tilde{\Omega}(x_1, x_2, \ldots, x_q)) \subset B) \quad p_0| < \varepsilon.$$

Thus the probability that the operator generates a representative of a point contained in any fixed open subset (B) of S must converge to a fixed value (p_0) as the operands (the x_i) converge to representatives of any fixed set of points (the a_i) in S.

Binomial minimal mutation

These definitions prompt us to redefine the binomial minimal mutation operator, BMM (see appendix A). As originally presented (Radcliffe & Surry, 1994), the operator made a number of minimal mutations chosen from a binomial distribution parameterised by the mutation probability, p_m, and the number of alleles in the genome, n. In order to preserve its behaviour as $n \to \infty$, we advocate that the binomial distribution be parameterised by an *effective* chromosome length, ℓ_n instead of the actual length n. This effective length should be chosen so that a sequence of ℓ_n randomly chosen minimal mutations randomises the chromosome. Typically $\ell_n = n$, but when the representation is highly non-orthogonal (so that the likelihood of "undoing" previous minimal mutations is high), we may have $\ell_n > n$. For example, with the Dedekind representation introduced below, we find that $\ell_n = n^2$.

5   Representations for real-parameter optimisation

In this section, we consider a number of different representations for discretised real-parameter optimisation. We first discuss traditional integer-coding and the related Gray coding, and then go on to develop two new representations and their associated operators based on formally characterising our beliefs about the structure of the search domain.

In generic real-parameter optimisation, the most obvious/general belief we would like a representation to capture is some form of Lipschitz condition (also known as Hölder-continuity)—that small changes in the parameters lead to small changes in the observed function values. Thus, neighbouring solutions in the search space are expected to have related performance. By capturing this idea on an "axis-by-axis" (parameter by parameter) basis, we develop the Dedekind representation, and by considering all possible axis orientations simultaneously we derive the Isodedekind representation. The operators we derive from these representations have been commonly used in evolution strategies, but are now seen to be formally equivalent to operators used in completely different discrete/combinatorial domains.

Traditional approaches to binary coding of real parameters is based (if on any explicit foundation) on the belief that more schemata are better than fewer (the notion of implicit parallelism, giving rise to the principle of minimal alphabets). This has repeatedly been shown to be little more than statistical sleight of hand: one sample is one sample, not many. There is also perhaps some idea that because binary coding "chops up the search space" in many different ways, it lets the algorithm discover useful patterns (Goldberg, 1989; Holland, 1975) but research has shown that is only true if the problem happens to coincide with the particular scaling and location captured in the binary coding. For example, Eshelman & Schaffer (1992) found that simply rescaling or shifting the coordinate axes could dramatically impact performance. (It is reasonable, however, to speculate about constructing a formal representation based on beliefs about periodicity in the objective function—or, indeed, on any other feature thought to be relevant—but this has not as yet been achieved, although an early attempt was made by Radcliffe, 1991a.)

5.1   Approximating the search domain

In evolutionary real-parameter optimisation, we face the problem of representing a discrete approximation to a continuous search space. Here the search space is taken to be a product of real intervals,

$$S \triangleq \prod_{i=1}^{m} [\alpha_i, \beta_i] \subseteq \mathbf{R}^m.$$

We consider a discretised approximation to the search space generated by the intersection points of a uniform lattice of planes along each co-ordinate axis, namely:

$$S_n \triangleq \prod_{i=1}^{m} \{\alpha_i, \alpha_i + \Delta_{i,n}, \alpha_i + 2\Delta_{i,n}, \ldots, \beta_i\} \subset S$$

where

$$\Delta_{i,n} = \frac{\beta_i - \alpha_i}{n - 1}.$$

It is thus clear that by using a simple linear transformation, it is sufficient to consider the case $S_n = \mathbf{Z}_n^m$. (For the traditional binary codings, we can, for simplicity, restrict n to powers of 2, but this is not a significant restriction.)

We begin by considering the case $m = 1$ (in which we represent a single parameter), and examine the traditional binary representations as well as developing the *Dedekind* representation. In section 5.4, we show that building up to higher dimensional search spaces is straightforward, and also introduce the alternative *Isodedekind* representation.

5.2   Traditional genetic algorithm representations

We first examine the traditional methods for coercing a genetic algorithm into a real-parameter optimisation domain. The two standard and variously-championed approaches are traditional integer coding, in which an integer is directly coded in its base 2 representation, and Gray coding, which alleviates one of the perceived problems with the first approach. We present formal definitions of the representations in forma analysis terms, in order that we will later be able to derive forms of generalised genetic operators and to examine their limiting behaviour as we approximate the continuous space more closely.

We will see that neither representation is based on explicitly characterising any particular structure of the underlying optimisation problem, and that this leads to pathological limiting behaviour.

Traditional integer coding

A common approach to representing n adjacent integer values is to use $k = \lceil \log_2 n \rceil$ bits. When such an approach is taken, there is a choice, in principle, of $2^k!$ mappings between the 2^k values and the 2^k strings used to represent them. In practice, almost all such work uses either "traditional" binary coding, in which the ith value is represented by the binary number i, or so-called *Gray coding* (explained below)

With traditional integer-coding, we can write the formal equivalence relations generating the representation as follows:

$$\psi_i(x, y) = \begin{cases} 1, & \text{if } x \otimes 2^i = y \otimes 2^i, \\ 0, & \text{otherwise.} \end{cases}$$

Value	Binary	$\square\square 1$	$\square 0 \square$	$\square 01$	Gray	$\square\square 1$	$\square 0 \square$	$\square 01$	Dedekind	ξ_5^0	ξ_2^1	$\xi_5^0 \cap \xi_2^1$
0	000	-	•	-	000	-	•	-	0000000	•	-	-
1	001	•	•	•	001	•	•	•	0000001	•	-	-
2	010	-	-	-	011	•	-	-	0000011	•	•	•
3	011	•	-	-	010	-	-	-	0000111	•	•	•
4	100	-	•	-	110	-	-	-	0001111	•	•	•
5	101	•	•	•	111	•	-	-	0011111	-	•	-
6	110	-	-	-	101	•	•	•	0111111	-	•	-
7	111	•	-	-	100	-	•	-	1111111	-	•	-

Table 2: The figure shows the way in which elements of $\mathbf{Z}_n$ (used to approximate a real-valued interval) are represented using traditional binary coding, Gray coding, and the Dedekind representation developed here. Several example formae are illustrated in each case. Note that in the first two cases, formae correspond to schemata and are global in extent (including intersections), while in the third case, formae correspond to intervals on the line and encapsulate the notion of locality, presumably important in real optimisation. These representations are used to mathematically derive genetic operators suitable for computational implementation—it is *not* necessary (or even feasible, in the case of Dedekind) to store solutions in the forms shown here.

where $i \in \{0, 1, \ldots, k-1\}$ and $\otimes$ denotes bitwise-and. These equivalence relations induce the basic formae (alleles) $\xi_0^0, \xi_0^1, \ldots, \xi_i^0, \xi_i^1, \ldots, \xi_{k-1}^0, \xi_{k-1}^1$ which we can identify exactly with schemata

$$\xi_i^0 \equiv \square \cdots \square 0 \square \cdots \square$$
$$\xi_i^1 \equiv \square \cdots \square 1 \square \cdots \square$$

with the 0 or 1 in the ith position. It is clear that through intersections of these basic formae we can build all higher-order formae (again, exactly the higher-order schemata), and can identify individual solutions by noting the equivalence class to which they belong for each of the basic equivalence relations. Examples of this coding indicating the membership patterns of several formae are shown in table 2. Qualitatively we see that formae are neither local nor purely periodic in extent. Further, it is clear that as we increase the number of formae in order to approximate S more and more accurately, there is no clear notion of the limiting properties of the formae. This will be made evident in section 5.6 when we examine the limiting behaviour of the genetic operators derived from this representation.

Gray coding

The principal motivation for considering Gray coding is the perceived problem of Hamming Cliffs with traditional integer coding. An example of a Hamming cliff is the transition from 7 to 8 in the traditional coding, where a relatively large number of bits change value with a small step in the search space (e.g. $\cdots 0111$ to $\cdots 1000$). The attraction of Gray coding (Caruana & Schaffer, 1988) is that the strings representing adjacent values always differ by exactly one bit. There are numerous possible mappings of the integers to binary strings that have this adjacency property, but the most commonly used one codes the integer x as the (binary) value of $x \oplus \lfloor x/2 \rfloor$ where $\oplus$ is the bitwise exclusive-or operator. If we write the binary value of x (the traditional integer coding) as $b_{k-1} \cdots b_1 b_0$ and the Gray-coded representation of i as $g_{k-1} \cdots g_1 g_0$ then we have the relationships

$$g_i = b_{i+1} \oplus b_i$$

and

$$b_i = b_{i+1} \oplus g_i,$$

which allow conversion from one form to the other (taking $b_k = 0$).

These relationships allow us to write the equivalence relations which define the Gray-coding representation:

$$\psi_i(x,y) = \begin{cases} 1, & \text{if } (x \oplus \lfloor x/2 \rfloor) \otimes 2^i = (y \oplus \lfloor y/2 \rfloor) \otimes 2^i, \\ 0, & \text{otherwise.} \end{cases}$$

where $i \in \{0, 1, \ldots, k-1\}$. As with traditional integer coding, the formae can be exactly identified with (now Gray-coded) schemata. An example of the coding scheme along with the members of several formae are shown in table 2. Although these formae never contain 'singleton' solutions, it is still clear that they are still highly non-local in extent. It will also be shown that the limiting properties of the genetic operators (as the level of approximation is improved) are no better than the traditional coding.

5.3 Representations that "capture" continuity

The Dedekind representation

We seek to define a representation for Z_n based on our beliefs about the structure of the problems we will be attacking. For the wide class of real-parameter optimisation problems, perhaps the simplest belief we might hold is some notion of continuity. That is, we believe that small changes in the parameter values will lead to small changes in the objective function. In evolution strategies, this belief is termed *the principle of strong causality*, and in real analysis functions with such a property are termed *Hölder continuous* or *Lipschitz*.

In order to quantify this belief, we seek to characterise groups of solutions (formae) with related performance. To do this, we will define equivalence relations that capture locality, based on the idea of *Dedekind cuts*:

> A Dedekind cut is a partitioning of the rational numbers into two non-empty sets, such that all the members of one are less than all those of the other. For example, the positive irrationals can be defined as Dedekind cuts on the positive rationals
> (e.g. $\sqrt{2} \triangleq \langle \{x \in \mathbb{Q}^+ \mid x^2 < 2\}, \{x \in \mathbb{Q}^+ \mid x^2 > 2\} \rangle$).

Thus the basic equivalence relations we define on Z_n are cuts

$$\psi_i(x,y) = \begin{cases} 1, & \text{if } x,y \geq i \text{ or } x,y < i, \\ 0, & \text{otherwise,} \end{cases}$$

where $i \in \{1, \ldots, n-1\}$. These equivalence relations induce half-space equivalence classes of the following type:

$$\begin{aligned} \xi_i^0 &\equiv \{0, 1, \ldots, i-1\}, \\ \xi_i^1 &\equiv \{i, i+1, \ldots, n-1\}. \end{aligned}$$

It is easy to see that intersections of these basic formae result in sets defining closed intervals, as illustrated in table 2. Note that, formally, this representation has $n-1$ highly non-orthogonal (constrained) binary genes coding a single approximated parameter, instead of the $k = \lceil \log_2 n \rceil$ orthogonal genes of traditional integer coding or Gray coding. However, we will see that the operators we derive from this representation and their limiting behaviour as we increase the level of approximation ($n \to \infty$) are much more natural with our new definitions.

While it is somewhat ironic that this formalism of the real representation utilises binary genes, we emphasise once again that we do *not* propose to store or manipulate solutions in this form, but only to apply our design principles to develop and analyse our genetic operators.

5.4 Extending the representations to multiple parameters

It is a simple matter to extend any of the representations to higher dimensions by forming products of the one-dimensional equivalence relations. For example, in a two-dimensional search space, approximated by $Z_n \times Z_n$, the basic equivalence relations for the Dedekind representation are of the form

$$\psi_{ij}(x,y) \equiv \psi_i(x_1,y_1) \times \psi_j(x_2,y_2) = \begin{cases} 1, & \text{if } (x_1,y_1 \geq i \text{ or } x_1,y_1 < i) \\ & \text{and } (x_2,y_2 \geq j \text{ or } x_2,y_2 < j), \\ 0, & \text{otherwise,} \end{cases}$$

with equivalence classes of the form

$$
\begin{aligned}
\xi_{ij}^{00} \equiv \xi_i^0 \times \xi_j^0 &= \{(0,0),\ldots,(0,j-1),\ldots,(i-1,0),\ldots,(i-1,j-1)\}, \\
\xi_{ij}^{10} \equiv \xi_i^1 \times \xi_j^0 &= \{(i,0),\ldots,(i,j-1),\ldots,(n-1,0),\ldots,(n-1,j-1)\}, \\
\xi_{ij}^{01} \equiv \xi_i^0 \times \xi_j^1 &= \{(0,j),\ldots,(0,n-1),\ldots,(i-1,j),\ldots,(i-1,n-1)\}, \\
\xi_{ij}^{11} \equiv \xi_i^1 \times \xi_j^1 &= \{(i,j),\ldots,(i,n-1),\ldots,(n-1,j),\ldots,(n-1,n-1)\}.
\end{aligned}
$$

The traditional binary and Gray codings can be similarly extended.

The Isodedekind representation

An alternative approach to extending the Dedekind representation to multiple parameters is to define new equivalence relations. Because it seems somewhat artificial to characterise locality only along the axis directions, we might think of devising a characterisation to capture locality more generally. Thus, we could define basic equivalence relations which partition Z_n^m using cut planes which have arbitrary orientation. This would require our conceptual chromosome to have alleles indicating on which side of a series of cuts it fell in each possible direction from the origin. Thus in the limiting case, the chromosome consists of a continuous infinity of continuous infinities of genes! We do not exhibit a precise discrete formulation here for reasons of space, but it is straightforward to visualise the limiting forms that the generalised operators take in such a case (see for example figure 5). The Isodedekind representation demonstrates convincingly that even extremely non-orthogonal characterisations can be used successfully.

5.5 Forma variance calculations

One measure which indicates how well formae succeed in grouping together solutions of related fitness is mean forma variance. By generating random formae of a particular size and measuring the fitness variance within them, we can estimate the mean variance for formae of a given size. This was shown to be a good qualitative indicator of relative algorithmic performance (Radcliffe & Surry, 1994).

For the Dedekind and Isodedekind representation, all formae can be represented as convex simplices in $\mathbf{R}^m$. For illustrative purposes, we consider the one-dimensional case in which formae become intervals (although it is not difficult to extend the results to higher dimensions). It is then a simple matter to write down an expression for the fitness variance of a forma (interval) of size τ, centered at $x = t$, with objective function $f(x)$. Namely,

$$\sigma^2(t,\tau) = \frac{1}{\tau} \int_{t-\tau/2}^{t+\tau/2} (f(x) - \bar{f}(t,\tau))^2 dx,$$

where

$$\bar{f}(t,\tau) = \frac{1}{\tau} \int_{t-\tau/2}^{t+\tau/2} f(x) dx.$$

It is straightforward to show that requiring the forma variance to decrease to zero as forma size (τ) decreases is closely related to making a Lipschitz assumption on the objective function.

For instance, assume that f is Lipschitz over an interval $[\alpha, \beta]$, that is,

$$x, y \in [\alpha, \beta] \implies |f(x) - f(y)| < \varepsilon|x - y|$$

for some $\varepsilon \in \mathbf{R}^+$. Now consider any forma of size τ contained in $[\alpha, \beta]$. By the mean value theorem, we know that $\bar{f}(t,\tau) = f(c)$ for some $c \in [t - \tau/2, t + \tau/2]$. We then have,

$$
\begin{aligned}
\sigma^2(t,\tau) \quad &< \quad \frac{1}{\tau} \int_{t-\tau/2}^{t+\tau/2} (\varepsilon(x - c))^2 dx \\
&= \quad \frac{\varepsilon^2}{3\tau}(x - c)^3 \Big|_{t-\tau/2}^{t+\tau/2} \\
&\leq \quad \frac{\varepsilon^2\tau^2}{3}
\end{aligned}
$$

Conversely, it is trivial to show that if f is nowhere Lipschitz on $[\alpha, \beta]$, that

$$\sigma^2(t,\tau) \geq \frac{\varepsilon^2\tau^2}{12}$$

Thus the notion that formae should group together solutions of related fitness has been shown to be closely linked to the characterisations on which we based the construction of the Dedekind and Isodedekind representations—namely that the functions of interest were in some sense smooth (satisfying a Lipschitz condition, or more loosely the principle of strong causality).

For the traditional integer coding and Gray codings used with genetic algorithms, there is no analogous limiting behaviour that can be extracted. We might speculate on some relationship to periodic behaviour of the function, but it is not simply that. It has been "discovered" several times that simply by shifting the origin or rescaling the axes, the behaviour of algorithms based on these representation can change radically. This is clearly very undesirable behaviour.

Fundamentally, we argue that this stems from the lack of a principled foundation for the traditional representations—they do not encapsulate particular beliefs about the problem domains of interest. In fact, many workers have taken the diametrically opposite approach of trying to discover what it is

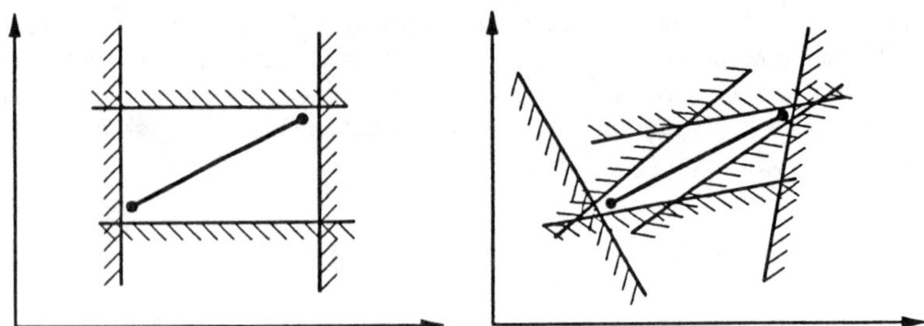

Figure 5: The figure illustrates two problem-specific forms of the random respectful recombination (R^3) operator for a two-dimensional real-parameter optimisation problem. (a) On the left, the Dedekind representation is defined by cut formae along each axis. Since R^3 requires that the child be a member of all formae to which both parents belong, the child must lie within the hypercube (square here) with its two parents at opposite vertices. Hence R^3 reduces to BLX-0 in this case. (b) On the right, the Isodedekind representation is defined by cut formae in arbitrary directions. Thus R^3 requires, in the limit, that the child lies on the line segment bounded by the two parents, so that R^3 is equivalent to line recombination in this case. It is also instructive to compare algorithms based on these different representations which incorporate R^3—see figure 1.

that these representations *are* characterising, for instance by constructing specialised functions over the integers which lead the algorithms in particular directions. While such research may be intrinsically interesting, it is far from clear that it bears on the problem of how algorithms based on these representations behave for "real" functions.

5.6 Derivation of operators

It is now straightforward to derive forms of the generalised genetic operators described in appendix A. The derivations are summarised in table 1. These operators can then be used to instantiate a fixed representation-independent algorithm for each of the four representations presented here. This is illustrated for a simple objective function in figure 1.

For the traditional binary and Gray codings, the generalised operators reduce to "standard" forms, since the representations are orthogonal (all combination of allele values are legal). Thus, RAR, RTR and R^3 reduce to uniform crossover, GNX reduces to N-point crossover, and BMM reduces to bitwise point mutation.

For the Dedekind representation, it is clear that both R^3 and RTR require that the child be uniformly selected to lie in the box determined by the parents (see also figure 5). Thus, in one dimension, the crossover operator $X : Z_n \times Z_n \times [0, 1) \longrightarrow Z_n$ acting on parents x and y (without loss of generality, $x < y$) and control parameter $\kappa \in [0, 1)$ results in the child $X(x, y, \kappa) = x + \lfloor \kappa(y - x + 1) \rfloor$. It is clear that in the limit of $n \to \infty$, this is equivalent to BLX-0 as defined by Eshelman & Schaffer (1992); see figure 2. For this representation, it is not difficult to see that RAR is also equivalent to BLX-0 (it is easy to show that the child must lie in the interval defined by the parents, and only slightly more difficult to demonstrate that the likelihood is uniform over the interval).

For the Isodedekind representation, R^3 and RTR reduce to line recombination as shown in figure 5, and RAR simply requires that we are able to generate any point in the search space.

Turning to mutation, if we analyse our representation-independent mutation operator BMM with the Dedekind representation, it is clear that a minimal mutation involves flipping the value of one of the two bits forming the transition from ones to zeros in the genome. Thus a fixed-length sequence of minimal mutations is equivalent to a random walk away from the original transition point. We will show that this reduces in the limit of $n \to \infty$ to standard gaussian creep mutation with width parameterised by the gene-wise mutation probability.

Proof: Assume that each parameter is represented by n genes in the Dedekind representation. Consider the action of BMM on a single parameter (as it is clear that genes in different parameters are orthogonal). Given a gene-wise mutation rate p_m, and an effective chromosome length ℓ_n (which we will find must be proportional to n^2), we make a binomial number s of minimal mutations, where s is chosen from the distribution $S \sim B(\ell_n, p_m)$. Now, we know that the binomial distribution $B(n,p)$ is asymptotically approximated by the normal distribution $N(np, \sqrt{np(1-p)})$ provided that $\sqrt{np(1-p)} \ll np$. In our case, we take p_m fixed, and $\ell_n \to \infty$ as $n \to \infty$ so that S is asymptotically approximated by $S \sim N(\ell_n p_m, \sqrt{\ell_n p_m(1-p_m)})$. Now, each minimal mutation results in a step of size $\Delta = L/n$ to the left or right of the current value, where L is the length of the interval in which the parameter lies. Thus once we have chosen a number of steps s, distributed according to $S \sim N(\ell_n p_m, \sqrt{\ell_n p_m(1-p_m)})$ we perform a random walk with step length Δ, so that the final displacement x is distributed conditionally on s, according to the normal distribution $X|S \sim N(0, \sqrt{s}L/n)$. Further, we can thus write the unconditional p.d.f. for X as:

$$p(x) = \int_{-\infty}^{\infty} p(x|s)p(s)\,ds.$$

Consider now the moment-generating function for X, $m_X(t)$, given by:

$$
\begin{aligned}
m_X(t) = E(e^{tx}) &= \int_{-\infty}^{\infty}\int_{-\infty}^{\infty} p(x|s)p(s)e^{tx}\,ds\,dx \\
&= \int_{-\infty}^{\infty} p(s)\int_{-\infty}^{\infty} p(x|s)e^{tx}\,dx\,ds \\
&= \int_{-\infty}^{\infty} p(s)m_{X|S}(t)\,ds.
\end{aligned}
$$

Now, since $X|S \sim N(0, \sqrt{s}L/n)$, a normal distribution, we know that $m_{X|S}(t) = \exp(0t + (\sqrt{s}L/n)^2 t^2/2)$, which yields

$$
\begin{aligned}
m_X(t) &= \int_{-\infty}^{\infty} p(s)\exp\left(\frac{s}{2}\left(\frac{Lt}{n}\right)^2\right)ds \\
&= m_S\left(\frac{1}{2}\left(\frac{Lt}{n}\right)^2\right).
\end{aligned}
$$

Finally, since $S \sim N(\ell_n p_m, \sqrt{\ell_n p_m(1-p_m)})$ we have $m_S(t) = \exp(\ell_n p_m t + \ell_n p_m(1-p_m)t^2/2)$, so that

$$m_X(t) = \exp\left(\frac{p_m L^2 \ell_n}{2n^2}t^2 + \frac{p_m(1-p_m)L^4 \ell_n}{8n^4}t^4\right).$$

We thus choose our length scale $\ell_n = n^2$ to make the limit finite, and see that $\lim_{n\to\infty} m_X(t) = \exp(p_m L^2 t^2/2)$. This is simply the moment generating function for $N(0, \sqrt{p_m}L)$ so the final displacement X must have the identical distribution. Thus BMM instantiated for the Dedekind representation is that operator which adds gaussian noise with width $\sqrt{p_m}L$ to each parameter.

Note that for the Isodedekind representation a sequence of minimal mutations involves a random walk with steps taken in arbitrary directions in $\mathbf{R}^m$. Thus BMM is likely to be equivalent to Gaussian mutation, but the precise scaling factors have not yet been derived.

6 Discussion

This paper has presented formal constructions for two genetic representations for real-parameter optimisation based on characterising the notion of locality—the Dedekind and Isodedekind representations. Generalised genetic operators are shown to reduce in these representations to standard forms, namely blend crossover, line recombination and gaussian creep mutation which are widely used in practice. Both of these representations are highly non-orthogonal, but this is seen not to present difficulties. Analysis of the limiting behaviour of discrete approximations to a continuous search space has shown that the more traditional binary and Gray codings have pathological behaviour. This is illustrated qualitatively when a fixed algorithm is instantiated for all four representations and radically different behaviour is observed (figure 1).

A Forma analysis

Holland (1975) identified subsets of a search space of strings using *schemata*—sets of strings that share certain gene values. His schema theorem shows how the *observed* fitness of any schema in a population can be used to bound the *expected* instantiation of the same schema in the next generation, under the action of proportional selection. Several authors have generalised the idea of schema and shown that the theorem applies to arbitrary subsets of the search space, provided that suitable disruption coefficients are chosen (Radcliffe, 1991a; Vose & Liepins, 1991).

In Radcliffe's work, subsets of the search space, S, are identified as *formae*. Typically, the formae are defined as the equivalence classes induced by a set of equivalence relations, Ψ. (An equivalence relation $\psi : S \times S \longrightarrow \{0, 1\}$ can be thought of as a function which returns 1 if a given pair of solutions are "equivalent" and 0 otherwise.) Any solution can then be identified by specifying the equivalence class to which it belongs for each of the equivalence relations. Loosely speaking, we identify genes with a set of basic equivalence relations (from which any member of Ψ can be constructed) and alleles with the corresponding equivalence classes. For instance, "same hair colour" and "same eye colour" might be two basic equivalence relations in Ψ, which would induce the formae "red hair", "brown hair", "blue eyes", etc. Higher order formae are then constructed by intersection, e.g. "brown hair and blue eyes".

The selection of an appropriate set of equivalence relations for a particular class of problem is an open problem. We assume that domain knowledge *characterised* by an algorithmic procedure which generates the required equivalence classes for any given problem instance. For example, in the travelling sales-rep problem, we might reasonably believe that tours sharing any given edge will have related performance (indeed this is clear in this case since the length of a tour is simply the sum of its edge lengths). Thus we might propose a characterisation which generates formae based on equivalence relations of the form 'has edge $\overline{xy}$' (although other characterisations are also possible; see Radcliffe & Surry, 1994).

However, several ideas have been previously proposed (Radcliffe, 1991a) which summarise the way formae should partition the search space. These permit the construction of representation-independent operators that manipulate solutions in effective ways.

- Correlation within formae. The formae should group together solutions of related fitness. One measure of this is the mean fitness variance over formae of a given size. This has been measured experimentally for four representations in the travelling sales-rep problem and shown to correlate well with performance (Radcliffe & Surry, 1994).

- Minimal degeneracy[1]. The number of genomes representing each member of S should be small.

- Computability. It must be possible to efficiently exhibit members of any given formae computationally (clearly equivalence relations based on tour length in the TSP could be mathematically specified, but it would be computationally infeasible to generate members of particular formae). These restrictions have not been investigated in depth, but have not been a problem with those representations investigated to date.

Representation-independent operators

The way in which formae are thought to group solutions of related performance suggests several *design principles* for constructing genetic operators. Such operators can be precisely defined independently of any particular representation, by specifying how they manipulate the formae-membership properties of their operand(s). For any given representation, we can use the definition of the operators to formally derive a problem-specific version of that operator. This leads in some cases to previously known operators in a given search domain, but in other cases leads to new insights about what form of recombination or mutation might be applicable to a given problem domain. The generalised operators are particularly relevant to non-orthogonal representations (in which not all combinations of alleles are valid), which often arise when the problem characterisation is based on beliefs which are not completely compatible. A number of these principles and related operators are summarised below.

Respect Respect requires that children are members of all formae to which both their parents belong. For example, if there were equivalence relations about hair colour and eye colour in Ψ, then if both parents had red hair and green eyes, so should all children produced by X.

More formally, a recombination operator $X : S \times S \times \mathcal{K}_X \longrightarrow S$ (where $\mathcal{K}_X$ is a set of control parameters such as cross-points or crossover masks) is said to *respect* the set of formae Ξ generated by Ψ iff

$$\forall \xi \in \Xi \; \forall a \in \xi \; \forall b \in \xi \; \forall \kappa \in \mathcal{K}_X : \; X(a,b,\kappa) \in \xi.$$

Random respectful recombination (R^3) is defined as that operator which selects a child uniformly at random from the set of all solutions which share all characteristics possessed by both parents (their *similarity set*).

Transmission A recombination operator is said to be *strictly transmitting* if every child it produces is equivalent to one of its parents under each of the basic equivalence relations (loosely, every gene is set to an allele which is taken from one or other parent). Thus, if one parent had red hair and the other had brown hair, then transmission would require that the child had either red or brown hair.

---

[1]The term *redundancy* has previously been used to mean the same thing, but we now urge that redundancy should be reserved for the situation in which chromosomes contain more information than strictly necessary to specify the solution they represent.

The *random transmitting recombination* (RTR) operator is defined as that operator which selects a child uniformly at random from the set of all solutions belonging only to basic formae present in either of the parents (their *dynastic span*).

Assortment Assortment requires that a recombination operator be capable of generating a child with any compatible characteristics taken from the two parents. In our example above, if one parent had green eyes and the other had red hair, and if those two characteristics are compatible, assortment would require that we could generate a child with green eyes and red hair.

Formally, a recombination operator is said to *properly assort* the formae generated by Ψ iff

$$\forall \xi_1, \xi_2 \in \Xi \ (\xi_1 \cap \xi_2 \neq \varnothing) \ \forall a_1 \in \xi_1 \ \forall a_2 \in \xi_2 \ \exists \kappa \in \mathcal{K}_X : \ X(a_1, a_2, \kappa) \in \xi_1 \cap \xi_2.$$

The *random assorting recombination operator* (RAR), a generalised form of uniform crossover, has been previously defined (Radcliffe, 1992). It proceeds by placing all alleles from both parents in a conceptual bag (possibly with different weights), and then repeatedly draws out alleles for insertion into the child, discarding them if they are incompatible with those already there. If the bag empties before the child is complete, which can happen if not all combinations of gene values are allowed (so that the representation is *non-orthogonal*) remaining genes are set to random values that are compatible with those genes already set.

A *generalised N-point crossover,* GNX, has also been proposed (Radcliffe & Surry, 1994). This proceeds in much the same way as standard N-point crossover, dividing the two parents with N cut-points, and then using genetic material from alternating segments. The alleles within each segment are tested in a random order for inclusion in the child, and any remaining gaps are patched by randomly selecting compatible alleles first from the unused alleles in the parents, and then from all possible alleles.

Ergodicity This demands that we select operators such that it is possible to move from any location in the search space to any other by their repeated action. (Typically a standard mutation operator is sufficient.)

Binomial minimal mutation, BMM, a generalisation of standard point-wise mutation, has been proposed in Radcliffe & Surry (1994). Minimal mutations are defined to be those moves which change the fewest possible number of alleles in a solution (in non-orthogonal representations it may be necessary to change more than one allele at a time to maintain legality). BMM performs a binomially-distributed number (parameterised by the genome length and a gene-wise mutation probability) of minimal mutations, and does not forbid mutations which 'undo' previous ones.

Work is also ongoing which investigates the ramifications of a principle of *disdain* in which formae non-membership is used to compare parent solutions. This leads to the development of search operators such as directed mutation and simplex-like recombination.

References

T. Bäck and H.-P. Schwefel, 1993. An overview of evolutionary algorithms for parameter optimisation. *Evolutionary Computation*, 1(1):1–24.

R. A. Caruana and J. D. Schaffer, 1988. Representation and hidden bias: Gray vs. binary coding for genetic algorithms. In *Proceedings of the 5th International Conference on Machine Learning*. Morgan Kaufmann (Los Altos).

L. Davis, 1991. *Handbook of Genetic Algorithms*. Van Nostrand Reinhold (New York).

L. J. Eshelman and D. J. Schaffer, 1992. Real-coded genetic algorithms and interval schemata. In D. Whitley, editor, *Foundations of Genetic Algorithms 2*. Morgan Kaufmann (San Mateo, CA).

L. J. Fogel, A. J. Owens, and M. J. Walsh, 1966. *Artificial Intelligence Through Simulated Evolution*. Wiley Publishing (New York).

D. E. Goldberg, 1989. *Genetic Algorithms in Search, Optimization & Machine Learning*. Addison-Wesley (Reading, Mass).

D. E. Goldberg, 1990. Real-coded genetic algorithms, virtual alphabets, and blocking. Technical Report IlliGAL Report No. 90001, Department of General Engineering, University of Illinois at Urbana-Champaign.

J. H. Holland, 1975. *Adaptation in Natural and Artificial Systems*. University of Michigan Press (Ann Arbor).

Z. Michalewicz, 1992. *Genetic Algorithms + Data Structures = Evolution Programs*. Springer Verlag (Berlin).

N. J. Radcliffe and P. D. Surry, 1994. Fitness variance of formae and performance prediction. In L. D. Whitley and M. D. Vose, editors, *Foundations of Genetic Algorithms III*, pages 51–72. Morgan Kaufmann (San Mateo, CA).

N. J. Radcliffe and P. D. Surry, 1995. Fundamental limitations on search algorithms: Evolutionary computing in perspective. In J. van Leeuwen, editor, *Computer Science Today: Recent Trends and Developments, Lecture Notes in Computer Science, Volume 1000*, pages 275–291. Springer-Verlag (New York).

N. J. Radcliffe, 1991a. Equivalence class analysis of genetic algorithms. *Complex Systems*, 5(2):183–205.

N. J. Radcliffe, 1991b. Forma analysis and random respectful recombination. In *Proceedings of the Fourth International Conference on Genetic Algorithms*, pages 222–229. Morgan Kaufmann (San Mateo).

N. J. Radcliffe, 1992. Genetic set recombination. In D. Whitley, editor, *Foundations of Genetic Algorithms 2*. Morgan Kaufmann (San Mateo, CA).

N. J. Radcliffe, 1993. Genetic set recombination and its application to neural network topology optimisation. *Neural Computing and Applications*, 1(1):67–90.

N. J. Radcliffe, 1994. The algebra of genetic algorithms. *Annals of Maths and Artificial Intelligence*, 10:339–384.

I. Rechenberg, 1973. *Evolutionstrategie—Optimierung technischer Systeme nach Prinzipien der biologischen Evolution*. Frommann-Holzboog (Stuttgart).

P. D. Surry and N. J. Radcliffe, 1996. Formal algorithms + formal representations = search strategies. In H.-M. Voigt, W. Ebeling, I. Rechenberg, and H. Schwefel, editors, *to appear in Parallel Problem Solving from Nature IV*, pages 366–375. (Springer-Verlag, LNCS 1141).

P. D. Surry, N. J. Radcliffe, and I. D. Boyd, 1995. A multi-objective approach to constrained optimisation of gas supply networks: The COMOGA method. In T. C. Fogarty, editor, *Evolutionary Computing: AISB Workshop*, pages 166–180. Springer-Verlag, Lecture Notes in Computer Science 993.

M. D. Vose and G. E. Liepins, 1991. Schema disruption. In *Proceedings of the Fourth International Conference on Genetic Algorithms*, pages 237–243. Morgan Kaufmann (San Mateo).

D. H. Wolpert and W. G. Macready, 1995. No free lunch theorems for search. Technical Report SFI–TR–95–02–010, Santa Fe Institute.

A Study of Fixed-Length Subset Recombination

Kelly D. Crawford
Amoco Corporation
kcrawford@amoco.com

Cory J. Hoelting
The University of Tulsa
hoeltc@euler.mcs.utulsa.edu

Roger L. Wainwright
The University of Tulsa
rogerw@penguin.mcs.utulsa.edu

Dale A. Schoenefeld
The University of Tulsa
schoend@utulsa.edu

Abstract

While bit-based, order-based and real-valued genetic algorithms have been well-studied in the literature, the fixed-length subset representation has received relatively little attention. We discuss various crossover operators for this representation and the pitfalls associated with each. In particular, we explore the ratio of the subset size to the set size. This important ratio is a major contributor to the rate of convergence.

1 INTRODUCTION

Given a set, S, of the integers from 1 to N inclusive, a fixed-length subset is defined to be any subset of S of cardinality n. For example, if $N = 4$ and $n = 2$, then $S = \{1, 2, 3, 4\}$, and the fixed-length subsets of size n are {1,2}, {1,3}, {1,4}, {2,3}, {2,4}, and {3,4}.

A fixed-length subset problem is one where candidate solutions are represented by fixed-length subsets. There are numerous examples of fixed-length subset problems in the literature. Radcliffe (1991, 1993) described improved crossover operators for fixed-length subsets. Radcliffe and George (1993) examined fixed-length subset recombination on a highly epistatic function they developed. Lucasius and Kateman (1992) developed crossover heuristics for a fixed-length subset problem in chemometrics. Crawford, Wainwright and Vasicek (1992, 1995), constructed a genetic algorithm to search for n outliers in a set of regression data of size N (Crawford and Wainwright, 1995). Hoelting, *et al.* (1995), used fixed-length subsets to find solutions to the p-median problem.

The effect of fixed-length subset crossover on convergence in genetic algorithms has not been studied in detail. This paper examines the problem. We begin with an overview of some existing representations and operators for fixed-length subset crossover. The problems with these representations and operators are then examined. Detailed analysis of the better operators leads to insight into the pitfalls of dealing with fixed-length subsets. Of particular interest is the ratio between the set size and the fixed-length subset size. Finally, we present a method that takes this ratio into account and show successful test results.

2   REPRESENTATION AND RECOMBINATION

There are numerous ways to encode a fixed-length subset. One could use a list of N bits, B, where $B_i = 1$ indicates that data point i is part of the subset. This representation requires exactly n 1-bits, and $N - n$ 0-bits. A permutation of N integers could also be used, where the first n elements (or some set of n elements) represent the subset. A simpler, more intuitive representation, referred to as the subset encoding, is to keep a list of n distinct integers from the set $\{1, ..., N\}$.

There are problems with recombination for any of these encodings. The 2-change operator is the simplest. Randomly select an element in the subset, randomly select an element outside the subset, and exchange them. This is a one-parent operator, however, and is more properly termed a mutation than a crossover. We will use the 2-change operator for comparison.

The permutation encoding can make use of many existing operators, making it an initially attractive representation. However, without modifications, there is no guarantee that the n elements in question will be changed after crossover. There are $N!$ possible permutations, but only $\binom{N}{n}$ possible subsets. Each subset is represented $n!(N - n)!$ different ways with the permutation encoding.

Bit encoding is 1-1 and onto. Subset encoding represents each subset only $n!$ times, rather than $n!(N - n)!$ times. However, in either case, standard crossover on these chromosomes usually produces invalid offspring. With the bit encoding, 1-point, 2-point, or uniform crossover will often produce offspring where the number of 1-bits is not equal to n. Similar crossover for the subset encoding often results in offspring that contain duplicate alleles, leaving less than n distinct alleles. Penalty functions or post-crossover fixups must be applied to address these problems. For example, using subset encoding, uniform crossover with fixup (UXF) lines up the parents and crosses them over in the typical uniform fashion. After this, duplicate alleles are removed from the offspring and replaced by alleles not already found in the offspring.

UXF is a *locus-based* crossover operator, only exchanging alleles between parents at fixed loci. To illustrate this, notice that an allele at locus i will never be moved to any locus j, $j \neq i$. The only exception to this is when duplicate alleles are removed from the offspring during the fixup stage, potentially resulting in offspring alleles not found in either parent. This is an example of an *implicit mutation*. An *explicit mutation* is the use of a mutation operator in the normal course of the genetic algorithm.

The first true subset crossover, RAR_w, was proposed by Radcliffe (1993). Using subset encoding, parents are compared for similarity. While only the members of the subset are stored, the members outside the subset, referred to as *barred* alleles, are also considered.

Four categories of alleles are identified. The subset of alleles common to both parents is denoted by w_2, those that show up in neither parent by $\bar{w}_2$ (i.e., those that show up as barred alleles in both parents), those found in only one parent by w_1, and those that show up as barred alleles in only one parent by $\bar{w}_1$. Note that $\bar{w}_1$ always contains exactly the barred versions of w_1.

RAR_w works by filling a "draw bag" with both regular and barred alleles. These alleles are then randomly drawn (without replacement) from the bag (or, *multiset*) and used to create new offspring. The w in RAR_w determines the ratio of the number of copies of w_2 and $\bar{w}_2$ alleles versus the number of copies of w_1 and $\bar{w}_1$ alleles to place into the draw bag. Note that in RAR_w, the order of alleles in the chromosome is ignored, making it a *set-based* operator (as opposed to a *locus-based* operator).

When a barred allele is drawn from the bag, it means that this allele cannot show up in the offspring. When a regular allele is drawn, it is placed into the offspring unless the matching barred allele has already been drawn. An interesting note is that after $N - n$ barred alleles have been drawn, the offspring is fully specified as the n remaining alleles. This special case can result in the offspring containing alleles not found in either parent (although the barred alleles are found in both parents). Complete implementation details can be found in Radcliffe (1993).

If the offspring is not fully specified after the bag has been emptied, alleles are randomly generated and placed into the offspring. Note that this can only happen for the special cases of RAR_0 and RAR_∞. In RAR_0, no w_2 or $\bar{w}_2$ alleles will ever be placed into the draw bag. In RAR_∞, no w_1 or $\bar{w}_1$ alleles will ever be placed into the draw bag. The only way a bag can be emptied without fully specifying an offspring is if it does not contain at least $N - n$ barred alleles. Thus, to empty the bag, we must have $|\bar{w}_1| + |\bar{w}_2| < N - n$. As long as the w in RAR_w is not 0 or ∞, this inequality never holds.

To illustrate a typical application of RAR_w, suppose $N = 6$ and $n = 3$. We have $\{1, 2, 3, 4, 5, 6\}$ as possible alleles, and $\{\bar{1}, \bar{2}, \bar{3}, \bar{4}, \bar{5}, \bar{6}\}$ as possible barred alleles. Given the parents $p_1 = \{1, 2, 3\}$ and $p_2 = \{2, 3, 4\}$ (which implies $p_1' = \{4, 5, 6\}$ and $p_2' = \{1, 5, 6\}$) we identify the following sets: $w_1 = \{1, 4\}$, $\bar{w}_1 = \{\bar{1}, \bar{4}\}$, $w_2 = \{2, 3\}$, $\bar{w}_2 = \{\bar{5}, \bar{6}\}$. Assume we are using $w = 2$ (i.e., RAR_2.) This means we will place 1 copy each of all w_1 and $\bar{w}_1$ alleles and 2 copies each of all w_2 and $\bar{w}_2$ alleles into the bag. Thus, we place 1 copy each of 1, 4, $\bar{1}$ and $\bar{4}$ into the bag, and 2 copies each of 2, 3, $\bar{5}$ and $\bar{6}$ into the bag. In fact, this is exactly one copy of each of the alleles (normal and barred) found in both parents, making RAR_2 an intuitive starting choice. The bag now contains $\{1, 4, \bar{1}, \bar{4}, 2, 2, 3, 3, \bar{5}, \bar{5}, \bar{6}, \bar{6}\}$. Finally, we randomly draw from the bag (without replacement) until we have constructed an offspring as illustrated in Table 1. The resulting offspring is $\{2, 3, 4\}$. As another example, suppose the first three draws were $\bar{1}$, $\bar{4}$ and $\bar{5}$. At this point we can quit drawing alleles from the bag. We have now fully specified the offspring as $\{2, 3, 6\}$. Note that the allele 6 is not found in either parent, making this an example of an implicit mutation.

A weakness of other operators is that they typically ignore anything outside the subset. This leads to loss of diversity in the population and premature convergence. RAR_w still suffers from this problem, but is a much improved operator due to the introduction of barred alleles.

$draw$	offspring				
3			3		
$\bar{5}$			3		$\bar{\bar{5}}$
$\bar{1}$	$\bar{1}$		3		$\bar{\bar{5}}$
$\bar{\bar{5}}$	$\bar{1}$		3		$\bar{\bar{5}}$
1	$\bar{1}$		3		$\bar{\bar{5}}$
4	$\bar{1}$		3	4	$\bar{\bar{5}}$
$\bar{4}$	$\bar{1}$		3	4	$\bar{\bar{5}}$
2	$\bar{1}$	2	3	4	$\bar{\bar{5}}$

Table 1: RAR_2 example

3 RECOMBINATION PITFALLS

In actual tests, we found the fixed-length subset operators lacking, with premature convergence as the most common problem. However, since the available literature on the subject reported a fair measure of success, further analysis was required. We surmised that crossover was the problem. To test this conjecture, we devised a method to study the crossover operators themselves. We termed this tool *static analysis* (Crawford, 1996).

Static analysis is the use of a genetic algorithm to study crossover in the absence of selection pressure, fitness and mutation. The objective is not fitness related, but instead is simply to see how long it takes for a population to unify when only crossover is a factor. Such an analysis will provide a measure of the inherent bias of a crossover operator. By using a fitness function that always returns 1, setting the crossover rate to 1 and setting the mutation rate to 0, almost any genetic algorithm package can be turned into a static analyzer. For our tests we used the LibGA package (Corcoran and Wainwright, 1993) under the generational model (subsequent testing of the steady-state model produced similar results).

To understand why a population would unify under static analysis, consider the nature of locus-based crossover operators. Viewing a population of bit strings as a set of columns, notice that an allele in column i (i.e., locus i), will only be exchanged with other alleles in column i. Now consider what happens when you randomly select alleles from one of these columns in order to create a new column. Over time, sampling error (because we have a finite population size) will unify the column. A single allele will begin to dominate the column, and eventually, the entire column will contain a single allele. Note that as the population size increases, the number of generations required for unification increases.

All bit-based crossover operators we tested eventually unified their populations under static analysis (the final chromosome was different for each initial random seed). Tests showed that in general, if it takes G generations to unify the population, between 80% and 90% of the alleles are lost after only $\frac{G}{2}$ generations. Explicit mutation operators never unify under static analysis. Without selection pressure, they simply produce random movement within the search space.

For bit-based and order-based crossover operators, testing showed that the rate of convergence under static analysis is a function of the operator, the population size and the chromosome length. For fixed-length subset crossover, however, it is a function of the operator, the population size, the set size N and the subset size n. This was our first indication

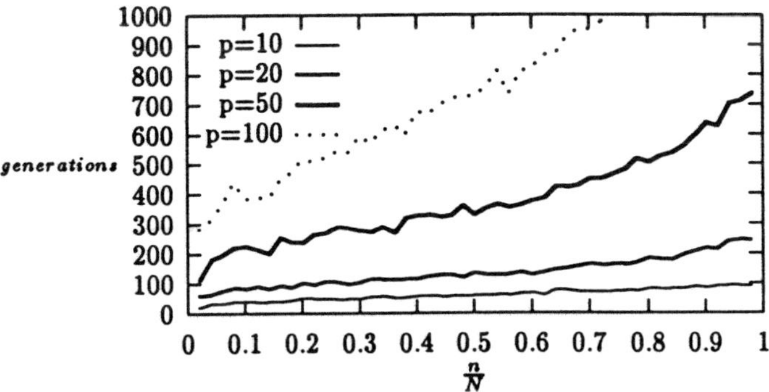

Figure 1: Static analysis convergence for UXF, $N = 100$

of the importance of the ratio between n and N.

The performance of each operator varied with respect to $\frac{n}{N}$. This variation is difficult to quantify since the behavior of the objective function also changes as n changes. Rather than behaving as a function parameter, changes in n tend to create new fitness landscapes. Nonetheless, this observation is critical to understanding and analyzing the behavior of fixed-length subset operators. We will limit this discussion to subset encodings using the crossover operators UXF and RAR_w.

3.1   UXF

Static analysis provided us with much insight into the behavior of UXF. As the ratio between $\frac{n}{N}$ varies, the number of generations required to converge the population also varies. Figure 1 shows results of static analysis tests for $N = 100$. The x-axis shows the different values of n expressed as a ratio with N, the y-axis shows the number of generations required for the entire population to unify, and the population size is represented by p. The same information is presented in Figure 2, but with the number of generations divided by the population size. Note the correlation between the different lines, especially for lower values of n.

Overall, empirical testing (see Section 4.3) showed very poor performance for small values of $\frac{n}{N}$, with somewhat better performance for larger values. Static analysis supports these results by showing that even in the absence of selection pressure, UXF converges quickly for small ratios. When selection pressure is added, premature convergence is the result.

It is important to note that although order is not important in a fixed-length subset problem, UXF still respects order, being a locus based crossover operator. Thus, rather than having $\binom{N}{n}$ possible subsets, UXF considers a search space of size $n!\binom{N}{n} = \frac{N!}{(N-n)!}$. In other words, there is a considerable amount of duplication in the search space imposed by UXF. There are two major implications of this analysis. First, since for larger values of n, $n! \gg \binom{N}{n}$, the search space is much larger than required (although proportionately, there is a like increase

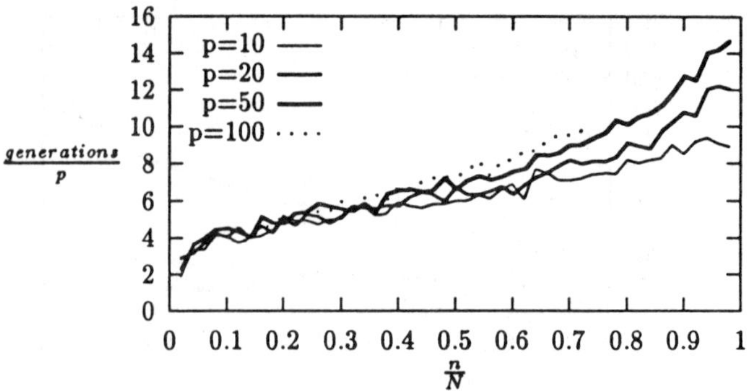

Figure 2: Static analysis ratio of convergence for UXF, $N = 100$

in the number of solutions). Second, while $n!$ continues to grow as n gets closer to N, $\binom{N}{n}$ reaches its peak at $n = \frac{N}{2}$. In fact, for all n, $\binom{N}{n} = \binom{N}{N-n}$. The result is more and more duplication as n increases.

Given the static analysis results, our empirical test results and the success reported in the literature for other fixed-length subset problems, it became clear that the culprit was the ratio between n and N. The tests shown in the literature always used $\frac{n}{N} = .5$, or very nearly so. Our tests were usually concerned with $\frac{n}{N} < .2$. This observation was the initial basis for our research into fixed-length subset crossover.

One might conjecture that since UXF performs better for $\frac{n}{N}$ close to 1, a complement encoding could be used for small n. In a subset encoding, the list of n integers corresponding to the subset is stored in the chromosome. In a complement encoding, the list of $N - n$ integers corresponding to the members outside the subset is kept in the chromosome. However, empirical testing showed the complement encoding to perform more or less the same as subset encoding.

UXF was a consistently poor performer in all of our tests, often being beaten by a simple 2-change operator. The locus-based nature of UXF together with the problem of the ratio $\frac{n}{N}$ combine to make it a poor choice for fixed-length subset crossover.

3.2 RAR_w

Given the effect of the ratio $\frac{n}{N}$ on UXF, we suspected the same for RAR_w. Static analysis, however, was initially inconclusive. After every crossover operator that was tested converged a population to a single chromosome under static analysis, it was initially surprising to find that RAR_w did not. However, the set-based nature of RAR_w prevented unification. Alleles would disappear and reappear in the population over time, with the total number of alleles lost at any one time hovering around a fixed number. This fixed number is a function of population size, w, N and n. Table 2 shows the results of static analysis tests for various n

Operator	n								
	10	20	30	40	50	60	70	80	90
$RAR_{0.5}$	2.78	0.11	0.01	0.00	0.00	0.00	0.00	0.00	0.00
RAR_1	3.21	0.17	0.01	0.00	0.00	0.00	0.00	0.00	0.00
RAR_2	4.55	0.61	0.11	0.02	0.00	0.00	0.00	0.00	0.00
RAR_4	13.45	6.79	3.87	2.14	1.01	0.46	0.10	0.01	0.00
RAR_8	43.37	35.77	28.65	21.96	13.39	8.86	4.68	1.62	0.17

Table 2: RAR_w maximum allele loss under static analysis for $N = 100$

sizes with $N = 100$ and a population size of 100.

Clearly, the ratio $\frac{n}{N}$ still plays a role in RAR_w. We define a difference measure (D) between parents that will assist us in our analysis (Crawford, 1996). Given two parents, each of length n, we count the number of alleles in common (this is $|w_2|$). The difference measure, D, is defined to be $n - |w_2|$. Assuming $\frac{n}{N} \leq 0.5$, identical parents will have $D = 0$, while parents with no alleles in common will have $D = n$.

We will refer to the four sets w_1, $\bar{w}_1$, w_2 and $\bar{w}_2$ collectively as w^*. The relationships between D and the cardinality of the w^* are shown in equations 1 through 4.

$$|w_1| = 2 * D \tag{1}$$
$$|\bar{w}_1| = 2 * D \tag{2}$$
$$|w_2| = n - D \tag{3}$$
$$|w_2| = N - (D + n) \tag{4}$$

Consider the case where $N = 8$. We can quickly calculate the cardinality of the w^* for $n = 2..6$. To demonstrate, we constructed representative pairs of parents in Table 3 to cover all values of D for $n = 3$. We can do likewise for the other values of n. From this, we can construct Table 4, Table 5 and Table 6, which show the cardinality of the w^* for $n = 2$, $n = 3$ and $n = 4$, respectively. For example, Table 5 shows that for $n = 3$ and $D = 2$ we will have 4 alleles of type w_1, 4 of type $\bar{w}_1$, 1 of type w_2 and 3 of type $\bar{w}_2$. Thus, we can quickly see the distribution of alleles in the bag for RAR_w based on the difference measure D and the subset size n. Note that the table for $n = 5$ will be the same as Table 5 (with $n = 3$), except that w_2 and $\bar{w}_2$ are switched. The same is true for $n = 2$ and $n = 6$.

It is clear that for $\frac{n}{N} \leq 0.5$ the largest D is n and for $\frac{n}{N} > 0.5$ the largest D is $N - n$. Figure 3 illustrates. Note that the largest maximum D value occurs at $\frac{n}{N} = 0.5$.

Initially, when the population is most random, the average D will be at its highest. Over time, as the population begins to converge, the average D decreases. When the average D reaches 0, the population has unified. When D is 0, RAR_w will always produce offspring identical to the parents (except for RAR_0, where w_2 and $\bar{w}_2$ alleles are never placed into the bag).

Again, with static analysis suggesting that RAR_w suffers less from allele loss when $\frac{n}{N}$ is close to 1, why not use a complement encoding when $\frac{n}{N}$ is small? The reasons for this are that the search space size is the same, i.e. $\binom{N}{n} = \binom{N}{N-n}$, the fitness landscape is the same, and the

D	parents					
0	a	b	c			
	a	b	c			
1	a	b	c			
		b	c	d		
2	a	b	c			
			c	d	e	
3	a	b	c			
				d	e	f

Table 3: Example parents representing all possible D values for $N = 8$, $n = 3$

	D		
	0	1	2
$|w_1|$	0	2	4
$|\bar{w}_1|$	0	2	4
$|w_2|$	2	1	0
$|\bar{w}_2|$	6	5	4

Table 4: $N = 8$, $n = 2$

	D			
	0	1	2	3
$|w_1|$	0	2	4	6
$|\bar{w}_1|$	0	2	4	6
$|w_2|$	3	2	1	0
$|\bar{w}_2|$	5	4	3	2

Table 5: $N = 8$, $n = 3$

	D				
	0	1	2	3	4
$|w_1|$	0	2	4	6	8
$|\bar{w}_1|$	0	2	4	6	8
$|w_2|$	4	3	2	1	0
$|\bar{w}_2|$	4	3	2	1	0

Table 6: $N = 8$, $n = 4$

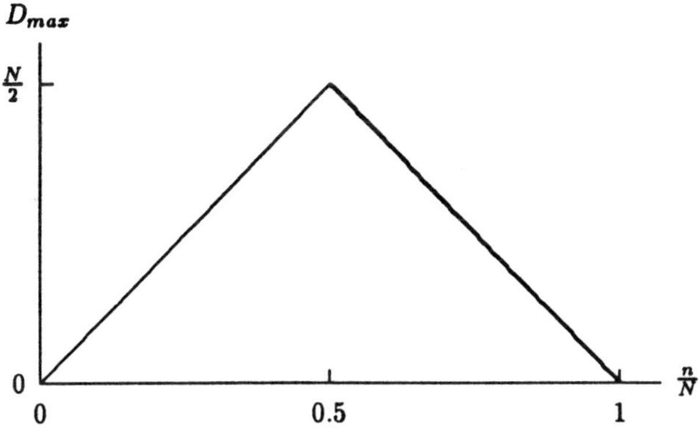

Figure 3: Maximum possible D values relative to n and N

maximum D value is the same. To illustrate, consider the following example. Let $N = 8$ and $n = 2$ for RAR_1. Assume we have $\{a, b\}$ and $\{b, c\}$ as our two subsets. These two subsets are represented by themselves in subset encoding. In complement encoding, these two subsets are represented by $\{c, d, e, f, g, h\}$ and $\{a, d, e, f, g, h\}$. When recombining the two subsets in subset encoding we have $w_1 = \{a, c\}$, $\bar{w}_1 = \{\bar{a}, \bar{c}\}$, $w_2 = \{b\}$, and $\bar{w}_2 = \{\bar{d}, \bar{e}, \bar{f}, \bar{g}, \bar{h}\}$. When recombining in complement encoding we have $w_1 = \{a, c\}$, $\bar{w}_1 = \{\bar{a}, \bar{c}\}$, $w_2 = \{d, e, f, g, h\}$, and $\bar{w}_2 = \{b\}$. Hence, over all sequences of random draws from the bag, we are just as likely to draw $\bar{d}$ in the subset encoding before the individual is fully specified as we are to draw d in the complement encoding. This can be said for any allele or barred allele in the subset encoding and its corresponding barred allele or allele in the complement encoding. Furthermore, the meaning of an allele in subset encoding is the same as the meaning of its corresponding barred allele in complement encoding. Therefore, subset encoding will have, on the average, the same performance as complement encoding. Our empirical tests agreed with this analysis.

4   RECOMBINATION MODIFICATIONS

We attempted several modifications to RAR_w in order to alleviate the problem with small ratios of $\frac{n}{N}$ (Crawford, 1996). We first noted that RAR_w mandated that the number of copies of w_1 and $\bar{w}_1$ would be the same. Likewise for w_2 and $\bar{w}_2$. Separate controls for all four allele types might prove useful. Second, we note that there is a symmetry of the distribution of the w^* cardinalities in the draw bag when $\frac{n}{N} = .5$. Other ratios show the bag more skewed, so perhaps a forced symmetry in the draw bag would be helpful. Lastly, as $\frac{n}{N}$ ratios approach 0 or 1, the maximum range of D decreases (as shown in Figure 3). If we could set an average D threshhold for a population, we might be able to delay convergence long enough to find a solution.

	D				
	0	1	2	3	4
$|w_1|$	0	2	4	6	8
$|\bar{w}_1|$	0	2	4	6	8
$|w_2|$	4	3	2	1	0
$|\bar{w}_2|$	96	95	94	93	92

Table 7: $N = 100$, $n = 4$

4.1 Extended RAR (ERAR)

$ERAR$ takes 4 arguments: $|w_1|$, $|\bar{w}_1|$, $|w_2|$ and $|\bar{w}_2|$. Rather than a ratio, as in RAR_w, the arguments to $ERAR$ are the actual number of copies of each w^* allele type to put into the bag. For all cases where $|w_1| = |\bar{w}_1|$ and $|w_2| = |\bar{w}_2|$, $ERAR$ is equivalent to RAR_w, where $w = |w_2|/|w_1|$. This additional flexibility allows us to experiment with decreasing the number of barred alleles for smaller ratios of $\frac{n}{N}$. Tests showed a modest improvement in a few cases. However, it was not clear how to properly set the arguments to $ERAR$ or whether this would actually be useful in the general case.

4.2 Adjusting RAR (ARAR)

Note the symmetry for $n = 4$ as shown in Table 6. Also note that the w_1 and $\bar{w}_1$ values, when reversed, are the w_2 and $\bar{w}_2$ values times 2. This symmetry disappears as n moves away from $\frac{N}{2}$. This is particularly striking for larger values of N. For example, consider Table 7 where $N = 100$ and $n = 4$. Under RAR_2, $\bar{w}_2$ always dominates the draw bag. In Table 7, for $D = 2$, we see that $\bar{w}_2$ has a total of 188 entries in the bag (2 copies of each of the 94 alleles). w_1, $\bar{w}_1$ and w_2 have 4 entries each. Most of the time is spent selecting values outside the subset that will not be considered for insertion into the offspring. In other words, most of the alleles in the offspring are primarily chosen by drawing barred alleles, and this is true regardless of D.

Using lower values of w (e.g., $RAR_{0.1}$) is one way to balance the bag distribution. Another is to construct an operator that will balance the bag as it is being constructed. We call this operator ARAR. We ran tests where the bag distribution was forced to be the same as when $\frac{n}{N} = 0.5$ (easily computed during an initialization step). As with ERAR, success was modest and varied with the fitness function. In most cases our testing did not support our initial assumption that a lack of symmetry in the bag distribution affects convergence.

4.3 Threshholding RAR (TRAR)

Our third modification was very successful. We observe that the genetic algorithm converges faster when w_2 and $\bar{w}_2$ alleles are selected from the bag. These alleles are selected more often as the population converges since most alleles will fall into these two categories as D decreases. Thus, convergence is accelerated.

We can detect when the population begins to converge by keeping track of the average value of D during crossover. When D_{avg} drops below a specified threshhold value, $TRAR$ temporarily sets the number of draw bag copies of the w_2 and $\bar{w}_2$ alleles to 0 until D_{avg}

Sequence	How Many Correct in the Sequence	Epistatic Credit
1:{0,1}	0	1
	1	0
	2	2
2:{2,3}	0	0
	1	1
	2	2
3:{4,5}	0	0
	1	1
	2	2
4:{6,7}	0	1
	1	0
	2	2
5:{8,9}	0	1
	1	0
	2	2

Table 8: Example credit for epistatic function with $N = 100$ and $n = 10$

climbs back above the threshhold.

To illustrate the success of threshholding we show empirical results on a slightly modified version of a function developed by Radcliffe and George (1993). Given a set of size N containing the integers modulo N ($\{0, 1, 2, ..., N-2, N-1\}$), the goal is to seek the size n subset containing the lowest n integers. Thus, the optimal solution will be $\{0, 1, 2, ..., n-2, n-1\}$ Each correct element of the subset is assigned 1 point, so the maximum fitness value is n.

As stated, this function is non-epistatic and quite easy for a genetic algorithm to solve. To add epistasis, the elements of the size n subset are grouped into pairs, namely $\{0,1\}$, $\{2,3\}$, $\{4,5\}$, etc. If both elements of a pair show up somewhere in the subset, 2 points are added to the fitness. The fitnesses for finding 0 and 1 elements of a particular pair will be randomly determined at the start of the run to be 0 and 1, or 1 and 0, respectively. Thus, having 0 elements of some pairs will add 0 to the fitness, while 0 elements of other pairs will add 1 to the fitness. This makes the function very deceptive.

For $N = 100$ and $n = 10$, Table 8 shows an example of the randomly generated function. Note that sequence number 2 (which corresponds to the set $\{2,3\}$), adds credit of 0, 1 and 2 points to the fitness when 0, 1 and 2 members of the sequence are found in the chromosome, respectively. Sequence number 4, however, adds credit of 1, 0 and 2 points to the fitness when 0, 1 and 2 members are found.

Table 9 illustrates how the function described in Table 8 is used to evaluate 5 sample chromosomes. Consider child 3 in the top section of Table 9. Row 3 of the bottom section shows how the allele sequences match up with the expected optimum. Sequences 1 and 5 have 1 match and are both assigned a credit of 0 according to Table 8. All others have a perfect match and are assigned a credit of 2 each. The combined fitness is 6.

Note how child 2 has 0 matches for all sequences. Even so, Table 8 shows a credit assignment

Child	Example Chromosomes										Fitness
1	0	6	8	10	11	13	22	33	70	84	0
2	11	54	70	78	92	93	94	96	98	99	3
3	1	2	3	4	5	6	7	9	10	20	6
4	0	1	2	3	4	5	60	61	62	63	8
5	0	1	2	3	4	5	6	7	8	9	10

Child	Seq 1		Seq 2		Seq 3		Seq 4		Seq 5		Fitness
1	0						6		8		0
2											3
3		1	2	3	4	5	6	7		9	6
4	0	1	2	3	4	5					8
5	0	1	2	3	4	5	6	7	8	9	10

Table 9: Example chromosomes and fitnesses for epistatic function

of 1 for the sequences 1, 4 and 5, for a combined fitness of 3. Child 1 with 3 matches has a fitness of 0, thus illustrating the epistatic qualities of this function. Incomplete sequences will often lead selection away from the solution. Complete sequences must be found and recombined intact in order to locate the optimum.

We ran a genetic algorithm on the epistatic function and gathered statistics. Each test was run 100 times with 100 different random seeds (the same seeds for each crossover operator, which guaranteed that the same 100 initial populations were used for each suite of tests). Other parameters included population size = 100, crossover rate = 1.0, mutation rate = 0.05 (per string), generational model and maximum number of generations = 200. Success was defined as finding the optimum. Over the 100 test runs, the percentage of time this optimum was found, as well as the average number of generations it took to find it, were used to benchmark the threshholding operator. Note that the average number of generations only includes those runs that found the optimal value. In cases where the optimal value was never found, the run either prematurely converged or was stopped after 200 generations.

Table 10 shows the results of the crossover tests on the epistatic function for $N = 100$ and $n = 10$. 2-change not only performs poorly, but the average number of generations was high relative to its poor performance. UXF was dismal, never locating the optimum value. The RAR_w variations showed a constant 9 to 10% success rate. When thresholding was added (in this case, the threshold = 6.5), the success rate climbed dramatically. Note that the iteration count increased, indicating that the non-threshold versions of RAR_w tended to prematurely converge. The addition of the threshold proved to be a significant aid in avoiding premature convergence.

5   CONCLUSIONS

We have examined a number of fixed-length subset recombination operators from the literature. A problem with the operators proposed to date is that none consider the important ratio $\frac{n}{N}$. We demonstrate analytically why this ratio is so important, and then support this with empirical tests. Analysis of the best fixed-length subset operator, RAR_w, provides us with insight into why it works well for $\frac{n}{N} = 0.5$, but struggles with smaller ratios. The

Crossover Operator	% of Time Optimum Found	Average Generations
2-change	7	42
UXF	0	-
$RAR_{0.1}$	10	18
$RAR_{0.25}$	9	16
$RAR_{0.5}$	10	16
$RAR_{0.75}$	9	17
$RAR_{1.0}$	10	18
$RAR_{2.0}$	9	17
$RAR_{3.0}$	9	15
$RAR_{4.0}$	9	16
$ERAR(20, 40, 20, 5)$	9	17
$ARAR(1, 2, 1, 2)$	24	17
T-$RAR_{0.1}$	63	61
T-$RAR_{0.25}$	65	55
T-$RAR_{0.5}$	68	57
T-$RAR_{0.75}$	76	56
T-$RAR_{1.0}$	63	50
T-$RAR_{2.0}$	76	55
T-$RAR_{3.0}$	68	52
T-$RAR_{4.0}$	75	52

Table 10: Epi10 test results

addition of threshholding to RAR_w showed significant performance improvements.

Acknowledgements

Special thanks to Michael Vose and Darrell Whitley for a helpful conversation at ICGA-6 that pointed us in the right direction on this work.

References

A. L. Corcoran and R. L. Wainwright. (1993) LibGA: A user-friendly workbench for order-based genetic algorithm research. In *Proceedings of the 1993 ACM/SIGAPP Symposium on Applied Computing*, pages 111–117. ACM Press.

Kelly D. Crawford. (1996) *The Role of Recombination in Genetic Algorithms for Fixed-Length Subset Problems*. PhD thesis, The University of Tulsa.

Kelly D. Crawford and Roger L. Wainwright. (1995) Applying genetic algorithms to outlier detection. In Larry J. Eshelman, editor, *Proceedings of the Sixth International Conference on Genetic Algorithms*, San Mateo, CA: Morgan Kaufmann Publishers.

Kelly D. Crawford, Roger L. Wainwright, and Daniel J. Vasicek. (1992) Detecting multiple outliers in multiple dimensions using genetic algorithms. Technical Report UTULSA-MCS-92-4, The University of Tulsa, July.

Kelly D. Crawford, Roger L. Wainwright, and Daniel J. Vasicek. (1995) Detecting multiple outliers in regression data using genetic algorithms. In *Proceedings of the 1995 ACM/SIGAPP Symposium on Applied Computing*. ACM Press.

Cory J. Hoelting, Dale A. Schoenefeld, and Roger L. Wainwright. (1995) Approximation techniques for variations of the p-median problem. In *Proceedings of the 1995 ACM/SIGAPP Symposium on Applied Computing*. ACM Press.

C. B. Lucasius and G. Kateman. (1992) Towards solving subset selection problems with the aid of the genetic algorithm. In R. Männer and B. Manderick, editors, *Parallel Problem Solving from Nature, 2*, Amsterdam. Elsevier Science Publishers, B. V.

Nicholas J. Radcliffe. (1991) Forma analysis and random respectful recombination. In Richard K. Belew and Lashon B. Booker, editors, *Proceedings of the Fourth International Conference on Genetic Algorithms*, San Mateo, CA. Morgan Kaufmann Publishers.

Nicholas J. Radcliffe. (1993) Genetic set recombination. In L. Darrell Whitley, editor, *Foundations of Genetic Algorithms 2*, San Mateo, CA. Morgan Kaufmann Publishers.

Nicholas J. Radcliffe and Felicity A. W. George. (1993) A study in set recombination. In Stephanie Forrest, editor, *Proceedings of the Fifth International Conference on Genetic Algorithms*, San Mateo, CA. Morgan Kaufmann Publishers.

Exact Uniform Initialization For Genetic Programming

Walter Böhm
Department of Mathematical Methods of Statistics,
Institute of Statistics,
Vienna University of Economics and Business
Administration, Augasse 2–6, A-1090 Vienna, Austria.
E-mail: boehm@wu-wien.ac.at

Andreas Geyer-Schulz
Department of Applied Computer Science,
Institute of Information Processing
Vienna University of Economics and Business
Administration, Augasse 2–6, A-1090 Vienna, Austria.
E-mail: geyers@wu-wien.ac.at

Abstract

In this paper we solve the problem of *exactly uniform* generation of complete derivation trees from k-bounded context-free languages. The result is applied and is used
for developing an exact uniform initialization routine for a genetic programming
variant based on an explicit representation of the grammar of the context-free language (simple genetic algorithm over k-bounded context-free languages) [Geyer-
Schulz, 1996b]. In this genetic programming variant the grammar is used to generate complete derivation trees which constitute the genomes for the algorithm.
For the case that no a priori information about the solution is available, we prove
that this (simple random sampling) algorithm is optimal in the sense of a minimax
strategy. An exact uniform initialization routine for Koza's genetic programming
variant [Koza, 1992] is derived as a special case.

1   INTRODUCTION

The random generation of combinatorial structures is of major theoretical and practical
importance for the design of randomized algorithms [Gupta *et al.*, 1994] and often leads to

difficult and unsolved combinatorial problems. In genetic programming the initialization of a population of programs is usually tackled by ad hoc methods. A few examples from the literature are:

1. Koza's "full method" (naive), Koza's "grow method" (naive) and Koza's "ramped-half-and-half" method [Koza, 1992, p. 93 and 597f]. Koza's "full method" is a recursive tree generation method which generates "full" parse trees whose leaves all have paths of the same length to the root. Koza's "grow" method generates parse trees whose leaves have paths of different length to the root. Koza's "ramped-half-and-half" method uses the "full" method for generating one half of the members of the population and the "grow" method for the other half with the maximum depth varying between 2 and a fixed upper bound.

2. A "naive" method with and without duplicates [Geyer-Schulz, 1995] and [Whigham, 1995a]. The "naive" method of generating a derivation tree from a grammar consists of expanding the nonterminal symbols of the frontier of a derivation tree with the symbols on the right hand side of a production rule for this nonterminal symbol until only terminal symbols are contained in the frontier. If more than one production rule is available for a nonterminal symbol, the production is chosen with equal probability. The process starts from the nonterminal symbol specified as the start symbol of the grammar and is usually terminated after some maximum number of "expansions" or derivation steps.

3. "Stratified sampling" with a rejection method [Geyer-Schulz, 1995] and [Iba, 1995], [Iba, 1996a] and [Iba, 1996b]. Trees are generated by any method and only trees satisfying a sampling plan are accepted as members of the population. The sampling plan specifies how many trees with e.g. a certain number of nodes or requiring a certain number of derivation steps for construction have to be in the population.

4. "Compound derivations" [Geyer-Schulz, 1996a] and [Geyer-Schulz, 1996b], or "grammar bias" [Whigham, 1995b], [Whigham, 1996]). The basic idea of this method is to find a grammar which generates the same language as the original grammar, but which favors the construction of larger parts of a derivation tree in a single derivation step. This effect can be achieved by simply adding redundant production rules. For example, in the grammar shown in Figure 1 the production rule <fe> := ” (” <f2> <fe> <fe> ”) ” ; may be added a second time.

```
S   := <fe> ;
<fe> := ”(” <f0> ”)” |
        ”(” <f1> <fe> ”)” |
        ”(” <f2> <fe> <fe> ”)”    ;
<f0> := ”D1” | ”D2” ;
<f1> := ”NOT” ;
<f2> := ”OR” | ”AND” ;
```

Figure 1: The Backus Naur Form of L_{XOR}

The genetic programming variant used in this paper, simple genetic algorithms over k-bounded context-free languages, is characterized by an explicit representation of the grammar of the context-free language and by a bound k on the number of derivation steps available for generating a derivation tree [Geyer-Schulz, 1996b]. Instead of bit strings as in the canonical genetic algorithm or parse trees as in Koza's genetic programming variant the algorithm works with complete derivation trees. For the definitions and results about context-free languages which are needed in this paper we refer the reader to section 2.

Figure 1 shows the grammar of a context-free language for solving the XOR problem in Backus Naur Form. For example, let us compute the probability of generating the program (NOT(D2)) from the grammar shown in Figure 1 by the "naive" method of [Geyer-Schulz, 1995] and [Whigham, 1995a]: We start by expanding the start symbol $<$fe$>$. For this substitution we choose either "(" $<$f0$>$ ")" or "(" $<$f1$>$ $<$fe$>$ ")" or "(" $<$f2$>$ $<$fe$>$ $<$fe$>$ ")". The probability of making the right choice is 1/3. Suppose, we picked "(" $<$f1$>$ $<$fe$>$ ")" and we continue by expanding $<$f1$>$. In this derivation step we have no choice. With probability 1 we get "NOT". From "(" "NOT" $<$fe$>$ ")" we expand $<$fe$>$ in the third derivation step. The probability of choosing "(" $<$f0$>$ ")" is 1/3. From "(" "NOT" "(" $<$f0$>$ ")" ")" we expand $<$f0$>$ and we can choose from either "D1" or "D2". In the fourth derivation step we get (NOT(D2)) with probability 1/2. To compute the probability of deriving (NOT(D2)) we multiply the probabilities of choosing the right production in each derivation step: $1/3 \times 1 \times 1/3 \times 1/2 = 1/18 = 0.05556$. In Table 1 we present a few examples of the probabilities of generating programs from the grammar shown in Figure 1 for an increasing number of derivation steps. (The examples shown have been selected arbitrarily.) In Table 1 we observe an exponential decay in the probability of generating long programs, when choosing production rules in Figure 1 with equal probability.

Table 1: Programs and the Probability of Derivation (n = Number of Derivation Steps Required)

Program	P(Program)	n
(D1)	0.16667	2
(NOT(D2))	0.05556	4
(NOT(NOT(D2)))	0.01851	6
(OR(AND(D2)(NOT(D2)))(D2))	0.00004	12
(AND(D2)(NOT(AND(NOT(D2))(NOT(D1)))))	$4.76 \cdot 10^{-6}$	16
(NOT(NOT(NOT(NOT(NOT(NOT (AND(D1)(D1))))))))	$6.35 \cdot 10^{-6}$	18
(AND(OR(NOT(NOT(D1))) (AND(D1)(D2)))(NOT(D2)))	$1.32 \cdot 10^{-7}$	20
(OR(D1)(NOT(AND(AND(D2) (NOT(NOT(OR(D2)(D2))))) (NOT(OR(D1)(D2))))))	$3.40 \cdot 10^{-11}$	30

These methods have the disadvantage that the population of programs ceases to be a simple random sample, where each population of n programs has the same chance to be selected. In the "naive" methods the skewed distribution of programs leads to a degraded genetic programming performance. Each of the authors quoted above has intuitively recognized this fact and tried to get a "better" mixture of programs by ad hoc methods. All authors report that these ad hoc methods resulted in improved genetic programming performance. However, the "best" mixture of programs is obtained by simple random sampling and intuitively this implies that – without additional information – simple random sampling is the best algorithm for initializing a population of programs.

In this paper we solve the problem of *exactly uniform* generation of complete derivation trees from k-bounded context-free languages. The resulting algorithm has all properties of simple random sampling. The tree generating algorithm is based on a k-bounded, recursive derivation tree generator and a nonlinear transformation on the probability of choosing the next production rule. The nonlinear transformation is based on the automatic derivation of a "word" counting function from the Backus Naur Form (BNF) of the (unambiguous) grammar of a context-free language from [Geyer-Schulz, 1996b]. For ambiguous grammars we count "complete derivation trees". We count distinct trees, which means different derivations of the same word are considered distinct. In Section 2 we introduce the notation, definitions and results for context-free languages. An example of "counting" is given in Section 3. The general technique is presented in Section 4 and its implementation in APL is deferred to the Appendix. In Section 5 the results of the previous sections are used to implement an exact, uniform initialization algorithm for k-bounded context-free languages. In Section 6 we show that the algorithm behaves as expected and in Section 7 we discuss the impact on genetic programming performance. For the case that no a priori information about the solution is available, we prove that this (simple random sampling) algorithm is optimal in the sense of a minimax strategy. Finally, in Section 8 an exact uniform initialization routine for Koza's genetic programming variant [Koza, 1992] is derived as a special case.

2 CONTEXT-FREE LANGUAGES

In this section we introduce the notation, definitions and results of context-free languages which are used in the rest of the paper.

By $L(G)$ we mean the language L generated by grammar G, this is the set of sentences (words) generated by G. By a *k-bounded* language $L(G)$ we mean the set of words generated by G with at most k derivation steps.

A *context-free grammar* G is a 4-tuple $G = (V_{NT}, V_T, P, S)$, where V_{NT} is a finite set of nonterminal symbols, V_T is a finite set of terminal symbols disjoint from V_{NT}, P is a finite subset of $V_{NT} \times (V_{NT} \cup V_T)^*$ called the production rules or productions of the grammar and S is a distinguished symbol in V_N called the start symbol of G [Aho and Ullman, 1972]. We denote the empty word by ϵ.

A *sentential form* of G is defined recursively: S is a sentential form and if xyz is a sentential form and $y \rightarrow u$ is in P, then xuz is a sentential form too.

A *sentence* or a *word* w of $L(G)$ is a sentential form without terminal symbols. Clearly, the *programs* in genetic programming are words or sentences of a context-free language.

For specifying small grammars a very compact notation is used (e.g. [Aho and Ullman, 1972]): Symbols from V_T are taken from the small letters $a, \ldots, z$, symbols from V_{NT} are taken from the capital letters $A, \ldots, Z$ and *derives* is denoted by $\rightarrow$. For the set of productions $P = \{S \rightarrow AB, S \rightarrow aS\}$ we use the production $S \rightarrow AB \mid aS$ as shorthand. $\mid$ denotes *or*.

For "real" grammars we use a version of Backus Naur Form (BNF) [Naur, 1963]: Symbols from V_T are delimited by ' ', for example ' 'D1' ', symbols from V_{NT} are delimted by $<$ and $>$, for example $<$fe$>$. *Derives* is denoted by $:=$, *or* by $\mid$, and *catenation* is denoted by juxtaposition of symbols. Whenever we want to represent *catenation* explicitly, we denote *catenation* as $\star$, for example aS corresponds to $a \star S$ with explicit representation of the catenation operation. For simplifying automatic processing of grammars in Backus-Naur form we use a semicolon ; as production rule separator and we include the specification of the start symbol as the *first* derivation. For example, S: = <fe> ; as first production specifies that <fe> is the start symbol of the grammar in Figure 1.

Both notations are isomorphic. However, in practice Backus Naur Form is more convenient for specifying large languages manually. By delimiting symbols no confusion about symbols and symbol strings can arise as for example in [Whigham, 1995b]. It is common practice to use informal names for syntactic categories to make grammars more readable. Figure 1 shows a grammar of a context-free language for solving the XOR problem in Backus Naur Form. For the syntactic categories we have used the following informal memnonic scheme: <fe> is short for functional expression, <f0> denotes variables (functions with 0 arguments), <f1> denotes functions with 1 argument, and <f2> denotes functions with 2 arguments.

A *derivation tree D* is a labeled ordered tree for a context–free grammar $G = (V_N, V_T, P, X)$ with the following properties: X labels the root of D. For all subtrees $D_1, \ldots, D_k$ of the sons of the root X with the root of the subtree D_i labeled X_i, $X \rightarrow X_1 \ldots X_k$ is a production of P. If X_i is a nonterminal symbol, D_i is a derivation tree, if X_i is a terminal symbol, D_i is the single node X_i. If the empty word ϵ is the root of D_1, the only subtree of D, then $X \rightarrow \epsilon$ is a production in P [Aho and Ullman, 1972, p. 139].

The *frontier* of a derivation tree is the string obtained by concatenating the leaves of the derivation tree (in order from the left) [Aho and Ullman, 1972, p. 140].

$\Longrightarrow$ denotes the relation *derives*, $\overset{k}{\Longrightarrow}$ denotes the k-fold product of the relation $\longrightarrow$ and $\overset{*}{\Longrightarrow}$ denotes the k-fold product of the relation $\Longrightarrow$ for an arbitrary but finite k.

Theorem 2.1 *Suppose $G - (V_{NT}, V_T, P, X)$ is a context-free grammar. Then $X \overset{*}{\Longrightarrow} \alpha$ if and only if there is a derivation tree with the sentential form α as frontier [Aho and Ullman, 1972, p. 143].*

Proof See [Aho and Ullman, 1972, p. 141] ∎

From theorem 2.1 the following consequences are obvious: For each word w of $L(G)$ there exists at least one derivation tree with frontier w. We can retrieve a word w from its derivation tree by extracting the frontier of the derivation tree.

A *complete derivation tree* is a derivation tree whose frontier is a word w of $L(G)$. All leaves of a complete derivation tree are terminal symbols and all interior nodes of a complete derivation tree are nonterminal symbols.

The leftmost (rightmost) derivation associated with a derivation tree is unique. If there exists at least one word in $L(G)$ which has two or more distinct leftmost (rightmost) derivations, we say that the grammar G is *ambiguous*. A language which has no unambiguous grammar is called *inherently ambiguous*. The counting algorithm presented in section 4 counts all complete derivation trees once. However, the implication that every word is counted once only holds for unambiguous grammars. How often a word will be counted for ambiguous grammars, depends on the degree of ambiguity of the grammar which may be infinite [Kuich and Salomaa, 1986, p. 296]. Consider for example the grammar G with the production $S \rightarrow S \mid a$. For G we count a, the only word in $L(G)$, infinitely often.

Unfortunately, in general it is undecidable whether a context-free grammar G is ambiguous or not [Aho and Ullman, 1972, p. 203].

The *signature* (of an algebraic specification) is defined as follows [Ehrich *et al.*, 1989, p. 14f]: A *signature* is a pair $\sum = <S, O>$ with S a set of *sorts* and $O = \{O_{\bar{s},s}\}_{\bar{s} \in S^*, s \in S}$ an $S^* \times S$ indexed set family of *operators*. For every word $\bar{s} \in S^*$ and every sort $s \in S$ exists a set $O_{\bar{s},s}$ of operators in O. $\bar{s} = s_1, \ldots s_n$ denotes the list of argument sorts, s the result sort of each operator $o \in O_{\bar{s},s}$. Instead of $o \in O_{\bar{s},s}$ we often write $o : s_1 \times \ldots \times s_n \rightarrow s$. For the case $n = 0$ we obtain the *constants* of sort s which are denoted by $O_{\epsilon,s}$. $X = \{X_s\}_{s \in S}$ is an S indexed set family. The elements of $x \in X_s, s \in S$ are called *variables* of the sort s. We assume that X_s and $O_{\epsilon,s}$ are disjoint for all $s \in S$. This implies that variables and constants are different. With $\sum(X)$ we denote the signature which results from adding all variables as constants to $\sum$ [Ehrich *et al.*, 1989, p. 19]: $\sum = <S, O \cup X>$ with $(O \cup X)_{\epsilon,s} = O_{\epsilon,s} \cup X_s$ and $(O \cup X)_{\bar{s},s} = O_{\bar{s},s}$ for all $s \in S$ and $\bar{s} \in S^+$.

3 COUNTING DERIVATION TREES

In Figure 2 we show, how the set of all complete derivation trees which we can generate in *exactly* 2 derivation steps from the grammar shown in Figure 1 can be counted.

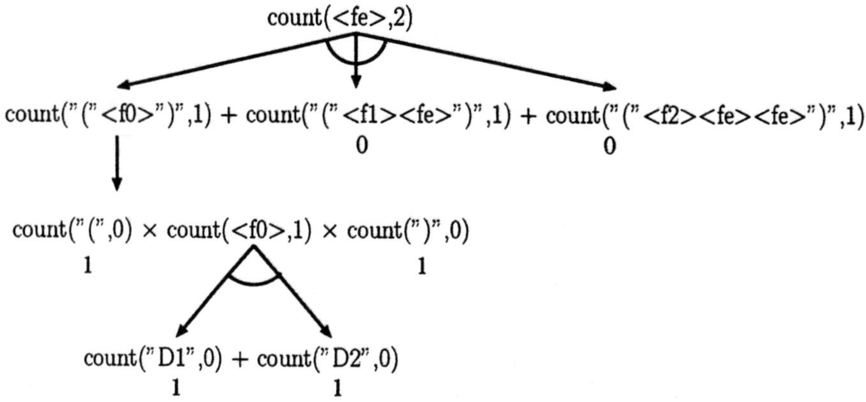

Figure 2: A Small Example

We use a *divide-and-conquer* approach in which the task of counting is successively split into smaller tasks. Starting from the start-symbol <fe> with 2 derivation steps, we write down the set of all possible derivations for this symbol. As a result, we add the results of counting the derivations from the three productions for <fe> with one derivation step. Next, each symbol in the production is assigned the number of derivation steps available. For "("<f0>")" this is easy. The terminal symbols receive 0 derivation steps, the only available derivation step is assigned to <f0>. For simplicity, whenever we allocate derivation steps to symbols, terminal symbols receive 0 derivation steps. The task of counting the number of different trees which can be generated starting from "("<f0>")" can be split into counting the number of trees starting with "(", <f0>, and ")", respectively. In our example, only one assignment of derivation steps is possible. In order to obtain the total number of trees we take the product of the number of trees starting with "(", <f0>, and ")", because the number of elements of the Cartesian product of the set of trees T_1 starting at position 1 with the set of trees T_2 starting at position 2 and the set of trees T_3 starting at position 3 is $|T_1| \times |T_2| \times |T_3|$. For proof, see [Berge, 1971, p. 16]. Not enough derivation steps are available in the remaining two cases to eliminate all terminals in the derivation, because in both cases the number of nonterminal symbols (2 in the second case and 3 in the third) is higher than the number of available derivation steps (1 derivation step). This implies that some nonterminal symbols remain in the frontier of the derivation tree and that no complete derivation tree could be derived with two derivation steps in both cases. Finally, for <f0> with 1 derivation step we repeat splitting the counting task. The total number of complete derivation trees in the example is 2.

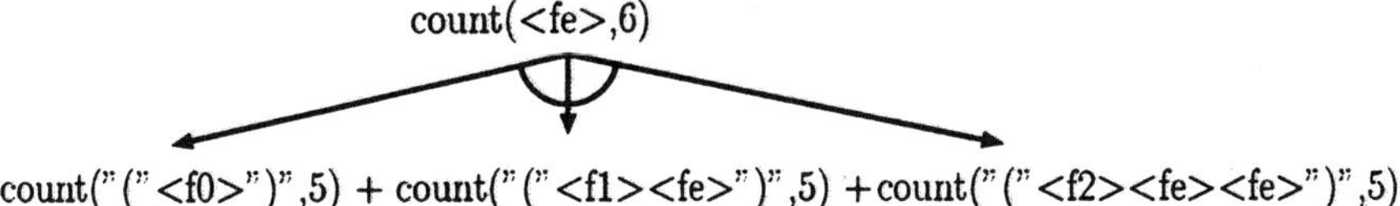

Figure 3: Substitution of <fe> by the Right-Hand Side of the Production Rule

The next example is large enough to illustrate all possible complications in search space counting. Now we count the set of all complete derivation trees which we can generate in exactly 6 derivation steps from the grammar shown in Figure 1. Figure 3 repeats the first step discussed above, this time with 6 derivation steps. Figure 4 shows how terminal symbols are counted, Figure 5 demonstrates the 2-partition case, and Figure 6 illustrates the 3-partition case. In Figure 7 the 3-partition case is derived from applying the 2-partition operation twice.

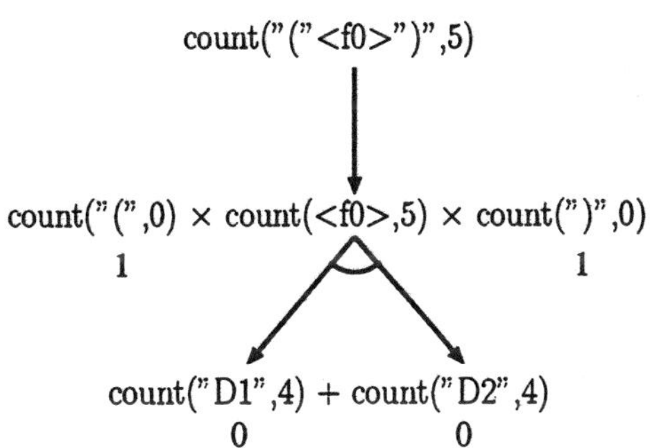

Figure 4: Counting Terminal Symbols (Case 1)

In Figure 4 we have 5 derivation steps which we have to assign to the symbols "(", <f0>, and ")". Terminal symbols do not need any further derivation steps. So, the number of derivation steps assigned to "(" and ")" is 0 and the remaining 5 derivation steps are assigned to <f0>. Because the right hand side of the production rule for <f0> consists of only one terminal symbol, we must assign all available derivation steps to these symbols.

Allocating derivation steps to a terminal symbol indicates that no derivation with exactly 5 derivation steps exists for <f0>. Compare this with the derivation from <f0> with exactly one derivation step shown in Figure 2. Counting terminal symbols with 0 derivation steps assigned results in 1. Counting terminal symbols with 1 or more derivation steps assigned results in 0.

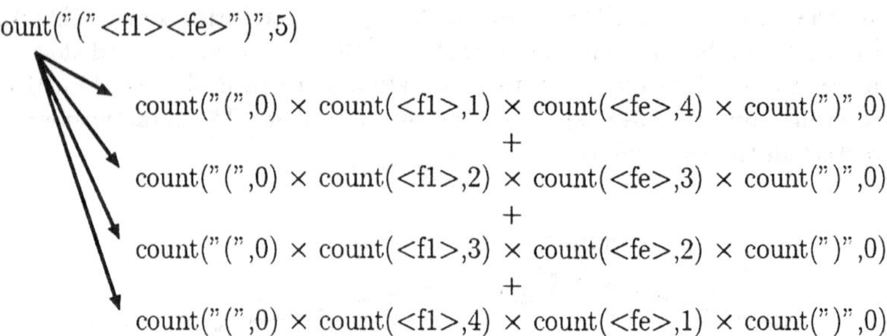

Figure 5: The 2-Partition Case (Case 2)

In Figure 5 there are 2 nonterminal symbols in the string and 5 derivation steps available. In order to count all complete derivation trees which can be derived in this setting, we have to consider all possible assignments of 5 derivation steps to 2 symbols. All possible ordered 2-partitions (compositions) of 5 are $(1, 4), (2, 3), (3, 2), (4, 1)$. These are all pairs (r_1, r_2) for which $r_1 + r_2 = 5$ holds. We have to count the number of complete derivation trees for each of these configurations and to sum over all configurations. Clearly, for a fixed configuration the total number of complete derivation trees is the number of complete derivation trees derivable from the first nonterminal symbol times the number of complete derivation trees derivable from the second.

count(" (" <f2><fe><fe>")",5)

count("(",0) × count(<f2>,1) × count(<fe>,1) × count(<fe>,3) × count(")",0)
+
count("(",0) × count(<f2>,1) × count(<fe>,3) × count(<fe>,1) × count(")",0)
+
count("(",0) × count(<f2>,3) × count(<fe>,1) × count(<fe>,1) × count(")",0)
+
count("(",0) × count(<f2>,1) × count(<fe>,2) × count(<fe>,2) × count(")",0)
+
count("(",0) × count(<f2>,2) × count(<fe>,1) × count(<fe>,2) × count(")",0)
+
count("(",0) × count(<f2>,2) × count(<fe>,2) × count(<fe>,1) × count(")",0)

Figure 6: The 3-Partition Case (Case 3)

In Figure 6 we have to allocate 5 derivation steps to three nonterminal symbols. Enumeration of the possible configurations results in $(1, 1, 3), (1, 2, 2), (1, 3, 1), (2, 1, 2), (2, 2, 1), (3, 1, 1)$.

In any context-free grammar, at most i nonterminal symbols may occur in the right hand side of a production rule. This implies that at most ordered i-partitions of integers are needed for our task.

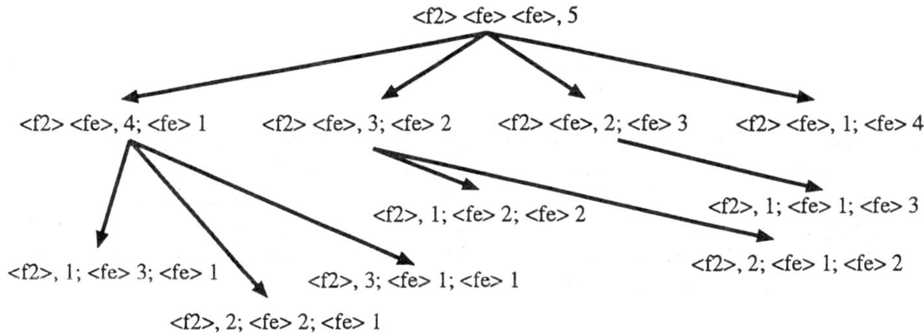

Figure 7: From the 2-Partition Case to the 3-Partition Case

Figure 7 illustrates how we can obtain a 3-partition by repeated applications of 2-partition operations. Because of the associativity of addition, we can combine a fixed collection of 2-partitions in any order we like to obtain the 3-partition. Verification of this for the example in Figure 7 is not included for the sake of brevity. However, we use this fact in generalizing from the 2-partition case in (5) to the k-partition case in (3).

4   FROM THE BNF TO THE WORD COUNTING FUNCTION

The number of words generated by an arbitrary context-free grammar is often infinite. However, we can partition the set of words S into an infinite number of subsets $S_{L,=,i}$. The members of $S_{L,=,i}$ are all words which can be generated in i derivation steps. The set S is then defined by $S = \bigcup_{i=1}^{\infty} S_{L,=,i}$.

Definition 4.1 *A k-bounded search space $S_{L,k}$ contains all words derivable in at most k derivation steps:* $S_{L,k} = \bigcup_{i=1}^{k} S_{L,=,i}$

We denote the size of a search space S by $|\, S\, |$. For a k-bounded search space $S_{L,k}$ the search space is then $|\, S_{L,k}\, | = \sum_{i=1}^{k} |\, S_{L,=,i}\, |$.

Finally, we can characterize the search space size $|\, S_{L,k}\, |$ of L for all $k \in N$ with $|\, S_{L,k}\, | = \sum_{i=1}^{k} \Pi(\langle \text{startsymbol} \rangle, i)$, where $\Pi(\langle \text{startsymbol} \rangle, i)$ denotes a recursive word counting function for $|\, S_{L,=,i}\, |$. (As usual, N denotes the integers $1, 2, 3, \ldots$ and $N_0 = N \cup \{0\}$.)

Definition 4.2 $\Pi(\langle startsymbol \rangle, i)$ *is a recursive word counting function for* $|\, S_{L,=,i}\, |$ *which is automatically derived from the grammar G of a context-free language L.* $\Pi(\langle startsymbol \rangle, i)$ *counts the number of words which can be derived from* $\langle startsymbol \rangle$ *in exactly i derivation steps. (Recursive word counting function.)*

In the following we show in detail how the recursive word counting function is derived from the production rules of the grammar of a context-free language.

For $L(G)$ the recursive word counting function Π can be automatically derived by a signature mapping $F_1 : \sum_{BNF} \to \sum_{WCF}$ from the productions P of G which are given in Backus-Naur Form. We assume, that all semicolons (rule separators) have already been stripped in a preprocessing phase. F_1 "compiles" a grammar into a word counting function.

$$\sum_{BNF} = \langle V_T, V_{NT}, :=, |, \star \rangle \tag{1}$$

is the signature of the language of the BNF grammar specification, with V_T denoting the terminal alphabet, V_{NT} the nonterminal alphabet, $:=$ denoting *derives to*, $|$ denoting *or* and $\star$ denoting *catenation* (usually catenation is denoted by juxtaposition of symbols). Since $y \in V_{NT}$ may appear on both sides of a production, y_{LHS} indicates its appearance on the left hand side and y_{RHS} its appearance on the right hand side of a production. The signature of the recursive word counting function language is

$$\sum_{WCF} = \langle \Pi(x, d), \Pi(y, d), =, +, \circ \rangle. \tag{2}$$

$\Pi(x, d)$ is the set of all invocations and definitions of the recursive word counting function Π with $x \in V_T$ and $d \in N_0$ as argument. $\Pi(y, d)$ is the set of all invocations and definitions of the recursive word counting function Π with $y \in V_{NT}$ and $d \in N$ as argument. $=$ denotes *is defined by* and $+$ denotes addition. $\circ$ is the ordered 2-partition function explained in Figures 5 to 7 which acts as a kind of a ternary function composition operation. $\circ(\Pi(y_1, d), \Pi(y_2, d), d)$ calculates the number of words derivable from the symbol string $y_1 y_2$ in d derivation steps.

The recursive word counting function scheme $\Pi : (V_T \times N_0) \cup (V_{NT} \times N) \to N_0$ is now derived by the signature mapping $F_1 : \sum_{BNF} \to \sum_{WCF}$ which is defined as follows:

1. For all elements x of V_T, x is replaced by a call to $\Pi(x, d - 1)$:

$$\forall x \in V_T : x \to \Pi(x, d - 1) \, .$$

   We add for all $x \in V_T$ a clause of the following kind to the recursive word counting function scheme Π:

$$\Pi(x, d) = 1 \cdot (d = 0), \qquad \text{where}(S) = \left\{ \begin{array}{ll} 1 & \text{if } S \text{ is true} \\ 0 & \text{else} \end{array} \right.$$

   for any statement S which can be either true or false. Therefore, for a terminal symbol x, $\Pi(x, d)$ is 1, if $d = 0$ and 0 otherwise.
2. For all elements y of V_{NT}, the substitution rules for y are given by:

$$\forall y_{LHS} \in V_{NT} : y_{LHS} \to \Pi(y_{LHS}, d)$$

$$\forall y_{RHS} \in V_{NT} : y_{RHS} \to \Pi(y_{RHS}, r_i)$$

For a nonterminal symbol y and $d < 1$, Π is undefined. Whenever Π is undefined, it takes the value 0. For r_i see Expression 3.

3. We replace := by =:

$$:= \; \rightarrow \; =$$

4. We replace | by +:

$$| \; \rightarrow \; +$$

5. We replace catenation $*$ by 2-partitions $\circ$:

$$\star \; \rightarrow \; \circ$$

In the BNF notation catenation $x_1 \star x_2$ is usually formed by writing the symbols immediately together: $x_1 x_2$. Each k-symbol string $y^k = y_1 \ldots y_k$ is therefore replaced by the function $\Gamma(y_1 \ldots y_k, d)$ defined below:

$$\Gamma(y_1 \ldots y_k, d) = \sum_A \prod_{i=1}^{k} \Pi(y_i, r_i), \tag{3}$$

where the summation runs over the set $A = \left\{ r_i \mid \sum_i^k r_i = d - 1, d > 0, r_i \geq 0 \right\}$. Function $\Gamma(y_1 \ldots y_k, d)$ is the ordered k-partition function as shown in Figure 7 for $k = 3$ (3-partitions).

We denote the number of words derivable in d derivation steps from a string $y_1 \ldots y_k$ for one specific partition $r = r_1 \ldots r_k$ of d by

$$\gamma(y_1 \ldots y_k, r) = \prod_{i=1}^{k} \Pi(y_i, r_i) \tag{4}$$

Note that $\Gamma(y_1 \ldots y_k, d) = \sum_A \gamma(y_1 \ldots y_k, r_i)$. Let us return to the string $x_1 x_2$ with the two symbols x_1 and x_2 with e derivation steps available. How many different words can we derive in e derivation steps from the start string $x_1 x_2$? The answer is found after having analysed the following four cases:

(a) Both symbols x_1 and x_2 are nonterminal symbols. In order to derive a string of terminal symbols we have to assign say r_1 derivation steps to x_1. For the partition of e into 2 parts (2-partition) the number of words derivable is the product of the number of words derivable from x_1 in r_1 derivation steps with the number of words derivable from x_2 in r_2 derivation steps. To find all words, we have to sum over all 2-partitions. By all ordered k-partitions of d derivation steps, we mean all k-tuples of integers $r_1, \ldots, r_k$ such that $r_1 + r_2 + \ldots + r_k = d$, with $r_i \geq 0$. This means, all partitions generated by pairs r_1, r_2 such that $r_1 + r_2 = e$ and $r_1, r_2 \neq r_2, r_1$ hold:

$$\circ(\Pi(x_1, e), \Pi(x_2, e), e) = \sum_{\substack{r_1 + r_2 = e, r_1 \geq 0, \\ r_2 \geq 0, e \geq 0}} \Pi(x_1, r_1) \cdot \Pi(x_2, r_2) \tag{5}$$

If $r_i = 0$, $\Pi(x_i, r_i)$ is undefined, because we cannot derive a string of terminal symbols and this implies that $\Pi(x_i, r_i) = 0$. For further information regarding the theory of partitions of integers see [Andrews, 1976].

(b) x_1 is a terminal symbol and x_2 a nonterminal symbol. With Expression 5 we obtain again our result. You can convince yourself that this is the case, because $\Pi(x_1, r_1)$ is 0 for all values of r_1 except for $r_1 = 0$.

(c) x_1 is a nonterminal symbol and x_2 a terminal symbol. The roles of x_1 and x_2 have changed. With Expression 5 we obtain again our result. You can see for yourself that this is the case, because $\Pi(x_2, r_2)$ is 0 for all values of r_2 except for $r_2 = 0$.

(d) Both symbols x_1 and x_2 are terminal symbols. Expression 5 is only defined, if e, r_1 and r_2 are 0. In this case, its result is 1.

In order to obtain Function 3, we only have to generalize Expression 5 to the n-partition case, taking terminal symbols into account. Obviously, by doing this we have generalized the $2 + 1$-ary operation $\circ$ to a $n + 1$-ary operation.

For example, by applying the signature mapping F_1 to the production rules for L_{XOR} shown in Figure 1 we obtain the recursive function shown in (6). Note, that we have folded the clauses for the terminal symbols into an "otherwise" clause.

$$
\Pi(y, d) = \begin{cases}
\Gamma("\,("\,<\!f0\!>")\,", d-1) + \Gamma("\,("\,<\!f1\!>\,<\!fe\!>")\,", d-1) + \\
\quad \Gamma("\,("\,<\!f2\!>\,<\!fe\!>\,<\!fe\!>")\,", d-1) & \text{if } y = \,<\!fe\!> \\
\Gamma("\,D1", d-1) + \Gamma("\,D2", d-1) & \text{if } y = \,<\!f0\!> \\
\Gamma("\,NOT", d-1) & \text{if } y = \,<\!f1\!> \\
\Gamma("\,OR", d-1) + \Gamma("\,AND", d-1) & \text{if } y = \,<\!f2\!> \\
1 \cdot (d = 0) & \text{otherwise}
\end{cases}
\tag{6}
$$

In Table 2 we show the search space sizes of $S_{L_{XOR},=,i}$ up to $i = 24$ and the probability that a word is drawn from $S_{L_{XOR},=,i}$ if we draw with equal probability from all words in $S_{L_{XOR},24}$. To increase the performance of the search space counting functions we recommend to use the corresponding memoizing functions [Geyer-Schulz, 1989]. A memoizing function computes the value of a function for an argument the first time it is called with this argument and stores the value in a lookup table. For all other function calls with this argument the memoizing functions return the value in the lookup table.

Table 2: The Search Space Sizes $S_{L_{XOR},=,i}$

Derivation Steps i	$\mid S_{L_{XOR},=,i} \mid$	$P(X \in S_{L_{XOR},=,i})$
2	2	0.0000006
4	2	0.0000006
6	10	0.0000032
8	26	0.0000082
10	114	0.0000360
12	402	0.0001269
14	1722	0.0005435
16	6890	0.0021745
18	29794	0.0094032
20	126626	0.0399640
22	556778	0.1757227
24	2446138	0.7720167

5   AN EXACT UNIFORM INITIALIZING ALGORITHM

In Table 1 we observed an exponential decay in the probability of generating words, as the number of derivation steps n increased. However, in the following we develop an exact, uniform sampling algorithm for initializing populations of words of k-bounded context-free languages. The algorithm has two phases:

1. From the sets $S_{L,=,i}$ of the search space of a k-bounded context-free language draw a partition $S_{L,=,i}$ to which the word we intend to generate belongs. (Draw a partition of the search space.)
2. Generate a derivation tree with exactly i derivation steps. (Generate a derivation tree.)

Draw a partition of the search space. In the first step of the exact uniform initialization algorithm we determine the partition $S_{L,=,i}$ to which the word we intend to generate should belong. The probability of drawing a complete derivation tree with (exactly) i derivation steps from start symbol S in a k-bounded context-free language L with grammar G with equal probability is trivially given as:

$$P(\text{tree in } i \text{ derivation steps}) = \frac{\Pi(S, i)}{\sum_{i=0}^{k} \Pi(S, i)} \tag{7}$$

For the grammar L_{XOR} bounded to 24 derivation steps the probability of drawing a word derivable in 20 derivation steps is 0.0399640. Column 3 of Table 2 shows the probability of drawing a word from partition $S_{L,=,i}$. Table 2 has been computed with the help of (6).

Generate a derivation tree. The function INIT_WORD_U (see Figure 8) implements an algorithm for generating a complete derivation tree from start symbol S in exactly i derivation steps with equal probability. However, for ease of use e.g. as part of other genetic operators, if no word can be derived in d derivation steps, a word from the non-empty partition $S_{L,=,i}$ with the largest $i < d$ is generated. In the initialization algorithm an invocation of the algorithm INIT_WORD_U on empty sets $S_{L,=,i}$ is not possible, because empty sets $S_{L,=,i}$ have probability 0. The algorithm consists of

1. a recursive tree generation algorithm without backtrack,
2. a randomized choice function for selecting the appropriate production rule for expansion,
3. and a randomized choice function for selecting the appropriate k-partition of derivation steps. This function assigns to each symbol in a selected production rule the number of derivation steps which are available for expanding this symbol on the next level of recursion.

The word generating function. In Figure 8 we present the pseudo-code for the word generating function.

In the pseudo-code we assume the existence of a generic list data type with the operations *new_list*, *add_list*, *head*, *tail* and the predicate *empty*. *new_list* generates an empty list, *add_list* appends its second argument to the list given as its first argument and returns the result, *head* returns the first element of the list given as argument, *tail* returns the list given

```
tree function INIT_WORD_U(symbol root, int d);
    int production;
    list_of_symbol production_symbols;
    list_of_int partition;
    list_of_trees subtree_list;
begin
    if TERMINAL(root) then
        begin
            return(new_tree(root, new_list))
        end
    else
        begin
            production := choose_production(access_ST(root), d-1);
            production_symbols := access_PT(production);
            partition := choose_partition(production_symbols, d-1);
            subtree_list := new_list;
            while not empty(production_symbols) do
                begin
                    subtree_list := add_list(subtree_list,
                        INIT_WORD_U(head(production_symbols),head(partition)));
                    production_symbols := tail(production_symbols);
                    partition := tail(partition);
                end
            return(new_tree(root, subtree_list))
        end
end
```

Figure 8: Pseudocode for the Word Generating Function

as argument without first element. The predicate *empty* returns *true* if its list argument is empty.

The derivation tree is of the form (*root, list of subtrees*). The only operation we need is *new_tree* which generates a new derivation tree with its first argument as *root* and its second argument as *list of subtrees*.

The predicate *TERMINAL* returns *true* if its argument is a terminal symbol of the grammar.

The access functions *access_ST* and *access_PT* access the symbol table *ST* shown in Figure 9 and the production table shown in Figure 10, respectively. Both figures are explained at the end of this section.

The choice function for production rules (choose_production). Suppose a nonterminal symbol y can be substituted by p_j, the right hand side of a production rule, $j = 1, \ldots, m$. Of course, each p_j is a k-symbol string $y_1 \ldots y_k$. If we know how many words can be generated starting from each string p_j, we can easily compute the probability to choose p_j so that we draw a complete derivation tree with equal probability. See (3).

$$P(p_j \text{ in } d \text{ derivation steps}) = \frac{\Gamma(p_j, d)}{\sum_{j=1}^{m} \Gamma(p_j, d)} \tag{8}$$

The choice function for k-partitions (choose_partition). For each symbol y_i in the right hand side of a production rule $y_1 \ldots y_k$ we have to assign the number r_i of derivation steps available for its expansion, so that $d = \sum_{i=1}^{k} r_i$. We call the vector r a k-partition of d. The number of complete derivation trees which can be generated in d derivation steps starting from $y_1 \ldots y_k$ with k-partition r is $\gamma(y_1 \ldots y_k, r) = \prod_{i=1}^{k} \Pi(y_i, r_i)$. See (4). The probability of choosing the k-partition r, so that complete derivation trees are generated with equal probability, is:

$$P(r) = \frac{\gamma(y_1 \ldots y_k, r)}{\Gamma(y_1 \ldots y_k, d)} \tag{9}$$

The symbol table used is shown in Figure 9. The first three columns contain the symbol name, a 1 for nonterminals, and the numerical identifier used in the implementation.

```
<fe>   1   1    1 2 3
<f0>   1   2    4 5
<f1>   1   3    6
<f2>   1   4    7 8
(      0   5
)      0   6
D1     0   7
D2     0   8
NOT    0   9
OR     0  10
AND    0  11
```

Figure 9: The Symbol Table ST

The production table is shown in Figure 10. The first column contains the left hand side of a production, the second the right hand side.

```
<fe>    ( <f0> )
<fe>    ( <f1> <fe> )
<fe>    ( <f2> <fe> <fe> )
<f0>    D1
<f0>    D2
<f1>    NOT
<f2>    OR
<f2>    AND
```

Figure 10: The Production Table in Symbolic Form

6 EXPERIMENTAL RESULTS

In order to test the implementation of the exact uniform initializing algorithm developed above we constructed the following experiments.

The simplest experiment to test the correctness of the implementation is to generate a large number of trees with a sufficiently small number of derivation steps and to test whether the trees are generated with equal probability by comparing the expected number of occurrences of each tree with the observed number in the experiment. We generated a population of $n = 1540$ complete derivation trees with at most 10 derivation steps for the grammar shown in Figure 1. Because at most 154 different complete derivation trees can be generated, under the hypothesis that complete derivation trees are generated with equal probability, we expect each complete derivation tree to occur 10 times in the population. In this experiment and in the three other experiments of this section we performed a standard χ^2-test of goodness of fit. See e.g. [Bhattacharyya and Johnson, 1977, pp 424]. For a confidence level of $\alpha = 0.05$ this hypothesis is accepted ($\chi^2 = 150.8$, $\chi^2 < c = 182.49$, degrees of freedom $DF = 153$).

However, for search spaces bounded with a larger number of derivation steps this approach is infeasible because of the rapid growth of the number of trees in the search space for most grammars. See Table 2. For the grammar shown in Figure 1 we generated a population of $n = 2000$ complete derivation trees with at most 30 derivation steps and we tested the following hypotheses:

1. The complete derivation trees are distributed uniformly over the $S_{L,=,i}$ with $i = 1, \ldots, 30$. The result of this experiment is shown in Table 3. Note that the number of derivation trees with an odd number of derivation steps is zero. At a confidence level of $\alpha = 0.05$ we accept this hypothesis ($\chi^2 = 4.67$, $\chi^2 < c = 7.81$, degrees of freedom $DF = 3$).

Table 3: Distribution of Derivation Trees over Number of Derivation Steps

Derivation Steps	Expected	Observed
< 24	22.22	23
26	76.65	92
28	343.81	361
30	1557.32	1524

2. The complete derivation trees are distributed uniformly over the following partition: Class 1 contains all complete derivation trees starting with <fe> $\Rightarrow$ ”(” <f0> ”)” or <fe> $\Rightarrow$ ”(” <f1> <fe> ”)” and class 2 contains all derivation trees starting with <fe> $\Rightarrow$ ”(” <f2> <fe> <fe> ”)”. The results of this experiment are shown in Table 4. Again, at a confidence level of $\alpha = 0.05$ this hypothesis is accepted ($\chi^2 = 1.36$, $\chi^2 < c = 3.84$, degrees of freedom $DF = 1$).

3. We further partitioned the classes according to length. Table 5 shows the results. Again, we accept the hypothesis that the complete derivation trees are uniformly distributed at a confidence level of $\alpha = 0.05$ ($\chi^2 = 6.33$, $\chi^2 < c = 14.07$, degrees of freedom $DF = 7$).

Table 4: Distribution of Derivation Trees over Class 1 and Class 2

Class	Expected	Observed
1	442.68	421
2	1557.32	1579

Table 5: Distribution of Derivation Trees over Classes and Derivation Steps

Class	Derivation Steps	Expected	Observed
1	< 24	5.07	5
1	26	17.15	20
1	28	76.65	73
1	30	343.81	323
2	< 24	17.15	18
2	26	59.49	72
2	28	267.16	288
2	30	1213.50	1201

7 THE IMPACT ON GENETIC PROGRAMMING PERFORMANCE

To show the impact of our exact uniform initialization procedure on genetic programming performance we tried an experiment. We repeated the genetic algorithm with each initialization algorithm 100 times for a population size of 50, a k-bound of 40 and with at most 50 generations with a mutation rate of 0.05, a crossover rate of 0.7 and elite selection on the XOR-problem.

The biased genetic algorithm succeeded 45 times in finding a correct solution for the XOR-function, the exact uniform genetic algorithm succeeded 61 times. A statistical comparison of these success rates is most conveniently performed by means of a 2×2 contingency table.

	Success	No Success
Biased GA	45	55
Uniform GA	61	39

The corresponding χ^2 test statistic is $T = 5.13$ which exceeds the critical value $c = 3.84$, $(DF = 1)$ at a significance level of $\alpha = 0.05$. For details see [Bhattacharyya and Johnson, 1977, pp 440].

Similar improvements are reported by Iba for his heuristic random tree generation algorithm for Koza's genetic programming variant for learning boolean functions with 3 arguments [Iba, 1996a], simple symbolic regression, trigonometric identities, and predicting a Mackey-Glass time series [Iba, 1995].

However, speculation based on a few simulation results always remains unsatisfactory. There is nothing more practical (and final) than a proof of what constitutes the best initialization algorithm for the case that no a priori information on the solution is available.

Because of the stochastic nature of genetic programming algorithms, their initialization is essentially a problem of statistical sampling theory. There are several ways to devise a rule or *sampling design* which determines the probability that a particular point of the search space is included into the initial population or not. One such rule is uniform initialization or *simple random sampling*, which assigns to each point in the search space the same probability of being sampled. An alternative would be stratified sampling which is based on a partition of the search space according to some reliable a priori information about the possible locations of the optimum. Here points belonging to different parts or strata are assigned different probability of being included into the initial population. Several other sampling designs have been proposed in statistics, the interested reader is referred to [Krishnaiah and Rao, 1988] for further details.

The decision which design to use should be certainly oriented on some measure of efficiency or optimality. Interestingly, it turns out, that simple random sampling is optimal in the sense of being a *minimax procedure*, provided that we do not have any useful a priori information about the possible locations of the optimum in search space. The result we are going to present is not new, it has in fact been known since 1954 and comes from [Blackwell and Girshick, 1954, Chapter 8].

In the sequel we will outline the basic ideas of Blackwell and Girshick, suitably adapted, however, to the situation we encounter when initializing genetic programming algorithms.

Let S denote the search space which we assume to be finite with cardinality M and define X to be the set containing S and all its permutations. Let the triple $(X; \Omega, p)$ denote a sample space in the sense of Blackwell and Girshick, where Ω is a parameter space being equal to X and p is the trivial probability measure

$$p(x|\omega) = \begin{cases} 1 & \text{if} \quad x = \omega \\ 0 & \text{if} \quad x \neq \omega. \end{cases}$$

Next let us define a space of actions A in the following way: A contains all possible initial populations of size $N < M$ which may be sampled from X, with the proviso that there are no duplicate individuals in $a \in A$. Thus we consider sampling designs without replacement. Observe that a violation of this restriction is very unlikely to have serious effects, as long as M is large compared to N, a situation which we typically encounter in practice. This point can be made more precise, see for instance [Pathak, 1988]. The action associated with $a \in A$ is simply: run the genetic programming algorithm GP with initial population a.

Let V denote a set of sampling designs which consists of all subsets of the form

$$v = (j_1, j_2, \ldots, j_N)$$

of the integers $1, 2, \ldots, M$, such that $N < M$ and all components in v are different. Choosing a particular $v \in V$ means, create the initial population consisting of the individuals $j_1, j_2, \ldots, j_N$.

On V we define a decision function which is the identity, i.e. $a = v$, where equality means, that a and v contain the same individuals regardless of order. The decision is: if v has been drawn from X, then run the genetic programming algorithm GP with initial population a.

Let $\phi(v, a|x)$ be a randomized procedure, i.e. a probability measure defined on $V \times A \times X$ as

$$
\begin{aligned}
\phi(v, a|x) \quad &= \quad P(\text{select } v \text{ and start GP with population } a) \\
&= \quad \begin{cases} \pi(v) & \text{if } \quad v = a \\ 0 & \text{else} \end{cases} \quad ,
\end{aligned}
\tag{10}
$$

where $\pi(v)$ is the probability that sample v is drawn. Observe that $\pi(v)$ is just the sampling design, which we are looking for. If $\pi(v)$ is equal for all possible samples v, then we have simple random sampling.

Note that $\sum_v \pi(v) = 1$ and observe also that by (10)

$$
\sum_{v \in V} \sum_{a \in A} \phi(v, a|x) = 1,
$$

furthermore, $\phi(v, a|x)$ depends only on the individuals of x contained in v and we assume that

$$
\sum_{a \in A} \phi(v, a|x)
$$

is independent of x for all $v \in V$.

To any particular choice of v and corresponding action a we associate a certain loss L, which is conveniently measured by the time complexity of the genetic programming algorithm GP initialized by population a. The loss function L is defined on $\Omega \times A$ and is assumed to be constant with respect to permutations of $\omega = x$. More formally we write

$$
L(\omega, a) = L(\omega, (v, a)).
$$

Let $\sigma = (\sigma_1, \sigma_2, \ldots, \sigma_M)$ denote a permutation of $1, 2, \ldots, M$, and let

$$
\sigma(x) = (x_{\sigma_1}, \ldots, x_{\sigma_M})
$$

and if $v = (j_1, j_2, \ldots, j_N)$, then define

$$
\sigma(v) = (\sigma_{j_1}, \sigma_{j_2}, \ldots, \sigma_{j_N}).
$$

Also let $\sigma(v, a) = (\sigma(v), a)$.

Now observe that the loss function is trivially invariant with respect to permutations, i.e.

$$
L(\omega, (v, a)) = L(\sigma(\omega), \sigma(v, a)),
$$

and note also that

$$
p(\sigma(x)|\sigma(\omega)) = 1 \quad \text{if} \quad \sigma(x) = \sigma(\omega)m
$$

and thus $x = \omega$ and $p(x|\omega) = 1$. Moreover

$$
p(\sigma(x)|\sigma(\omega)) = 0 \quad \text{if} \quad \sigma(x) \neq \sigma(\omega),
$$

and therefore $x \neq \omega$ and $p(x|\omega) = 0$.

The risk associated with the random procedure $\phi(v, a|x)$, i.e. the risk induced by starting the genetic programming algorithm GP with a particular initial population, will be denoted by $\rho(\omega, \phi)$ and is defined by

$$\rho(\omega, \phi) = \sum_{x \in X} \sum_{a \in A} L(\omega, (v, a))\phi(v, a|x)p(x|\omega).$$

Obviously, the risk function is invariant with respect to permutations σ applied to both, ω and (v, a). It follows from theorem 8.6.4 of Blackwell and Girshick (1954), that there exists a minimax procedure ϕ^*, such that

$$\sup_{\omega \in \Omega} \rho(\omega, \phi^*) \leq \sup_{\omega \in \Omega} \rho(\omega, \phi).$$

Furthermore, we have by invariance that

$$\sum_{a \in A} \phi^*(v, a|x) = \sum_{a \in A} \phi^*(\sigma(v), a|\sigma(\omega)),$$

and both sides are independent of x by definition and equal to $\pi(v)$, the probability of selecting sample v.

Thus it follows that

$$\pi(v) = \pi(\sigma(v)).$$

If we sum both sides of this equation over all $M!$ permutations, then we obtain

$$M!\pi(v) = (M - N)!,$$

since $\sum_v \pi(v) = 1$ and since there are to each sample v $N!$ permutations which represent the same initial population. Hence we finally get

$$\pi(v) = 1/\binom{M}{N}. \tag{11}$$

However, equation (11) states, what the minimax sampling design is: draw samples uniformly or apply simple random sampling.

These results are in accordance with theoretical results of [Strasser, 1978] and [Strasser, 1976] which prove in a (Bayesian) setting that choosing the non-informative prior distribution improves the speed of convergence of a Bayesian learning algorithm.

In addition, sampling theory (e.g. [Hansen *et al.*, 1953]) requires simple random sampling for the usual sample statistics to be unbiased estimators of the population statistics. In a Bayesian setting simple random sampling constitutes the obvious noninformative prior or the "most uncertain" or maximum entropy prior [Berger, 1988].

8 EXACT UNIFORM INITIALIZATION FOR KOZA'S GENETIC PROGRAMMING VARIANT

Because of recent interest and a large number of applications of Koza's genetic programming variant ([Koza *et al.*, 1996] and [Koza, 1996]), it is desirable to apply the algorithms developed above to Koza's genetic programming variant too. By using a well-known mapping between signatures of algebraic specifications to context-free grammars (which is the foundation of the algebraic semantic of programming languages) we show that we can express Koza's specification of programming languages in terms of a "terminal set" (parse tree leaves) and a "nonterminal set" (interior nodes of a parse tree) in terms of a signature $\sum(X)$ and that this signature can be transformed into a context-free grammar.

Next, we show how Koza style specifications of programming languages can be converted into a signature $\sum(X)$. Because of the closure property of Koza's genetic programming variant (all functions must accept as arguments the results of any other functional expression of the language) the signature has only one sort, namely *functional expressions*. Koza's "terminal set" corresponds to the set of variables and constants $O_{\epsilon,s} \cup X_s$ of the sort and the "nonterminal set" corresponds to the set of operators O.

Now we are again on familiar ground. For each signature $\sum(X) =< S, O \cup X >$ we obtain an S-indexed set family $G(\sum) = \{G(\sum)_{s_0} = (N, T, s_0, P)\}_{s_0 \in S}$ of context-free grammars by the following mapping [Ehrich *et al.*, 1989, p. 16]:

1. The nonterminals are $N = S$.
2. The terminal are $T = \overline{O} \cup \{(,)\} \cup \{,\}$ with $\overline{O}$ the disjoint union of all sets $O_{\overline{s},s}$ for $\overline{s} \in S^*$ and $s \in S$.
3. The start symbol of $G(\sum)_{s_0}$ is s_0.
4. The productions are defined by $P = \{s \to o(s_1, \ldots, s_n) \mid o \in O_{s_1 \ldots s_n, s}\}$.

For every context-free grammar $G = (N, T, P, X_0)$ a signature $\sum(G) =< S, O >$ can be allocated as follows:

1. The sorts are $S - N$.
2. The operators in $O_{\overline{s},s}$ are the productions with left hand side s and the string $\overline{s}$ of nonterminal symbols on the right hand side.

As a corollary we immediately see that the programming languages used in Koza's genetic programming variant form a proper subset of context-free languages, namely those context-free languages which can be generated with exactly one nonterminal symbol.

In our practical example we use a (slightly) modified version of the mapping from signatures to context-free grammars:

1. The nonterminals are $N = S$.
2. The terminal are $T = \overline{O} \cup \{(,)\}$ with $\overline{O}$ the disjoint union of all sets $O_{\overline{s},s}$ for $\overline{s} \in S^*$ and $s \in S$.
3. The start symbol of $G(\sum)_{s_0}$ is s_0.
4. The productions are defined by $P = \{s \to (os_1 \ldots s_n) \mid o \in O_{s_1 \ldots s_n, s}\}$.
   (For those reader who prefer PostScript (an interpreter with postfix notation) we change P to $P = \{s \to (s_1 \ldots s_n o) \mid o \in O_{s_1 \ldots s_n, s}\}$.)

To apply the exact uniform initialization algorithm presented in Section 5 all what remains to be done is to explicitly derive the context-free grammar $G(\sum)_s$ induced by the signature $\sum(X)$ which is implicitly defined by Koza's genetic programming variant.

For example, [Iba, 1996b] considers the following specification of a language in Koza's style by defining a "terminal set" T and a "nonterminal set" F. The subscripts of a "nonterminal" represents the arity of the "nonterminal":

$$T \;=\; \{D_0, D_1, D_2, D_3\} \tag{12}$$
$$F \;=\; \{\text{AND}_2, \text{OR}_2, \text{NAND}_2, \text{NOR}_2\} \tag{13}$$

From (13) we can easily see that all functions are of arity 2. Let A be the arity set which in this case is $A = \{2\}$. By applying the mapping presented above to Iba's example, we obtain the grammar shown in Backus Naur form in Figure 11.

```
S  := <fe> ;
<fe> := "(" "D0" ")" | "(" "D1" ")" | "(" "D2" ")" | "(" "D3" ")" |
        "(" "AND" <fe> <fe> ")" | "(" "OR" <fe> <fe> ")" |
        "(" "NAND" <fe> <fe> ")" | "(" "NOR" <fe> <fe> ")" ;
```

Figure 11: The Backus Naur Form for Iba's Example

This mapping enables us to compare the exact uniform initialization algorithm with the random tree generation heuristic developed by Iba in [Iba, 1995] and [Iba, 1996b] for Koza's genetic programming variant. Iba treats Koza's parse trees as unlabeled structures.

Table 6: Counting Labeled and Unlabeled Trees

n	Catalan(n)	Unlabeled, $A = \{2\}$	Labeled
1	1	1	4
2	1	0	0
3	2	1	64
4	5	0	0
5	14	2	2048
6	42	0	0
7	132	5	81920
8	429	0	0
9	1430	14	3670016
10	4862	0	0

As a first estimation for the number of parse trees with n nodes for a language he proposes the n-th Catalan number

$$Cn(n) = \frac{1}{n} \binom{2n-2}{n-1}$$

which counts the number of unlabeled trees with n nodes. This is shown in column 2 of Table 6. However, not every unlabeled tree is a valid parse tree for Iba's language. In [Iba, 1995] a method of counting all unlabeled trees which respect the arity constraints is presented. The number of these trees can be shown to be

$$\frac{1}{n} \left(\begin{array}{c} n \\ \frac{n-1}{2} \end{array} \right)$$

for Iba's example with the proviso that this binomial coefficient is 0, whenever n is an even number. See Table 6, column 3. The general case is covered in [Goulden and Jackson, 1983, pp. 111]. The last column in Table 6 gives the number of derivation trees for the language specified by (12) and (13).

The interested reader will certainly recognize a striking difference between columns 3 and 4 of Table 6. This discrepancy can be explained by the simple fact that derivation trees are labeled ordered trees for context-free grammars. As we have shown above, the language specified in (12) and (13) gives rise to the context-free grammar shown in Figure 11.

9   CONCLUSION

The algorithms in this paper solve the problem of exact uniform generation of complete derivation trees from k-bounded context-free languages. They are the basis for an exact uniform initialization routine for simple genetic algorithms over k-bounded context-free grammars, a variant of genetic programming. It is important to note that, in principle, uniform initialization may be used as a starting point for the design of initialization algorithms for genetic programming which utilize a priori information about the search space and thus require biased initialization procedures. However, it seems that the practical implementation of these algorithms is, in general, highly non trivial, because such issues like balance of trees, depth, number of inner nodes, ... have to be taken into account. Furthermore, the result of Section 4 gives prerequisites for the combinatorial analysis of crossover and mutation operators on complete derivation trees. This is of crucial importance for deriving a schema-theorem, the corresponding loss function, and for the comparison with other stochastic optmization methods. This task is left for further research.

The complexity of our algorithm depends on the following:

1. The signature mapping $F1$ which compiles a grammar into a word counting function has complexity O(number of the symbols in the grammar).
2. For the tabulation of $\Pi(y, d)$, $\Gamma(y_1 \ldots y_k, d)$ and $\gamma(y_1 \ldots y_k, d)$ the complexity is dependent on the recursive structure of the grammar and on the number of ordered partitions (compositions) including zeroes $c(k, d)$. See [Andrews, 1976, p. 54].

$$c(k, d) = \left(\begin{array}{c} d + k - 1 \\ k - 1 \end{array} \right) \sim O(d^k), \text{for fixed } k \text{ and } d \to \infty.$$

For most of the grammars used in practical applications of genetic programming, the largest k is very small, because function arities are seldom larger than 4. However, there is still hope that further complexity reductions can be achieved with the help of normal-form theory and formal power series techniques. For example, each context-free grammar can be transformed to Chomsky normal form [Aho and Ullman, 1972, p. 151f]. In this case k will be equal to 2 and the number of ordered partitions is linear in the number of derivation steps. However, currently we do not know how the transformation to Chomsky normal form affects the recursive structure of the grammar. This requires further research.

3. The complexity of the word generating function shown in Figure 8 is of $O(d)$, the number of derivation steps, provided $\Pi(y, d)$, $\Gamma(y_1 \ldots y_k, d)$ and $\gamma(y_1 \ldots y_k, d)$ have been tabulated.

Acknowledgements

We gratefully acknowledge the help of Hitoshi Iba, William B. Langdon, Peter Whigham, and four anonymous referees. Their comments and suggestions as well as their help in getting papers otherwise inaccesible to us over the internet have considerably improved this work.

References

[Aho and Ullman, 1972] Alfred V. Aho and Jeffrey D. Ullman. *The Theory of Parsing, Translation and Compiling, Volume I: Parsing*, volume 1. Prentice–Hall, Inc., Englewood Cliffs, N.J., 1972.

[Andrews, 1976] George E. Andrews. *The Theory of Partitions*. Addison Wesley, Reading, 1976.

[Berge, 1971] Claude Berge. *Principles of Combinatorics*, volume 72 of *Mathematics in Science and Engineering*. Academic Press, New York, 2nd edition, 1971.

[Berger, 1988] James O. Berger. *Statistical Decision Theory and Bayesian Analysis*. Springer Series in Statistics. Springer Verlag, New York, 2nd edition, 1988.

[Bhattacharyya and Johnson, 1977] G. K. Bhattacharyya and R. A. Johnson. *Statistical Concepts and Methods*. Wiley, New York, 1977.

[Blackwell and Girshick, 1954] David Blackwell and M. A. Girshick. *Theory of Games and Statistical Decisions*. John Wiley & Sons, New York, 1954.

[Brown *et al.*, 1988] James A. Brown, Sandra Pakin, and Raymond P. Polivka. *APL2 at a Glance*. Prentice–Hall, Inc., Englewood Cliffs, N.J., 1988.

[Ehrich *et al.*, 1989] Hans-Dieter Ehrich, Martin Gogolla, and Udo Walter Lipeck. *Algebraische Spezifikation abstrakter Datentypen*. Leitfäden und Monographien der Informatik. B. G. Teubner, Stuttgart, 1989.

[Geyer-Schulz, 1989] Andreas Geyer-Schulz. Memo. *APL Quote Quad*, 20(2):12–27, December 1989. ACM, New York.

[Geyer-Schulz, 1995] Andreas Geyer-Schulz. *Fuzzy Rule-Based Expert Systems and Genetic Machine Learning*, volume 3 of *Studies in Fuzziness*. Physica-Verlag, Heidelberg, 1995.

[Geyer-Schulz, 1996a] Andreas Geyer-Schulz. Compound derivations in fuzzy genetic programming. *Proc. NAFIPS'96*, pages 510–514, July 1996.

[Geyer-Schulz, 1996b] Andreas Geyer-Schulz. *Fuzzy Rule-Based Expert Systems and Genetic Machine Learning*, volume 3 of *Studies in Fuzziness and Soft Computing*. Physica-Verlag, Heidelberg, 2nd revised edition, 1996.

[Goulden and Jackson, 1983] Ian P. Goulden and David M. Jackson. *Combinatorial Enumeration.* John Wiley & Sons, New York, 1983.

[Gupta *et al.*, 1994] Rajiv Gupta, Scott A. Smolka, and Shaji Bhaskar. On randomization in sequential and distributed algorithms. *ACM Computing Surveys*, 26(1):7–86, March 1994.

[Hansen *et al.*, 1953] Morris H. Hansen, William N. Hurwitz, and William G. Madow. *Sample Survey Methods and Theory.* John Wiley & Sons, New York, 1953.

[Iba, 1995] Hitoshi Iba. Random tree generation for genetic programming. Technical Report ETL-TR-95-35, Electrotechnical Laboratory (ETL), 1-1-4 Umezono, Tsukuba Science City, Ibaraki, 305, Japan, November 14th 1995.

[Iba, 1996a] Hitoshi Iba. Random tree generation for genetic programming. In Koza [1996], pages 75–82.

[Iba, 1996b] Hitoshi Iba. Random tree generation for genetic programming. *Parallel Problem Solving From Nature (PPSN'96)*, 1996. to appear.

[IBM, 1985] IBM. *APL2 Programming: Language Reference.* IBM Corporation, San Jose, 1985.

[Koza *et al.*, 1996] John R. Koza, David E. Goldberg, David B. Fogel, and Rick L. Riolo, editors. *Genetic Programming 1996: Proceedings of the First Annual Conference*, Cambridge, MA, July 1996. MIT Press.

[Koza, 1992] John R. Koza. *Genetic Programming: On the Programming of Computers by Means of Natural Selection.* The MIT Press, Cambridge, Massachusetts, 1992.

[Koza, 1996] John R. Koza, editor. *Late Breaking Papers at the Genetic Programming 1996 Conference*, Stanford, July 1996. Stanford University Bookstore.

[Krishnaiah and Rao, 1988] P. R. Krishnaiah and C. R. Rao, editors. *Handbook of Statistics: Sampling*, volume 6, Amsterdam, 1988. North-Holland.

[Kuich and Salomaa, 1986] Werner Kuich and Arto Salomaa. *Semirings, Automata, Languages*, volume 5 of *EATCS Monographs on Theoretical Computer Science.* Springer Verlag, Berlin, 1986.

[Naur, 1963] P. Naur. Revised report on the algorithmic language ALGOL 60. *Communication of the ACM*, 6(1):1–17, 1963.

[Pathak, 1988] P. K. Pathak. Simple random sampling. In Krishnaiah and Rao [1988], pages 97–110.

[Rosca, 1995] J. Rosca, editor. *Proceedings of the Workshop on Genetic Programming: From Theory to Real-World Applications*, San Mateo, July 1995. Morgan Kaufmann.

[Strasser, 1976] Helmut Strasser. Asymptotic properties of posterior distributions. *Zeitschrift für Wahrscheinlichkeitstheorie und verwandte Gebiete*, 35:209–282, 1976.

[Strasser, 1978] Helmut Strasser. Admissible representations of asymptotically optimal estimates. *The Annals of Statistics*, 6(4):867–881, 1978.

[Whigham, 1995a] Peter A. Whigham. Grammatically-based genetic programming. In Rosca [1995], pages 33–41.

[Whigham, 1995b] Peter A. Whigham. Inductive bias and genetic programming. In Zalzala [1995], pages 461–466.

[Whigham, 1996] Peter A. Whigham. Search bias, language bias, and genetic programming. In Koza et al. [1996], pages 230–237.

[Zalzala, 1995] A. M. S. Zalzala, editor. *First International Conference on Genetic Algorithms in Engineering Systems: Innovations and Applications, GALESIA*, volume 414, London, September 1995. IEE.

A THE APL COMPILER

As executable notation which allows the reader immediate experimentation we add the APL2 implementation of the algorithms presented in the paper. For an introduction to APL2 we refer the interested reader to [Brown et al., 1988] and [IBM, 1985]. The APL2 source code is available from http://mortadelo.wu-wien.ac.at/usr/genetic/.

The signature mapping $F1$ is implemented by the APL function PI_COMP which takes a BNF as argument and returns the canonical representation of the APL function PI which implements the recursive word counting function $\Pi(y, d)$ shown in (6). The function PI_COMP calls the function BNF_COMP given in [Geyer-Schulz, 1996b, p. 242f] which returns a four column symbol table ST (symbols of the language, nonterminal/terminal symbol, symbol identifier, list of indices of symbol in production table PT), a two column production table (symbol identifier, production) and the identifier of the start symbol START.

```
      ∇Z←PI_COMP BNF;ST;PT;START;HEAD;NT_CODE;T_CODE;NT
[1]    (ST PT START)←BNF_COMP BNF
[2]    HEAD←'Z←PI A;X;D' '(X D)←A' ' ⍕ ' ' →LABEL' ',⍕X' 'Z←' '
       ERROR''' ' →0'
[3]    T_CODE←'Z←1×(D=0)' ' →0'
[4]    T_CODE←(((⊂'LABEL'),¨(⍕¨(0=ST[;2])/ST[;3])),¨':'),T_CODE
[5]    NT_CODE←((((⊂'LABEL'),¨(⍕¨NT←(1=ST[;2])/ST[;3])),¨':')
[6]    NT_CODE←,(NT_CODE,[1.5](NT_ARG¨NT)),[2]⊂'→0'
[7]    Z←HEAD,NT_CODE,T_CODE
      ∇
```

The implementation of the function PI_COMP is straightforward. We know that the body of the function PI consists of one large case-statement which provides a clause for each symbol in the grammar. So, we have to generate the function header of PI and the branching code (line 2 of PI_COMP), the clauses for the terminal symbols (lines 3 and 4 of PI_COMP), and the clauses for the nonterminal symbols (lines 5 and 6 of PI_COMP).

```
      ∇Z←NT_ARG NT;B
[1]    Z←'Z←+/(⊂D-1)(YK MEMO ''YK'')¨'
[2]    →(1=+/(B←ε'(',¨(⍕¨PT[εST[NT;4];2]),¨')')ε'(')/PUSH
[3]    Z←Z,B
[4]    →0
```

```
[5]    PUSH:Z←Z,',⊂',B
     ▽
```

The code generator for a nonterminal symbol is shown in function NT_ARG which applies
the function YK to the symbol string $y_1 \ldots y_k$ on the right hand side of a production rule.
From the number of derivation steps d given as left argument and the sentential form $y_1 \ldots y_k$
as right argument, YK computes the number of words which can be generated with exactly
d derivation steps starting from $y_1 \ldots y_k$. Of course, we have to apply YK to each possible
right-hand side of the nonterminal and to take the sum over all possibilities.

By all ordered k-partitions of d derivation steps, we mean all k-tuples of integers $r_1, \ldots, r_k$
such that $r_1 + r_2 + \ldots + r_k = d$, with $r_i \geq 0$. For one k-partition of d the number of words
is the product $\prod_{i=1}^{k} \Pi(y_i, r_i)$. In [Geyer-Schulz, 1995] an elegant, but highly inefficient
implementation of the function YK for $\Gamma(y_1 \ldots y_k, d)$ has been presented which computes
all products for all k-partitions of d. However, a less elegant, but more efficient algorithm for
computing $\Gamma(y_1 \ldots y_k, d)$ is shown below. The strategy of this algorithm which is due to H.
Hörner relies on the elimination of all products $\prod_{i=1}^{k} \Pi(y_i, r_i)$ with at least one $\Pi(y_i, r_i) = 0$.

```
     ▽Z←D YK Y;M
[1]    →(0>D)/Z←0
[2]    Z←+/2⊃D YKF MEMO 'YKF' Y
     ▽
```

Function YKF starts by retrieving all search space sizes for words starting with nonterminals
in $y_1 \ldots y_k$ for all derivation steps up to d (line 1). Next, in line 2 we generate a list of all
combinations of derivation steps $j = 1, \ldots, d$ starting with y_i, $i = 1, \ldots, k$ with non-empty
search space. In line 3 we select those combinations which are k-partitions of d and we test
if k-partitions of d exist. In line 4 we compute the index structure for accessing the search
space sizes in our vector list A and in line 5 we return the existing k-partitions and the
products.

```
     ▽Z←D YKF Y;MAX;A;I
[1]    A←PI MEMO 'PI' ((Y←,Y)∪.,∪,⍳D)
[2]    Z←,⊃(∘.,)/((0<⊂[2]A)SEL¨⊂0,⍳D)
[3]    →(0=ρZ←(D=+/¨Z)/Z)/END
[4]    I←⊂¨¨((⊂⍳1↑ρA),¨¨1+Z)
[5]    Z←Z P←×/¨I PICK¨⊂A
[6]    →0
[7]    END:Z←(0ρ0)0
     ▽
```

The functions SEL encapsulates the APL primitive selection, the function PICK implements
a scatter index function.

```
     ▽Z←A SEL B
[1]    Z← A/D
     ▽
```

```
     ▽Z← I PICK A
[1]    Z←I⊃¨⊂A
     ▽
```

B   THE ALGORITHM

```apl
      ∇Z←INIT_UNIFORM A;W;D;S
[1]   (W D)←A
[2]   Z←INIT_WORD_U W(((?(¯1+2⋆31))÷2⋆31)IN+\S÷+/S←(PI MEMO 'PI')
      ¨W,¯ιD)
      ∇
```

The right argument of the word generating function INIT_WORD_U consists of the start symbol and the number of derivations drawn according to (7).

```apl
      ∇Z←N IN F
[1]   Z←1↑(N≤F)/ιρF
      ∇
```

The word generating function

The pseudocode of the word generating function INIT_WORD_U is shown in Figure 8.

```apl
      ∇Z←INIT_WORD_U A;S;D;W;N;I;R;DN
[1]   Z←1⊃(W D)←A
[2]   →(~ST[W;2])/0
[3]   S←PI_TF_OR(,⊃ST[W;4])(I←D−1)
[4]   R←0ρDN←0,,⊃PI_TF_AND(1↓N←0,,⊃PT[1↑S;2])(I)
[5]   LOOP:→(0=ρN←1↓N)/END
[6]   R←R,⊂INIT_WORD_U(1⊃N)(1⊃DN←1↓DN)
[7]   →LOOP
[8]   END:Z←(W R)
      ∇
```

The choice function for production rules

The probability of choosing the right hand side of a production rule is computed in lines 3 to 5 of PI_TF_OR according to (8).

```apl
      ∇Z←PI_TF_OR ARGS;SUM;PSUMS;D;S;P
[1]   (S D)←ARGS
[2]   →(1=ρZ←S)/0
[3]   PSUMS←(0,ιD)∘.(YK MEMO 'YK')(,¨⊃¯PT[S;2])
[4]   P←,(¯1,(1↓ρPSUMS))↑(0≠+/[2]PSUMS)/[1]PSUMS
[5]   Z←S[(((?(¯1+2⋆31))÷2⋆31)IN+\P÷+/P]
      ∇
```

The choice function for *k*-partitions

The probability of choosing a partition is computed in lines 3 and 4 of PI_TF_AND according to (9).

```apl
      ∇Z←PI_TF_AND ARGS;M;Y;D;P
[1]   Z←2⊃(Y D)←ARGS
[2]   →(1=ρY)/0
[3]   (M P)←(¯1↑(0≠(ιD)YK MEMO 'YK'¨⊂Y)/ιD)YKF MEMO 'YKF' Y
[4]   Z←M[(((?(¯1+2⋆31))÷2⋆31)IN+\P÷+/P]
      ∇
```

C COUNTING FOR L_{XOR}

The function PI implements the recursive function $\Pi(y, d)$ shown in (6). This function has been automatically generated by the function PI_COMP of Appendix A. Lines 1 to 4 of PI contain the branching code for the case-statement. The four clauses of the nonterminal symbols of L_{XOR} are coded in lines 5 to 16 of PI. The clauses for the terminal symbols of L_{XOR} are shown in lines 17–25 of PI. In Definition 6 this is the otherwise case.

For readers who want to verify that PI really corresponds to the (mathematical) Definition 6, the symbol table used is shown in Figure 9.

```
      ∇Z←PI A;X;D
[1]    (X D)←A
[2]    ⍋'→LABEL',⍕X
[3]    Z←'ERROR'
[4]    →0
[5]    LABEL1:
[6]    Z←+/(⊂D-1)(YK MEMO 'YK')¯(5 2 6)(5 3 1 6)(5 4 1 1 6)
[7]    →0
[8]    LABEL2:
[9]    Z←+/(⊂D-1)(YK MEMO 'YK')¯(7)(8)
[10]   →0
[11]   LABEL3:
[12]   Z←+/(⊂D-1)(YK MEMO 'YK')¯(9)
[13]   →0
[14]   LABEL4:
[15]   Z←+/(⊂D-1)(YK MEMO 'YK')¯(10)(11)
[16]   →0
[17]   LABEL5:
[18]   LABEL6:
[19]   LABEL7:
[20]   LABEL8:
[21]   LABEL9:
[22]   LABEL10:
[23]   LABEL11:
[24]   Z←1×(D=0)
[25]   →0
      ∇
```

Stochastic Context-Free Grammar Induction with a Genetic Algorithm Using Local Search

Thomas E. Kammeyer and **Richard K. Belew**
Cognitive Computer Science Research Group
Computer Science and Engineering Dept. – Mail Code 0114
University of California, San Diego
9500 Gilman Drive
La Jolla, CA 92093-0114
{tkammeye,rik}@@cs.ucsd.edu

Abstract

We have previously used grammars as a formalism to structure a GA's search for simple programs called sorting networks (SNets) (Kammeyer, Belew, and Williamson, 1995). In this paper we restrict ourselves to stochastic context-free grammars which, while more analytically tractable than our SNet grammars, are more difficult than others previously considered by the GA community. In our approach, the production rules of a grammar are encoded as genes of a genome; this grammar is used as a recognizer of strings and assigned a fitness measure that reflects the probability that it captures the structure of a restricted sample of strings generated by an imagined stochastic target grammar. Our GA introduces a novel encoding of grammars as genotypic strings, and uses a local search component to aid in learning rule probabilities. Both fitness evaluation and the local search algorithm depend on a "chart parser". We give results for two grammars whose nonstochastic equivalents have been used in previous studies. We also present arguments about the degree of testing needed for GA-based grammar induction.

1   INTRODUCTION

Genetic algorithms (GAs) are now regularly being applied to much more difficult problems than originally conceived. Much of this advance has been towards extending

GA performance on "classic" function optimization problems, for example on problems with very difficult or even perverse "GA-hard" characteristics, on problems of much higher dimensionality than have been attempted in the past, etc. This paper is part of a second extension of GA research, to problems outside the standard function optimization formulation.

Most ambitiously, we seek a way of evolving arbitrary *programs*: functions that produce appropriate outputs for all possible inputs. Recent empirical results arising from LISP-oriented "genetic programming" and related techniques have made this prospect much more tantalizing than we might have imagined even a few years ago. A fundamental obstacle to theoretical progress on the evolution of programs is due to the enormous variability introduced by the program's dependence on its input. For most problems of practical interest, the space of possible inputs is infinite, or at least too large to be exhaustively tested as part of each individual's fitness evaluation.

We have previously used grammars as a formalism to structure a GA's search in a particular class of programs called sorting networks or "SNets" (Kammeyer, Belew, and Williamson, 1995). Briefly, production rules of a grammar are encoded as genes of a genome; this grammar is used as a generator of a string which can be interpreted as an SNet specification; the SNet is then tested against a small set of input vectors; and finally the individual's fitness measures how successfully it has sorted them. While the goal of evolving a sorting program is obviously much more restricted than a search for an arbitrary function, it does retain the characteristic that the solution must sort correctly for *any input vector*, despite the fact that this space of potential inputs is exponentially large.

In this paper we restrict ourselves still further to much simpler but analytically tractable grammars. Our goal is to apply the background of research regarding the computational power of various grammatical classes and the problems inducing these from finite samples of their corresponding languages. We focus particularly on the task of stochastic, context-free grammar induction. We encode production rules of grammars as genes of a variable-length genome, and we use a fitness measure that reflects the probability that a grammar assigns to restricted samples from a stochastic target language. Our main results explore the effect of a local search algorithm for tuning production probabilities on GA performance. Previous GA-based grammatical inference studies have concentrated on nonstochastic context-free grammars (CFGs) (Lankhorst, 1994; Wyard, 1991; Langdon, 1996), or stochastic regular grammars (Ost and Schwehm, 1995), but we believe this to be the first attempt to induce stochastic CFG's with a genetic algorithm.

The rest of this paper is organized as follows: the next section presents some background regarding stochastic grammar induction. Section 3 covers some relevant aspects of our genetic algorithm, detailing our representation and fitness function. Section 4 presents our test languages and our results. Section 5 discusses the results, further work currently in progress, and extensions and other aspects of our algorithm. Section 6 briefly states our conclusions.

2   BACKGROUND

2.1   DEFINITIONS

We begin by defining the nonstochastic version of the grammar induction problem and then step up to the definition of the stochastic version. We use a very simple example in each case to illustrate some of the definitions, but assume some formal language theory background on the part of the reader. In grammar induction generally, we are searching for a grammar which characterizes an unknown target language, generated by some unknown target grammar Γ^*. The target language is usually infinite or at least very large and we must assume that the learner can only observe a small, finite sample. We also assume that the finite sample we can see was generated by Γ^*. If, for example, we are trying to learn a grammar for the set of strings consisting of some number of a's followed by the same number of b's, an appropriate grammar choice for Γ^* is:

$$\text{start symbol} = A$$
$$A \rightarrow aAb$$
$$A \rightarrow ab$$

which generates all such strings by repeatedly applying the first rule and then ending with the last one.

Let Σ be the alphabet over which languages are defined ({a,b} for the previous example), so that Σ^* is the set of all strings. Then the data available is some subset of the target language, $S \subseteq L(\Gamma^*) \subseteq \Sigma^*$, and $|S| < \infty$[1]. Given the sample S, a given learning algorithm $\mathcal{A}$ returns a grammar as a best guess at the correct grammar. $\mathcal{A}$ may be randomized and thus may not always return the same grammar for a given sample – this is certainly true of our GA, as will be seen below. Thus it makes sense to talk about the probability that $\mathcal{A}$ returns a hypothesis grammar Γ when given some sample S, notated $\Gamma = \mathcal{A}(S)$.

In terms of the theory of "probably approximately correct" (PAC) learning, we want the probability that $\mathcal{A}$ returns an erroneous grammar to be small for all possible samples, S (Anthony and Biggs, 1992). That is, if μ is a distribution from which each training example in S is drawn and $P_{\mathcal{A}}(\Gamma \mid S)$ is the probability that $\mathcal{A}$ returns Γ when given sample S, then we want the following to be true:

$$\sum_{S} P_{\mathcal{A}}\left(\Gamma : \mu\left(L(\Gamma) \Delta L(\Gamma^*) \right) \geq \varepsilon \mid S \right) \mu^{|S|}(S) \leq \delta \qquad (1)$$

where "Δ" denotes symmetric difference on sets and $\mu^{|S|}$ is the distribution over samples with each element of the sample drawn from μ. In other words, we want the probability that $\mathcal{A}(S)$ and Γ^* differ, under μ, by ε or more to be less than δ.

The stochastic grammar induction problem is very similar to the nonstochastic problem. The main difference is that μ disappears because stochastic grammars specify not only a set of strings, but also a probability distribution over those strings. By P_Γ we denote the probability distribution over Σ^* induced by *stochastic* grammar Γ. We consider only grammars for which no productions have probability zero, since these could be thrown out without affecting the distribution induced by Γ. Thus, P_Γ assigns nonzero probability to $x \in \Sigma^*$ if and only if the productions of Γ generate x. Equivalently, P_Γ assigns nonzero probability to all strings x such that $x \in L(\Gamma)$. A stochastic grammar generalizing our former example would be:

---

[1] This particular formulation assumes that S contains only positive examples, which will be the case in all of the work which we report here.

$$\text{start symbol} = A$$
$$A \to aAb \qquad (0.5)$$
$$A \to ab \qquad (0.5)$$

This grammar assigns probability $(0.5)^{|x|/2}$ to each string x generated by the productions shown, and would be an appropriate choice of $\Gamma^\bullet$ if we were trying to learn this distribution over strings consisting of some number of a's followed by the same number of b's. A stochastic grammar Γ assigns a quantity of probability to $x \in L(\Gamma)$ equal to the sum of the probabilities of all derivations of x from Γ's rules[2]. The probability of a derivation is the product of the probability of the rule used at each step taken over all steps of the derivation. We use $L(\Gamma)$ to denote the set of strings derivable from the rules of the stochastic grammar Γ. The distribution $P_\Gamma(x)$ is thus nonzero only for $x \in L(\Gamma)$.

With this definition we can define the sample, S, almost as before: $S \subseteq L(\Gamma^\bullet) \subseteq \Sigma^*$, where $\Gamma^\bullet$ is now stochastic. The difference is that S is a multiset – it may contain duplicates of strings from $L(\Gamma)$. The relative frequencies of strings occurring in S is all the probability information that is available to $\mathcal{A}$. The definition for $\mathcal{A}$ applies mutatis mutandis – $\mathcal{A}$ must now return a *stochastic* grammar, and it uses frequency information from S to estimate probabilities. We can then state our learning criterion, modified for stochastic language learning as:

$$\sum_S P_{\mathcal{A}}\left(\Gamma: \mid P_\Gamma - P_{\Gamma^\bullet} \mid \geq \varepsilon \mid S\right) P_\Gamma^{|S|}(S) \leq \delta \qquad (2)$$

the intuition is the same as that behind the nonstochastic formulation in equation (1), but in this case, we measure error according to some (here unspecified) distance metric over probability distributions, as can be seen by the change from $\mu(L(\Gamma) \Delta L(\Gamma^\bullet)) \geq \varepsilon$ in the nonstochastic case to $|P_\Gamma - P_{\Gamma^\bullet}| \geq \varepsilon$ here. Also, as mentioned previously, the target language now specifies a probability distribution over Σ^*, and so we must use it to measure probability for samples since it is the distribution used to generate them, as evidenced by the change from $\mu^{|S|}$ to $P_\Gamma^{|S|}$.

It can thus be seen that the main difference between the nonstochastic and stochastic problems is that in the nonstochastic case we *introduce* some distribution used to generate the sample, and try to learn the correct grammar productions. In the stochastic case, the distribution over examples is part of the target and we must learn it as well, by learning the appropriate production probabilities.

The problem of grammar induction, or grammatical inference, has been studied for quite some time. Fu and Booth present an excellent survey of the basics (Fu and Booth, 1975). Many of the methods, such as the k-TAIL method for regular grammar induction, are based on the idea of constructing a "canonical" grammar which generates only the strings in S and then replacing pairs of nonterminals with a single nonterminal repeatedly to attempt generalization. The successor method, also for regular grammar induction,

---

[2] A derivation starts from the grammar's start symbol and applies rules of the grammar to replace symbols until a string is derived which contains only "terminal" or non-replaceable symbols.

uses a set of simple rules to construct a grammar that will cover and also generalize the sample. Other methods are specialized to a particular subset of regular grammars, such as the k-TLSS method. Context-free grammars are much harder to induce and the methods mentioned by Fu and Booth are usually restricted to a subclass of grammars. In general, context-free grammar induction seems to be approached mostly via heuristic methods. Another idea in Fu and Booth uses a "structural information sample", which is a sample derived from the target grammar after all productions have had their right-hand sides surrounded with extra "bracketing" terminals. Each example thus carries brackets making its exact derivation apparent. All of these grammar inference algorithms create nonstochastic grammars. To induce a stochastic grammar using them, one first builds the corresponding nonstochastic grammar and then approximates the probabilities.

There is a well-known algorithm, the inside-outside (Charniak, 1993) algorithm, for approximating the production probabilities for a stochastic context-free grammar given a sample. This algorithm is sometimes used on its own as a grammar induction method. First, a grammar is produced by sampling randomly from the space of possible productions with some fixed length. Next, the inside-outside algorithm is used to tune production probabilities and all productions whose probabilities have dropped to zero, or below some threshold, are deleted from the grammar. At this point, we either stop with the grammar thus found or introduce new productions and retune .

2.2   GENETIC ALGORITHMS FOR GRAMMAR INDUCTION

In this work, we wish to apply a GA to the problem of stochastic context-free grammar induction. Figure 1 shows a schematic form of our genetic algorithm. We will use it below to discuss previous research in this area, and then describe our own GA in terms of it. This pseudo-code shows the GA as a procedure taking one parameter, the sample S from which it is to learn. The execution of a GA depends on a variety of other parameters, such as mutation and crossover rates, but we have elided these here since we are interested only in the information about the learning problem given to the GA. Another form of information which might be given to the GA is less directly implied in figure 1; the genotypic representation of grammars could be chosen to usefully restrict the search.

```
1.      procedure GA( S )
2.          forall i do
3.              Geno[i] := randomly generated genotype
4.          end forall
5.          for gen from 0 to MaxGen do
6.              Choose test set, R ⊆ S,  for this generation
7.              forall i do
8.                  Pheno[i] := interpret genotype Geno[i] as a  grammar
9.                  [Optional:  tune Pheno[i]'s production probabilities using
                         local search]
10.                 Fit[i] := evaluate fitness Pheno[i] on R
11.             end forall
12.             apply selection, genetic operators to form the next generation
13.             replace Geno[i]'s with next generation's genotypes
14.          end for
```

Figure 1: Pseudo-Code For A Grammar-Inducing GA

Figure 1 supplies a "template" for a grammar-inducing GA. Instantiating this template involves making several choices. First, we must decide how to represent grammars as genotypes for the GA, and along with this choice we must decide on genetic operators. An important issue here is the extent to which the operators are specialized for the grammar induction task. Also, the "granularity" of encoding can vary, as we will see below.

Second, we must decide on some fitness function. Part of this will almost certainly involve determining which strings in S are derivable from each grammar in the population. For stochastic grammars we will also generally want to know for a given phenotypic grammar Γ = Pheno[i], the quantity $P_\Gamma(x)$ for each $x \in R$. The choice of R in figure 1 at each generation is important as well. The obvious approach is to exhaustively test each generation, using R=S for all generations. Our results below demonstrate that this is not needed. Such complete testing is potentially very expensive since general parsing algorithms cost $O(n^3)$ when applied to strings of length n. Note that in figure 1, R is shown as being kept constant across all individuals for a given generation. It is certainly possible to choose a new R for every individual, but none of the earlier approaches we cite below did this, and our experience with it to date doesn't show it to be obviously superior. Further, we will later give some a-priori reasons why we might *not* wish to take this approach.

2.2.1   Three Previous Approaches

Here we give a brief description of each of three previous studies in the use of GA's for grammar induction. Wyard's early work on nonstochastic grammar induction used samples of 20-100 each of positive and negative examples, and drew a new sample each generation (Wyard, 1991). Of the two test languages, only one was inferred correctly, and then only in 2 out of 5 runs. Wyard's representation used Greibach normal form, and allowed up to four nonterminals on the right-hand side of each rule. No hard limit on genotypic length is mentioned, but the initial generation is produced to have the same number of productions as the target grammar. Each rule in Greibach normal form begins with a single terminal which is followed zero or more nonterminals. Wyard used this feature of his representation: crossovers were only allowed between productions, between the left-hand and right-hand sides (LHS and RHS respectively hereafter) of a production, *and* between the leading terminal of an RHS and the rest of a production. Wyard's fitness function was based on the number of strings derivable from the grammar being evaluated. The fraction of strings in R which an individual grammar generated determined fitness: every positive example derived or negative example not derived by the grammar contributed +1 to fitness and the opposite circumstances resulted in a contribution of -1 to fitness. Since R was completely recreated by classifying random examples at each generation, the effective size of S, which was not explicitly represented in Wyard's study, was very large.

Wyard's latest work makes significant improvements on his 1991 publication (Wyard, 1995). His basic representation is the same: a series of productions on the genome written using sets of allowed terminals and nonterminals plus two delimiter symbols. One delimiter separates the RHS and LHS of each rule, and the other separates rules from one another. As before, crossover is restricted to occur on these "punctuation marks". Unlike his previous work, the choice of R in this case is fixed at R=S for the entire GA run, and contains 150 each of positive and negative examples.

The results in this second paper are impressive. Wyard is able to induce the harder of his previous paper's two target languages, as well as a 3-palindrome language and a subset of a grammar for English verb and noun phrases. Two potential concerns are that Wyard used knowledge of the target grammar to initialize the population at the beginning of each run, and penalized each individual grammar by 1 for each RHS nonterminal it contained over the total number occurring in the target grammar. Despite these biases, Wyard's paper makes two important points about the importance of the choice of normal forms for grammars as encoded on the genotype and about the dramatic impact which he observed population size to have on his GA's success. As Wyard did in this paper, we avoid restricting our grammars to a particular normal form in what follows.

Two other studies in genetic algorithm-based grammar induction are currently known to us. Ost and Schwehm studied induction of stochastic regular grammars (Ost and Schwehm, 1995). They attempted to infer a stochastic grammar which correctly captured ftp file transfers. They used a structured population consisting of a 32 by 32 grid of individuals, and tested their grammars on samples of size 284 and 4000, the smaller from actual network event traces and the larger from a hand-designed grammar, using a supercomputer. They were able to find an almost-correct grammar in terms of the set of strings generated, and compared their approach to several reference methods for stochastic regular grammar induction. It should be noted that the authors were *not* attempting to find an exact match to the grammar they used to generate the larger sample. Rather, it was sufficient for their purposes to find grammars that were very similar in form and generalized slightly from the target grammar.

Because Ost and Schwehm were inducing stochastic *regular* grammars, they were able to considerably optimize their representation by using previous results regarding finite state automata. They investigated two close variants in which they represented finite state machines, corresponding to regular grammars, in their genotypes. In both cases, the basic encoding used bit strings which encoded indices into sets of terminals and nonterminals; the authors mention no particular constraint on crossover. This was a fairly "low-level" representation since bit strings were used to encode individual symbols, and thus a single grammar symbol corresponded to multiple alleles.

The fitness function in this study was a linear combination of three terms. The first captured the ability of a given grammar to generate the training sample's strings, the second was meant to reward low-complexity grammars, and the third was designed to reward strings that could generate prefixes of the training sample successfully, even if they could not generate any whole string from the sample. Ost and Schwehm's GA used exhaustive testing: every generation, every individual was tested against all of S, meaning that R was chosen as R=S at each generation in terms of our GA in figure 1. Recall that the population was a 32x32 geographically structured population. The authors do not report the number of generations for which they ran their actual experiments, or a hard limit on number of generations, but assuming that their sample runs are representative, they ran for about 160 generations. If this is the case, their GA performed about 46.5 and 655 million parses in the course of a run using their small and large samples, respectively. It should be noted, however, that their use of a parallel processor made this a reasonable strategy and that their genotypic parsing algorithm was for *regular* languages, which are much cheaper to parse than context-free languages.

Finally, a technical report by Lankhorst discusses his extensive grammar induction experiments using a CM-5 multiprocessor. For the regular and context-free formal languages he induced, Lankhorst used 100 negative and 100 positive examples. As in the case of Ost and Schwehm, exhaustive testing was used at each generation, meaning again that R=S for every generation. For the more complex "micro-NL" language[3] he induced, he used 250 positive and 250 negative examples (Lankhorst, 1994). These experiments often resulted in discovery of the target language but generally required millions of parses before the first discovery of a correct grammar. Lankhorst's genetic representation was also in terms of bit strings encoding indices into ordered sets of nonterminals and terminals. Lankhorst, however, encoded the sequence of integers encoding each production using an "interval encoding" which reduced a sequence of integers representing a production to a sequence of bits, though not by directly encoding the integers in binary. Crossover and mutation were unrestricted. Fitness evaluation was based on the number of strings generated or not by an individual grammar Γ_i. As in Ost and Schwehm's work, Lankhorst tried to reward Γ_i if it could generate a large substring of a given $x \in R$.

3 A NEW GA FOR GRAMMAR INDUCTION

Our genetic algorithm, called "EvoGrams" (for "Evolving Grammars"), operates on variable-length strings which encode stochastic grammars as described below. One consequence of our representation is that the two most common genetic operators, crossover and mutation can be used directly, with no special considerations made for the grammars being represented. Crossover is two-point crossover, where the cross points are chosen independently in the two parent genomes; thus, crossover can dramatically change the lengths of the genomes on which it operates.

The mutation operator implements three simple point mutations: insertion, deletion, and modification. At a given location, 1, where a mutation is to occur in a genome, insertion inserts a random symbol from the alphabet before 1, deletion deletes the symbol at 1, and modification replaces the symbol at 1 with a randomly chosen symbol. The crossover rate is 0.8 per genome and the mutation rate is 0.005 per character. Tournament selection with tournament size 3 is used in all experiments.

Finally, initialization of the first population is done by choosing random characters for each location in each genotype. The genotypes are all initialized to the same number of characters, usually 128. By contrast, the maximum length to which they may grow is 512 characters. The character at each location is chosen as follows: with probability 0.5, it is the "punctuation" symbol discussed in the next section, and with probability 0.5 it is a uniform choice over the terminals and nonterminals the GA is allowed to use in the simulation. We stress that there is no guarantee of so much as a well-formed grammar in the initial population, but that typically several decodable productions occur that account for fragments of strings from the data set when the genotypes are initialized randomly with length 128, as specified above.

3.1 GENOTYPIC REPRESENTATION OF GRAMMARS

To represent a complete stochastic grammar in a genotype, we must encode the grammar's start symbol and then encode each production in turn. To encode a production, we must encode its LHS, a single nonterminal for context-free grammars, its RHS, a sequence of nonterminal and terminals, and its probability, a real number in (0,1]. Our earlier work with sorting networks (Kammeyer, Belew, and Williamson, 1995) used a highly structured genotypic representation. Crossover occurred only

---

[3] This context-free language was a fragment of English generated by a simple grammar.

between grammar productions and mutations was custom-designed to work with just the representation we chose for encoding grammars to build SNets. In designing our new representation, we were motivated to consider making more of the genome accessible to crossover. Also, we sought to avoid custom-fitting the operators to the representation since in the previous study this made changing the representation more difficult and time-consuming than we would have liked.

Our representation shares some features with each of the three previous studies mentioned above. As in the latter two studies, crossover is unrestricted. As in the first study, we do not use bit strings but instead represent the various symbols directly on the genotype. Unlike any of the cited studies, our representation does not require that all parts of the genotype code for productions, and does not require that the LHS, RHS, and probability (PROB hereafter) components of a given production be immediately adjacent on the genotype. Below, we will refer to this as "looseness" in the representation. It attempts to combine the virtue of restricted crossover, lack of disruption of grammar productions, with the virtue of unrestricted crossover, better exploration of the search space with the nonlocal moves which crossover can generate.

As mentioned above, part of the motivation behind our representation is the desire to use "standard" genetic operators which operate on character strings while allowing the operators to respect boundaries between important pieces of the genotype, such as the boundary between the end of one production and the beginning of the next one. To this end, our encoding allows for "junk" regions between productions on the genotype whose size range is not set in advance but which may expand and contract under the action of mutation and crossover. This is accomplished by introducing a single punctuation symbol, "|" which marks off regions in our genotypes which code for pieces of grammars, or "coding regions".

```
Gram   ::=  junk Start (junk Prod)+ junk
Start  ::=  | N |
Prod   ::=  | LHS | junk | RHS | junk | PROB |
LHS    ::=  N
RHS    ::=  (N ∪ T)i, 1 ≤ i ≤ MaxRHSLen
PROB   ::=  Ti, 1 ≤ i ≤ MaxProbLen
junk   ::=  (N ∪ T)*
junk   ::=  "anything that can't decode as what's
            expected next"
```

Figure 2: BNF Characterization Of Genotypes In EvoGrams[4]

Genomes are strings of symbols whose lengths can vary from zero to **MaxLength**. The symbols allowed are the terminals, T, nonterminals N, and the single special character "|". The "|" symbol delimits the start symbol of the grammar, and the LHS, RHS, and PROB of each production. Our representation is given in somewhat loose BNF form as figure 2. Note that a junk region can contain a decodable segment as long as its of the wrong "type". Thus an LHS segment could allowably occur between an

---

[4] It is important to note that the "|" symbols in this diagram are *not* BNF disjunctions, but instances of our punctuation symbol – there are no BNF disjuncts in figure 2. We have also used some regular expression notation.

RHS segment and a PROB segment, since it contains a nonterminal and would not be mistaken for a PROB segment. Similarly, anything to long to be an RHS, even if offset by "|" characters, could occur between an LHS and RHS harmlessly. Note that segments of a production are never allowed to be empty and that we don't use epsilon productions.

In words, the start symbol is the first singleton nonterminal bracketed by |'s. Each production is then encoded as a sequence of |-delimited fields specifying the LHS, RHS and PROB of that production. The LHS must contain only a single nonterminal, the RHS may have length up to **MaxRHSLen**, and probability fields may have length up to **MaxProbLen**. The probability field must contain only terminal symbols. Half of all terminal symbols are arbitrarily interpreted to encode 1 and the other half encode 0[5]; the symbols are then treated as the most significant bits of a fixed-point binary fraction. This encoding of production probabilities allows us to use genotypes which are simply strings of symbols over an alphabet of grammar symbols plus a single punctuation symbol, "|". No special symbols to encode *digits* need be added, and our genotype need not contain a mixture of real-valued and string-valued sections. This is in keeping with our desire to use, as much as possible, "standard" versions of the genetic operators, without special knowledge about the representation built into them.

One more detail concerning the interpretation of probability fields is important. Obviously the numbers encoded on individual productions with the same LHS are not guaranteed to sum to one, and cannot therefore be interpreted directly as probabilities. After having interpreted the genome as a grammar, we normalize all probabilities associated with the same LHS by summing the raw "probabilities" from the genotype over all productions with the same LHS and then dividing these probabilities by their sum. This is done for each distinct LHS in the grammar. Further, we coalesce genotypic duplicates of productions into single productions whose probabilities are the sums of the coalesced probabilities. This does not change the meaning of the tested grammar, but improves the efficiency of our chart parser which would otherwise engage in a redundant parsing activity as it formed parses using each copy of each multiply-represented rule.

An important feature of our representation is that between any two coding regions, any number of terminals and nonterminals can occur as "junk". Further, any sequence that doesn't contain a valid encoding of a start symbol may occur before the start symbol, and "failed production segments" may occur between the end of one production and the beginning of the next one or in some cases between segments of a valid production. We call these non-coding regions "junk" regions, even though we suspect that they might play some role in the search, as discussed in Section 5 below.

As an example of how a grammar is represented in our scheme, consider the short genome in figure 3a, defined over the terminal alphabet T={a,b}, the nonterminal set N={A,B}, and interpreting "a" as the one bit and "b" as the zero bit. Ellipses have been used to indicate the continuation of the genome across lines.

In this figure, **boldface** is used to denote regions coding for correctly specified start symbols and productions, and underlining to highlight an "illegal" segment which doesn't decode to anything. This genotype encodes the stochastic grammar in figure 3b.

---

[5] In the event of an odd number of terminal symbols, one is simply not used for encoding probabilities. Typically only about 10 iterations are needed to adequately tune the grammars considered in this paper.

When the decoding algorithm reaches the underlined region, it is looking for a PROB segment. None of the underlined segments can be decoded as such, but each "|" in the underlined area causes an attempt to match a valid PROB segment beginning at that location. Since all of these contain a nonterminal, they are unsuitable. Further, the second "|" underlined begins an empty segment since it is immediately followed by another "|". As mentioned earlier, empty segments are disallowed.

```
||ababbAABB|A|abABBb|A|aaABabbB|aB|bbaa|bBAa|A||abA|Ba|aa
|aaA|A||ba||ba|ABBba|B|abbBAA|Ab|abABBaA|a|abbaaaAABabAB
aAaaa
```

Figure 3a: Sample genome

```
Start = A
A -> aB        (0.75)
A -> ba        (0.25)
B -> Ab        (1.0)
```

Figure 3b: Interpretation as SCFG

3.2   FITNESS EVALUATION

At each generation, the first activity in evaluating the entire population is to construct R. |R| is fixed across all generations in the experiments reported here. Each genotype is decoded into a grammar as described in section 3.1. If nothing at all can be decoded, the grammar is "nonviable" and is assigned a fitness value lower than any viable grammar will have, -10^{50}. This extremely low value was picked so that even if a viable grammar, Γ, assigned the lowest representable probability (in our machine's double-precision floating point format) to every example in R, its fitness would still be higher than that of a nonviable, as will be seen below.

Before being evaluated, the grammar can have its probabilities tuned using the inside-outside algorithm. This algorithm modifies the grammar's probabilities to make the training data it is given as likely as possible. It is at heart an EM-based ("expectation maximization"-based) local search and thus converges quickly[6]. The training data given to the inside-outside algorithm is always the same R used for fitness evaluation. This essentially means that we are allowing a grammar to make the examples on which its fitness will be evaluated more likely, thus increasing its fitness. Since the inside-outside algorithm only applies to those examples which can be parsed by a given grammar, Γ_i, this means that Γ_i will only increase its probabilities for those examples which its productions can already generate.

Next, the grammar being evaluated, Γ, is used to attempt to parse each string in R using a chart parsing algorithm (Charniak, 1993). This parsing algorithm also allows us to assess the probability of each $x \in R$ according to Γ, $P_\Gamma(x)$, and these probabilities are used as the basis for fitness evaluation. Provided that the grammar was viable, the fitness of a the grammar is the sum of the fitness contributions to it from the examples in R. The

---

[6] Note that the inside-outside algorithm is, like any local search method, only guaranteed to find a *local* maximum.

fitness contribution for grammar Γ from $x \in R$ is referred to as the "credit" due to Γ for x, and is written $f(\Gamma, x)$. The fitness of a viable genome tested on the strings in R is then $\sum_{x \in R} f(\Gamma, x)$, where:

$$f(x, \Gamma) = \begin{cases} \log(P(x|\Gamma)), & \text{if } \Gamma \text{ generates } x \\ \text{partial credit}, & \text{if } \Gamma \text{ generates a substring of } x \\ -10000 = \log(10^{-10000}), & \text{if } \Gamma \text{ does not generate } x \end{cases}$$

Note that when $P_\Gamma(x)$ is zero in this definition, we substitute a minimum of 10^{-10000}. That is, the minimum value under the log function in f is 10^{-10000}. This allows us to tolerate but heavily penalize failure to parse an example. This only applies to *complete* failure. If the grammar can account for any substring of the data, then we give it partial credit.

Partial credit is awarded to a given grammar for a given string by find the length of the longest segment of the string derivable from the grammar. Then the average probability assigned by the grammar to substrings of that length is calculated. Substrings of length zero are discounted. We then assume that the parse of the rest of the string is accomplished as if we added productions to the grammar. These productions are all assumed to have right-hand-sides of length two, the minimum possible to account for nontrivial strings, and probability equal to half the minimum probability representable on a genotype. Given these assumptions, *any* grammar that completely generated the string with genotypically represented productions would do better. The contribution for the string is computed as if these productions completed the partial parse, giving a value of $P_\Gamma(x)$ which is used to produce a fitness contribution.

Essentially, we complete parses in the least charitable way possible whenever only part of a string is parsed.

Since our fitness function is a sum of log-probabilities, maximizing this is the same as maximizing the product of those probabilities. Thus we are maximizing the probability of the sample given the grammar in this case. The reader may recall that in section 2.1 we pointed out that, in the stochastic grammar learning case, we need to minimize, over representable grammars, some difference measure over on the distribution of strings in S and the distribution over strings induced by a hypothesis grammar. Cross entropy is one of the standard methods for measuring such differences for grammars. In fact, among grammars that generate all of S, our fitness measure accomplishes minimization of cross entropy.

If all strings can be parsed and assigned non-zero probabilities[7] by a given grammar, it's fitness is:

$$\sum_{x \in S} \log P_\Gamma(x)$$

Now if unique(S) contains all of the unique strings in S and string x occurs $n_S(x)$ times in S, we can rewrite this as:

---

[7] For us, the events of being parsed and having a non-zero probability grammar are the same since we do not allow zero-probability productions to occur genotypically.

$$\sum_{x \in \text{unique}(S)} n_S(x) \log P_\Gamma(x)$$

dividing through by $-|S|$ gives us the cross entropy between the distribution of strings in the sample and the probabilities assigned by the grammar:

$$- \sum_{x \in \text{unique}(S)} \frac{n_S(x)}{|S|} \log P_\Gamma(x)$$

Since we divided by a negative constant during this derivation, we have the result that maximizing our fitness function minimized cross entropy.

For large enough $|R|$, we hope that sampling from S is sufficient to maximize the probability of all of S over several generations, even though only a fraction of $|S|$ is seen by any single genome at any given generation. We return to this point in section 5, where we give reasons to believe that this is true, even when local search is used to tune individual grammars to R. In addition to the issue of the accuracy of fitness evaluation, we also must depend on the GA's ability to retain promising grammars and productions in the population long enough for them to be tested on enough distinct choices of R that the average probability of strings over those R is highly representative of S.

3.3 CROSS-GENERATIONAL SUB-SAMPLING

An important advantage of using a GA for grammar induction is that each individual grammar is tested several times if it proves fit enough to last for more than one or two generations. Though the fitness function needs to be able to distinguish good grammars from bad ones, it need not test on all of S at each generation. In particular, if stochastic grammars Γ_i and Γ_j occur in the population at least once each at generation g, and if Γ_i generates a larger fraction of the strings in S than Γ_j, then successfully distinguishing between them requires that we draw an R containing more strings in $L(\Gamma_i)$ than strings in $L(\Gamma_j)$. If selection isn't strong, this sampling process can be spread across more than one generation, so long as both grammars remain in the population across those generations

Here, we briefly analyze the probability of misjudging the fitnesses of two grammars in this way. While this discussion is in terms of the abilities of grammars to *generate* strings from S, .it is very relevant to our work on stochastic grammar induction since we heavily penalize failure to account for example strings. Also note that because our simulations use a form of rank selection (viz., tournament selection) it is the *ordering* of fitnesses which is important to us. Finally, whenever specific numbers below, we are citing them for the case $|R|=10$, which is used in the simulations reported later.

Divide S into four subsets: those strings which are derivable from exactly one, both, or neither of Γ_i and Γ_j. In the following diagram, we show these four regions graphically, with further labels indicating S and the subsets of S derivable from each of the two grammars:

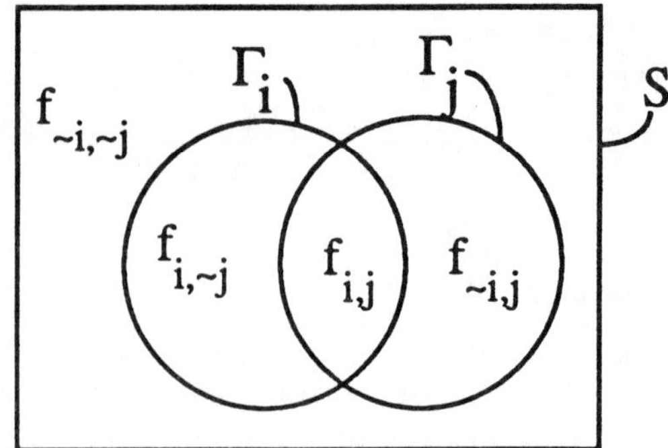

The probability of either not being able to tell the two grammars apart, or of judging the better grammar as worse is just the probably of drawing an R which contains the same number or more strings from $L(\Gamma_j)$ than strings from $L(\Gamma_i)$, rendering the grammars indistinguishable according to R. This occurs according to the probability of selecting samples from a multinomial distribution:

$$\sum_{\substack{m+n+o=|R|,\\ m\le n}} \binom{|R|}{m,n,o} f_{i,\sim j}^{m}\, f_{\sim i,j}^{n}\, \left(f_{i,j}+f_{\sim i,\sim j}\right)^{o}$$

where m is the number of strings drawn that fell in $f_{i,\sim j}$, n is the number of strings drawn which fell in $f_{\sim i,j}$, and o is the number of strings drawn which fell in $f_{i,j}\cup f_{\sim i,\sim j}$. The above expression can be written as:

$$\sum_{n=0}^{|R|}\sum_{\substack{m=0,\\ m+n\\ \le|R|}}^{n}\binom{|R|}{n}\binom{|R|-n}{m} f_{i,\sim j}^{m} f_{\sim i,j}^{n}\left(f_{i,j}+f_{\sim i,\sim j}\right)^{|R|-n-m}$$

Note that $f_{i,\sim j}^{m}$ is never zero since this would mean that Γ_i did not in fact derive more of the strings in S than Γ_j.

When both $f_{i,\sim j}^{m}$ and $f_{\sim i,j}^{n}$ are close to zero, however, the probability above is close to one: there will be few strings which distinguish the two grammars. This means that early in a run, when most grammars will fail to account for most of the training data, it will be very hard to distinguish grammars and drift becomes likely. This motivates our use of a "partial credit" mechanism, discussed later.

The worst case occurs when all strings in S are generated by exactly one of the two grammars, which means the two grammars partition the space between them and differ as little as possible in the number of strings from S each can derive. That is, the above expression reduces to the case where:

$$f_{\sim i,\sim j}=f_{i,j}=0 \text{ and } f_{i,\sim j}-f_{\sim i,j}=\frac{1}{|S|}.$$

Setting $f_{\sim i,\sim j}=f_{i,j}=0$ simplifies the previous double summation to:

$$\sum_{\substack{n=0 \\ m=0, \\ m+n \\ =|R|}}^{|R|} \sum_{n}^{n} \binom{|R|}{n} f^{m}_{i,\sim j} f^{n}_{\sim i,j}$$

since these are the only members of the earlier sum that will remain under the conditions given. This is the same as:

$$\sum_{m=0}^{\lfloor |R|/2 \rfloor} \binom{|R|}{m} f^{m}_{i,\sim j} f^{|R|-m}_{\sim i,j}.$$

From the constraints, we know that each string in S is derivable from either Γ_i or Γ_j. Thus, we have:

$$f_{i,\sim j} - f_{\sim i,j} = \frac{1}{|S|} \text{ and } f_{i,\sim j} + f_{\sim i,j} = 1$$

which is easy to solve to get:

$$f_{i,\sim j} = \tfrac{1}{2} + \tfrac{1}{2|S|} \text{ and } f_{\sim i,j} = \tfrac{1}{2} - \tfrac{1}{2|S|}.$$

If we plug these values into the formula we derived by setting $f_{\sim i,\sim j} = f_{i,j} = 0$, we get the worst-case estimate of the probability of a "fitness mistake" when each string is generated by exactly one of our two grammars:

$$\sum_{m=0}^{\lfloor |R|/2 \rfloor} \binom{|R|}{m} \left(\frac{1}{2} + \frac{1}{|S|}\right)^{m} \left(\frac{1}{2} - \frac{1}{|S|}\right)^{|R|-m}.$$

For $|S| = 1000$ and $|R|=10$, the parameters we use in our simulations reported below, this yields a probability of about 0.62 of misjudging the order of the fitness of the two grammars. Even in this case, the probability of failing to distinguish the two grammars for two generations in a row is $(0.62)^2=0.38$. For three generations in a row, it is only $(0.62)^3=0.24$. These numbers remain valid if $|R|$ is fixed at 10 and $|S|$ is increased. Note that these are probabilities for the case where Γ_i and Γ_j are as hard to distinguish using S as we can make them: since we examined the case where $f_{\sim i,\sim j} = f_{i,j} = 0$, there are no strings from S which are simply non-distinguishing. Every string in R that doesn't support the belief that Γ_i has higher true fitness will instead support the belief that Γ_j has higher true fitness.

Generally, however, two grammars will differ in their extensions by more than just one string if they differ in the amount of S they can derive. This is especially to be expected when S, as will often be the case, contains many duplicates. If the two grammars differ in their ability to generate the sample by a number of strings equal to 10% of the sample size $|S|$, then, using the same calculation as we just employed, but with the slightly different constraints:

$$f_{i,\sim j} - f_{\sim i,j} = \frac{(0.1)|S|}{|S|} = \frac{1}{10}$$

and, as before, $f_{\sim i,\sim j} = f_{i,j} = 0$, we find that the probability of a fitness mistake falls to about 0.5 for on generation and about 0.25 for two generations. Larger differences in the grammars' abilities to generate the sample will lead to probabilities of less than 0.5 in one generation. If the difference between the two grammars' abilities to generate S amounts to half of |S|, then the probability for even one generation falls below 0.1.

A final interesting case is that in which the better grammar, Γ_i, accounts for a subset of S that is a proper superset of those strings accounted for by the worse grammar, Γ_j. Assuming that all strings in S are derived by at least one of the two grammars, the worst case for the purpose of distinguishing them is when the two differ by just one string:

$$f_{i,-j} - f_{i,j} = \frac{1}{|S|}, \text{ and } f_{-i,j} = f_{-i,-j} = 0.$$

In this case, again with |S|=1000 and |R|=10, the probability of a fitness mistake falls to less than 0.001. In this case, there is no chance of actually getting the fitnesses of the two grammars backwards, only one of judging them to be equivalent in fitness. This is encouraging, since it means that if the genetic operators produce a grammar which is a marginal improvement over its parents, it is unlikely to be misjudged as no better than either parent.

The above discussion suggests that "subsampling" a small number of strings from S and testing each genome on them might suffice. That is, testing each genome on a set $R \subseteq S$ strings should allow correct induction of grammars as long as |R| is big enough so that the fitnesses of any two grammars are more often than not correctly ordered.

Our simulations do such subsampling; at the start of testing for each generation, R is drawn from S and this choice of R is frozen for the entire generation's fitness evaluations. R is used both as the test set and local search algorithm's training set. Each element of R is drawn from a uniform distribution over S. The reason for freezing R within each generation instead of redrawing R for every fitness evaluation is that it keeps the fitness function consistent within each generation. Thus, if an R is drawn at some generation which is not representative of S, the grammars rewarded according to the skewed R will all receive punishment at the next generation in which R is more representative of S.

|R| must be large enough to insure that several generations will not pass, all with particularly unfortunate subsamples, since this might lead to the complete elimination of the current best grammars from the population. Our above discussion and our results, reported below, suggest that even for |R|=10 when |S|=1000, this is not a serious problem.

4   TEST LANGUAGES AND EXPERIMENTS

4.1   THE BRACKETS LANGUAGE

Our first test language is a stochastic generalization of one used by Wyard in his earlier study on genetic grammar induction (Wyard, 1991). The "brackets language" contains all strings over a binary alphabet that are properly nested and balanced, where one of the letters of the alphabet is considered to be an "open bracket" and the other a "closed bracket." Our grammar for this target language is shown as Figure 4. It is identical to Wyard's nonstochastic version, except of course that his grammatical rules have no associated probabilities.

```
Start = A
A → aAb        ( (1-α)/2 )
A → AA         ( (1-α)/2 )
A → ab         ( α )
α = 0.6
```

Figure 4: Our Grammar For The Brackets Language

The probabilities in figure 4 were chosen to ensure that the strings in the sample would not take too long to parse. Note that as α decreases, the probability of generating longer strings increases. We intend our results for this grammar as a simple demonstration of our methods, and we thus present the results of a single run.

Before proceeding to the results, we make a few observations about our simulations and Wyard's. Wyard generated a new sample against which to test his population every generation. Our simulation used a base sample, S, of size 2000, but only tested on $|R|$=25 strings per individual per generation. Further, it is easy to see from the grammar in figure 4 that on average 60% of these test strings were just the string ab! Finally, the results of this section used a slightly earlier version of the simulator than that described above. The main difference was that when decoding, any failure to find an LHS, RHS, PROB for a given production when a "|" was found resulted not in further attempts to identify the absent segment, but rather in a discarding of the offending production. Further decoding from the genome sought the beginning of the LHS of a new production. Another difference was that the initial population contained random, but well-formed, grammars. Lastly, and importantly, these simulations used no partial credit.

We ran our simulator for 500 generations using the sample S just mentioned and with $|R|$ set as indicated. **MaxLength** was 256, **MaxRHSLen** was 3, and **MaxProbLen** was 5. The nonterminal set was N={A,B,C}. The population size was 100. No local search was used for this language. The maximum genome length allowed many more productions than were needed to be explored. For example, the best of generation for the initial population contained 11 productions[8]. Even if we only count grammars with no more than 8 productions, the search space size for this task is about $5.9 \cdot 10^{28}$.

In all, we performed five runs with this grammar and since all of the results were qualitatively similar, we look at one in detail. Figure 5 shows the best of generation for several generations of this run. By generation 500, the GA has learned both the correct grammar structure (the correct grammar productions), and the correct probabilities to associate with those productions. The grammars shown have had probabilities normalized as described in section 3. If duplicate productions occurred in the genotype, they are aggregated into a single production in the figure.

---

[8] The number 11 is after duplicates of the same production are coalesced. Thus, there is room for at least 11 productions. In this run, one could fit, with no junk regions, 16 productions into a genotype even if all had the longest RHS and PROB components possible.

Generation 100		Generation 120		Generation 180	
A → ab	(0.333)	A → Bb	(0.333)	A → Bb	(0.2)
A → bA	(0.167)	A → ab	(0.333)	A → AA	(0.2)
A → ba	(0.167)	B → aA	(1)	A → ab	(0.6)
A → aA	(0.167)	A → AA	(0.333)	B → aA	(1)
A → aAb	(0.167)				
Generation 280		Generation 360		Generation 500	
B → a	(0.993)	A → ab	(0.608)	C → CBb	(1)
A → aAb	(0.142)	A → aAb	(0.217)	A → aAb	(0.2)
A → ab	(0.428)	A → AA	(0.173)	A → ab	(0.6)
A → Bb	(0.285)			A → AA	(0.2)
B → aA	(0.006)				
A → AA	(0.142)				

Figure 5: Best Of Generation Grammars For Several Generations From A GA Run That Learned A Stochastic Version Of The Brackets Language. The Start Symbol Is "A" In All Cases.

In the very first generations, many grammars generate all possible strings. At generation 100, we see for the first time a grammar that has found the basic structural element of the brackets language, the production A → aAb. Note that although the grammar still generates the incorrect string ba and also generates most of Σ^*, it concentrates more probability on correct strings than would a simpler grammar covering Σ^* uniformly. At generation 120, we see the first grammar with all correct productions but not probabilities. Generation 180 is the first time we see a grammar matching the one which generated the data set. Observing the grammars from generation 280 to generation 500, we see that more than one solution remains in the population. One form uses two productions to produce the effect of the production A → aAb, and the other simply uses that production.

It is important to note that with any finite subsample, R, individuals in the population late in the run can have incorrect probabilities or productions. These individuals do not dominate the population, because they do not *reliably* obtain high fitness across many generations.

4.2 A MORE DIFFICULT TASK AND LOCAL SEARCH

4.2.1 A Second Target Language

Our second set of experiments is aimed at assessing the effectiveness of our local search algorithm in guiding evolution. A grammar for the target language used here is shown in figure 6. This grammar generates all of Σ^*, but concentrates the most probability on strings with the same numbers of a's and b's.

```
Start = A
    A → a    (0.09)   (*)   0.3α/2
    A → b    (0.09)   (*)   0.3α/2
    A → ab   (0.21)         0.7α/2
    A → ba   (0.21)         0.7α/2
    A → aAb  (0.14)         0.7β/2
    A → bAa  (0.14)         0.7β/2
    A → AA   (0.12)   (*)   0.3β/2
```

Figure 6: A grammar for our second target

The probabilities were chosen by first considering the grammar with only the productions marked "(*)" in figure 6. These were assigned probabilities $\alpha/2$ each for the first two and β for the last one, where $\alpha+\beta=1$ and $\alpha=0.6$. Next, the formulae at the far right of figure 6 were used to assign probability to the non-(*) productions. The grammar consisting of only the (*) productions generates all of Σ^*. We added the other four productions to place extra probability mass on strings with the same numbers of a's and b's. Note that in each case, 70% percent of the probability mass on old productions is shifted to the new productions. This places emphasis on the structure of strings with the same numbers of a's and b's. The $\alpha=0.6$ value was chosen so that the longest string in S could be parsed in a reasonable amount of time given our computational resources and the need to run several repetitions of the experiment.

These choices had the unfortunate side-effect of making the problem a bit harder than it might otherwise be, since S is "diluted" with many short strings. Essentially, we are trying to learn a stochastic variant of the language of strings over {a,b} with the number of a's and b's the same, but generalized to all of Σ^*, where the generalization assigns relatively low probability to strings where the numbers of a's and b's are different.

This last move, to generalizing the stochastic target over all of Σ^* has the potential to give us an important advantage. Local search should never hurt us for this problem, since R is fixed within each generation! Imagine comparing, for some choice of R, the target grammar's fitness with the fitness of a grammar which contains only the (*) productions. Both grammars cover all of Σ^* with nonzero probability on every string. With no local search, a particular R might reward the (*)-only grammar more than the target, if it contained a disproportionate number of strings whose numbers of a's and b's differed. If local search is used, however, and is deep enough to allow both grammars to fully tune to the choice of R against which they're to be evaluated, then the target grammar should do no worse than the (*)-only grammar, since at worst it could simply tune the probabilities of the non-(*) productions arbitrarily close to zero if this made R as likely as possible.

Conversely, assume some choice of R which more accurately reflects S. Than the target grammar should be favored, since it contains productions allowing it to capture the correct nonuniform distribution of probability over Σ^*. Thus, the correct grammar should be favored when found, and grammars like the (*)-only grammar but with a subset of the target's "extra" productions thrown in should also be favored for reasons similar to those above. Thus, we expect that the GA with local search will, on the whole, do as well or better than the GA without local search on this problem.

4.2.2 Results For The Second Target Language

For the simulations here, we used a fixed sample S with $|S|$=1000 and $|R|$=10. The simulations were run to 1250 generations for the GA-only (GA) runs, and 625 generations for the GA-plus-local-search (GALS) search runs. These numbers of generations were chosen to keep the CPU time for runs with and with local search close together. The maximum number of inside-outside algorithm iterations was 10 and the probability per individual of applying local search was 1.0. **MaxLength**, the maximum genome length, was 512, and the length of the initial population's genotypes was 128. **MaxRHSLen** was 3 and **MaxProbLen** 5. The genome was able to accomodate up to about 32 productions. The terminal set was T={a,b}, and the nonterminal set N={A,B,C,D,E,F,G,H,I,J}. Assuming that the search space included grammars with only up to 16 productions, the number of grammars in the search space is about $1.4 \cdot 10^{79}$. Ignoring probability fields, the number of grammars is $1.1 \cdot 10^{55}$.

We ran 10 of the GA simulations and 10 of the GALS simulations. To measure each run's performance, we evaluated each final population on a test set of 1000 strings, which was the same for all runs and was generated separately from the training sample S. Evaluation on the test set did not use subsampling, but computed fitness over the entire collection of 1000 strings to achieve a good estimate of true fitness. Our performance measure for all runs is the best fitness on the test set of all individuals in the final population. This measurement is made both with and without local search, even for runs which used no local search, since it would be unfair to compare two final populations of grammars when only one was tuned using the inside-outside algorithm on the test sample.

Initially, we ran a set of simulations to demonstrate the need for frequency information in the sample. These stripped all frequency information by including only one copy of each distinct string from the original learning sample. When this reduction was done, the size of the sample was only $|S|$=152. None of these runs learned the correct grammar or anything close with or without local search.

Consequently, all subsequent runs made use of the full $|S|$=1000 sample containing replicated strings. These results are summarized in figure 7a and 7b. These show that populations that had benefit of local search throughout the GA run are more successful than those without benefit. It is interesting to note, however, that individuals in these final populations are not immediate, genetic successes but only succeed after they are subjected to the same training that shaped their ancestors. Conversely, the final generation of individuals of the populations, which did not enjoy the benefit of local search are able to improve their performance only marginally from just one final exposure to training.

The difference between the GA and GALS runs in figure 7a, when no local search was performed in final evaluation (left-hand side of figure) was not significant (Mann-Whitney U test, Uobs=28). When local search was performed, the runs trained with local search did significantly better than those not trained with local search (Uobs=93, significance level 0.01, nondirectional test). Final testing seems to have made *some* difference for the GA runs in figure 7a, since the difference between the fitness scores in figure 7a before and after local search is significant (Uobs=79, significance level 0.05). Local search, as one might guess from the figure, was used much more effectively by those runs trained with it, and the difference was significant at the 0.01 level (Uobs = 98).

The above results indicate that the difference between GA and GALS runs was based on the use of the local search operator during simulations, as opposed to only during final

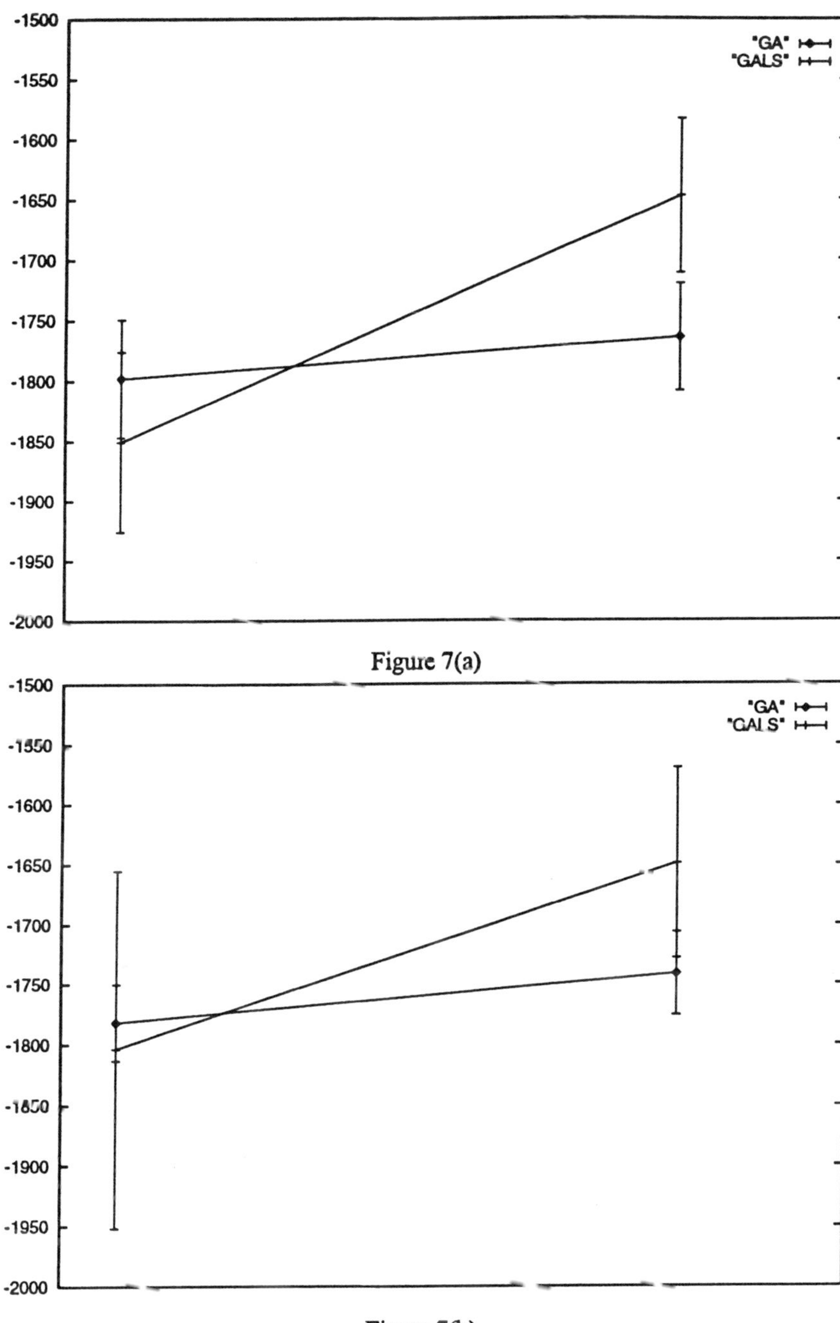

Figure 7(a)

Figure 7(b)

Figure 7: Final population true fitness averaged over ten runs both with and without local search during the run itself. The best individual, averaged over final populations, is shown before and after local search (left and right, respectively) connected by a line. Error bars are one standard deviation in each direction.

testing. An obvious question that arises is: Did we need to do ten iterations per individual per generation, or would fewer have sufficed to produce the effect in figure 7(a).

We ran the GA and GALS runs again, but this time we only allowed 1 iteration of the inside-outside algorithm per individual per generation. The results are summarized in figure 7(b). In addition, the number of generations was higher and was the same for both sets of runs, 2000. One iteration of local search turns out to result in negligible overhead; the CPU times of GA and GALS runs in this case showed no significant difference using a t-test[9]. Once again, the non-local-search final evaluations were not statistically different across the two sets of runs. With local search in the final evaluation, however, the GALS runs performed better (Uobs=85.5, significance level 0.01). Both sets of runs improved significantly at the 0.01 level this time when their final evaluations used local search (Uobs=91 for GA, Uobs=86 for GALS). Note that the only difference between the GA runs in this case and those in the previous case was that these runs were 750 generations longer.

Finally, figure 7(b), and figure 7(a) to a lesser extent, shows more variation in the GALS runs than in the GA runs, as seen in the size of the error bars. Note that this is the variation in the true fitness of the best of final population over ten runs, *not* the amount of variation in the final population. In both cases, the range of variation of outcomes is wider for GALS runs, but these runs are almost always better than the GA runs.

For the runs corresponding to figure 7(a), we performed a Mann-Whitney test to check whether the standard deviations of the whole final populations were different between the GA and GALS runs both with and without local search in the final testing. No statistically significant results were found. We also performed such a test for the right-hand side of figure 7(b), and found weak significance (at the .1 level). We lacked the data to do this test for the left-hand side of figure 7(b), the case where final testing does not use local search. The GALS runs may show a wider dispersion in the figures, but this does not indicate a larger ending population variance for those runs.

5 DISCUSSION AND FUTURE WORK

5.1 OTHER RECENT SCFG INDUCTION RESEARCH

An important difference between our work and that of others cited is that we attempt to evolve stochastic context-free grammars, another increment up the ladder of complexity either from stochastic regular grammars or nonstochastic context-free grammars. In the case of nonstochastic grammatical inference, the examples will be drawn, usually, from some fixed but unknown distribution. In this light, the stochastic and nonstochastic versions of the problem appear similar. But in the case of nonstochastic grammatical inference, the algorithm need only learn the form of the strings with which it is presented. In the stochastic variant of the learning problem, the algorithm must also estimate correct probabilities for the grammar productions, so that the "fixed but unknown distribution" used to generate the training data must also be acquired.

---

[9] There must be *some* overhead from doing even one iteration of the inside-outside algorithm. Probably, either we can't see the difference over a sample of ten runs each with and without this local search, or the GALS runs in this case are making up some time by somehow throwing out grammars that have useless productions that add to the cost of parsing.

Imagine a set of grammar productions like those of our second learning target from the previous section. The productions generate *any* string of a's and b's. The target is defined not only by the rules themselves but also by their probabilities, which arc assigned to concentrate probability mass on strings with the same numbers of a's as b's. A nonstochastic grammatical inference algorithm given a sample generated from this target grammar might well consider the grammar given by just the *'d productions of figure 6 to be an adequate answer, unless it treated the data set as containing noise.

Another recent approach to SCFG induction is available in a recent paper by Stolcke and Omohundro (Stolcke and Omohundro, 1994). Their approach is based on a technique called "Bayesian model merging". The paper discusses other models as well but here we discuss only the aspects of the paper that are relevant to SCFG induction.

Stolcke and Omohundro use an approach called "Bayesian model merging" in which an initial model, a grammar, is constructed which explicitly incorporates all of the data, S in our discussion here. Then a merging operator is applied until some stopping point is reached. Actually, two operators are used in the SCFG experiments: "merging" replaces two nonterminals with one new nonterminal, and "chunking" takes a sequence of nonterminals and replaces it with a new nonterminal (and introduces a rule from the new nonterminal to the old sequence). The authors report successfully discovering several grammars from sample data, using best-first search in some cases and beam search in others, but do not report the amount of time or the number of chunking and merging steps required by their algorithm. Also, the authors work with samples of very high-probability and very small size[10]. Thus, even though one of their test languages is structurally equivalent[11] to our first test language, we find it difficult to compare our results with the results reported in their paper.

Stolcke and Omohundro do claim to be mainly addressing the problem of finding the structure of a probabilistic model and not just that of tuning the probabilities on a known structure. Underlying this focus is an assumption that the rules will generally be apparent given the sample data strings. Our second test language does not seem amenable to this assumption, since the structure present in it is only made apparent in light of the extra probability mass placed on strings with the same number of a's as b's.

5.2   INTRONS

One novel aspect of our genotypic representation is that it allows evolvable "junk" regions analogous to introns. Levenick used fixed introns in the context of a more typical GA task and noticed a marked improvement in GA performance using them (Levenick, 1991). In that study, the introns essentially provided neutral crossover points and reduced the probability of disruptive crossovers. Levenick also showed that requiring different orderings of information on the genotype made the task harder again in spite of introns. Another study has explored the issue of fixed introns in greater detail (Wu and Lindsay, 1995). Further work on intron exists also within the genetic programming community. We deal with the previous two papers here because they discuss a

---

[10] In fairness, it should be mentioned that they are discussing previous results and thus used the same data as that used in the previous study.

[11] The sets of distinct strings derived from their grammar and our first one are the same. Stolcke and Omohundro do not report the actual probabilities used on their grammar. This appears to have been the easiest problem tackled in both studies.

representation more obviously like ours than the tree-structured geneotypes used in genetic programming.

Unlike Levenick's, our crossover operator causes lengths to vary, as is the case in most of the previous work cited above. The length and position of the introns can change over time in our representation, however, as can the ordering of the genotypic information (The order in which productions occur on our genotypes doesn't matter). Further, our junk regions can potentially contain "damaged" or "deactivated" productions, which mutations could conceivably "fix" or "turn on" by causing a "|" to appear where one was needed and did not occur. If present, these would be similar to pseudo-genes, which Wu and Lindsay mention (Wu and Lindsay, 1995). In figure 3a, for example, a single insertion of a "|" in the underlined region would suffice to create a valid PROB field, and would result in it being "expressed" in the phenotypic grammar of figure 3b.

An important question which we have yet to answer is: Do these introns play a role in search?. That is, do high-fitness productions or parts of productions generally occur separated by "small" junk regions, with less-related productions farther apart? More generally, does the length of junk regions between coding regions for a particular genome reflect, after many generations, the relative fitness of the substrings of the genome in which those regions occur? A reasonable start on such an analysis would be to examine the lengths of junk regions between various types of coding regions (following, for example, a start symbol, LHS, RHS, or PROB) and track changes in the distribution across a run. Also important would be to examine the relative rates at which coding and noncoding ("junk") regions accumulate mutations (the latter ought to change more quickly). More importantly, our representation needs to be more closely studied to see what the building blocks are. We certainly know what we probably *want* them to be: coding segments that form fragments of productions, perhaps up to entire productions. Whether these are being reliably recombined and tried with one another is an interesting question. The question is, "How well do our intron regions locally tune crossover to keep pieces of productions or pairs or groups of whole productions together on the genotype?"

5.3 THE EFFECTS OF SUBSAMPLING

An important issue in using our fitness evaluation technique is whether the fitness function is maximal for the same solutions in both cases. Fitzpatrick and Grefenstette discuss issues surrounding sampling to evaluate fitness (Fitzpatrick and Grefenstette, 1988). In their discussion, the fitness function is viewed as the mean of some random variable that is repeatedly sampled to estimate fitness. Here, we discuss the fitness of an imagined "ideal" grammar, capable of perfectly modeling the distribution implicit in S. That is, we imagine that we have some grammar Γ such that $P_\Gamma(x) = n_S(x)S^{-1}$ for all x in S. We further imagine that Γ can be tuned to match any subsample R's distribution of strings exactly, so that if string occurs in some choice of R k times and the inside-outside algorithm is run to change the probabilities of Γ, the probability of x under the grammar after tuning will be $k \cdot r^1$.

We will consider "true" fitness to be fitness averaged[12] over all of S:

---

[12] In our actual runs, we don't average, since this doesn't effect the maximization of the function.

$$\frac{1}{|S|} \sum_{x \in S} \log\left(\frac{n_S(x)}{|S|}\right)$$

as opposed to the fitness estimated by subsampling, averaged over all choices of R:

$$\sum_R \left(\frac{1}{|R|} \sum_{x \in R} \log\left(\frac{n_S(x)}{|S|}\right)\right) P(R)$$

this is the mean of the sampling distribution of the mean for the numbers

$$\log\left(\frac{n_S(x)}{|S|}\right)$$

with sample size $|R|$. Thus, we know that this number converges to the true mean of these numbers over all of S, which is the true fitness as given above.

A more challenging problem arises when we consider the problem of applying local search, the inside-outside algorithm, to our grammar using strings in R. As we mentioned above, we assume that the "ideal" grammar can have its probabilities tuned to exactly capture frequencies of strings in R. For our imagined ideal grammar, with its probabilities tuned exactly to the choice of R:

$$\left\langle \frac{1}{|R|} \sum_{x \in R} \log\left(\frac{n_R(x)}{|R|}\right) \right\rangle_R$$

In the above expression, we have changed the notation under the log so as to reflect x's frequency in R instead of S. Ideally we would like the fitness contribution for each individual string to be the same as it would be for standard fitness as R becomes large. A weaker but still desirable condition would be for this expression to assign the maximum fitness to a grammar that exactly captures the distribution of example strings in S. We can separate the contribution of a given string by taking its expected contribution for samples of size k summed over k from 1 to $|R|$. This reduces to the following:

$$\frac{1}{|R|} \sum_{k=1}^{|R|} \left(k \log\left(\tfrac{k}{|R|}\right)(u-1)^{|R|-k}\left(\tfrac{n_S(x)}{|S|}\right)^k\left(1-\tfrac{n_S(x)}{|S|}\right)^{|R|-k}\binom{|R|}{k}\right)$$

where $u = |\text{unique}(S)|$ is the number of distinct strings in S.

5.3.1   Sampling Fidelity And PAC Learnability

$|R|$ also has an important correspondence with the formulation of the goal of learning given in terms of variable ε and δ in section 2. As $|R|$ is increased, the fidelity of the information in the fitness function increases, in the sense that it more reliably reflects the relative frequencies of strings in S. This should drive δ downward, ε upward or both. That is, with larger and larger $|R|$, we should expect to more reliably find better hypotheses. A variety of basic learning theory results are available relating $|S|$, the "sample complexity" of the set of possible targets, to ε and δ. Given a fixed large $|S|$, we would like to know, for example, how small we can make $|R|$ for the GA. The better our GA does at maintaining high-fitness grammars in the population, the more likely it is that those grammars will persist across enough generations to receive adequate testing via several choices of R, and the smaller $|R|$ can, in theory be made. An interesting general question is how well a learning algorithm can do when it only sees a random selection of strings from an a-priori fixed training sample at any given time, where the size of the fixed sample (S in our notation) would be much smaller than the number of (not necessarily distinct) examples examined by the algorithm. This is the case with our GA simulations cited above. The authors are unaware of results concerning the performance of, for example, consistent algorithms in this context[13].

5.4   GENERALIZATION ABILITY AND DESCRIPTION LENGTH

One concern in machine learning generally is that of overfitting. Our fitness measure as stated contains no explicit term which punishes overly-specific grammars. Overfitting is, however, a potential problem since our fitness measure would assign maximal fitness to a grammar which generated *only* the data of S. This can be done by building a "definite grammar" for S, one that has a set of productions explicitly designed to generate each $x \in S$. If there is no limit on RHS length, such a grammar could contain a single production to expand the start symbol to each x. Such a grammar could assign to each string a probability exactly equal to its frequency in S.

We considered such a grammar in our discussion of subsampling above because we were asking whether the fitness function still provided information about all of S when each grammar was tuned to R, and the grammar we have just described would be perfectly tunable to any choice of R precisely because it is "perfectly overfitted". One would not, however, want the GA to arrive at such a grammar as a solution since it doesn't generalize from the training data at all. In machine learning generally, there are a variety of strategies for rewarding hypotheses for generalization ability, and a good deal of effort is often invested in testing generalization. The question that arises here is, "Why wasn't overfitting a problem here?"

One possibility is that the problems considered were not complex enough. That is, the number of productions, for example, in the target language was not very large and the data set was large enough to make the structure of the language being learned clear. Another, related possibility is that the GA as implemented is punishing grammars with large numbers of productions by disrupting them with crossover. The longer a genotypic grammar, the more likely it is to have a production eliminated by crossover. Perhaps crossover is discouraging long grammars by pulling them apart to often for them to take over the population. It might be that the target grammars used in this study were short enough that individuals in the population could encode them with many production duplications or long noncoding regions which could absorb many potential deleterious crossovers. If this were the case, we could be concerned that attempts to evolve grammars for languages whose minimal description length was large might founder since any grammar long enough to accurately capture that target might be cut to pieces by crossover unless the genotype was allowed to be long enough that significant protection from crossover would be possible. In such a situation, we might find ourselves encouraging, seemingly perversely enough, higher-complexity grammars.

The above discussion, though hypothetical, raises questions for any grammar-inducing GA which we believe must be addressed. It is not enough to propagate individual productions of the grammar from one generation to the next. We must remember that

---

[13] Consistent algorithms are defined in most introductory texts on computational learning theory (Anthony and Biggs, 1992).

propagating building blocks is not of great interest unless highly fit *combinations* of building blocks can be maintained once discovered.

6 CONCLUSION

Previous work as well as ours suggests that genetic algorithms show promise as grammar inducers. Using our representation, we were able to evolve stochastic versions of two target languages, both of which are well known in the field of grammatical inference.

The use of the inside-outside algorithm as a means of tuning production probabilities of stochastic grammars aids the discovery of better solutions. In fact, only a single iteration of the inside-outside algorithm was necessary for a noticeable benefit to occur, as evidenced by figure 7b. When a new production is introduced into a grammar by, for example, crossover, it disrupts the distribution of probabilities for productions having identical LHS's. The inside-outside algorithm gives us an assurance that the new production will be integrated into the new "phenotypic" grammar, and that it will have its probability tuned to zero if it cannot participate in any complete parse. One particularly intriguing facet of the results from section 4.2 is that no or only weak Baldwin learning seems to be happening. That is, as demonstrated in figure 7, rather than having the GA "pull" the evolved genotypes closer to the best solutions, these remain a significant distance (in terms of performance) from their ultimate, post-inside-outside training phenotypic form. The grammars, as far as we can see, seem to remain dependent on the inside-outside algorithm. Whether evolutionary convergence eventually occurs in much longer runs, and the sensitivity of these results to the amount and frequency of local search remain interesting questions for future work.

References

Anthony, M. and Biggs, N. (1992) *Computational Learning Theory: an introduction.* Cambridge University Press, New York.

Charniak, C. *Statistical Language Learning.* The MIT Press, Cambridge, MA, 1993.

Fitzpatrick, J.M. and Grefenstette, J. J. (1988) *Genetic Algorithms in Noisy Environments.* Machine Learning, vol. 3 no. 2/3, pp. 101-120.

Fu, K. and Booth, T. (1975) Grammatical Inference: introduction and survey, parts 1 and 2. *IEEE Transactions on Systems, Man, and Cybernetics SMC-5.* 95-111, 409-423.

Gazdar, D. and Mellish, C. (1989) *Natural Language Processing in LISP: An Introduction to Computational Linguistics.* Addison-Wesley Publishing Company, Reading, MA.

W. Hart, T. Kammeyer, and R. Belew. (1995) The Role of Development in Genetic Algorithms. In *Foundations of Genetic Algorithms 3.* Morgan Kaufmann, Inc., San Francisco, CA. pp. 315-332

Hopcraft, J. and Ullman, J. (1979) *Introduction to Automata Theory, Languages, and Computation.* Addison-Wesley Publishing Company, Reading, MA.

Thomas E. Kammeyer, Richard K. Belew, and S. Gill Williamson. (1995) *Evolving Compare-exchange Networks Using Grammars*. Artificial Life, vol. 2 no. 2, pp. 199-237.

Langdon, W.B. (1996) *Using Data Structures within Genetic Programming*. Genetic Programming 1996: Proceedings of the First Annual Conference. MIT Press.

Lankhorst, M.M. (1994) *Breeding Grammars: Grammatical Inference with a Genetic Algorithm*. Computing Science Report CS-R 9401, Department of Computing Science, University of Groningen, The Netherlands.

Levenick, James R. (1991) Inserting Introns Improves Genetic Algorithm Success Rate: Taking a Cue from Biology. *Proceedings of the Fourth International Conference on Genetic Algorithms*. Morgan Kaufmann Publishers, Inc., San Francisco, California.

Schwehm, M. and Ost, A. (1995) Inference of Stochastic Regular Grammars by Massively Parallel Genetic Algorithms. *Proceedings of the Sixth International Conference on Genetic Algorithms*. Morgan Kaufmann Publishers, Inc., San Francisco, California.

Sakakibara, Y., Brown, M., Hughey, R., Mian I.S., Sjölander, K., Underwood, R.C., and Haussler, D. (1993) *Stochastic Context-Free Grammars for tRNA Modeling*. UCSC Technical Report Number UCSC-CRL-94-14, November.

Stolcke, A. and Omohundro, S. (1994) Inducing Probabilistic Grammars by Bayesian Model Merging. *Proceedings of the International Conference on Grammatical Inference*.

Wu, A.S. and Lindsay, R.K. (1995) *Empirical Studies of the Genetic Algorithm with Noncoding Segments*. Evolutionary Computation, vol. 2 no. 3, pp. 121-147.

Wyard, P. (1991) Context Free Grammar Induction Using Genetic Algorithms. *Proceedings of the Fourth International Conference on Genetic Algorithms*. Morgan Kaufmann Publishers, Inc., San Francisco, California.

Wyard, P. (1995) Representational Issues for Context-Free Grammar Induction Using Genetic Algorithms. Technical Report, British Telecom.

Fitness Functions for Multiple Objective Optimization Problems: Combining Preferences with Pareto Rankings

Garrison W. Greenwood
Dept. of Electrical & Computer Engineering
Western Michigan University
Kalamazoo, MI 49008

Xiaobo (Sharon) Hu
Dept. of Computer Science & Engineering
University of Notre Dame
Notre Dame, IN 46556

Joseph G. D'Ambrosio
General Motors R&D Center
Warren, MI 48090-9055

Abstract

Traditional approaches for solving multiple objective optimization problems attempt to sketch out the Pareto optimal front. This approach presumes that all Pareto optimal solutions will be considered equally valuable by the decision maker. However, in many real-world problems some attributes are preferred over others. In this work we use preferences given *a priori* by a decision maker to construct fitness functions for evolutionary algorithms. These fitness functions help to direct the search operation towards solutions which match the decision maker's preferences.

1   Introduction

A large number of problems require the simultaneous optimization of several objectives. Such problems define the class of *Multiple objective Optimization Problems* (MOPs). Conventional optimization techniques such as gradient search or simulated annealing do not typically perform well for this class of problems.

Recently there has been a growing interest in solving MOPs using *evolutionary algorithms* (EAs). Schaffer was one of the first researchers to propose using EAs to search for multiple nondominated solutions (Schaffer, 1985). His vector evaluated genetic algorithm (VEGA) is similar to a conventional genetic algorithm except a fraction of each population chosen to survive was selected according to each objective. Richardson *et al.*, showed that VEGA essentially performed a linear combination of the objectives to assign fitness (Richardson *et al.*, 1989). This results in a bias against some nondominated individuals with respect to survival. Goldberg (Goldberg, 1989) suggested the use of a Pareto optimality ranking scheme to address this problem and empirical evidence suggests that the resultant EA will outperform VEGA (Hilliard *et al.*, 1989 and Liepins *et al.*, 1990). For certain classes of deceptive problems, it has been shown that Pareto optimal genetic algorithms outperform stochastic hill-climbers (Louis *et al.*, 1993). Pareto optimal EAs have been successfully applied to MOPs ranging from atomic emission spectroscopy (Ritzel *et al.*, 1994) to groundwater pollution containment (Wienke *et al.*, 1992).

The focus of a significant amount of this research in using EAs to solve MOPs has dealt with techniques for locating Pareto optimal solutions[1]. When searching for these solutions, the goal is to locate all of those solutions whose attribute levels (which indicate the degree to which an objective has been met) are not dominated by any others. The search for Pareto optimal solutions assumes that all attributes are of equal importance. In other words, there are no preferences between attributes.

The lack of preferences poses problems for EAs. Fonseca and Fleming (Fonseca, *et al.* 1995) put it this way:

> ...in the total absence of preference information, the EA will face the "impossible" task of finding a satisfactory compromise in the dark, which can only occur by pure chance.

On the other hand, an aggregated approach represents fitness in MOPs by combining the multiple objectives into a single, scalar quantity. One popular aggregated approach is to form a weighted sum of the attribute levels where larger weights are assigned to more important attributes. However, these weights (which may significantly affect the final solution) can be difficult to exactly specify.

We have chosen a compromise between no preference information and the aggregated approach. In our work we use elements of *imprecisely specified multi-attribute value theory* (ISMAUT) to perform imprecise ranking of attributes (White *et al.*, 1984).

Our approach to using EAs for solving MOPs is unique in two respects. First, rather than asking a decision maker to explicitly rank the attributes, we ask for the ranking of a small number of candidate solutions to the MOP. This ranking of solutions implicitly defines a ranking of the attributes. Thus, we are able to avoid the difficulties associated with the aggregated approach. Secondly, we incorporate preference information into the survival criteria used by the EA. Our goal is not to just find *any* Pareto optimal solution, but rather to find specific Pareto optimal solutions which reflect the decision maker's preferences.

The concept of "directing" the search towards a desired set of optimal values has been

---

[1]The interested reader is referred to (Fonseca, *et al.* 1995) for an excellent survey of this work.

previously suggested. For example, the COMOGA method, in addition to the problem constraints, also incorporates a cost function (Surry *et al.*, 1995). During each iteration of the EA, a proportion p_{cost} of the parents are chosen for reproduction based upon cost while the remainder are chosen according to constraint ranking. (p_{cost} can be adaptively modified.) Our approach bases survival upon a decision maker's preferences. Hence, it also provides the capability of directing the search operation but without the explicit definition of a cost function. This aspect is discussed in greater detail in Section 6.

2 Definitions & Mathematical Preliminaries

The definitions and concepts presented in this section are used in later sections for discussion of fitness functions for MOPs. More detailed information can be found in a number of sources (*e.g.*, Keeny *et al.*, 1976 or Murty, 1983).

Optimization problems are essentially search problems. Each individual in the population of an EA constitutes a potential solution or *alternative* within the problem space of an optimization problem. *Objectives* define desirable properties of a good alternative and *attributes* are used to determine the degree to which a specific objective is met. An objective is normally formulated as an *objective function* with the attributes as the function's arguments. In the terminology of EAs, attribute levels are used to quantify the fitness of an alternative and the objective function is equivalent to a fitness function. The goal of the EA is to find an alternative which optimizes the fitness.

Suppose we are given a MOP with $\mathcal{X}$ representing the set of all feasible alternatives. Further, let $\mathcal{A}$ represent the set of n attributes. Each alternative $x \in \mathcal{X}$ has an assigned level for each $a_i \in \mathcal{A}$. We let $\mathcal{A}_x$ denote the set of attribute levels associated with the alternative $x \in \mathcal{X}$. Our goal is to represent the fitness of x by defining an appropriate objective function $f : \mathcal{A}_x \to \Re_+^0$ where $\Re_+^0 \in [0, \infty)$.

Let x and x' be two alternatives from $\mathcal{X}$ with their associated attribute level sets $\mathcal{A}_x = \{a_1, ..., a_n\}$ and $\mathcal{A}_{x'} = \{a'_1, ..., a'_n\}$, respectively. We say x *dominates* x' if $\forall i\ a_i$ is better than or equal to a'_i and, in addition, there exists at least one a_j such that a_j is strictly better than a'_j. Let $x \succ_D x'$ denote that x dominates x'. The set of non-dominated alternatives lies on a surface in attribute space known as the *Pareto optimal frontier*[2]. In each generation of an EA there exists a set of non-dominated alternatives (with respect to all other alternatives in the current population). We call this set of alternatives the *Phenotypical Pareto Front* (PPF).

Two important aspects of dominance are worth noting. First, dominance applies only to the *ordinal* characteristics of a_j and a'_j and not to their *cardinal* characteristics[3]. Second, dominance does not require that a_i be compared against a'_j for $i \neq j$.

Given two non-dominated alternatives, a decision maker may still prefer one over the other. This concept is expressed with the following two relationships:

R1: $x' \succ x$ (read as "x' is preferred-to x")

---

[2] Some authors refer to this as the Pareto optimal set.

[3] In other words, one only needs to know that the attribute level of a_j is greater than that of a'_j. How much greater is of no importance in determining dominance.

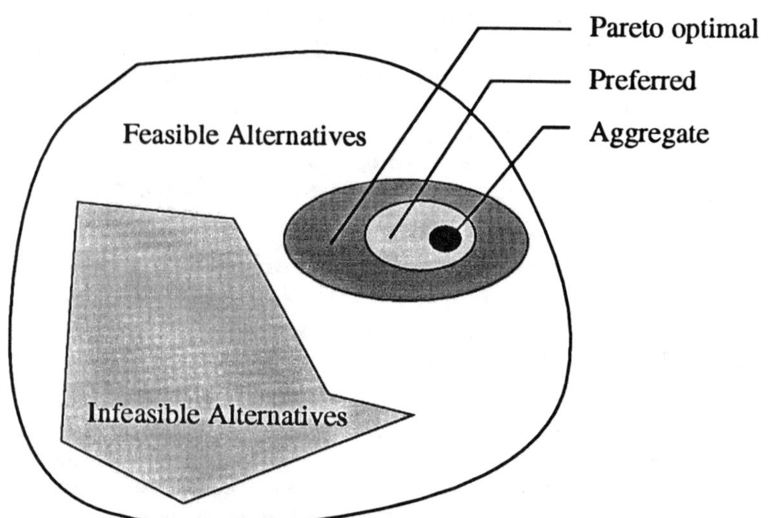

Figure 1: A picture of alternative space. The Pareto optimal, preferred, and aggregate subsets may actually be the union of a number of disjoint subsets of the same type.

R2: $x' \sim x$ (read as "x' is indifferent-to x")

x and x' are indifferent when $x \not\succ x'$ and $x' \not\succ x$ indicating that there is no clear preference between them. Relationships **R1** and **R2** together establish a *partial order* on $\mathcal{X}$. If relationship **R2** does not exist (*i.e.*, $\forall\, x, x' \in \mathcal{X}$, either $x \succ x'$ or $x' \succ x$), then a *total order* on $\mathcal{X}$ is established. Preference is purely subjective and thus is different from dominance (which is purely objective). In a later section we will show how dominance and preference are related.

Figure 1 depicts alternative space. Notice that some of the alternatives may be infeasible because they violate design constraints. A subset of the feasible alternatives are Pareto optimal. Only a subset of these Pareto optimal alternatives are preferred since they coincide with the decision maker's preferences. This preferred subset has a "fuzzy boundary" since the attribute weights are imprecisely specified. (This aspect will be discussed further in the next section.) The smallest subset of the Pareto optimal alternatives is the aggregate subset which can only be identified if the attribute weights are precisely specified. Our objective is to identify example alternatives from within the preferred subset.

3   Evaluating Alternatives

Evaluating alternatives requires the resolution of conflicting objectives. These conflicts arise because of the physical relationships between objectives as well as resource limitations. For example, reducing the production cost of a system may adversely affect its performance. Therefore, a decision maker must identify a set of measurable attributes for evaluating alternatives, and then apply a consistent set of preferences that quantify how the tradeoffs among the attributes are to be made.

Our problem is thus one of choosing an appropriate function format so that tradeoffs between alternatives can be represented as a measure of fitness. An intuitive format for this fitness function may be a weighted sum

$$f = \sum_k w_k \, a_k \tag{1}$$

where a_k is the k-th attribute and $w_k > 0$ is its associated weight. (Higher weight values reflect greater importance.) The weights must satisfy $\sum_k w_k = 1$. Unfortunately, this format for a fitness function is a bit naive and has a number of problems. Specifically,

1. Attributes are expressed in different units of measure which makes direct summation not possible.

2. There is no step-by-step procedure for precisely specifying the attribute weights.

3. There is no convenient way of capturing any decision maker's preferences between alternatives.

We replace the objective function of Equation (1) with an *imprecise value function*, which does not require direct specification of the attribute weights. In this section, we describe how the imprecise value function is created and applied to evaluate alternatives.

A scaling of the attribute levels may be necessary whenever fitness sharing is used to prevent genetic drift (Goldberg, 1989). This scaling process maps each raw attribute level to a convenient subset of $\Re^0_+$ (normally $[0,1]$). As before, let $\mathcal{A}_x = \{a_1, a_2, \cdots, a_n\}$ represent the set of n attributes associated with the alternative $x \in \mathcal{X}$. Suppose there exists a set of real-valued functions $\{v_1, v_2, ..., v_n\}$ on $\mathcal{A}$ such that $v_i : a_i \to [0, 1]$ where v_i monotonically increases towards 1 as the attribute level of a_i improves. The set of real-valued functions are referred to as *attribute value functions*[4].

Let a_i^{max} and a_i^{min} denote the maximum and minimum levels, respectively, of the attribute a_i. In our work we chose the "more-is-better" attribute value function to be

$$v_i(a_i) = \frac{a_i - a_i^{min}}{a_i^{max} - a_i^{min}} \tag{2}$$

and for the "less-is-better" attribute value function

$$v_i(a_i) = \frac{a_i - a_i^{max}}{a_i^{min} - a_i^{max}} \tag{3}$$

Note that $v_i(\cdot)$ is not restricted to a linear form as shown in Equations (2) and (3). Indeed, any arbitrary nonlinear function can be used as long as it satisfies the monotonicity requirements.

The ISMAUT preference model we use assumes that all attributes are mutually, preferentially independent. This independence property means that the value function associated with the attribute a_i is not affected by the values of some other attribute a_j ($j \neq i$). Of course, it is possible that for some problems attributes are mutually, preferentially dependent which dictates that a more complex value function is needed. Our approach would still be valid (except perhaps a nonlinear program may have to be solved). Yet, for many real world problems the ISMAUT perference model is sufficient and simple enough to be applied and it is for this reason it was chosen.

---

[4]Some authors in this context will refer to v_i as a "utility function".

An imprecise multi-attribute value function corresponding to the alternative x has the following form:

$$V_x = \sum_k w_k \, v_k(a_k) \tag{4}$$

where a strictly positive w_k is the weight and $v_k(a_k)$ is the attribute value function for attribute a_k. All weights must satisfy

$$\sum_k w_k = 1 \; ; \; w_k > 0 \tag{5}$$

V_x is imprecise in the sense that each w_k does not have a specific assignment, but is constrained by preferences among attributes. Such constraints can be formulated based upon preferences between distinct alternatives. (These alternatives can be provided by the decision maker or generated by an EA.) For example, let $x, x' \in \mathcal{X}$ be two alternatives with corresponding attribute level sets $\mathcal{A}_x$ and $\mathcal{A}_{x'}$ for which the decision maker has decided that $x \succ x'$. By definition,

$$x \succ x' \implies V_x > V_{x'} \implies \sum_{k=1}^{n} w_k[v_k(a_k) - v_k(a'_k)] > 0. \tag{6}$$

Such an expression defines a constraint for the attribute weights. When several alternative pairs are ranked by the decision maker, a series of such constraints are defined. The set of all such constraints confines the w_k's to a subspace $W \subset \Re_+^n$ where $\Re_+^n$ is the n-dimensional space of positive real numbers.

Using the attribute value functions and the constraint subspace W, other configurations created from running an EA may be evaluated. More specifically, by definition

$$V_x - V_{x'} = \sum_k w_k[v_k(a_k) - v_k(a'_k)] > 0 \implies x \succ x' \tag{7}$$

It follows that alternatives x'' and x can be compared by solving the following linear programming problem:

$$\text{Minimize (w.r.t. } w_k\text{):} \qquad \sum_k w_k[v_k(a''_k) - v_k(a_k)]$$
$$\text{Subject to:} \qquad w_k \in W \tag{8}$$

Then x'' is preferred to x if Equation (9) is true.

$$z = \min_{w_k} \sum_k w_k[v_k(a''_k) - v_k(a_k)] > 0 \tag{9}$$

However, knowing that $z \leq 0$ is not sufficient to determine preference, we must reverse the terms in Equation (9) as shown below.

$$\bar{z} = \min_{w_k} \sum_k w_k[v_k(a_k) - v_k(a''_k)] > 0 \tag{10}$$

Now, if Equation (9) is false and Equation (10) is true, then $x \succ x''$. If both equations are false, then x and x'' are pairwise indifferent (*i.e.*, $x'' \sim x$.

Table 1: Feasible Alternative of Example Design Problem

Alternatives	Attributes			Preference
	$v_1(a_1)$	$v_2(a_2)$	$v_3(a_3)$	
x_1	0.75	1.0	0.4	2
x_2	0.5	0.0	0.8	1
x_3	0.0	1.0	1.0	–
x_4	1.0	0.0	0.0	–

It is important to emphasize that the ranking of the selected alternatives is done merely to obtain the constraint subspace W. W is then used in the series of linear programming problems that must be solved to conduct pairwise comparisons between alternatives.

To illustrate some of the above concepts, consider the following example problem. Table 3 shows 4 alternatives and their corresponding attribute levels. The first two of these were randomly generated and ranked by the decision maker (x_2 is the most preferred). Alternatives x_3 and x_4 were identified by the optimization process (e.g., using an EA). Since $x_2 \succ x_1$, substituting into Equation (6) yields

$$w_1[0.5 - 0.75] + w_2[0.0 - 1.0] + w_3[0.8 - 0.4] > 0$$

Or,

$$-0.25w_1 - w_2 + 0.4w_3 > 0$$

This constraint (in conjunction with Equation (5) and Table 3) completely defines the imprecise value function. Suppose now that we wish to determine if $x_2 \succ x_4$. This preference exists if the following equation is true:

$$\min_{w_k} \sum_k w_k[v_k(a_k^2) - v_k(a_k^4)] > 0 \tag{11}$$

where a_k^j denotes the k-th attribute for the j-th alternative. Solving the following linear program

$$\text{Minimize (w.r.t. } w_k): \quad z = \sum_k w_k[v_k(a_k^2) - v_k(a_k^4)]$$

Subject to:

$$-0.25w_1 - w_2 + 0.4w_3 > 0$$
$$\forall k, \; w_k > 0$$
$$\sum_k w_k = 1$$

will determine the relationship between x_2 and x_4. It is easy to show that for the above example $z > 0$ and so $x_2 \succ x_4$.

We conclude this section with an important theorem that establishes the link between our precedence relationship ($\succ$) and the dominance relationship ($\succ_D$). Specifically, it proves that preference relationships will preserve existing dominance relationships.

Theorem: $x \succ x' \Rightarrow x' \not\succ_D x$.

Proof: *(By Contradiction.)* Let $x \succ x'$ and assume $x' \succ_D x$. By Equation (6), $V_x > V_{x'}$ which means there must exist at least one j such that $[v_j(a_j) - v_j(a'_j)] > 0$. But this means a_j is strictly better than a'_j which contradicts the assumption that $x' \succ_D x$. $\square$

4   Representing Fitness in an EA

Figure 2 shows a canonical form of an EA. The initial population is randomly generated. A small number of these alternatives can be used for the preference ranking discussed in the previous section. The stopping criteria can be either 'an acceptable solution has been found' or 'a fixed number of generations have been produced'. Offspring (new alternatives) are produced each generation using a suite of genetic operators. Each alternative explicitly specifies the attribute levels which can be mapped to the interval [0,1] on the real number line using Equation (2) or (3) as appropriate. The evaluation of alternatives requires that their fitness be computed; alternatives with high fitness should, with high probability, survive and reproduce while alternatives with low fitness should die out.

```
Procedure EA
      Randomly generate initial population of alternatives
      Evaluate population
      While stopping criteria not met do
            Select parents for reproduction
            Apply genetic operators to produce offspring
            Evaluate offspring
      End while
End EA
```

Figure 2: A Canonical EA for MOPs

We use the preference ordering discussed in the previous section to assign fitness to each alternative. Alternative x is said to have a higher fitness over alternative x' if $x \succ x'$. Equation (7) can be used to determine these preference relationships. However, this will typically establish only a partial order. Ranking all of the alternatives can be done with a technique described by Goldberg (Goldberg, 1989, pg 201). Assign rank 1 to all preferred alternatives and then remove them from further contention. A new set of preferred alternatives can then be found, ranked 2, and so on until all alternatives have been ranked. Survival can be determined using a variety of techniques (*e.g.*, tournament selection). It is important to note that a fitness assignment based upon preference relationships will preserve existing dominance relationships. It is also important to emphasize that the decision maker need only establish preference relationships for a small number of alternatives from the initial population[5].

---

[5]Three alternatives are sufficient for most problems. Indeed, ranking more than three may prove to be difficult.

Our use of imprecise value functions for establishing a survival criteria is what differentiates our approach from conventional Pareto optimal searches. Complete enumeration of the entire Pareto optimal set is not practical.

The goal in most other Pareto optimal approaches is to "sketch out" the set by finding a (hopefully) uniformly distributed subset of samples from it. While certainly laudable, this assumes that all Pareto optimal solutions are equally preferable which is often not the case. Using preferences to influence the probability of survival allows the decision maker to drive the search process of the EA. This helps to prevent the EA from conducting a simple blind exploration of the tradeoff space.

Independent of the survival criteria chosen, there is a non-zero probability that genetic drift will occur[6]. Fitness sharing (Fonseca, *et al.* 1995) and equivalence class sharing (Horn *et al.*, 1993) are two methods which help to avoid this problem. Diversity can be maintained within the PPF by sharing in attribute space rather than decision variable space. Sharing techniques do require a distance metric for which we have chosen the Holder metric. Given two alternatives x and x' be two alternatives with attribute sets $\mathcal{A}_x$ and $\mathcal{A}_{x'}$, we form the two *attribute vectors* $V = [v_1(a_1)\ v_2(a_2)\ \dots\ v_n(a_n)]^T$ and $V' = [v_1(a_1')\ v_2(a_2')\ \dots\ v_n(a_n')]^T$. The Holder metric (of degree p) is then given by:

$$\text{distance}(x, x') = \left(\sum_{i=1}^{n} |v_i(a_i) - v_i(a_i')|^p \right)^{1/p} \tag{12}$$

Notice that instead of using the raw attribute values (which can introduce niching bias), we use the real-valued functions for the attribute values (*c.f.*, Equations (2)and (3)). Also, varying p modifies the shape of the niche. It has been suggested that values of $p < 2$ be used as this tends to form niches which more accurately reflects the tradeoff between attributes (Horn *et al.*, 1993).

5   Some Example Problems

We begin with a simple problem that was described in a paper by Horn and Nafpliotis (Horn *et al.*, 1993). This will be followed by a problem from the hardware/software codesign domain[7].

Problem 1:

Let S_l denote a binary bit string of length l. Associated with S_l are two attributes *unitation* and *pairs*. Unitation $U[S_l]$ returns the number of ones in the string S_l while pairs $P[S_l]$ returns the number of adjacent complementary bits in S_l. For example, with S_8=11110101, $U[S_8]$=6 and $P[S_8]$=4. The objective is (for some given l) to find a S_l which maximizes both attributes.

Intuitively, if we increase the number of ones, $U[S_l]$ should increase and $P[S_l]$ should decrease. Horn and Nafpliotis claim that there exists a tradeoff between these attributes for unitation

---

[6]Critical relationships between mutation rate, population size and selection pressure determine how significant this genetic drift will become (Harvey, 1993).

[7]The interested reader is referred to (Wolf, 1994) for an excellent introduction to this subject.

$\geq l/2$. For example, let $S_8 = 11111110$. Clearly increasing the ones causes $U[S_8]$ to increase and $P[S_8]$ to decrease. However, such is not always the case as a simple counter-example will illustrate. Suppose $S_8 = 11111000$ which gives $U[S_8] = 5$ and $P[S_8] = 1$. Complementing the least significant bit yields $U[S_8] = 6$ and $P[S_8] = 2$. Nevertheless, in general some tradeoff will exist between these attributes.

As a test case we consider $l = 28$. Horn and Nafpliotis used a *niched Pareto genetic algorithm* to identify stable subpopulations on the Pareto front. The population distribution they were able to achieve after 200 generations is shown in Figure 4. Notice that there is a reasonable distribution across the Pareto front. We attempted to solve the same problem using the EA shown in Figure 3.

1. Randomly generate $\mu = 100$ alternatives for the initial population. Set $\Gamma = 200$ and $k=1$.

2. Randomly select 3 alternatives from the population and rank them to establish preferences. Use Goldberg's technique to rank all alternatives (including the 3 previously selected) according to the preferences.

3. Construct niches and compute the niche count for each alternative. Increment the niche count of alternative x for each alternative $x' \neq x \mid \text{distance}(x, x') < 5$.

4. Conduct a tournament to select parents for reproduction. Use equivalence class sharing if necessary. Apply crossover or mutation operators (with probabilities 0.7 and 0.3, respectively) to generate μ total offspring.

5. Use Goldberg's technique to rank the 2μ alternatives according to preferences.

6. Select the μ best alternatives for survival and discard the rest.

7. $k = k + 1$. If $k < \Gamma$, go to step 3. Otherwise, exit.

Figure 3: The EA used for problem 1.

For initial ranking by the decision maker, we randomly selected the alternatives shown in Table 5 from the initial population.

Table 2: Alternatives used for problem 1

No.	Alternative	$P[S_{28}]$	$U[S_{28}]$
1	1011101101010101110110001001	0.667	0.571
2	0110010110111011010101111001	0.630	0.607
3	0010101000000110101101010101	0.704	0.429

For the first test we decided that $A_3 \succ A_1 \succ A_2$. This choice says that we consider generations of pairs more important than ones. The population distribution after 200 generations is shown in Figure 5. Notice that the alternatives have a large number of pairs.

We then chose a ranking of $A_2 \succ A_1 \succ A_3$ This choice says that we consider generations of ones more important than pairs. The population distribution after 200 generations is shown in Figure 6. Here the alternatives found all have a large number of ones. Indeed, all

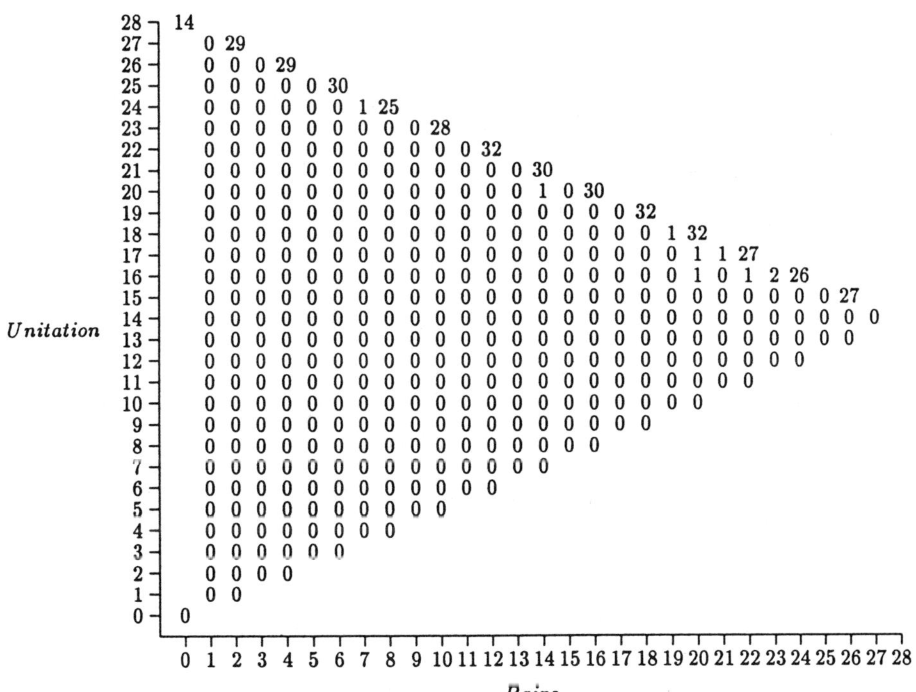

Figure 4: Stable subpopulations after 200 generations for problem 1 with l=28, as given by Horn and Nafpliotis. Population size was $N = 400$. Locations without a number represent infeasible alternatives.

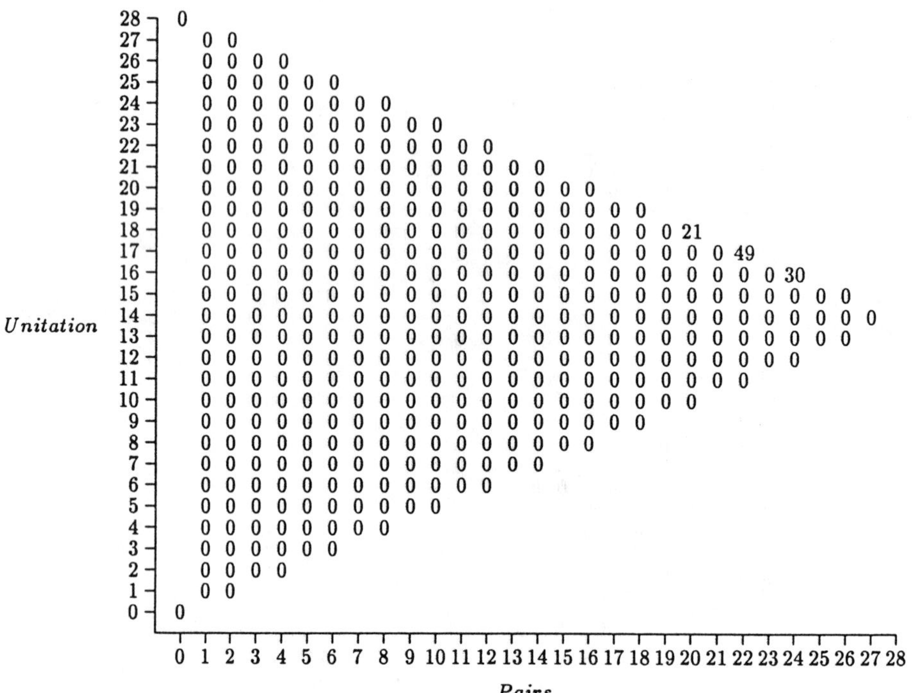

Figure 5: Stable subpopulations after 200 generations for problem 1 with $l=28$. Initial ranking emphasized production of pairs. Locations without a number represent infeasible alternatives.

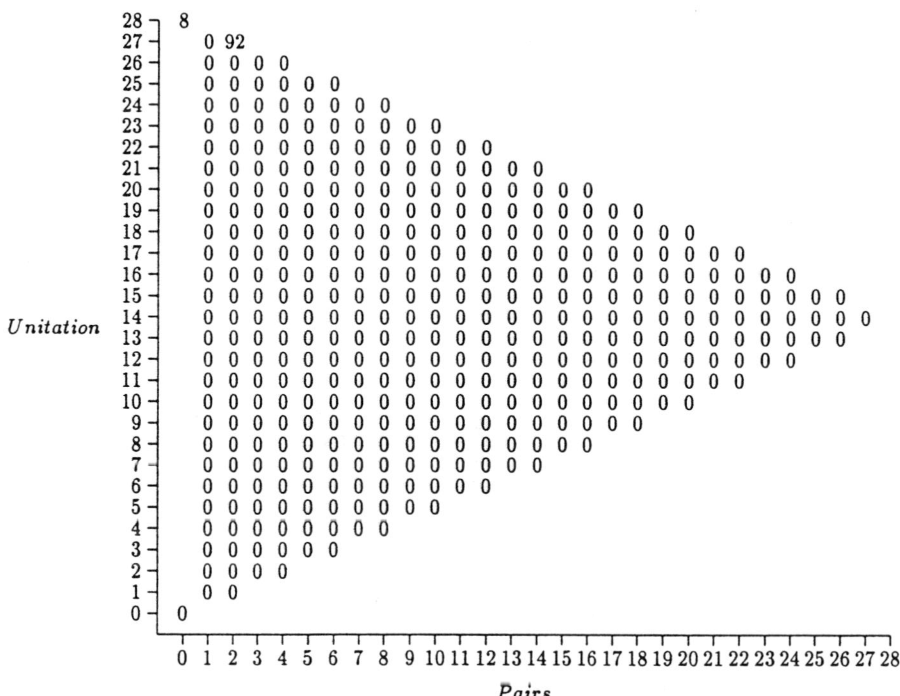

Figure 6: Stable subpopulations after 200 generations for problem 1 with $l=28$. Initial ranking emphasized production of ones. Locations without a number represent infeasible alternatives.

alternatives found were Pareto optimal. Ninety-two of these alternatives had only a single zero bit. Scanning these alternatives showed an extensive diversity since the position of this zero bit varied considerably.

Problem 2:

We now present a hardware/software codesign problem with an application in the automotive industry. For brevity, only an outline of the problem is given as more detailed information is available in a forthcoming paper (Hu *et al.*, 1996).

The system specification contains nine periodic functions with real-time constraints, which are given in Table 5. Associated with each function is a known computation time, a deadline for completion and the time period between successive activations. Each function may be implemented either as a software module executing on a processor or as a hardware module (*e.g.*, an application specific integrated circuit).

For simplicity, we have assumed that communication between hardware components in the resultant system is carried out through a zero-delay shared memory area. Software

Table 3: Primary set of functions to be implemented.

No.	Name
1	DigitalFilter1 (DF1)
2	DigitalFilter2 (DF2)
3	DecodeSPUB (DSB)
4	DecodeSPUA (DSA)
5	ReadCAM (RC)
6	ServiceRoutine (SR)
7	FuelCalc (FC)
8	SparkCalc (SC)
9	ReadMAP (RM)

modules are listed in Table 4. Each software module is characterized by the number of instructions executed and the amount of RAM and ROM required to implement the module. For this example, we assume the software characterization given in Table 4 is valid for every processor. Although all functions may be implemented in software, functions DF1, DF2, DSA and DSB may also be implemented in hardware. Table 5 lists some of the hardware modules available for this system. The modules include: microcontrollers (MC), processors (P), application-specific components (ASIC), standard peripherals (PIO), RAM, and ROM. For example, three derivatives of microcontroller four (MC4a-H, MC4b-H, MC4c-H) are available, and MC4a-H has 2K bytes of RAM, fourteen timing channels (TC), and custom circuits to implement functions 1 through 4.

The system's attributes are component cost, critical excess MIPS (Δ_c), and feasibility factor (λ). Critical excess MIPs indicates the amount of computational power yet available for future expansion. Feasibility factor reflects the ability of an implementation to meet all temporal requirements. λ is dependent on the scheduling algorithm used and indicates the probability that the target processor has sufficient computational power to meet all of the timing requirements of the tasks assigned to it. A methodology for calculating λ and Δ_c can be found in (D'ambrosio *et al.*, 1996).

Table 4: Software modules to implement functions. RAM and ROM are measured in bytes.

Name	Function Implemented	Instructions Executed	RAM Required	ROM Required
DF1-S	DF1	64	100	100
DF2-S	DF2	32	100	100
DSB-S	DSB	30	200	300
DSA-S	DSA	30	200	300
RC-S	RC	30	100	100
SR-S	SR	20	200	200
FC-S	FC	480	500	400
SC-S	SC	100	400	300
RM-S	RM	40	100	100

Table 5: Hardware modules to implement functions.

Name	Functions Implemented	Cost	MIPS Available
MC1-H	CPU, RAM(2K), ROM(2K), DF1,DF2,DSB,DSA	3.50	1.30
MC2-H	CPU, RAM(2K), ROM(2K), TC(32)	3.25	1.50
MC3a-H	CPU, RAM(4K), TC(16)	5.25	2.50
MC3b-H	CPU, RAM(4K), DF1,DF2, DSB,DSA	6.25	2.50
MC4a-H	CPU, RAM(2K), DF1, DF2, DSB, DSA, TC(14)	3.75	1.70
MC4b-H	CPU, RAM(2K), DF1, DF2, DSB, DSA, TC(14)	3.25	1.35
MC4c-H	CPU, RAM(2K),TC(16)	2.50	1.70
P1-H	CPU, RAM(2K), ROM(2K)	2.00	1.43
P2-H	CPU	13.00	13.50
ASIC1-H	DF1,DF2,DSB,DSA	2.50	-
PIO1-H	TC(16)	1.00	-
RAM1-H	RAM(2K)	2.00	-
ROM1-H	ROM(2K)	1.00	-

The only constraint used for this problem is that λ must be greater than or equal to zero which insures the design will meet real-time constraints. This size problem is small enough that exhaustive search can be used to enumerate the Pareto optimal set within a reasonable amount of computational time. There are a total of 12 Pareto optimal alternatives which are identified in Table 5.

Table 6: Pareto optimal set of alternatives found by exhaustive search. Note that all alternatives also include: RM-S,SC-S, FC-S, SR-S, RC-S.

Number	Part Set	Cost	Feasibility Factor (λ)	Critical Excess Req. Ratio (Δ_c)
1	DF1toTC, DF2toTC, DSB-S, DSA-S, P1-H, PIO1-H	3.00	0.013	0.011
2	DF1toTC, DF2toTC, DSB-S, DSA-S, MC2-H	3.25	0.094	0.081
3	MC1-H	3.50	0.706	0.183
4	DF1toTC, DF2toTC, DSB-S, DSA-S, MC4c-H, ROM1-H	3.50	0.325	0.281
5	MC4b-H, ROM1-H	4.25	0.899	0.233
6	P1-H, ASIC1-H	4.50	1.000	0.313
7	MC4a-H, ROM1-H	4.75	1.000	0.583
8	DF1toTC, DF2toTC, DSB-S, DSA-S, MC3a-H, ROM1-H	6.25	1.000	1.081
9	MC3b-H ROM1-H	7.25	1.000	1.383
10	DF1-S, DF2-S, DSB-S, DSA-S, P2-H, RAM1-H, ROM1-H	16.00	1.000	11.460
11	DF1toTC, DF2toTC, DSB-S, DSA-S, P2-H, PIO1-H, RAM1-H, ROM1-H	17.00	1.000	12.080
12	P2-H, ASIC1-H, RAM1-H, ROM1-H	18.50	1.000	12.380

Two tests were conducted using an EA with a population size of $\mu=20$. Three mutation operators were used. Operator M_1 changed a hardware (software) assignment to a software (hardware) assignment. Operator M_2 changed the main processor while operator M_3 changed the device used to implement a hardware function. The EA was run for $\Gamma=50$ generations with mutation probabilities of $p_1 = 0.8$, $p_2 = 0.05$, and $p_3 = 0.15$, respectively. In both test cases three design alternatives were randomly selected from the initial population for ranking according to a designer's preferences. Five alternatives were randomly chosen in each generation for conducting a tournament selection to ascertain which alternatives are chosen for reproduction. After Γ generations had been processed, alternatives with rank 1 were output.

The first test ranked the three given alternatives according to cost (lower cost implies higher ranking). **EvoC** correctly identified alternatives 2 and 4 from Table 5. The second test ranked the three given alternatives according to Δ_c (higher value implies higher ranking). The EA consistently identified alternatives 10, 11, and 12 from Table 5.

6   Final Remarks

Complete enumeration of the Pareto optimal frontier $\mathcal{P}$ is rarely possible due to the high dimensionality of the tradeoff surface. Even sketching out $\mathcal{P}$ is often unnecessary as a decision maker's preferences really only demand enumeration of $\mathcal{P}' \subset \mathcal{P}$. This means that the progression of the PPF should hopefully be towards $\mathcal{P}'$ rather than to some arbitrary subset of $\mathcal{P}$. (This progression concept is shown for a 2-dimensional attribute space in Figure 7. ζ_i represents the PPF in the i-th generation of the EA.)

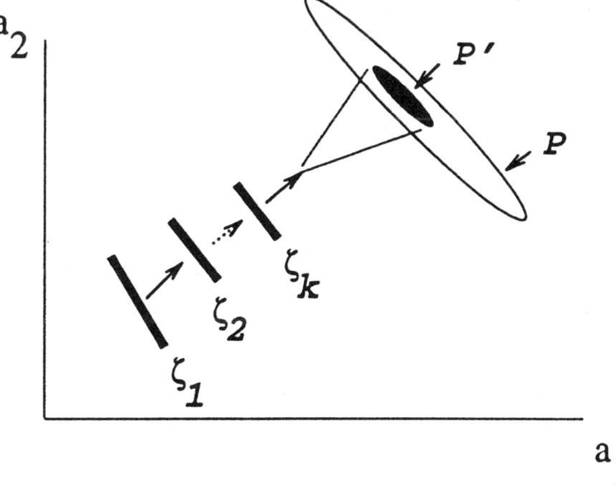

Figure 7: Progression of the PPF

So how do we achieve this progression of the PPF? Recall that in each generation the alternatives are ranked according to the decision maker's preferences. It has been shown that this preference relationship preserves Pareto optimality. Then, if we choose these preferred alternatives for survival with a high probability, we are letting a decision maker's preferences drive the search process of the EA. This is exactly what we are trying to accomplish.

Since we are only interested in finding a particular subset of $\mathcal{P}$ (the one which matches the decision maker's preferences), it might be argued that sharing is unnecessary; genetic drift may even be desirable. However, it is important to realize that the set of preferred alternatives in alternative space can actually be the union of several disjoint subsets. This requires one to maintain a diverse population and justifies the need for sharing.

Finally, we assumed it was always possible to find solutions to the linear programming problem which satisfy all of the constraints imposed on the $w'_k s$. However, if a user specifies an inconsistent set of preferences, there will be no solution to the linear program containing the resulting w_k constraints. We have implemented an exponential time algorithm (White et al., 1984). for identifying the inconsistent preference statements This algorithm identifies minimum sets of preference statement, that if removed, would result in a feasible solution to the linear program. In all cases to date, our implementation has been able to identify the inconsistent preferences in a trivial amount of time, and we expect to achieve the same level of favorable performance on any other problems we encounter in the future.

454 Greenwood, Hu and D'Ambrosio

Acknowledgements

The work by Garrison Greenwood and Xiaobo Hu was supported in part by an External Research Program Grant from Hewlett-Packard Laboratories, Bristol, England. This support is greatly appreciated.

References

J. D'Ambrosio and X. Hu. (1994) "Configuration-level hardware/software partition for real-time embedded systems," *Proc. of Third Int'l Workshop on Hardware-Software Codesign*, 34-41

C. Fonseca and P. Fleming. (1995) "An overview of evolutionary algorithms in multiobjective optimization," *Evolutionary Computation*, Vol. 3, No. 1, 1-17

D. Goldberg. (1989) *Genetic Algorithms in Search, Optimization, and Machine Learning*, Addison-Wesley Pub. Co.

I. Harvey. (1993) "The puzzle of the persistent question marks: a case study of genetic drift," in S. Forrest (Ed.), *Proc. of Fifth Int'l Conf. on Genetic Algorithms*, San Mateo, CA: Morgan Kaufmann, 15-22

M. Hilliard, G. Liepins, M. palmer and G. Rangarajen. (1989) "The computer as a partner in algorithmic design: Automated discovery of parameters for a multiobjective scheduling heuristic," in R. Sharda, B. Golden, E. Wasil, O. Balci and W. Stewart (Eds.), *Impacts of Recent Computer Adv. on Operations Res.*, New York: North-Holland

J. Horn and N. Nafpliotis. (1993) " Multiobjective optimization using the niched Pareto genetic algorithm," IlliGAL Report 93005, University of Illinois at Urbana-Champaign

X. Hu, G. Greenwood and J. D'Ambrosio. (1996) "An evolutionary approach to hardware/software partitioning," in H.M Voigt, W. Ebeling, I. Rechenberg and H.P. Schwefel (Eds.), *Parallel Prob. Solving from Nature IV*, Lecture Notes in Computer Science 1141, Springer-Verlag, 900-909

R. Keeny and H. Raiffa. (1976) *Decisions with Multiple Objectives: Preferences and Value Tradeoffs*, John Wiley & Sons, NY

G. Liepins, M. Hilliard, J. Richardson and M. Palmer. (1990) "Genetic algorithms application to set covering and traveling salesman problems," in D. Brown and C. White (Eds.), *Oper. Res. and Artificial Intelligence: The Integration of Problem-Solving Strategies*, Norwell, MA: Kluwer Academic, 29-57

S. Louis and G. Rawlins. (1993) "Pareto optimality, GA-easiness and deception," in S. Forrest (Ed.), *Proc. of Fifth Int'l Conf. on Genetic Algorithms*, San Mateo, CA: Morgan Kaufmann, 118-123

K. Murty. (1983) *Linear Programming*, John Wiley & Sons, NY

J. Richardson, M. Palmer, G. Liepins and M. Hilliard. (1989) "Some guidelines for genetic algorithms with penalty functions," in J. Schaffer (Ed.), *Proc. of Third Int'l Conf. on Genetic Algorithms*, San Mateo, CA: Morgan Kaufmann, 191-197

B. Ritzel, J. Eheart and S. Ranjithan. (1994) "Using genetic algorithms to solve a multiple objective groundwater pollution containment problem," *Water Resources Research*, 30(5), 1589-1603

J. Schaffer. (1985) "Multiple objective optimization with vector evaluated genetic algorithms," in J. Grefenstette (Ed.), *Proc. of First Int'l Conf. on Genetic Algorithms*, Hillsdale, NJ: Lawrence Erlbaum, 93-100

P. Surry, N. Radcliffe and I. Boyd. (1995) "A multi-objective approach to constrained optimisation of gas supply networks: the COMOGA method," *Evolutionary computing: AISB Workshop*, Springer-Verlag, Lecture notes in comp. sci 993, 166-180

C. White, A. Sage, and S. Dozono. (1984) "A model of multiattribute decisionmaking and tradeoff weight determination under uncertainty," *IEEE Trans. Syst., Man, Cybern.*, Vol SMC-14, 223-229

D. Wienke, C. Lucasius and G. Kateman. (1992) "Multicriteria target vector optimization of analytical procedures using a genetic algorithm," *Analytica Chimica Acta*, Vol. 265, 211-225

W. Wolf. (1994) "Hardware-software co-design of embedded systems," *Proc. of the IEEE*, Vol 82, No 7, 967-991

Author Index

Key Word Index